Contents

Management

A contemporary approach

Prof. dr Doede Keuning

PROFESSOR OF MANAGEMENT AND ORGANIZATION
DIRECTOR OF POSTDOCTORAL COURSE
MANAGEMENT CONSULTANT
FREE UNIVERSITY, AMSTERDAM

PITMAN
PUBLISHING

London · Hong Kong · Johanne … ngton DC

PITMAN PUBLISHING
128 Long Acre, London WC2E 9AN
Tel: +44 (0)171 447 2000
Fax: +44 (0)171 240 5771

A Division of Pearson Professional Limited

Visit the Pitman Publishing Website at
http://www.pitman.co.uk

First published in Great Britain 1998
First published in 1995 in Dutch by Stenfert Kroese/Educatieve Partners Nederland
under the title *Grondslagen van het Management*
with the assistance of drs. R de Lange.

ISBN 0 273 62591 8

British Library Cataloguing in Publication Data
A CIP catalogue record for this book can be obtained from the British Library

Translated by drs. C.A.A. Keuning.

10 9 8 7 6 5 4 3 2 1

Typeset by Pantek Arts, Maidstone, Kent
Printed and bound in Great Britain by Clays Ltd, St Ives plc

The Publishers' policy is to use paper manufactured from sustainable forests.

Preface

Every type of organization – whether profit making or non-profit making – requires some form of management if it is to operate effectively. As a result management is of importance to everyone who comes into contact with organizations, as employees, managers, suppliers or clients.

This book is intended as a comprehensive introduction to management. It acquaints the reader with all aspects of the subject and, by using examples and case studies from the world of business, enables the reader to relate the theory of management to everyday situations.

Every chapter starts with a *Management in action* and ends with a *Management case study*. These extended case studies give the reader the opportunity to consider the practical application of the concepts discussed in the chapter.

The organization is examined in the context of its environment – that is, the outside world in which the organization operates and which influences the organization's performance. The challenges currently facing managers are discussed, as are those confronting the managers of the twenty-first century.

This book is arranged according to the process approach to management.

Part one deals with the role of managers and organizations in society, the history of management theory and the stages of development of individual organizations. In addition, the interrelationship between society and organizations is introduced.

Part two looks at the questions that every organization must address: What is our direction? Do we have to change? These are questions of mission and strategy formulation, decision making, creativity and learning.

In *Part three*, the structuring of organizations and the ways in which work can be divided are covered. The organizational structure that is chosen needs to fit the organization's strategic positioning. The formulation of tasks, departmentalization, organizing around processes and the ways in which employees work – for example, in group structures or autonomous teams – are all described.

Part four deals with issues regarding people in the organization – the motivation of employees, as well as that of managers and their leadership styles. Human resources management, development of talent, and the distribution and execution of power are described, as is the shared expectations of the members of the organization concerning work behaviour – that is, the organizational culture.

Part five explores the control of organizational processes. Planning and corrective action are discussed, and special attention is given to the possibilities and pitfalls of

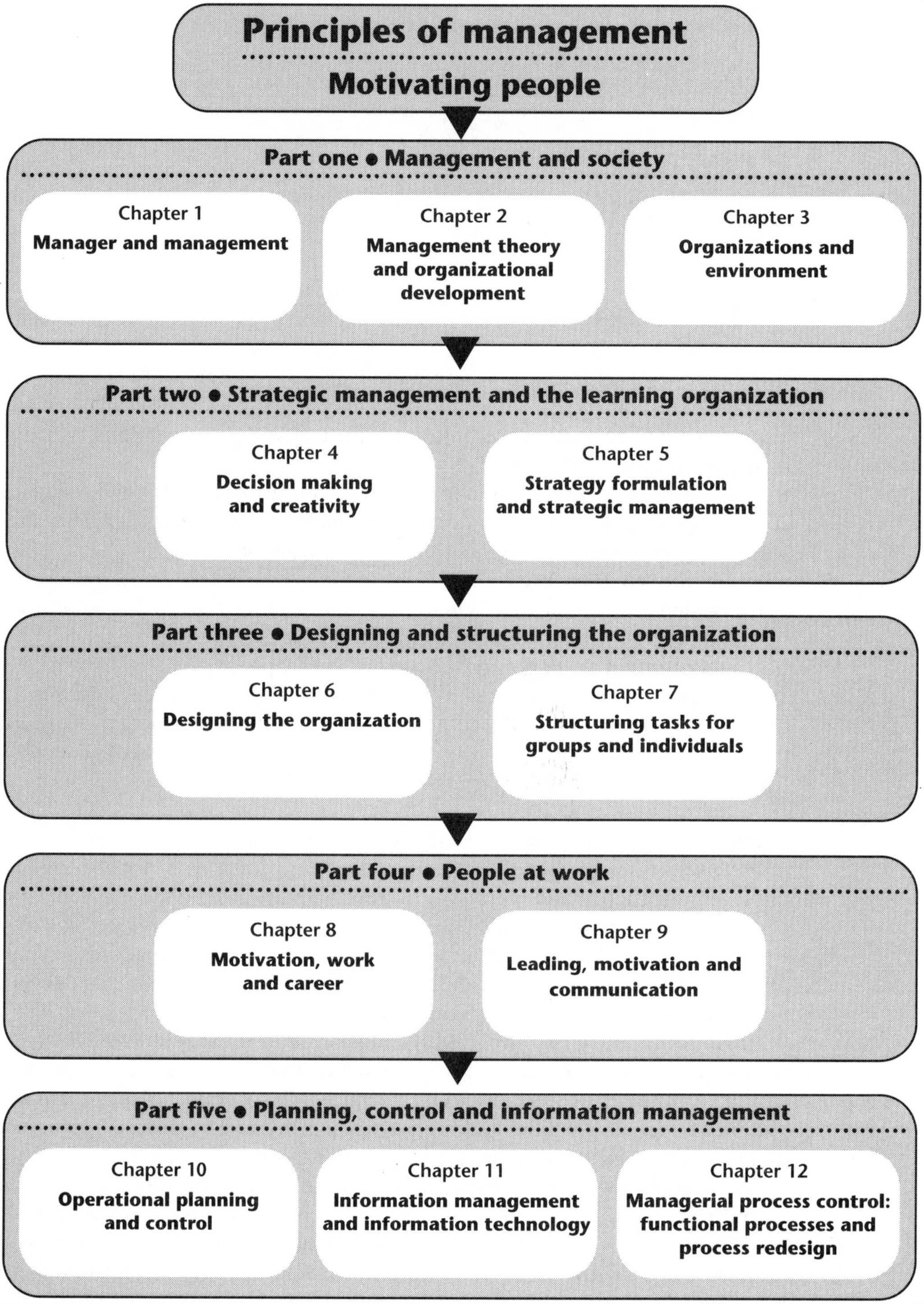

Principles of management

Motivating people

Part one • Management and society

Chapter 1
Manager and management

Chapter 2
Management theory and organizational development

Chapter 3
Organizations and environment

Part two • Strategic management and the learning organization

Chapter 4
Decision making and creativity

Chapter 5
Strategy formulation and strategic management

Part three • Designing and structuring the organization

Chapter 6
Designing the organization

Chapter 7
Structuring tasks for groups and individuals

Part four • People at work

Chapter 8
Motivation, work and career

Chapter 9
Leading, motivation and communication

Part five • Planning, control and information management

Chapter 10
Operational planning and control

Chapter 11
Information management and information technology

Chapter 12
Managerial process control: functional processes and process redesign

Fig A ● The 'step-by-step' process model

information technology in relation to management and organizations. The management aspects of several functional processes such as logistics and human resources are covered. This part concludes with a look at the organization in relation to business process re-engineering (BPR).

As an introduction to the discipline of management and the organization, this book can be seen as a 'guided tour' through the different aspects of management, as depicted in the step-by-step process model in Fig A. It is important to stress two points with regard to this approach. First, organizations and management are always concerned with people and their motivation (that is why we have positioned motivation at the top of Fig A). In every aspect of management (and in every step of the model) the motivation of the people concerned must be taken into account. Second, the person who acts as 'manager' must not lose sight of what a manager actually is and does. In both a symbolic sense and in Fig A, the reader has to start the tour at the beginning.

Students on management and organization courses and programmes of study at universities, colleges and MBA schools will find this book useful. It can also be used in higher level management courses.

To accompany this book, an *Instructor's Manual* has been produced, which contains additional guidance for lecturers using this book with students. This all helps to enhance the learning process.

A new book is always open to improvement: comments and suggestions are very welcome.

Doede Keuning
October 1997

Foreword

Having had the privilege of working with Professor Keuning in several management seminars, it is a bonus that his verbal insights have been committed to this book for wider dissemination. The book reflects Doede Keuning's personality – thoroughly comprehensive in the breadth of relevant issues considered; meticulous in its focus as a learning vehicle and reflective as to potential solutions.

The book demonstrates just how far business academics have converged with the reality of business. Some three decades ago Fred Fiedler wrote an article in the Harvard Business Review entitled 'Organize the job to fit the manager, not the manager to fit the job'. Contemporary academics laughed: this was not 'scientific' management. Theories were propounded but, like the mountebanks in medieval times, had little effect. The connection between theory and practice failed to be made.

It is not so with this book. Each chapter begins with an example of real business which is related to apposite theory and empirical testing and the reader is placed in a managerial situation of decision with an international case study of current relevance. Successful implementation is the focus: balancing the kaleidoscope of external environmental trading conditions with internal managerial motivation, the canvas.

I wish this splendid book very well.

Professor David Norburn,
Director, Imperial College Management School
London University

August 1997

Acknowledgements

Example on p. 20 and Exhibit 1.3 extracted from *Directors: Myth and Reality* by Myles Mace. Reprinted by permission of Harvard Business School Publishing. © 1971, 1986 by the President and Fellows of Harvard College, all rights reserved.

Exhibits 1.4, 3.9, 4.1, 5.3, 8.5, 9.4, 10.6, 11.1, 12.2, 12.3, 12.4, Management in action and Management case studies in Chapters 3 and 8 reproduced from *International Management* by permission of Reed Business Information Ltd.

Fig 3.4 reproduced from *Management* by Stoner, J.A.F. and Freeman, R.E., © 1993, by permission of Prentice Hall Europe.

Exhibit 3.6 reproduced from 'Spider versus Spider' by John Hagel, III, *The McKinsey Quarterly*, Vol. 1, 1996. © McKinsey and Company, 1996.

Fig 4.6 reproduced from *The Shape of Automation* by Simon, H.A. (1965), Harper & Row, by permission of the author.

Figs 4.8, 4.9 and 4.10 reprinted from 'The Link Between Individual and Organizational Learning' by Kim, D.H., *Sloan Management Review*, Autumn 1993, by permission of publisher. © 1993 by Sloan Management Review Association. All rights reserved. Fig 4.8 reproduced as adpated from *Experiential Learning: Experience as the Source of Learning and Development* by Kolb, D.A., © 1984, by permission of Prentice-Hall, Inc. Upper Saddle River, NJ.

Fig 5.4 adapted with the permission of The Free Press, a Division of Simon & Schuster from *Competitive Strategy: Techniques for Analyzing Industries and Competitors* by Michael E. Porter. © 1980 by The Free Press.

Figs 8.1, 8.2, 8.3, 8.11, 9.12 adapted from *Organizational Behaviour* by Robbins, Stephen, © 1979. Reprinted by permission of Prentice-Hall, Inc. Upper Saddle River, NJ.

Exhibits 8.1, 8.2 from 'Use Transnational Teams to Globalise Your Company' by Charles Snow, *et al.* are reproduced by permission of the publisher from *Organizational Dynamics*, Spring 1996, © 1996. American Management Association, New York. All rights reserved.

Exhibits 8.3, 8.4, 8.6, 9.1, 9.3, 9.5, 9.7 and 10.2 reproduced from *Transnational Management* by Bartlett and Ghoshal (1992). By permission of The McGraw Hill Companies.

Fig 9.1 reproduced from 'The Paradox of Mangerial Leadership' by Nicholls, J., *Journal of General Management*, Summer 1993, with permission from the Braybrooke Press.

Fig 12.4 adapted with the permission of The Free Press, a Division of Simon & Schuster from *Competitive Advantage: Creating and Sustaining Superior Performance* by Michael E. Porter. © 1985 by Michael E. Porter.

Every effort has been made to trace and acknowledge ownership of copyright. The publishers will be glad to make suitable arrangements with any copyright-holders whom it has not been possible to contact.

Management and society

We begin with a general introduction and examination of some of the basic concepts of management and the organization. In later chapters we deal with particular aspects of the management process itself. In today's world 'management' is an important social phenomenon. In Chapters 1 to 3 we look at management and its place in society and address the following questions:

- What are managers and organizations, and what is management all about? (Chapter 1)
- How has the theory of management developed and what are the stages in the growth of an individual organization? (Chapter 2)
- What is the relationship between an organization and the environment in which it operates? (Chapter 3)

Principles of management

Motivating people

Part one • Management and society

Chapter 1
Manager and management

Chapter 2
Management theory and organizational development

Chapter 3
Organizations and environment

Part two • Strategic management and the learning organization

Chapter 4
Decision making and creativity

Chapter 5
Strategy formulation and strategic management

Part three • Designing and structuring the organization

Chapter 6
Designing the organization

Chapter 7
Structuring tasks for groups and individuals

Part four • People at work

Chapter 8
Motivation, work and career

Chapter 9
Leading, motivation and communication

Part five • Planning, control and information management

Chapter 10
Operational planning and control

Chapter 11
Information management and information technology

Chapter 12
Managerial process control: functional processes and process redesign

Chapter 1

Manager and management

LEARNING OBJECTIVES

After studying this chapter, you should be able to:

- describe the concepts of management and organization and explain why these are important;
- identify the levels of management in the organization and explain why, at each level, different knowledge and skills are required;
- list the core activities of the management process and show how they relate to each other;
- name the characteristics of the modern manager;
- indicate the criteria, requirements and standards that are or should be met by effective and healthy organizations;
- distinguish between the concepts of effectiveness and efficiency and explain why these are important for reviewing an organization;
- give examples of instruments for assessing or evaluating management performance.

Management in action

Europe's most respected companies

FT

The quality and implementation of corporate strategy are high on the list of attributes admired by top managers.

Europe's top managers are, it seems, remarkably consistent when it comes to judging corporate excellence. For the third year running they have voted ABB, the Swedish-Swiss engineering group, Europe's most respected company in a survey carried out by the Financial Times and Price Waterhouse.

Though ABB again achieved an impressive score on a wide range of criteria, it is not alone in establishing itself as a firm favourite. Nine of this year's 10 most respected companies also featured in last year's top 10 – though there were some changes in the ranking order.

British Airways moved up a place to second position, nosing ahead of Nestlé of Switzerland. Siemens of Germany rose two places, while British Petroleum entered the top 10 for the first time. Britain's Marks & Spencer and the Anglo-Dutch Unilever slipped slightly, while Fiat of Italy – joint No. 10 last year – tumbled out of the league table.

However, the survey also yielded some surprises, which cast an interesting perspective on its other findings. Asked which company they respected most, regardless of its country of origin, European managers plumped by a substantial margin for General Electric of the US. ABB was relegated to second position, shared with Microsoft of the US.

Furthermore, no fewer than six of the 11 top-ranked companies in this category are US-based, while companies from other non-European countries barely rate a mention. That suggests not only that many of Europe's top executives look across the Atlantic for inspiration but that Japanese corporate prowess no longer enthrals them as it did in the 1980s.

Widening the survey to include views on companies based outside Europe is one of several innovations this year. The questionnaire has been refined and expanded to pinpoint more precisely the most highly-prized corporate attributes – and which companies are perceived to possess them.

Respondents were also asked to name the European business leader they most respect, the companies they use as performance benchmarks, and the main challenges confronting business. Finally, the survey was sent to chief executives and presidents of more companies – more than 1,400 compared with 1,000 last year.

Differences in methodology mean that too much should not be read into variations or contrasts between the findings this year and last. Nor does the survey pretend to be a scientific exercise. Nonetheless, it points to some clear conclusions about the values and priorities of European managers.

Overall, the most highly-prized corporate attributes emerge as quality and implementation of corporate strategy, management of complexity, and skill at balancing the interests of customers, employees or shareholders. Branding, basic financial measures of success, innovation and corporate ethics are all considered less important.

These perceptions are borne out by ABB's score. As well as being the overall winner, it is rated exceptionally highly for business performance, corporate strategy and maximising employee potential. It is also cited most frequently as the benchmark against which other companies measure their performance.

Indeed, admiration for ABB's achievements is overshadowed only by esteem for Mr Percy Barnevik, its president. Named Europe's most respected business leader, he attracted more votes than were cast for his company in the overall rankings: he was particularly praised for strategic vision and focus.

The ability to achieve sustained success by adopting long-term strategies, while adjusting quickly to changing market conditions, is especially highly regarded. The findings suggest that companies which score well on these criteria can ride out short-term reverses or blemishes to their reputation.

In this context, two findings are striking. Despite controversy over the disposal of its Brent Spar oil rig, Shell was named as the company which deals best with environmental issues. Meanwhile, adverse publicity over BA's "dirty tricks" campaign against Virgin Airlines did not prevent BA taking joint sixth place among companies respected for demonstrating the highest standards of ethical conduct.

The findings also suggest that the European companies most likely to be held in high esteem are large and involved in manufacturing or heavy industry. Despite the growing economic importance of services businesses, these are poorly represented at the upper levels of the overall rankings. Honourable exceptions include BA, Marks & Spencer, ING, Swissair, Deutsche Bank and Reuters.

Furthermore, the most highly respected companies tend to be long-established. Virgin, the only genuinely young company in last year's top 30, failed to make the grade this year, though it is ranked first for innovation.

The only other youthful concern to attract wide support is SAP, a fast-growing German software company. It is rated highly for innovation and maximising long-term value to shareholders.

But if that suggests that European managers can be cautious about the new, they had no hesitations about naming Novartis – a company which does not yet formally exist – as the best-judged recent merger or acquisition. As of early September, consummation of this planned merger of Ciba and Sandoz, two Swiss pharmaceuticals companies, was still awaiting US anti-trust clearance.

Though the survey sample was geographically broadly based, the most highly regarded companies are overwhelmingly from northern Europe. Companies from the south are conspicuously absent from the overall league table, and poorly represented in rankings by specific attributes.

Among the few exceptions are Benetton of Italy, respected for innovation, Spain's Repsol, whose privatisation is judged a success, and El Corte Inglés, a Spanish retailer admired for balancing the interests of shareholders, employees and customers.

Some of the detailed findings confirm national business stereotypes. Germany is strongly represented in engineering and chemicals, while the most highly ranked European companies in aviation, retailing and information services are all British.

A number of UK companies, including BA, BP, and Marks & Spencer, perform well on criteria normally associated with the kind of long-termism for which German companies have traditionally been renowned.

That suggests that negative perceptions of Anglo-Saxon capitalism as irredeemably "short-termist" are waning – a point reinforced by the high regard in which many European managers now appear to hold US companies.

Furthermore, the successful "stakeholder" company is no longer viewed predominantly as a German phenomenon. Indeed, the list of companies judged to balance best the interests of shareholders, employees and customers is headed by BA and Marks & Spencer.

Though companies such as Nestlé, BMW and Siemens also score highly on this measure, Air Liquide and L'Oréal of France, Astra of Sweden, Body Shop, BP, Rentokil, Reuters and Tesco all obtain honourable mentions.

By definition, most of the survey's findings are based on perceptions of past performance. But what of the future? Asked what they considered the biggest challenges facing European business, almost half the respondents named competition, particularly from the Far East, and pressure on costs.

Roughly a fifth singled out regional issues, such as European monetary union and the growth of protectionism in Europe, while almost as many picked on the globalisation of markets.

No one company is perceived as best-placed to tackle all these challenges. However, BA, Shell and Nestlé are all rated highly for their ability to deal with cost pressures, while ABB is considered the best bet to handle the implications of globalising markets.

Rank				
1	**Company**	**ABB**	**1996**	1
	Country	Sweden/Switzerland	**1995**	1
	Sector	Engineering	**1994**	=1
	Turnover ($m)	33,738.00**	**ROCE***	33.84%
2	**Company**	**British Airways**	**1996**	3
	Country	United Kingdom	**1995**	1
	Sector	Transport	**1994**	4
	Turnover ($m)	12,033.00	**ROCE**	11.44%
3	**Company**	**Nestlé**	**1996**	3
	Country	Switzerland	**1995**	2
	Sector	Food processors	**1994**	6
	Turnover ($m)	46,972.10	**ROCE**	15.50%
4	**Company**	**BMW**	**1996**	4
	Country	Germany	**1995**	4
	Sector	Automobiles	**1994**	8
	Turnover ($m)	31,130.00	**ROCE**	4.49%
5	**Company**	**Royal Dutch Shell**	**1996**	5
	Country	Netherlands/UK	**1995**	=5
	Sector	Oil, gas and mining	**1994**	3
	Turnover ($m)	107,916.00	**ROCE**	14.59%
6	**Company**	**Siemens**	**1996**	6
	Country	Germany	**1995**	8
	Sector	Electronics	**1994**	21
	Turnover ($m)	58,881.90	**ROCE**	2.4%

* Return on capital employed is based on profit before interest and tax, after exceptional items

** The average exchange rates for August 1996 have been used for currency conversions

Source: *Financial Times*, 18 September 1996.

Management in action continued

US top of the table

Executives hold up American companies as models of management

It is not that long ago that many European business people – and some of their transatlantic counterparts – viewed corporate America with ill-concealed disdain. Prey to financial markets apparently fixated with short-term returns, out-manoeuvred by Japanese competitors and often wrestling with obsolete working practices, many big US companies seemed on the road to oblivion.

What a difference a few years can make. From the survey findings in the world table, it appears that European managers not only believe that US companies are on the comeback trail, but hold them up as models of impressive management.

None more so than General Electric, which is held in higher respect than any European company.

Respondents particularly praised its long-term business performance, exceptional profitability and its success in defying the current bias against corporate diversification.

Microsoft won plaudits for successfully riding the roller coaster of the information economy, while Coco-Cola was applauded for pursuing a long-term global strategy and a firm commitment to shareholder value.

More than 90 per cent of executives responding to the survey nominated one company which they most respected, regardless of its country of origin. However, the geographical pattern of support for individual companies varied considerably.

More than half the votes for GE were from executives in Germany and Italy. ABB won more than half its votes from Finland and Britain and won only one vote from Germany. More than half of Microsoft's votes were from Germany and Britain, while BA attracted more support from Italy than from the UK.

At least as striking as the strong showing of US companies is the virtual absence in the table of contenders from any other non-European country. Asia, the only other region mentioned, by respondents, won a mere 3 per cent of the votes, divided between Sony and Mitsubishi of Japan and Singapore Airlines.

Yet survey respondents also named intensifying competition, particularly from the Far East, as one of the biggest challenges facing European business in the future.

Another oddity is that Fiat of Italy achieved a relatively high ranking in this part of the survey, while losing its place among the top 30 European companies which command the greatest respect overall.

Most respected companies in the world

Rank	Company	Country	No of countries voting	% votes
1	General Electric	US	8	14.5
2	ABB	Swe/Switz	8	9.9
2	Microsoft	US	6	9.9
4	British Airways	UK	5	7.6
5	Coco-Cola	US	8	6.9
6	Nestlé	Switzerland	5	3.8
7	BMW	Germany	4	3.0
7	Procter and Gamble	US	4	3.0
9	Fiat	Italy	2	2.3
9	General Motors	US	3	2.3
9	Hewlett-Packard	US	3	2.3

Source: *Financial Times*, 18 September 1996.

INTRODUCTION

When people work together to achieve something, management of some kind is always involved. Until the middle of the nineteenth century management was never seen as a specific defined task, let alone as a profession or discipline. In the past the possession of almost absolute power over people and other resources meant that 'managers' worked towards their own personal objectives and goals and could realize these as they wished. Major and frequent failures were allowed; experience was the only way to learn. Changing power structures, especially after the Industrial Revolution, set limits to the managers' power. It was no longer acceptable for capital and labour to be used at will or wasted. This created a new concept and style of management in which the first societal goal was, and still is, the effective and efficient use of people and other resources.

Social change and scientific development have launched us into a new era in which management is, so to speak, at the service of the community. Rational use of people and resources involves more than simple administration and the implementation of direction and control alone. The main characteristic of the 'new' profession of management is the making of decisions that enable many diverse, externally oriented objectives to be reached while taking continuity and societal interest into account. Furthermore, management remains a people-oriented activity. To a large extent, it is based on the personality of the manager and the capabilities of employees. The diverse nature of modern management provides many people with the opportunity to participate in the process of management, each according to his or her own abilities, skills and knowledge.

1.1 ORGANIZATION AND MANAGEMENT

In everyday life, we all come into contact with organizations, operating as companies and institutions. We use the products and services which are made available to us through organizations such as factories, schools, hospitals and travel companies – bread, dairy products, clothes, education, health care, public transport, and so on.

Organizations ... an integral part of our daily lives

We all work and live in a society of organizations. When we go to work, we are dealing with an organization – for example, an industrial firm or an institution in the service sector. Even our spare time and vacations are based around organizations: think of travel agencies, camp sites, hotels and restaurants, sports clubs and so on. In fact, organizations are such an integral part of our daily lives that we rarely consider what organizations are, how they are designed or how they are managed or governed.

Organizations ... a problem

This all changes when we have to accomplish something with the co-operation of other people, when we want to start up a company, when something goes wrong in the company we work for, or when the daily supply of goods and services is disrupted. *Then* we start to notice something of the importance of good management and organization. *Then* we appreciate the problems of a manager and an organization – namely the design, the functioning of processes and the management of the company or institution.

In most cases we conclude that 'they' should have done things differently or better, but what happens if we are directly involved ourselves? *Then* we realize that things are not as self-evident and straightforward as we considered them to be. *Then* it becomes clear how important it is to have insights into the problems of management and organizations. *Then* we also find out how useful it is to be able to draw on techniques, tools and instruments that help us to set up and design an organization and to manage resources and people effectively.

Minicase 1.1

The Perrier Affair – a case of product recall

After an accident has happened, it often turns out that certain signals were given which warned of the disaster to come – signals which were ignored. This can be explained by the so-called 'cry wolf' syndrome which is based on the story of the little boy who warns the guards that the wolf is coming. Time and time again, when the guards come out to have a look, it appears to be a false alarm. When the wolf actually turns up, the guards hear the boy calling, but take no action. It is often difficult for organizations to judge how important a particular warning or signal may be. However, companies should always take signals, such as near-accidents, seriously because these are precisely the events from which they can learn a great deal.

Nowadays, producers may quickly decide to recall a product from the market. A threat to a brand name in a brand-oriented firm can render all statistical calculations irrelevant. In 1990, for example, the soft drink manufacturer, Perrier, decided to take its Perrier Water off the market, despite the fact that there existed no direct danger to public health. The paramount importance of protecting the brand name was reason enough for the company to recall the product. If a company refrains from market recall and the problem recurs, the carefully built-up reputation of a recognized brand name – the ultimate marketing instrument – can be badly damaged in a short period of time. Technological developments have made it possible to track down relatively small imperfections in products quickly. More than ever before, we are making increasingly high demands of products.

Source: Adapted from *Elan*, January 1994.

1.1.1 Managers: what kind of people are they?

Is the word 'manager' simply a new word for a supervisor or a boss? Is 'the management' simply a group of people who tell others what to do? Certainly, the word 'manager' is a relatively new addition to the English language. It comes from the Latin words *manus*, which means 'hand' and *agere* which means 'to set in motion, to carry along, to act'.

Defining management

A manager is someone who directs processes. We can state that a manager is someone who gets work done through other people by initiating and directing actions. As an executive, a manager takes decisions time and time again about what work has to be done, how it has to be done, and who has to do it. As a result, the manager has to be prepared to give explanations at any time. All levels of management – the managing director, supervisor, foreman or boss – sit at the cross-roads between work group, team, department, company, parent group and the societal environment.

The word 'management' can have three different meanings in common usage. In this book, which is intended as a review and discussion of practice as well as a means of preparing for that practice, all three meanings are used, so it is important to be familiar with them.

1. The word 'management' indicates all the employees in an organization whose job it is to set in motion, prepare and control the actions of other people and resources, given the objectives – implicit or explicit – of the organization. This meaning is expressed in sentences like: 'The management had a meeting at 10 am.'
2. The word 'management' means the process or activities (thinking as well as acting) which have to be executed in order to get something done. This meaning is expressed in sentences like: 'The management of a world tour involves a vast amount of work.'
3. 'Management' is a specific field of knowledge and discipline in which the everyday work and the phenomena of 'managers' and 'organizations' are studied. This meaning can be found in sentences like: 'I am taking an exam in management next week.'

This book is intended as a basic introduction to the study of management (Definition 3) in which management is considered both as a group of employees in an organization (Definition 1) and as a process made up of discrete but interrelated activities (Definition 2).

Characteristics of managers

It is the responsibility of managers to accomplish tasks and goals through other people, often without being able to exert direct or substantial influence over what those people do and how they do it.

Dependency on others

In principle, a manager is dependent on the dedication and contributions of other people. This applies as much to top managers as it does to all other managers in the organization. Often this dependency relates to colleagues with whom there is a direct line of authority. However, it can also involve reliance on employees from other parts of the company, departments or divisions, with whom there is no direct line of authority. Managers then need to develop ways of working through which they can gain the co-operation of all those from whom a contribution is required in order to reach the specified goals and objectives.

Responsibility for the working climate

As the leader of a company, department or division, a manager is responsible for creating a good working climate. The manager has to stimulate co-operation. There has to be a certain degree of harmony between the work that has to be done and the needs of the individuals and groups. A manager also has joint responsibility for the staffing of his or her department, division or working unit, for education and training, assessment, promotion and for motivating employees.

Receiving and transmitting information

A manager has to be well informed at all times about what is going on both outside and within the organizational unit. If problems are to be spotted and dealt with in time, information is required. The organizational unit must receive sufficient and timely information in order to be able to react to events effectively.

Decision making

All managers will face unexpected situations even though they may strive for and prefer planned action. Sometimes, problems are ignored for a long time and this can result eventually in an acute crisis – for example, a conflict between departments or divisions, or between subordinates in work groups, or a sudden disruption to the supply of essential resources. Managers have to find solutions and take decisions regarding these problems. As a first priority they have to implement immediate short-term measures, so that work can be resumed as soon as possible. They then have to look in depth for more fundamental adjustments or changes in aspects of the organization, such as structure and policies, to prevent the same problems from happening again.

Time management

Managers need to possess good time management skills. The need for joint consultation and participation in various work situations, for example, makes it important for the manager to learn the 'art' and skills of effective meetings and communication. Setting priorities and delegating to others, whenever possible, are very important. Prioritizing is a key skill for everyone who wants to work effectively.

Field knowledge and focus on results

Managers need to have knowledge of the specific field in which they work and should be results-oriented, for themselves as well as for the company as a whole.

Minicase 1.2

Prize for the messiest desk

Priority Management is a Dutch company providing training directed at improving on-the-job performance. For the second year in a row, Priority Management is holding a competition to find the messiest desk in the Netherlands. In association with an international 'Clean Up Your Desk Day', the competition draws attention to the unholy mess of some desks. In many organizations huge piles of paper on a desk are still mistakenly considered to be a sign of the occupant's diligence and prestige. Nothing could be further from the truth. A messy desk is bad for productivity and a cause of stress.

It has become evident from research that many people in management and data processing positions have over 30 hours of work on their desk. On average it will take three hours to sort through such a pile of work.

Everyone at Priority Management can enter the competition or they can nominate someone else by sending in a picture or a description of the desk, with details of the occupant. The winner is rewarded with an appropriate prize – a free management training course!

Source: Adapted from *Noordhollands Dagblad*, 28 December 1994.

1.1.2 Organizations and organizing

In companies or institutions, people work together, with technical, information and financial resources all being used in order to reach specific goals.

An *organization* is a *co-operative goal-realizing unit* in which participants consciously enter into a mutual relationship and work together in order to attain common goals. These goals can often be best realized by means of joint effort rather than when individuals act alone. Thus, an organization is the 'instrument' used to make products or provide services which meet the needs of society and of individual people.

An organization does not come into being by chance. Organizations are always the result of *conscious decision making* and *actions*. This is what we call *organizing*. Organizing as an activity is the *creating of effective relationships* between available people, resources and actions in order to attain certain goals.

A good organization ... effective and efficient

A good organization is one in which people work purposefully, are goal-oriented and try to make efficient use of available resources. In organizations where people work at cross-purposes, strive for different goals, or use up more resources and time than is really necessary, we then talk of actions and behaviour that are *ineffective* (that is, failing to attain multiple goals) and *inefficient* (that is, wasting skills and resources). Specified goals are not reached or, when they are reached, more resources have been used and more time taken than would have been necessary in an organization where work is carried out effectively and efficiently.

In this case goals are reached according to plan, on time, and at the lowest possible costs, and the people who work in such an organization experience high levels of job satisfaction. They like their work and derive *intrinsic* satisfaction from it. In this sense, good organizing and a good organization constitute the most important conditions for success.

Organizations ... in all shapes and sizes

Organizations come in all sorts of shapes and sizes: profit and non-profit organizations and institutions; industrial companies and service industries; private and government-controlled firms; large, medium-sized and small companies; national and multinational companies; charities and voluntary organizations; unions, political organizations and so on. Whatever grouping we choose, all organizations have certain common features:

- *people* who
- *work together* and *co-operate*
- in order to reach a *specific set of goals*.

Why do they do this? For the 'simple' reason that an organization is a powerful instrument which performs actions that can never be matched by an individual working alone and through which it is possible to accomplish goals which could not be reached otherwise.

As with the word 'management', the word 'organization' can be defined in three different ways:

1. It can be used in the *institutional* sense – for example, when we want to identify a company or association, such as Philips, IKEA, Marks & Spencer, Volvo, The Red Cross.
2. It can have an *instrumental* meaning, referring to the internal arrangement, especially the structure, of a company or institution. An example of this use is: 'We are going to improve the organization of the company as it does not currently contribute to the realization of our goals.' This concerns elements such as division of work, co-ordination, decision-making processes and planning and policy procedures.
3. It can be used in the *functional* sense, by which we mean the process of carrying out a set of activities. For example: 'The organization of the party was very poor.'

1.1.3 The nature of today's management

When we look at the past, it becomes clear that management was involved whenever people wanted to accomplish something by means of joint effort. Think, for example, of the building of the pyramids in Egypt, the Coliseum in Rome or the Great Wall of China. When we consider how the stones were cut and transported over great distances in order for them to be used in such impressive construction projects, it is clear that leading and masterminding these projects must have demanded excellent management skills. No wonder that in the ancient documents of philosophers like Plato and Xenophon, we find passages which are devoted to management. In one of his debates on management, Socrates says, for example:

> *. . . if a man knows what he wants and can get it, he will be a good controller, whether he controls a chorus, an estate, a city or an army. Don't look down on businessmen . . . For the management of private concerns differs only in point of number from that of public affairs . . . neither can be carried on without men . . . and the men employed in private and public transactions are the same . . . and those who understand how to employ them are successful directors . . . and those who do not, fail in both . . .*
>
> Taken from: Socrates' debates as noted by Xenophon in: *Memorabilia* (III.IV. 6–12) and *Oeconomicus.*

These statements are still valid today, because they are based on experience. The same applies to a number of management principles which were already in use in ancient Rome and which will be covered later in this book – for example, **unity of direction**, **hierarchy**, **chain of command** and **unity of command**, **centralization/decentralization**, **line relations** and **staff relations** (*see* Chapters 6 and 7).

Developments over the last 200 years have given us the following important elements of modern management:

- the interrelationship between business and society;
- business growth and internationalization;
- changes in power/authority relations;
- the role of science and technology;
- marketing 'philosophy'.

The interrelationship between business and society

The time when a business enjoyed an almost totally autonomous position in society is long gone. Never before has there been so much influence exerted by society on what happens within a business and other forms of labour organization as is the case at the end of the twentieth century. The extent of this influence is apparent from contemporary ideas about the objectives and goals of a company and the way in which people think these should be realized. In their roles as societal stakeholders, people now make demands with regard to:

- the *optimal satisfaction* of the needs, wishes and requirements of the consumer;
- the *spending* of profits;
- the provision of appropriate *employment*, which suits the qualitative and quantitative supply and demand in the region;
- the promotion of the well-being of every employee through the creation of a *favourable working environment*, as well as a contribution to the upkeep of that environment;
- the guarantee of reasonable *compensation* to suppliers of capital and employees for their contributions to the company.

Other demands on organizations include governmental policies on health, safety and welfare, regulations concerning the environment, regulations with regard to minimum wages and the social security system, not to mention the efforts of consumers' associations and trade unions. In addition, there are government policies with regard to the realization of economic markets like the European Union (EU) and regulations concerning wages, pricing policy and so on.

Business growth and internationalization

In recent times many organizations have transformed themselves by increasing the size of their business (either through internal growth or through acquisitions and mergers) and by arranging their operations on an increasingly international basis.

After the Second World War, a large number of countries and continents became increasingly interdependent in the economic, social and strategic sphere. Within Europe, a supranational co-operation was created (the EU) and, after the disappearance of the so-called Iron Curtain in the late 1980s, all kinds of relations became possible between the former Eastern bloc countries and the West. In addition, Japan and South-East Asia became new economic superpowers. Continents like Africa, parts of Asia and South America, because of their relative poverty, played less of a role in international trade.

Enormous technological developments have encouraged international co-operation. Many small, national companies could not afford the enormous investments that the developments involved so they merged. Internationalization and the increase in business size mean that new problems have arisen in the cultural–technical sphere, which have been a big influence on present-day entrepreneurs and managers.

Changes in power/authority relations

It is important to make the distinction between authority and power. **Authority** is the legal or official right to exert a certain influence. **Power** is the capacity to influence the behaviour of others and to get others to act in a certain manner, possibly even forcibly. The number of people who exert influence or authority over others without having the legal authority to do so has greatly increased in recent times. Within a company, the formal authority is still with the shareholders, but in reality a number of people can 'pull the strings'.

Prestige is paramount. Acceptance of authority through personal prestige is crucial to effective implementation. Having prestige means that employees are spontaneously willing to co-operate and accept the exerted authority without objections (and without the necessity to invoke the legitimate possibilities of punishment that are anchored in the formal entitlement).

To clarify, it might be wise to speak of '*positional authority*' (formal competence) and '*personal prestige*' as the basis of power instead of authority. People have power when they possess or have at their disposal the resources and characteristics with which they can motivate others to do things that they otherwise would not do, or with which they can at least influence the behaviour of others. To speak of the exercise of power means for someone to use his or her authority and prestige, and thereby influence (for example, by means of communication) the behaviour and ideas of others.

All this means that the influence which managers can exert partly depends on *the willingness of others to listen*. When managers have little or no prestige at their disposal, then the simple fact that they have a degree of authority will not be enough to determine the way work is carried out in the organization. The relatively high level of education and development of the average employee means that the exercise of power is less and less likely to be based simply on the possession of resources of production and formal authority. Real influence has to be supported by ability and competence, and has to be experienced as being useful and fair in relation to the task.

Role of science and technology

Areas of management science, such as **operations research**, **cybernetics** and **information technology** have gradually developed into management tools. These areas of study are so sophisticated and powerful that some believe that one day the taking of decisions will be one of the jobs of a computer. Others refute this on the basis that the human brain is too complex to be completely simulated with the aid of digital technology. After all, it will be people who pose the problems, interpret the information and set priorities. In management today and tomorrow, the emphasis will be on the accurate timing of decisions crucial to the survival of the organization. Central to this will be the creativity which makes this possible and which stimulates new developments.

The development of a marketing philosophy

The development of a marketing philosophy has helped management to realize that the actual goal of the organization lies outside the organization itself, namely in the market. The customers or clients who buy products or services will eventually decide if an organization is to reach its goals and survive.

1.1.4 The nature of labour organizations

The organizations featured in this book are all labour organizations in which work in terms of paid labour is being carried out. Such organizations have the following features.

Specific goals

Companies and institutions have specific goals such as making a profit, working to a budget, attaining a market share. Small organizations often have a limited (not formally established) but still clearly recognizable goal. In larger organizations, goals are formally established for purposes of clarification.

Exhibit 1.1

Most admired attributes of Europe's most respected companies

Business & management performance

ABB	Swe/Switz	Engineering
British Airways	UK	Transport
Nestlé	Switzerland	Food processors
BMW	Germany	Automobiles
Bertelsmann	Germany	Media, printing & advertising
British Petroleum	UK	Oil, gas & mining

Effective corporate strategy

ABB	Swe/Switz	Engineering
British Airways	UK	Transport
Nestlé	Switzerland	Food processors
BMW	Germany	Automobiles
Reuters	UK	Media, printing & advertising
Royal Dutch Shell	Netherlands/UK	Oil, gas & mining

Impressive improvement in performance

British Airways	UK	Transport
British Petroleum	UK	Oil, gas & mining
ABB	Swe/Switz	Engineering
Philips	Netherlands	Electronics
ASDA	UK	Retail & distribution
Ericsson	Sweden	Electronics
ING	Netherlands	Banks & financial institutions

Strongest corporate brand image

BMW	Germany	Automobiles
Nestlé	Switzerland	Food processors
British Airways	UK	Transport
ABB	Swe/Switz	Engineering
Daimler	Germany	Automobiles
Royal Dutch Shell	Netherlands/UK	Oil, gas & mining

Maximum long-term value to shareholders

Royal Dutch Shell	Netherlands/UK	Oil, gas & mining
ABB	Swe/Switz	Engineering
Nestlé	Switzerland	Food processors
Roche	Switzerland	Pharmaceuticals
Glaxo-Wellcome	UK	Pharmaceuticals
SAP	Germany	Computers, office equip.
VEBA	Germany	Oil, gas & mining

Maximises potential of its employees

ABB	Swe/Switz	Engineering
British Airways	UK	Transport
Bertelsmann	Germany	Media, printing & advertising
Marks & Spencer	UK	Retail & distribution
Nestlé	Switzerland	Food processors
Unilever	Netherlands/UK	Food processors

Best at satisfying its customers

British Airways	UK	Transport
Marks & Spencer	UK	Retail & distribution
BMW	Germany	Automobiles
Virgin	UK	Transport
Daimler	Germany	Automobiles
Reuters	UK	Media, printing & advertising
ABB	Swe/Switz	Engineering

Best balances stakeholder interest

British Airways	UK	Transport
Marks & Spencer	UK	Retail & distribution
ABB	Swe/Switz	Engineering
Nestlé	Switzerland	Food processors
Royal Dutch Shell	Netherlands/UK	Oil, gas & mining
BMW	Germany	Automobiles
Siemens	Germany	Electronics

Best response to privatisation

British Airways	UK	Transport
BT	UK	Telecoms
PowerGen	UK	Electricity & water
KPN	Netherlands	Telecoms
Repsol	Spain	Oil, gas & mining
BAA	UK	Transport

Completed the best-judged recent merger or acquisition

Novartis	Switzerland	Pharmaceuticals
Glaxo-Wellcome	UK	Pharmaceuticals
BMW	Germany	Automobiles
Granada	UK	Entertainment & leisure
Rentokil	UK	Diversified holding companies
ABN Amro	Netherlands	Bank & financial institutions
Fortis	Bel/Neth	Insurance
ING	Netherlands	Bank & financial institutions

Most innovative in its business approach

Virgin	UK	Transport
ABB	Swe/Switz	Engineering
Benetton	Italy	Household textiles & clothing
British Airways	UK	Transport
Nokia	Finland	Electronics
SAP	Germany	Computers, office equip.

Most effective use of technology

Nokia	Finland	Electronics
Reuters	UK	Media, printing & advertising
Ericsson	Sweden	Electronics
ABB	Swe/Switz	Engineering
BMW	Germany	Automobiles
Siemens	Germany	Electronics
Philips	Netherlands	Electronics
SAP	Germany	Computers, office equip.

Highest standards of ethical business conduct

Marks & Spencer	UK	Retail & distribution
Royal Dutch Shell	Netherlands/UK	Oil, gas & mining
ABB	Swe/Switz	Engineering
Nestlé	Switzerland	Food processors
Body Shop	UK	Retail & distribution
British Airways	UK	Transport
Bayer	Germany	Chemicals, rubber & plastics
Bosch	Germany	Automobiles
Volvo	Sweden	Automobiles
Swissair	Switzerland	Transport
Unilever	UK/Netherlands	Food processors

Deals best with environment issues

Royal Dutch Shell	Netherlands/UK	Oil, gas & mining
Nestlé	Switzerland	Food processors
British Petroleum	UK	Oil, gas & mining
ABB	Swe/Switz	Engineering
Ciba	Switzerland	Pharmaceuticals & healthcare
ICI	UK	Chemicals, rubber & plastics

Serves as a benchmark

ABB	Swe/Switz	Engineering
British Petroleum	UK	Oil, gas & mining
Royal Dutch Shell	Netherlands/UK	Oil, gas & mining
British Airways	UK	Transport
Reuters	UK	Media, printing & advertising
Siemens	Germany	Electronics
Marks & Spencer	UK	Retail & distribution

Source: Financial Times, 10 September 1996.

Deployment of trained labour

Much of the work in organizations is performed by people who have been especially educated/trained for that purpose. In the 'staffing' of the organization, special attention is given to skills, so selection, education and training are important in this context.

Formalized communication

In a company or institution, people need to communicate, to consult each other, and to exchange information for the sake of co-ordination and the resolution of problems in decision-making processes. When companies become larger, informal communication will eventually not be adequate and the exchange of information will need to be organized by way of consultative and communication structures – for example, regular consultation, committee meetings, interdepartmental consultation, work group meetings, meetings of departmental heads or supervisors, etc.

Formal rules of behaviour, procedures and control

In organizations, a certain standard of labour behaviour needs to be in place. Procedures need to be used (for the sake of co-ordination) and results controlled and compared by feeding back or feeding forward information. In the light of the goals or objectives of the organization adjustments may have to be made in the cycle of planning, execution and control.

Layers of authority

In labour organizations, certain people have the authority to issue instructions for the execution of activities to other employees. Authority means the right (based on a formally assigned competence) (*see* section 1.2) to give orders. This right can be given by the organization's board of directors or by another person who is in turn authorized to do so. In this way authority can be seen as *positional power*.

Division of labour

In labour organizations, the work that has to be carried out needs to be divided in such a way that each employee (taking into account, among other things, individual competences and skills) can perform a range of tasks without being overloaded. In other words, a formal system of labour division and structuring of work and tasks needs to exist.

1.2 ● THE COMPANY: ITS GOVERNANCE STRUCTURE AND MANAGEMENT

A *company* or *corporation* is a distinct entity in society with its own 'personality' and 'identity' formally distinguished from those of its owners. The owners are not personally liable for the company's debts; it can hold property and can do business in its own right. A company continues to exist as an entity even though the individuals who own it may change time and time again. In contrast, a *partnership* is automatically dissolved on the death or departure of one of the owners, unless special arrangements have been made in the agreement.

The holders of common stock (that is, the shareholders) are the true owners of the company and have the power to control it. Directors are elected by shareholders; they select and nominate the president and other executive officers of the company, who together make up the senior management team or board of management. The precise structure and the terms used to identify the levels of the organizational structure vary according to whether the system adopted is a 'one-tier' or 'two-tier' system (*see* section 3.5.5).

The governance structure of a large company whose shares are widely held by the public is sometimes pictured like an hour-glass (*see* Fig 1.1). At the top are thousands and thousands of shareholders. The structure then narrows down to the board of directors. (In a two-tier system (*see* section 3.5.5) this would consist of non-executives only and there would be a second tier of senior management in the form of a board of management or executive committee headed by the Chief Executive Officer (CEO) as president.) Below the president is a rather small group of executive managers, a larger group of **middle managers**, an even larger group of **front-line managers** or supervisors and, last but not least, all the other employees at the operational core of the organization.

The board of directors constitutes the bridge between the shareholders and society on the one hand and the managers of the corporate organization on the other. They are supposed to exercise broad supervision in terms of setting objectives, establishing policy and appraising the results of actions.

As representatives of shareholders and other societal stakeholders – such as employees and unions, consumer organizations and banks – the directors must pay sufficient attention to the business, show interest in the company – from a certain distance in the case of non-executive directors – and exercise prudent control in the management of

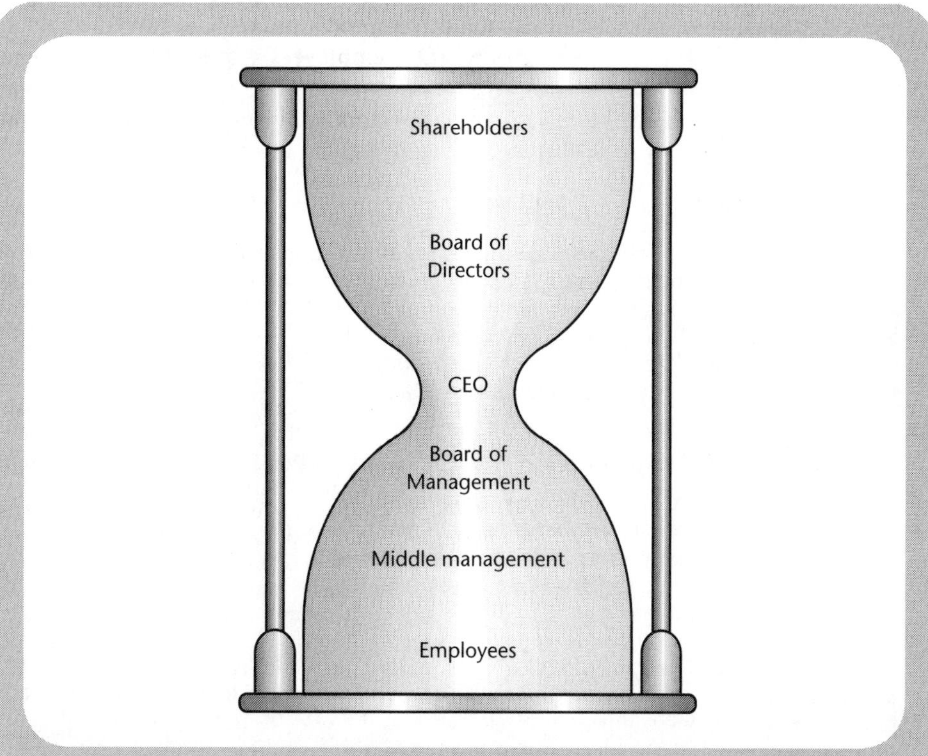

Fig 1.1 ● Hour-glass model of the company, indicating governance structure and management levels in the organization

the company's affairs. In a publicly quoted company the board of directors consists of anything from three to twelve members, although it could be even larger. Small companies tend to have rather small boards; some companies, such as banks and public government organizations, have larger boards – sometimes 20 or more members.

Directors select and nominate (and eventually dismiss) the chief executive and other executive officers, determine their remuneration and act as a court of the last resort when managers disagree. They can issue new stock on to the market; they must authorize capital spending over a certain amount; and they concern themselves with corporate objectives and with strategy, such as the type of business the company should be in, develop, enter or leave. They determine what proportion of the company's profits will be paid out in dividends and what proportion will be retained by the company. Under a system of co-option they would normally nominate their own successors, with the formal nomination subject to election by shareholders.

Exhibit 1.2

How high can CEO pay go?

In a year of downsizing and layoffs, compensation rose by 30%, on average

CEO PAY	CORPORATE PROFITS	WORKER PAY	WORKER LAYOFFS
+92%	+75%	+16%	+39%
1990	1990	1990	1990
$1.95 million	$176 million	$22,976	$316,047
1995	1995	1995	1995
$3.75 million	$308 million	$26,652	$439,882

Angry voices. Yet back in the factories and offices of the far-flung conglomerate, some employees are stirring – as they are at companies large and small across the country. In an era of massive downsizings, stagnant wages, and ever more burdensome workloads for layoff survivors, employees are feeling disenfranchised, discouraged, and angry.

Despite consistently good performance reviews, a $64,000-a-year manager with nearly two decades of service to the company has averaged a mere 4% pay raise in each of the past three years. 'At the same time, the CEO is paid millions, and his salary is going up much higher than anyone else's,' he adds. 'It makes me angry and resentful.'

The average salary and bonus for a chief executive rose by 18% last year, to £1,653,670 – slightly above the 15% gain in corporate profits. But throw in gains from long-term compensation such as stock options, and the CEO's average total pay climbed 30%, to $3,746,392. The boss's pay not only outstripped last year's 2.8% inflation rate, but also the pay of both white-collar professionals, who averaged a 4.2% gain, and of factory employees, who received a 1% raise.

Those are the primary conclusions of BUSINESS WEEK'S 46th annual Executive Pay Scoreboard, compiled with Standard & Poor's Compustat Services, a division of The McGraw-Hill Companies. The survey examines the compensation of the two top-paid executives at 362 of the largest companies.

While workers express anger over rising CEO pay, many have benefited from the runup in stock prices through investments in mutual funds and pensions saving plans for retirement. And more companies are handing stock options and incentive bonuses to workers further down in the organization.

Source: *Business Week*, 22 April 1996.

The CEO, generally the company president in European-based companies, is likely to be the chief policy maker in the company although others are expected to make recommendations and will influence decisions. The CEO has probably the final word on most of the important questions that arise. Even in companies where organization charts show a group of apparent equals at the top, there is often one man or woman who is first among the equals – *the primus inter pares*.

In the case of group control and group decision making at the top, some executives may be freed from day-to-day operational duties (or at least a proportion of them) in order to devote themselves entirely to overall policy issues. Such a top management structure can address itself to issues concerning strategy, planning, organization and control and may also deal with specific functional issues which need overall co-ordination, thus bringing more than one mind to bear on the company's most serious problems. It is easier to consider problems with an open mind when not operationally involved and committed to previous decisions and, since members of the top management group are more or less equals, this stimulates free discussion.

This group structure may work well in some companies; in others it will be less successful. Success depends largely on the personalities of group members. On the one hand, some work well together, supplementing each other's knowledge and experience and stimulating ideas. For others, the group structure might dilute the sense of responsibility and perhaps give rise to a tendency to postpone necessary actions.

Against this background three important functions of a board of directors can be identified:

- The board provides advice and counsel.
- The board serves as a source of discipline.
- The board acts in crisis situations.

A typical meeting of a board of directors might have some of the following items on the agenda:

- Consideration of a refinancing plan
- Liquidation of obsolete or surplus plant
- Dividend action
- Consideration of an acquisition proposed by top management
- Company's position and risk of devaluation abroad
- A report on research and development programmes and products.

In a one-tier system, such as that common in UK companies, few if any questions are usually asked during the meeting by external non-executive directors, and questions are only rarely asked by internal executive directors. It is generally accepted that it is the role of the board of directors:

1. to establish the basic objectives, corporate strategies and broad policies of the company;
2. to ask discerning questions; and
3. to select the president.

Assessing management – that is fulfilling the key function of deciding whether management is doing a good job – and facing the difficult question of whether management has to be changed are difficult tasks for an external director.

For example ...

... in a company with 15 board members, eight of whom were insiders, earnings had declined steadily for 18 months. Concerned about the company's leadership, the seven external directors met to discuss what, if anything, should be done. Most of the directors reluctantly concluded that the president had to be replaced, but two directors put forward alternative solutions. They suggested that the president be promoted to a post created for the occasion – vice-chairman of the board; that the president be appointed head of the finance committee; or that the president be retained and the vice-president be asked to take over as chief executive officer. These suggested compromises were rejected by the other five external directors and the president was forced to resign.

For example ...

... according to one president: 'The board of directors serves as a sounding board, a wall to bounce the ball against. It is a kind of screen on major moves, whether it be acquisitions, or whether it be major shifts of policy or product line – the broad decisions of the business. Board members serve as sources of information ... The decision is not made by the board, but the directors are a checkpoint for the management in adding their experience and knowledge to the programme.'

According to another president: 'Let's be honest. My board is a group of advisors and they know it. I select and throw up ideas, opportunities and problems to them and they respond. The board is not a decision-making body. Although there may be times when it could rise up and say no, this would be foolhardy. But I hope that we in management are never stupid enough to come up with such a proposal.'

A third president had this to say: 'One of my outside directors is a real "pro" on acquisitions and he has been most helpful to me. He does not know much about our operations or our problems, but he does know a lot about the process of identifying and acquiring other companies. Also he knows the people involved, and this is useful. There is a lot of stuff on acquisitions that is common to all acquisitions. He has been through a bundle of them and has helped me out of some tight spots – in negotiating, for example.

(*Source*: Adapted from Directors: Myth and Reality by Mace, 1986)

Owner–managers of small corporations possess and exercise *de jure* powers of control, because for them ownership is the same as management. Owner-managers, therefore, determine what directors do or do not do. This is also often the case in family-owned companies.

In large and medium-sized companies where ownership is spread and dissipated among thousands of shareholders, the powers of ownership, while theoretically equivalent to those of the small company owner–managers, are actually minimal and almost non-existent.

Presidents of these companies have assumed and do exercise *de facto* powers of control over the companies for which they are responsible. To them the shareholders constitute what is in effect an anonymous mass of paper faces. Thus, presidents in these situations determine what directors do or do not do. As was found by Myles L. Mace (1986), most presidents choose to exercise their powers of control in a moderate and acceptable manner with regard to their relationships with boards of directors. They do communicate, however, either explicitly or implicitly, that they, as presidents, control the enterprise they are heading and this is generally understood and accepted by the directors. Many non-executive directors are presidents of companies themselves and they thoroughly understand the existence and location of powers of control.

Exhibit 1.3

Directors in family corporations

... In family-controlled corporations the board of directors does serve as sources of advice and counsel, but the advice and counsel are deemed to be primarily for the benefit of the family. If a member of the family is president, the directors' advice was found to be useful to the president. But if the family members in control of the company have employed a nonfamily professional manager as president, the directors' advice-and-counsel role then was deemed to be primarily for the benefit of the family group, and secondarily for the nonfamily president. Generally it was found that dominant family members communicated to the outside-the-family board members that one of their important roles was to advise the family of their opinions of the company.

It was found that directors of family enterprises, in addition to serving as sources of advice and counsel to the family, served as arbitrators and conciliators in helping to resolve the high-emotion crisis issues sometimes encountered in family situations. The conflicts, rivalries, guilt feelings, ambitions, loyalties, prides, resentments, and interrelationships of family members in the same organization inevitably result in controversies which mature and skillful outside directors can, and do, help resolve.

Because of family suspicions, it was found to be extremely important for the outside director to maintain the utmost calm and objectivity under the tension and stress perpetrated by emotional family combatants. Family business differences and quarrels are distinctive from differences and quarrels encountered in nonfamily companies. In family companies members of the group feel privileged, and it seems in some cases almost obligated, to be as personally offensive and insulting as possible. Comments below any respectable standard of social behavior are exchanged among family members, and it is the wise director who hears but does not visibly react, and who restrains from approving or disapproving the points made by any of the participants. Blood – for those who have not served as directors of family corporations – is thicker than water. One effective way of unifying the antagonistic members of a family business conflict is for the nonfamily director to be critical or disapproving of the behavior of some member of the family. While this is an effective device for the reunification of feuding family business executives, the outside director may find the price high in that the usual next step is that he is asked to resign from the board.

In family-controlled companies the selection and deselection of corporation presidents typically was found to be made by the dominant representative of the family in control of the company. It was found that fathers generally – especially entrepreneurial-type company-founding fathers – are incapable of making an objective evaluation of the qualifications of their sons or relatives as candidates for the position of president. In some cases the members of the board were able to advise and counsel the dominant family member, but in most cases the decision-making power was in the family members, whether they were numerically in the majority on the board or not.

As was the case in large companies, there were a few family-controlled companies in which the dominant family member chose to treat the enterprise like a publicly held company, and to regard the board of directors as the controlling layer of top management. In these situations the board of directors did, in fact, select, appraise, and evaluate the president; determine corporate objectives, strategies, and broad policies; ask discerning questions; and perform the other advisory and discipline roles. But, these situations were rare.

Source: An extract from *Directors: Myth and Reality* by Mace, 1986.

Our firm

Predominance of family companies in local economy, 1994 estimates, %

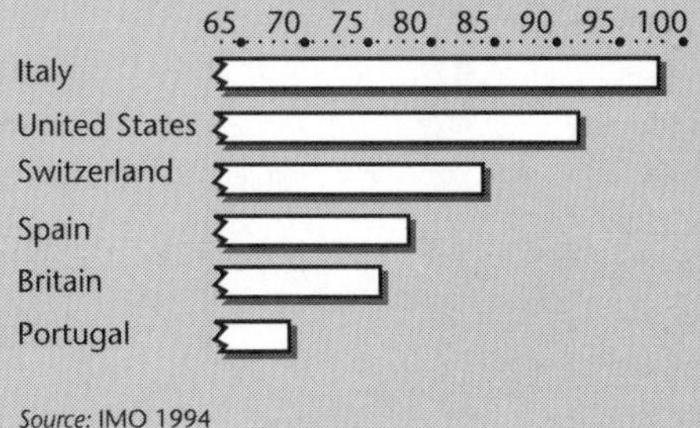

Source: IMO 1994

1.3 ● LEVELS OF MANAGEMENT IN AN ORGANIZATION

Having considered what managers and organizations are (*see* section 1.1) and how they are built up in layers in the governance structure (*see* section 1.2), we will now examine the different levels of management within the organization in greater detail. The levels that can usually be distinguished within companies and institutions are:

- top or senior management;
- middle management; and
- front-line management and operational employees.

In the hierarchy of a company each of these layers has its own job specification with corresponding responsibilities.

If a large number of management layers is discernible with limited scope of control and little delegation, we speak of a '*tall*' or '*steep*' organization. If, on the other hand, only a few management layers are present with extensive scope of control and a high degree of delegation, we speak of a '*flat*' organization (*see* Fig 1.2).

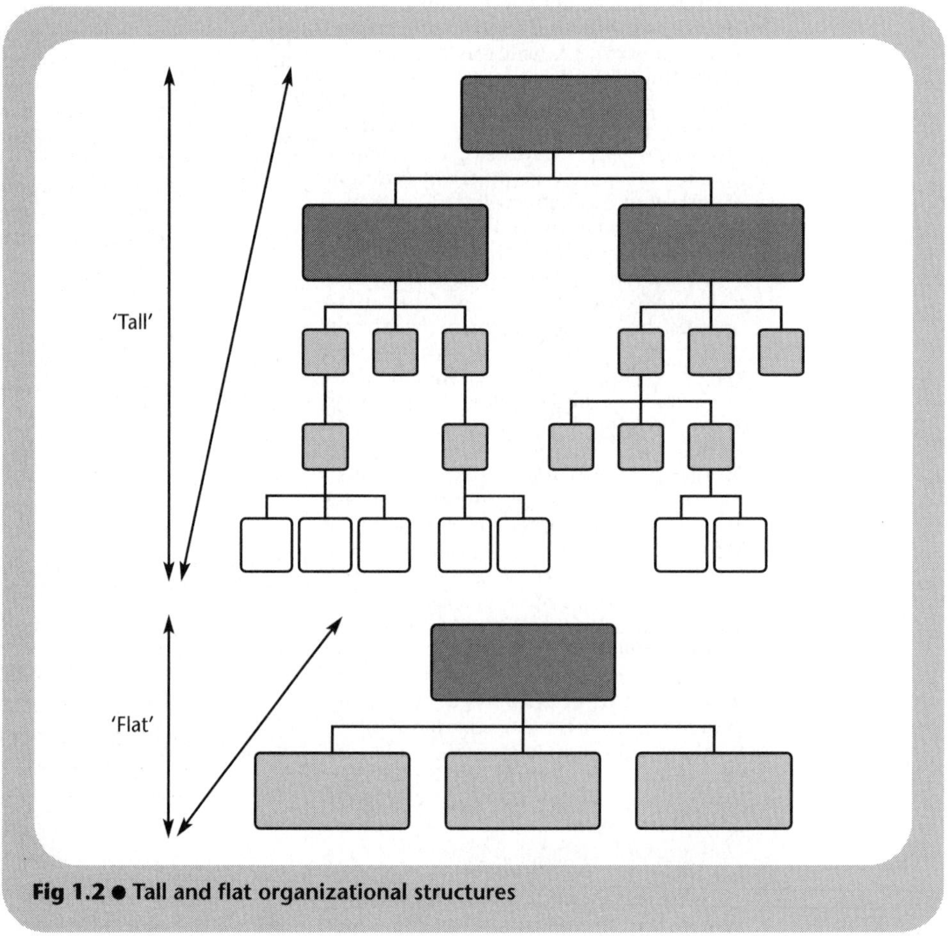

Fig 1.2 ● Tall and flat organizational structures

1.3.1 Top management tasks

By **top management** we mean, for example, the owner–leader–manager of the company, the chief executive, the board of directors or the board of management of a hospital or a union. Figure 1.3 shows the position of top management in relation to the wider external environment and the other levels of management in the internal organization of the company.

The task of top management in the organization is to give content to the relationships between the organization and the market and the wider societal environment in such a way that the continued existence of the organization is secured. To do this, strategic decisions are needed. These decisions concern the long-term mission and the route to be followed by the organization in its external positioning. Furthermore, all those measurements need to be taken at the top that allow the implementation of the decisions about the products and services in relation to the markets and consumer groups. Organizational and administrative arrangements must be made. Middle management can then make the required detailed organizational and operational decisions. In a company, the assignment of responsibility, tasks and authority to managers further down the line and to specialists in staff and support services takes place by means of delegation. Nevertheless, top management retains its own responsibility for the management of the entire operation of the company.

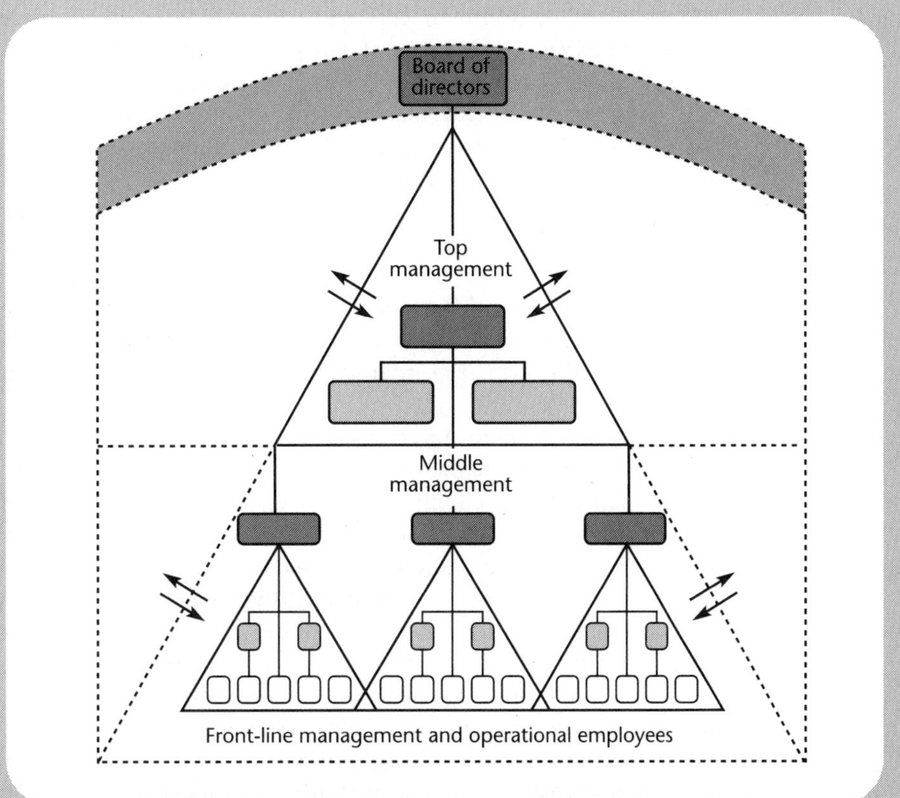

Fig 1.3 ● Position of top management in relation to the board of directors, lower levels and the societal environment

The management of a Public Limited Company (PLC) in the United Kingdom – Societé Anonyme (SA) in France, Naamloze Vennootschap (NV) in the Netherlands, Aktiengesellschaft (AG) in Germany – has to periodically render an account with regard to the fulfilment of tasks and the results reached. After audit and approval, *discharge* is granted. Discharge means that, after a review of policy and auditing of results and procedures, management is discharged of further obligations for the period in question. In other words, it is established that top management has done everything possible to attain a satisfactory result. Owners (shareholders) are then expected to be satisfied. On behalf of the shareholders, the board of directors exercises the ultimate supervision over management as specified in section 1.2.

1.3.2 Middle-management tasks

As top management cannot concern itself with all the activities of the organization, middle management has responsibility for the timely and accurate execution of operational activities.

In the organization, middle management has both an executive function 'towards the top' and a managerial function 'towards the bottom'. This means that middle management is positioned at the point where the interests of the different layers of the organization cross. In principle, the term 'middle management' refers to the managers positioned 'in the line' under top management – that is, assistant directors, production managers, marketing managers and sales managers – and above the front-line managers – for example, the heads of department, team leaders and supervisors.

In an organization which is built up on a division basis, the divisional managers are also considered as middle management. In large organizations, therefore, a number of layers of middle management can be found. These can be referred to as 'higher middle management' and 'lower middle management'.

Higher middle management directs the activities of lower management and sometimes that of executives. The most important responsibilities of these higher middle managers are translating the strategic decisions and policy of top management and assisting in directing the operational activities. In this respect, it is particularly important for them to strike a balance between the demands from the top and the capacity of the front-line management to satisfy these demands. They perform a kind of buffer function.

Middle management has increasingly come under fire in recent years. Its function varies according to the manager's position relative to top management and operations. As the managers move higher up the hierarchical ladder, they will have more planning and organizing to do, while at the lower levels they will be more concerned with instructing, motivation and operational control. As a result the position of managers in the middle is particularly difficult; they are, so to speak, pinned between the top layer and the lowest levels, and are under pressure from both. From a leadership perspective (that is, from the point of view of maintaining and developing good relations, motivating and stimulating) these middle managers seem to have a considerably tougher task than the managing director at the very top of the ladder.

Middle management has to translate the plans of top management into the daily execution of tasks. It has the authority, to a greater or lesser degree, to direct operational activities. Operational execution is directly supervised and operational problems are identified on the spot. If these involve several departments, higher management needs to be called in.

Middle managers spend a great deal of their time on managerial activities (motivating and operational execution) and on organizing the activities of other people.

Responsibilities of middle management include formulating departmental policies, making departmental plans, maintaining network contacts for the company (both internally and externally), the timely gathering of information to help assess and amend operational results, and reporting to the higher management on the execution of operations.

1.3.3 Front-line management and operational employees

Front-line managers at the operations level are directly responsible for the work carried out by other operational employees.

For example ...

... Harry Jones is responsible for a machine in a door factory. At his machine, two panels are glued together to form a door. The panels pass through a stretch of 12 metres. Three employees who have to be directed and coached by Harry work along the stretch of this machine. Harry is responsible not only for the quantity and quality of the doors, but also for the correct supply of materials, the correct supply and mix of glues and the maintenance of the machine.

The front-line managers coach and have management authority over the operational staff. The front-line manager is the immediate supervisor or 'boss' in the factory, office, or research department. To the operational staff the front-line manager is their 'real' and most direct boss. Other 'higher' bosses are indirect and often hardly visible, leading to questions concerning their contribution. The front-line positions are the key players in keeping the company in action and production. For this reason it is important that front-line managers know the problems of managing and organizing, are able to analyse the situations that can arise, to talk about these with higher management, and to translate solutions into terms of operational assignments and tasks.

'*Self-steering*' or *autonomous process-oriented teams* are increasingly taking the front-line management task into their own hands. In operations, resources (raw materials, components, information, etc.) are transformed into products and services. The management levels discussed earlier can be seen in this context as *formulators of policy* and *facilitators of conditions* with respect to the operational execution of tasks. They have a regulative and supportive relationship to the operational processes of production or to the rendering of services by which, for example, cars are assembled, machines are manufactured, reports are drawn up or patients are treated or cared for.

Operational staff have to concentrate on achieving the specified level of production or demanded level of service. The required output level and the way in which the work is to be done can be decided through consultation with operational staff. The allocation of tasks and the style of leadership are major determining factors in the commitment and motivation of operational staff. (In Chapters 7 and 8 we will cover this subject in more detail.)

Having examined the levels of management in an organization, for the remainder of this chapter we will consider the demands that are made of managers. Among other issues, attention will be given to decision making, time management, the workload of managers, and the *culture* of the organization.

1.4 CORE ACTIVITIES OF MANAGERS

So far we have considered management as a group of managers in an organization, placed above the operational staff, and have separated them into top management, middle management and front-line management. In principle these layers apply to all forms of organization – for example, in both profit-oriented and non-profit-making organizations.

1.4.1 Similarities between management levels

The most important task common to all managers is the direction of people and resources in an organization. According to Mintzberg (1973), managers divide their time between:

- interpersonal activities
- information-related activities and
- decision-making activities.

Interpersonal activities

Managers manage people. They are responsible for progress and for the results from processes which are under their authority. By maintaining network relations, they are able to control the processes as well as promote the interests of the group, both inside the organization at a higher level as well as to the outside. The building up of a formal and informal network of relationships inside as well as outside the organization is an integral part of this activity.

Information-related activities

To control an organization, managers need to have information at their disposal. That is why managers need to be kept informed of changes in the organization and the performance of the department. In turn, managers communicate with other members of the organization, stakeholders and other interested parties. Information is essential to enable managers to act and intervene appropriately in an ever-changing environment.

Decision-making activities

As head of a department, group or unit of the organization, the manager will have to give direction to the policies that are to be implemented. Based on information gathered and by maintaining personal contacts, the manager will take opportunities and threats in the environment and, with due consideration of the strengths and weaknesses of the organization, will translate these into management decisions. Over and over again, the manager has to be prepared to take decisions about the optimal use of people and resources in order to realize the goals. Managers cannot oversee everything, however; managers need their employees.

1.4.2 Differences between management levels

From the activities mentioned above, it appears that the manager spends a significant amount of time *communicating* with organization members and people and institutions outside the organization. However, this varies at each management level.

Top management

The demands made of top managers vary. From research involving 1500 top managers from 20 different countries, a new management profile can be outlined. The top management of tomorrow will have to excel in the following areas:

- strategy formulation
- human resources management
- marketing/sales
- conflict resolution/negotiating.

Marketing and sales are considered to be of lower importance than human resources management. This implies that more and more attention has to be paid to the 'people' aspects of the organization. Furthermore, researchers indicate that, in the twenty-first century, hostile takeovers, protectionism and company espionage will make the life of a top manager more difficult. This explains in part the relevance of negotiating and conflict resolution.

The top manager will have to be a 'great communicator' who can inspire employees. Furthermore, he or she will have to display *creativity*, *enthusiasm*, and an *open mind*. The top person will also have to have a 'clean past' in the ethical sense; and last but not least, the top manager will have to know how to behave like a politician, both inside and outside the company.

Middle management and front-line management

The largest group of managers is the layer under the top management of the organization – middle management. Middle management is important since it has to execute general policies and give direct **leadership** to the implementation of operations.

The most important tasks of middle management are:

- **leading** and **controlling** activities
- taking operational decisions
- passing on information from the top down and from the bottom up
- planning
- organizing activities
- motivating employees
- maintaining internal and external contacts
- reporting
- generating new activities.

With the tendency of top management to delegate authority, more and more policy formulating tasks are placed with the higher middle-management ranks. In organizations where change is taking place, middle management has a key position. After all, top management can think in terms of ambitious plans, but middle management will have to take these to the employees and motivate them to put the plans into action.

1.4.3 Managers and types of decisions

We have already stated that managers spend a certain amount of their time on decision-making activities (*see* section 1.4.1). We now consider the link between the position of a manager in the organization and the nature of the decisions to be taken and the amount of time spent on decision-making activities. (Decision making is discussed fully in Chapter 4.)

The decisions that need to be taken in organizations are widely varying in nature. In principle, we can distinguish three types of decisions in the management process:

- strategic decisions
- organizational (or administrative and tactical) decisions
- operational decisions.

Strategic decisions

Strategic decisions concern the selection of the objectives or goals of an organization, the choice and positioning of product–market activities, the choice of resources and the route by which the goals are attained. (*See* Chapter 5 for more detail.)

Since these decisions concern the entire organization, they need to be taken at the highest level. This does not mean, however, that employees at the lower managerial levels can be excluded from these decisions. On the contrary, they are a necessary source of information. The final decisions are nevertheless taken by the board of directors (or board of management in some companies). These decisions are characterized by a large degree of uncertainty and a lack of available information. They are mostly one-off decisions with far-reaching implications, such as a big investment in a new production process, a merger, the closure of a subsidiary or the development of a new product.

Organizational decisions

Sometimes referred to as administrative or tactical decisions, organizational decisions concern choices in the design of an organizational structure and the allocation of the firm's resources – that is, structuring the flows of information and tasks and responsibilities in relation to the members of the organization. (*See* Chapters 6 and 7 for more detail.) The structure of an organization may need to be changed as a result of changes in strategy, or due to problems which arise during implementation of operational tasks. In searching for the most appropriate design of organizational structure, choices have to be made from different forms of division of work and co-ordination. Tasks and authority may have to be allocated under changing conditions – for example, due to technological developments. It may be necessary to set up a new information system or to develop new procedures and guidelines.

Operational decisions

These decisions concern the daily arrangements for the operational execution of tasks and optimization of potential resources in the organization. Operational decisions can be made at lower levels in the organization. Were this not the case, overloading would result at the top and delays would occur in the decision-making process. These decisions include those which relate to the repetitive operational problems, possibly of a routine nature. Operational targets and levels have to be determined and operational (day-to-day) plans made. Finally, there are the daily regulation and control elements of recording and reporting – for example, in terms of inventory levels, sales figures and cost budgets. (These aspects will be discussed in more detail in Chapter 10.)

In Fig 1.4, the types of decisions and the time and attention devoted to them are related to the levels of management.

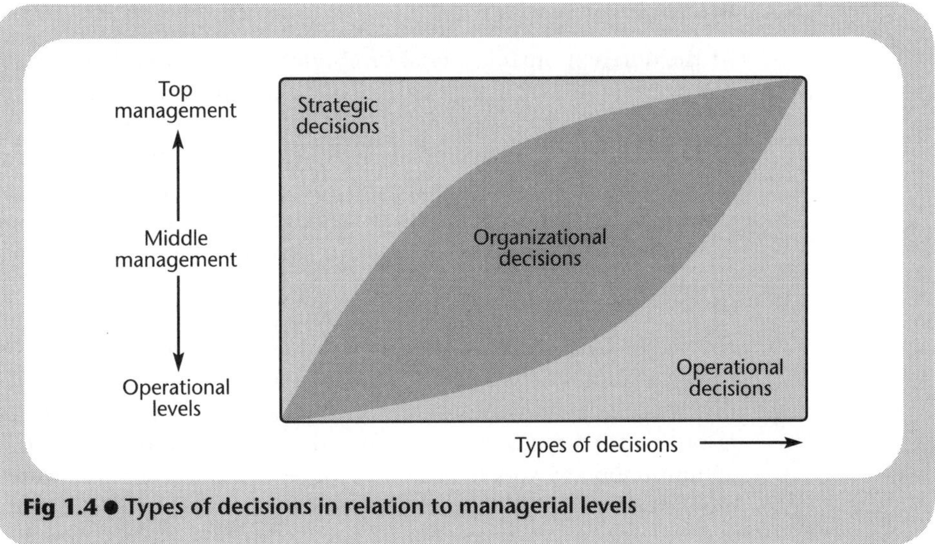

Fig 1.4 ● Types of decisions in relation to managerial levels

The preparation for, the eventual taking of, and the ability to implement decisions usually call for deliberation, consultation and participation. Whether the decision results in its intended goal depends on the quality of the decision as well as on the degree of its acceptance by the members of the organization. This can be expressed as:

$$\textbf{E(ffect)} = \textbf{Q(uality)} \times \textbf{A(cceptance)}$$

In Chapters 4, 8 and 9 aspects of the acceptance of decision making and management will be discussed in more detail.

1.5 ● MANAGERS: BORN OR MADE?

It is often said that 'leaders are born, not made.' There is certainly an element of truth in this statement as some leadership qualities are, of course, part of our genetic make-up. However, leadership always takes place within a socio-cultural context. As a result, in the area of policy development and the daily operational control of the organization, a great deal can be learned.

An important responsibility of the manager is helping the organization to realize its goals. At the same time, the manager has to see to it that the personal ambitions of fellow workers are utilized to optimum advantage and that the expectations of team members are met. However, staff can be satisfied and content, but this does not say anything about results. The manager has to always strike the right balance between the efforts of employees and the attained results.

In assessing a manager, the issue is always *management effectiveness* – that is, the ability to use and handle resources and instruments which contribute to the attainment of organizational goals. This requirement holds true for all managers at the different levels of management. At each organizational level, the relative differences in the capabilities of managers are then of further importance.

1.5.1 Manager or leader?

At the different organizational levels, different managerial skills are required in different degrees. As far back as 1916, Fayol explained how the relative importance of the manager's different skills was related to the manager's position in the company hierarchy and the size of the company itself. Fayol stated that for lower company managers, their *technical capability* was of prime importance, while for the higher managers it was their *management capability* that was significant. In a small company the technical capability will dominate; as the company becomes larger, the managing capabilities become relatively more important.

The differences between managers and leaders – the subject of many studies – will be covered in detail in Chapter 9. For now, we will simply make a few comments. According to some studies, leaders work actively and are idea-generating. They are emotionally involved, create tension, are focused on ideas, are visionary and evoke feelings of appreciation and hatred. Managers, on the other hand, concentrate on the careful administration of work to be done. If necessary, they consciously use manipulation. They are focused on people and are settled in their working environment. Managers are compromising when directing efforts towards the objectives of the organization, whereas leaders may want to break up and transform that same organization. The manager keeps things going and controls the working of the company; the leader strives for change.

When managers appear to show shortcomings or even fail, the cry for a charismatic leader becomes louder and louder. In other words, a leader carries an inspiring vision and offers such a lively and appealing image of the future that employees are motivated by it in such a way that they are prepared to accept change. In his book on leadership, Kotter (1988) considers that even the leader will have to have knowledge of the field and will have to have demonstrable attained results from the past. In this respect perhaps the differences between the leader and the manager are fading.

1.5.2 Management capabilities: knowledge, skills and attitude

In the execution of the different management tasks, the main issues are: *directing and control*, *communication* and *interpersonal effectiveness*.

- In *directing and control*, we need to make time for 'managing from behind the desk': reading notes and extracting key points from them, making choices in the drawing up of the annual budget, putting on to paper the headlines for a business plan, drawing up and reading letters, sorting and prioritizing, etc.
- In *communication*, all forms of oral and written language skills are involved: attending meetings effectively or leading them efficiently, giving presentations, writing speeches, conducting a follow-up conversation, drafting notes and many other forms of non-verbal communication.
- *Interpersonal effectiveness* has to do with leadership, persuasive power, influence and assertiveness.

In the assessment of managers, five skills can be identified on which ideally a positive score should be registered: namely, thinking power, social power, achievement power, willpower and balance.

- *Thinking power* does not just involve the passive 'knowing in the head', but also the ability to think creatively. In other words, what is needed is not only the skill to

Exhibit 1.4

Women's progress in the business world has been likened to the advance of the next ice age. There are few clear signs of a thaw.

The newest, and most controversial, reason cited for giving women a break is a change in management culture. Women in management used to be criticized for their inability to behave like men in the corporate world, but now management gurus such as Peter Drucker, Tom Peters and Robert Waterman are saying that corporate cultures must move towards a style that in the old days would have been thought of as typically feminine. The buzzwords are co-operative leadership, teamwork, an emphasis on quality, intuitive problem-solving and light control.

A major EC study showed that in 1987 women made up 4% of middle management in the Netherlands and Ireland, 7% in Belgium, 8% in Denmark, West Germany and Italy, and 9% in France. The proportion of women in top management was even lower – less than 3% everywhere except in France, which headed the European league table at 7%.

Yet women across Europe account for between 36% and 48% of the labour force. There is ample evidence that most of them are no longer content with what the Germans call the three Ks – *Kinder*, *Küche*, *Kirche* (children, kitchen and church). Many are looking for managerial opportunities; few are getting them.

When male bosses are pressed on the question of unequal promotion chances for female managers they will usually admit, slightly shamefacedly, that it has 'something to do with babies'. They mean that women's careers are liable to be interrupted, at least temporarily, by childbirth and child care. It is this expectation, as much as the fact itself, that will affect promotion prospects. Some of the most high-powered women in business get round the problem by remaining childless, or even husbandless, but if that solution were widely adopted the population would plummet.

One solution to the problem of combining job and family is part-time work. But in many employers' eyes management is a full-time and continuous job that is incompatible with divided attention. Women, both in management and in lower-grade jobs, have taken the hint: most women workers are employed full-time, says the OECD.

If academic qualifications were the main key to Europe's boardrooms, women would be entering in droves. The large gap between numbers of male and female university graduates in the 1940s and 1950s has narrowed dramatically in most European countries over the past few decades. Women now make up more than 40% of graduates in business, economics and law, although they remain severely underrepresented in engineering and natural sciences.

In a few European countries – Germany, Italy, the UK – governments have mandated some form of positive discrimination within public administrations, but there are few sanctions for non-compliance.

In a survey covering 500,000 employees, one in every three companies in the European Community was found to be discriminating in favour of female employees and searching out women candidates to fill top jobs. More than two fifths of companies were providing general management training specifically for female staff to help them crash their way through the 'glass ceiling' on their promotion prospects.

If promotion is not coming their way, corporate life proves too inflexible for their needs or unemployment looms, women are increasingly setting up their own companies. In Germany a third of all new business start-ups involve female entrepreneurs; their total number has risen to 600,000. Several European governments, including the Netherlands and Sweden, have introduced policies to encourage women entrepreneurs.

Is all this enough to make a real difference?

Source: *International Management*, March 1992.

Why Europe Is a Man's World

Women make up 41% of the workforce:

BUT EARN LESS THAN MEN

- Up to 40% less in manufacturing jobs
- Up to 35% less in service jobs

AND HOLD FEWER TOP JOBS

- 29% of all management jobs*
- Less than 2% of senior management jobs**
- Less than 1% of board seats**

* Including voluntary organizations and local and state governments
** Private sector

Source: Data: Eurostat, International Labor Office, Business Week, 15 April 1996.

analyse the pieces of a puzzle and put it together in a perfect solution (analytical capability), but also the ability to draft a new puzzle (systematic ability combined with creativity). The analysis should not only lead to a precise, numbered and classified explanation of the problem, but should also result in the different elements being assimilated into a new goal-oriented package: a proposal, a plan, an idea that is new (creative but also attainable.

- *Social power* refers to all the activities involved in contributing to the organizational goal together with, by means of, on behalf of, or even in spite of, people. Managers with well developed social powers are able to get others to adopt their points of view and then realize the organizational goals of the company in co-operation with this group.
- *Achievement power* refers to the ability to bring plans to fruition, through thick and thin, in spite of logistical, financial or social resistance. This involves operational power, the practical skill of planning, guarding and controlling projects, and the ability to monitor both personal and other people's agendas.
- *Willpower* concerns both ambition and motivation. *Ambition* is built up out of four elements:
  1. *Initiative*. Managers need to get started with something by and through themselves instead of waiting passively for an assignment to come up.
  2. *Persistency*. Once started, managers are not supposed to quit quickly. Managers have to push through their initiatives even under extreme pressure.
  3. *Stress resistance*. In this respect, managers have to keep going, even if pressured by factors over which they have no control. (The difference between persistency and stress resistance is that, in the first case, the manager is the one who causes the tension, while in the second case, stress has an external cause.)
  4. *Energy*. This relates to the question of whether the manager is vital, enthusiastic and has visible work spirit.

  Motivation refers to the dedication of managers. What do they do it for? In this respect we distinguish three types of motives: performance driven, socially driven and power driven. The performance-driven manager feels especially committed to work because it provides opportunities for action. The socially driven manager finds satisfaction in the network of social relations which has to be built up, maintained and renewed continuously. The power-driven manager wants to be the boss – to be (visibly) better than others in all respects.
- *Balance* refers to the degree to which the four powers mentioned above are in mutual harmony and equilibrium with each other. Here, the *internal balance* is what counts – the personal maturity of the manager. Insight and personal control are determining factors.

Areas of management

Characteristics of higher middle management cannot be considered in isolation from the area of activity which the managers are supposed to influence. This concerns the area of responsibility in which they operate and refers to competences and skills (*see* Table 1.1).

Table 1.1 ● Typology of management situations

Management point of view	Competences
General	Planning Goal setting Organizing Supervising/Giving instructions Co-ordinating Decision making Investigating
Financial	Drawing up budgets (including analysing and evaluation) Budget control and registration Administration (especially management-related)
Social	A range of staffing situations (job interviews, performance reviews, bad news talks, etc.) Drawing up social policies and plans Meetings Assessing the quality of staff and keeping them up to standard Negotiating
Commercial	Giving lectures/presentations Conducting sales talks (direct communicative contacts) Negotiating Drawing up a business plan (analysing, developing vision, technological know-how, marketing) External representation Internal salesmanship (selling ideas; political behaviour)

Source: Adapted from Jansen, 1991

1.6 ● THE MANAGEMENT PROCESS AND CORE ACTIVITIES

In this introductory chapter we have clarified the concepts 'organization', 'manager' and 'management', in that we have shown what 'organizations' are and what 'managers' can experience at different levels of the organization. We have been considering 'management' as a group of people. We now move on to consider 'management' as a process and to draw up a picture of the different management tasks. (These will be discussed in greater detail in Chapters 5 to 12.)

1.6.1 Management as a process

Henri Fayol (1841–1925) is considered to be the founder of the modern management-process theory. Fayol stated that management could be learned. However, the problem was that in his time no theory existed on which management education could be based. With the first systematic analysis of the elements of the management function, Fayol met this need himself in 1916. Fayol broke down management (as an activity) into five essential parts:

- policy making and planning (*prévoir*);
- organizing/designing organizational structure (*organiser*);
- giving instructions and assistance during the execution of tasks (*commander*);
- co-ordinating (*coordonner*);
- checking and making adjustments, if necessary (*controler*).

Taking Fayol's idea as a starting point, management can be said to always contain the elements depicted in Fig 1.5.

The figure shows that management in its broad sense is a logical series of activities. The concept of 'leading' refers especially to giving orders, motivating people and checking activities which have been performed by other people – that is, managing in the 'narrow' sense (as it is only one of the management functions). Managing in the 'broad' sense also includes other management functions, such as determination of the *mission* and the course, positioning and the maintenance of external contacts. By seeing management as a process, we are better able to study the activities of 'the management' as a group of people and gain insight into the function of management and the role and position of the manager in the organization.

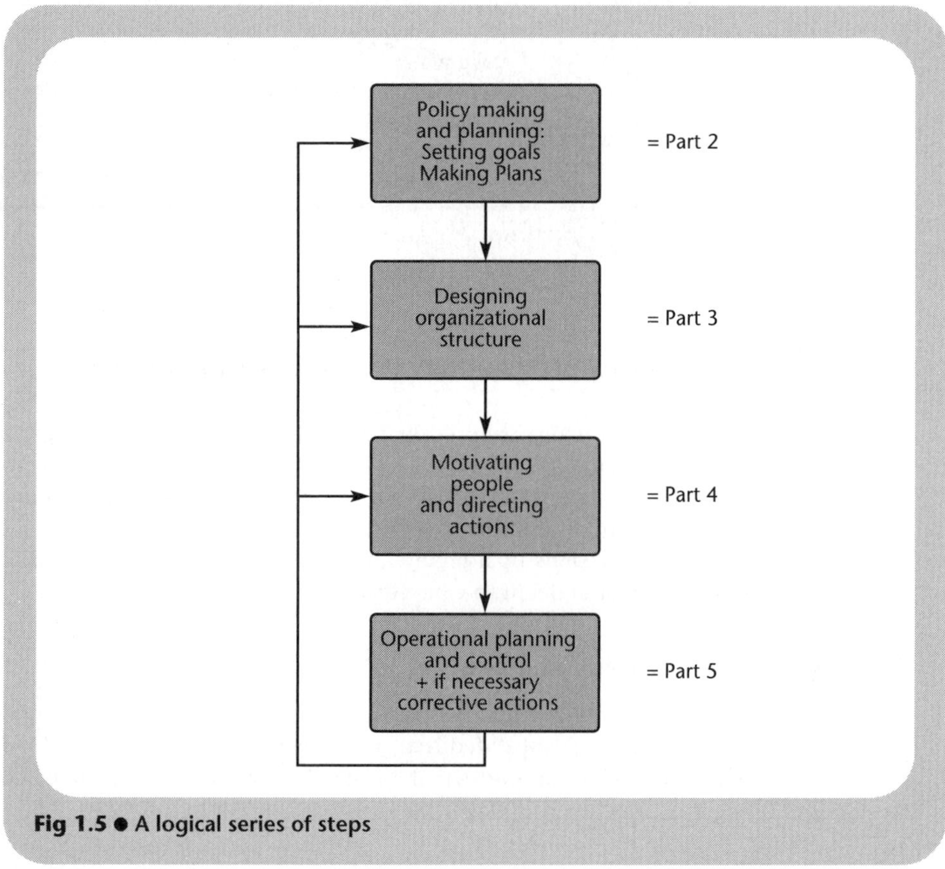

Fig 1.5 ● A logical series of steps

In management, we concern ourselves with a process of planning, organizing, governing and controlling – a process in which the skills and talents of the management team play an important role.

1.6.2 Core tasks and activities

In the management process we can distinguish two core tasks: namely, *constituting* and *directing*. These tasks are characterized by the authority to make decisions and take initiative.

Constituting

Constituting is creating a setting in which operational activity can take place. Constituting tasks include determining the goals that have to be attained by an organization or by a department, the formulation of the general lines of policy, the drawing up of policy guidelines and the action plans and procedures that go with them in order to realize plans for the short, medium or long term. Constituting tasks also involve the creating of conditions to enable goals to be attained – for example, the building up and design of an organizational structure, the structuring of functions and tasks, the assignment of decision-making authorities over departments and employees, the determination of procedures, and the design of the necessary channels of co-ordination and communication and ways of consultation and participation. In summary, the constituting tasks refer to proactive capabilities like forecasting, planning and organizing. With reference to Fayol, these are the first two activities: policy making (looking ahead, setting objectives and goals, making plans (*prévoir*)) and building up and designing the organization (organizing (*organiser*)).

Directing

Directing involves stimulating actions, setting the direction in which work has to be carried out, as well as checking on and, if necessary, redirecting the actions which are performed by the operational staff. When handling people and resources, the first concern is to motivate the staff and give directions and orders. To ensure that goals are attained, it is necessary to check whether the orders are being executed in accordance with the norms, rules and procedures. In terms of Fayol, the directing tasks are concerned with the last three elements of the management process: giving instructions and assistance during the execution of tasks (*commander*), co-ordinating (*coordonner*) and checking and making adjustments, if necessary (*controler*).

Readjusting activities as a 'step' in the management process can refer to renewed constituting as well as to renewed directing.

The higher the manager is in an organization, the more time and attention will be allocated to constituting tasks. These tasks can be described as *policy intensive*. At the lower levels, more and more attention is given to the directing tasks. Directing becomes increasingly *operationally intensive*. This is depicted in Fig 1.6. At all levels, constituting is, so to speak, only half of the job. *First think and prepare, then execute, act and do.* If the right thinking has taken place in advance, then it should only be necessary to give specific orders and, in principle, few problems will occur when the tasks are carried out. Operational implementation then seems possible in terms of time estimates, budgets and so on.

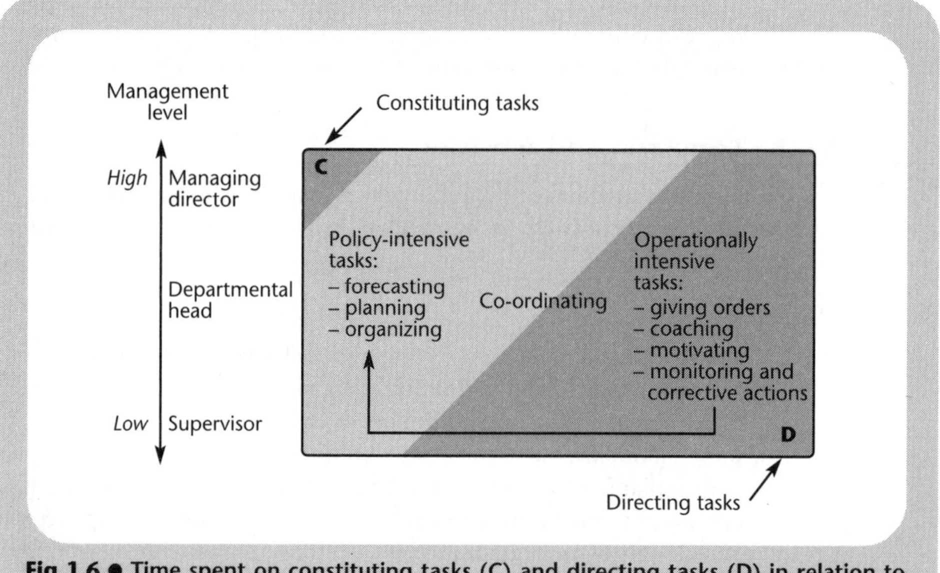

Fig 1.6 ● Time spent on constituting tasks (C) and directing tasks (D) in relation to management position or level

1.6.3 Constituting tasks

Goal-oriented action can be described in a number of ways – for example:

- as a conscious striving for the attainment of specific goals with specific means in a specific time scale;
- as well thought out, effective, efficient and systematic management;
- as the art of converting the present not-preferred situation into a preferred future situation.

In section 1.1.2, in which we talked about the characteristics of the organization, we stated that the organization is a co-operative, goal-realizing unit; management is therefore a set of rational actions by managers aimed at controlling the organization or institution as a co-operative, goal-realizing unit. Central to the actions of managers are the *objectives* and *goals* of the organization – the most important elements of 'policy making', together with the resources and the time scales involved.

If goals are to be realized, actions have to be taken in order to move from the existing situation to a target and more desirable situation. This process is illustrated in Fig 1.7.

Primary objectives are broken down into partial goals in order to identify a number of specific activities. This has to be done in such a way that, eventually, a goal is formulated for every activity. The goals need to reflect the way the organizational structure is built up and relate to the broader objectives of the organization's mission.

The myriad of objectives and goals needs to be brought together to form one coherent picture – a picture that reflects the aspirations not only of *all* layers of the organization, but also those of *all* employees at each of the levels of that hierarchy.

The objectives and goals of the organization must match society's needs with the capabilities of the organization. The organization also derives its *raison d'être* from the

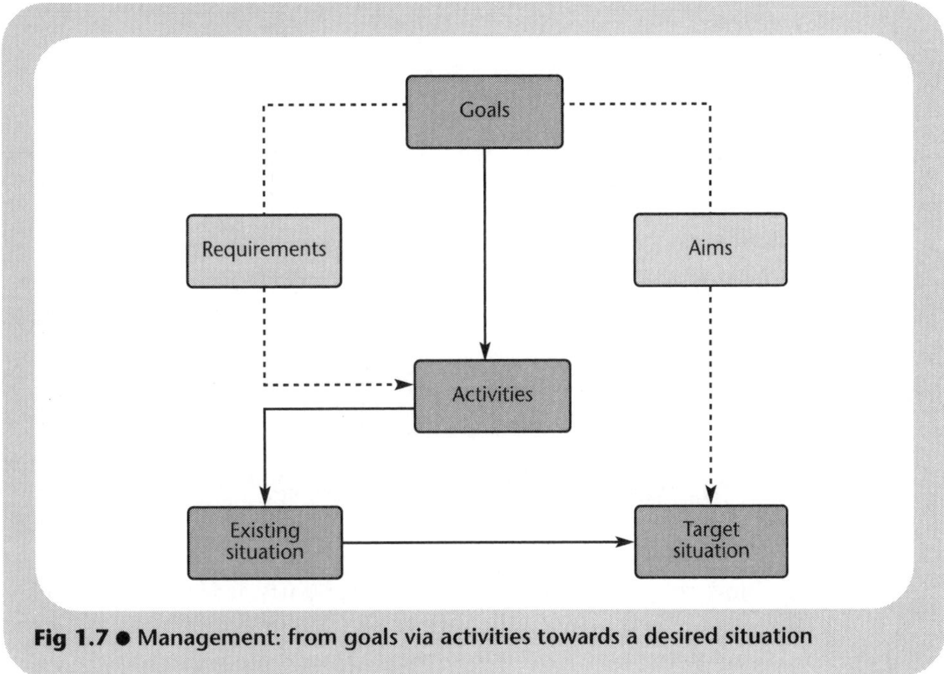

Fig 1.7 ● Management: from goals via activities towards a desired situation

goals which it strives for. The main objectives and goals of an organization need to meet three important criteria:

1. The objectives which are set need to be *acceptable* to all those involved, both internal and external. The degree to which goals can be accepted determines to a great extent the willingness of those involved to contribute to their realization.
2. The objectives and goals which are set need to be *attainable*. Thorough research into the possibilities of the organization with regard to available human skills and resources can give insights into attainability.
3. The objectives and goals have to be *clear*. Poorly formulated objectives and goals often lead to difficulties in interpretation resulting in a lower level of activity directed at attaining the goals and objectives.

Organizing as an activity can be defined as:

> *the purposeful and directed development of an effective relationship between people, other resources, and their actions to attain specific goals.*

This is depicted as a triangle in Fig 1.8.

From Fig 1.8 we can see that there are three factors that a manager, as an organizer, has to bring together – people, resources and actions. At the same time this means that it is not only the task of the manager to see to it that in practice everything goes according to a specific organizational formula, but also to design the formula itself. (The design activity will be covered in greater detail in Chapters 6 and 7.)

This design activity involves careful consideration of the effective relations between people and resources. Decisions have to be made on the division of work (who does what). In this respect decision-making authority has to be explicitly stated and mutual relationships determined. The manager has to understand the organization as a whole

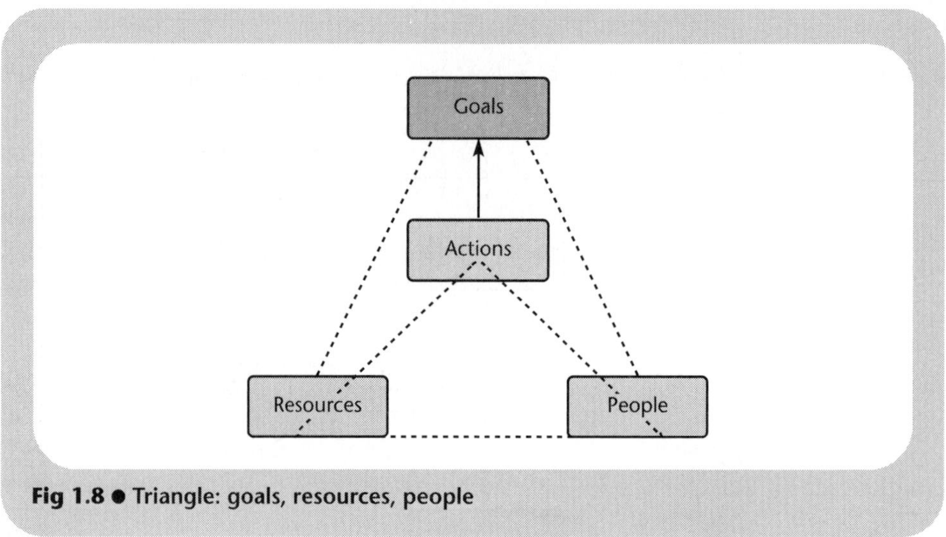

Fig 1.8 ● Triangle: goals, resources, people

and not as a few more or less isolated parts; it is important to know the functional connections between the various parts of the organization and to be aware of the relationships or interdependencies.

1.6.4 Directing tasks

Managers need to spend a large part of their time directly managing employees and supporting and coaching them in the execution of their tasks. This is managing in its 'narrow' sense and it involves, among other things, managers having to derive tasks from medium- and long-term plans and relate these to short-term targets and budgets. This is followed by the giving of orders, the provision of support during the execution of tasks, and the motivation of employees. Managers then need to ensure that tasks are executed properly (evaluating). In giving day-to-day direction, middle managers are in direct contact with subordinate employees, influencing their behaviour in such a way that the goals which are set for the organization, the department, or the work unit are attained as far as possible. Since organizations mostly revolve around people, the style of managerial leadership is an important factor.

Making plans

In practice, operational staff can often be involved in the drawing up of departmental plans and operational norms – for example, the sales plan and quota for the sales department. Involvement in drawing up attainable goals can be very motivating and stimulating.

Motivating and directing

An important part of management is treating people in such a way that they want to and are able to perform a task. That is why managers need to be able to stimulate or even force employees in their organization to act effectively and according to a plan. This area of management involves activities such as motivating, directing and instructing/commanding, which are necessary to ensure that people in an organization are performing their activities effectively. To do this, managers have to be able to make good decisions, communicate well and inspire others. Furthermore, they have to be able to choose the right people for the many functions of an organization. It is part of the task of the manager to see to it that people use their capacities to the full, by improving or maintaining their knowledge, skills, attitude and behaviour.

Controlling and correcting actions

Management has to see to it that plans are executed. With this in mind, management will have to check whether the activities performed by the organization have gone according to plan, in order to be able to evaluate, intervene, and/or make adjustments or arrange new procedures.

To keep track of the progress in the execution of tasks, the manager can use different tools. Sometimes, discrepancies can be avoided by *direct control* or, alternatively, can be spotted by simply walking around. Most of the time, however, there is a kind of *indirect control* and the manager perceives discrepancies afterwards by means of a report on the implementation or the status of operational factors such as time, cost or quality.

The adjustment and readjustment procedures in the process of control are illustrated in Fig 1.9. The plan, which contains a number of decisions on actions for the future, has to be broken down in order to come into effect and lead to results. Working methods and results are compared to norms, and, when there are non-allowable differences, this gives rise to additional or corrective actions. These adjustments need to be made in order for the desired performance and results to be attained.

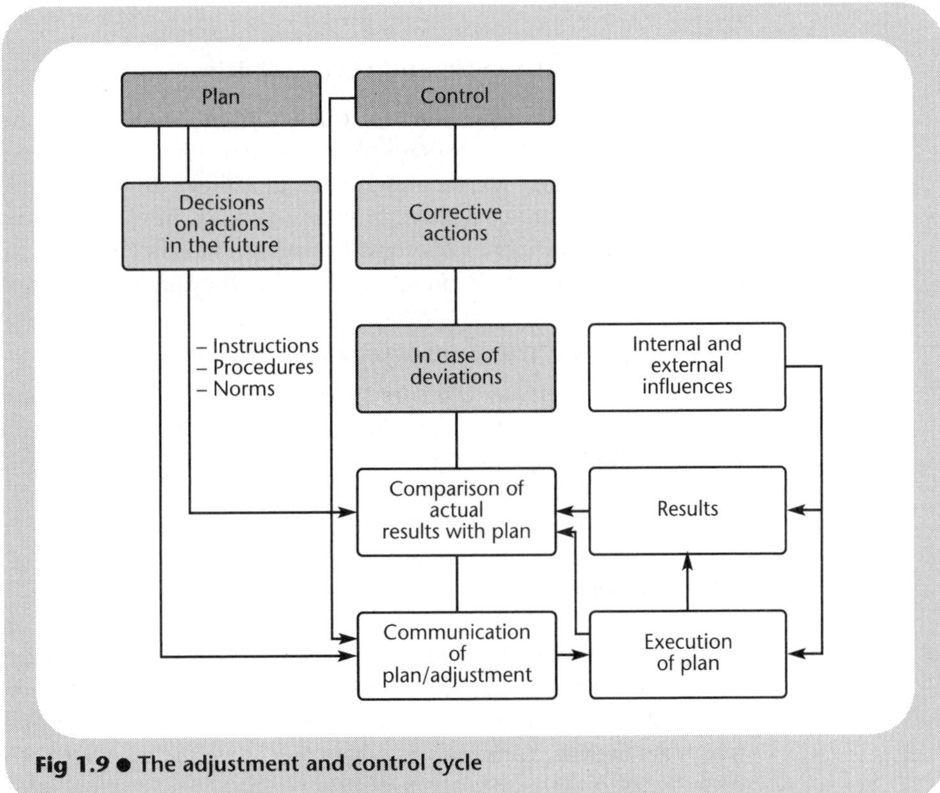

Fig 1.9 ● The adjustment and control cycle

Planning and control is a continuous process that involves setting standards, measuring results and making adjustments. Even though there is a general adjustment and corrective process, this has often to be revised to fit specific situations.

A number of rules can be mentioned in this context:

- The adjustments and corrections need to be adapted to the specific requirements. The managing director will have a system that works in a different way to that of a head of department. The size of the organization or department will also be an influence. The need for a control system is the central question.
- Information on discrepancies needs to be obtained in good time. Record systems which give good but late information are of little or no use – for example, if a trading company received information on a loss that occurred in a transaction six months previously.
- The control data need to be objective and should leave as little room as possible for multiple interpretations.
- The system needs to be flexible – that is, it has to be possible to adjust and correct when necessary.
- The process needs to be profitable, which means that the related costs of control and adjustment have to be covered.
- The process needs to be simple and easy to understand. Managers may not be specialists; they need access to concise and clear reports.
- In addition to recording and identifying discrepancies, the process has to indicate which corrective measures and/or additional actions are demanded.

1.6.5 The management cycle and core activities

Communication is demanded for the execution of all management tasks. All managers have to be able to explain to others their reasons, intentions and decisions in such a way that they will be understood. To achieve this in practice, managers need to have an insight into communication as a process. In the future, communication will become more and more important to managers as they practise their function. Managers will have to understand others as well as they understand themselves.

The management cycle: areas of knowledge for managers

We can never consider the core tasks of the management process as independent activities, even though they are described separately. Effective performance of each of these functions depends on the way in which the others are also being performed. Effective co-ordination, for example, is impossible without good planning, while good communication is strongly dependent on good organization. However, there is a logical time scale for the sequence of planning, organizing, giving orders, controlling and adjustment.

A business plan is the basis for organizing, while task implementation and output are, in their turn, the basis for the daily adjustment in the control cycle. The results of the adjustment and corrective process, in their turn, give information on the necessity to revise plans. Decision making, co-ordinating and communicating are functions which are used in planning and organizing as well as managing. The interrelationship between the functions is depicted in Fig 1.10.

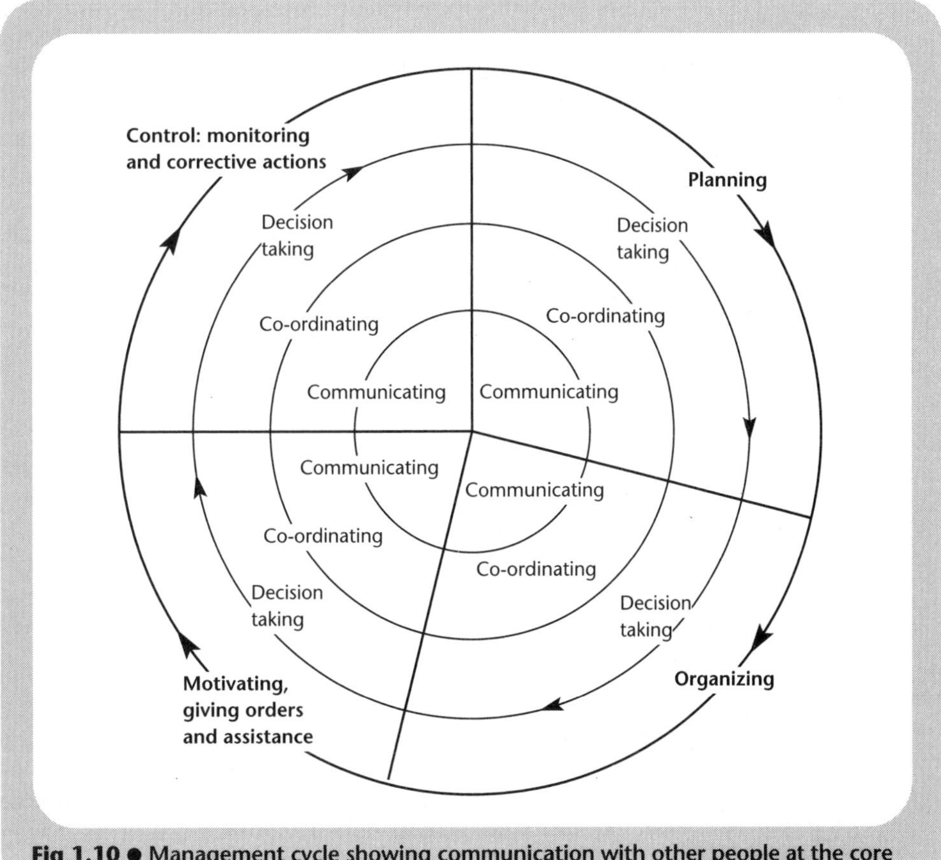

Fig 1.10 ● Management cycle showing communication with other people at the core

1.6.6 What competencies does a good manager need?

It will already have become clear that managers, in order to be able to do their job successfully, need to have many, sometimes extremely diverse qualities. Some people still believe that these qualities can only be developed by trial and error. Although this statement is partly based in truth, it is important to realize that this way of learning is the most difficult, most time consuming and most costly imaginable. It is far better if, at an early stage, the manager can draw on existing knowledge and experience based on the best practices of others. The areas of knowledge which managers need to cover can be divided up as follows:

- *Knowledge of planning, organizing and governing an organization.* Managers need to have knowledge of the areas of *planning*, *organizing* and *governing* an organization or part of it, otherwise their management will be of little use. They may be able to hide their weaknesses on these points for a long time with an enormous effort, but in the end they will always fail.
- *Knowledge of people and organizational behaviour.* Managers work among and with people and are to a great extent influenced by the behaviour of other people. In turn the behaviour of managers influences those with whom they work. They

should therefore at least be able to recognize normal behaviour patterns of people in the work environment and know how people are likely to react to their actions. Only then can managers expect their actions in the areas of co-ordinating and motivating to be generally effective.

- *Knowledge of technology and the field.* Managers cannot completely do without knowledge of the specific field in which they work. The head of accounts will need to have some knowledge of book-keeping. It is impossible to imagine a successful marketing manager with no knowledge whatsoever in the areas of sales, distribution and advertising. Managers need to have, as is often mentioned in recruitment advertisements, some demonstrable technical knowledge of the department which they will be managing and of the sector in which they will work. As the manager climbs further up the hierarchical ladder, the work becomes less operational and the importance of specific technical knowledge diminishes.
- *Knowledge of the organization in which they work.* It speaks for itself that managers without knowledge of their own organization, its goals, and its way of operating, can hardly operate successfully. They have to be fully informed about the history of the organization and also of its policies, philosophy and culture, strengths and weaknesses, problems, place in the sector, image, etc. It is clear that the only source of this kind of information is the organization itself. When the initiative for gathering this information does not come from the institution, the wise manager will acquire it through his or her own initiative.

Other characteristics of good managers

The manager has to be incorruptible – to have a certain measure of self-knowledge and sincerity. Employees will expect that promises and expectations are met. Managers have to set an example. Employees will not so much do as managers *say*, but rather they will do as they *do*.

Creativity and the ability to innovate are necessary, especially in a changing environment where the manager will always be expected to solve new and unfamiliar problems. Creativity will help to generate new ideas, solutions and approaches.

As we have mentioned more than once already, thorough expert knowledge is of importance. In this respect, of course, a great deal can be learned: managers have to intervene, make proposals, come up with solutions and give instructions. When employees recognize a manager's expertise, they will be accepted as leader more quickly and their motivational influence on employees will be greater.

The social abilities of a manager are also important. It is necessary to be able to manage relationships, especially in teams in which employees work closely together, as conflicts, disappointments, tensions and rivalry will occur. The manager needs to have social skills in order to resolve these situations tactically or find ways of avoiding or reducing them.

Managers need to be driven by and totally devoted to the task of managing. Their active acceptance of the organization's goals should be seen as an example to employees. The steps which they take to serve the organizational goals – even if not popular – have to be accepted by employees without regard for their own interests.

The manager needs to have a certain degree of self-confidence. He or she needs to support organizational policies and send out an aura of calm and confidence. The courage to take risks, the ability to delegate and readiness for action are all important skills. No 'one' best solution exists; there are always other possible solutions. Once a manager has decided on a solution, he or she will have to take the risks associated with that choice.

1.7 CHARACTERISTICS OF AN EFFECTIVE ORGANIZATION AND SUCCESSFUL MANAGEMENT

In their book, *In Search of Excellence*, Peters and Waterman (1982) described eight characteristics of successful management:

- *A bias towards action* – preferring to undertake something actively instead of endlessly studying and analysing a concept.
- *A customer-directed attitude* – knowing the customer's preference and serving that preference.
- *Autonomy and entrepreneurship* – dividing the company up into smaller units and encouraging an independent and competitive working attitude.
- *Productivity through people* – making employees aware of the fact that effort is essential and that they profit from the success of the company.
- *Hands-on and value-driven* – showing personal commitment and keeping in touch with the essence of the company, stimulating a strong company culture.
- *'Stick to the knitting'* – stick to the activities that the company performs best.
- *'Simple forms and lean staff'* – few administrative and managerial layers and few people at the top.
- *Simultaneous loose–tight properties* – freedom from constraints, which means taking care of the central values of the company, combined with respect for all employees who accept these values.

These eight characteristics were observed in very well functioning ('excellent') organizations, although the degree to which these characteristics were present differed. Furthermore, it is known that some years after the research, not all of these 'excellent' companies were still functioning as well. Sometimes, the explanations for successful management are very complex. Meeting these eight characteristics is no guarantee of continuous success. Such success requires hard work and commitment to attaining and improving the company's performance in changing times and market conditions.

1.7.1 Criteria for measuring the effectiveness of an organization

Organizational effectiveness is a characteristic which is difficult to identify because it concerns *the degree to which and the means through which goals are attained.*

The *measuring* of effectiveness is only possible if an instrument exists for this purpose. The organization can be seen as a 'lasting complex of people and resources for realization of specific, but in time shifting, goals.' Criteria for effectiveness can be derived from this. Keuning and Eppink (1979, 6th edition 1996) drew up four main criteria:

- *Efficiency* is the degree to which a set of goals is achieved while using up a minimum of resources, leading to *technical and economic efficiency.*
- *Satisfaction* is the degree to which the needs of the members of the organization are satisfied by means of labour-intrinsic and labour-extrinsic factors, leading to *psycho-social efficiency.*
- *Fulfilment of stakeholders' needs* is the degree to which the demands and needs of the stakeholders from the external environment are met, leading to *societal efficiency.*

Exhibit 1.5

Sector rankings of Europe's most respected companies

FT

Sector	Rank	Company	Country
Automobiles/trucks & parts			
	1	BMW	Germany
	2	Robert Bosch	Germany
	=3	Volkswagen	Germany
	=3	Fiat	Italy
Banks & financial institutions			
	1	Deutsche Bank	Germany
	2	Lloyds TSB	UK
	3	ABN Amro	Netherlands
Beverages & tobacco			
	1	LVMH	France
	=2	Carlsberg	Denmark
	=2	Heineken	Netherlands
Construction			
	1	Holderbank	Switzerland
	2	Lafarge	France
	=3	Caradon	UK
	=3	Skanska	Sweden
Electronics			
	1	Siemens	Germany
	2	Electrolux	Sweden
	3	Nokia	Finland
Electricity & water			
	1	PowerGen	UK
	2	RWE	Germany
	3	Lyonnaise Des Eaux	France
Engineering			
	1	ABB	Sweden/Switzerland
	=2	Atlas Copco	Sweden
	=2	Kvaemer	Norway
	=2	Smiths Industries	UK
Food processors			
	1	Nestlé	Switzerland
	2	Unilever	Netherlands/UK
	3	Danone	France
Household			
	1	Max Mara	Italy
	2	Hugo Boss	Germany
Insurance			
	1	Allianz	Germany
	2	ING	Netherlands
	3	Münchener	Germany
Media, printing & advertising			
	1	Reuters	UK
	=2	Bertelsmann	Germany
	=2	Reed Elsevier	Netherlands/UK
	=2	WPP	UK
	=2	BBC	UK
Oil, gas & mining			
	1	Royal Dutch Shell	Netherlands/UK
	2	British Petroleum	UK
	3	VEBA	Germany
Pharmaceuticals & healthcare			
	1	Roche	Switzerland
	2	Novartis	Switzerland
	=3	Glaxo-Wellcome	UK
	=3	Smith & Nephew	UK
Retail & distribution			
	1	Tesco	UK
	2	Carrefour	France
	3	Marks & Spencer	UK
Telecoms & communications			
	1	British Telecom	UK
	2	PTT Post	Netherlands
	3	Telia	Sweden
Transport & transport services			
	1	British Telecom	UK
	2	Swissair	Switzerland
	3	Lufthansa	Germany

Source: *Financial Times*, 10 September 1996.

- *Self-preservation through flexibility and responsiveness* is the degree to which an organization can speedily adjust its short-term strategy, structure and operational goals in reaction to changing external circumstances, leading to *managerial efficiency*.

In an evaluation of an organization, all these aspects of an effective and healthy organization can be observed and scored. The organization has to show positive scores in relation to these criteria if it wants to be assessed as effective.

Exhibit 1.6

Respected, but short on excellence

In terms of shareholder value, top US companies are ahead of Europe's leaders

The definition of excellence in companies will always be partly subjective. But there is one measure which is, within its narrow limits, purely objective: how far a company has created value for its owners, in the form of increased dividends and a rising share price.

This question was touched on in the survey, but in an indirect way. Respondents were asked which European company was best placed to provide maximum long-term value to shareholders. Put that way, the question is one of forward-looking opinion, rather than a bald appeal to the record.

The difference is subtle, but important. Shareholders naturally prefer to emphasise past share price performance, since it leaves less room for excuses on the part of underperforming managers, And in Europe, it is often argued, shareholders tend to occupy a less important place in the scheme of things than in the US.

The typical survey respondent was the chief executive of a large European corporation. Most of those executives would probably work on longer planning horizons than five years. Many, one suspects, would regard the shareholder's interest as only one component – sometimes a minor one – in a much larger whole.

This touches on a wider debate. It is a cliche to say that continental European companies place more emphasis on stakeholder relationships – suppliers, bankers, employees – than do their competitors in the US and UK. It is also a cliche to accuse the US–UK approach of resulting in a short-term attitude to business and investment.

But the debate is shifting ground. The recent ousting of Carlo de Benedetti as head of Olivetti, for instance, bears some of the hallmarks of a shareholders' revolt.

Equally, it is notable that the survey respondents named General Electric of the US as their favourite company worldwide. Jack Welch, GE's chairman, is certainly a long-term strategist. But he is also an explicit champion of shareholder value.

Indeed, he has said that rewarding his managers in stock – as GE increasingly does – is an important way of channelling their competitive instincts into working for the good of the corporation as a whole. European managers plainly admire Mr Welch's results. It might also pay them to emulate his methods.

Source: *Financial Times*, 18 September 1996.

1.8 THE MANAGER AND THE ORGANIZATIONAL CULTURE

Whenever a newly appointed employee is getting to know an organization, or a recently recruited manager wants to make changes in the organization, it is important to realize that an organization is more than just a structure and a system of behaviour according to guidelines and procedures. Upon further acquaintance, we usually experience 'something' in the organization which is, to a certain degree, elusive. This 'something' seems to pervade all aspects of the organization, including statements, ways of thinking and the actions of the people in the organization. In recent years, we have started calling this 'something' **organizational culture**.

In the first place, an organizational culture is formed by the prevailing ideas which are disseminated by a large proportion of the members of the organization who carry those ideas with them in terms of operative values, norms and convictions.

Values are the things that people consider to be important and which consciously – but often unconsciously – determine human behaviour. In organizations, values are expressed in the way in which the organization is managed and the way in which people associate with each other, in things that the members of the organization do or do not do, and in choices that are made. Underlying this behaviour are the values and norms, expectations, convictions and attitudes which play an important role. This is the existing organizational culture. For example, 'loyalty to the company' (a value) results in 'wanting to be on time' (a norm) and finding this to be important.

Convictions are expressed by members of the organization, whether asked for or not. Convictions are the notions and opinions of reality which are shared by the members of the organization. These convictions cause them to show certain types of behaviour, disseminate information in a certain way, and so on. From one perspective, a conviction brings order to a specific experience; however, it can also lead to distortions or discord – for example, in statements such as '... those staff, they are far too theoretical' or '... research managers, they are always late'.

Organizational culture is important because it makes organizational life predictable and clearly structured; it creates a relationship between the members of different parts of the organization; and it means that it is not always necessary to adapt or make new decisions to fit individual circumstances. Organizational culture can be considered as the mutual understanding between the members and stakeholders of the organization.

In those positions in the organization where examples are being set, it is important to be aware of the organizational culture. At first sight, this may seem 'vague' and 'elusive', but it shows itself in all forms of organizational practice, such as different forms of sanctions, rewards and 'punishments', traditions and habits, and norms and rules which are in force at different levels or within different parts of the organization. The culture of an organization expresses itself, for example, in the use or otherwise of first names, in the physical environment and corporate image, in the communication between employees, in the way in which customers are treated, in the work effort and the degree of commitment shown by employees, in the dress code and in the language and attitude to time keeping. It is therefore important to 'know' an organization and the 'determined' relationships and interrelationships within it.

1.8.1 Functions of an organizational culture

Organizational culture involves the way in which members perceive the organization, its nature and ways of working, and their contribution to it. It is the result of a mutual understanding and is influenced by the organization's past just as the structure and strategy of the organization reflect the mutual understanding and the experiences of those in authority with regard to the execution of power, the allocation of responsibility and the reaction of the organization to events in its external environment.

Organizational culture is considered to have two important functions:

1. *To provide relatively fixed patterns for handling and solving problems* – relating to the organization's ability to cope with changing external and internal factors. Reactions which proved to be an effective way of solving problems in the past are used again. Mutual understanding takes the form of a 'recipe book' for the solution of external and internal adjustment problems.
2. *To reduce uncertainty for the members of the organization when confronted with new situations.*

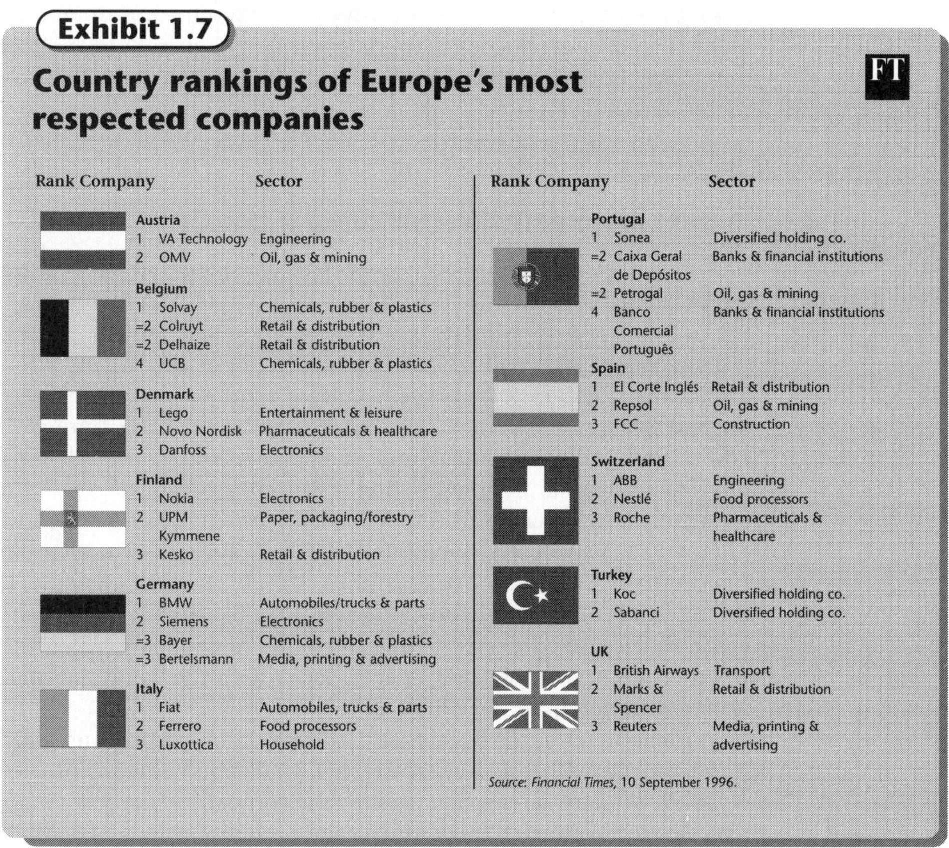

Exhibit 1.7

Country rankings of Europe's most respected companies

FT

Country	Rank	Company	Sector
Austria	1	VA Technology	Engineering
	2	OMV	Oil, gas & mining
Belgium	1	Solvay	Chemicals, rubber & plastics
	=2	Colruyt	Retail & distribution
	=2	Delhaize	Retail & distribution
	4	UCB	Chemicals, rubber & plastics
Denmark	1	Lego	Entertainment & leisure
	2	Novo Nordisk	Pharmaceuticals & healthcare
	3	Danfoss	Electronics
Finland	1	Nokia	Electronics
	2	UPM Kymmene	Paper, packaging/forestry
	3	Kesko	Retail & distribution
Germany	1	BMW	Automobiles/trucks & parts
	2	Siemens	Electronics
	=3	Bayer	Chemicals, rubber & plastics
	=3	Bertelsmann	Media, printing & advertising
Italy	1	Fiat	Automobiles, trucks & parts
	2	Ferrero	Food processors
	3	Luxottica	Household
Portugal	1	Sonea	Diversified holding co.
	=2	Caixa Geral de Depósitos	Banks & financial institutions
	=2	Petrogal	Oil, gas & mining
	4	Banco Comercial Português	Banks & financial institutions
Spain	1	El Corte Inglés	Retail & distribution
	2	Repsol	Oil, gas & mining
	3	FCC	Construction
Switzerland	1	ABB	Engineering
	2	Nestlé	Food processors
	3	Roche	Pharmaceuticals & healthcare
Turkey	1	Koc	Diversified holding co.
	2	Sabanci	Diversified holding co.
UK	1	British Airways	Transport
	2	Marks & Spencer	Retail & distribution
	3	Reuters	Media, printing & advertising

Source: Financial Times, 10 September 1996.

The two functions of organizational culture – the standardization of problem solution and the reduction of uncertainty – will crystallize over time. The form the culture takes will depend on the way in which the 'leaders' find solutions for problems and on the ways in which they interpret the events and activities that go on around them. The reduction of uncertainty and the giving of meaning to daily actions can only take place when there is a connection between the individual values of the members of the organization and the core of the organizational culture. A company in western Europe, for example, will need to give employees the opportunity for relatively individualistic value patterns, when compared with the more collective value patterns of employees working in other economies.

The values of the organization's employees will be especially determined by the kind of people that the organization recruits – their nationality, education and age. The company can only influence the values of its employees to a limited extent after they have been appointed; a company can rarely 're-educate' its members on the level of values. For most people values are developed in the first ten years of life. A company can only inform new employees of existing rituals, heroes and symbols and ask that they adopt these so as to comply with existing patterns of work behaviour.

1.8.2 Professional cultures

In addition to national and company cultures, there are also the so-called professional or job cultures, whose values are usually picked up and developed by professional staff during their training for the job they perform – for example, certified accountants, medical specialists. Of course, this is particularly apparent in the professional organization – one in which most people are employed with the same professional training, such as an accountancy practice, a hospital, a faculty within a university, a consultancy or an engineering firm.

1.8.3 Culture preservation versus cultural change

The organizational culture is an important consideration with regard to the survival of the organization. It is important to constantly question the degree to which the existing culture is still appropriate, given the goals to be attained.

For those placed and working at the centre of the organization, it is not easy to answer this question; the company culture determines to a high degree the things they see and the way they react. The culture can become a self-preserving cycle of values and norms. For example, the instruments used in the personnel function are largely directed at maintaining the existing organizational culture: recruitment and selection, induction, assessment, succession in management positions and management development. These processes guarantee that the values of future employees and those of the company as a whole rarely conflict. In selection, for example, this is expressed in the question of whether the candidate will 'fit in with the organization'. In assessment, this is also addressed, either implicitly or explicitly, when the question is asked whether the person 'behaves in accordance with the values, norms and beliefs' of the unit or department of the company.

In the long term, all this can also mean that an existing organizational culture is no longer in line with the desired strategy, goals and demands of the organization with regard to primary processes crucial to the company's survival. Change is then imperative. Adjustments to strategy and to the design of the organization structure will not be enough. Sometimes, cultural change will be necessary and may even be a condition which will enable strategic renewal to take place and will allow the organizational structure to function in quite a different way.

SUMMARY

- In this chapter we have introduced the basic concepts of 'management'.
- Management is both a very old and very modern field of study. This is because management has to do with the co-operation of people.
- An organization is defined as a 'goal-realizing co-operative unit of people'.
- In this book we cover the management of labour organizations in which paid work is carried out.
- Every person in a labour organization who is in control of others and has to make decisions is a manager. This is what distinguishes a manager from other employees. In every organization, different levels of management can be recognized; each level has its own tasks and responsibilities.
- The core tasks of management are in constituting and directing. The constituting tasks enable the frame to be created within which the executive actions can take place. The directing tasks are concerned with the initiation of operational actions and the controlling and adjusting of these.

- A manager has to make decisions and co-ordinate activities and for these tasks good communication in the organization is essential. Management can be described as a process of planning, organizing, giving orders and controlling and adjusting.
- The management cycle depicts the management process as being set in motion and maintained by the manager by means of decision making, co-ordination and communication. From this we can derive the demands that are made of modern managers, which include:
  - reacting to internal and external developments;
  - achieving acceptance, quality and effectiveness in decision making;
  - efficient use of own time;
  - working according to the organizational culture.
- Criteria for the effectiveness of the organization are:
  - efficiency
  - satisfaction
  - fulfilment of stakeholders' needs and
  - self-preservation through flexibility and responsiveness.

DISCUSSION QUESTIONS

1. With reference to Management in Action at the beginning of this chapter:
   (a) Give your comments on the ranking of Europe's most respected companies.
   (b) Choose from this list a company that you know well and comment, giving more precise examples, on the most highly prized corporate attributes which are described in the article.
   (c) Why is it that European executives hold American companies up as models of management? What would be your own model?
2. Does a manager have power, or does a manager depend on others?
3. When a group of university students is waiting at a bus stop, do we have an organization?
4. 'When we refer to companies or hospitals we can speak of "organizations" whereas we cannot speak of organizations when we refer to forms of co-existence such as families or people co-habiting.' Discuss this comment.
5. Give your responses to the following questions: 'Why would organizational culture be important to management? Isn't management only concerned with time and money?'
6. 'Managers are men in three-piece suits.'

   'Managers sit behind desks.'

   'Managers are driven around in big cars by chauffeurs.'

   Give your opinion on each of the above statements and try to indicate:
   - whether the image presented is in accordance with the topics covered in Chapter 1;
   - where the image originates;
   - how the image relates to the increasing number of women in management?

Management case study

A Woman's place is in her own business

A big crop of entrepreneurs springs up in eastern Germany

When the Berlin Wall fell, Cornelia Pfaff exploited her new-found freedom by opening a boutique in the east German city of Erfurt. Women jammed in to snatch up the latest in West German fashions. Six years later, the 38-year-old Pfaff runs a chain of five stores with 21 employees, and plans to expand to nearby cities. 'It was supposed to just be for fun,' she says. 'But I did it with so much love, it has become a success.'

Companies started by women are becoming important players in the burgeoning service sector in eastern Germany. With unemployment among women around 20% in eastern Germany, female entrepreneurship is surging. More than half of self-employed professionals such as doctors, architects, and lawyers are female. Nearly a third of all businesses launched in eastern Germany since 1990 were founded by women, compared with 21% in western Germany. Altogether, economists estimate, the 150,000 new female-run companies in eastern Germany have created about 1 million jobs and contribute about $15 billion to Germany's annual gross domestic product. Some are key additions to the *Mittelstand* – the small and medium-size manufacturing companies that make up Germany's economic backbone.

Necessity forced many east German women into business. As the region's old-line industries stumbled and folded after reunification, women were hit especially hard. Lay-offs in factories in the textile and electronics industries and in agriculture put more than 750,000 women out of work. Compared with western Germany, where 38% of women work, 94% of eastern Germany's adult women had worked before reunification. While many held menial jobs, others built up careers as administrators, economists, and physicians. When the wall came down, women borrowed money under scores of government-sponsored programs designed to kick-start growth in eastern Germany.

Take Käte Lindner. Under the old regime, she was economic director for a collective of 21 state-owned packaging companies in the southern part of eastern Germany. 'Women were equipped with management skills,' says the 59-year-old grandmother. Just months after the wall fell, she managed to purchase from the still-extant East German government what remained of the *Mittelstand* boxmaking company her grandfather had started in the village of Mühlau in 1909. After buying new machinery and replacing the rundown former dance hall that served as a production facility, Lindner now employs 72 people and produces glossy packaging for such clients as CompuServe Inc. and *Reader's Digest*. Sales have quadrupled since 1991, to $3.5 million.

Not all female-run companies are so bent on expansion. Researchers who study new business growth in Germany say that companies run by women develop more slowly than those managed by men. One reason is that the profit motive isn't as strong among women entrepreneurs. According to government surveys, women cite earning profits as a fourth or fifth reason for setting up their own companies, after their desire to be self-sufficient and develop their own ideas. Male entrepreneurs cite profits as the No. 1 motive.

Laid-back approach

Gunhild Haase, for example, is content to see her kitchen-design and -installation company grow at a modest 2% annual rate. 'I don't want to immediately make a huge profit,' says the former optical engineer, who set up her business in two houses she bought in the cobblestoned city of Jena in 1992. She makes sales calls in her eight-year-old Mercedes and employs just five people, two more than when she started. 'I'm happy with my business. It's exactly as I imagined it,' she says.

To be sure, such a laid-back approach means that the female-owned *Mittelstand* and service sector of eastern Germany will hardly be able to absorb the region's 1.3 million surplus workers on their own. In addition to small service companies, the region needs to create more manufacturing jobs in order to bolster employment, economists say. Nevertheless, the explosion in female-owned businesses has provided an important cushion against devastating joblessness – and has emerged as a surprising consequence of communism's collapse.

Source: Business Week, 18 March 1996.

CASE QUESTIONS

1. Why is it that companies started by women are becoming increasingly important players in European economies (and not only in the burgeoning service sector in Eastern Germany (*see* also Exhibit 1.4, p 31)?
2. Whereas male entrepreneurs cite profit as the number one motive, the profit motive is not as strong among women entrepreneurs (according to this case). Comment on this statement.
3. Does your role model of a good manager fit the idea of equal opportunities for men and women in the management ranks in organizations?
4. What competences and characteristics does a successful entrepreneur need? Are these different for male and female entrepreneurs?

Chapter 2

Management theory and organizational development

LEARNING OBJECTIVES

After studying this chapter, you should be able to:

- explain why a study of management and organizational theory is important;
- summarize the most important schools of thought;
- understand the nature of industrial democracy and the functioning of works councils in Europe;
- describe the different stages in the growth and development of a company;
- identify the main problems experienced by an organization at each stage of development;
- consider the relative merits of a strategic and policy orientation to management on the one hand and a goal and planning orientation on the other.
- discuss the management implications of organizational development;
- describe how the relative importance of managerial considerations for growth and development changes, as the external demands made on the organization change.

Management in action

The application of a new management theory

Neil O'Conner recently enrolled himself on a three-day management course entitled 'Modern Management'. O'Conner is 47 years of age and is Chief of Technical Staff in a large public transportation company. The course addressed the subject of 'decision making in organizations'.

O'Conner was especially impressed by the sessions on the benefits of group discussions and having decision making based in smaller groups. This was stressed over and over again during the lectures. O'Conner experienced this for himself during the problem situations which the course participants had to deal with. O'Conner knew of research into the advantages of group discussion and decision making, but only when he experienced the effects himself, did he become convinced. After in-depth discussions with two of the speakers, his initial objections seemed untenable.

According to the speakers, employees, when given the opportunity to consult together in meetings, will produce sensible and well considered proposals. Furthermore, when future decisions are made on the basis of the proposals of the employees, these will be implemented without resistance or obstructions. This is because employees no longer feel that they are having decisions passed down to them, but rather they are participants in decisions themselves; as a result effective operational implementation is almost guaranteed.

O'Conner planned to put into practice some of the maxims that were brought up in the course. On his return to his department, he called a meeting in the department's canteen of the 32 mechanics working in Repair Workshop C. He told them that he was of the opinion that the norms for maintenance, repair and revision of components and the regular technical check-ups, which had been set five years earlier on the basis of time studies, were now set too widely. Recently acquired testing equipment and more modern tools had now rendered these norms inappropriate.

O'Conner told this group of employees that they were to be given the opportunity to discuss specific factors with regard to the setting of norms, and further proposed that in the future a group would be responsible for setting the norms. O'Conner left the canteen, confident that his people would not let him down and without a doubt would introduce much stricter time norms than he himself would ever have dared to propose.

INTRODUCTION

It was during the Industrial Revolution that large-scale, paid labour forces first performed work in the workshops of others of their own volition. The emergence of mechanization forced them to work for those who had enough money to buy machines. Mechanization and the new work communities it produced made completely new demands: direction had to be given and a form of 'management' was established. Industrial management meant that available resources were being used in a far more rational way than ever before. Entrepreneurs, however, by allowing others to carry out the work for them, came up against problems due to the fact that they 'only' had economic power.

During the Industrial Revolution, studies were already being carried out which made recommendations on ways of improving the competitive position of firms – the first contributions of technology and behavioural science to organizational and management theory.

Descriptive and prescriptive management theory

Organization and management theory not only addresses the *structure* of organizations, the *functioning* of organizations as a whole and the *behaviour* of the members of the organization, but also examines the *managing* and *controlling* of the processes by which the organization attains its objectives and goals.

The theory of organizations and management has two forms:

- an analytical element, and
- an application and control element.

In its analytical form, it allows us to *understand the reality* of an organization and the environment in which it operates. We can recognize and be aware of all the aspects of the world around us.

By means of observation, description and the ordering of facts and empirical data, and by testing a hypothesis in relation to real-life fact and our own experience, we try to identify the factors and discover the interrelationships and interdependencies which determine the course of what happens in the organization.

Once we know what something is and how it works, the next step is usually to put that 'something' to work and to influence its functioning, even to construct and control it – whether it is a car, a human being or an organization. This area of study is management theory in its application and control form. It is aimed at *reproduction, manipulation* and having full *control* over the things we construct.

In almost every scientific field we are rarely satisfied with just a description, explanation or analysis; we strive for *managerial knowledge* so that we can control the world around us. For example, in the field of medicine, scientists working in the area of genetics seem to be striving towards the objective of being able to fully construct and control a human being.

This applies equally to organizations and to the problems of management. Using insights into cause-and-effect relationships, management will try to bring about the desired results by controlling the activities that have been carried out in order to realize the goals of the organization. Management and organizational theory aims to provide *instruments, tools* or *techniques* and wants to be able to make *recommendations* and prescribe *guidelines for behaviour and best practice* which can be used daily in the organization in determining goals and attaining them efficiently and effectively.

In this book, we describe management and organizational theory using both dimensions. It is *descriptive* in that we use notions and concepts, categorizations and other factors to analyse, explain and order reality in such a way that it is tangible. At the same time, methods, guidelines and recommendations for action involving skills and abilities are *prescribed.*

However, the prescriptive or normative character of the theory should not be seen in absolute terms. For example, in contingency theory (a recently developed contribution to theory) it is stressed that there is *no single best way of management and organization* which can be applied to every possible situation. That is why recommendations and guidelines have always to be seen and applied according to the specific *situation.*

The choice of which theory to apply is an issue that depends upon *people*. Individuals – managers and employees – will be influenced by various factors:

- *Practical considerations* – the organization involved, its particular management and control systems.
- *Theoretical considerations* – the notions and concepts selected for attention, either implicitly or explicitly, and those aspects of theory which are expected to produce results in a particular situation.
- *The value system* – the individual's personal interpretation of the theory and practice of management and the organization, based on personal values, expectations, ideas and convictions.

In short, application of management and organizational theory is always person-dependent.

2.1 THE FIRST MANAGEMENT THEORIES

2.1.1 The rise of 'scientific management'

During the Industrial Revolution in the USA, management was based for the first time on scientific principles and experimentation – the so-called 'scientific management', as developed by F.W. Taylor. Problems addressed included:

- raising productivity;
- organizational problems in production;
- production management, cost analyses, payment systems (e.g. Taylor's 'differential piecework' plan);
- time studies, motion studies, method studies.

With the development of industry, *efficiency* became a central issue. Opportunities to raise productivity levels were being sought. Inefficient working methods (those which took up too many resources and too much time) were being replaced by objective and scientifically based norms which indicated the level of performance expected of the labourer. In this period, it was mostly engineers who laid the foundations of 'scientific management'. Names like Taylor, the Gilbreths, Emerson and Gantt are inextricably linked with this area. F.W. Taylor (1856–1915), as the 'father of scientific management', was determined to find an answer to the question of how productivity could be raised. He focused his first research on what constituted a 'fair day's work' – that is, a 'feasible, normal labour performance' for a first-class worker. He did this by using 'new' techniques such as time, motion and method studies.

For example ...

... one of Taylor's later and best known experiments – the so-called Bethlehem experiment – concerned the loading of pig iron into train wagons. His first observations showed that about 47 tons of pig iron had been loaded instead of the 12.5 tons that had previously been the average daily capacity of a worker. To prove this, Taylor experimented with working times, rest times, weight per unit of time, working methods, tools, etc. To establish the 'fair day's work' Taylor selected the so-called 'Pennsylvania D(e)utchman', a very strong, diligent and thrifty man who had to carry out in detail what he was told to do. As compensation he was promised a higher wage per unit of performance. The performance was delivered and many other labourers then followed suit and appeared to achieve the same level of performance.

In applying his methods, Taylor met a degree of hostility which can be explained to a great extent by the belief at that time that higher productivity would lead to unemployment. By a 'systematic soldiering' and a reduction in performance, the employees tried to protect themselves against 'arbitrary management' in the form of 'cutting the rates'.

To improve the organization's production function, Taylor proposed a division of work between the management and the workmen – the establishment of the management concept. In addition, the processes of planning and work preparation were separated and an operations function was introduced for the first time. Finally, Taylor introduced the manager who had a specialized task as part of a more complicated, wider set of tasks – that is, a 'narrow' task specialization and 'functional foremanship'.

With the introduction of the differential piecework wage plan, Taylor appealed to the human need for higher wages. He supported this view by paying extra to those with enhanced performance levels, with percentages increasing the nearer workers got to top performance In this way, he made it clear that the worker, as well as the entrepreneur, could profit from higher productivity.

In terms of a 'motivational theory', Taylor considered only one stimulus to be dominant and relevant – namely, the money stimulus (via a form of piecework wage). According to the workings of this stimulus, a maximum performance would be reached. This solution to the motivational problem, as advocated by Taylor and his followers, was to prove to be too simplistic.

2.1.2 The rise of 'human relations' theory

The founder of human relations theory was the psychologist, Mayo (1880–1949). This theory was based on the research in the Hawthorne factories of the Western Electric Company during the years from 1924 to 1932. (Mayo was in charge from 1927 onwards.)

In the research at the Western Electric Company, studies were made of the effects of changes in working conditions on productivity. Without exception, production appeared to rise after a change in the working conditions, regardless of the nature of that change. When, in the last phase of the study, employees returned to the original working conditions – that is shorter rest breaks, no refreshment and longer working times – the highest performance to date was registered. It became clear that the rise in productivity had to be explained by a changed attitude to the working situation, involving the following factors, among others:

- The workers were consulted on the nature and the design of the experiments.
- A new style of management was introduced.
- A higher degree of personal freedom was experienced.
- There was personal recognition of the performances delivered.
- Workers had control over their own work.
- Workers got the feeling of being an 'elite', as they were considered interesting enough to warrant study.
- Loyalty developed, workers helped each other and there was an element of social contact.

From the experiments at Western Electric Company, Mayo concluded that the morale of the workers could be affected by the method of management. Furthermore, Mayo was convinced that satisfaction in the work place was strictly dependent on the informal social group pattern. In other words, Mayo came to the conclusion that a great number of socio-psychological factors influence the functioning of an organization and as a result managers needed to acquire social skills in order to be able to make positive use of human relationships in production groups. Technological knowledge and technical skills alone, as stressed by Taylor and others, were insufficient if the process of management was to attain optimal production results. As a result, the importance of a socially oriented style of leadership and management was placed at the forefront of management theory.

Later theories of motivation

Theories on management and motivation, based on the notions of scientific management and the human relations theory, were further developed in the years after 1950. This will be covered in more detail in Chapters 8 and 9.

2.1.3 The rise of management process theory

Henri Fayol (1841–1925) was introduced in Chapter 1 as the founder of management theory. Fayol was of the opinion that management skills could be learned. The problem was that, in his time, there was no theoretical model available that could be seen as the basis for management education. The contribution of Fayol from 1916 onwards filled the gap and can be seen as the first systematic analysis of the elements of management behaviour in governing a business. Fayol broke down the management function into five essential parts, as indicated in section 1.5:

1. policy making and planning (prévoir);
2. organizing (organiser)
3. giving instructions and support during implementation (commander);
4. co-ordinating (coordonner);
5. control and if necessary adjustment (controler).

2.1.4 Characteristics of the first management theories

The first management theories had the following features in common:

- They were derived from what happened in practice on a day-to-day basis. Actual daily activities were scientifically analysed and then systematized; normative actions were not subject to the same level of discussion.
- They arose out of a situation in which it was assumed that the employer enjoyed a great deal of autonomy, being rarely affected by the world outside the organization. (In those days the employer pretty well 'ran the show'.)
- They were directed at finding a single best solution and method which could be applied to every situation which seemed to lead to a preferred, uniform way of management.

2.2 THE MODERN SCHOOLS OF MANAGEMENT AND ORGANIZATIONAL THEORY

In addition to the first three founding schools of management theory, described in section 2.1, a further nine areas of development in management and organizational theory can be distinguished. These are:

- Structure theory
- Revisionism
- Decision-making theory
- Communication and information theory
- Systems theory
- Strategy theory
- Environment theory
- Theory of the growth and development of organizations
- Contingency theory.

The contributions of these schools of thought are described in the course of this book, as we follow the development of management and organizational theory (without necessarily making direct and repeated reference to each of them). A brief description of each of the nine schools follows, with an indication of where a more detailed discussion can be found.

2.2.1 Structure theory

The structure theorists focus attention on the rules and principles of designing – that is, building up and extending – the organizational structure. In addition, they often provide further insights, by way of empirical research, into the internal functioning of the 'organization as an instrument'. Obviously, sociological considerations will play an important role in this approach. Although organizational structure was covered in the preceding schools of thought, the subject was given far greater emphasis from 1945 onwards. (*See* Chapters 6 and 7 on effective organization structure for more detail.)

2.2.2 Revisionism

Bennis (1961) once characterized the scientific management movement as a way of thinking through the theme of 'organizations without people', while the human relations movement concerned the theme of '*people without organizations*'. Revisionism can be described using similar terms as an approach whereby the theme of '*people and the organization*' becomes the focus of problem formulation. In the 1950s, earlier elements of organizational theory were being reviewed, expanded and enriched. For example, Argyris (1964) referred to an 'individual integrated into the organization'. This integration can be given a concrete form by means of task enlargement, task enrichment and task rotation (*see* section 7.2), as well as by developing a new, more appropriate style of leadership (*see* Chapter 9). In the contributions of the Revisionism school *internal democracy* and the *humanization of work* are placed at the forefront. This direction of thought is especially relevant to the handling of problems of organizational design and leadership style.

2.2.3 Decision-making theory

Decision making becomes a problem if the view is held that the individuals concerned have limited cognitive abilities and are also affected by subjective or emotional (i.e. irrational) factors. Individual decision makers cannot know all the possible alternatives for action, while subjective and irrational influences play a role in the consideration of alternatives. Since the late 1940s, the postulate of complete *'objective rationality'* that characterized the *'homo economicus'* as a decision maker has been changed by Simon (1947) into *'bounded rationality'* or *'subjective rationality'*. The notion of 'one omniscient decision taker' in an organization at the top of the hierarchy is also no longer considered valid. The focus is now on the total process of decision *making* instead of decision *taking* in the narrow sense of the word. Now, the decision-making process is broken down into its constituent parts in a complex organization and is conceived as a process that consists of a series of steps (*see* Chapter 4).

2.2.4 Communication and information theory

This area of management theory concentrates on the key role of communication and information systems. Such systems have many similarities with cybernetics. Communication is a process of which *feedback* is considered to be an integral part. A system of 'two-way traffic' is emphasized. The feedback principle is also an essential ingredient in the managing of other processes including the setting of targets and operational norms, regulation, adjustments and corrective actions – in short, planning and control. Communication can take different forms – oral, written, electronic, horizontal, vertical, lateral – with different structures and patterns. (Communication structure and the effectiveness of communication and decision making are covered in Chapters 4, 8, 9, 10 and 11.)

2.2.5 Systems theory

The influence of systems theory on management and organizations is said to have developed around 1950 (although systems theory was applied to biology as far back as 1932). In principle, the theory is based around the general concept of a 'system' which can be applied in all sorts of scientific fields. In organization and management theory, the system model is used by considering organizations as 'open' systems – that is, systems which are in interaction with their surrounding environment (for example, the acquisition of energy, information and other resources and the provision of goods and services). This approach calls for renewed attention to be focused on the relationships of the organization's constituent parts and for the *control of processes* in the context of the whole organization. Business process redesign (BPR) – sometimes referred to as process re-engineering or business network redesign (*see* Chapter 12) – can be seen as a 1990s revival of these concepts from the 1950s in the era of information technology.

2.2.6 Strategy theory

The central issue in strategy theory is the striving for the survival, self-preservation or continuity of the organization in an ever-changing and complex environment. This school focuses further attention on the relationship between the organization and the surrounding environment with which it is interacting on a continuous basis. This relationship was first given prominence in the early 1960s during a period of dramatic change in the nature of the technological, societal and market environment. The relation between organization and environment has been investigated further in the intervening years (*see* Chapter 5).

2.2.7 Environment theory

From 1965 onwards, the external environment of the organization was seen as an 'independent' entity, laying down the rules of engagement for the organization, in stark contrast to earlier views which had seen the organization as autonomous and setting its own rules. Environment theorists try to develop models whereby events in the environment can be observed and can become manageable. In organization and management theory, it is important not only to study the features of the environment, to which the structure and behaviour of the organization can be related, but also to study the links and dependencies that exist in a network of organizations. The concepts of 'the organization as a network' and 'organizational webs' relate to inter-organizational co-operation between intelligent organizations (*see* Chapters 3 and 5 for further detail).

2.2.8 Theory of the growth and development of organizations

This school of thought, which has emerged since 1970, is concerned with both the various phases of growth and development in the economic–technological sense, as well as the problems of growth in the socio-psychological sense. (For economic–technological aspects of management, *see* Chapters 2 and 6; for socio-psychological aspects, *see* Chapters 2 and 9.)

2.2.9 Contingency theory

The starting-point for organizational contingency theory can be summarized in the phrase '*situationally dependent*'. In other words, no single best way can be advocated or given at the outset, for example, for structural design or for style of leadership. Recommendations, 'laws' or principles on planning, organizing and leadership have to be adapted to fit specific situations. These contingency contributions to theory, which emerged after 1960, were intended as a means of reviewing and enhancing earlier insights and theories, and they were mostly based on empirical research results. Contributions to the development of theory from this school of thought appear in every chapter of this book.

Figure 2.1 relates the different schools of management and organizational theory to the core tasks of management.

2.2.10 Management and organizational theory: an interdisciplinary field

By definition, the theory of organization and management is interdisciplinary in nature. *In theory*, human behaviour can be divided into areas of study which can be researched as single disciplines (for example, economics, psychology, sociology). *In reality*, however, human behaviour can only be viewed as a unity and a whole.

Those seeking practical solutions to specific problem situations will find only limited support in those single disciplines or subject-specific theories. Managers and specialists in the field need to realize that the direct application of insights from just one of the single disciplines carries risks. It means that only one aspect of a problem is put under the microscope, while other aspects get little or no attention. This does not reflect reality; it gives an unbalanced and biased view. An example would be a head of department who spent too little time acting as a leader during the evaluation of

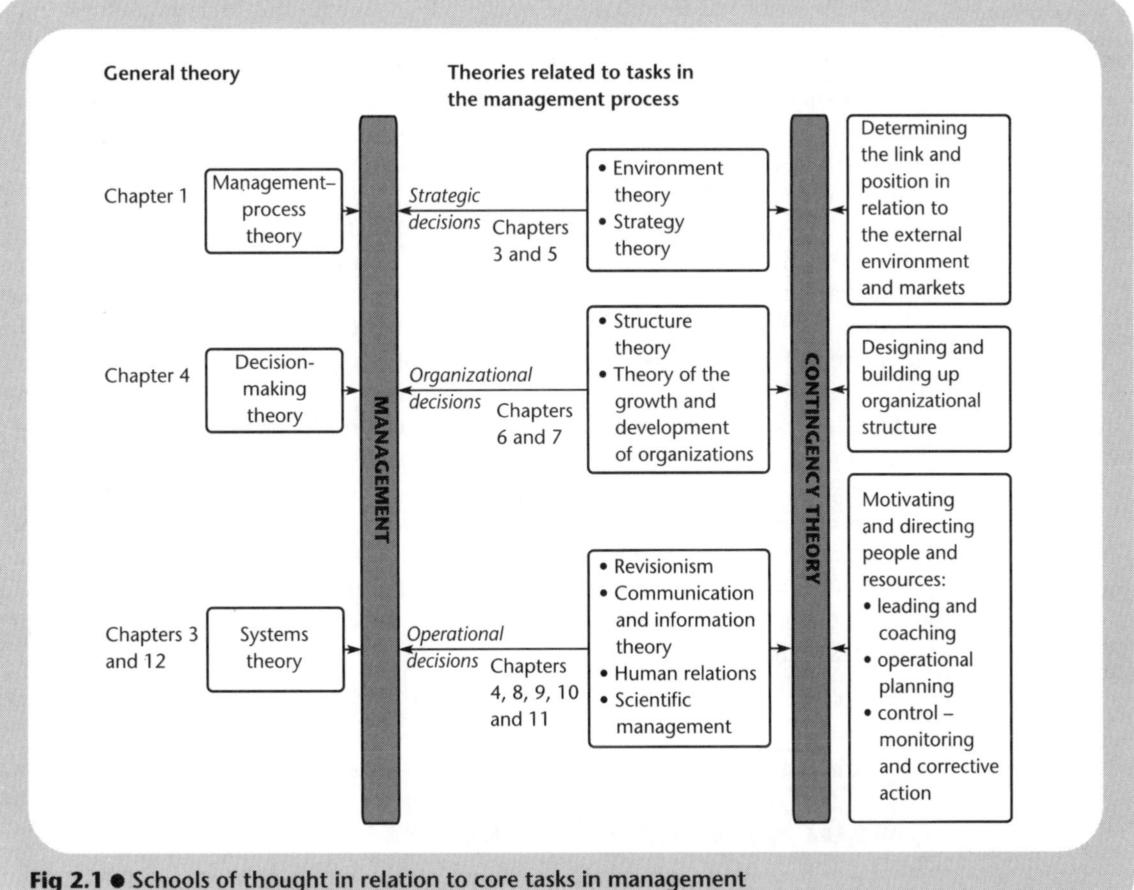

Fig 2.1 ● Schools of thought in relation to core tasks in management

results, and too much time as a psychologist or lawyer. The different aspects of the problem need to be related to each other – that is, the 'demands' that are made by the different factors first have to be integrated into the thoughts and actions of the manager. Only then can we do justice to reality.

2.3 ● INDUSTRIAL AND ORGANIZATIONAL DEMOCRACY IN A EUROPEAN CONTEXT

Flatter organizations with less of a hierarchy, participative decision making and increased self-determination by workers seem to be irreversible steps in the organizational development of firms. Sweden, Norway, Germany, the Netherlands and Denmark lead the way with such developments; Finland, Ireland, United Kingdom, France, Belgium and the Latin-European countries like Italy, Greece, Spain and Portugal follow some distance behind these north-west European countries. Increasing industrial democracy enables firms to better realize their societal responsibilities and to act in a more ethical way. Participative arrangements are often implemented with the belief that participation will improve productivity and performance.

The move towards the different forms of organizational democracy (which began after the Second World War) continues, albeit slowly, along different lines and in a somewhat piecemeal fashion. Students and worker uprisings in France, Germany and the Netherlands in the late 1960s and early 1970s gave new momentum to legislative processes in several European countries. Industrial democracy might again become an issue and could be somewhat accelerated by European Union (EU) legislation which permits and promotes different styles of participation and democratic processes. Respecting existing differences in national cultures and value patterns and acknowledging pluralistic national regulations seem likely to be important in future EU legislation.

At the Maastricht Summit (December 1991) the EU member countries – with the exception of the UK – agreed to strengthen employee participation rights in the states of the European Union and to further harmonize employment practices and laws. British firms, operating in other EU countries or doing business with clients in EU member countries, will of course be affected by these socio-political decisions of the EU.

The notion of joint decision making is already accepted and established as a feature of corporate life in the majority of countries in Western Europe (*see* Table 2.1 for a Europe-wide overview). Managers in Germany, Sweden and the Netherlands, for example, already work in the institutional and legal framework of joint consultation with works councils, on the one hand, and boards of directors which include worker representatives on the other.

Exhibit 2.1

Works councils total up in EU

More than 140 companies operating in the European Union have already set up works councils, three months before the controversial European Works Council Directive takes effect, according to research by the European Commission.

The list includes 13 UK companies, even though the directive does not cover the UK because of its opt-out from the Maastricht treaty's social chapter. The directive says every company operating in the EU employing over 1,000 people, with 150 of them in at least two member states, must establish a workers' information and consultation committee.

Many companies have acted early, as concluding agreements before the directive takes effect on September 22 avoids certain formal requirements, such as establishment of a special negotiating body.

German and French companies make up half the list, with 43 and 31 respectively. The US and Japan appear seven times each, while of EU members only Spain and Greece are not represented.

Source: *Financial Times*, 5 July 1996.

Exhibit 2.1 continued

EU unions to push 800 companies for councils

European trade union leaders plan to target more than 800 multinational companies and demand they set up consultative works councils for employees under the European Union law that came into force this weekend in 17 EU and European Economic Area countries.

An estimated 20 per cent of the multinational companies covered by the legislation have already negotiated voluntarily with trade unions to create such an information and consultation body at the corporate level of their business. From today employers will be compelled by law to create a works council if asked to do so by their workers.

Estimates by both the Warwick University Business School in the UK and the EU-funded European Foundation for the Improvement of Living and Working Conditions suggest that over 200 out of an estimated 1,152 companies covered may have negotiated agreements with their employees or trade unions. The EU legislation requires every company (including those which are US- and Japanese-owned) which employs more than 1,000 workers in the 17 countries, with over 150 in at least two member states, to establish an employee consultation and information committee.

The largest number of European works councils so far negotiated have been in Germany (27 per cent of them, more than 41) followed by France (22 per cent or over 25). But 14 per cent of agreements are with UK companies, despite the UK's opt-out from the social chapter of the Maastricht treaty which does not require those companies to create works councils to include their UK workers. Only one agreement – the Dutch-owned banking and insurance group ING – explicitly excludes its British workers from its works council.

The European Foundation survey found a third of all works council agreements included countries outside the area covered by the law, such as Switzerland, the Czech Republic, Hungary and Poland.

As many as 35 per cent of the existing agreements (61) are in the metalworking sector, followed by 25.4 per cent in chemicals (44) and 14.5 per cent in food, hotels and catering (25), according to the Warwick report, compiled by Mr Mark Hall from its industrial relations research unit. By contrast, only one retail company has negotiated a European works council, and there is one in telecommunications, A study of 111 voluntary European works councils published today the European Foundation found at least one in four French companies and one in six of UK companies had signed such an agreement voluntarily.

It also said that although trade unions were not specifically mentioned in the directive they had been 'heavily involved' in their creation, with 55 per cent of agreements signed by a trade union organisation. The survey suggests only about 15 per cent of works councils have been created without trade union influence.

The study has also found full-time trade union officials are directly taking part in half of the works councils so far created, and more will participate as so-called experts in an advisory role on the new bodies. Two thirds of all the negotiated councils provide for trade unions to nominate employee representatives in all or some of the European countries covered.

Three-quarters of the works councils are joint management-employee bodies and 80 per cent cover all the operations of the multinational, with the rest providing for divisional-level structures. Their average size is 25 on the workers' side, with size ranging between seven and 70. Around half have smaller select committees created to prepare for the council meetings which 90 per cent of companies hold once a year.

In 84 per cent of agreements, worker representatives are allowed to meet without the company management being present. Over half provide for a report back to the workforce as a whole in the operation of the works councils.

Source: Financial Times, 23 September 1996.

2.3.1 Organizational democracy

Organizational democracy in its broadest sense encompasses a considerable variety of interpersonal and/or structural arrangements which link organizational decision making to the interests and influence of employees at all levels of the organization. It determines the degree to which employees can influence the decision making of the firm or institution in which they work.

Examples of relatively weak forms of organizational democracy, where employees have only a small measure of influence over decision making, include quality circles or informal work consultation during meetings on certain aspects of work. However, many people only use the word 'democracy' to describe circumstances involving substantial influence on important decisions – not only consultation with workers at the operational core or via a works council, but also decision making at top management or board level. Supervisory boards – with members elected by employees or nominated by a union to represent the views of employees – as a form of decentralized decision making from the top of the organization, as well as a vehicle for initiatives on safety, health care and working conditions at the bottom of the organization can indeed be seen as forms of organizational democracy.

Research among British managers and shop stewards has shown almost unanimous (95 per cent) support for work group meetings and job design with a large majority considering these to be of interest to employees as well as management in organizations. These findings are consistent with further research which showed that employees welcomed direct participation – as well as indirect participation – in every respect, and at the same time recognized that such participation was of advantage, not only to themselves, but also to the company for which they work.

It is significant that the great majority of workers do not expect participation (both direct and indirect) to affect power differences between management and workers. These findings therefore indicate that it is functional democracy that is beneficial from the workers' perspective.

Various studies have produced circumstantial evidence to support the fact that participation not only influences the atmosphere of an organization in a positive way, but ultimately also has a positive influence on efficiency and effectiveness. Research studies into US experiences (Crouch and Heller 1983, Wilpert and Sorge 1988) with the Scanlon plan and the Quality of Working Life (QWL) programmes, the long-term effects of socio-technical reorganization in Indian textile mills, Swedish organization development (OD) programmes and Norwegian industrial democracy experiments all point to the successful implementation of functional democracy, and an accompanying increase in performance and improvement in the working climate of the organization.

2.3.2 Future EU legislation and directives on industrial democracy

On 22 September 1994, the EU member states agreed a directive (Directive 94/95 Concerning the Institution of the Euro Works Council) that could lead to fully fledged employee participation across Europe. The directive states that employees in companies and institutions (which meet certain criteria) have to be informed and/or consulted on cross-border affairs. This EU directive was to be included in national legislation not later than 22 September 1996. Negotiations to establish a European Works Council (EWC) are continuing. It must be said, however, that EU harmonization, not to mention unification, in this respect is still a long way off. The somewhat unrealistic belief in EU political circles is that the four models of employee participation which can be distinguished in the EU at this point in time and which reflect the degree of workers' influence in the diverse corporate governance structures are equivalent to each other. These are:

1. A minimum of one third and a maximum of one half of the members of the supervisory board are nominated by the employees (the German '*Mitbestimmungs*' variant).

2. The members of the supervisory board are all nominated according to the system of controlled co-option (the Dutch variant).
3. An employee representative body is installed at the highest level of the organization and has to be kept informed and consulted on all matters which are on the agenda of the supervisory board (the French–Italian variant).
4. There is compulsory regulation of employee participation through collective labour agreements (the so-called Swedish collective bargaining variant).

These official models can be seen, more or less, as a reflection of three dominant patterns of thought, which are recognizable in the different structures of industrial relations at corporate levels in the EU member states – *negotiation, opposition* and *integration* – currently applied most unambiguously and coherently in the United Kingdom, France and Germany respectively. In other countries we often see combinations of these three approaches (*see* Table 2.1).

2.3.3 The German and Dutch system

The German and Dutch system of industrial democracy is regarded as the most comprehensive in Europe. The system comprises a works council (*Betriebsrat/Ondernemingsraad*), a representation on the board of directors or supervisory board (*Aufsichtsrat/Raad van Commissarissen*) and the executive board or board of management (*Vorstand/Raad van Bestuur*).

Works councils exist in organizations in all areas of both the private and public sectors. Representatives on works councils are elected by their fellow workers. The works council has three basic rights:

1. the right to receive information concerning the financial position, performance, future prospects and strategic position of the organization;
2. the right to be consulted by top management on decisions of strategic importance like major investments, reorganization, changing location, acquisitions or closing down subsidiaries, etc.;
3. the right of co-determination concerning essential aspects of the management of personnel. The works council by law has discretionary power in policies concerning work regulations, regulations on pensions, profit sharing or savings, working day and holiday arrangements, regulations concerning safety, health care and the welfare of personnel, regulations on appointment, dismissal or promotion, salary policy, position of the younger workers in the organization, etc.

The works council also has the right to be consulted on any decision to appoint or dismiss an executive manager at board level and to veto board appointments.

The formal authority to appoint members of the board of management lies at the level of the supervisory board (or board of directors). The supervisory board, if necessary, can veto policy decisions of the board of management – for example, in the case of a merger or an excessively risky acquisition – or can urge the board of management to abandon a policy.

Representatives on the supervisory board – whether nominated by shareholders, workers or unions – are always supposed to act and take decisions on behalf of the company or the institution as a whole. Supervisory board members are not supposed to simply represent the interest of a specific group.

The board of management in German organizations (*Vorstand*) includes a so-called '*Arbeitsdirektor*' – a personnel director. This *Arbeitsdirektor* cannot be appointed without the consent of the majority of worker representatives on the '*Aufsichtsrat*' (the supervisory board), according to the *Mitbestimmungsgesetz* 1976. The chosen *Arbeitsdirektor* has the same rights and legal status as the other members of the board of management. Of course, the works council is an important point of reference for the execution of the *Arbeitsdirektor*'s duties.

Exhibit 2.2

Austrian tyre workers fight plant removal

Workers at an Austrian tyre company yesterday threatened to use force to stop its German owners removing machinery from the plant to another of their factories in the Czech Republic.

The works council at Semperit, a subsidiary of the German tyre company Continental, was reacting to plans by the Hanover-based group to shift half its tyre production from Traiskirchen to the Czech Republic and to make 1,100 of the 2,300 employees in Austria redundant.

Continental's plans have set off a heated controversy in Austria about employment practices by foreign investors, especially German companies. It has become a key issue in the European Parliament election campaign on October 13.

The Austrian government has made several efforts to prevent the redundancies, but was criticised by the opposition for not doing enough. Austrian industry experts fear the plant will not be viable at a reduced annual capacity of 2m car tyres and will eventually be shut. Continental dismissed these predictions and cited the 500,000 truck tyres it will continue to make.

Mr Rudolf Neubauer, chairman of Semperit's works council, said he would personally block the removal of equipment and even chain himself to the machines. Management responded by threatening to sack resisting workers and even to shut the plant down.

Observers fear that a physical confrontation could spark violence and deter other foreign companies from investing in Austria. By law, local police would be obliged to assist the removal of machinery, for Continental is the legal owner of the plant. But as the public is nearly united in its support for the Semperit staff, the authorities would probably shy away from any drastic measures.

The Traiskirchen region south of Vienna is economically depressed and offers little alternative employment to redundant workers.

Once the flagship of Austrian industry, Semperit was nearly bankrupt when acquired by Continental in 1985. But the Traiskirchen plant generated solid profits in recent years, and even some conservative public leaders have suggested that international investors should be prevented from putting a healthy enterprise at risk for the sake of even higher profits.

But some economists point out that Semperit's high labour costs and the decline in its sales to Japanese car-makers after Austria joined the European-Union in 1995 gives Continental a good reason to move production to lower-cost sites.

Source: *Financial Times*, 1 October 1996.

2.3.4 Industrial democracy in Europe: a comparative survey

The range of attitudes to work councils across the European Union is shown in Fig 2.2, with more detail of the individual approaches to industrial democracy included in Table 2.1. Germany and the Netherlands are influenced by a different view of the organization (it is considered as a co-operative working organization rather than as an arena) and a different concept of the works council (as a meeting point between the entrepreneur/owner and the unions – the works council is seen as the representative body of the employees).

The countries in the upper boxes of the matrix in Fig 2.2 – Belgium and Denmark, Germany and the Netherlands – have in common the notion of joint decision making

	Works council as meeting point of entrepreneur and unions	Works council as representative of employees
The firm as a co-operative working organization; not as an arena	Belgium Denmark	Germany The Netherlands
The firm as an arena	France	Spain

Fig 2.2 ● Position of works councils in relation to different views of the organization in some EU countries

through co-operation with the works council; they are different with regard to the position of the works council vis-à-vis the unions and vis-à-vis the owner/entrepreneur. In the lower boxes, this notion is less developed; the firm is organized as an arena where the entrepreneur meets with the unions. The works council is still a 'strange intruder', although in several ways regulations are similar to those in the countries in the upper boxes.

The left-hand column indicates the dominance of unions in the works council. The works council is not the most important instrument for democracy and participation; that remains union representation. In the right-hand column the works council is rather independent of union influence. It enjoys greater autonomy with respect to the unions compared to those in the left-hand column, but not complete autonomy as regulations concerning the nomination of candidates for the works council might show.

In the right-hand column, the formal authorities of the works council are more extensive, but this is balanced out as a rule by the weaker presence of unions in the firm's organization – something that applies more to Germany and the Netherlands than it does to Spain.

Table 2.1 ● Diversity in patterns of industrial democracy in EU countries

Austria, Germany, Luxembourg and the Netherlands (North-west European model)

- Legislation exists concerning participation and joint decision making in enterprises and public institutions.
- The instrument for joint decision making is the works council (*Betriebsrat/comité mixte d'enterprise/Ondernemingsraad*) with a varying level of influence (more in Austria, Luxembourg and Germany; less in the Netherlands) through the supervisory council and/or board of management. The influence of employees is enhanced through representation on the supervisory council and board of management.
- There is a right of co-determination in personnel affairs and a right of consultation and information in economic and organizational affairs.

continued overleaf

Table 2.1 ● Continued

Ireland and the United Kingdom (the Anglo–Irish model)

- No legislation exists concerning participation and joint decision making in enterprises and public institutions (voluntarism).
- The instrument for employee participation is the union through the shop steward. No participation or representation of employees on the board of directors (the two-tier system of supervisory board/board of management is rare), with the exception of Ireland where in public institutions employee representatives have been nominated to the board of management since the end of the 1970s.
- There is no right of co-determination; negotiations are the way to influence social policy and the economic affairs of an organization (including conditions of employment).

Denmark, Finland, Norway and Sweden (North-west European/Anglo–Irish mixed model)

- Legislation exists concerning participation and joint decision making in enterprises and public institutions in Sweden and Norway; in Denmark the existence of works councils (*Samarbejdsudvalg* (SU)) goes back to a gentlemen's agreement between employers' organizations and unions (*Dansk Arbejdgiverforening* (DA) and the *Landsorganisationen* (LO) in Denmark in 1947, renewed in 1986). The degree of statutory participation is a step behind that of the other Scandinavian countries.
- Instruments for employee participation are the unions through the shop stewards, in Denmark the representation of employees on the supervisory council (the *Bestyrelse*), in Sweden the appointment of two workers' directors on the board of directors and in Norway the election of one third of members of the board of directors and supervisory board by employees, after nomination by local unions.
- There is a right of co-determination in social policies, conditions of employment, pension fund administration and the organization of the production function. Only rights of information and consultation apply in economic affairs.

Belgium, France, Greece, Italy, Portugal and Spain (Latin-European model)

- Legislation exists concerning participation in enterprises and public institutions.
- Instruments for employee participation in two- or three-way structures include:
  (a) union representation through syndical delegation (Belgium, Greece, Italy, Portugal and Spain);
  (b) works councils in all countries (in Belgium *Ondernemingsraad*; in France *comité d'enterprise* (CE); in Spain *comite de empresa* (CE); in Italy *consiglio di farica dei delegati*; in Portugal *comissoes de trabalhadores* (CT).
  (c) personnel council (in France *delegues du personnel* and in Spain the *delegados de personal*)
- No worker representatives on supervisory councils in Belgium; in France a CE member has the right to attend a meeting of the board of management or supervisory council (*conseil d'administration*); in Italy, there are no legal obligations to have employee representatives on the boards. On the basis of so-called protocol some major industrial groups like IRI, ENI, EFIM created in 1984 bilateral committees to be consulted on economic affairs and social strategies of the firms. In Greece, Portugal and Spain employees are represented on the board of management of government enterprises and public institutions.
- No prescribed rights of co-determination, with the exception of the conditions of employment; rights of information and consultation exists concerning social and economic policies, pension funds and production organization.
- In all these countries (with the exception of Portugal) there are health and safety committees prescribed by legislation. In Portugal, existing health and safety committees in the bigger firms are installed on the basis of collective bargaining.

In Fig 2.2, Germany and the Netherlands are placed in the same box because of the common logic behind the formal works council regulations and legislation. However, there are substantial differences between these two countries, the most important of which is the representation of the employees and the unions on the supervisory council, which is not particularly strongly and explicitly regulated in the Netherlands.

2.4 ORGANIZATIONAL AND MANAGEMENT CONSIDERATIONS FOR GROWTH AND DEVELOPMENT

Organizations are always in motion and the world around the organizations never rests. As a result, different and often new management problems arise. It is often the case that the stage of development of an organization will determine the way in which problems are handled. When an organization becomes larger and more complex, problems are approached more and more systematically and with reference to policy. Those factors which receive special attention at each stage of growth and development will become clear when we start to examine the relationship between the different management factors and growth.

In all organizations – whether an established company, a business starting up or a firm which has been recently taken over – questions of a strategic, organizational and operational nature are always under discussion. However, the stage of development of a business will dictate which factors receive the most urgent attention. Whether the situation involves a new business or an existing business with a solid reputation, it remains important to consider in advance *what* has to be done, *where* the activities will be performed and *how* they will be carried out. The goals and plans for the coming period need to be constantly under review.

In other words, from the business point of view, it is not sufficient simply to know what is required; it is important to know the ways in which and the resources with which the goals set or proposed are going to be attained.

2.4.1 Starting up a business

In principle there are three ways of starting a business:

- setting up a new firm;
- a company takeover (or management buyout);
- company succession.

Setting up a new firm

For the **entrepreneur** who is just starting out, the setting up of a new firm has the advantage that many matters can be determined by the entrepreneur. The founding entrepreneur determines among other things:

- *which products* the company will be supplying;
- the *location* where the company activities will be performed;
- the *legal form* in which the company will be managed;
- the *size* of the company;

- the *scope* of the activities, not only in a technological terms, but also in the sense of financial and human resources;
- the *design of production methods, the production line* and the *organization.*

On the negative side, the starting costs are pretty high and it may be some time before revenue starts to be generated.

For example ...

What are the services our fellow human beings require? More and more entrepreneurial Europeans are trying to find out. The shoeshiner has made a comeback. Even ironing is not necessary anymore, for those who can afford to pay someone to do it for them. From the comfort of one's own home, one telephone call is all it takes to send for a Greek meal or a pizza. 'Kitty litter', videos, breakfast in bed even, a new cover for a worn-out chair or just a filled shopping bag – one telephone call and somebody will bring them to your doorstep.

More and more people are starting up their own businesses. Often these have to be built up from scratch, by one person or one family. In the past entrepreneur was a dirty word, or so it seemed. An entrepreneur got rich on the backs of other people and contributed to the pollution of the environment. Some entrepreneurs are just people who have been looking for work for some time and who want to see whether they can work for themselves. Most entrepreneurs also prefer not to have a boss looking over their shoulders all the time.

For example ...

Rick Meyer of a dog service company, Paw, describes himself as 'pig-headed' – which is why being his own boss suits him. 'When you think of something at night, it is more profitable. A boss appreciates you thinking after working hours, but that is that.' For the last four years he has run a dog-walking service, together with his partner Jenny Lane.

It started out in a very modest way. 'The starting capital was spent on an answering machine,' Rick comments. They picked up and dropped off the dogs with their own car. The dog service developed out of a hobby of Rick's: dog training. Every now and then he walked other people's dogs. After an advertisement about the dog service in the local newspaper, customers came flocking in. After a while, he resigned from his old job as a distributor of newspapers. Jenny gradually gave up hers too. The couple have now even hired somebody to help them. The customers are usually 'dinkies' – dual-income, no kids – shift workers or elderly people who want their dogs to receive more exercise.

Entrepreneurs starting out in business for the first time might find the following points useful.

- Be open to advice.
- Let someone from a bank look over plans and make comments on them.
- An ideal entrepreneur can associate well with other people.
- Sales skills are useful, as are strategic thinking and the ability to make deals.
- A new entrepreneur doesn't need to be superhuman.

Company takeovers

The takeover of a company often requires a large initial investment. The entrepreneur, when purchasing an existing company, will have to research thoroughly the true value of the company involved. Sometimes it is necessary to be mindful of the loss of customers when the company changes owner; sometimes the range of products needs to be revised, or the essential company functions like marketing and sales, production and purchasing are not carried out adequately.

In the past few years, *management buyouts* have become more common. In these cases, the ownership of the company is transferred to its management – often with the help of venture capital from (private) investment companies. In some cases, the personnel will also be involved in the transaction. It is often the case that large companies, after reviewing their current activities, may decide on a strategic reorientation and repositioning of the company which involves a return to core activities. This may involve the liquidation of assets or privatization of peripheral parts of the business in the form of a management buyout or acquisition by another company (for example, ITT, ABB, Philips or Unilever).

Company succession

Company succession provides the new starter with the opportunity to acquire knowledge of business matters and make use of the **goodwill** of the retiring entrepreneur.

When looking to take over a company or take over management of a company by means of gradual succession, where the company is in private hands, it is important to know the true value of the company. In this respect the expertise of an accountant and bank manager are certainly of value. The purchase price can be seen as the sum of the equity of a company and the value of possible goodwill. Goodwill is an extra amount of money which is paid, in the case of a takeover, for the good name of the company that is to be taken over, which has arisen from the unique product or service offered.

Depending on the line of business, different calculation methods are used; the amount of money to be paid for goodwill is determined by opportunities to make future profits from the company that is to be taken over. The total profit then needs to stay above the normal entrepreneurial income (in that particular line of business) plus a normal compensation for the equity capital. This extra profit capacity forms the added value (that is, goodwill) which gives rise to 'extra' value and in the event that this profit potential can be continued in the future. The takeover price which eventually needs to be paid is a matter for negotiation. As well as factors such as location, directory of customers, clients, market product and so on, subjective matters also play their part, especially future expectations of profitability and potential for development.

2.4.2 Questions of policy after the start

Once a company has got underway and shows a certain degree of growth, or when a company has gained an established position, policy questions on the route to expansion and growth have to be addressed – for example, changes in the legal form, methods of financing (possibly by means of stock exchange flotation), whether or not to co-operate with other companies (partially by alliance and joint venture, or completely by means of takeover or merger).

When a company does not have all the necessary resources at its disposal (for example, finance, new products, distribution channels, etc.), it can perhaps look for external financial resources; it can also seek co-operation with another company. These questions can be looked into further by distinguishing the individual stages in the growth and development of companies and by determining which factors require especial attention at each stage.

2.4.3 Stages in the growth and development of a company

The problems facing a particular company will to a certain extent be a function of the company's position in the cycle of organizational growth and development.

Compare, for example, the growth and development problems of a six-month old company with 20 employees, to the growth and development problems of an established company which has existed for 30 years and has 600 employees. In the former case, for example, the planning of cash flow may be vital, while in the latter case, co-ordination and control of company activities by means of explicit strategic planning and budgeting are perhaps most important. In order to gain a better insight into the problems of small and growing companies, five *stages of growth* can be distinguished:

1. build up;
2. survival;
3. success;
4. take-off and expansion;
5. resource maturity and optimal position.

Companies can be considered in more detail by positioning them according to two axes – young–mature and small–large – using an index of size, number of locations, diversity and complexity and by considering five factors in relation to management: managerial style, **organizational structure**, extent of formal systems, major strategic goals and involvement of the owner(s) in the company's business. This cycle of development is described by Churchill and Lewis (1983) as shown in Fig 2.3.

Stage 1: build up

The main problems with which a company is confronted during build up are obtaining customers/clients and meeting obligations with regard to the delivery and supply of products and services. The most fundamental questions for the new business include:

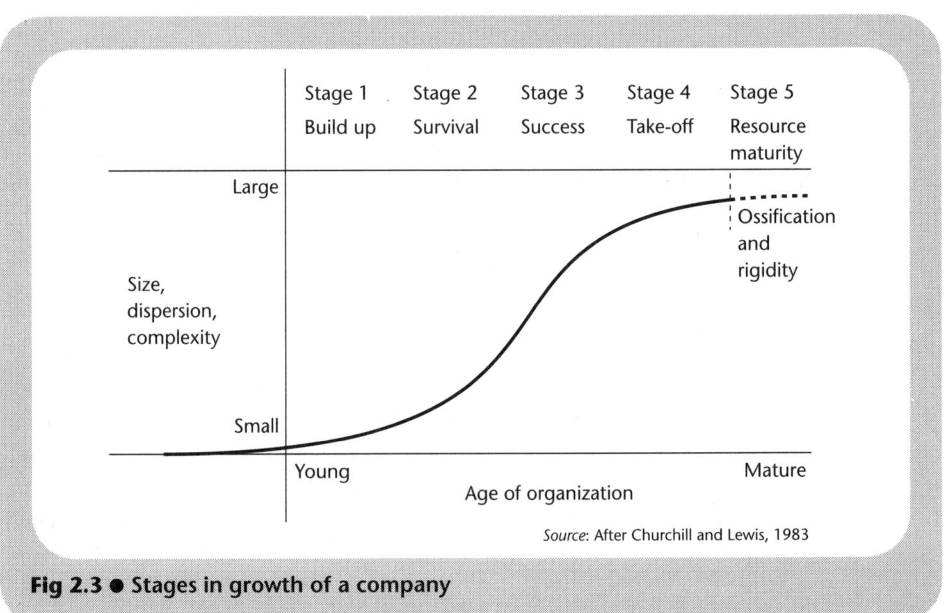

Fig 2.3 ● Stages in growth of a company

- Will we be able to fulfil our orders? Is our service good enough? Can we find enough clients to make our company viable?
- Will our customer base ever expand beyond that of one key account or will our one pilot production process move onto a much broader sales base?
- Do we have enough money to cover the considerable cash demands needed to start up activities and build up business?

The organization's structure is simple: the owner directly supervises employees, who should be, at least, of average competence and fit for their task. Systems and formal planning are rarely referred to. The strategy of the company is to stay operational. The owner *is* the business, performing all the important tasks, acting as the major driving force, determining the course which the company follows and, perhaps together with relatives and friends, taking on the role of a major supplier of capital. Companies which are in the build-up stage can vary from new restaurants or retail shops to companies in a high-tech industry in which the production or quality of products has yet to stabilize.

Many of these companies will not gain sufficient customer acceptance or bring about an effective enough product capability to become viable. In such cases, the owner will close down the company, once the initial capital has run out and – if lucky – will sell the business for its asset value. The owner may also pull out for other reasons, for example because the company takes up too much time, money and energy. Those companies that remain in business become Stage 2 enterprises.

Stage 2: survival

When a business makes it to Stage 2, it has shown itself to be viable and a workable business entity. There are sufficient customers and the quality of the delivered products or services is of a high enough standard to keep them as clients. The key problem now shifts from mere existence to the bringing about of a proper balance between revenues and expenses. The main issues include:

- Can we generate enough cash to break even in the short term (in order not to suffer a loss) and to cover finance of the repair or replacement of capital assets as they wear out?
- Can we, as a minimum, generate enough cash flow to keep things going and stay in business and to finance the company's expansion to a size that is large enough, given the industry and the market niche, to earn an economic return on the investment in assets and labour?

The organization is still simple in form. In some cases there will be a sales manager or a supervisor who is responsible for a limited number of employees. However, these people will never take important decisions on their own, but will rather carry out the well defined orders of the owner. Systems development is minimal and formal planning is, at best, limited to the forecasting and estimating of cash flow. The main goal is survival and the owner is still synonymous with the business. In this survival stage, if successful, the enterprises will be growing continuously in size and profitability and eventually will end up in Stage 3.

Many companies never proceed further than Stage 2, however, earning a marginal return on the invested time and capital, and eventually going out of business when the owner gives up or retires. Small family stores and many manufacturing businesses that cannot sell their products or processes as planned belong in this category. Some of these marginal businesses have developed enough economic viability to be sold on, often at a slight loss; others simply disappear.

Stage 3: success

At this stage, the owner has a choice of options: to further exploit the company's accomplishments and expand; to keep the company stable and profitable, providing a basis for the owner to undertake other activities; or even to pull back from the company partially or totally. An owner may wish to pull back from the company in order to start up a new company or to spend time on other activities.

At this stage, companies experience true financial success. Their size, market share and market penetration are large enough to ensure economic well-being and an average or above-average profit. If the competitive position is not weakened through ineffective management, and if there are no changes in the economic situation resulting in the loss of market share, a company can maintain itself at this stage for an unlimited period of time.

The company is now of such a size that, in many functional areas, such as production and sales, managers have taken over certain duties from the owner. These managers should be competent, but do not necessarily have to be of top calibre since their upward potential is limited by the corporate goals. Cash is plentiful and the main concern is to avoid a cash drain in prosperous periods which affects the company's ability to withstand the inevitable rough times.

Furthermore, for the first time, professional staff are employed – usually a controller in the office and often a production scheduler in the plant. The introduction of basic financial, marketing and production systems begins as does the delegation of functions – all supported by planning in the form of operational budgeting. Owners, and to a lesser degree, managers, need to monitor the implementation of the strategy, the main goal of which is to maintain the status quo. As the company continues to develop, the relationship between the owner and the company will loosen up, perhaps because the owner may become involved in activities elsewhere or perhaps because of the presence of other managers in the company.

Many companies stay at this stage of development for a long time. In some cases, this is because the market situation makes further growth impossible. This applies, for example, to a number of service companies in small or medium-sized communities, and to *franchise holders* in a limited area. In other cases, however, the owner deliberately chooses this situation. As long as the company keeps adjusting itself to changes in the economic climate, it can continue on its chosen path, be sold with a profit or merged. Alternatively, it can move to the next phase.

The owner may consolidate the position of the company and arrange resources to realize expansion plans, perhaps even putting up all the cash resources and taking advantage of the company's full borrowing capacity. The major tasks are to see that the core of the company stays profitable so that it will not outrun its source of cash, and to attract developed and trained managers who can meet the needs of the growing business – managers with a vision for the future of the company, rather than just the capacity to consolidate its current position.

Any systems which are to be installed need to take into account future needs, such as planning and budgeting. Strategic planning needs to be introduced and this demands a high level of commitment by the owner, including involvement in all aspects of management. When all goes according to plan, the company moves on to Stage 4. In practice there may be some initial attempts at growth and expansion before definite commitment to a growth strategy is made.

Minicase 2.1

McDonald's drive for international expansion

In 1994 there seemed to be no limit to the growth of the McDonald's empire. In the Netherlands, where McDonald's had first begun its international expansion outside the US, McDonald's was talking big: 'We took the past 22 years to set up the first 100 restaurants. In the next five to six years we will set up the next 100.'

The McDonald's Drive Thrus are now located in areas where people work and live. McDonald's were already established in areas where people shop, so all of the three main locations are now covered. There are ample opportunities for expansion. In Germany and Switzerland, the chain has restaurants in trains. Furthermore, McDonald's is now operating on ferries, in hospitals, stadiums, airports and since more recently on United Airlines aircraft. According to the McDonald's spokesperson: 'McDonald's is strong in establishing a system and we want to and can expand that further than just restaurants.'

The base of McDonald's is a system of franchising. Three quarters of all the restaurants in the world are run by franchisees. The company's own restaurants are used to train personnel and test new products. 'We need our own businesses to help the organization grow. But we want to have as few of our own restaurants as possible.'

Prospective franchisees need to meet a number of criteria. 'Many people have the wrong idea about this. Investors come to us regularly thinking they will invest money in a restaurant, put someone else in charge and then draw the profits from it. We don't want that. A franchise holder not only invests his business sense and his money, but must also be present on the floor.'

The financial demands are pretty high. The franchise holder has to put up about \$60 000 of equity in the business and that is only the first step. McDonald's calls this the 'BFL concept' – the *Business Facility Lease* – which means that, within two or a maximum of three years, the licensee makes enough money on that restaurant to convert the BFL into a *straight lease*. It is also possible for franchise holders to commit themselves to this straight lease from the beginning. The input of equity is about \$240 000.

The most important difference between these two arrangements is that the straight-lease partner, in addition to managing the personnel, also owns the inventory. At the outset, therefore, McDonald's expects an investment of over \$300 000 in the restaurant in order to meet the quality norms. Besides bringing in their own equity, franchise holders may also need to seek other sources of funding, for example from a bank.

'The McDonald's organization of course invests a fair amount of money in the building itself and the grounds. We expect the same of the franchise holder. It is our growth scenario: you enter as a BFL-partner and you grow into a straight lease ... Worldwide, we see it as a *partnership* to make the McDonald's system grow. We have a wide variety of franchise holders: former greengrocers, bank directors, dentists. Their background and experience aid the total organization in different areas, for example, with new ideas for advertising and marketing, but also with regard to the products.'

All potential franchise holders have a training period of one to two years. 'Such a man or woman needs to fit in with us. We offer freedom from constraints and so, in one person, we look for both a leader and a follower. The only constraints are the *system* and the *standard*. That sounds terribly rigid but it is because we are talking about food; it has to be 100 per cent identical, safe and hygienic.'

continued overleaf

Minicase continued

The belief in the power of collectivity is high. The franchise holders pay for the training which is given to employees during working hours. Worldwide, the licensee pays, as defined in their contracts, a minimum of 4 per cent of their revenues for marketing efforts, which is why the organization can spend 1.2 billion dollars on it.

The collective ethos also means that ideas put forward by employees can be exploited by all. 'When one country introduces something like a particular advertising campaign, and it is picked up by other countries, the original country does not get paid for it. We look at the collective advantages. All our entrepreneurs believe in McDonald's. More restaurants mean that all our entrepreneurs are better off. The commitment is there from this point of view, but not based on a desire for more personal honour and glory.'

The franchise holders are essential to the expansion of the hamburger chain, but employees are not actively encouraged by the organization to climb up the hierarchy. Opportunities are offered, but that is all.

'In the company-businesses, managers may be thinking of becoming franchise holders. If people really want this, we welcome it, but we do not actively encourage it. If people are not able to take responsibility for putting money aside, they will not be a good partner in the future. They exist at McDonald's – those self-made entrepreneurs who started out preparing hamburgers and now control several restaurants. But it is quite hard to get together your first $60 000. Once you get that far, you invest your money in your own business. The financial demands are a significant pressure. Each partner needs to achieve a good profit on his or her investment in money, time and energy. But the same goes for the McDonald's Corporation. The starting point of our formula is that the *return on investments* of the partners is the same as that of McDonald's. We do not earn more than they do.'

McDonald's entrepreneurs do not have personal control over everything. They are committed to the conditions of the lease, the yearly payment for marketing policy and recommended prices. They are allowed to raise the price of a product, but this does not happen in practice. 'The crux for the franchise holder is to improve sales and keep costs of personnel and purchases stable. Besides common marketing efforts, each licensee can arrange local marketing activities to raise sales. When they succeed, they can earn a great deal out of it.' At McDonald's they call this *local store marketing*. At the level of the individual countries the possibility exists to adjust the menu choices to the taste and culture of the country – for example, in some European countries the vegetable burger is offered, in Norway you can buy a salmon burger and in Hawaii a rice burger.

Source: Adapted from *FEM*, 29 Oct 1994

Stage 4: Take-off and expansion

It is crucial at this stage for a company to be able to grow rapidly and to find and acquire the financial resources to fund the rapid growth. Related to those needs are the following key issues:

- *Delegation*. Can the owner delegate a certain number of duties (plus the responsibilities that go with them) to others in order to improve the managerial effectiveness of the company which is growing fast and becoming increasingly complex? If so, will there be true delegation, with controls on performance and a willingness to see mistakes made, or will this involve abdication by the owner?

- *Cash.* Is there enough cash to meet the great financial demands which the growth process makes on the company? (This often means that the owner has to accept the fact that the debts largely exceed the equity, i.e. there is a high debt/equity ratio.) Is the cash flow eroded by inadequate control of expenses or ill advised investments as a result of the impatience of the owner?

By this stage, the organization is further decentralized and at least partially divided up into departments, mostly in the fields of sales and production. Managers in key positions need to be very skilled and competent in managing a growing and more complex organization. Under the pressure of growth, the systems become more and more refined and extensive. Both operational planning and strategic planning are carried out and involve specialists in these fields. Even though the relationship between the company and the owner becomes less rigid and more distant, the company is still often dominated by the owner as a result of his or her presence and major ownership of shares in the company.

This stage is a pivotal period for the organization. If the owner measures up to the demands which the expansion makes, managerially as well as financially, the business can grow into a big company. If not, then the organization can often be sold at a profit, provided the owner recognizes his or her limitations in time. Too often an owner makes it to the success stage, but fails at Stage 4, because he or she is not capable of delegating effectively in the way that is demanded in a well functioning company (the 'omniscience' syndrome).

Of course it is possible that the organization goes through this high-growth stage without the original management. Often, the entrepreneur who founded the company and brought it to the success stage, is replaced voluntarily or involuntarily by the company's investors or creditors.

If the expansion plans do not succeed, the strategy can sometimes be changed so that the company can continue to exist as a successful and substantial company in a state of equilibrium. In other cases, the company may drop back to Stage 3 or, if the problems are very extensive, may even end up in the survival stage or fail and go bankrupt. High interest rates and unstable economic conditions in the early 1980s made the last two possibilities all too common outcomes.

Stage 5: Resource maturity and optimal position

The greatest concerns of a company and its management entering this stage are the consolidation and control of the financial gains which flow from rapid growth and the retention of the advantages of small size which include flexibility and an entrepreneurial spirit. The management needs to be expanded fast and it needs to become more professional in the use of budgeting, strategic planning, 'management by objectives' and standard cost systems. It is important that all this does not take place at the expense of the entrepreneurial qualities.

A company in Stage 5 has the staff and financial resources to engage in detailed operational and strategic planning. The management is decentralized, adequately staffed and experienced, and use is made of extensive and well developed systems. With regard to finance as well as company activity, the involvement of the owner with the company is limited. The company has arrived and 'made it'. It has the advantages of size, ample financial resources and managerial talent at its disposal. When the entrepreneurial spirit can be preserved the company is a formidable force in the market and can achieve a strong competitive position.

Exhibit 2.3

Italian group's sweet smell of success

Ferrero is the company which makes the world's largest confectioners lick their lips. It is not so much the Italian company's products which invite admiration – although its Nutella spread, Kinder and Ferrero Rocher chocolates, and Tic Tac mints are among the world's best-selling sweet things – but the Italian group's ability to go on growing, at a time when most of its competitors have had their share of hard times. It is a quality which has made it Italy's second most admired company in this year's list, behind Fiat.

Last year, the Ferrero holding company – registered in the Netherlands – increased worldwide consolidated turnover by 7.3 per cent to Fl 17.23bn ($4.35bn) in a difficult market. Not surprisingly, as one food analyst puts it: 'People like Cadbury would really like to get their sticky hands on Ferrero.'

The frustration for fellow confectioners is that whereas Ferrero's products are marketed with style and aggression, Ferrero the company is emphatically not open to offers. The group, which celebrates its 50th anniversary this year, is as discreet as only a family-owned Italian company can be. It is entirely self-financing, has never made an acquisition, and does not publish holding company profits.

The Ferreros themselves rarely talk publicly about the company, which now claims to be one of the world's top five confectionery groups, up there with Mars, Suchard, Nestlé and Cadbury. Perhaps unsurprisingly, one of Ferrero's closest allies is that other soul of Italian discretion, Mediobanca, the powerful and secretive Milan-based merchant bank, of which the chocolate company is a core shareholder.

The group is headed by Michele Ferrero, son of Pietro, one of two brothers who launched the group in 1946 in Alba, in Piedmont, where the family owned a cake manufacturing business.

The technical key to postwar success was the invention of Pasta Gianduja – a mixture of cocoa, sugar, milk, nuts and coconut butter which cost a quarter of pure chocolate, and became a mass-market alternative almost immediately. Within a year, Ferrero had transferred production to a larger factory and increased the number of employees from five or six to more than 50. Soon it had expanded from the surrogate-chocolate market into manufacturing the real thing, at prices which challenged Italy's traditional confectioners.

Ferrero claims the keys to success have always included strong attention to distribution and marketing – the company started almost immediately to cut out intermediaries and sell products direct to shopkeepers using its own fleet of vehicles – development of innovative new product lines, and the strong loyalty of the staff.

Workers have twice rescued the group's Alba plant from floods which submerged the production facilities. In February 1948, the factory was up and running again within 10 days. In autumn 1994, when the company was working towards the busy Christmas period, employees helped restore partial production in the much larger Alba factory within two weeks. Net profit at the Italian operating company halved to L65.6bn ($43.5m), but recovered last year to L100.5bn.

Michele Ferrero – who, with his mother, took over the full running of the group in the 1950s after the deaths of his father and uncle – began expansion into the rest of Europe as early as 1957, with the construction of a factory in Germany. In the 1970s, Ferrero pushed into the Americas, south-east Asia and Australia, and, in the 1990s, started to build its presence in eastern Europe.

Ferrero now claims to produce the best-selling praline and liqueur chocolate in Europe (respectively Ferrero Rocher, launched only in 1981, and Mon Cheri), and the world's best-selling mint, Tic Tac. As a group, Ferrero employs 14 000 people worldwide, and has 14 production plants, with new factories under construction in Poland and in Argentina.

So where does Ferrero go from here? It would be out of character for the company to join the acquisition trail, so the most likely route is expansion into new markets. Of the group's Fl 7.23bn turnover, Fl 1.8bn is made in Italy, Fl 4.57bn in the rest of Europe and only Fl 817bn in the rest of the world.

As for the possibility of the family selling out to one of those hungry rivals, that looks even less likely now that Michele Ferrero is handing more power over to his sons, both only in their early 30s.

Source: *Financial Times*, 18 September 1996.

Alternatively, rigidity and ossification can occur and threaten to bring the company down to a sub-optimal position. Ossification and rigidity are characterized by a lack of innovative decision making and the avoidance of risks. This phenomenon arises sometimes in large companies which stay viable thanks to their sizeable market share, buying power and/or financial resources, until major shifts in the economic climate or in technology occur.

2.4.4 Size and quality of the organization

When setting up a company or considering expansion or downsizing, decisions have to be taken on the size of the company with the aim of optimizing the company size. At the point where the costs per unit of product (or service) are lowest, and so the relationship between costs and company size (expressed in capacity units) is optimal, the *optimal company size* is reached. The determination of the size of the necessary technological and personnel capacities will of course have to be based on the sales expectations of the products and services; it is not just a matter of buildings and machinery, but also of the number of employees.

Technological and organizational considerations

When sales expectations are uncertain, it is desirable to have flexibility in planning capacity. This can be achieved, for example, by setting up a relatively small capacity with expansion possibilities.

Productivity or servicing on a larger scale can bring about cost advantages, for example, through better use of production resources, better division of labour, more efficient allocation of production resources, more expertise, better purchase contracts.

Business growth, in the organizational sense, also means change. A growing company needs to remain controllable. In practice this means that management needs to be supported by professionals in so-called staff and service functions (*see also* Chapters 6 and 7). This is where the ratio of 'direct' (the operational staff and the front-line managers) to 'indirect' personnel (including the professionals and service employees on the support staff and in specialized support functions) starts to shift.

Furthermore with business growth all kinds of extra measures are taken in planning and the supply of information (*see also* Chapter 11). Management needs to make use of more resources in order to be able to control the business with the inevitable cost implications. The way the organization is managed changes as a result. The personalized and informal character of the small organization is adapted into a more distant and formal method of management. In this way the advantages of being large bring extra costs of more indirect personnel and resources in order to control the company activities. Furthermore, becoming larger and gaining a stronger market share often means a loss of personal contact between the company and the client. These advantages and disadvantages need to be faced when making decisions on company size and the scope of the company activities.

Later we will see that these kinds of changes do not always run smoothly and cannot be implemented in an organization without problems. During the various stages of development, problems can arise which can result in a crisis of one form or another. Interventions in strategy and policies, structure and culture are then inevitable.

Personnel considerations

During the growth and development of an organization, it is also important to monitor continuously the areas of expertise (and types of personnel) which need to be recruited and the degree to which these may have to be drawn from what is already available in the organization. Personnel decisions in this respect are concerned with ensuring suitable *quantities* of staff, both management and operational workers, and a satisfactory level of *quality*. A personnel plan will have to contain statements on recruitment of personnel, training and development and, if necessary, about issues such as early retirement, dismissals and so on (*see also* Chapters 7, 8 and 12).

Financial considerations

A company or institution is always financially dependent on people and other institutions that supply the necessary resources to start up a business or finance or subsidize company activities. Financial planning involves looking into areas such as the sources of funds, the allocation of resources to different investment projects and the control of working capital and asking questions like 'Should this machine be financed by equity or debt capital, or should it be leased?' 'Which policy of profit sharing and dividend payment should be followed?'

It is the task of management to control the incoming and outgoing flows of financial resources in an organization. First, the financial need has to be estimated based on the product and market development plans. In this, the choice of investment projects is important. Next, ways in which financial resources can be obtained have to be explored. A choice has to be made between equity and debt finance in its various forms. Suppliers of equity are the owner(s) or the shareholders. Suppliers of debt capital are, for example, commercial banks, building societies or other financial institutions who are willing to extend the company a loan under specified conditions.

2.4.5 Policy decisions and business goals

The owner–manager or the appointed managing director has to take policy decisions with regard to product range, direction of growth, location, legal company form, company size (including personnel and financial considerations), investment in and the acquisition of production resources, spatial planning in terms of technical layout and possible co-operation with other companies. In the preparation of these decisions, a mature company will have staff specialists available within the company it may be necessary to consult external professionals as specialists. Through consultation, answers can be given to questions like:

- Do we strive for growth? To what extent and in which direction do we want to grow?
- Will we devote ourselves to a specific product, to a specific market segment/niche, or to a specific geographical market area?
- Do we focus on low prices, low costs or superior quality?
- Do we stay small and independent, or do we look for some form of co-operation?

These statements form the basis of the business policy which is to be implemented. In mature companies such statements are often made explicit, are written into the mission statement and company objectives, and are worked out in a strategic plan (*see* Chapter 5). In small companies the goals such as the proposed direction and size of the business are often implicit; they are in the head of the owner–entrepreneur–

manager and are instantly recognizable in actions rather than being established in words in formal company documents. However, in small and medium-sized companies, for the purposes of getting company credit or financing expansion activities, a plan needs to be drawn up. Furthermore, external directors in 'small' companies may 'force' the management, through questioning, to make company policy explicit in its plans and budgets for the medium and long term.

It is the ongoing task of management to see to it that relations with the organization's external environment, and also with the forces inside the organization are such that the survival of the company is assured as far as possible. This means that the management in the organization has to take continuous account of what is happening in and around the organization and has to react to changes such as conflicts between department, a slow down in decision making, a rise in staff turnover, increases in the prices of resources, a scarcity of labour, the supply of new materials and substitutes or technological breakthroughs.

In this the management has to realize that these kinds of changes and forces occur in an existing organizational framework and within a societal and market environment in which, for example, departments, a works council, unions, suppliers, banks, and local and national governments or action group may or will exercise their influence. Taking all this into account, an owner–manager in a small company or the professional management in a large company has to state a mission, has to determine goals and set out a course of action, choose the design of the organization and obtain and employ resources required for the task.

2.4.6 Objectives, goals, policies and planning

To ensure the effective and efficient functioning of an organization, it is necessary for all relevant commercial, technological, financial and personnel considerations to be taken into account. *Policies* have to be formulated and *planning* has to take place at different levels of the organization.

The drawing up of a business policy involves the *formulation* and *passing down* of the ways and means by which the management wants to realize their goals. Once the goals are set, a plan has to be formulated which sets out the methods, time scale and resources with which the goals are to be attained.

The difference between a company's success and failure is often its ability or inability to appreciate the demands of its markets and its own limitations with regard to what it wishes to achieve. This appreciation of the demands of the market (*external appraisal*) and the organization's own capabilities and will (*internal appraisal*) is the essence of company strategy (*see* Chapter 5). A strategy includes statements about the goals a company wants to attain, the ways in which this will be achieved, and the resources that will be required. In the process of strategic decision making and policy making in companies, goals are determined and policies are drawn up, which relate to, among other things:

- market position – ranges of products or services, nature of customers and clients and geographical markets;
- productivity and added value;
- profitability or relationship between costs and revenues;
- societal responsibility – employment, the environment, etc.;
- growth and continuity;

- income, working conditions, prestige, status and authority of the managerial and operational staff of the organization.

In a strategy and business plan, management states the *objectives*, *goals* and the *guidelines* for the activities which will have to take place. A *policy* states the methods and resources which will be needed if the company goals are to be attained. It is also necessary to determine which *organizational structure* will be best for the attainment of the company goals. In this respect, planning precedes the commercial, technological, financial and personnel consideration. Planning is the systematic preparation and adjustment of decisions which are directed at realizing future goals. Plans have the following functions:

- They *describe the goals* which need to be attained by a company and company departments.
- They *establish the measurements* for attaining these goals.
- They pass down the personnel and financial *resources* which are necessary for attaining these goals.
- They *state in which time span* the set goals will have to be attained.

When drawing up a plan, decisions have to be taken regarding *what* has to be produced, *where* this will happen, *how* this will happen, *when* this has to happen, *how much* has to be made and *who* will do this and *with what resources* (*see also* Chapter 10).

When an organization does not have all the necessary resources itself, it has to look externally, perhaps through measures such as co-operation with another company. Decisions will have to be made on the way in which the resources can effectively and economically be spent.

Plans need to be based on adequate and reliable data with regard to the future. During the operational implementation, plans need to be monitored and adjusted. Unexpected developments and sudden changes naturally give rise to reviews and adjustments.

Exhibit 2.4

No lovefest at Birkenstock

A labour dispute rips the family company as the sons step into the patriarch's shoes

No shoe makes more of a political statement than the Birkenstock, the comfortable, German-made sandal with the clunky sole. Hippies popularized it in the U.S., while German Greens are still recognizable by their Birkenstocks-and-socks. A pair of Birks – which can cost up to $110 – radiates a liberal image.

Until recently, so did the company that makes them. Run by Karl Birkenstock, 59, fifth-generation owner of the 222-year-old shoemaker, the company recycles materials and soles, pays workers' commuting costs, and gives free shoes to employees. So it may come as a nasty surprise to Birk lovers to learn that the company is locked in a bitter labor dispute.

Flex time

While the family is now trying to contain the damage and move on, the showdown causing so much turmoil involves the same generational trends threatening others in Germany's *Millittelstand* sector of family companies. Throughout the sector, the postwar generation of patriarchs is stepping aside and their sons and daughters are trying to assert their own leadership. At the same time, Germany's unions are struggling to replace lost membership at giant companies by making inroads in smaller ones. The result, says Stefan Behr of *Mittelstand* consultant DGM, unleashes 'a dash situation.'

If a clash could occur at Birkenstock, it could happen anywhere. Birkenstock – organized as a group of companies that make different shoe parts – employs 2,000 workers, all of them in Germany. All belong to small teams whose members willingly swap jobs with each other. This flexibility allows for higher productivity, says the family, which supports a wage scale that's generous by industry standards. The highest wage negotiated by the leather union is $9.68 per hour, while the lowest hourly wage at Birkenstock is $11.30. The family won't disclose financial data but says that sales, now around $600 million, have grown between 10% to 20% every year since the 1970s.

About five years ago, Karl started preparing his sons for the succession. Stephan, 28, handles logistics; Alex, 27, runs sales and marketing; and Christian, 23, who left school at 16 to work full-time, manages production. They grew up next door to headquarters in Bad Honnef, a small, picturesque town on the Rhine. Alex attended his first trade fair at age 10, wearing his First Communion suit to serve drinks to guests.

But through the early 1990s, tensions were building at the plant in St. Katharinen, a nearby town. There, some 700 workers in Birko Schuhtechnik, one of the family companies, assembled straps, buckles, and soles into complete sandels. Ulrike Köster, who had joined Birko in 1976 and rose to team leader, felt the brisk rise in sales was creating too much pressure on workers. To boost productivity, Alex had introduced bonuses linked to the number of shoes teams turned out. Yet workers claimed that the task of operating complicated new machines was affecting productivity. 'It got worse when the sons came,' says Köster, who has since left.

Gridlock at Birkenstock

April, 1993 Concerned about a production speedup, employees at the Birko Schuhtechnik division elect a works council
December, 1993 Backed by an outside union, the council clashes with owner Karl Birkenstock over bonuses and pay scales
June–August, 1994 Karl's sons open non-union shops to take away work from Birko
February, 1995 A proposed settlement to close Birko collapses
August, 1995 Most of Birko's remaining workers are moved to a rented hall
March, 1996 Stalemate as the Birko workers are left idle while costing the Birkenstock family $138,000 a month

In April 1993, the frustrated employees decided for the first time to elect a works council to represent them in discussions with management. The family wanted nothing to do with outside unions but had no objection to a council. Then, however, the council allowed the Union for Woodworking & Plastic Materials to recruit members at Birko.

In December 1993, all hell broke loose. At a companywide meeting that included the family, the council demanded equal pay for men and women and a review of the bonus system. Christian alleges that an outside union representative humiliated his father by calling on him to be less extravagant in his personal finances. For a man who rises at 5 am, wears cheap gray suits and Birks, and has no secretary, this was too much. In tears, Karl was too devastated to speak.

Birkenstock cancelled the bonus system at Birko. Then, to meet brisk summer demand in 1994, Alex wanted to run the plant overtime, but the council refused to approve it, fearing layoffs later. Delivery delays cost millions of dollars in sales, says Alex.

'Idiots'

The turmoil enraged Karl. He started at the company in 1954 when just 30 people worked there, made the sandal a global icon, and saw no reason any employee should oppose his family. 'Karl Birkenstock is a fantastic businessman, but he still operates as if it were the early 1900s,' says Ulrich Schmulz, a local politician who tried to mediate the dispute. 'He has to have the last word.'

Both sides filed numerous complaints against each other with labor authorities and the prosecutor's office. Karl was fined $10,300 by a public prosecutor in Koblenz for calling council members 'idiots' in April 1994. Alex was fined $11,700 for obstructing a council meeting where he argued the need for overtime. 'The [council members] are puppets of the union,' says Alex. Greater strife exploded among the workers themselves, many of whom wanted the bonus system back. Council members felt so harassed they carried weapons.

Determined to end the problem, in 1994 the sons started shifting some production from Birko to newly opened plants nearby. Some 450 workers quit Birko to work at the new plants. About 130 held on. Others quit Birkenstock altogether in anger either over the demands of the works council or the family's hostility.

Then in early 1995, Karl tried to shut Birko down by paying the workers to leave. But the workers demanded $2 million – three times more than what the company says is legally required. That's when the feud took a Dickensian twist: The family, refusing to cave in to more demands, decided to keep the workers employed but isolated. The Birko employees were moved to another building and Christian put in charge. When the workers complained that there weren't enough toilets, he shipped in portable construction-site restrooms.

Now Christian communicates by mail or through a security guard with the 98 remaining workers, who have nothing to do. As Christian walks in unannounced one morning, one woman ditches her knitting, another hides her book, while three more stubbornly go on playing cards. Boss and rebels glare at each other. No one speaks.

'Just jealous'

Isolating the renegades in their legal yet dreary conditions has triggered a spate of articles in the German press, sporting headlines like 'Psychoterror' and painting the company in a terrible light. But neither side is giving in. 'We have power as long as we can hang on,' says Marion Rahm, head of the council. Birkenstock is equally stubborn – it costs $138,000 per month to keep the ghost company open.

Across the road in another Birkenstock company, workers seem content. 'They're just jealous we have good work without them,' says Sigrid Sieg, 30, as she paints glue onto leather straps, seated in a spacious room with splendid views of a snowy valley. Business is nearly back to normal, too, with only a few German Greens and hospital workers kicking off their sandals in protest. But the behavior of the Birkenstock family risks further backlash. And the confrontation daily wounds the soul of a proud family company.

Source: *Business Week*, 25 March 1996.

2.4.7 Management factors and growth

There are several factors which significantly influence the ultimate success or failure of an organization; their relative importance changes depending on the stage of growth and development of a company. Research by Churchill and Lewis (1983) identified eight factors of which four relate to the company and its organization and four to the owners.

The factors that relate to the company and its organization are:

- *Financial resources*: **liquidity/solvency**, including cash and borrowing capacity.
- *Personnel resources*: number, specific knowledge and depth or expertise and quality of people within the organization, particularly in staff and management positions.
- *Systems resources*: nature, size and degree of development and sophistication of information, planning and control systems.
- *Business resources*: in general, all factors which determine the market position and industry position, including customer relations, market share, manufacturing and distribution, supplier relations, state of technology, reputation of the company, and so on.

The factors that relate to the owner–leader–managers are:

- *Goals of the owners, both personal and business*: a comparison of business and personal plans.
- *Operational abilities of the owners*: the degree to which they are capable of carrying out important duties in the field of marketing, innovation, production, distribution, etc.
- *Managerial ability and willingness of the owners to delegate responsibilities* (including the tasks and the authority that goes with them) and *to manage the activities of others*.
- *Strategic abilities of the owners*: the ability to look beyond the present, to match strengths and weaknesses of the company with personal goals and opportunities and threats in the external environment.

Minicase 2.2

Troubled times at Saatchi & Saatchi

By the end of 1994, Maurice Saatchi had left the management of the famous advertising agency, Saatchi & Saatchi, which he founded in 1970 with his brother Charles, to consider the setting up of a new agency with that same brother.

Saatchi had been given a warning by a large group of shareholders in the agency, who were especially angry about a plan which would have allowed share prices to almost double in three years and would have resulted in an income of almost $12 million for Maurice Saatchi. Other managers would have profited less from the possible rise in share prices. Earlier that year, Saatchi's salary had been reduced from £650 000 ($1.1 million) to £200 000 ($330 000).

Saatchi & Saatchi grew very fast in the 1970s and 1980s but has done less well subsequently and the agency even experienced financial problems in 1989. The departure of Saatchi, who could at best have expected to continue with an honorary position in the agency, was expected to have implications for the future prosperity of the organization, particularly if major clients like Mars, British Airways and Mirror Group Newspapers, who together account for 8 per cent of Saatchi & Saatchi revenue, chose to look for an alternative agency.

2.4.8 Factors that relate to the stage of growth

As a business moves from one stage of development to another (*see* section 2.4.3), the relative importance of the individual factors changes. At each stage, the factors can be divided into three categories based on their relative importance:

1. key factors for the success of the company and to which high priority should be given (referred to as critical success factors);
2. factors which are clearly necessary for success and which certainly must receive attention; and
3. factors which are of little immediate concern to top management.

When categorizing each of the factors according to their importance at each stage in the development of the company, a clear picture of the demands made on management is formed (*see* Fig 2.4). The stage of development of the business will determine what changes in managerial demands are necessary and which factors should be given priority. Figure 2.4 shows the changing nature of managerial challenges.

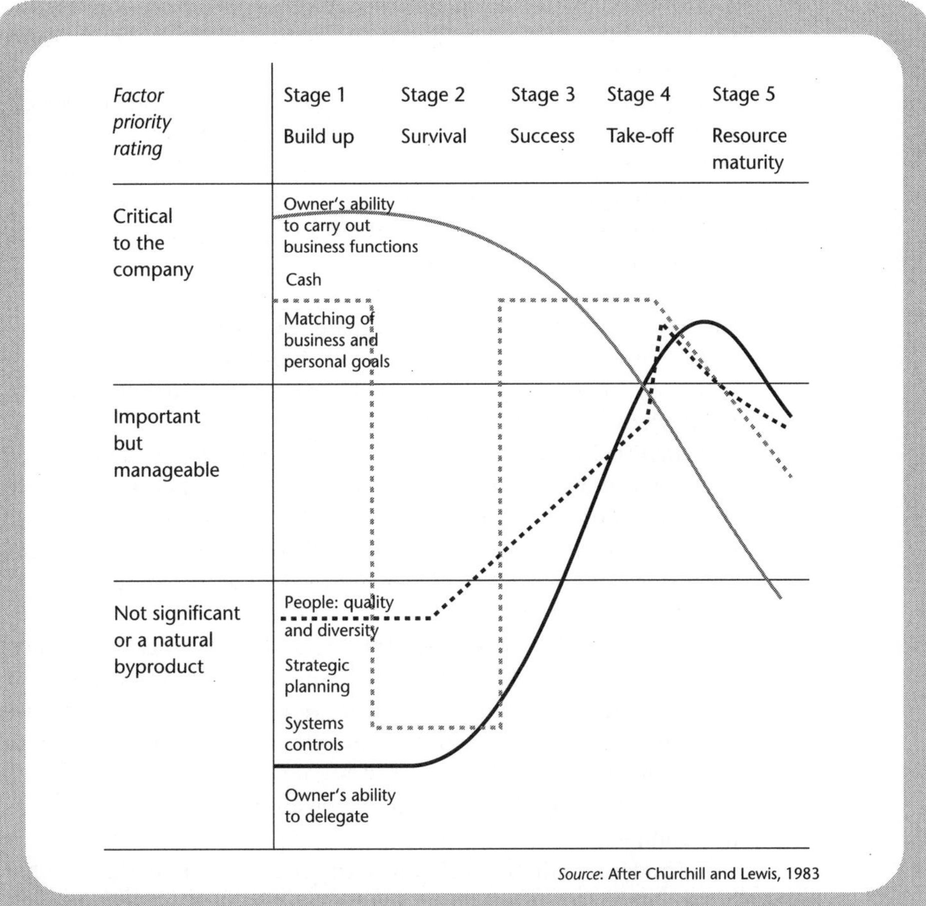

Fig 2.4 ● Factors and their relative importance at difference stages of growth and development

In the early stages, the ability of the owner to do the job gives life to the business. Small businesses are built and dependent on the talents of the owners – for example, their abilities to sell or produce. These factors are of vital importance therefore at Stages 1 and 2. The ability to delegate, however, is at the bottom of the scale since there are few, if any, employees to delegate to.

The more a company grows, the more people there are who will specifically devote themselves to sales, production or engineering and technology. At first they will support and then complement the owner, but later they will take over the owner's duties partly, if not completely, thus reducing the relative importance of the owner's capabilities. At the same time, the owner can spend less time on a diverse range of duties and more time on management. He or she will have to leave more and more work activities to others, and that means delegating. The inability of founders to stand back from operational activities and to begin managing and delegating is a common cause of company failure at Stages 3 and 4.

An owner who is contemplating a growth strategy must understand that changes in personal activities within the company will become necessary as a result of such a decision and has to consider the managerial demands depicted in Fig 2.4. Similarly, an entrepreneur setting up a new business should appreciate that during the initial stage all the sales, manufacturing and engineering activities will need to be done as well as the planning and managing of cash – with a corresponding cost in time, effort, energy and commitment.

The importance of cash also changes depending on the development of the business. At the start, cash is extremely important; this becomes easier to manage in the success stage, but becomes a crucial factor again when the business begins to grow. At the end of Stage 4 or 5, when the pace of growth slows down, cash becomes a manageable factor again. Companies in Stage 3 need to recognize the financial needs and risks entailed in a move to Stage 4.

The issues of people, planning and systems gradually increase in importance when the initial slow growth of the company in Stage 3 converts to the fast growth of Stage 4. The entrepreneur needs to see to it that these resources are already present in the company in advance of the growth stage or are developed so that they are already there when the need for them arises.

Matching business goals and the personal goals and ambitions of the owner is especially crucial in the first stage because the owner then has to recognize and accept the high demands which the company makes on his or her financial resources, time and energy. For some, these demands appear to be higher than they can handle. In the survival stage, however, the owner has reconciled these demands and survival is at the top of the list of priorities.

The matching of goals is of little importance at Stage 2, but becomes very important again in the success stage. Owners then have to decide whether to risk the company's accumulated equity built up in order to realize further growth, whether they are prepared to commit all their time to growth, or whether they want to enjoy a few of the advantages which the success already gained has to offer. All too often an owner wants both, but it is very risky to expand a business and at the same time build a new house, for example.

To make a realistic decision with regard to the direction that is to be followed, owners need to consider both the personal as well as the business demands of the different strategies and should try to evaluate their own abilities to meet and live up to these demands and challenges.

Factors affecting business resources – such as market share, customer relations, sources of supply and technological base – are very important in the early stages. In later stages, the loss of, for example, an important customer, supplier or technological source can be borne more easily. As shown in Fig 2.4, the relative importance of this factor declines in line with growth.

The changing priority of the individual factors clearly illustrates the need for owner flexibility. In the first two stages, the company should strive not to pay tax until it is obliged to do so; in the period of growth and success the late payment of tax would seriously distort accounting data and use up too much management time. Furthermore, the conversion from 'doing' to 'delegating' requires flexibility. Holding on to old strategies and methods will not serve a company that is entering the stages of growth and in some cases can prove fatal.

2.4.9 Avoiding future problems

Even a passing glance at Fig 2.4 reveals the demands that the take-off and expansion stage make on the organization. Almost all factors except the owner's 'ability to do' are crucial. This is a stage of action and of potentially high rewards. An owner who wants to realize such growth must address the following questions (Churchill and Lewis, 1983):

- Do my managers and I have the quality and diversity to fulfil the demands of managing a growing company?
- Do I have or will I have shortly the systems in place to handle the needs of a larger, more diversified company?
- Am I prepared to and do I have the ability to delegate decision making to my managers?
- Do I have enough cash and is my borrowing power big enough to finance fast growth, and am I prepared to risk everything to pursue rapid growth?

In a similar way, a potential entrepreneur can see that starting a business demands the ability to do something very well (or an idea that is very marketable), a large amount of energy and a favourable 'cash flow' forecast (or a large sum of cash directly to hand). These requirements are less important in Stage 5, when management skills, good information systems and budget controls have the highest priority. Perhaps this is the reason why some experienced people coming from large companies fail to make it as entrepreneurs or managers in a small company; they are used to delegating and are not good enough at carrying out operational tasks themselves.

SUMMARY

- In this chapter we have looked at the historical development of organizational and management theory, with particular reference to the development of theory on industrial democracy in relation to the stages of development and growth in an organization.
- Management and organizational theory is, on the one hand, analytical and descriptive knowledge which we need in order to understand reality. On the other hand, the theories that have been developed can be seen as a collection of

continued overleaf

ground rules and examples of best practice which can be used in specific practical situations. Such theories are not only *descriptive*, but also *prescriptive* and therefore normative in nature.

- The application of the theory depends on the norms and values of the manager who operates in specific circumstances with a specific cultural context. It is important that the manager's vision of people matches reality and societal developments.
- The development of management and organizational theory – from the first theories of scientific management to the more recent contingency theory – has always reflected a corresponding social change.
- Employees in an organization are a resource and, as such a 'means of production', but at the same time they are a 'factor' with norms and ideas which will change with the passing of time, just like the society of which the people and the organization are a part as illustrated by the development of industrial democracy in Europe.
- The way in which an organization handles the problems which it identifies – even the identification process itself – depends on that organisation's stage of growth and development. The stages of growth and development of a company are: build up, survival, success, take-off and expansion, resource maturity and optimal position.
- With regard to the expansion of business activities, attention is focused on policy decisions, goals and the necessity of planning and control. In growth, factors relating to the company and the company organization play an important part, as do factors relating in particular to the owner–leader.

DISCUSSION QUESTIONS

1. With reference to *Management in action* at the beginning of this chapter, describe how you would expect the maintenance department to be affected by the 'sudden' new style of management introduced by O'Conner.
2. Comment on the following statement: 'As soon as the organization has more than 70 employees, every founding entrepreneur should leave and start up another organization.'
3. Are there aspects of management which lend themselves to the approach of 'management from behind a desk'? If so, what are they? If not, why not?
4. Comment on the following statement: 'Automation always means reorganization, and so this always has to be on the agenda of a works council or of normal work meetings.'
5. Respond to the statement: 'Safety, health and well-being are to do with your private life and are your own personal responsibility; they are not really of importance in the development of a business.'
6. 'The different management theories mirror the time in which they arose.' What is your opinion of this statement? Which of the theories do you find most convincing?
7. How would you 'score' Ferrero (*see* Exhibit 2.3) as a company in terms of the five stages of growth and development and their associated factors?
8. With reference to Exhibit 2.4, what would you advise Birkenstock as a family company to do?

Management case study

Cleaning up in Poland

Stephen and Kerry-Jane Martin spent three weeks travelling around Poland investigating the possibility of starting up a furniture importing business to the UK.

But it was their growing pile of washing that provided the inspiration for their first business venture together. Kerry-Jane searched for the nearest launderette but could find nothing resembling a western one, even though many people lived in huge tower blocks with little space or money for their own washing machines.

The couple saw their opportunity. Five years on, they run six dry-cleaning shops, have eight agents, several industrial contracts and takings last year reached £294,789.

Stephen, 40, a former commodity broker and management consultant, had been made redundant in March, 1991, from his job as director of a Midlands-based management consultancy. Kerry-Jane, 30, worked as a political lobbyist but the two were keen to work together on their own ventures.

A friend who had gone to Poland with a school party returned full of enthusiasm and recommended a visit.

Stephen remembered: 'We went out with the idea of buying a product, such as furniture, and importing it into the UK as a nice, simple business venture. But so many of the things we looked at were just too badly made.

'After we had the launderette idea, a contact we knew carried out a survey for us of 1,000 people in Lodz, Poland's second city, and the response was very positive.

'It seemed a terrific plan and we thought we were going to be millionaires in three years,' he said wryly.

They returned to England and approached the chief executive of the commodity company Stephen had worked for and he agreed to invest in their idea.

The couple set up a Dutch holding company with £100,000 capital, 90 per cent from their investor and 10 per cent from their savings, and called it East European Holdings. This became the parent company of their Polish limited liability company Luxomat, of which they are both directors. Once in Poland, the company provided them with a rented house in Warsaw, a car, flights home and a basic salary.

Stephen said: 'We learnt about the launderette business as fast as we could and bought the best equipment from Belgium and America. We gave up our rented house in England and returned to Poland with our two dogs in September 1991. We took on a full-time assistant/translator and found premises in Warsaw in a very good tower block area where there were 250,000 people living on top of each other.

'This building was going to be the first western-style launderette in Poland and we wanted it to be our super flagship which we would then replicate all round Poland.'

It was opened in June 1992 by the Irish ambassador and featured on television. During the first week, they offered a special deal and the local people were very enthusiastic. 'It was all music to our ears,' said Kerry-Jane. The couple had an office in the basement, just under the water pipes. They began their second week expecting to hear water gushing through them – but they heard not a drip. The launderette stayed empty.

'We discovered just how family-minded the Poles are. They often have a mother or grandmother at home during the day to do the washing, and are distrustful of outsiders. So the idea of sitting around in a launderette with a lot of strangers did not appeal.'

continued overleaf

Management case study continued

Luckily, the couple had also bought a small dry cleaning machine and ironing table and, bit by bit, demand took off.

So, the two set about restructuring the business, concentrating on the dry cleaning. They bought new dry cleaning equipment and retraining their staff. It was a difficult time. 'The cash flow was so bad at times we had to take money out on our credit cards to pay the staff bill.'

They found a factory to use as a central processing plant. It now services their six shops and agents, all in Warsaw and its outskirts. It also does the dry cleaning for several industrial contracts with embassies, the armed forces, restaurants and hairdressers. Luxomat now has a staff of 35.

The couple were determined the shops would stand out as modern, efficient and competitive. But marketing was a problem as they did not want to appear just another foreign organisation looking for a quick profit. However, their Polish manager convinced them it was important the shops had a western cachet and so the shop signs now announce they are The British Dry Cleaners. 'The difficulty is, the people expect a superior service because it is western but do not expect to pay more than for using their old local service which left their clothes smelling of old cabbages,' Stephen said.

Turnover for their first two quarters' trading in 1992 was £15 669. The following year, takings reached £85 500. Turnover doubled to £174 181 in 1994 and again in 1995 to £294 789. Takings in the first two quarters of 1996 reached £141 156. Operating profits are about 20 per cent. They say they now need to open more shops and look at the opportunities in other cities.

There is a very strong labour code and little is done to help employers.

The couple, who have a daughter Venetia, nearly two, and a second baby due in October, lived in Poland until last Christmas when they felt their general manager was ready to take responsibility for the shops.

Kerry-Jane spends between two and three days there every six weeks and is in weekly telephone contact. They are now living in the Cotswolds after spending three months in France to 'clear their heads of Poland'. The two found working in Poland very frustrating at times. Stephen said: 'The people are very money and commercially-minded with plenty of entrepreneurial spirit but everyone is struggling against the state. There is also a very strong labour code and little is done to help employers.

'Many problems arise from the Poles' habit of non-co-operation with each other. In government offices and utilities, they still treat the consumer like a supplicant who should, in many cases, be obstructed.

'In business, a contract is readily discarded if the terms no longer suit and employees have a low sense of personal responsibility for their work or conduct. All this stems from having been an enclosed society. Things have improved in the past five years but only in the upper echelons of the capital's business community.'

Wages are low – the average salary of the laundry staff is £175 a month – but the company has to pay a further 68 per cent of that amount on top to cover tax and social security. It means the company's average monthly staffing bill is about £10 000.

'Our rents are also high – an average of about £1 900 a month – and we have to get everything from the chemicals and bags to cover the clothes to the tagging guns and safety pins from abroad,' Stephen said.

'The bureaucracy is a complete nightmare. Getting permission to open an outlet at one of the city's supermarkets took written permission from 14 different authorities.

'We even had to get permission from a major and a captain in the army. They had no idea why but, aided by a gift of a bottle of vodka each, they said "fine".'

The couple are now looking for new ventures. 'We were asked to set up something in Lithuania but this time we want to do something in Britain or in western Europe,' they say.

Source: *Financial Times Weekend*, 28–9 September 1996.

CASE QUESTIONS

1. Does the growth rate in this case follow a 'standard pattern'? Are the founders looking to achieve too fast a rate of growth?
2. What specific problems were complicating the take-off phase in Poland as a result of it having been a rather 'enclosed' society?
3. What managerial and other arrangements should the couple make, when delegating responsibility for their shops to their general manager?

Chapter 3

Organizations and environment

LEARNING OBJECTIVES

After studying this chapter, you should be able to:

- identify the different stakeholders who both influence the organization and make a specific contribution to it;
- describe the contribution of each of the stakeholders to the organization and the inducement or incentive each wishes to receive in return;
- distinguish the different environmental factors and external developments to which the organization is exposed and to which the organization has to react;
- understand the concepts of 'external environment' and 'external adaptation', 'internal environment' and 'internal adaptation';
- explain what is meant by organizational equilibrium as a basis for the survival of an organization;
- describe an organization's place in the societal system;
- identify the consequences for the organization of the relevant trends in the environment;
- examine the interrelationships between developments in moral and organizational behaviour;
- discuss the links between societal responsibility, external reporting and corporate governance;
- be aware of the effects of national cultures on organizations.

Management in action

Market winning product hazardous to employees?

Karl Schwartz, senior medical officer with Koenig AG, an industrial heating and insulation manufacturing firm in West Germany, asked to see the chief executive, Hans Weiss, and handed him a document. 'It's a thesis on atmospheric health hazards produced by one of our sponsored research students,' he explained. 'I think you ought to read it.'

'Is it urgent?' Weiss asked.

'He has researched, by chance, one of the chemicals used in our new compound for improving insulation. He suggests that surfaces impregnated with the chemical can give off fumes that may be harmful to health.'

Weiss looked at Schwartz sharply. '*Can* give off fumes. *May* be harmful to health," he echoed. "Our own research department didn't come up with anything. You can check with them, but I think they decided that the compound emitted only harmless fumes when sprayed on to insulating walls, screens and furnace linings."

Schwartz said that he had already shown the paper to Franz Braun, the head of research, but that he had been dismissive. 'The thesis suggests,' Schwartz said, 'that when this chemical is heated through a certain temperature range, as it has to be when it is applied to our products, it emits small quantities of vapour that can cause a skin condition conducive to cancer.'

'The student has proof, of course,' Weiss said sarcastically.

'He has done experiments with rats,' replied Schwartz.

'Who hasn't done experiments with rats! What's your reaction to this thesis?'

'I think that on medical grounds we ought to look into it,' Schwartz said. 'I know the chemical is not on anyone's list of dangerous substances, let alone carcinogenic ones. But can we ignore this finding? I'd like your permission to repeat the student's experiments in our own laboratories. The thesis hasn't been published yet, but its findings will not be secret for ever.'

'You have my permission,' Weiss said. 'But the production line on the new super insulation board has been running for six months. It has given us a real competitive edge in the market-place. That one product has turned the company round and I'm not going to throw it all away because a research student wants to get his doctorate.'

When Schwartz had left, Weiss summoned Braun to his office and asked him to read the thesis thoroughly and come back with a full evaluation within three days. When Braun reported, he avoided making any judgement on the student's thesis. But he restated that the chemical involved was an essential ingredient in the process Koenig had patented and that the search for any substitute would be lengthy, costly and probably hopeless.

Weiss was inclined to share in the general complacency. It was not until four months later that Schwartz reported that several rats which he had exposed to heavy doses of vapour from the compound containing the suspect chemical had developed incipient skin cancer. He also produced a research report from an Indian medical journal which said that the chemical was suspected of causing illness in the paint-spraying department of an electric motor manufacturer in Bombay.

'The fact remains,' Braun said at an executive meeting which Weiss called, "that none of this is even remotely conclusive. I must repeat that this chemical is not on any list of dangerous substances."

continued overleaf

Management in action continued

'This is primarily a question of protecting our own employees,' Weiss said. 'One quarter of the items in our product range are now being impregnated with this compound, and as you know, social pressures on environmental health and pollution are steadily increasing.'

He turned to the works manager of Koenig's biggest factory. 'What would it cost to seal off the chemical application areas completely, instal monitoring equipment and add more sophisticated extraction and filtering devices?'

'As you know,' the works manager replied, 'the new plant was designed to meet in every respect the environmental health standards demanded by law. But we did not believe this compound to be dangerous. To instal every possible safeguard in both our plants would cost perhaps $10 million. It would also mean halting production for at least two months.'

'Intolerable,' the marketing director butted in. 'We cannot meet all our commitments to customers now. The competition is reacting to our success in the market. Stopping production would put us back five years.'

'Realistically, how big is the health risk to our workers?' Weiss asked Schwartz.

'However big or small,' the doctor replied, 'is it a risk we can afford to take?'

Weiss pondered. Should he continue to market the product, as though nothing had happened, and risk serious consequences later? Or should he put in safety devices that might wreck the company's revival?

Source: *International Management*, July 1979.

INTRODUCTION

In this chapter we examine the environmental factors which influence organizations and their operations. Organizations are always subject to influences from external groups and stakeholders, situations and events in the markets and society as a whole. Organizations, in turn, influence others in their business environment. Organizations have to consider the environmental factors which influence the way in which they operate and have to react to changing demands and needs. Relevant trends in the environment have to be recognized and the consequences for future operations have to be explored.

3.1 AN ORGANIZATION IN ITS ENVIRONMENT

Companies and institutions are organizations which derive the reason for their existence from the function which they fulfil in society as a whole. As such, organizations are part of our society; society can be seen as the environment in which organizations operate. As a result the functioning of organizations is always subject to influences from the societal and market environment and the organization influences in turn the environment in which it operates. This applies not only to industrial and agricultural companies and financial institutions, like banks and insurance companies, but also to institutions like schools, hospitals and nursing homes.

3.1.1 The organization and its external influences

An organization's environment consists of *stakeholders* or interest groups and of *situations* – events and circumstances which are determined by environmental factors. The main stakeholders/groups and environmental factors which influence the functioning of an organization are shown in Fig 3.1.

Stakeholders or interest groups are *tangible*, *visible* and *approachable* groups or institutions which can exercise direct influence on the functioning of an organization – for example, customers, investors, suppliers, competitors, government institutions, interest groups such as consumer associations, unions. These groups exercise *direct influence* on the individual organization, for example, by buying products and services, offering labour, creativity and knowledge, by supplying resources and components or by offering financial resources.

Furthermore, influence is exercised by societal demands, setting constraints and defining responsibilities and other limitations on the products and services which are to be supplied and the processes by which these arise – for example, environmental regulations, health and safety legislation, price constraints, quality demands.

An organization exercises influence itself on potential interest groups and stakeholders in the business environment by advertising, by information supplied with products and services or by maintaining contact with these groups by means of direct negotiations and by making deals. Furthermore, organizations supply the external

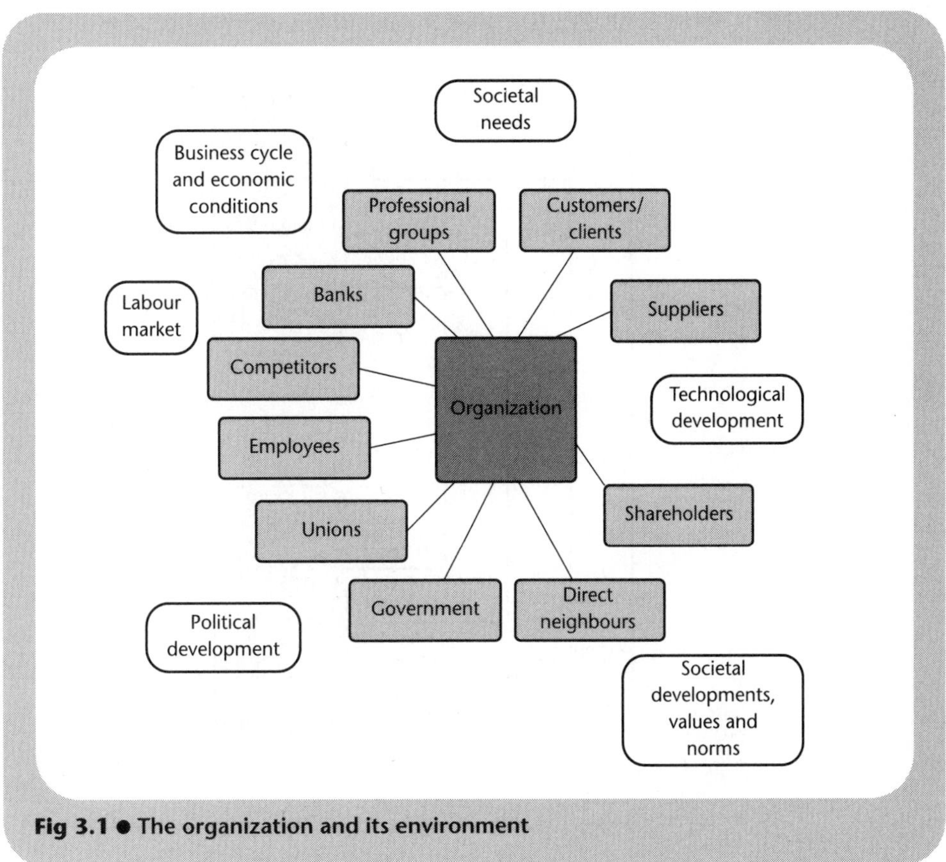

Fig 3.1 ● The organization and its environment

environment with information and account for their business operations – for example, annual reports to shareholders, government and banks, on environmental issues.

Situations, events or circumstances arise from all sorts of developments in the environment which affect the organization – for example, inflation and interest rates, unemployment levels and scarcity of supply in some parts of the labour market and the development of technology.

Organizations respond to environmental influences, but in many cases cannot really influence the actual macro-environment factors themselves. Other important environmental factors which organizations have to take into account include demographic factors, ecological factors and political factors.

3.1.2 Organizations and their environments as a cycle of events

In order to survive, an organization must be constantly interacting with its environment. On the input side, for example, the organization must interact with the markets for labour, capital, information, components, energy, raw materials and other resources. An individual organization's relationship with its environment is shown in Fig 3.2.

The diagram illustrates how an organization influences its environment and its markets and how the organization in its turn is influenced by society and market developments. Society as a whole exercises influence on the organization by, for example, laws, values and norms. This has consequences for factors such as the way in

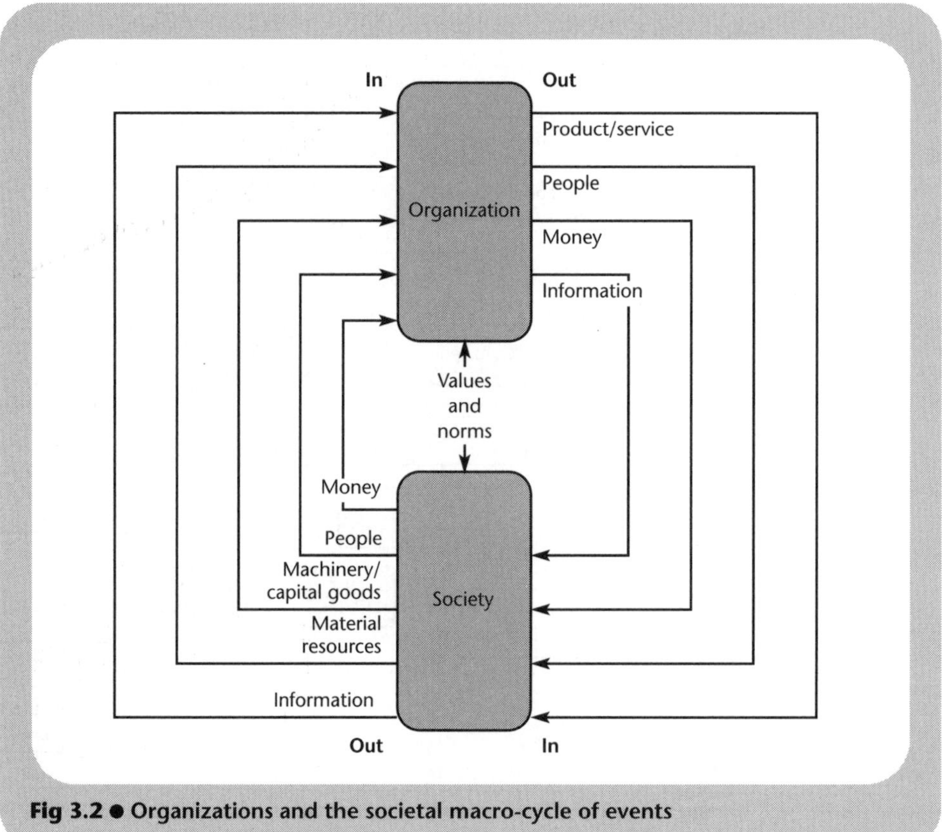

Fig 3.2 ● Organizations and the societal macro-cycle of events

which the production function is organized and working conditions. Unemployment levels in the community also have an effect on the functioning of an organization because of the influences on wage levels, while societal pressure can influence the company in the case of a reorganization. In some cases, this can lead management to postpone a reorganization or have it take place in another subsidiary in a different country or region.

Societal forces are always interrelated, but can be grouped as follows:

- *economic influences*: state of the economy, employment situations, price and wage relations, situation in the capital markets, specific markets in the sector or industry in which the company is active (oligopoly, monopoly, etc.);
- *technological influences*: new tools, new production methods, innovation, new or improved products, degree of automation, substitutes, etc.;
- *cultural/societal influences*: development of people, changes in power structures and power relations, external and internal influences through unions and works councils;
- *political influences*: wages and pricing policy, legislation on labour conditions and working conditions, industry and investment policy, tax policy, subsidies, etc.

Over time, environmental forces can differ in the degree of their influence. New situations can also arise which bring new forces into play. Higher wages, for example, as a result of new governmental policy, can make the costs of labour rise. This can in turn lead to increased demand for automation which in turn can influence the political ideas.

Taking in materials, energy and information from society

Just as the human body takes in oxygen, food and information from its environment, the organization takes in resources – such as machines, money, energy, raw materials – from its environment (*see* Fig 3.2). In addition, people are recruited to the labour force on the basis of their abilities to carry out certain skills, such as thinking and being creative. At the same time, an organization needs to take in a steady supply of external information on societal developments in general and on purchasing resources and sales markets in particular. The organization also needs a good supply of accurate and timely internal information. This is necessary to *plan* the activities, to *control* the progress and for possible *adjustment* of norms and/or *corrective actions* in current activities (*see* section 1.5.1).

Processing resources, energy and information

The organization transforms resources into specific products or services. Organization and management are required to set such a transformation process in motion and to maintain it. The activities which have to be conducted demand a rational approach within a consciously chosen organizational design. Raw materials are used up during production processes. Other resources, like people and machines, are subject to ageing and wear and tear. The *flow of people and resources* is directly connected to the continuous *flow of information*. By combining human abilities with other resources and with internal and external information, the transformation process delivers products and services which can be sold on to external markets.

Giving back a range of products and services

By producing a range of goods and services, organizations provide for external societal needs. On the output side, there are people who retire, who take early retirement, resign or get fired, and worn out and obsolete machines that are cast aside. The incoming energy and materials are either completely or partially used up or may end up in the form of smoke or refuse. Furthermore by means of instruments such as advertising and public relations, information is given out about the company and its products and services. Some organizations are obliged to render accounts of their operations and results to the outside world – for example, in the form of external annual reports to shareholders, the government and banks.

This cycle of activities continues due to the output of the products or services. The revenues generated allow the organization, in often, by then, changed circumstances to purchase the same or other raw materials, labour and machines depending on the needs of society and specific markets.

3.1.3 External adaptation and matching

A company or institution always has to be fully aware of what goes on in the outside world. It has to react to changes in the market, such as the demands for new products or services, fluctuating prices of raw materials, reduction of labour supply, availability of substitute components or raw materials and new technological findings. In this outside world, stakeholders also play a part. They invariably make additional demands and set new conditions and attempt to exercise influence from their position and changing interests. Examples include unions, government, shareholders and environmental interest groups.

If an organization wants to have and maintain a *'raison d'être'*, a match with its external environment is the first step. The direction of the business to take into account interest groups/stakeholders and circumstances/events in the external environment is referred to as **external adaptation**. Sections 3.2 and 3.3 cover in more detail the groups and situations which exercise influence over an organization and, as a result, determine its position and actions.

3.1.4 Internal adaptation and matching

An organization has been described as a *co-operative, goal-realizing unit*. In a company or institution, people and resources are *consciously and purposefully* brought together and co-operate to achieve an *efficient and effective* realization of those goals. In this way, resources are used up while the goals which have to be attained are expected to justify the right of the organization to exist in society.

Within the organization we have to pay special attention to the internal stakeholders, such as the managers and the operational staff. In addition to the external environment, therefore, we have to take into account the internal environment – that is the organization as an *economic*, *social* and *technical* system consisting of *social components*.

The most important components that form the internal environment are the managers and other members of the organization, the company culture, the machines, buildings and the financial resources. As a result, an organization can be seen as a subsystem or a more all-encompassing societal system.

Internal adaptation and the matching of components refers to the question of how the organization, the individual members of the organization and the components (people and financial resources, organizational systems and culture) have to match with each other.

3.1.5 Organizations and 'organizational equilibrium'

When an organization wants to survive, it has to see to it that both the external and internal stakeholders are and remain satisfied, for it is their requirements, needs and demands or wishes and their striving, ambition and expectations that will determine the basis for survival of an organization.

Each of these groups has its own 'stake' in the survival of the organization. As a result, every stakeholder is prepared to make a certain *contribution* to the organization. Of course, in exchange for their contribution a certain form of *incentive, inducement* or *reward* is expected, and as long as the inducement is in *reasonable proportion* to the contribution, the stakeholder will be prepared to continue participation.

The phrase '**organizational equilibrium**' can be used when an organization succeeds in rewarding its external and internal stakeholders in such as way that they remain motivated to play a part in the organization, in exchange for their contributions. Despite having all sorts of possible contradictory interests, stakeholders have one *common interest* – namely, the survival of the organization. The organization allows them to realize at least some of their own goals (needs and wishes) directly or indirectly, in exchange for their contributions. The management of the organization needs to see to it that the contributions which are made and the inducements or rewards received are and remain in balance.

Organizational equilibrium is certainly not a static concept; it is more a matter of shifting and dynamic equilibrium which has to be attained over and over again under changing circumstances and the shifting needs and demands of external and internal stakeholders, and as the organization goes about its activities.

Table 3.1 describes the contributions stakeholders make and the associated rewards.

Table 3.1 ● Contributions and rewards of stakeholders

Stakeholders	Contribution	Inducement/Reward
Owners, funders of equity, interest, and debt capital, fee payers	Money, equity capital	Ownership, rent, dividend
Members of the organization: managers and other employees	Labour, knowledge and expertise	Wages, prestige, status, social contacts, markets, self-realization
Suppliers	Raw materials, services, energy, information, other resources of production	Market prices, clientele
Customers/clients	Market prices, clientele	Products, services
Unions	Work and working environment, labour satisfaction and labour conditions	Employment, industrial democracy, participation and control
Government	Social, economic and legislative framework, infrastructure	Taxes, impositions and refunds

3.2 EXTERNAL STAKEHOLDERS

The external stakeholders who are dependent on the results of the business management and who are concerned as a group with the continued existence and survival of an organization include:

- customers/clients;
- suppliers;
- suppliers of equity and debt capital such as shareholders, banks, fee and contribution payers;
- government;
- competitors;
- societal stakeholders and interest groups, like unions, consumers' organizations, action groups, sector organizations.

These groups of stakeholders are capable of directly influencing the organization by their purchase decisions or, for example, by their decisions to put resources at the disposal of the organization. In many cases the groups themselves will have obtained a certain degree of organization, will be visible and will represent a particular interest. In any event, these groups show a certain organizational behaviour, are representative and approachable for the purposes of negotiating, lobbying, etc.

3.2.1 Customers/clients

The customers or clients buy the products of a manufacturing company, on payment, or make use of the services offered by, for example, a hospital, bank or consultancy agency. If the customers are to stay loyal and to continue to demand the product or service, the company or institution always has to provide quality supplies for fair and acceptable prices and rates. It is also important to deliver products or services on time. All of these considerations will help to ensure that an organization earns its revenues. When an organization does not apply itself to the changing needs of the buyers or its products or services, or does not do so to a satisfactory standard, the existing products will no longer be bought and the organization will lose the basis of its existence.

3.2.2 Suppliers

Every organization uses products or services from other organizations and as a result conducts relationships with external suppliers. As their contribution, suppliers deliver the raw materials, services, energy, information, machinery or components which the company orders. In return, they expect to receive the invoiced market prices on the agreed terms of payment. In case of non-payment by the client, future supplies can be stopped. Most of the time, both parties are keen to continue the relationship. To an increasing degree, demands are made with respect to quality, delivery times, flexibility and fair price setting.

3.2.3 Suppliers of equity and debt capital: shareholders, banks, contribution payers

The owner–shareholders, banks and other suppliers of equity or debt capital, and fee or contribution payers have all put money at the disposal of the organization in order to finance its operations. Their contributions consist of the provision of equity or debt capital in the form of shares, loans or mortgages. In return, they expect to have a certain degree of control in the organization and, in the financial sense, receive interest, a dividend or a rise in the value of the shares. If the organization underperforms, then the capital suppliers can shut off the flows of money, demand reorganization or intervene in the management of the board.

3.2.4 Government

The government provides the socio-economic and legislative framework within which organizations fulfil their functions. Furthermore, the government is responsible for the provision of infrastructure, such as roads, shipping routes and the railway network. The government also provides legislation in all sorts of fields (labour, wages, working conditions, opening and closing times of shops, etc.). Both national and regional government exercises influence in macro-economic terms by means of national and regional budgets, subsidies, and wage and price conditions. In return for its contribution, the national, regional or local government receives a reward in the form of taxes on, for example, profit, income or property at various rates. At the international level, the decisions of organizations are influenced by decisions from bodies such as the European Union, the Organization for Economic Co-operation and Development (OECD) and the Organization of Petroleum Exporting Countries (OPEC).

3.2.5 Competitors

Important factors with regard to competition are the number of competitors, their positioning and market share. To compete with other organizations, advertisements are published, offers of products and services are made, prices and quality levels are determined, and use is made of distribution channels. Sometimes, organizations make certain deals with each other, like wage and price deals, or activities are undertaken together in alliances or through collective advertising or joint research and development.

To protect the interests of the general public, government often introduces restrictions, for example, on price agreements, unfair competition and monopoly situations. In other circumstances, government may even promote co-operation, for example, in health care and in small businesses.

3.2.6 Societal interest groups

A growing number of interest groups have arisen in recent years with the aim of promoting certain points of view or defending interests in negotiating processes – for example, unions, employers' organizations, etc.

'Action groups' sometimes hold very strong views in relation to the decision making of companies and institutions and as a result cannot be ignored (think of Greenpeace and the World Wide Fund for Nature). Each group will try to bring attention to and present its own position and interests with arguments and, if necessary, by means of specific actions. Sometimes, legal action is taken or strikes are organized. Sometimes, from a societal 'stake', influence can be exercised on other organizations.

To counterbalance this influence effectively a certain degree of *organization* and *representation* is almost always required. In this way the interests of individuals, be they employees, employers or consumers, can be joined together and can become an effective force that can bring about shifts in power positions. In certain cases, these representative organizations can, for example, restore disrupted equilibrium and 'neutralize' discrepancies between powerless individuals and over-powerful organizations. In principle, consultative bodies and sector-based co-operative arrangements between competitors will do the same.

3.3 ENVIRONMENTAL FACTORS

In principle, every organization is influenced by factors and developments in the environment. When an organization experiences the force of environmental factors, we call these *macro forces*; the organization has little influence over them. Sometimes, some influence can be achieved by co-operation between organizations but technological and societal developments are not easily influenced by one organization. The organization cannot escape these macro forces, however, and so it is important to look at these key environmental considerations in more detail. These macro forces can be grouped into:

- demographic factors;
- economic factors;
- societal factors;
- technological factors;
- political factors;
- ecological factors; and
- market and industry factors.

3.3.1 Demographic factors

Demographic factors include considerations such as the growth, size, structure and composition of the population. In many cases, these factors determine how large a sales market will be. For example, changes in these factors will have consequences for companies in the building industry. Changes in the growth rate of the population will have implications for the sales of bread, detergents and so on. When the number of children between the ages of five and ten decreases, this will have consequences for the toy industry.

An important recent demographic development is the growth in total population. The number of households is on the increase in most countries. This has been caused, for a large part, by the increase in the number of two-member households and an explosive growth in the number of people living on their own. A large proportion of the people who are living on their own will, by around 2013, be elderly people, in particular women. The average age of the total population continues to rise. Within the EU, the proportion of people 60 years of age and over will, in 2010, have grown to 23 per cent of the total population. Alongside the so-called 'ageing' population is the remarkable fact that the number of young people is decreasing, both in relative and absolute terms.

In comparison with 30 years ago, the European population is better educated. During the same period, a large number of jobs has disappeared from agriculture and industry and reappeared in other sectors. Job-directed education has had to make way for general education. When we project the theme of education to the trends described above, it can be noted that in the future the proportion of elderly people participating in education will increase spectacularly.

Another demographic factor which is of importance in this regard, is the change in the ethnic composition of the population of some countries in Europe, for example in Germany, France, Belgium and the Netherlands.

Exhibit 3.1

Conflict between age groups looms

FT

By 2030, the over 60s in the world population will have tripled to 1.4bn.

Percentage of the population over 60 years old

OECD countries
Transitional socialist countries
China
Latin America and the Caribbean
Asia (excluding China)
Africa and the Middle East
World

Between 60 and 75 Over 75
1990
2030
Between 60 and 75 Over 75

0 5% 10% 15% 20% 25% 30%

Japan is included with the OECD countries, not with Asia

Source: World Bank

Karl Marx famously believed that all world history had been the history of class struggles. The signs are that the biggest economic battles of the next few decades will not be between classes, but between generations,

As the world's population gets older, governments are realising that meeting the demands of the over 60s means higher taxes and reduced spending and investment on services for the young. Younger generations have a strong interest in demanding that the cost of rapid ageing is spread more evenly. But so far they are losing the battle.

As Marx would have predicted, the root cause of the conflict is technological and economic progress. Better health care has increased life expectancy in nearly all countries over the past 30 years. At the same time, many fast-growing developing countries have slowed their rates of population growth to developed country levels in a fraction of the time it took early industrialisers such as the UK.

The net result of these advances, according to the World Bank, will be a tripling of the number of people in the world over 60, from nearly 500m, or 9 per cent of the world's population, in 1990 to 1.4bn, or 16 per cent, by 2030. Most of this rise will be in developing countries – again, particularly Asian ones.

What crisis? **Pension payments and contributions, as % of GDP***

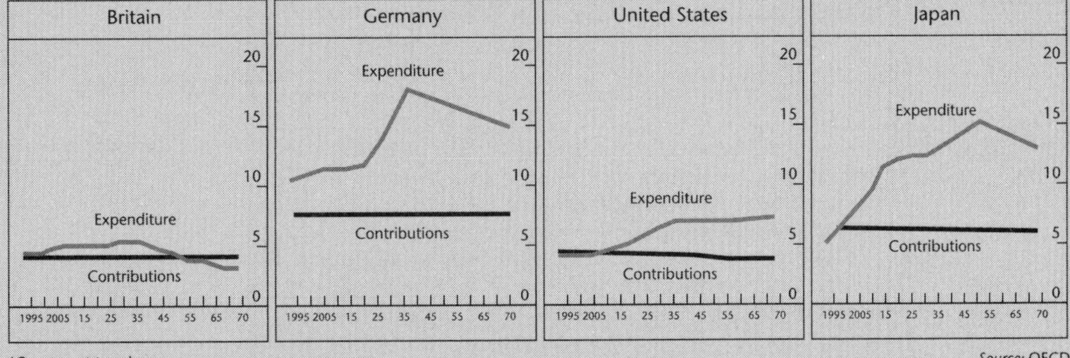

*On current trends

Source: OECD

Source: *Financial Times*, 27 September 1996.

3.3.2 Economic factors

Economic factors, such as the size of a person's disposable income, play an important role for organizations which are directed at the consumer/user. Trends in national income, the state of the economy, interest rate fluctuations, costs of labour, exchange rates and so on, are all important points of attention for organizations. Together, these factors determine the competitive position and the investment climate – that is, the attractiveness of investment. This is important for companies if they want to expand further in their own country or for companies that want to start up or expand in other countries.

A steady growth in the Gross National Product (GNP) normally leads to more spending from customers, and logically offers chances for new companies and supports the growth of existing companies. In addition to national economic factors, international economic developments are also important. The rise of the Japanese economy, which started in the 1960s, has had major consequences, first for the shipbuilding industry and then for companies producing cameras, watches, computers and cars. Also remarkable is the rapid rise of the Asian economies: South Korea, Taiwan, Hong Kong and Singapore. The relative costs of labour and the relative rise in labour productivity are equally significant.

Fluctuations in the exchange rates have a major influence on the competitive position and profit of companies operating internationally, so strong fluctuations in the dollar rate have enormous consequences for companies which export to or import from the United States. With an increase in the dollar rate, exports from European countries are stimulated and imports slowed down; in the case of a decrease, the reverse is true.

Exhibit 3.2

Korea's big leap into Europe

The *chaebol* are poised to pour in billions

LG like Korea's other *chaebol*, has decided this is the moment for dramatic expansion in Europe, especially in sophisticated products such as cars and custom-made chips. For many reasons, such as rising wages back home, saturated markets in the US, and a desire to go global, Korean giants are spending billions in Britain and on the Continent. Fierce protests are certain from such companies as Peugeot that have already suffered from a Japanese incursion. Yet the hugely ambitious Koreans won't stop until they have grabbed big chunks of Europe's markets.

The *chaebol* sometimes find it cheaper to produce in Europe than to ship goods from home. 'In certain parts of northern England, labor costs are lower than they are in Korea,' says LG's Kong, whose company has expanded a TV and microwave plant in Britain employing 475.

Source: *Business Week*, 18 March 1996.

3.3.3 Societal factors

Consumerism is a key feature of the business world of the late twentieth century. More and more consumers wish their personal needs and requirements to be met. Sometimes these wishes are expressed via action groups, or more usually via consumers' organizations. Adjustments to the working environment are also demanded as a response to changing human and societal needs – for example, the striving for more participation and joint responsibility.

Consumerism has also yielded views and demands relating to products (about safety and environmental impact, for example). Action groups have sprung up expressing societal wishes and demands; the media play their part in making these known. No organization can afford to ignore these factors. On the contrary, when after evaluation and review these demands appear to be justified, it is important to react positively to them.

The increasing complexity of society can be partly explained by a trend towards individualization – the desire of people to live their lives in their own way – and this demands a more personal approach to servicing and tailoring needs.

3.3.4 Technological factors

Technological developments have important consequences for the modernization and renewal of production processes and the arrival on the market of new products, like the development of the transistor, electronic calculators and quartz watches. Such products quickly became a serious threat to more traditional products or in some cases they replaced them completely. The rise of substitutes – for example, synthetics like plastics – made major inroads into the market shares of producers of more natural products.

Technological developments have accelerated in the past decade. The development of the electronic chip has made possible, with increasing acceleration, a number of new products which, in turn, form a basis for the development of more new products and services.

The development of technology has a major effect on labour as a factor of production. Countless jobs have disappeared. New functions – like systems developers and engineers, programmers and a new generation of electronic maintenance engineers – have made their entry and to a certain extent have disappeared again in some cases. The individual functions or parts of a company can now operate at a physical distance from each other, while still remaining in direct contact through a web of information systems. These developments have allowed ideas like *teleworking* to come to the fore (which in turn make a contribution to reducing traffic congestion and the resulting impact on the environment).

3.3.5 Political factors

Societal factors in some cases lead to legislative processes and new laws which mostly involve a limitation on the freedom of the organization to implement plans in an unrevised form – for example, the location of a certain industry in a densely populated area. Furthermore, government also directly intervenes in economic life – for example, by setting maximum and minimum prices, establishing working conditions or fixing minimum or maximum wage levels. In a number of countries, government influences economic life through forms of transfer payment/minimum wage support or by the commissioning of large infrastructure works via the public expenditure budget.

Besides fiscal legislation, dividend and interest policy is important for trade and industry. The government can also design special tax arrangements, such as stock options, through which, for example, saving becomes more attractive.

Organizations should also keep abreast of jurisdictional developments which result in judges awarding substantial compensation claims.

There are also certain international bodies whose work influences the decisions within organizations – for example, the EU, the OECD, OPEC, the World Bank and the International Monetary Fund (IMF).

3.3.6 Ecological factors

Care for the environment has become more and more important in recent years with the onset of increasing levels of water, soil and air pollution. It is expected that regulations will be tightened – for example, governing the dumping of toxic materials. Stricter environmental protection has consequences for the production processes. For certain products, like CFCs, it can even lead to production being prohibited. Such demands can also create opportunities, however. For companies in the field of environmental technology and in the fight against 'noise pollution', more severe regulations can result in more sales opportunities.

Government and industries have joint responsibility for the environment. The sacrifice of natural beauty due to economic necessity is becoming less and less acceptable. Government is confronted with this in the form of public outcries and legal action, for example, whenever the plans for the construction of roads and railways are published.

Exhibit 3.3

Green warrior in gray flannel

Like the Greenpeace radicals who recently paddled kayaks into a French nuclear testing zone off Tahiti, Jeremy Leggett is a fierce environmental campaigner. The difference is in tactics. Instead of paddles and flares, the pinstriped director of Greenpeace International's solar campaign uses slides and statistics to bring about change. His mission: convincing insurance executives that global warming could bankrupt their industry. And he's getting results.

So far, some 50 European and Asian insurers have signed an accord with the UN pledging to consider the issues of climate change and other environmental problems in all business practices. Dozens of banks have signed a similar UN pledge, fearing that many of the industries they lend money to – such as coastal resorts could be devastated by climate change. That would leave the banks with devalued or stranded assets.

Latest word on global warming

The UN's Intergovernmental Panel on Climate Change (IPCC) has concluded:

- That temperatures worldwide will rise by 1 to 3.5 degrees centigrade by 2100.
- that higher temperatures will lead to more severe droughts and floods in some places – and to less severe droughts and floods in others.
- That sea level will rise about 50 centimeters by 2100 – which is 25% less than the group had forecast in 1990.
- That the balance of evidence suggests a discernible human influence on global climate.

Data: IPCC

Source: *Business Week*, 6 May 1996.

3.3.7 Market and industry factors

Market factors are determined by the size and composition of the market. There are problems in measuring the size of the market, however. It is important to have an idea of the market which will be targeted, and a useful starting point is the *function* of the product. The technological aspects of the product are of less importance.

For example ...

... a car has the function of transportation. This means that when an automobile manufacturer defines its market as the transportation market, it defines its competitors as not only cars, but also products like trains, trams, planes and ships. Clearly this description of the market is too wide. Even the total car market is too wide a definition – for example, a Rolls-Royce does not compete with a standard saloon car. It is useful to look at certain market segments of the market which are determined, among other factors, by price, income of the buyer and optional extras.

In determining the size of the market, demographic and economic factors are highly relevant. Competition between existing companies within an industrial sector is influenced by four groups of factors:

- the bargaining power of the supplier;
- the bargaining power of buyers/clients;
- the threat of substitute products;
- the threat of new entrants.

Together these factors determine the rivalry among existing firms in an industry (Porter, 1980). The intensity of competition within an industry depends on factors, such as:

- the number and size of the competitors (in relative market shares);
- the costs the client has to incur if switching suppliers; and
- the costs of withdrawal from an industry.

Are there, for example, a few large giants or are there a large number of small organizations active in a specific market? What costs would be incurred if the organization ceased trading (redundancy payments, extra depreciation)? Does the leader–owner actually want this?

3.4 RELEVANT TRENDS IN THE ENVIRONMENT

The main underlying trends in an organization's environment which can lead to operational problems are outlined in Fig 3.3. These trends will make it necessary for adjustments to be made to an organization's procedures.

Increasing competition and internationalization of markets

In a number of markets there is evidence of increasing competition.

Christopher Columbus said, 'the world is smaller than the average human being assumes' even before he discovered America and this statement is still applicable today. The single European market, the GATT agreements, the increasing sophistication of

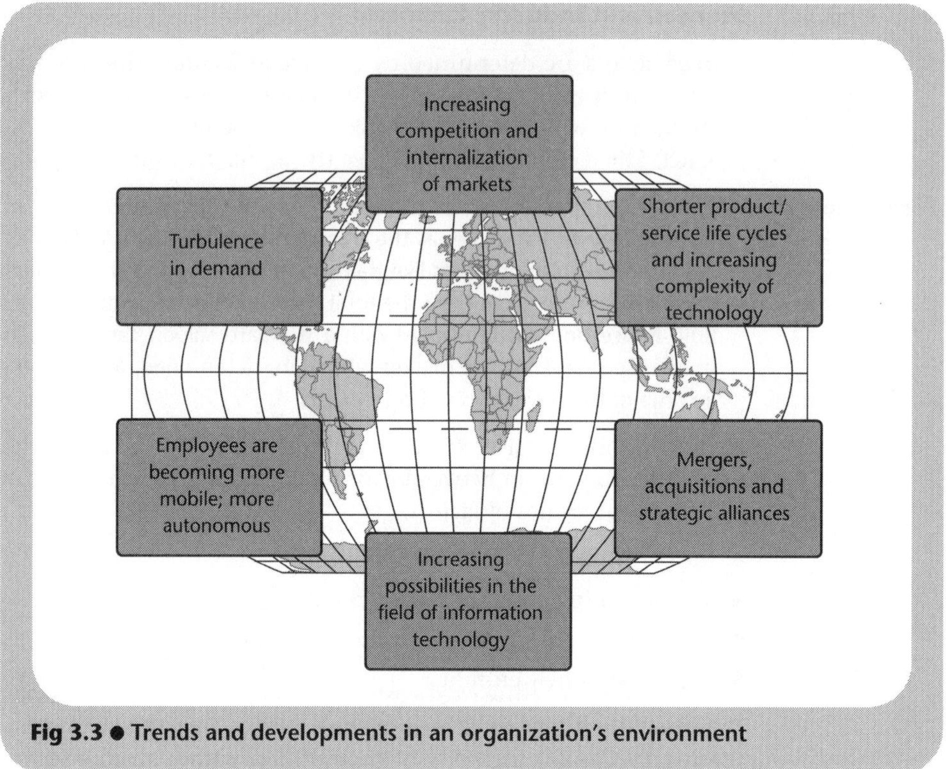

Fig 3.3 ● Trends and developments in an organization's environment

communication technology and improvements in the transportation of people and products mean that companies can now operate and indeed compete on a truly international basis.

The creation of a single European market in 1992, for example, was part of a continuing process started with the Treaty of Rome in 1956 and involves the breaking down of physical, psychological and cultural borders. The removal of trade barriers intensifies competition and puts margins under pressure. At the same time societies get to know each other better and exchange customs and habits. Similar patterns of consumption and methods of production arise, which enable companies to sell their products all over the world. The internationalization of markets will be intensified when Japan, China and the Eastern European countries increasingly open up their markets and become more involved with western economies.

Companies operating on a global basis do still encounter trade barriers and have to become efficient at coping with them. For example:

- differences in culture and language;
- tax and legislative procedures;
- banking systems;
- stock exchange regulations;
- exchange rate risks and foreign bill restrictions;

- differences in social climate and regulations concerning industrial democracy and participation;
- environmental regulations;
- subsidy and government regulations which provide incentives.

Shorter life cycles of products/services and increasing complexity of technology

New technologies are being developed at an ever-increasing pace, and as a result products are becoming obsolete more quickly. Organizations are being forced to develop their products further or to introduce new products at more regular intervals. This reduction in the **product life cycle** means that there is hardly time to earn back the often high production and development costs. Companies have to be alert and flexible in response to new technologies and market developments in order to stay ahead of their competitors.

The reduction in the product life cycle forces organizations to remove the remaining internal barriers between research and development, manufacturing and marketing and to make the contributions and responsibilities of each as clear as possible in direct communication between these functions. In some cases, the formation of business units is a solution, bringing functional specialist closer to the market (*see also* Chapters 6 and 7).

Mergers, acquisitions, takeovers and strategic alliances

In order to finance the high costs of product development and worldwide operations, many organizations tend to co-operate in alliances or even merge. In such large organizations, there is then a movement towards decentralization as autonomous units encourage more appropriate decision making.

The organization which is large enough to produce efficiently and to overcome any barriers to trade it encounters – for example by forming a **strategic alliance** or joint venture with a local entrepreneur – will occupy the most competitive position in an international market.

Exhibit 3.4

The age of mergers

There's no escaping globalization now

No one is sure what the shape of Corporate Europe will be, though at least one big car combination, a series of airline deals, and lots of action in banking and pharmaceuticals seem likely (table). Immense turmoil could result. Restructuring designed to ready industry for the European Union's single market has already helped push EU unemployment to 11%, double the U. S. level. Further consolidation will mean more joblessness, which could prompt a populist backlash. Ciba and Sandoz, for example, will cut 10% of their workforce.

Higher-tech industries aren't being spared, either. The megamerger of Switzerland's Ciba-Geigy and Sandoz 'really put the cat among the pigeons.'

The deal showed that even high-quality pharmaceutical producers face intense pressure to forge partnerships that can limit costs and satisfy investor demands for higher returns.

continued overleaf

Exhibit continued

Corporate Europe may look very different in 2001

Autos

Europe's biggest carmaker results from a merger between Fiat and either Peugeot or Renault. Volvo finally ends its independence, succumbing to a bid by joint-venture partner Mitsubishi or joining Saab at General Motors. Overall, excess capacity in Europe shrinks after the mergers.

Airlines

After deregulation in 1997, the weaker and smaller national carriers either team up, get bought out or disappear. Belgium's Sabena joins Swissair and SAS. A giant results when Air France merges with Alitalia. Iberia is bought out by a healthy competitor, possibly British Airways or Lufthansa.

Banks

The stronger players pick up the banks with the weakest balance sheets. Union Bank of Switzerland picks up Crédit Commercial de France. Deutsche Bank restructures German banking by buying Commerzbank. Spain's Banco Central Hispano Americano merges into Argentaria.

Defence/Aerospace

France's Aerospatiale joins with Dassault. Britains GEC and BAe also team up.

Pharmaceuticals

To focus on pharmaceuticals, BASF, Bayer, and Hoechst separate their drug and chemicals operations. A wave of consolidations follows in each business. Swiss giant Roche takes over Zeneca Group.

Source: Business Week, 15 April 1996.

For example ... ... automobile manufacturer Peugeot/Citröen and steel producer Hoogovens have worked together in the development of new materials – in particular a substitute for steel – for the bodies of future cars. Suppliers and clients work together in research and development activities without giving up their autonomy and independence.

The increasing complexity of technology makes it very unlikely that one company has the necessary knowledge and skills for all its research and development programmes. Even the largest companies will be confronted with a lack of knowledge and skills in specific fields. Furthermore, the costs and risks associated with research and development are so high that a very large market share is required if the investments are to be earned back in time. The combining of complementary knowledge and the sharing of risks are important reasons for engaging in a strategic joint venture or alliance. Such ventures are also engaged in for the purpose of maintaining or intensifying market share – for example, Lufthansa–Delta Airlines, British Airways–American Airlines, Northwest–KLM.

Developments in information technology

Developments in the field of information technology offer opportunities to improve efficiency and effectiveness. More sophisticated telecommunication networks and management information systems have improved the possibilities for decentralized decision making, while at the same time allowing management to maintain an overview at the centre. If organizations are to exploit these opportunities, change will be inevitable.

Greater employee mobility and autonomy

There is a trend in organizations towards increasing the involvement and the autonomy of employees. They wish to have a say in the allocation of work and are also prepared to change jobs. As a result the mobility and quality of employees have become important issues for management.

Exhibit 3.5

Downsizing, outsourcing: now hotelling is the vogue

The key to miximising the efficiency of buildings is the ability to respond to variable demand. First came downsizing and outsourcing as companies shed staff and peripheral activities in the campaign to reduce liabilities and overheads.

Next came a reappraisal of the space requirements of the core operations and personnel to be retained. Here the buzz words are hot desking and hotelling. The old pattern, in which each employee had a permanent desk space, may be over. Sales staff who are usually on the road, for example, may only need to borrow a desk temporarily vacated by a colleague. Senior managers who spend much of their time visiting branches may not need permanent offices but, like hotel guests, could book a room and assistants. With a laptop and a password they can create a virtual office anywhere, with access to all company information.

The hotel principle is mostly applied internally as companies exploit their existing stock of buildings. But it has also spawned a new property sector: the business centre. These offer serviced suites of offices on flexible leases.

Source: *Financial Times*, 20 September 1996.

Turbulence in demand

Consumer behaviour is constantly changing and consumer needs are becoming more and more varied. Organizations are thus forced to provide different customer groups with a variety of products. They also need to react more and more quickly to changes in taste and preferences.

Some of these developments – namely, internationalization, cultural differences, strategic alliances and network organizations – will now be examined in some detail. The influence of IT and the changes in employee attitudes are covered in Chapters 8, 11 and 12.

3.4.1 Internationalization of industrial life

The decision of an organization to target international markets and/or operate on a global basis may be taken for a variety of reasons. Sometimes, growth in the home market is no longer possible and so further growth is dependent on the organization operating beyond its own national borders. In other cases, profits can be increased and the costs of production lowered by embarking on a large-scale investment programme. The spreading of activities over more countries or regions makes a company less vulnerable to the effects of specific developments and risks in one region or country.

The internationalization of company activities may start out with the execution of an order which 'accidentally' ends up abroad, leading on to the formation of an export/import section within the sales department and later perhaps even to licensing or franchising. In other cases, internationalization may develop through a 'daughter' company or via a strategic alliance.

This growth in the importance of international activities means an increase in the complexity of business considerations as well as the need for a greater level of management involvement. International operations may take many different forms:

- the export of products/services;
- the export of technology, patents and licences;
- franchising of the export formula;
- investments in own foreign subsidiaries or manufacturing facilities;
- acquisitions, joint venture and alliances;
- worldwide operations in a so-called 'global' company.

In the case of the global company, great emphasis must be placed on the co-ordination of activities in different countries (*see* Fig 3.4). For example, the designs may be made in Country A, produced in Countries B, C and D and eventually sold in a number of different countries. The activities of individual countries have to be co-ordinated and

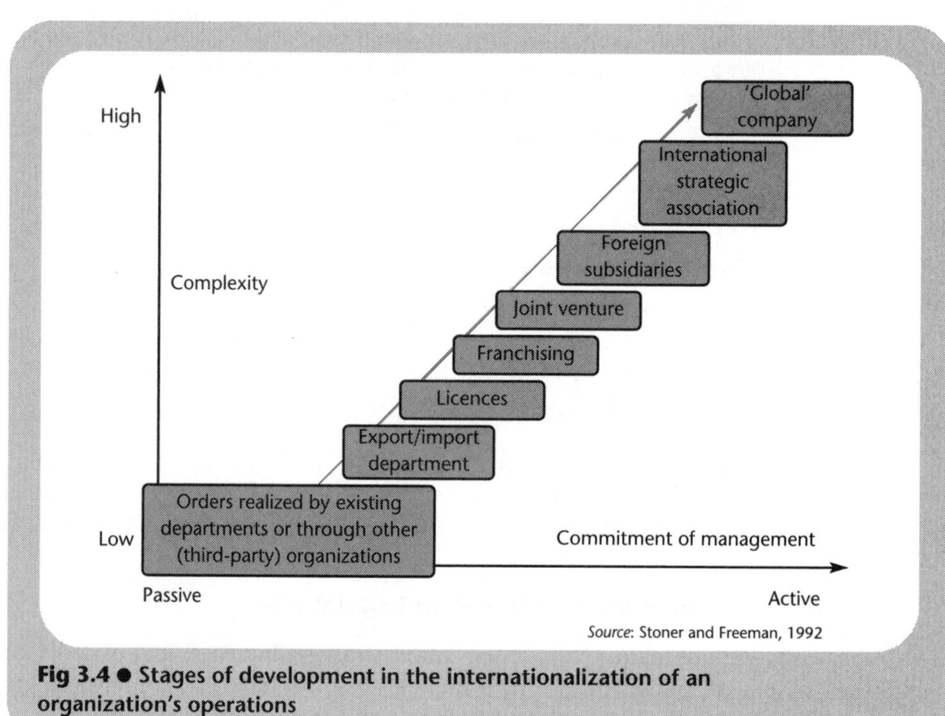

Fig 3.4 ● Stages of development in the internationalization of an organization's operations

the flow of goods and information between the countries has to be controlled. In the case of a multinational company, operating on an international basis, the company has autonomous subsidiaries in different countries, each with its own products, brands and markets.

The slogan 'think global, act local' refers to the necessity for the organization working on a global scale to balance the specific needs of the local market with the overall need for a high degree of efficiency and impeccable co-ordination. This poses a great challenge for management. Operating on an international basis means that managers must appreciate the significance of differences in culture and their role in determining the relative success or failure of projects worldwide.

Minicase 3.1

Investments in Central and Eastern Europe: mere adventure or real opportunities?

More and more companies have been, and still are, investing in Central and Eastern Europe.

The costs of entry to these geographical regions as potential markets are still relatively low, whereas the chance of attaining a high or dominant market position is reasonably high. In some product groups, market shares of between 25 and 75 per cent have been won relatively easily. Central and Eastern Europe with its 425 million inhabitants is not only seen as an attractive potential market, however, but also as a potential centre of production, since this region has rich natural resources and still offers relatively low labour costs.

When doing business in Central and Eastern Europe, several important factors must be given careful consideration – for example, technical communication problems, political instability, inadequate infrastructure, environmental problems, a tiring and often irritating bureaucracy, low quality standards and low productivity standards, a different work ethic, corruption and high losses at the start of business activities. More than 25 per cent of joint ventures with Russian companies have failed due to inadequate initial research into local market conditions.

A thorough examination of investment opportunities is equally important when preparing to do business with other regions of the world – for example, the Far East, South and Central America.

Organizations operating on a global basis will provide a 'local' dimension to its operations in a number of ways. For example, the involvement of local representatives seems to be a prerequisite for successful market entry in Central and Eastern Europe. This local dimension may take the form of a complete takeover of a local existing business, joint venture, the opening of a wholly owned local subsidiary or simply the contracting of a local representative. Each solution has its problems.

In practice, the following options should be given serious consideration.

- Local management may need to be supplemented with western management at the top of the local enterprise, giving a better basis for quality, financial control and technical expertise and ensuring the standard of day-to-day management activities.

- A business plan and the implementation of tools and techniques to measure results in quality improvement are essential.
- Gaining the full commitment of the partners is also of great importance. If this is not realized, the only basis for co-operation is the signed contract or the formal takeover agreements.
- A thorough understanding of the cultural differences and the attitudes prevailing in the country and among the local people is crucial to success. This is often the cause of persistent problems (*see* section 3.4.2).

A long-term vision is a basic condition of investing in certain countries or parts of the world such as Central or Eastern Europe, China or Mexico. The desire for short-term gains results time and time again in costly misadventures. A solid, well thought out, long-term perspective might prevent this type of business failure. It gives a sound basis for developing a network of contacts essential to keeping abreast of business developments and information in the informal business environment which often exists in these countries.

3.4.2 Effects of national cultures on organizations

Cultural differences are reflected in national variations in consumer behaviour and consumption patterns – for example, in terms of the way people dress or the food they prefer.

For example ...

Tea is served in different ways in different parts of the world. The British like to drink their tea as a light brew diluted with milk; the Americans prefer iced tea and regard it primarily as a summer drink to be served over ice; the Saudi Arabians drink theirs as a thick, hot brew, heavily sweetened.

To succeed in a world of such diversity companies often have to modify their plans for global efficiency through worldwide standardization so that they can respond to the needs and opportunities created and demanded by cultural differences.

Research by Hofstede (1980), Trompenaars (1995) and others shows that there is a relation between the culture of a nation and the specific organizational models which prevail in that country. Hofstede's study also demonstrates how distinct cultural differences across countries result in wide variations in social norms and individual behaviour in areas such as respect for elders or response to the pressure of time which are also reflected in the effectiveness of different organizational forms and management systems.

Figure 3.5 indicates how organizations are characterized in different countries around the world. The countries' position on the matrix is determined by the level of power distance and uncertainty avoidance within the organizational environment. Power distance comprises the difference in the extent to which one person can determine someone else's behaviour, and a variety of factors can lead to different countries having a different attitude towards power distance in all types of social relationship (parent and child, teacher and pupil, boss and employee, *etc.*). Different societies also deal differently with the uncertainties of life, with some cultures attempting to minimise or avoid uncertainties so far as possible. In countries where people tend to avoid uncertainties there is a greater need for clear oganizational structures with clear procedures and a clear hierarchy.

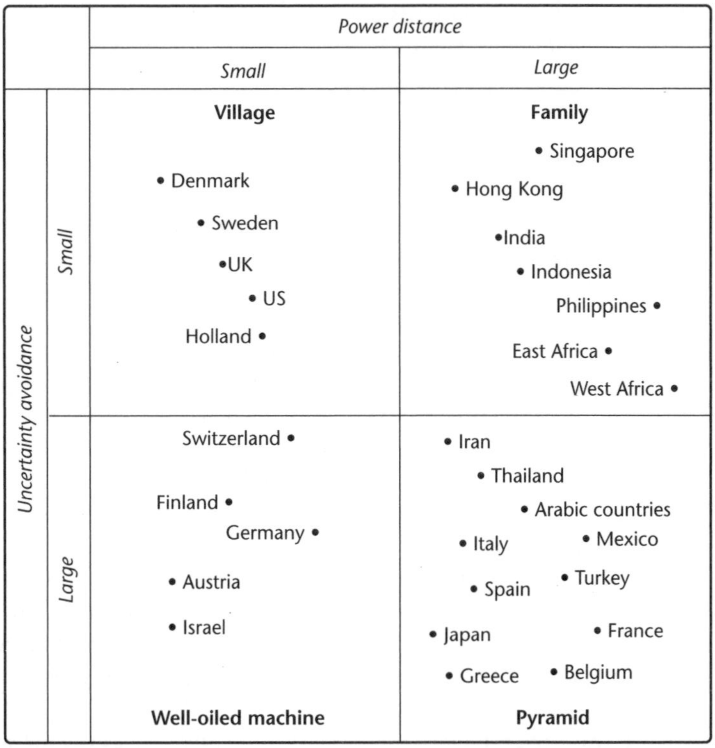

Uncertainty avoidance	Power distance: Small	Power distance: Large
Small	**Village** • Denmark • Sweden • UK • US Holland •	**Family** • Singapore • Hong Kong • India • Indonesia Philippines • East Africa • West Africa •
Large	Switzerland • Finland • Germany • • Austria • Israel **Well-oiled machine**	• Iran • Thailand • Arabic countries • Italy • Mexico • Spain • Turkey • Japan • France • Greece • Belgium **Pyramid**

Source: Hofstede, 1980, p319

Fig 3.5 ● Characterization of countries and organizations

1. Organizations in Scandinavia, Anglo-American countries and the Netherlands (small power distance and a low degree of uncertainty avoidance) are generally pretty informal and the degree of labour division and formalization is comparatively low. There is relatively little hierarchy, reflected in the limited number of levels. This form of organization is sometimes referred to as the *'village model'* (*implicit structure*).
2. At the other cultural extreme, we find Japan and Latin America, Islamic and some Asian countries. Organizations in these countries are often characterized by a *'pyramid'* with one person at the top and many layers of employees supporting the leader from below (*full bureaucracy*). The interrelationships between individual employees on the one hand, and between employees and the work process on the other are strictly prescribed according to formal rules and laws or by tradition. Great emphasis is placed on the hierarchy of the organization.
3. In countries like South-East Asia (low degree of uncertainty avoidance behaviour and relatively large power distances) the relations between people are strongly determined by rules, hierarchy and tradition, but the work process is not so strictly structured. The most common organizational form can be compared with a *'family'* (*personal bureaucracy*).

4. In German-speaking countries, Finland and Israel, the work processes are strictly structures, but there is little power distance and formulation of relations between people (in Germany the group or team often has the central authority). Such an organizational structure is often referred to as a *'well-oiled machine'* (*workflow bureaucracy*).

It is particularly interesting to compare the relative positions of Germany and France in this respect, according to Hofstede. In contrast with Anglo-American and Scandinavian countries and the Netherlands, power distances in French organizations appear to be very large. This is seen in the large number of layers within the organization and an extensive and powerful 'cadre'. The power distance in German organizations is similar to that in the Anglo-American and Scandinavian countries. Indeed in Germany there is a stronger need for rules and procedures in avoidance of uncertainty (the 'well oiled machine').

In a comparison of industrial companies, French companies had an average of five organizational levels and the German companies an average of three. The ratio of management and specialists in relation to total personnel in the French companies was 26 per cent compared with 16 per cent in German companies.

Finally the wage differential between the highest and lowest paid employees in the French companies was many times larger than that of the German companies. The employees on the lowest level got paid more in the German companies and were better trained.

Research by Lincoln and others (1985) showed that Japanese companies tended to have one and a half more organizational levels than their American counterparts (average number of levels was five). The number of managers per level was smaller in the Japanese companies and the Japanese companies had more sub-groups. In one respect, therefore, the Japanese companies seemed more centralized because of the larger hierarchy and yet at the same time more sub-groups were involved in the decision-making process.

Cultural differences in international firms

In organizations with subsidiaries in several countries or with significant numbers of immigrant employees in their workforce, it is important that managers (and of course also researchers and consultants) take into account the effect of differing value patterns. Some examples may illustrate this further.

Sweden and the United Kingdom

One analysis showed that the Swedish management of a Swedish subsidiary of a British company was strongly characterized by competitive values – a more common feature of British culture than of Swedish culture. The Swedish subsidiary had been founded by someone from the UK and although senior management within the organization had recently changed from being British to being Swedish, a process of selection and succession had meant that those Swedish managers who had best adapted to the British style of work were the ones who had reached the top.

The average Swedish employee, however, was not happy with this style of leadership, but until recently this had not affected the effectiveness of the company to a significant degree. Suddenly a large number of skilled workers and respected middle managers left the company. Those who stayed showed a low degree of motivation and loyalty. This was due to the fact that the company culture was perceived as closed and because workers felt treated as a technical factor of production instead of as human beings with flesh and blood. In this case national cultural difference had an indirect, negative effect on the organizational culture of the Swedish subsidiary.

France and the Netherlands

A worldwide investigation relating to the organizational culture of a multinational company asked employees, among other things, whether, when they disagreed with their superiors, they communicated their disagreement to their superiors directly. In France and the Netherlands many employees gave a negative response – not surprising given French culture, but definitely so given Dutch culture. In France the decisions of a superior will not be questioned as a rule. Although employees may be critical of superiors, they would not make a habit of opposing them too often. In the Netherlands, on the other hand, employees do not generally hesitate to disagree openly with their boss.

Germany

In another investigation it was asked whether a sense of humour was expressed in the organization. In the case of a German company, the answer was a whole-hearted 'yes'. However, when employees were asked whether this was desirable, their response was negative. It seems that in Germany pleasure at the misfortune of others (*Schadenfreude*) is more prevalent than in other European countries, for example. While elsewhere a joke at the expense of the organization does not immediately have a negative connotation, this was definitely the case in the German company. If an organization operating on an international basis was unaware of this aspect of German culture, misunderstandings might easily occur.

USA

In the United States it is seen as important that a person is assertive in a way which in Europe would be regarded as exaggerated or excessive. In the US it is also very important that every person can show how much he or she contributes to the success of the organization. A typical American employee is a conformist, extremely motivated by his or her career and by serving the public. There is a subconscious fear that non-conformist behaviour could result in missing out on a career, a promotion, a salary increase or public recognition and acknowledgement. This seems somewhat inconsistent with the individualistic value patterns of Americans. These cultural issues were once described as follows:

> *Money creates uniformity. American employees wear the same Wall Street suits or fast-food aprons, as if they belong to one and the same religious order. Secretaries all wear the same blouse or jersey, their superiors the same ladies' suits with pearl necklace*

Source: *NRC*, 10 June 1995.

International mergers and cultural differences

When considering mergers or acquisitions, companies should take into account not only financial and market-oriented considerations, but also the culture of the organizations. It is widely known that one of the main reasons for unsuccessful mergers is the failure to bridge the existing cultural differences. Although such cultural differences can exist in mergers of two companies within the same country, they are particularly problematic with countries originating from different countries. It is often the case that even many years after a merger has taken place, people in the merged organization still regard themselves as members of a specific 'blood group', with all the negative images that such an attitude brings with it.

It is not always the case that groups of people originating from the same cultural region will necessarily have fewer problems relating to each other than groups of people from totally different cultural regions. Think, for example, of the people of the different republics of the former Yugoslavia, the Roman Catholic and Protestant people of Northern Ireland or the Flemish and Walloon communities of Belgium.

In cases where the cultural differences are well known, people are less able to get along together when these differences are deeply rooted in the past. This of course does not necessarily mean that people from different cultural regions are unable to co-operate effectively. For example, despite negative impressions and political problems between the Flemish and the Walloons, people from both sections of the community seem to be able to work together very well.

Hofstede's research results make it possible, to a certain extent, to predict whether an international merger will cause problems related to national cultural differences or not. Mergers between British and French companies are fraught with difficulties due to the major cultural differences. Mergers between German and Dutch companies and between Belgian and Dutch companies seem to experience similar difficulties. Mergers between Dutch and British companies are relatively straightforward in comparison.

In the light of the possible consequences of cultural differences, it is important for an organization to devote a great deal of time and effort to the development of its own company culture and to the selection and training of employees who will fit into this.

Minicase 3.2

Heineken moves into China

'We assume that Heineken is known all over the world. In large parts of China, however, this is not the case,' says Eric Nelissen, General Manager in China of the Dutch beer manufacturer. 'In Chinese script, Heineken is called He-Lic. It means both powerful and happy.'

Spreading the name He-Lic in the People's Republic is not a straightforward process. As Eric Nelissen confirmed: 'Local TV advertising in Shanghai and in Changshu is just as expensive as it is in the West. But in China you have no say in the decisions regarding the time at which your ad is broadcast. For all you know, this could be at four o'clock in the morning.'

Heineken has high expectations. China is already the largest beer market in the world after the United States, although individual consumption is still low.

'A Chinese person drinks on average 8 litres of beer per year,' says Nelissen. Compare that to Germany (154 litres per year) or the US (92 litres per year). For the time being Heineken does not want to brew in China. 'We have to be careful with our image as a top brand,' states Nelissen.

But is China a single market? 'Absolutely not. The People's Republic is divided up into many individual markets. We aim at the top hotels and karaoke bars in the large cities. In Shanghai alone there are already thousands of karaoke bars. Furthermore, the number of supermarkets in China is rising at an impressive pace. Makro will shortly open its first store.'

Distribution seems to be the big bottleneck. 'The distribution sector has not yet been liberalized and it is not permitted for a foreign brand to be distributed by the owner company.'

Finally, Heineken is not putting all its eggs in one basket. Besides its own brand, the company has interests in breweries in Shanghai and the province of Fujion with the Tiger Beer brand in a joint venture with Asia Pacific Breweries.

3.4.3 Network organizations

In the transition to the twenty-first century it is possible to see the beginnings of a new type of organization with new roles and assignments for managers and employees (and also, for example, for unions). This new organization form is called the *'dynamic network' model* (sometimes referred to as *'inter-organizational networks'* or *'organizational webs'*).

What is a dynamic network?

The most straightforward means of defining a dynamic network is to consider a practical example of one.

For example ...

... consider the following situation. A piece of ice hockey equipment is designed in Scandinavia, made ready for production in the United States, adapted according to the demands of the total North American market, manufactured in Korea and distributed by a multinational sales network with first deliveries originating from Japan. Where and what is 'the organization' in this case? The product design, the process development, the production, the sales and the distribution functions each take place in a different location, in a number of different organizations, which may only be linked for this particular project.

This sequence of events is said to be taking place in a **network organization** (*see* Fig 3.6) made up of discrete but interrelated parts consisting of a number of co-operating organizations. The role of the centre as an 'intermediary' does not have to be an independent function; it can be taken over by any of the other participants. The co-ordination of the whole network of important components is the main issue.

'Networking' – the building up of contacts, connections – becomes increasingly important in fast developing economies. Whether this concerns the tracking down of the right materials, the bringing together of the designers and an appropriate location for manufacturing or the hiring of temporary personnel, the ability to bring together people and components fast and efficiently (often with the help of a computer) is the key factor for the flexibility of the organization.

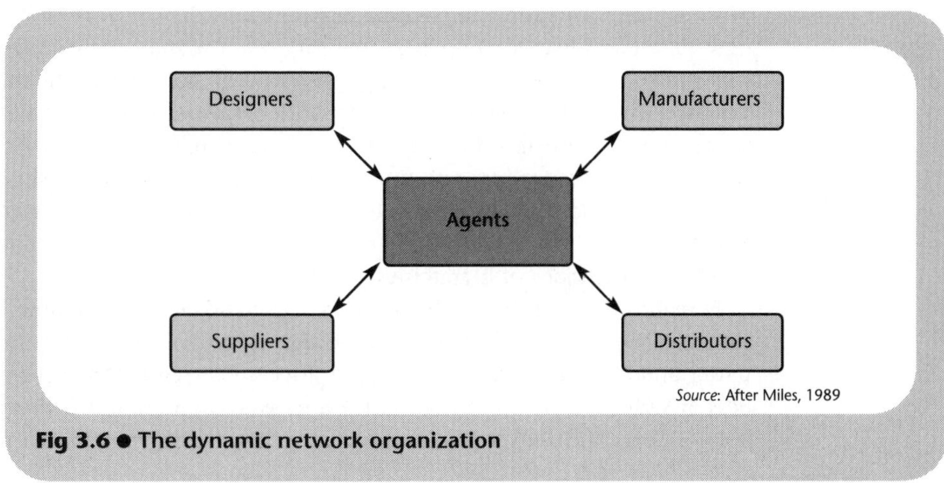

Fig 3.6 ● The dynamic network organization

The more networks are used, the more refined and efficient they become. This means that they can be used more often as a useful tool for expansion, supply and outsourcing. With this network approach, organizations can be more flexible and can adapt more quickly to innovations and shifts in the demand for products or services.

The network is not new in itself. In many lines of business relatively stable networks of suppliers, manufacturers and distributors already exist. What is new is the speed with which the network can now be composed.

The disadvantages of networks

The main concern of most managers is that the dynamic network structure does not offer the degree of direct supervision and control that is possible when all activities take place 'under one roof'. The organization, whose name appears on the final product, may not be involved in its manufacture at all (as in the case of Nike) and thus relies on the other partners in the network living up to the quality and delivery conditions. If one element of the network falls short in its task, all of the remaining partners in the project suffer, especially the one directly responsible to the end customer.

There is also a concern that the smaller scale and flexible structures within the network will lead to higher staff turnover (with more employees crossing over to other functions in other companies) and that the loyalty and devotion of managers and employees will diminish. With the possibility of higher staff turnover, the further uses of supplies and the temporary hiring of specialists, there is also a danger of loss of company secrets and patents.

The advantages of networks

When a dynamic network functions well, however, it gives a higher flexibility, a better use of human capital and an improvement in overall efficiency.

For example ...

... more products can be produced more quickly when a company is not tied to the limited capacities of its own manufacturing units, designers, technicians and distributors. The provision of contract-based services can expand the range of a small business. The hiring of temporary specialist support can increase the availability of expertise without a substantial rise in overheads.

Often middle managers spend a large part of their time on internal, procedural matters at some distance from the clients, suppliers and distributors of the company. In the new, flatter and leaner companies there are fewer management functions, but the ones that are there are more demanding, present a greater challenge and often give more satisfaction. The managers in these network organizations have a wider vision. In contrast, most of the middle managers in larger and integrated firms have to fulfil co-ordinating, controlling and linking functions. They have to keep together the giant pieces and ensure that numerous bits and pieces come together at the right time. This type of function is less important in a network system, where contracts and agreements take the place of hierarchies.

Furthermore, employees in network organizations will be able to expect more of their jobs and employees will derive a higher level of satisfaction from it. In the new, flatter and less complex structures, employees can see for themselves how their products or services develop in the market and as a result are more directly involved. Most network organizations will probably have fewer managers and as a result more knowledge and skills will be expected of the employees, both with regard to working with ever more complex technology and with regard to building up and maintaining a wider circle of clients.

The notion that employees have to be more responsible for managing themselves and more involved in the decision-making processes is not new (*see* Chapters 4, 6, 7 and 8). In many modern factories and offices, almost completely self-controlling and autonomous work groups set their own deadlines, assign work and their members can switch quickly from one task to another. Such groups also have responsibility for quality and internal co-ordination. The network structure strengthens this approach and introduces even more flexibility with greater opportunities for 'self-management' and autonomy.

One can expect this trend to continue. In the flexible world of dynamic networks and webs, in the future work teams may switch from one company to another on a temporary basis. In such a situation, the training and development of employees will have to be directed at complete systems, not only at the characteristics and special features of one single process within the system. As systems become more flexible and automated, the basis of training must be widened.

Of course, more training makes the employee more mobile. Such mobility will be an asset when employees outgrow their functions and teams, even when these have an extremely wide base. Promotion may involve gaining experience and knowledge in certain technologies and fields of work. This will imply mobility and acceptance of career paths in flat and network organizations where the motto is 'horizontally up' (*see* Chapter 8) and added value is supplied along these new lines.

Networks within a single organization

In the case of a network of different business units within one organization, each of the individual parts of the organization needs to be in tune with the others, and the abilities of each unit are exploited in order to improve overall performance. Programmes or employees who can contribute to that process are brought together.

For now a 'business unit' can be defined as a unit of a company which is responsible for and operates in a discrete product market. Each unit has guidelines in the form of company procedures, priorities and investment decisions which have been established by central management.

In a network structure within a single company the assignment of work of the individual business units will have to be more clearly defined and data on the respective performances will have to be exchanged. The links and communication between the different business units will also increase. Furthermore, a wider range of process and communication skills will be expected from managers.

In the network model, central management's role involves areas like taxes, financial administration, collective purchasing (if appropriate), the relation with the shareholders, the public relations strategy of the company and important group initiatives (new alliances or the taking over or the selling off of companies). Senior management is concerned with problems which can be better resolved by one central unit rather than by a combination of units. The most important role of senior management is to function as a kind of 'switch', an intermediary at the centre that delegates responsibility for specific assignments to the individual managers or to a combination of managers because they are closer to the customers, the competitors and the production processes than the staff at the central head office.

Local managers are given much more responsibility therefore; they are the 'centres of excellence' of the group. They participate in the project groups in which all parts of the organization are represented; they have the authority to take decisions which directly influence local results; and they are also responsible for the supply of information to review and evaluate the work in progress.

Double challenge

In the years to come, the greatest challenge by far will be in the building up of a closer relation with customers and in competing on both a regional and worldwide basis. To realize these two goals, not only will new organizational procedures be necessary, but also new strategies for the management of a company. Dynamic networks in strategic co-operation or within one larger organization make it possible to develop and execute some of these strategies in an effective way. They also offer new possibilities for personal rewards both for employees and for managers.

Exhibit 3.6

Organizational webs

An **economic web** is a set of companies that use a common architecture to deliver independent elements of an overall value proposition that grows stronger as more companies join the set. Before a web can form, two conditions must be present: a technological standard and increasing returns. The standard reduces risk by allowing companies to make irreversible investment decisions in the face of technological uncertainty. The increasing returns create a mutual dependence that strengthens the web by drawing in more and more customers and producers.

Webs are not alliances, however. They operate without any formal relationships between participants. Each company in a web is wholly independent; only the pursuit of economic self-interest drives it into web-like behavior. It prices, markets, and sells its products autonomously.

Within economic webs, **technology webs** organize around specific technology platforms. One prominent example of a technology web is the desktop computing business. In the desktop computing business of the 1980s, highly specialized participants acted both independently and interdependently to assemble a complex package of technology components and services.

Within technology webs, clusters of players participate in competing **value webs**, which seek to capture a disproportionate share of the value-creation opportunity. Whereas economic activity in technology webs focuses on maximizing value to the customer, value webs add a second objective: to create value for a specific group of companies that have adopted a common technology platform. In the desktop computing technology web, for example, at least two major value webs are in competition. One is organized and shaped by Apple, and promotes the Macintosh as the standard desktop computing platform; the other is controlled by Microsoft and Intel, and champions an alternative standard defined by the use of the Intel microprocessor and the Microsoft operating system.

Market webs represent a third form of web. Unlike customer webs, which focus on the behavior and preferences of an individual customer segment, market webs are organized around a specific type of transaction. The customer web shaper wants to develop the broadest possible relationship with its chosen segment, and to serve these customers across a wide range of needs. The market web shaper tries to build the deepest possible relationship with all the buyers and sellers involved in a particular kind of market transaction.

What strategic roles are created by webs?

Two different strategic roles may be played in webs: adaptation and shaping. Each has the potential to generate considerable value.

In companies that opt for an **adapting** role, senior management deals with uncertainty by trying to stay one step ahead of other players in anticipating and responding to changes in the business environment. Rather than attempting to influence events, these companies endeavor to stay at the edge of them, and to

Winning strategies for major web players

	Web formation	Web mobilization	Web evolution
	Get into the flow →	Build momentum →	Encourage lock-in
Shaper	Pick the right technology platform	Manage perceptions actively	Enhance platform technology frequently
	Enter market quickly	Create economic incentives for others	Promote standardization
	Accelerate adoption	Evangelize opportunity	Link and leverage
Adapter	Identify winning web early	Compete aggressively for web share	Exploit customer lock-in
	Focus on near-term profit opportunities	Link up with web shaper's strategy	Undermine supplier/shaper lock-in or diversify into new webs
	Establish dense information links with other web participants		

capture value by spotting opportunities earlier and moving more quickly than the competition.

Shapers, on the other hand, focus on the fluidity of events and on opportunities to determine or influence outcomes. They believe it is possible to mold the environment in such a way that it enhances their ability to create value.

Web strategies demand a completely different mindset from that employed in traditional strategic thinking. For one thing, they tend both to narrow and to broaden management focus. The former, because they encourage unbundling and the outsourcing of undifferentiated business activities. (The extreme form of this is the virtual corporation, where the scope of activities conducted within the enterprise and subject to direct management control is radically reduced.) The latter, because the context for defining strategy expands from maximizing value for the enterprise to maximizing value for the web. If the web does not maximize value, neither can the enterprise within it.

Webs represent a whole new way of thinking about industry structure, relationships between companies, and value creation. Though not monopolies, they are just as powerful. For the rest of this decade – perhaps much longer – we shall see industries being shaped by competing webs that relentlessly devour one another.

Source: From "Spider versus Spider" by John Hagel, III, 1996.

3.4.4 Strategic partnering

In recent years, an increasing number of strategic partnerships have been set up between American, Japanese and European-based companies. This rise in the incidence of partnerships can be explained by the need for increased flexibility in organizational structures due to developments such as:

- the increased internationalization of markets which introduces new competitors to existing geographical markets;

- the ever increasing complexity of technology which increases the amounts of money needed for investment in research and development; and
- the increase in the speed with which successive innovations are launched, shortening the pay-back period of these investments.

The funding of research and development thus requires a strong market position. Companies with large market shares should be able to raise the required funding quite easily. Small companies have to find ways to resist such competition. This is sometimes possible by adopting a strategy of specialization in co-operation with other companies in a strategic partnership arrangement. In other cases a company has to become an international competitor itself.

Strategic partnering is the only way in which a company can ensure that it is able to react in a flexible way to the fast changing circumstances in the organizational environment or even to survive. With strategic partnering the partners undertaking the co-operation agreement keep their independence and their own identity and the effect on the competitive position of the partners will be noticeable in the long term. Strategic partnering and mutual co-operation can take many forms (*see* section 5.4). We covered the strategic alliance of Hoogovens and Peugeot/Citröen earlier. In Chapter 5 we will cover strategic alliances in more detail.

For example ...

... the telecommunication industry is an industry which is profoundly affected by worldwide developments. The large number of strategic joint ventures in this industry can be cited as evidence of this. Think of the joint venture agreement between Philips and Sony in which they agreed to co-operate on the product development of audio-visual compact discs. Think of the agreement between Olivetti and Canon to develop jointly copiers and image processors, and of the announcement by American Telephone and Telegraph (AT&T) that it is buying a 20 per cent stake in Sun Microsystems (*see also* Fig 3.7).

Strategic partnering can be the key which opens the doors to new technologies, skills and competences. At the same time there is a danger that knowledge and skills will be 'borrowed' by a better organized partner. Partnering with a (potential) competitor can bring significant advantages, but at the same time caution is vital. From a longer term perspective, there is a real danger that one of the partners will lose out in the end (*see* section 5.5).

Each partnership, in whatever form this is realized, has both advantages and disadvantages. It is important to investigate these thoroughly before taking a first step on the road to partnering. (Joint production, licensing and outsourcing are covered in greater detail in section 5.5.)

3.5 SOCIAL RESPONSIBILITY, EXTERNAL REPORTING AND CORPORATE GOVERNANCE

An organization is a goal-realizing unit through which people and resources come together to strive for survival in a socio-economic and technological market environment. A condition of this is that the rewards of the stakeholders – employees, consumers, shareholders and others – are such that they are willing to continue their contribution to the organization. In this way an organization has to justify its societal

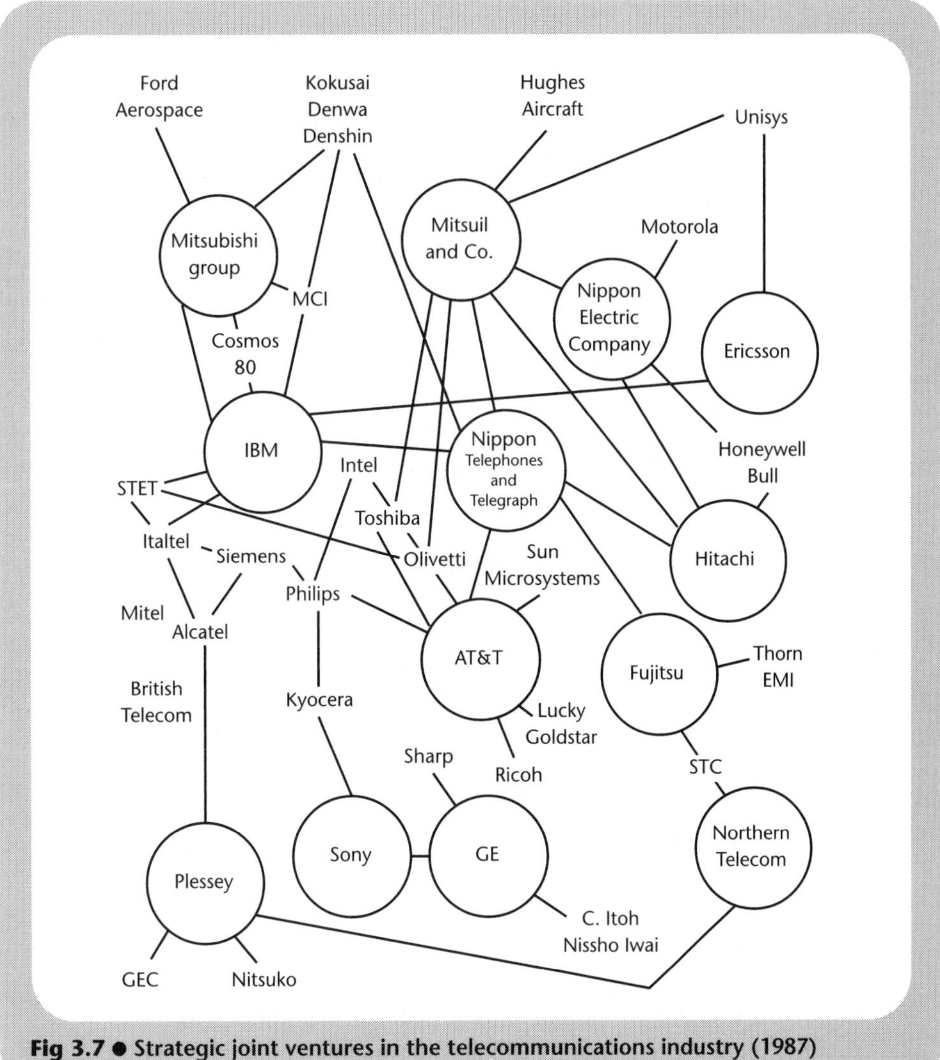

Fig 3.7 ● Strategic joint ventures in the telecommunications industry (1987)

function and *'raison d'être'* over and over again. Nowadays, this involves society as a whole and the actions of organizations are followed with close critical interest.

3.5.1 External information and reporting

Companies and other organizations are more or less separate and distinct entities in society, each with its own 'personality' and 'identity' and an ability to grow, survive or die. To function effectively, organizations have to communicate with persons or groups of stakeholders which have no direct access to the internal organizational information system. They must apply the information they have available to questions that may arise from external interested parties. If this is not carried out properly, problems will arise – for example, societal criticism, negative reports in the press – and there will be reactions from specific interest groups such as unfavourable stock market performance, a fall in stock prices, problems with raising external finance, labour unrest, etc.

3.5.2 Target groups

It is a legal requirement for most organizations to account for their actions and performance to their stakeholders – that is, their *external* stakeholders such as shareholders, banks, unions, government and their *internal* stakeholders in the shape of its employees – and provide information to these parties which will give them an insight into the workings of the organization.

An employee is not only a supplier of labour, but is also willing and able to participate in organizational problems and to take joint responsibility. Just because a person has a specific role and occupies a subordinate position, this does not mean that he or she does not want to be informed about the whole organization's affairs.

The employee as a participant is often prepared to subject his or her personal goals to the goals of the organization as a whole to a certain degree. At the same time the employee wants to have influence over the way in which the organization is directed. Internal stakeholders, therefore, not only wish to receive information, but also want to participate in the decisions about important organizational affairs.

Insight into the internal affairs of an organization is necessary for the shareholders as financial stakeholders if they are to form an opinion about the equity capital, the solvency, liquidity, and profitability of the company. At the very least, shareholders have to approve the annual reports based on this opinion; it is for this reason that the needs of financial stakeholders are given such priority.

Other stakeholders such as governmental agencies and creditors also have to be able to form an opinion about the organization's affairs. Based on this, they have to decide whether they want to continue their co-operation and contribution.

All participants, agencies or groups, therefore, which are directly involved with an organization have to know how things are going.

- Entrepreneurs have to be able to determine whether there has been a profit or a loss. In the case of non-profit-making organizations, it has to be determined whether there is a budget or credit balance.
- When considering an application for debt funding, a bank would want to know what the financial position of the organization was.
- Unions which negotiate on labour conditions of the employees have to determine their constraints and starting points for deliberation, based on the company results in a particular line of business.
- Members of a works council have to be able to determine their point of view about organizational policies which are partially based on the annual figures.

It is important therefore that manageable financial information is available about the organization. It is for this reason that ordering of financial data is governed by legislation and regulations set by the accountancy profession. There are also rules which prescribe that certain types of information have to be included and made available to parties other than direct stakeholders.

Balancing the demand and supply of processing (external) information by companies and other types of organizations is thus a rather complicated affair. There is no market mechanism to set a form of equilibrium, but there are opposing interests. The supply side of information gathering consists of more or less autonomous organizations and as a result they display a form of reluctance to the giving of information and a desire for privacy. The board of directors of a company requires a certain degree of autonomy and is therefore unhappy about communicating too much about its area of responsibility. This seems to be particularly the case with organizations operating in the free market where the provision of information could work out as a competitive disadvantage.

On the demand side there is also a need for limitations on the flow of free information: too much information confuses issues as it is difficult for outsiders to discriminate between what is important and what is not. Furthermore, the demand side is in general of a rather heterogeneous nature. It can include many different groups with individual interests varying according to their relations with the specific organization. For example:

- stockholders
- suppliers/creditors
- suppliers of capital, bankers
- employees and their unions
- competitors
- fiscal authorities
- governmental institutions for reasons of economic policy, environmental protection, etc.
- financial press and analysts
- scientific research
- pressure groups

The diversity of interests means that it is almost impossible to satisfy every external interested stakeholder with regard to the scope and contents of the information. It would be totally impractical to tailor the information given to the specific demands of individual groups of stakeholders and this is why the process is governed by legislation, complemented by generic rules, agreements and conventions, so that the parties concerned know what they can expect.

3.5.3 National and international directives

Several bodies exist which set standards for the provision of business information on behalf of national governments and supranational associations such as the European Union. At first these were especially concerned with the provision of periodic external information to shareholders, but have come to encompass the provision of information to all stakeholders.

In the EU member states legislation is strongly influenced by directives which harmonize the prescribed external information throughout the EU (with special directives for banks, insurance companies and investors). In some countries there are special (national) directives for information to works councils.

External reporting in EU countries has to be based on the 4th and 7th Directives. For example:

- In *Germany* this is included in the *Aktiengesetz* (for public limited companies (*Aktiengesellschaften*, AG)) and in the *Handelsgesetzbuch* (for private companies (*Kapitalgesellschaften*, KG)). The EU legislation is closely linked with traditional German practice of external reporting.
- In *France*, there has been legislation since the Second World War which comprises both directives on external reporting and a system of company accounting. Through

the so-called *plan comptable* the French government tries to promote a uniform accounting system which facilitates the aggregation of figures from annual reports.

- In *the Netherlands* the aggregation of figures from companies and other organizations are separate information-gathering activities, for which the Central Bureau of Statistics has the overall responsibility.
- The legislation on external reporting in *Belgium* is quite similar to the French regulations. The aggregation of figures from officially published annual reports is one of the objectives since this data is input into a central databank.
- In the *United Kingdom* the legislation concerning the external reporting of companies is included in several Companies Acts.
- In contrast, in *the USA*, there is hardly any legislation. The US government uses a form of self-regulation. It is mainly the concern of stock exchange authorities (SEC) and private organizations to organize their own regulations (within certain limits set by federal laws).

It is quite common, both in the US and European countries, for legislation and directives concerning external reporting to be drawn up by representatives of relevant societal interest groups, like users of information (associations of financial analysts, consumers and employee organizations), suppliers of information (employers' associations) and auditors (associations of certified public accountants).

For international companies quoted on the stock exchange and for readers/users of their annual reports, it is especially important that the international harmonization of external reporting continues. This will not only facilitate cross-border comparability of annual reports, but will also reduce costs for these companies. Further harmonization of external reporting seems to be less important to small businesses. There is a generic obligation of publication of annual figures for this type of company in the EU, but this does not necessarily mean that these companies will be included in the ongoing process of harmonization.

3.5.4 International organizations

The ever increasing internationalization of business operations and the movement of capital has made the harmonization in standards of external reporting at both regional and global levels a priority.

Within the EU, harmonization is implemented through directives (as mentioned in section 3.5.5). At global level, harmonization is being worked on by the International Accounting Standards Committee (IASC), an association of national organizations of certified public accountants. The IASC is striving to come to an agreement with the international umbrella organization of supervisors on stock exchanges (IOSCO) to acknowledge the International Accounting Standards (IAS) as the basis for the requirements which have to be met by all corporations in their financial reporting systems.

The United Nations (UN) and the Organization for Economic Co-operation and Development (OECD) are also working on international regulations, especially as part of an ethical code for multinational companies.

3.5.5 Corporate governance

In its broadest sense corporate governance concerns the way in which firms are managed and the way control is executed. The phenomenon of corporate governance exists because of the separate identities in law of the professional managers of an organization on the one hand and the shareholders with their financial interests in the organization on the other. It is a phenomenon which manifests itself as soon as one person does business with someone else's money.

Today corporate governance is a keenly debated issue all over the world, especially in relation to the big corporations which are owned by a large number of shareholders. The wider society also has an interest in the effective management and control of such organizations and so the quality of management and both internal and external control are coming under closer scrutiny. Internal control concerns the whole process by which the company's board of directors, management and other personnel aim to provide reasonable assurance regarding the achievement of objectives in the following categories:

- effectiveness and efficiency of operations;
- reliability of financial reporting;
- compliance with applicable laws and regulations.

In more precise terms, this process not only involves the role of management, but also the role of the board, and especially the role and the duties of executive and non-executive directors. Some form of independent control has to be in place.

In practice two types of board system have developed: the '*monistic*' or '*one-tier*' system and the '*dualistic*' or '*two-tier*' system. On the European continent the dualistic system is the most common form, while the monistic system is the most prevalent in Anglo-Saxon countries.

In the dualistic system, the task of objectively monitoring the activities of the company are assigned by the board of directors to a separate, independent body, such as a supervisory council. In the monistic system there is no separate supervisory body; the supervisory tasks are carried out by special members of the main board, referred to as 'non-executive directors' in the United Kingdom and 'outside directors' in the United States. No US or UK legislation exists which obliges boards to nominate supervisory board members; this has simply developed from business practice. In the recent debate on corporate governance, criticism was especially targeted at those companies with no non-executive directors or in which non-executive directors formed a minority and could not therefore stand up to executive directors.

3.5.6 Corporate governance: an international perspective

The governance systems in mainland Europe (and those in Japan) differ from those in the United Kingdom and the United States not only with regard to their structure, but also in relation to the importance of capital markets and the effects of market-oriented mechanisms – for example, raider threats, takeovers, buyouts, etc. – stock market reactions and so-called 'Wall Street Talk'.

The different legal requirements currently in force in EU countries stem from two basic models of corporate structure: the Anglo-Saxon model and the Continental model. On closer examination, the Continental model can be further divided into two models: one for the so-called Rhineland countries (Germany, Austria, Switzerland and the Netherlands) and another for countries like Italy, Spain, France and Belgium which can be grouped together under the heading of Latin European countries. The Japanese corporate structure differs in many important respects from those listed above.

These models of corporate structure can be characterized as follows.

Exhibit 3.7

Europe's corporations finally get It

European companies are under growing pressure from US pension and mutual funds and an increasing number of European funds to raise their share prices. For several years, the strategy of these new investors has been to push for better corporate governance. They are finally getting results and meeting with far more success than anyone predicted even a year ago.

Most blue-chip European companies are part of a web of cross-shareholdings, controlled by other industrial conglomerates or banks, which historically have not been bothered by low returns. If this sounds like Japan, it is – it closely resembles the *keiretsu*. This protective shield of cross-ownership, made bulletproof by uneven voting rights, makes most companies immune to takeovers. The result: entrenched, unresponsive management. Financial disclosure laws are lax enough so that company accounts can hide major problems, from underfunded pensions to financial irregularities.

But pressure from new investors is changing the European corporate system. Companies all over the Continent are disclosing more information, tying executive pay to performance, spinning off unrelated assets to boost shareholder value, and forming investor-relations departments.

In the case of Daimler Benz, a new generation of leaders is reforming corporate governance because of the need to tap global capital markets and maintain competitiveness. Without transparency in its balance sheets, Daimler cannot raise capital in US equity markets. In addition, by refusing to pump more cash into money-losing Dutch airplane maker Fokker, CEO Jürgen E. Schremp showed he is far more attuned to the concept of shareholder value than was his predecessor, Edzard Reuter.

True, some companies talk the talk but don't really seem willing to change, yet. Deutsche Bank is Germany's largest and most powerful institution, with seats on the boards of more than 100 large German companies in which it holds major stakes. It holds 24% of Daimler Benz. Company officials often speak in favor of strong corporate governance, yet Deutsche Bank can't seem to police the companies it has large stakes in. The latest fiasco centers on its 49%-owned engineering company, Klöckner-Humboldt-Deutz, which faces collapse after revealing on May 28 that it hid hundreds of millions of dollars in losses.

The global market for capital means money will flow to the places that offer the highest returns for the least amount of risk. European companies are right to worry that they will lose out in the race to attract this footloose money. It means they should try and hold on to those features that work for them, such as apprenticeship programs, but adapt to the new Anglo-Saxon model of corporate governance. It would be wrong for European companies to become obsessed with quarterly results, as many US companies have in recent years. But opening their books, focusing on core businesses, and dumping losers can only boost productivity profits.

European companies feeling the heat

BRITISH AEROSPACE	At May 1 annual meeting, shareholder groups force British Aerospace to put directors' fees to an annual vote and to publish proposed shareholder amendments to resolutions in advance.
COMPAGNIE D'INVESTISSEMENTS DE PARIS	Dissident shareholders have extracted a buyout offer from Banque Nationale de Paris, which controls the poor-performing investment company.
DAIMLER BENZ	At May 22 annual meeting, shareholders lambaste management for last year's $3.7 billion loss
EUROTUNNEL	Small shareholders are fighting a debt-to-equity swap that will dilute their holdings
MONTEDISON	Fund manager Codelouf & Co. proposed a breakup of the Italian maker of foods and chemicals

Source: *Business Week*, 10 June 1996.

The Anglo-Saxon model (UK and USA)

In the United Kingdom and the United States the financial markets are long established and well developed. The 'open' corporation has assumed enormous proportions and share ownership is widespread. Legislation has resulted in banks not developing into shareholders with substantial packages of shares in non-financial companies in contrast to the systems in countries like Germany and Japan.

In the Anglo-Saxon model the enterprise is seen as an extension of the shareholder. The objective is first and foremost profit maximization. Companies often raise finance via the stock exchange. The internal organization and the external environment of the corporation are characterized by competition and are wary of corporatism. Management is considered to be somewhat short-term oriented; the results for the next financial quarter are the main focus of interest. External financial reporting is in accordance with the highest international standards.

Widespread share ownership results in potential conflicts of interest between corporate governors and shareholders which are often difficult to control and can manifest themselves in high drama during takeover negotiations.

The Rhineland model (Germany, Austria, Switzerland, the Netherlands)

In these countries we see substantially fewer companies listed on the stock exchange. There are also conceptual differences in the nature of the enterprise and/or corporation. Instead of 'corporate enterprise' as an extension of the shareholders, this is a more institutional form of corporation. The organization shows characteristics of corporatism and is more concerned with consensus than with competition. Goals and time scales are oriented more towards the long term. The main objective is continuity.

The corporate interest has to be balanced and integrated with the interests of the other participants in the corporation – for example, those of the managers, employees, suppliers of capital and suppliers of resources, customers/clients. The stock exchange is of secondary importance. Internal funding and financing through banks are the preferred source of finance.

Traditionally banks have played an important role in financing the expansion of the company. In Germany, in particular, the rise of the big industrial banks ('*Universalbanken*') has been instrumental to industrial development. Nowadays the big banks like Deutsche Bank, Commerzbank and Dresdner Bank still play an important role in financing and the corporate governance of big German corporations, not only as suppliers of debt, but also as financiers of equity capital and shareholders. There are often different forms of share, which facilitate the concentration of control. External financial reports are of limited use, in that they are not always published at regular intervals and the information contained in them is often out of date and superficial.

For example ...

... in Germany the '*Aufsichtsrat*' (or supervisory council) was created shortly after the Second World War. The '*Mitbestimmung*' (the right of both labour and capital to participate in joint decision making) was introduced by the allied forces not only to ensure the equal representation of the providers of labour and the providers of capital, but also to ensure that the unions shared responsibility.

All companies were given a 20-member supervisory council in which employees and shareholders were equally represented in terms of seats. As a result the labour representatives in the German supervisory councils are very well informed and the representatives of management and the providers of capital cannot openly and critically discuss the core problems of the company without reference to them. Banks have a strong representation on supervisory councils in Germany. The role of the management team in the German system is also given due prominence.

The Latin-European model (Italy, Spain, France, Belgium)

Ownership in Latin-European countries is especially characterized by family ownership, financial holding companies, cross-financial participation, and state ownership. Important families (like the Agnelli family in Italy) and multinational industrial groups control ownership and management in almost every corporation quoted on the stock exchange. In Spain cross-participation and bank participation play an important role. Furthermore, the state has an influence over corporate structure. In France there are several forms of financial holding (competing financial groups with cross-participation and 'interlocking directorships', that is, companies are inter-linked at board level by virtue of the fact that one of their directors also holds directorships in other companies), bank participation (*'banques d'affaires'*) and state ownership. In recent years there has been a marked tendency towards privatization. In Belgium financial holdings and family property are most common. The *'Generale'* controls a large number of Belgium's top companies and as a result some important industrial sectors.

Japan

Industrial life in Japan is characterized by the presence of a number of major industrial groups, the *'keiretsu'*. Each group can comprise hundreds of companies, which are interconnected through cross-participation, with one bank functioning as the primary

Exhibit 3.8

Shareholders better off with UK companies

UK companies treat their shareholders better than other European companies, a survey of corporate governance practice at large public companies published today shows.

UK companies such as GEC, Glaxo Wellcome, and Marks & Spencer are picked out as having particularly good corporate governance-practices. Dutch companies' corporate governance structures are ranked last after companies in France, Germany and Belgium.

UK companies scored particularly well on disclosure of directors' pay, due to the Greenbury code of best practice, and the operation of board committees, a Cadbury code recommendation.

The survey of 140 of the largest companies traded on five European stock exchanges was carried out by Déminor, a Brussels-based consultancy which specialises in advising minority shareholders. Companies in Italy and Spain were excluded because of their poor response to requests for information.

The UK confirms its advance in the field of corporate governance, the Déminor's report states.

Using publicly available information such as companies' annual reports, Déminor judged companies on five different corporate governance tests. They included:

- Do board committees exist and do they work in a democratic, independent and effective way?
- What is the quality and accessibility of information for institutional and private shareholders?
- Has the company or one of its subsidiaries initiated financial operations against the interests of minority shareholders?

Déminor also compared the corporate governance ranking of each company with its financial performance and found a 'slight correlation' only for UK companies.

Source: *Financial Times*, 8 October 1996.

source of finance, especially with regard to the supply of debt capital. This bank is also active in corporate governance, as a consultant, supervisory body and supplier of management expertise in areas such as career development, crisis management and corporate turnarounds.

The Japanese structure is comparable to the German structure as far as the role of the industrial banks is concerned and to the Latin-European structure with regard to the industrial corporate groups.

The separation of the interests of management (and employees) from the interests of shareholders in all these models leads to problems of communication and control. As a result effective independent supervision and external control are crucial. The differences between the models are due not only to their respective structures, but also to the patterns and level of industrial democracy in the different countries (*see* sections 1.2 and 2.3).

3.5.7 A Code of Best Practice

All forms of governance structure are currently under close scrutiny. The Anglo-Saxon model sees the company as an extension of its shareholders with the objective of serving shareholder needs. However, this approach also accepts that in the long run the creation of economic value is only possible when the interests of all stakeholders are adequately taken into account and that the company must also heed its wider societal responsibilities in terms of the 'common good of the community'.

At the same time the Rhineland model is beginning to lose its sparkle. This system of ownership has shown serious weaknesses. For example, in Germany, the 'Metallgesellschaft' has suffered from major governance problems, despite the presence of long-term shareholders. The equal representation of employee directors and other forms of directors (for example, from banks or shareholders) on the supervisory councils seems to make effective monitoring and discussion of the real issues at stake more difficult.

Furthermore, the position of the banks with regard to proxy voting is under discussion – a mechanism which allows banks to vote on behalf of clients who deposit their stock with them – as it is an important way of influencing corporate decision making.

In the United Kingdom the Cadbury Committee was set up to make recommendations for better guidance and control of directors. The committee's report, *Cadbury: The Code of Best Practice*, was published in December 1992 and has three essential elements:

- The board of directors should meet regularly and no decisions should be made by a single person alone. In the monistic system in the United Kingdom there should be within the board a strong countervailing power in the form of independent, non-executive directors with objective opinions and judgement on the corporation's strategy, results realized and nominations for key management posts.
- It is preferable for the functions of chief executive and chairman of a corporation to be kept separate.
- From 1995 corporations must make statements in their annual reports concerning their systems of 'internal control' and the 'continuity' of the corporation.

More recently statements of directors' responsibilities have also been included in the annual reports of large corporations.

3.5.8 The advantages and disadvantages of the one-tier system

The Anglo-Saxon model for a publicly quoted company features a single layer of top management. Senior managers are chosen by the owners of the company – the shareholders. An important characteristic of this model is that there are a number of committees – for example, the audit committee, the nomination committee (for the selection of senior managers) and a remuneration committee (for salaries, bonuses, etc.). The most important decisions are taken by the executive committee (the top management team) and are later verified by the board as a whole.

Advantages

- There is widespread ownership of shares in these countries. Shareholders have a number of powers.
- The Anglo-Saxon system is more fair. No one plays hide and seek. Board members are known to be closely involved in the firm itself. Board members, whether executive or non-executive, share joint responsibility. They are colleagues, without losing sight of the supervisory role of the non-executive directors.
- The executive directors and non-executive directors occupy the same legal position. They provide joint leadership of the organization.

Disadvantages

- When it comes to the selection of new directors, the board and/or chairman/CEO can use a 'proxy statement' to propose a shortlist of candidates to the shareholders' meeting. The choice is confined to this list. In practice this means that the board has the power to dictate who is selected.
- When earnings per share, price/earnings ratios, stock exchange quotations and other indicators change, Anglo-Saxon boards intervene much more quickly than their European counterparts. As a rule, when the need for short-term profits per share is weighed against the desire for long-term continuity, short-term profits will generally win the day. This is mainly due to the formidable, looming risk of hostile takeovers in the United States.

3.5.9 The advantages and disadvantages of the two-tier system

Advantages

- The Rhineland model puts less power in the hands of any single individual. Responsibilities are shared by the management team and the advisory supervisory board resulting in a more balanced approach. In this model, it is possible for the same person to have both an operational and a supervisory function.
- Discussions on the supervisory board tend to be more in-depth and direct than those in the one-tier system. Formal discussions about strategy are rarely on the agenda of board meetings in the US. This system also seems to provide a more satisfactory system of feedback and approval.
- Decision making is more efficient and effective with the combination of management team and supervisory board.

Disadvantages

- The power of the shareholders has waned. In the large publicly quoted companies, shareholders have almost no power at all. The question of ownership has become somewhat obscure. Institutional investors rarely appear at shareholders' meetings.

- It is unclear 'who controls the controllers'. When problems arise, the supervisory council cannot take over operations. The result is a potential power vacuum which can be very dangerous. The members of the supervisory councils have fewer options than those directors with supervisory roles on the one-tier boards.
- The role of the supervisory council can be unclear in some cases. Its dual function as a source both of advice and control can sometimes lead to conflicts of interests.
- Supervisory council members choose who will be admitted as new members of the council – a system of co-option – and this has several disadvantages:
  1. The supervisory council is not under the control of any part of the corporation.
  2. The stimulus for maximizing economic and market value of share equity is removed.
  3. The supervisory council sets its own salary, which inevitably results in substantial remuneration packages.
  4. There is a risk that inappropriate members will be selected.
  5. Supervisory councils tend to favour maintaining the independence of the corporation even in situations where a merger or takeover would be economically advantageous.

3.5.10 Recent developments in one-tier and two-tier models

Despite the considerable cultural differences, the two systems are coming closer together. The EU is encouraging this trend, for example by enabling the Netherlands to change its laws to allow the establishment of one-tier systems. This will mean that financial vulnerability alone will determine the way in which the corporation functions.

In practice there is no longer any significant difference between the decision-making function of the management team/supervisory council in the two-tier system and that of the board of directors in the one-tier system. The management team is still clearly dominant in the two-tier system due to the fact that it has the opportunity for more thorough preparation, quicker access to information and operational responsibility.

There are two approaches to overcoming the disadvantages of the co-option system in the supervisory councils: the supervisory council could be made more open and more accountable with regard to its supervisory role, or the supervisory council could be reorganized so that the claim that it is nothing more than an 'old boys' club' is no longer valid.

3.6 MANAGEMENT AND ETHICS

Ethics involves a whole range of unwritten rules and habits which society uses to judge whether something is decent or fair.

The current trend towards the development of such codes of conduct reflects society's concern in recent years regarding business practices and crime. In 1992 a report was published by the US Committee of Sponsoring Organizations of the Treadway Commission (COSO) on the possibility and the desirability of a common frame of reference with regard to monitoring internal controls. To be effective, such a system would have to be efficient and reliable and the company would have to abide by the laws and regulations. The COSO Report defined five discrete elements:

Minicase 3.4

Crime prevention

What can management do to prevent crime and fraud? Internally, many organizations have thick tomes which they refer to as handbooks and which contain all the norms, rules and procedures of the organization. But to what extent are these standards applied to the organization? There is no external test or an international standard for corporate integrity at the present time although steps are being taken in that direction. In the United Kingdom, the management of companies quoted on the stock exchange have for some time now used a set of 'model' or standard declarations in the annual report, not only to render account to shareholders regarding financial and related matters but also to inform them of the measures the organization takes to prevent fraud, tax evasion and corruption. In the United States, similar standard declarations are being studied.

- a control environment;
- an evaluation of risks;
- internal control measurements;
- information and communication;
- a focus on the well functioning.

At just about the same time, the Cadbury Report was published in the UK on which the stock exchange and the accountancy organizations worked together. The significance of the Committee's findings was increased by two business scandals which gained a great deal of international publicity in the early 1990s: The Maxwell Affair and the BCCI Affair. The Committee addressed the question of whether it was possible to draw up a code of conduct which could be monitored by accountants and that would commit the management of a company to operating a good system of internal control which would prevent abuse. The Committee published a preliminary Code of Best Practice with the following recommendations:

- There has to be a clear division of tasks at the top of the organization, resulting in *a good balance of power and authority*.
- There should be no ambiguity with regard to the authority of management.
- The board of directors should be independent and impartial. It should meet regularly, should participate in the audit committee and should participate in decisions regarding appointments and their duration.
- The remuneration of board members should be published, and the extent to which this is performance-related should be made clear.

The London Stock Exchange urged all quoted companies to endorse and publish such a code of conduct. The head of a central anti-fraud unit at the accountants, Coopers & Lybrand could see advantages in such a code, and also limitations:

> *To start with, you will never be able to cover every business with a statement like that. There will always be room for different interpretations of norms and deviations. There is no way that an auditor can cover everything.*

However, it is essential that crime prevention is taken seriously. This is only possible if there has been a thorough analysis of the risks involved – perhaps as a joint responsibility of government, employers' organization and accountants. The notion of the *management audit* which was first mooted in the 1970s but failed to materialize, is now being given more serious consideration, now that the auditor is expected to uncover fraud and report it to the authorities. Once again questions are being asked regarding how strictly these internal rules are applied, what the procedures are for auditing the application of the rules and who is responsible for overseeing this.

Ethics needs to be distinguished from justice. The law can enforce certain types of behaviour, while ethics tries to convince with arguments. Ethics involves thinking about the unwritten rules which regulate human society. Ethics encompasses a voluntary rather than a formal set of rules which are required if a good society or a good organization is to survive. A society or organization can be maintained because the members keep more or less to the universal rules of behaviour, written or unwritten.

New moral stances arise out of major events that are considered to be of importance (for example, Live Aid in the 1980s) as well as disasters, both personal (for example, the infection risk of HIV by means of sexual intercourse) and collective (for example, environmental pollution). Moral development proceeds by its own initiative as well as public debate in the media. 'Safe sex' and 'recycling' are part of the generally subscribed group moral of our society at the end of the twentieth century.

Individual morals deviate from the universal moral and may as a result cause it to change. Setting rules and norms and living according to them in practice are two completely different things. Deviation from the norms is perhaps only human: the difference between the 'ideal' and 'reality'.

Many organizational and managerial problems have an ethical dimension – for example, the implementation of social policy, the relocation of manufacturing abroad, the handling of chemical waste, etc. Organizational ethics or business ethics is concerned with what happens in an organization when moral problems arise. Morals are expressed in the way organizations conduct themselves. For example, the tax moral is the actual attitude of the organization with regard to the payment of tax to the fiscal authorities. It is possible that tax avoidance or evasion is the actual tax moral of the organization. Ethics is concerned with making choices from a given set of alternatives. Why do people not want to pay taxes? How do they justify this? In this context, the choice is not between legal and illegal. Obeying the law will in most cases be the most 'normal' course of action. The moral problem lies in the interpretation of 'good citizenship'. Is the exercise of rights and the avoidance of duties morally acceptable? The field of ethics is concerned with these and other problems.

According to Professor Kimman (1991), organizational ethics is a reflection on how organizations should act. In an organization individuals have a certain responsibility for their own actions and there is often talk of shared responsibility between the employees and the organization. However, in many cases individual contributions are such a small part of the whole product or service which the organization creates, that it is the organization as a whole which has to take responsibility for the final outcome.

Organizational ethics are closely linked with the organization process: the divisionalization, co-ordinating and execution of tasks and duties in pursuit of a specific goal. Organizational ethics can be used in formulating the goals of the organization, in allocating the resources to be used, in the assignment and execution of tasks and also to ensure the integrity of controls on the execution of tasks. What are the implications of investing in one country and divesting in another? What are the effects of firing people in one country and employing people in another, perhaps a low-wage, country? Many managers are aware of management practices that are not right. Ethical considerations must help managers by giving them a moral platform from which they can do something about it and come to a decision. This should result in what Kimman referred to as 'decent management'.

Exhibit 3.9

Companies clean up

European businesses are trying to put corruption scandals behind them and adopting new codes of ethics. They hope to see virtue rewarded in the bottom line.

Few subjects bring out the sceptics as much as corporate ethics. 'Business ethics ... isn't that a contradiction in terms?' goes an old saw.

The sceptics seem to have a point. Volkswagen's struggle to extricate itself from Europe's biggest industrial espionage scandal is only the latest addition to an apparently endless list of corporate misbehaviour: the collapse of fraudulent empires built by Drexel Burnham Lambert, BCCI and Robert Maxwell; British Airways misuse of Virgin Atlantic's confidential computer records; illegal share manipulation at Guinness and County NatWest in the UK; widespread accusations that French and Spanish companies contributed to political parties in exchange for public favours and, of course, the wholesale indictment of Italy's corrupt business and political class.

Companies are looking more closely at their own ethical underpinnings. The trend is strongest in the US, but UK companies have also woken up to the issue. Written codes of ethics, once rare, are becoming common.

Not all codes are created equal, of course; efforts range from vague commitments to honesty and integrity to specific lists of what may and may not be done. Most outline policy on conflicts of interest, bribery and other criminal activities, and accepting entertainment. Increasingly, integrity and fairness in dealing with suppliers, employees and customers, and in marketing and sales tactics, are also stressed. Some codes commit companies to paying suppliers within 30 days, for example, or outline principles to follow in laying off staff.

The movement has been slower to catch fire in continental Europe, but there is a spark of interest.

Source: *International Management*, October 1993.

Abuse of power

The astonishing tale of sexual harassment at Astra USA

When does a company become a cult? A six-month investigation by *Business Week* into Astra USA Inc., the American arm of Swedish pharmaceutical company Astra, reveals that the transition can occur when a corporate culture gets hijacked at the top. A bizarre case of abuse of power appears to have taken place at Astra, where a 15-year pattern of sexual harassment emanated from the president's office and worked its way down through the organization. On Apr. 29, the president was suspended by the Swedish parent just days before *Business Week* went to press with the story.

Astra is a striking example of how vulnerable a corporate culture can be to its leaders' cues. To many who worked there, Astra was a cult led by an autocratic, charismatic leader who established an almost militaristic atmosphere at headquarters. Staff had to eat lunch at precisely the same time each day. Permission was needed to hang anything personal on cubicle walls. A nine-week training period cut people off from their families.

Then there was the drinking and partying. Bar nights were part of training and sales conferences. Managers, led by the president and including visiting Astra officials from Europe, asked young women to bars and back to their hotel. Advancement in Astra appeared to go to those who co-operated. Women who responded favorably to the attention from senior managers were called The Chosen.

To the outside world, Astra was a successful corporation. Because most of the women who felt sexually harassed didn't go to the Equal Employment Opportunity Commission, the company appeared to be in good standing. Because the sales force was effective, the home office perceived it as a winner.

What lessons can be drawn from this strange situation? In the recent case of Mitsubishi Motors Corp., alleged victims of sexual harassment went to the EEOC, which sued the company. An investigation will reveal what really happened there. But at Astra, there was no government intervention. Female employees didn't have the financial resources, resolve, or courage to risk their jobs and reputations battling harassment.

In the end, harassment is simply bullying by another name. One can see why its victims, in this case, might wish to remain silent. After all, it appeared to be encouraged from the top down. One cannot, however, absolve Astra in Stockholm, owned largely by the Wallenbergs, who failed to supervise its subsidiary adequately as it careened out of control.

It may be mere coincidence that two foreign companies in the US in recent weeks experienced serious problems with the alleged sexual harassment of their employees. But in this era of economic globalization, where companies operate in dozens of cultures around the world, corporations everywhere must look beyond the financials in supervising their far-flung operations. Corporations, not governments, are primarily responsible for the people who work for them – and they must act to protect their dignity wherever they live.

Source: *Business Week*, 13 May 1996.

The green problem: the environment

To what degree do environmental problems influence actual organizational behaviour? Do we accept that there is a problem? If so, do we expect government to supply the solution? Do we, as an organization, continue to dispose of waste materials, which are generally accepted to be harmful?

In business life, one of the major ethical considerations is the 'green problem' – that is, the formidable number of environmental issues. More specifically, this is concerned with the consideration and setting of limits regarding the processing, disposal or dumping of waste, the use of energy, the choice of materials, etc.

Quality in products and services

Is decent building, construction and manufacturing a matter for the legislator – as the 'social problem' was in the nineteenth century – or are the industrial companies addressing the issues of quality and the environment?

Some will say that with new development, the first step is for new rights and rules to be drawn up by government. Sometimes company scandals can be held up as examples where regulations have fallen short, but mostly they are characterized by the inadequacy or the total absence of a moral notion. In a positive sense, raising the profile of ethical considerations is appealing to the ability of people, business firms and all sorts of organizations to regulate themselves.

Financial policy

How do we handle mass dismissals when the long-term outlooks are gloomy, but the present financial situation is not too bad? Do we accept a somewhat lower profit when higher investments have to be made due to environmental measures? Financial criteria in the 'narrow' sense do not offer solutions to these problems. The eventual decision will be affected by both moral and in some cases somewhat idealistic considerations. Decent financial policy needs to be viewed alongside other production factors. It is not only a matter of having a business 'conscience'.

Social policy

A good social policy from the ethical point of view is one in which the rights of individuals are not secondary to the rights of the organization. This involves problems regarding autonomy, the relative degree of dependency of individual employees, loyalty and organizational norms.

Organizations should not promise more than they can deliver. Even in large companies, school-leavers in their first jobs cannot be promised 'jobs for life'. Nevertheless, loyalty is an important consideration, based on trust between the employer and the employee. This has to be reflected in the way in which the organization conducts itself, in good times as well as bad. For example, a wage decrease in bad times does bestow obligation on the organization, although this might not apply in a situation in which employees are considered to be 'just passing through'.

3.7 COMMUNICATION WITH EXTERNAL GROUPS

How does an organization get what it wants? How does an organization – whether in the private, public or voluntary sector – make the customer, client or citizen behave the way the organization wants? How does the organization handle pressure groups? In trade and business, 'public relations' is an area of activity that is especially directed at the handling of problems relating to the organization's external environment. It is especially concerned with the image and the identity of an organization.

Image and identity are about the mission of an organization and its strengths and weaknesses. Many organizations are alarmed to learn that in practice there is quite a difference between how employees judge their organization (*identity*) and how the organization is valued by others (*image*). Incidents can often have negative long-term effects and do great damage to the reputation of the organization. It is crucial that these incidents are handled properly. Consistent information is essential both towards the inside of the organization (to employees) and towards the outside (to customers/clients, government, suppliers, etc.) but is often very difficult to realize.

In principle, image and identity need to be in harmony. Many organizations are unaware of the fact that they can play an active role in influencing their image; it is a matter of communication. Ideally, the desired and experienced reality (identity) within an organization should be consistent with the reality which is observed from the outside of the organization (image). In practice this does not always appear to be the case.

Minicase 3.4

The power of rehabilitation

The problems of Omo Power were big news; the rehabilitation was ignored. The press seems to be fixated on business misery. Good news is no news.

The vast majority of newspaper readers and TV viewers have formed the rather negative, but totally accurate impression that only bad news is worthy of note. This is somewhat unfair for companies which have many experiences of a positive nature, but which also perhaps suffer a single calamity. The bad will be widely covered by the press; little or no attention will be given to the good.

For example, in the summer of 1994 the newspapers and television programmes highlighted the attack by Proctor & Gamble on the safety of a new wash powder, Omo Power, manufactured by its arch-rival, Unilever. Unilever quickly changed the composition of Omo and again offered it up for testing. By mid-July, results were published which declared that the product was now safe for use.

However, the damage had been done. That summer's battle between the two detergent giants had already been analysed in the media and had been incorporated as a classic marketing case in the notes of many a college lecturer. It was a marketing disaster for Unilever.

Unilever used all its marketing expertise and power to try to launch the product's rehabilitation. In full-page ads it announced that 'the independent institute TNO' had achieved 'unexcelled results' during tests of the revised Omo Power. The press was provided with careful summaries of the new test results. However, the test results received far less exposure in the media than the original story. The newspapers ran articles, but rarely more than a few lines; television disregarded the story completely.

3.7.1 Active management of image and identity

Identity (how we see ourselves) and image (how we are seen by others) can in many cases be quite contradictory. Many organizations are disappointed to learn that there is a difference between the self-image of the employees and how they are seen and valued by others. Unless this mismatch is addressed, personnel and management problems may arise. In the light of this, management strives, by adapting the activities of the organization, to achieve:

- a better match of activities and image for specific target groups; and
- a better match of activities and identity for specific employees.

The communication function has an important role to play. Research into image and the setting up of a programme to improve an organization's image are well known tools. Identity can also be managed and structured. An organization can develop more than one image or identity, each connected to a particular target group or a group of employees. This is more common in business life than it is in government circles. A common house style can also support a desired overall feeling of identity.

3.7.2 Lobbying or problem management

Problem management or lobbying – an everyday feature of business life in the US – is the directed 'steering' to a desired result or, in the case of a particular incident, to a desired outcome. The following instruments can be used:

- Written documents (letters, memos)
- Oral contacts (personal conversations, telephone calls)
- Company visits, work visits
- Internships or work experience with Members of Parliament
- Receptions
- Informal lunch meetings with Members of Parliament (exchanging points of view, exploring political ideas)
- Speeches at congresses and symposia
- Hearings
- Calling in of specialists

- Exploiting possible contradictions between ministries or sectors within a ministry
- Publicity (public reactions, giving opinions in newspapers and magazines)
- Own media (annual report, personnel news).

The following seem to be the 'golden rules' of the lobbying industry:

- Always know your business (both with regard to content and procedures). Define the problem in terms that are clear and brief. Keep letters short and to the point. Leave one or two sheets of paper with your position or other relevant information after the meeting.
- Always intervene in time and approach the right person. Adopt an open attitude. Acknowledge self-interest, but explain why the problem is so important. Government officials and politicians are often grateful for information.
- Top management should always be seen in the thick of the action and should always talk and negotiate. Widen the lobby as far as possible by approaching allied organizations at industry/sector level or employers' organizations.
- Always consider the arguments of opponents. Never underestimate them.
- Always ensure a co-ordinated approach (not more than one contact from the same company). With a certain degree of causation, make use of publicity.
- Always make sure you have room to manoeuvre. Be flexible.
- Never give incorrect information. Never offer expensive or unnecessary dinners or display any behaviour which could be misinterpreted as corrupt. Never whine. Never aim too high. Never hire a lobbyist when it comes to negotiating. Never have nothing to offer.

Source: Adapted from *SMO-Informatief*, 94–5

3.7.3 Crisis management

A crisis can overwhelm the best companies with the most skilled managers. It can have technical, natural or human causes. It can have minor, considerable or fatal consequences. Crises can arise from bad investments, acid rain, toxic waste, a hostile takeover, inferior products, accidents or strikes, legislation which has a negative effect on the interests of the company, a smear campaign in the media, hostile actions by third parties, like threats, kidnapping or sabotage.

If an organization is perceived to be withholding information, this can become a crisis in itself, in which the right of the public to 'know the facts' will become the most important issue.

Minicase 3.5

Nestlé's negative publicity

The Nestlé organization has been burdened for some years with a stream of negative publicity which began when interest groups, the media, health organizations and politicians questioned the company regarding its methods of selling baby food in developing countries. It was alleged that under certain circumstances these selling practices led to malnutrition or even death. There were suggestions that this was a less than decent way of doing business.

Crises may vary in nature, size and intensity, but the consequences of a crisis are almost always far-reaching and never pleasant. Crises often strike at the very heart of a company and organization; credibility is affected, reputations are at stake, the business is rocked to its foundations.

Most crises have the following characteristics:

- Decisions have to be taken quickly.
- Doing nothing has undesirable consequences.
- There are a limited number of options.
- Wrong decisions have far-reaching consequences.
- Groups involved have conflicting interests.
- Top management has to become directly involved.

Electronic media have become the most important source of information in the industrialized world. News is sometimes compared to an avalanche. A small report – perhaps on a company closure, merger, stock exchange flotation, demonstration, accident or inferior product – can lead to a reaction from the unions, which in turn can provoke a reaction from an employers' organization. This can, in turn, lead to reactions from other groups wishing to make a social-economic contribution. A small snowball can very quickly become an avalanche. When an avalanche is out of control and leaves its preset course, it becomes a crisis.

3.7.3 The crisis action plan

Communication and planning are the key to good crisis management.

It can make an enormous difference when a company has an action plan which it has worked out in advance for the type of crisis that can occur in its line of business. There are teams ready which can take on the strategic and tactical lead on the issue at stake. An emergency plan that is tailor-made to an organization and the specific problems that can occur in it, usually stops the problems from taking on outrageous proportions.

If someone is looking out for signs of trouble, a threatening crisis can be averted. Mass resignation of employees, a suspicious pattern in customer order cancellations, the arrival of a group of activists who set up camp in the neighbourhood are all unmistakable signs that trouble is at hand. The real problem is that people do not usually pay attention to these early warning signs, because they do not wish to see them.

It is important to keep in contact with external groups, to actively search out sources of information and to remain alert at all times.

In her book Ten Berge (1989) comments: 'The interesting thing about crises, which occur in a wide variety of circumstances, is that they are awfully similar.'

Common external factors include:

- Damage has been done.
- There is a series of escalating events.
- Time is not on the company's side.
- The news media bear down upon it.
- Rumours and speculation threaten to take the upper hand.

Common psychological reactions to these factors are:

- disbelief;
- the drawing in of horns;
- a narrow-minded vision;
- panic-based kamikaze actions;
- the attribution of blame;
- hurt feelings.

Having a crisis plan worked out and ready for implementation can save valuable time, when crisis hits. The situation can only deteriorate if names and phone numbers of important people have to be looked up or logistical problems have to be solved. An organization can estimate the probability of a particular crisis occurring and can use these calculations to draw up a programme of advance crisis management.

3.7.4 Crisis management procedures

The following recommendations for good crisis management were suggested by Ten Berge in her book (1989).

The handling of a crisis

- When a crisis occurs, take immediate action in order to gain control over the situation as fast as possible and limit the harmful consequences. You have 24 hours at most to set the tone.
- Contact the members of the board, union leaders, the appropriate authorities or other stakeholders.
- Ensure that you are well informed about the different communication techniques beforehand.
- Make sure that the organization, if appropriate, has the necessary resources to communicate immediately and effectively with the interest groups and the general public.
- Bring all stakeholders – employees and their family members, shareholders, suppliers, distributors, local or regional governments and neighbours – up to date with developments as quickly and as fully as possible.
- See to it that the content of the message is exactly in tune with the needs of the target group. For example, television needs pictures which require no explanation; the financial world needs figures and forecasts.
- Be open and fair when you present the news.
- Publish an official statement as quickly as possible. Rumours and speculation thrive in an information vacuum.
- Seek the support of independent third parties and make use of this when clarifying your message to the public.
- The best solicitor is one who does not have a clear interest in the case.
- It might be necessary to cancel immediately any planned advertising campaigns and abandon any plans for forthcoming campaigns, because people might otherwise unconsciously relate the bad news of the crisis to the contents of the ad.

The handling of the press

- Be human.
- Announce the bad news promptly and fully.
- Explain how you are going to resolve the problem.
- Tell the truth.
- He who is silent admits his guilt.
- 'No comment' is probably the worst comment to make. Always give the reason why you cannot answer a question. For example, it could be that you have not yet informed your own people, or that you yourself do not yet know the facts.
- When you do not know the answer, admit it and commit yourself to finding out.
- See to it that there is an information pack ready for the press with information and pictures.
- Centralization of the information function is important. Appoint one spokesperson. When there is more than one spokesperson, make sure that there is good co-ordination with regard to the statements which are made. Everyone should be 'speaking the same language'.
- Give clear instructions to your personnel that all questions should be passed on to the appointed spokesperson.
- Allocate a central point which can serve as a press centre, where journalists can work and from where they can gather information.

Source: Adapted from Ten Berge, D. (1989) *De eerste 24 uur Handbook voor crisis management*, Tirion, Baarn

SUMMARY

- Organizations and managers operate in a societal environment, never in a vacuum. An organization can only survive when it supplies the products and services the environment wants.
- All kinds of environmental factors have an influence on organizations. These environmental factors can take the form of situations and events or groups and interested parties, such as stakeholders who contribute to the survival of the organization in return for a particular reward or incentive.
- There are environmental factors over which the individual organization has no influence. These are the forces and developments in the macro-environment which can be observed in an analysis of demographic, economic, technological, societal, political, ecological, market sector or business factors.
- The organization is also affected by trends in the environment such as the internationalization of markets (with the knock-on effects of differing national cultures), the shortening of life cycles, strategic joint ventures and network organizations.
- An organization always has to account for its operations to its external and internal stakeholders.

continued overleaf

- Based on the information provided – which can take the form of an annual report and a social report on personnel matters and health and safety – the stakeholders have to judge whether they want to continue to make their contribution to the organization in the future.
- Every society can only continue to function when the members of that society live by written and unwritten rules – that is, by laws and regulation on the one hand, and the rules of the generally accepted group moral on the other.
- New technologies, such as the digital storage of personally sensitive data, and major events, such as environmental pollution, can lead to changes in the generally accepted group moral. Individual ideas of morals can deviate from the 'ruling' group moral.
- Variations and developments in the generally accepted moral mean that managers, internal and external stakeholders of the organization must ask themselves 'What is decent management in relation to our organization?' This area of study is referred to as organizational or company ethics.
- It is possible that an organization is perceived differently by its external environment (image) than it is by its own members (identity). In principle, image and identity should be consistent. When these differ too much, communication plays an important role in resolving the situation.
- A crisis is a sudden and undesirable change in the relation between an organization and its environment. A crisis is unpredictable in nature and intensity.
- Sound crisis management is based on the existence of a crisis action plan and good communication with the internal and external interest groups.
- A manager should keep abreast of both macro-environmental factors and the developments discussed above.
- It is important for an organization to determine the contribution it is to make to the societal environment. In other words, it must have goals and a strategy. This is covered in more depth in Chapter 5.

DISCUSSION QUESTIONS

1. With reference to *Management in action* at the beginning of this chapter, consider the following questions:
   (a) Should the firm continue to use possibly hazardous materials in the successful new product?
   (b) What would you suggest as the best policy both to the general public and to the company's workforce?
2. Why does an organization have to be studied in the context of its markets and society?
3. To what extent can an organization be depicted as a 'spider in a web'?
4. Developments in the environment give the impression that today there is a faster replacement of existing products and that customers have more diverse needs and make greater demands. What does this mean for the management of business affairs? List some of the consequences of such a development.

5. How can innovation, specialization and exporting contribute to an improvement in results?
6. It is sometimes suggested that development and manufacturing problems can be passed on from individual manufacturers to the so-called 'network organizations'. What does this mean?
7. Is it acceptable for a company to use a hazardous production process, forbidden in the company's home country, in a so-called low-wage country where environmental legislation is not in effect?

Management case study

Trouble at mill

Bowing to environmentalists' demands could drive a paper maker to extinction. The letter from the environmental pressure group leaves no room for doubt: it is threatening to cause the Venlo Paper Company a lot of unspecified trouble unless immediate steps are taken to use recycled pulp in its paper manufacture, and to stop using chlorine to bleach it. Martyn Lievaart, manager responsible for environmental affairs, stares at it in horror: he has only just been promoted to the management board, and does not yet feel his colleagues' support to be strong enough to face a challenge of this size.

The company has made high-quality writing and business papers in the southern Dutch town for more than 80 years. It has a reputation for making prestige products, but in truth, margins are slim and the paper mill, although reasonably modern, is below the standards now imposed upon such operations by the Dutch government and the European Commission.

The management board is not insensitive to the environmentalists' demands – as Lievaart's appointment suggests. The company has tried to conform to legislation and to buy its pulp from sustainable sources in North America, but the quality required cannot be achieved with ordinary recycled pulp using its existing equipment. Meanwhile, public pressure is growing for the industry to use more of the paper waste being collected for recycling, and to clean up its effluent.

At the moment, as Lievaart is aware, Venlo has no chance of being awarded an 'eco-label' for its stationery, and sales are starting to suffer as a result.

The investment in plant that will enable recycled pulp to be used for high-quality papers and the bleaching process to be modified will, he calculates, amount to more than FL3 million (Ecu 1.4 million) – at least two years' profits, with no additional turnover. Lievaart's colleagues on the board are mostly traditional paper makers, whose long experience of the struggle to survive commercially has given them a robust view of investment, pressure groups, public opinion – and of enthusiastic young environmental managers.

He knows that if he tries to push his colleagues too hard, particularly in a recession, he risks hardening their attitudes to the environmental issue and, indeed, to his job. On the other hand, he realizes the letter is a straw in the wind of public opinion. If the company does nothing, sales, and its reputation, will be damaged, and the gradual tightening of regulations will in the end threaten its very existence. Meanwhile, what to do about that letter?

Source: *International Management*, November 1993.

continued overleaf

Management case study continued

CASE QUESTIONS

1. Do you think that it is possible for Lievaart to persuade his colleagues on the management board that a positive green policy will benefit the firm as a whole?
2. How would you handle this problem?

Part two

Strategic management and the learning organization

In Part one we were introduced to organization and management, the history of this discipline and the societal environment within which organizations function. In Part two we will be looking at the strategic management process within an organization. Every organization needs to address the question: What is our actual contribution to society? An organization's response to this question will determine its mission, goals and strategy.

The strategy process is both a creative and a decision-making process and this is discussed in Chapter 4. In the search for new opportunities to ensure the continued survival of the organization, management has to ask whether current policies are to be retained or change is necessary. When an organization conducts a systematic review of its members' experiences and adapts its operations as a result, it is said to be a 'learning organization'.

Chapter 5 deals with the actual formulation of strategy and the management of the strategy process.

Principles of management

Motivating people

Part one • Management and society

- Chapter 1 — **Manager and management**
- Chapter 2 — **Management theory and organizational development**
- Chapter 3 — **Organizations and environment**

Part two • Strategic management and the learning organization

- Chapter 4 — **Decision making and creativity**
- Chapter 5 — **Strategy formulation and strategic management**

Part three • Designing and structuring the organization

- Chapter 6 — **Designing the organization**
- Chapter 7 — **Structuring tasks for groups and individuals**

Part four • People at work

- Chapter 8 — **Motivation, work and career**
- Chapter 9 — **Leading, motivation and communication**

Part five • Planning, control and information management

- Chapter 10 — **Operational planning and control**
- Chapter 11 — **Information management and information technology**
- Chapter 12 — **Managerial process control: functional processes and process redesign**

Chapter 4

Decision making and creativity

LEARNING OBJECTIVES

After studying this chapter, you should be able to:

- identify the different kinds of decisions;
- describe the phases of the decision-making process;
- discuss the problems which can arise in the different phases of the decision-making process;
- recognize the pitfalls which make decision making difficult;
- specify the different levels of learning;
- explain the concept of the 'learning organization';
- evaluate the contribution of consultative groups in decision making;
- explain why managers decide to call in management consultants.

Management in action

Omo Power dies a silent death – Unilever as a learning organization

The parallel is too good to ignore. When Philips and Sony, in the mid-1980s, concluded that their VCR systems – V2000 and Betamax – were not going to make it in the competitive battle with VHS, they decided to bring out VHS themselves. This did not mean, of course, that they would withdraw their own systems from the market – so they shouted at the top of their voices. However, within two years those systems had silently disappeared from the market; with no advertising for V2000 and Betamax, consumers simply bought what they perceived to be the 'winning' system.

Is the same happening at Unilever? The company continues to have the 'highest of confidence' in its Omo Power, but the product has been pushed from a prominent place towards the side lines. This looks like the beginning of the end. Omo Power becomes a 'special detergent' and New Generation Omo, together with Color – which has never contained that infamous ingredient, accelerator – becomes the flagship of the company. Considering the marketing effort with which the product will no doubt be surrounded, Omo Power will be reduced to just another product in Unilever's detergent range.

In the meantime, Unilever is licking its wounds. Morris Tabaksblatt, the most important man in the company, admits that the company made a mistake with the introduction of Omo Power. Unilever had strongly disputed the damning test reports and had insisted that Omo Power was a good product. The problem was that Unilever was the only one who believed it. Tabaksblatt blamed the company itself:

> *We were so very enthusiastic about the product, too positive about the positive aspects, but we thought too lightly of the negative aspects of it. Something must have gone wrong somewhere between the research and the marketing process. Why? We wanted to be the first, in order to win.*

Tabaksblatt is referring to the haste with which the marketing departments at Unilever had wanted the new Omo Power launched, in order to deliver a destructive blow to Proctor & Gamble, which was to introduce Ariel Futur several months later. The doubts and observations of the R&D department had been abruptly brushed aside. Omo Power was a miracle detergent, and that was that.

According to a Unilever spokesperson, the company has learned from its experience. Communication between marketing and R&D has been improved.

> *With Omo Power, it was the first time Unilever had worked with multidisciplinary teams with representatives from all the involved departments. We learned that good communication is essential. The 'systems' have been carefully examined and adapted. We are convinced that what happened with Omo Power cannot happen again.*

Source: Adapted from *Het Financieel Dagblad*, 13 January 1995.

INTRODUCTION

Before addressing the formulation of strategy in Chapter 5, it is important to first examine the decision-making process in the organization. The choice of a strategy is one of the most fundamental decisions an organization will take.

In this chapter we describe the different stages of the decision-making process (referred to as the phase model of decision making). We then identify the factors that influence decision making and give recommendations as to how decision making can be improved.

Decision making and the resulting *planning* and, if necessary, *adjusting* of business activities are key elements of managerial and operational functions. A *good supply of information* is of crucial importance to these functions, for, without it, no decision can be made and potential problems will not be spotted. Information needs to be gathered in time and has to be presented in a clearly structured way. Transmitting information, receiving back signals from the organization and relaying decisions are all *communication processes*. This means that decision making, planning, the supply of information and communication are all elements which are directly linked to each other in the management and control of business processes.

All of these elements are examined fully in this book. In this chapter, we consider the decision-making process itself and, in so doing, introduce the influencing factors such as communication, information and motivation.

In Chapter 9, communication is discussed in greater detail, and information management and information technology are covered in more depth in Chapter 11.

4.1 THE NATURE OF DECISION MAKING

Every manager has to make decisions in order to solve the problems that arise in the working environment. The analysis of problems and the search for solutions are an integral part of the management function.

If an organization increases its output, for example, by offering more products or delivering more services, resulting in a higher level of product–market activities or if the production process becomes more sophisticated, this often means that more complex problems will arise within the organization. The preparation for decision making, the decision making itself and the implementation of these decisions usually involve three procedures: *consultation*, *deliberation* and *participation*.

It is important that decision making involves not only the specialists from the staff departments, but also the line managers from the different levels and departments in the organization, as they will later have to deal with the repercussions the decisions will have. In this respect, the line managers also possess important operational know-how and expertise, which should not be underestimated. The successful implementation of the decision depends as much on the degree of acceptance by the employees involved as it does on the quality of the decision itself. It is therefore paramount that all those involved are included in the preparation and the making of the decision.

Many decisions are often preceded internally by a consideration of the legal obligations of the organization with regard to consultation with employees (in particular through the works council). This will involve much advance deliberation – for example, in staff meetings, consultative groups, task forces, project groups (temporary) or committees (permanent). In an organization, consultation and deliberation in groups can take place at different levels in order to solve problems, give advice and propose decision alternatives. These groups can be established on either a permanent or temporary basis, depending on the nature and size of the problems. It is important to always take into account the consultative and communication structure in relation to the decision-making process.

4.1.1 Types of decisions

As we stated in section 1.4.3, three types of decisions can be distinguished in the process of management:

- strategic
- organizational or administrative
- operational.

In Fig 4.1, these three types of decisions are related to the job duties and the input of the different levels of management and operations in the organization.

A large number of decisions have to be made in organizations every day, but they are all very different in nature. Decisions will vary with respect to the following factors:

- how much money is involved (the decision to purchase 100 ball-point pens, for example, being very different from the decision to purchase a highly automated production line);
- the number of people affected by the decision;
- the scope of responsibility;
- the time span within which the effects of the decision become noticeable;
- the level of risk or uncertainty involved;
- the emotional reactions provoked by the decision.

As the decisions become increasingly complex and their importance increases, more specialists (from the organization's staff departments) may be consulted in the preparatory phases of the decision-making process. A decision about the introduction of flexible working hours in a bank or about early retirement in an industrial company has technical, as well as economic and social-psychological aspects. All these considerations, of course, have to be taken into account before the actual decision can be made.

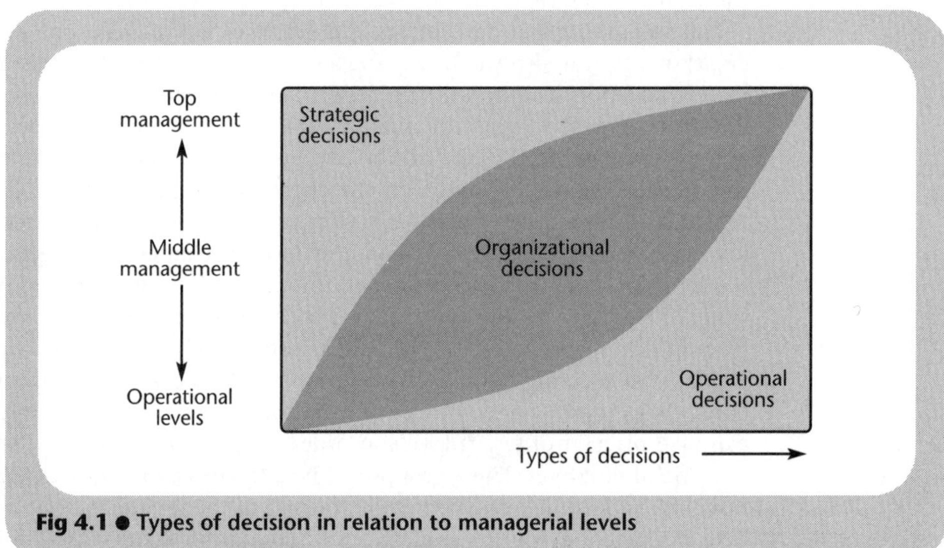

Fig 4.1 ● Types of decision in relation to managerial levels

4.1.2 Consultation and participation

Consultation, deliberation and participation occur in an organization by means of regular consultation (*see* section 7.5) and through consultative groups, such as work groups, project groups and/or committees. There is also a legal requirement in many countries for consultation and participation to take place in works councils (*see* section 2.3.3).

4.2 ● THE DECISION-MAKING PROCESS

Decision making can be described as a process which is made up of successive phases which begin the moment the information becomes available that indicates a problem and lasts until the chosen solution is implemented. The four phases of the decision-making process are presented in Fig 4.2.

This model applies to all types of decision, even though the content and the availability of information at each stage may vary. The order in which the decision-making process should occur is important if the organization is to make as good a decision as possible. Adequate attention should be paid, therefore, to the different phases in this process. It is not uncommon for the participants in meetings where decisions are being taken to be situated at different phases of the decision-making model. This often leads to confusion and certainly does not result in optimal decision making.

There are three golden rules for good decision making:

- Don't skip a phase.
- Go through each phase in depth.
- In joint decision making, proceed from one phase to the next in groups.

This phase model of the decision-making process is also characterized by a 'feedback' element. Indeed, we cannot rule out the possibility that a manager will have to return from Phase 2 or 3 to Phase 1, when the conclusion is reached that in earlier

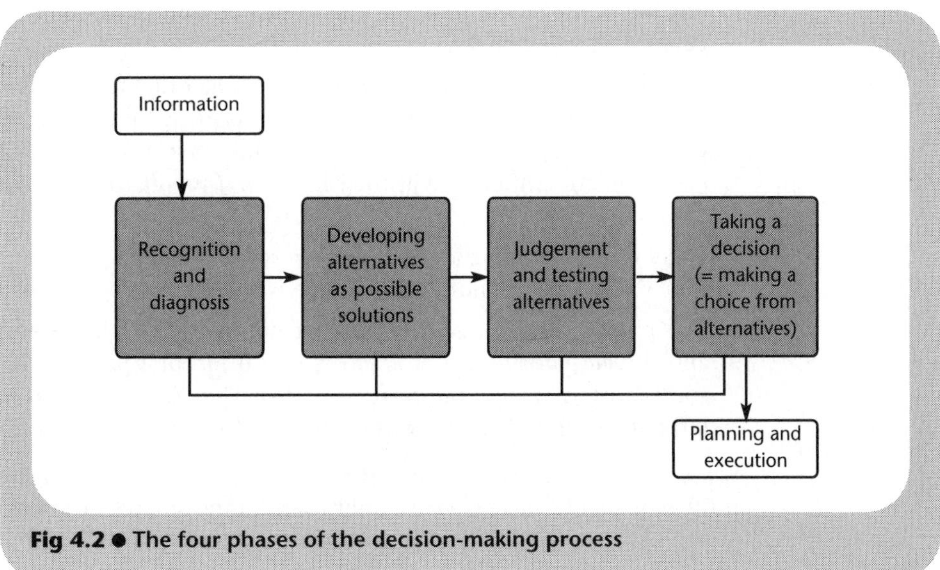

Fig 4.2 ● The four phases of the decision-making process

phases the problem was not tackled correctly or completely. The analysis of the problem in Phase 1 will have to be given renewed attention before the manager can proceed. This is referred to as an *iterative* process – that is, a process which is repeated over and over again.

4.2.1 Phase 1: recognition and diagnosis

As a first step, it is important to gain a clear impression of the problem which needs to be solved. The problem should be described in as much detail as possible, identifying the individual issues which come together to make up the *main problem*. This can be done, for example, by asking questions, by studying a problem in depth in small work groups or by means of a joint discussion.

It is always tempting, for the sake of convenience, to suppose that the problem is clear to everybody involved. Starting off with an inaccurate definition of a problem only leads to far greater problems at a later stage. When a problem is not properly or completely identified, there is little chance that a good solution can be found in the further course of the decision-making process. On the contrary, *a well defined problem is already well on the way to being solved.*

For example ...

... suppose that in a certain company the stock of finished products of a specific item has been seen to rise by a substantial margin. Management spots this from weekly or monthly reports and must find out what is going on. Is this a temporary decrease in demand? Or is this of a more structural nature? What is the cause? Too high a price? Too little direct advertising?

Before these questions can be answered, the problem has to be stated clearly, as there are a number of corrective measures which management has at its disposal – for example, a temporary price decrease, an improvement in services, the intensifying of direct advertising, doing nothing as the sales are expected to recover eventually, the dismissal of some representatives who are selling too little in the region.

Investigation will therefore have to precede a decision. This involves several elements:

1. The *root cause* of the problem has to be determined. *Symptoms* have to be distinguished from the causes.
2. It is important to reach *a mutual agreement* regarding the definition of the problem. This is not always easy. Sometimes, this process is hindered because a manager has gone 'company blind' and as a result is not open to new developments. For example, he might still believe in the success of a product because he was the one who originally developed it.
3. There is often a tendency to keep expressing problems in terms of past experience. A new problem is handled in the same way as all past problems.
4. This phase, which is also called the *identification phase*, involves both the *recognition* and the *diagnosis* of the problem. Recognition of a problem is an admission that something is wrong and that something has to be done about it. Diagnosis is directed at describing the precise nature of the problem in practical terms.

At the end of this phase, it is important that the problem is described in such a way that in the next phases there is a clear and 'guided' direction to the search for solutions.

Minicase 4.1

Scenario for a disaster

In most cases, disasters only occur as a result of an unexpectedly large number of things going wrong. This is what happened when the ferry, The Herald of Free Enterprise, *capsized on 6 March 1987 as it left the harbour of Zeebrugge in Belgium. 193 people were killed.*

What went wrong? The bowdoors were not closed. The sailor who should have taken care of this had fallen asleep. There was no alarm light on the instrument panel on the bridge to indicate opened bowdoors during sailing, because it was cheaper to have this checked by an officer; on this occasion the officer had some other very urgent matters to take care of. The ship had been designed for the height of the quay walls in Calais. The quay at Zeebrugge was lower so the cars could not drive in there. That is why ballast tanks had been filled so that the bow of the ship was lowered. There was a shortage of time and as a result the ballast tanks were not emptied before departure. The captain gave full speed ahead. A high bow-wave rose up and swept in through the lowered, and then the standard position, opened doors.

On 14 December 1982, four men drowned in Hold 6 of the ship, *Farmsum* when the partition wall with Hold 5, which appeared to be full of water, shattered. How was it that no one knew about the water in Hold 5? With hindsight, we know that Hold 5 was filled with water because of ballast water that had leaked from Hold 4. Indeed, the helmsman saw the level of water in Hold 4 drop, but assumed another cause. He had been pumping slops from Hold 6, when he noticed that the valve was in the wrong position. In that position, the pump would have been emptying Hold 4, not Hold 6. He concluded, incorrectly, that ballast water had been pumped out of Hold 4 instead of the slop from Hold 6. The valve supplied the helmsman with a hypothesis and the wasted water affirmed it.

People accept a hypothesis based on affirmed information without submitting the hypothesis to a critical test. In practice, often the most obvious hypothesis will be correct, and so this approach is seldom questioned.

The acceptance of a diagnosis prevents the search for other possible causes. Experience shows that, just like the helmsman, we tend to reason from (assumed) causes to (manifest) consequences – that is, forward in time. In nuclear technology, efforts have been made to develop forward-thinking systems (by feeding forward from information impulses to consequences) which would allow the consequences of disorders to be predicted on the basis of an idealized, technical model. However, the operator knows only the effect of the disorder, not its nature. It is important that the system helps the operator to reason back from the effect to all possible causes. Only then, can we think forward from each of the possible causes to trace which causes lead to the diagnosed effect.

Source: Adapted from *De Ingenieur*, 23 August 1994.

The first phase of the decision-making process is of enormous importance for the successful completion of later phases. An incorrect or incomplete diagnosis can mean that later in the process there is no longer a clear image of what the problem actually is. This will involve a loss of time (as it will be necessary to return to Phase 1 for further investigations), or even the choice of inappropriate solutions. It is therefore crucial that all the involved parties are in agreement with regard to the formulation of the problem.

4.2.2 Phase 2: developing alternatives as possible solutions

Only once the first phase of the decision-making process has produced as clear and as complete a definition of the problem as possible, can potential solutions to the problem be considered. Solution possibilities or *alternatives* have to be developed. In this phase, for example, the employees of the organization involved with the problem can be asked to offer as many solution proposals as possible – a process known as *brainstorming*. The problem may not be a new one and a previous solution can be suggested. In other cases, however, the decision makers are confronted with new problems and new solutions will have to be developed, taking full advantage of the *creative abilities* of the organization.

Unfortunately, there are a number of factors which could stifle such creativity – for example, traditional ways of working or an authoritarian manager who always knows best. If creativity is to develop, conditions must allow the free exchange of thoughts (*see also* section 4.5). It is also important that consideration should not be restricted to only one possible solution – for example, one the boss has chosen earlier or one for which someone has a particular (unconscious) preference. It is advisable at this stage to put down all alternatives on paper, to gather extra information to support these alternatives, and perhaps to examine these further in smaller work groups.

In Phase 2, therefore – the development phase – a direct search is carried out for solutions to the problems which were clearly defined in Phase 1. This phase can consist of two discrete activities:

1. *The search for an existing solution.* This can involve research into alternatives which have been used successfully in the past with a similar or related problem. An existing solution can be adjusted to suit the problem in question.
2. *The development of a new solution.* When there is no ready solution to be found, it is necessary to develop a new solution.

These processes take time. This phase cannot be rushed, as this may otherwise lead to an inappropriate solution. In practice, new solutions seem to work well. In most cases only one alternative will be developed. However, it is advisable to search for or to develop several alternatives at this phase, as this will enable the working party to weigh up the pros and cons of each alternative in the next phase of the process, and thus make the best possible choice.

4.2.3 Phase 3: judgement and testing alternatives

Once alternative solutions to the problem have been suggested, it is then necessary to consider the *consequences* of each of the alternatives. This will form the basis of the eventual choice.

In contrast with Phase 2, at this stage a *critical approach* is what is required – just like playing 'the devil's advocate'. The decision maker must check that the consequences have been mapped out as fully as possible, and that the analyses are all correct. When considering the consequences of the alternatives, it is important to map out the changes that are to be expected if a specific alternative is followed. In this way, not only should the *desired* and *possible* consequences be taken into account, but also the *undesired* consequences of every solution alternative.

In Phase 3, therefore, the decision maker considers which of the proposed alternatives solves the problem best. A possible solution is tested based on the available information, but also based on experience, feasibility and so on. It is important that the influence of one team member does not result in the absence of testing. In some cases, a proposal will not be critically tested because of pressure of time, bad management or because of power differences existing in a work group or committee. This can also be caused by inadequate explanations of the proposals, or by the overwhelming pressure of work group members unwilling to consider anything other than their own proposals. Sometimes, proposals are discounted unjustifiably, because of a personal dislike of the employee putting forward the proposal.

Once again this *selection phase* can be divided into two separate activities:

1. *Screening*. This involves the comparison of alternative solutions as the result of which the less satisfactory alternatives can be rejected. This can often be carried out on the basis of rather superficial criteria.
2. *Evaluation and selection*. The remaining alternatives are subjected to an even closer evaluation and those with the best results are then selected as preferred alternatives.

In this phase, it is important to create a good and open conversational climate and to call in specialists to look over proposals, in order that the relative quality and effectiveness of each alternative can be determined.

4.2.4 Phase 4: taking a decision

The final choice can only be taken when the consequences of the solution shortlist are measured against certain *choice criteria*.

A first criterion is the degree to which each of the alternatives results in the desired solution of the original problem, as specified in Phase 1. It is possible that two alternatives will lead to the same end result, be it in different ways. For example, a company wishing to enter a foreign market could either establish its own sales office in the area or could enter into an agreement with a foreign sales agent. In both cases the same end result is expected. At this point, the decision maker must take into account other factors affecting his choice – for example, the relative costs, the time scales within which the goals must be reached, the risks involved, the resources the organization wants to commit.

The choice is made more difficult if more than one goal needs to be attained at the same time. In such a situation, it is unlikely that all the alternatives will be realized to the same degree. There has to be a *list of priorities*. For example, there could be two possible ways of addressing a problem: one in which efficiency is raised but at the expense of relatively low labour satisfaction; another possibility involves increasing job satisfaction, but incurring an expected decrease in productivity. Each of the alternatives has its merits. Such a dilemma can often be overcome by a compromise involving consultation with the involved members of the organization.

Decision making usually takes place under less than perfect conditions. The decision maker will be unsure of many details and the data on which decisions are based may be incomplete or unclear. In many cases, there is a lack of information on future developments. Further information could be gathered to limit the degree of uncertainty, although this will involve extra time and expense and there is no guarantee that all relevant information can be gathered. It may be that the decision cannot be postponed because otherwise a chance in the market may be lost or an expected result may not be attained at all. All these factors must be taken into account at this stage.

Endless hesitation and prolonged investigation of the 'ifs and buts' should be avoided. The final choice is often made by a single person.

For example ...

... when considering decision making in a business context, it is worth taking a look at decision-making theory, as part of the discipline of psychology. The following examples offer some interesting insights.

When people were asked to choose between a certain profit of 800 Swiss francs or an 85 per cent chance of a profit of 1000 Swiss francs, most of the people chose the first option, in spite of the fact that the expected profit was 850 francs in the second case. The opposite happened when a loss was involved. Given a choice between a certain loss of 800 Swiss francs or an 85 per cent chance of a loss of 1000 Swiss francs, the second option was taken. In the former case, there is a flight or aversion from risk; in the latter case risk is welcomed.

Consider the following scenario. You have been to the cinema to buy a ticket in advance for £5. You lose the ticket. Will you buy a new ticket? In the majority of cases, the answer is 'no'. Now consider a slightly different case. You arrive at the cinema to buy a ticket and discover that you have lost a £5 note. In these circumstances, almost everyone will go ahead and buy the ticket regardless.

Where alternative solutions have quite different consequences for the interests of those involved, procedures such as negotiations can be implemented. After the solution to the problem has been decided, the next step is the *authorization* or *formulation* of the decision.

In this phase, good judgement, as clear as possible an image of the consequences of the solution alternatives, and a desire to reach an agreement or solution are all of importance if a justified decision is to be made. Careful comparisons, a review of the available information and a final check that all phases of the process of decision making have been completed all contribute to this.

4.2.5 Planning and implementing the decision

When all the steps in the process of decision making have been worked through and a solution has been chosen, a plan has to be made in order that the decision can be successfully implemented.

At this point the responsibility for the implementation of the decision should be assigned. This responsibility should not lie with just one individual. It is extremely important that there is commitment to the decision at all levels of the organization and that the decisions are supported by the members of the organization, who now have to work with the consequences of the decisions that have been made. In this respect, it is useful to examine the degree to which the individual goals are consistent with the goals of the company as a whole. If these are in conflict, an employee may try to give his or her own goals priority by failing to implement aspects of the decision taken. A consideration of the motivation of the employees involved is therefore crucial to the successful implementation of the decision.

Once the effects of the measures are known, a decision may be taken to carry out a part of the decision-making procedure again, to see whether the goals which are set are being attained. In some cases, there are advantages in repeating one of the preceding steps. However, if during implementation there are still a number of practical operational problems or undesired effects, it is wise to question the desirability of continuing along the chosen path. Perhaps, the course of direction will have to be changed after all.

4.2.6 The phase model of the decision-making process

As we have seen, the phase model covers the whole decision-making process from the initial signalling of the problem, through the searching for alternative solutions, to the actual choice and the authorization of a solution.

Each of the four phases – identification, development, selection and decision making (plus authorization) – involves a certain number of specific activities, which, when carried out in a structured way, lead to the development of a solution to the problem.

The phase model of Fig 4.2 can now be extended to include all aspects of the decision-making process (*see* Fig 4.3).

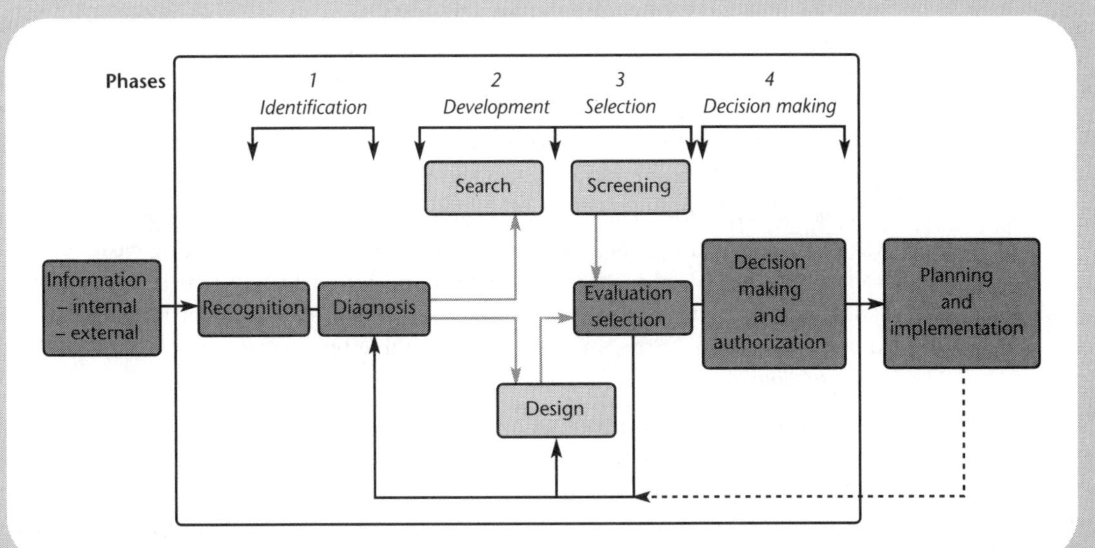

Fig 4.3 ● The extended phase model of the decision-making process (combining the models of Staerkle, Keuning–Eppink and Mintzberg)

4.3 ● FACTORS INFLUENCING DECISION MAKING

The phase model in Fig 4.3 depicts the process of decision making as a succession of discrete steps arranged in a logical order, and can therefore be used as a practical aid to structuring the process. However, the model does not take into account the factors which can influence the course of such a process in practice. For example, the interests of the individual stakeholders will affect the decision-making process. Conflicts of interest may arise. In practice, progress in the decision-making process may be subject to complications or delays. Even with these limitations, however, the phase model continues to fulfil the important function of highlighting the stage in the process which the decision makers have reached in the resolution of their own particular problems.

In practice, however, it is important to realize that the processes of decision making are enacted in a complex organizational environment. To understand these decision-making processes fully, we need to examine them in the context of the three factors which have an important influence over them:

- *The structure of the organization.* This involves the division of the organization into departments and/or divisions, the degree of centralization or decentralization and the degree to which, for example, individual employees are involved.
- *The quality of communication.* In decision making, communication takes place between people in their roles as members of the organization. This means that the decision-making process is influenced by a number of behavioural factors, such as biases, fear, frustration, ambition, cognitive dissonance, forgetfulness, etc. Decision making is therefore subject to a number of *non-rational* or *irrational factors*. The absence of good and open communication channels and the censoring or disruption of messages can mean that decisions are based on misconceptions or a distortion of reality. It is also important that communication takes place at the right time. The premature notice of certain plans can be problematic. On the other hand, the late or inadequate involvement of certain managers in the decision-making process can have serious consequences, especially when they are involved in the operational implementation of the decision.
- *The motivation of the members of the organization.* The role of employee motivation in the decision-making process cannot be underestimated. By making clear the behaviour which is desired in the organization and by rewarding that behaviour (*positive sanction*) the behaviour of individuals can be guided, to a certain degree, in the desired direction. At the same time, undesirable behaviour can be 'punished' (*negative sanction*).

(The problems of communication, motivation and conflict handling are covered in more detail in Chapters 8 and 9. Problems concerning organizational structure are discussed further in Chapters 6 and 7.)

It is therefore important to take into account the factors which influence and complicate the decision-making process if we are to understand how the process works in practice. This involves the irrational aspects of organizational behaviour and the political factors relating to the company, such as the division of power, reasons for conflict and use/misuse and absence of information.

The use of information is not a 'neutral' issue in this context; it is an important 'source of power' in the realization of goals. In many cases the use of information is dependent on the information supporting the interests of the decision maker (O'Reilly, 1983). It is more likely to be used under the following conditions:

- The source is powerful.
- There is no other source and therefore verification is impossible.
- The information is important to the functioning of the decision maker.
- The information is accessible.
- The source is credible.
- Desired visions are supported.
- Use of the information does not lead to conflict.
- The information is offered directly (not via third parties).

Exhibit 4.1

An intuitive move

Mogren AB is making profits but something doesn't add up

Call it intuition, a sixth sense or just gut feeling – Bertil Nilsson somehow knows that all is not well with two of the product divisions in his group, Mogren AB. He can't put his finger on it, and there's nothing in the figures to suggest it, but his subconscious warning bells have been ringing for a while now.

The divisions manufacture and distribute a range of automotive components, mainly electrical and electronic. Their customers are the big car and truck groups. It is a tough, highly competitive business, and Nilsson, from his office overlooking Gothenburg's port, does not interfere – out of policy as well as personal choice.

Mogren's origins were in shipping, but it has long since diversified. It still retains some maritime interests among its present seven divisions, but it is highly decentralised, and Nilsson's head office team consists of no more than 50 staff, mostly in the finance and legal sections. The accounts they prepare every month show him that all the divisions are making reasonable profits. Although auto parts have been hit hard by the recession, the losses have been contained and are slowly being turned into profits.

So why the alarm bells? At the monthly meetings Nilsson quizzes the divisional bosses about their performance. They explain their current problems on costs and inventories logically enough, and are resolutely optimistic about achieving their five-year targets once recovery is under way. Growth will still not be exciting, they say, but pruning the product range and rationalising production on a European basis will yield big savings.

Nilsson is not satisfied. Friends outside the company tell him the product quality may not be keeping pace with Japanese standards, and that important products are losing ground to competitors. But the evidence is anecdotal and he cannot prove it. He has confidence in the two divisional bosses, who have between them 25 years' experience with the group. Anyway, in a decentralised group, he cannot afford to be second-guessing his lieutenants – they would be demotivated, and he would end up running businesses he did not understand.

After talking it over with his finance director and confidant, Anders Heberg, who is able to compare margins, cashflow and return on investment across the group, the pair agree to demand more detail on the figures from the divisional accounts departments. Heberg's team of analysts can then provide a clearer picture of performance, and Nilsson will see whether and where his hunch is justified.

The following month, a deluge of information arrives over the fax. Every nut and bolt that moves, every krona is faithfully accounted for, but in spite of the analysts' best efforts, the picture is more obscure than ever. Nilsson still feels that decentralisation is right, but he must somehow regain control. His warning bells have never given a false alarm in the past.

Source: International Management, July/August 1994.

4.3.1 The organization as a political arena

Power and conflict need to be given special attention when it comes to decision making. An organization is a kind of coalition of participants to which each person brings his or her own specific demands. In this respect decision making is a political process.

Conflict arises because of the way in which the company is split into divisions and departments and the complex interdependencies between these groups. Scarcity in resources only serves to reinforce this. Whether these potential conflicts lead to actual 'control problems' of the diverse 'players' and interest groups depends on the importance of the subject concerned and the degree to which power is spread in the organization.

In the 'arena' model of decision making, there is so little agreement among the main players of the organization and such pre-occupation with power and politics, that consensus on the main issues facing the organization is very difficult to achieve.

To understand fully the dynamic nature of the decision-making process, four basic elements can be recognized.

1. Conflicts which arise in the organization due to the diversity of interests and preferences of the coalition partners are most often not totally resolved, but are instead reduced to acceptable proportions by means of a variety of procedures. To reconcile the various partial or quasi solutions, the organization can use the mechanism of optimizing, rather than maximizing results, and paying attention to the attaining of goals which are actually in conflict with each other in succession, using time as a buffer.
2. Organizations try to control the environment as far as possible, by means of agreements, contracts and traditions. Furthermore, they adjust their decision-making procedures all the time as a result of reactions from the environment.
3. Organizations keep searching for solutions to specific problems and only when a problem has been solved or seems to have been solved, does the searching stop. The search proceeds according to three patterns: searching around the problem, searching around known alternatives, and trying to pass the problem to organizationally 'weak' sectors of the organization.
4. Organizations seem to 'learn'. In the course of time, they appear to be able to adapt to changed circumstances. There are, of course, irrational aspects of organizational behaviour, but organizations almost always work along traditional lines. The organization operates according to an obvious hierarchy of preferences and a number of choice rules: avoid uncertainty, maintain rules and keep rules simple. An organization makes decisions in such a way that the results are satisfactory for the decision makers in that they attain a desired or target level (optimizing, rather than maximizing behaviour).

4.3.2 The organization as a garbage can

According to the 'garbage can model' of decision making, organizations are seen as 'organized anarchies' characterized by unclear and inconsistent goals, complex and little understood technology, as well as a varying degree of participation by the members of the organization. Universities and colleges are considered to be 'prototypes' of such a model.

The garbage can model views organizations as consisting of four elements: problems, solutions, participants and selection opportunities. Selection opportunities are situations in which participants are expected to match a particular problem and a particular solution and in so doing, make a decision.

These four elements exist in many different and totally unpredictable combinations. Solutions can precede problems, or problems and solutions can await the right occasion for a decision. In this model of decision making, the phase model described in section 4.2 – identification, development, selection and decision making – is completely turned on its head.

In the 'garbage can model' the organization is seen as a collection of rather autonomous departments and interest groups whose only link is the overall budget to which each must adhere. This does not mean, however, that there is no system at a ll to the decision making in this type of organization. On the contrary, from the decision-making point of view, the apparent anarchy has a structure which eventually forms a fairly good, if not optimal, response to the insecurities from the environment with which decision makers and departments have to deal.

Decision making can only progress if the organization's stakeholders appreciate the problems involved. Usually, the stakeholders have more to worry about and decisions are put off or are taken without due consideration of the problem by the stakeholders. However, it is the task of the board of directors or the divisional or departmental management to involve the stakeholders in the decision-making process and to direct decision making along the path desired by the organization.

4.3.3 Recommendations for better decision making

The degree to which decision making in an organization is rational, ordered and logical depends on all sorts of factors. Koopman *et al.* (1988) compiled a list of the most important limiting factors.

- *Lack of information.* Decision makers seldom have all the relevant information at their disposal. In many cases they will not have the time, tools, techniques or resources to gather all the relevant information.
- *Lack of courage and internal stability.* Information of a negative nature often leads decision makers to close their eyes to important aspects of reality. Stress can result in decision makers avoiding problems and risks as a defensive action. Both will lead to bad decision making. Group thinking can reinforce this further. The perception of the environment is false; deviating views are not taken into account.
- *Lack of consensus.* In the 'arena model' of organization the opposite of group thinking occurs – that is, a total lack of agreement on the main issues tears the organization apart. Power processes and conflicts between the important players or coalitions threaten the rationality of the decision making.
- *Lack of policy and insight into organizational processes.* According to the 'garbage can model' of organizations, decision makers often have to work with unclear and inconsistent goals and an insufficiently understood technology, resulting in a wide range of problems in decision making. Insufficient vision and a lack of policy can reinforce this.
- *Lack of guidance and control.* Highly complex decision-making processes demand well considered phasing and process handling. This involves good management skills, both in diagnosing the problem and handling the politics of the organization. Logical and political aspects must be carefully integrated.
- *Lack of tuning into the strategic situational factors.* Some situations will demand an approach that is directed towards participation and negotiations; others will require a one-sided policy direction, formulated at the top. In some cases, a flexible, step-by-step approach is necessary; in other cases, detailed planning and supervision of time and cost constraints will be the most important factors.

With these limitations on decision making in mind, we can draw up a list of recommendations for improving decision making in the organization.

1. Define the problem and plan the decision-making process carefully.
2. Consider all the alternatives.
3. Use your intuition, when necessary (a high level of uncertainty, little experience, no objective data).
4. Adopt group decision making, when appropriate (complex problems requiring specialist knowledge, need to build up trust and acceptance).

5. Otherwise avoid group thinking; use the 'devil's advocate' technique.
6. Delegate, wherever possible.
7. Strive for consensus as far as possible.
8. Pay attention to diagnostic and political skills of decision makers.
9. Adapt the decision-making strategy to the demands of the situation.
10. Ensure the choice of decision-making process gives equal weight to the technical content on the one hand and the social-political side on the other.

4.4 DECISION MAKING: TECHNIQUES AND APPROACHES

In the individual phases of the decision-making process, different techniques can be used to help solve the problems at hand. Some techniques promote creativity and so can be of help in Phase 2. Others can be used in Phase 4 to ensure a responsible choice will be made from the available alternatives.

4.4.1 Techniques for improving creativity

When there is an 'open' organizational culture, several techniques can be used to stimulate creative ability and to make optimal use of it. We will cover two of these techniques: *brainstorming* and *lateral thinking*. These techniques are based on the premise that human beings are more creative, the less they feel pressured by others.

Brainstorming

The purpose of brainstorming is to generate as many solutions to a problem as possible, in as short a period of time as possible. The aim is not to work out the ideas or to make a choice from them. During a brainstorming session, suggestions should not be criticized at all. This interferes with the development of new, daring and unconventional ideas. Spontaneity should not be impeded. Participants need to stimulate each other.

To be effective, a group needs to consist of 10 to 15 people. Attention should be given to ensuring an appropriate spread of knowledge, experience and background, as this will encourage contributions from different points of view. Experience shows that brainstorming is especially suitable for clearly defined problems – for example, in the field of product development or the improvement of production methods – and is less appropriate for problems which are difficult to describe or very complex, or for problems which assume in-depth specialist knowledge.

Lateral thinking

In lateral thinking, the aim is to change existing ideas and procedures. Vertical or logical thinking follows ready-made paths and obvious patterns and for this reason will not generate new insights or ideas. Vertical thinking is based on common sense and logical reasoning and involves proceeding one step at a time. Each step has to be justified. Mistakes are not allowed. At the end of the thinking process, the best solution is chosen or the conclusion drawn.

Lateral thinking is not meant as a replacement to vertical thinking. Its function is complementary. Lateral thinking is the searching for side entrances to problems which cannot be solved via the front door. The founder of lateral thinking, De Bono, states that 10 to 15 minutes of lateral thinking a day can make an important contribution to the development of creativity.

It is important to first map out existing ideas concerning a particular problem. Only then can we start searching for new points of view. Several methods of lateral thinking have been developed. These involve following an illogical path and taking a creative leap into new ideas. The basic starting point is to 'look at things differently' – for example, to turn the reasoning around, to mix up the procedure, to choose a random word and see whether it offers a new starting point.

For example ... ... consider the problem of shoplifting. A challenging 'lateral' idea is to give all the articles away – that will definitely solve the shoplifting problem. This 'interim' solution generates, in turn, the ideas of charging an entrance fee or letting people pay a contribution according to revenue received. With some adjustments these ideas might lead to a practical suggestion at a later stage. An idea that sounds strange at first can often lead on to useful thoughts.

Lateral thinking can be used to develop new ideas or points of view. It is not appropriate for systematically working out and evaluating ideas. This involves the field of logical, vertical thinking.

4.4.2 Decision-making techniques

In the decision-making process, different methods can be employed in Phase 4 to ensure that a responsible choice is made from available alternatives. Two of these methods will be covered here – the decision tree and the decision matrix.

The decision tree

The decision tree allows us to visualize a series of choice possibilities and their respective consequences under externally determined circumstances. We will clarify the principles of this technique by means of an example.

In Fig 4.4 we see an example of a decision tree with the features: choice, external determined circumstances and results. This can be applied to relatively complex situations. Suppose that a company has to make the choice between investing £3.5 million in order to bring a new product to the market, and placing this sum in the bank at an interest rate of 10 per cent. If it chooses the first option, there is always a chance that a competitor will bring a similar product to the market. The company can react to this by means of a price setting: high, medium or low. However, the competitor also has these possible choices. This situation can be depicted by means of a decision tree (*see* Fig 4.4).

In this, we see that each combination of choice possibilities and externally determined circumstances results in a certain profit or a certain loss. This example can be further supplemented by calculating the probability of each external circumstance arising (competition and the price setting of the competition). The probability value of each branch of the decision tree can be calculated and this can be used as the basis of determining whether the money will be invested in the launching of a new product or whether it will be put in the bank.

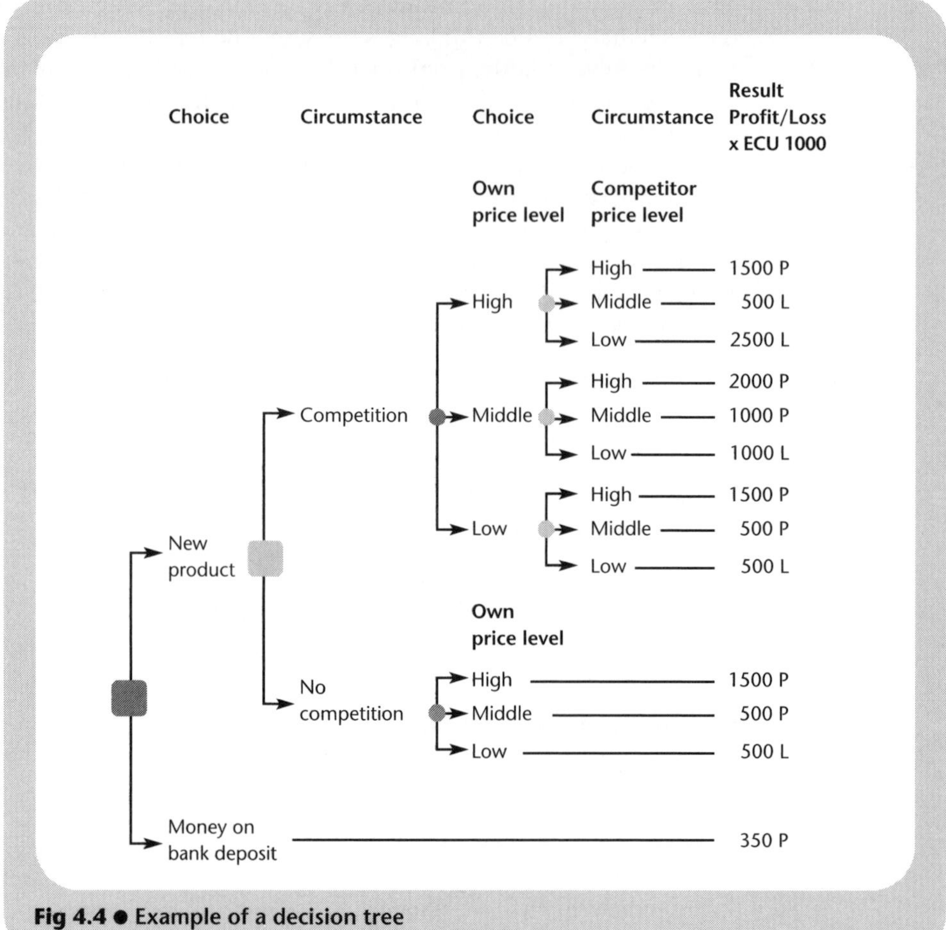

Fig 4.4 ● Example of a decision tree

The decision matrix

Usually, choice possibilities have consequences in different fields. Sometimes, these consequences will be in conflict with one another. Nevertheless, a decision will have to be made. The decision matrix allows us to map out the consequences and compare the alternatives. For example, suppose that the management of a company has to take a decision about the location of a factory which is to be built. For each alternative, a calculation is made of the expected return on investment (ROI). In addition to this key measure, however, a number of qualitative factors have to be taken into account. For example:

- the accessibility of potential clients;
- the accessibility of the most important suppliers;
- the availability of enough qualified personnel;
- subsidies and taxes.

Each factor is then assigned a weighting (1 to 5) according to its perceived importance relative to the other factors. In addition, each of the alternative locations is given a

	Customers	Suppliers	Personnel	Subsidies	Total score	ROI(%)
Weighting	*5*	*3*	*4*	*5*		
Location						
1	4 x 5=20	4 x 3=12	5 x 4=20	4 x 5=20	72	14.5
2	3 x 5=15	2 x 3= 6	2 x 4= 8	4 x 5=20	49	17.5
3	5 x 5=25	3 x 3= 9	3 x 4=12	4 x 5=20	66	19.5
4	4 x 5=20	4 x 3=12	2 x 4= 8	4 x 5=20	60	12.5

Fig 4.5 ● Example of a decision matrix

score (also 1 to 5) according to how appropriate each is in relation to the four factors. The multiplication of the score and the weighting gives the total score for each of the factors. Addition of the total scores gives an overall score for each of the locations. This calculation is summarized in the decision matrix in Fig 4.5.

With the help of such a decision matrix, management can gain a clear insight into the consequences of the different alternatives. The alternatives can now be compared with each other. The eventual choice will depend on the relative importance given to the quantitative consequences of each alternative.

Effectiveness of decision methods

Decision methods allow us to 'calculate' the best alternative. In addition, their application produces a very important side effect in that those involved gain a deeper insight into the problem, because the problem situation has to be systematically analysed. The application of decision methods forces those involved to ask critical questions about key factors of the decision-making process.

4.4.3 Types of decisions and procedures/techniques

It is important to distinguish the different types of decisions (as mentioned in section 4.1.1), because general statements and guidelines about one type of decision do not necessarily apply to another type. This is also true for the use of techniques in the decision-making process. The relative importance of a decision depends on factors, such as:

- the amount of money involved;
- the number of persons the decision affects;
- the time span within which results will have to be reported and within which the effects of the decision will be noticeable.

Decisions can be categorized into strategic, organizational and operational decisions (*see* section 4.1.1). Simon (1965) makes the distinction between programmed and non-programmed decisions (*see* Fig 4.6).

Types of decisions	Decision-making techniques *Tradition*	 *Modern*
Programmed: Routine, repetitive decisions Organization develops specific processes for handling them	1 Habit 2 Clerical routine: – standard operating procedures 3 Organization structure: – common expectations – a system of subgoals – well-defined information channels	1 Operations research: – mathematical analysis – models – computer simulation 2 Electronic data processing
Non-programmed: One-shot, ill-structured novel, policy decisions Handled by general problem-solving processes	1 Judgement, intuition, and creativity 2 Rules of thumb 3 Selection and training of executives	Heuristic problem-solving technique applied to: – training human decision makers – constructing heuristic computer programs

Source: Simon, 1965

Fig 4.6 ● Matrix of decision-making techniques and types of decisions

Programmed decisions

Programmed decisions are decisions of a routine-like nature. When a problem has been tackled once, experience is gained and any future recurrence of such a problem will result in the appropriate solution being immediately implemented without any further consideration.

Non-programmed decisions

Problems in this category are new and unstructured. Usually, they have major consequences for the organization. Given these characteristics, the approach cannot be programmed in standard procedures with advance solutions/routines. There is no cut-and-dried method set for handling such problems. Tailor-made solutions are required in this context.

In this grouping, Simon also makes a distinction between traditional and modern methods (*see* Fig 4.6). Simon suggests the use of heuristic methods as a modern approach to making non-programmed decisions. Heuristics is the *theory of solving problems methodically*. Simon states that heuristic methods can be used in two different ways:

1. People can *learn* to solve problems better or to handle them differently. In order to achieve this it is important to gain a better insight into human thinking processes. On this basis, decision makers can teach themselves alternative and better ways of working by means of *education* and *training*.
2. Computer programs can be developed which can help us solve complex problems in much the same way as computers play games of chess. Such programs should not

only be able to process quantitative information, but also qualitative information. The development of such programs and artificial intelligence is in its early stages.

4.4.4 Information technology, computers and decision making

Uncertainty and the reduction of uncertainty to acceptable and workable levels are recurring themes in decision making. With the aid of computer technology, it is possible to bring uncertainty under control to a certain degree because a large number of variables can be taken into consideration, consequences can be calculated and information can be gathered more quickly and more accurately. Computer technology addresses the practical problems of decision making in a number of management areas. For example:

- office automation;
- decision support systems (DSS);
- artificial intelligence (AI).

Office automation especially influences the productivity and efficiency of management. DSS and AI go further: they contribute to the problem identification, the generation of alternatives and the setting of priorities. The value of these last techniques is that they help to improve the whole decision-making process, not only the processing of information.

Decision support systems were first developed at the end of the 1960s by the opportunities the computer offered in the form of databases and direct access to information for manipulation purposes. The goal of DSS is contributing to the effectiveness of semi-structured decision-making processes, like production and inventory planning, strategic planning, financial planning and investment decisions.

If bottlenecks exist in the current approaches to decision making in the generation of alternatives, the designing of solutions and the selection of these, then DS systems can offer support. *Artificial intelligence* goes one step further than DSS in that the application possibilities of DSS are limited to situations in which the decision-making process can be represented by a formal model. AI can cope with conflicting or missing data. It is concerned with the processes that produce intelligent action – that is, involving decisions which are goal-oriented, attained by means of a logical reasoning process and which are underpinned by rules of thumb.

Artificial intelligence consists of three discrete fields: senses systems, natural language systems and expert systems. The *senses system* is, for example, concerned with the interpreting of, and the retrieving of as much information as possible of two dimensional pictures. *Language systems* are directed at the interpretation, for example, of English as it is spoken. *Expert systems* or knowledge systems are defined as programs which solve the most difficult problems which demand specialist knowledge. This area will without doubt have the greatest impact on management. Applications exist in diagnosis, medical information systems, process control, planning and industrial processes.

Some developments and consequences for organizations

Automation will continue to reduce the amount of time spent on analysis and document handling, for example, by staff and line managers. In addition, a further decrease in time spent on non-productive tasks will be possible. Not only will efficiency be increased but job satisfaction and quality should also be further enhanced.

Another important development in this field concerns the new telecommunication technology. To a certain degree, these techniques make the physical work place unimportant. Personal computers, perhaps linked to an electronic mail system, a central database or the office automation network of the organization, make it possible for employees to work at home or while travelling. The advantages of telecommunications are obvious: flexible working hours, less office space required, opportunities for disabled people and employees with domestic commitments.

The diminishing of personal contact may be a shortcoming. The latest figures on the expected improvement in efficiency as a result of automation are not very reliable. In addition, it is evident that managers have been slow to adopt these techniques.

Middle management has come under increasing pressure (as already stated in section 1.2.2) by the new possibilities of automation. It is predicted that more and more organizations will replace the layer of permanent middle-management functions with special units and temporary work groups within flatter, delayered structures in order to solve problems and to influence markets.

4.4.5 Problem solving and decision making: situational or contingent approaches

Situations sometimes arise where the nature of the problem is all too clear, but those involved have differing or even contradictory views on what should be done to resolve it (*see also* sections 4.3.1 and 4.3.2). The only way in which a solution can be found is for all concerned to make compromises. Of course, this is not the ideal approach, but at least an attempt is being made to improve the existing situation. Experience shows that the best solution is often a solution which is acceptable to all those involved and which seems to be practicable in the given situation.

Thompson (1967) states that decision making demands an approach that is appropriate to *the situation*. Two basic situational factors influence the choice of decision strategy:

- insight into the structure of the problem (cause–effect relations); and
- the preferences regarding possible outcomes.

When we summarize this in a matrix, four different approaches or strategies can be distinguished (*see* Fig 4.7).

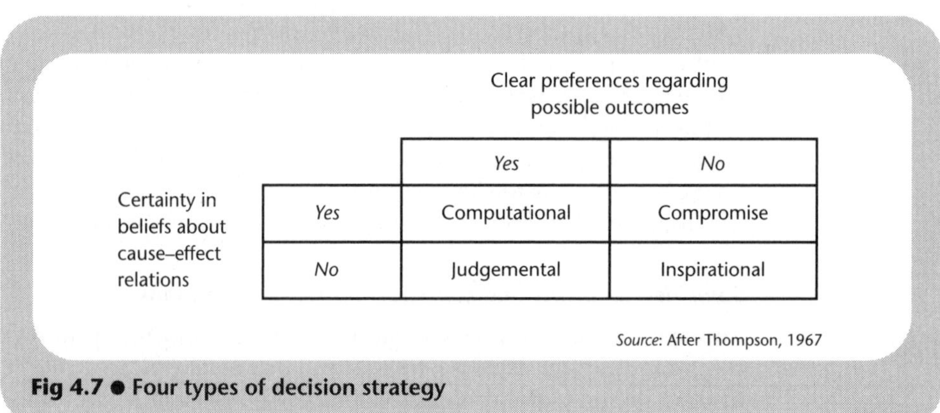

Fig 4.7 ● Four types of decision strategy

1. A good insight into the problem and certainty on causation and outcome preferences mean we are dealing with a *calculation problem* and should adopt a *computational strategy* for decision making. Such a problem can be converted into a formula or arithmetical terms.
2. Where outcome preferences are clear, but cause-effect relationships are uncertain, a *judgemental strategy* for decision making is required. The decision makers will have to *judge* the problem and relevant factors. With such problems, the decision makers, given their lack of insight into the problem, fall back on their judgemental abilities.
3. If those involved have a clear insight into the problem, but have differing goals, then a *compromise* will be required. This *compromise strategy* will involve negotiations, during which all the parties, depending on their negotiating abilities, will have to shift their positions to a certain extent.
4. When there is no insight into the problem and no agreement on the preferences or goals, a solution can only be attained by *inspiration*. First and foremost, the *inspirational strategy* assumes that there is a belief and trust in someone's vision. This way of approach assumes that the solution is found in the confidence each of the involved decision makers has in a particular approach inasmuch as everyone is inspired to see that the approach is implemented successfully. In such a situation, the *charisma* of the management is of decisive importance.

It is not only the interests and goals of the department or organization of the decision maker that are of importance in the decision-making process, but also those of other decision makers in other departments and/or organizations. A number of different approaches can be distinguished depending on the relative importance attached to personal preferences or goals over those of others. These will be covered in Chapter 9 when we discuss negotiations and the resolution of conflict.

Exhibit 4.2

Competitive intelligence pays off

Do your homework. It's amazing how many companies don't. Lazy, complacent, or simply unaware, thousands of corporate executives routinely make critical business decisions – from whether to build a plant to whether to start producing a new product – based on incomplete information about the competition. What they should be doing is systematically gathering 'competitive intelligence'. Best guesses are that only 10% of all companies in the US do so today. Although multinationals are better at it overseas.

Competitive intelligence isn't industrial espionage, and while it may sound cloak-and-dagger, it isn't. Competitive intelligence (CI) is, quite simply, the gathering of every bit of legally obtainable information that will help a company do better than its rivals. More than anything else, it requires persistence and ingenuity. Depending on your business, the sources of useful information can be both unusual and bountiful. Some corporations, such as Monsanto and Eastman Kodak, have formalized this process through CI departments, and not a few have even employed former Central Intelligence Agency analysts to conduct competitive intelligence.

Outside the US, of course, tough players have long pursued every avenue – sometimes illegal – in their attempt to outsmart the competition. In the US, industrial espionage and theft are crimes that now carry heavy penalties, and rightly so. But if executives at American companies were more assiduous about legally ferreting out intelligence on their competitors – information that very likely is right before their noses, on the Web or in obscure uniform commercial code filings, for instance – they'd go a long way toward putting their companies on a stronger footing globally. They'd be more efficient in their spending and investing. Ultimately, consumers would profit, too.

Source: *Business Week*, 28 October 1996.

4.5 ● THE CREATIVE AND LEARNING ORGANIZATION

An organization which is not capable of tapping creative resources will slowly be eliminated from the market by its competitors who either manufacture better products at lower costs, or who employ managers with more imaginative power and more of an eye for alternative solutions.

When creativity results in new inventions, an organization needs to devote time and resources to processing and co-ordinating its introduction. Often, products are indeed improved and adjusted, but it is rare for new goals to be formulated. However, an organization which wants to stay healthy and productive and to continuously adapt itself to the changing needs of society, will have to use all its creative power and learn from experience, in particular from its past 'mistakes'. This involves the creativity and learning abilities of employees, managers and the organization as a whole. It is important for managers to set a good example by being creative themselves, while encouraging creativity, learning behaviour and learning abilities in all areas of the organization. Only in this way, can the organization gain the optimum from its employees.

Training in techniques which stimulate creativity is very important (*see* section 4.4.1). However, very few organizations have permanent programmes which aim to expand the creative abilities and the learning behaviour of all employees. Employees often think of valuable ideas, but these are rarely acted upon. Many employees who have good ideas, lack the authority or the responsibility to implement them. In many case, such ideas are not even made known.

It is important to set up systems so that valuable ideas can be picked up and put into practice – not an easy task. Creative thinking is rather unstructured, undisciplined and often does not seem logical. However, it is the basis for the generation of the new ideas the organization needs. It is often the case, however, that the creative ideas affect the 'status quo'. This creates resistance from those who do not endorse or appreciate the importance of such ideas. The ultimate goal of creative thinking and of learning is to discover and put into practice something which the organization does not currently possess and which will enable the organization to function better.

4.5.1 The creative organization: some characteristics

What is the difference between a creative organization and an organization which works under creative management? An organization can be an effective instrument for the implementation of ideas and yet not be creative itself – for example, an orchestra which is conducted by a creative conductor, a firm managed by a creative director.

At this point, it is important to identify the specific characteristics which contribute to the creativity of an organization. We can start by considering the overall image of an organization. When the organization has an outstanding name in the field of growth, product development, renewal and problem solution, it can create the image of a very creative institution. Whether this overall image is the product of the influence of a few individuals or, alternatively, is the result of the creative contribution of all, or most of the members of the organization, does not seem to be relevant: the organization is generally seen to be creative. The characteristics of creativity, as they apply both to individuals and to the organization are described below.

The creative individual:

- can quickly produce a large number of ideas;
- is original;

- has unusual ideas;
- looks at ideas based on their merits, not on their origin;
- is motivated by the problem itself (follows it, wherever it may lead);
- postpones personal judgement, avoids premature acceptance of a solution;
- spends a lot of time on analysis and explanation;
- is not high-handed/authoritarian;
- is flexible;
- accepts own impulses;
- often investigates without too much discipline;
- is independent in personal judgements;
- is a non-conformist;
- often deviates from established ideas;
- sees him- or herself as being different;
- has a rich and fanciful fantasy and a clear insight into reality.

The creative organization:

- has human ideas;
- has open communication channels;
- encourages contacts with resources outside the environment;
- employs different types of persons;
- lets non-specialists help in the solving of problems;
- allows eccentricity;
- has an objective, factually based approach;
- evaluates ideas on their merits, not on the status of their creator;
- selects ideas on their merits;
- does not show short-term satisfaction with the financial and material aspects of the present products and policy;
- invests in basic research;
- has flexible planning in the long term;
- experiments with new ideas and does not judge these in advance based on rational grounds;
- gives everything a chance;
- is more decentralized;
- allows time and resources for mistakes;
- tolerates and expects the taking of risks;
- has employees who have high job satisfaction and the freedom to discuss ideas, choose problems and work on them;
- is autonomous and independent;
- has original goals;
- does not encourage the belief that the leader should always be followed, no matter what;
- finds enough certainty in fixed rules;
- provides groups with the opportunity to generate and evaluate ideas.

From this comparison, we can conclude that creativity in the organization is not necessarily dependent on having very creative employees. In principle, creativity is spread out among all company personnel. That is why it is not important to recruit a large number of very creative people. It is important, however, for the organization to be structured in such a way that everybody's input is shown to full advantage. This can only be done when there is a climate which does not suppress or smother originality. A creative management is essential. Even the most creative individuals become helpless in an environment which is indifferent or hostile to new ideas.

There are a number of features which can negatively influence creative thinking in an organization:

- Extreme structuring and formal planning result in barriers being raised between the functional units of an organization.
- Individual responsibilities in the work situation are seldom based on the particular talents of the personnel working there. The task has been structured in the past; the person has to adjust to that. This means that work units are being formalized into fixed positions.
- The work is controlled by a hierarchical authority structure. Even with appropriate co-ordination such an authority structure can result in a number of negative consequences.
- The communication pattern is determined according to the characteristics of the formal organization and not according to the demands of the task. A good communication process plays a key role in stimulating the initiative.

In these situations, a clearer separation of fields of authority is required; as a result the 'barriers' between the functions become even more difficult to overcome, especially with regard to initiative and co-ordination.

Promotion of creativity in organizations

All members of the organization should be encouraged to use their creative abilities, regardless of function or status. Not everyone will determine the goals of the organization, but they do have to think about how these are reached. Managers should be called upon to be creative in any decisions regarding the organization's function especially with regard to the setting up of innovations.

The creation of an 'open atmosphere' is dependent on conditions such as:

- *The centralization of activities directed at innovation*. This could involve, for example, the formation of a core group whose function is to actively encourage creativity.
- *The selection of generalists*. Specialists will be hindered by their tendency to relate their own abilities and experiences to problems in other fields.
- *Access to support services*. The availability of all necessary information is crucial.
- *The breaking down of barriers*. The effects of authority, status and specialities and other forms of behaviour which erect barriers should be minimized.
- *Minimization of interlinks*. Interlinks in terms of interlinking positions/functions often function as buffers between groups.
- *The encouragement of innovations*. In organizations which are not innovation-oriented, there is often resistance to change.

These conditions relate to the structure of an organization. Creativity can also be encouraged by taking into account the following considerations:

1. All employees should be encouraged to observe the principles of creative thinking, and to train themselves in the skills involved. For example:
   - Be wary of conditions which inhibit creative thinking.
   - Be flexible.
   - Hold back before criticising.
   - Allow thoughts to run free.
2. Managers should strive to create a climate in which creativity can thrive, for example:
   - by showing respect for unusual questions;
   - by showing respect for unusual ideas;
   - by showing employees that their ideas are valued.

4.5.2 Learning and the learning organization

The essence of an organization is in its people, not in its systems and procedures.

Organizations make mistakes; the important question is whether they learn from them. This obviously depends on the attitudes of the people who work there. The *learning organization* is much more than just a collection of 'learning individuals', however. It involves both individual learning and the learning of the organization – that is, the transfer and integration of knowledge between individuals, groups and the organization. As a result, a structure of individual and collective learning is created.

The experimental learning model

According to Lewin (1957) (and later Kolb (1984) and Kim (1993)) a human being follows a particular cycle of learning:

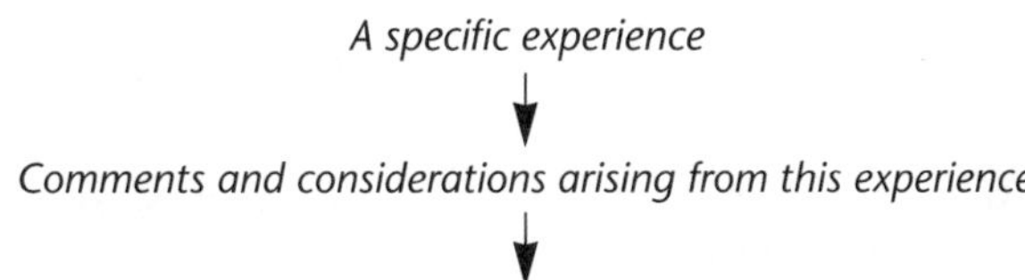

Formation of abstract notions based on the comments and generalizations of these comments

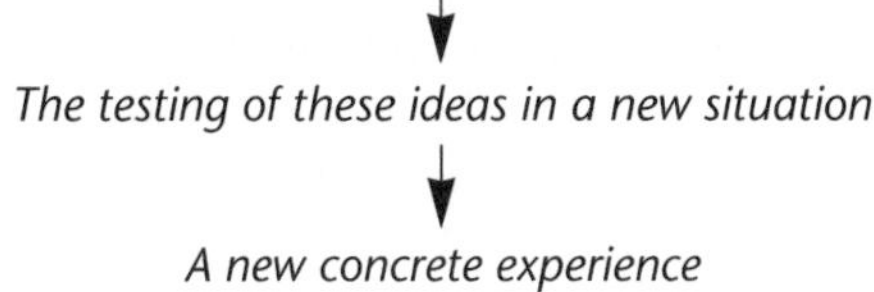

This basic cycle emerges in different contexts, both in the private and in the work environment. It can be expressed as:

observing – judging – designing – applying

and as such resembles the activities in an organization. In the OJDA-cycle (*see* Fig 4.8), people have a specific experience and they actively observe the events in relation to that. Next, they evaluate that experience – either consciously or unconsciously – by thinking about what they have observed. Next, they design a concept which supports this evaluation and test this by implementing it specifically. This then leads to a new specific experience and the cycle starts all over again.

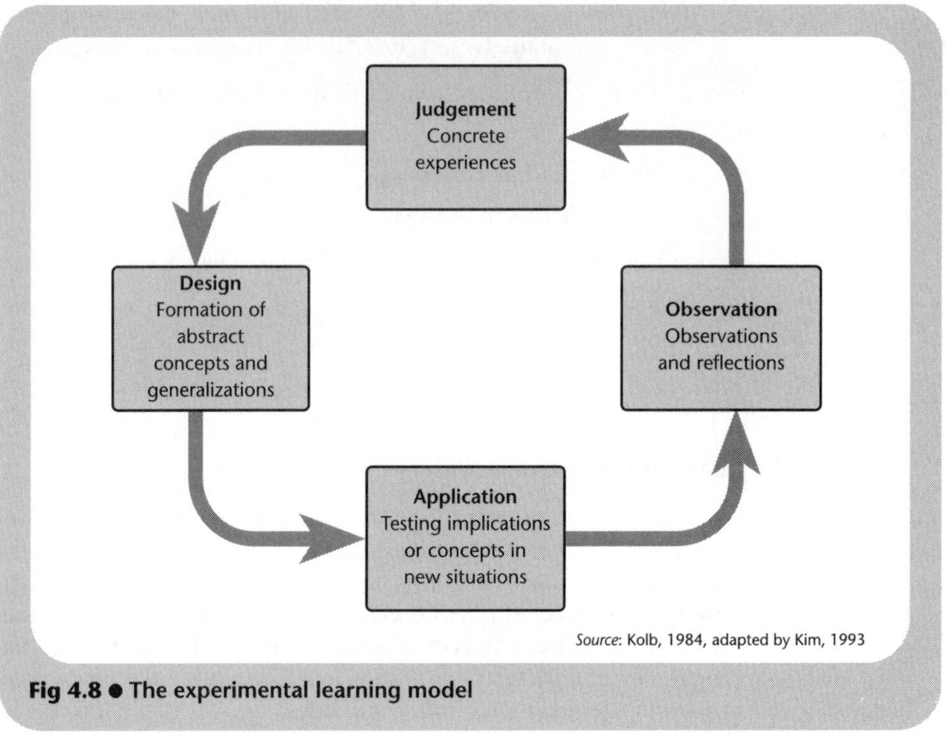

Fig 4.8 ● The experimental learning model

The operational and conceptual levels of learning

'Learning' can be described as the *enhancing of the ability to act effectively*. Learning as a concept has two components:

- *the acquiring of abilities or directly applicable knowledge* – that is a physical ability to act; and
- *the acquiring of rational knowledge* – that is, the ability to understand the reasons for an experience.

In this context there is a link between thinking and doing. Both parts of the definition are of importance: acquiring the knowledge of how something needs to be done on the one hand, and understanding and applying this knowledge on the other. These two components of learning can be expressed as *operational* and *conceptual learning*.

The role of memory

In the experimental learning model, no explicit attention is given to the memory, and yet the memory plays such a key role in the learning process. When considering the role of the memory, however, it is important to consider conceptual and operational learning separately.

In learning psychology, a distinction is made between learning and memorizing. Learning has to do with gathering knowledge, while memorizing has to do with storing that which has been gathered. In theory, these two activities can easily be presented as being separate, but in practice this is more difficult, due to the fact that what someone learns depends on what that person already knows and vice versa. The memory is assumed to be a form of storage room in which everything we observe and experience is neatly stored. In this context, however, it is important to distinguish two issues; on the one hand, stored knowledge – like soccer results, and similar trivial details – and on the other hand, the 'active' memory structures which influence the learning process.

These active structures in the learning process can be explained using the concept of mental models or mindsets. A mental model is an image of the world anchored deep within the individual personality which offers a basis for the interpretation of reality and, as a result, exercises a great influence over actions. In this way, the *mental model* is a form of basic code for decisions with regard to new information – what is being gathered, what is being stored and what is not, what is being used and what is being kept or 'erased'.

Furthermore, mental models are also responsible for programming that basic code. They have the conceptual ability to decide which code should receive priority in a specific situation. Mental models can have a limiting effect in that a person only sees what is understandable within the boundaries of the existing code.

Frameworks, routines and learning

Operational and conceptual learning are related to different parts of the individual mental model (IMM). *Operational learning* is enacted at the procedural level in the learning of the different steps which are necessary in order to complete a specific task. This might involve learning how to control certain routines such as filling out a form, operating a machine or handling a switch panel. *Conceptual learning* asks questions. Why is a particular procedure being carried out? Do I see what I think I see? The nature and existence of the prevailing situation, procedures and notions are being questioned. New interpretation frameworks can arise within the individual mental model (IMM) as a result, which in turn can lead to improvements due to the fact that the problem is being viewed in a totally new framework (*see* Fig 4.9).

For example ...

...consider the journey of John Smith when returning home from work by car in the evening. He knows several routes home. Based on his experience of what a 'good' route is, he chooses one. These ideas will depend on specific systems and frameworks within which the choice arises – for example, the route with the fewest traffic lights or the route with the best view. As soon as the choice is made, John will drive the same route every day. A routine is born, which is implemented as soon as he gets in the car after work in order to drive home. He can turn on automatic pilot, so to speak, in order to drive home. However, if the normal route is blocked by roadworks or there is a traffic jam on a regular basis, then John will consider again the criteria for a 'good' route and may choose a new route. This illustrates our model for individual learning: a cycle of conceptual and operational learning, which supplies information for mental models and also derives information from them.

The learning of the organization cannot simply be seen as individual learning on a more extended scale. When we move from the learning of one person to the learning of a large collection of individuals, there is a disproportionate increase in the complexity and dynamics of the process involving elements such as motivation and rewarding. Learning is still learning, of course, but the process is fundamentally different at the level of the organization. We have to accept the fact that a non-human unit – that is, the organization – has intellectual capacities and can learn.

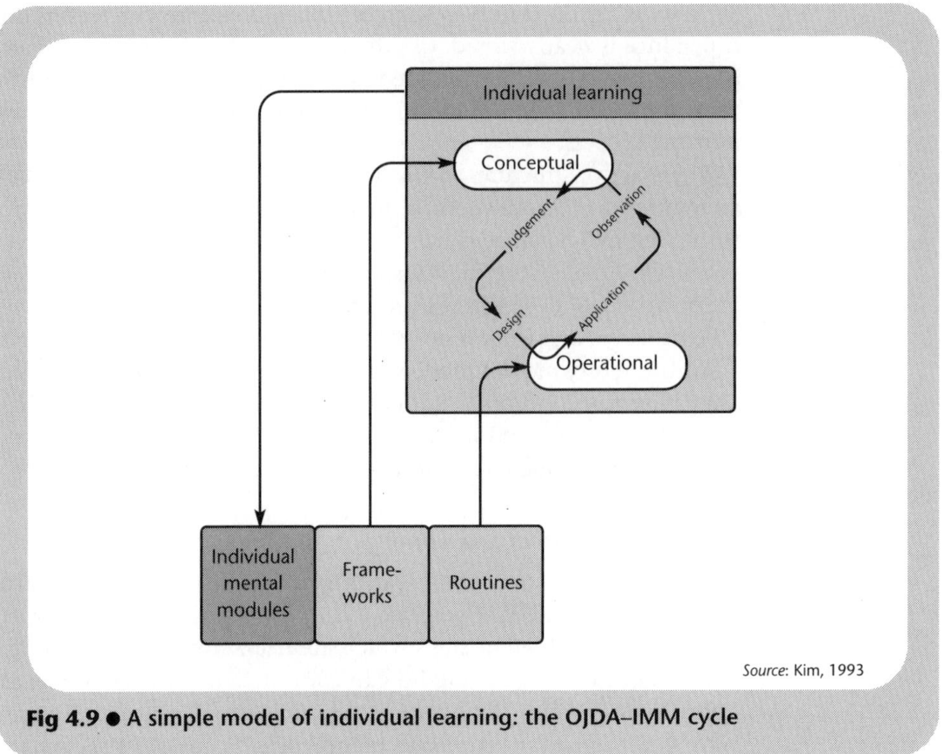

Source: Kim, 1993

Fig 4.9 ● A simple model of individual learning: the OJDA–IMM cycle

A model of organizational learning can help to clarify this. Such a model should also take into account the transfer of learned knowledge and the storing of knowledge and experience in the organization, as well as the possible fields of tension between individuals and the organization. It should also be acknowledged that an organization loses learning capacity/knowledge when specific people leave the organization.

This integrated model of the 'learning organization' uniting all the elements in a coherent scheme is referred to as the *OJDA–CMM cycle* (observing, judging, designing, applying – common mental models) (*see* Fig 4.10). The model is directed at the transfer of learned knowledge by means of and exchange of *individual common* and *shared mental models*. The definition of learning by the organization is therefore a variation on the definition of individual learning, that is, *the enhancing of the ability of an organization to act effectively*.

How strong the link between individual mental models and common mental models is depends on the way in which influence is exercised by a group or a specific member of the organization. The chief executive or the management team have influence because of the power which is inherent in their position. An autonomous group of people who work on an hourly basis can exercise influence simply by its size.

The 'world picture'

Mental models are not simply places of storage for data picked up by the senses. They play an active role because they contribute to the 'image forming' which is based on experiences. Every mental model forms a collection of data, which prescribes a point of view or a procedure. Conceptual learning leads to changes in the framework which result in a new image of the world. Operational learning yields new routines which replace the old ones. The changed mental models not only contain the new frameworks and routines, but also the 'science' of how these routines can be fitted into the new framework. These eventually become a part of the world picture itself, of the culture of the organization. The way in which the organization sees the world undergoes a gradual change, so, in time, the way of thinking of the members of the organization will more or less fit into that.

The 'world picture' is also a reflection of the organizational culture, the basic premise of the organization, material issues and explicit behavioural rules. All these factors can have a positive or a negative effect on the decision-making process, due to the continuous incidence of unexpected, non-routine events. Standard procedures, on the other hand, will involve aspects such as the marketing plan to launch a new product, payment procedures for suppliers, evaluation criteria for employees and the conditions of employment for new personnel. These are all ready for use. In this way, an organization can cope with recurring problems in a predictable manner.

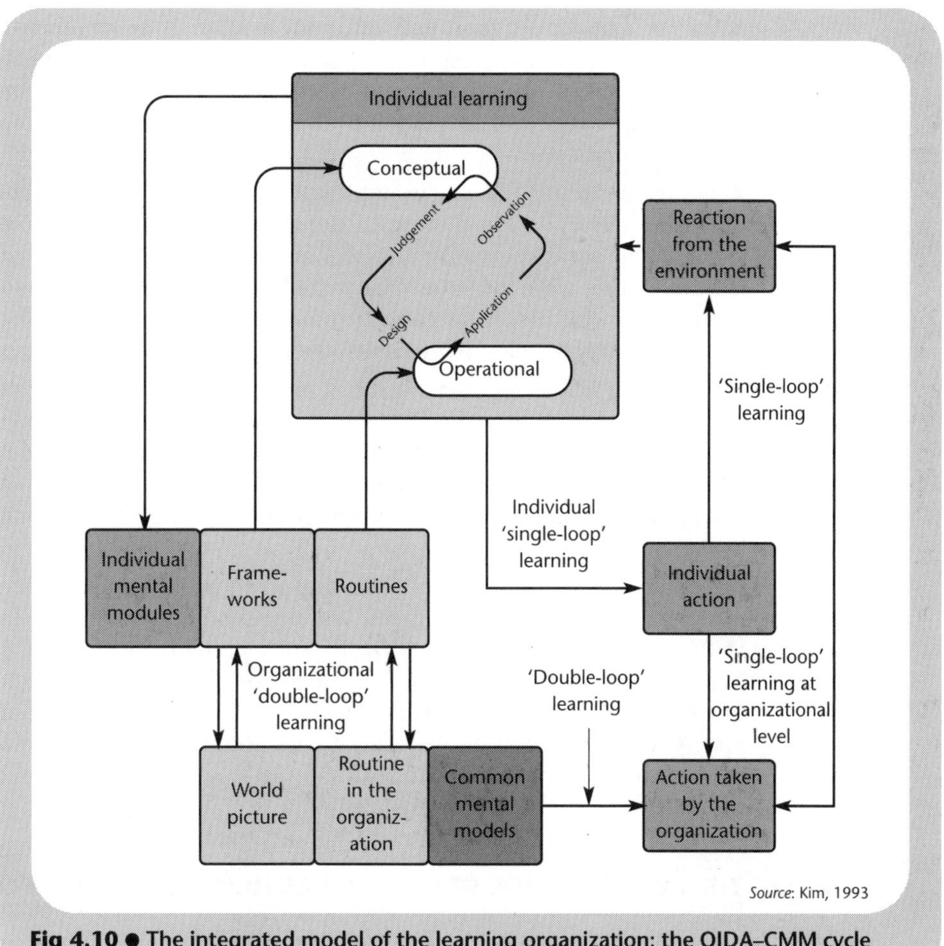

Fig 4.10 ● The integrated model of the learning organization: the OJDA–CMM cycle

'Single-loop' and 'double-loop' learning

The OJDA–CMM model involves the concepts of 'single-loop' and 'double-loop' learning, at both an individual and an organizational level. Single-loop learning is when one activity leads on to another actively and there is no direct feedback from the second activity to the first. Double-loop learning concerns a set of implicit assumptions and norms deeply rooted in the organization and presumed incapable of change. This learning with a double link – the 'double loop' – is depicted in Fig 4.10 in the form of a process in which individual learning influences individual mental models, which in turn have consequences for future learning.

Double-loop learning occurs in an organization when individual mental models become part of the organization via common mental models, which in turn influence the actions of the organization. In both cases, learning with a double loop creates important opportunities for improvements in that it provides a new framework for a known problem which can open up a totally new direction for solutions.

A 'learning organization' is one that operates according to this model as a whole. If such procedures are not in place, then the organization learns 'only' in an *ad hoc, dissipated* or *opportunistic* manner.

- *Ad hoc learning.* A good example of this is crisis management. Each problem is solved when it arises, but what is learned from the experience is not transferred to the next problem. The opposite of this is *quality improvement* in which situational learning is kept to a minimum by the systematic collecting of data, analysis and standardization.
- *Dissipated learning.* Classic examples of dissipated learning are provided by universities. Professors within their walls can be the world's leading experts in the fields of management, finance, operations and marketing, but the universities cannot employ that eminent knowledge in order to manage their own organization. Organizations with highly decentralized management structures, which do not offer the opportunity to build up internal networks, suffer from the same problem.
- *Opportunistic learning.* Organizations sometimes try to deliberately bypass their own standard procedures, because the normal course of working is becoming obstructive. Such an organization needs to break the link between common mental models and action – for example, to be able to take advantage of a once-in-a-lifetime opportunity. Waiting for the organization to undergo the necessary changes would take much too long.

Opportunistic learning occurs in an organization as a consequence of actions of one person or a small group of persons, and not as a result of the common mental models of the organization – that is, its values, culture, myths or standard procedures. A good example of opportunistic learning is the use of separate work units in the development of the IBM PC. IBM bypassed the overall bureaucratic structure and formed a completely separate, very dedicated team to develop the PC. Indeed, this was accomplished in a relatively short period of time.

4.6 THE ROLE OF WORK GROUPS IN PARTICIPATION AND DECISION MAKING

Within an organization, consultation, deliberation and participation take place in work groups. These are appointed as project groups (temporary), task forces or as committees (permanent) at all levels of the organization. Work and consultation groups are created in order to bring together expertise and information in the analysis of problems and the development of solutions and thus *improve the quality of the decision making*. Furthermore, such groups offer the opportunity for participation in decision making, as a result of which, *the basis of decisions is extended and their acceptance stimulated.*

The tasks of such groups vary – for example, innovation, automation, organizational changes, personnel policy, long-term planning. The problems will involve different types of decisions. The groups may be referred to as 'higher' or 'lower' depending on whether the decisions taken are strategic, organizational or operational. The nature of the assignment will also determine whether the groups have an *advisory, co-ordinating* or even *executive authority*.

It is important to choose the members of consultation and work groups with care. A good result is dependent on the necessary information and expertise being present in sufficient quantities. Attention must therefore be paid to the information and expertise of individual members. In addition, it is important to assign authority within the groups clearly and satisfactorily. When different levels and different departments are represented in a team, the members have to be given the mandate to address the relevant issue if a meaningful contribution is to be made. The team has to be able to make decisions or make recommendations.

The *will* and the *capacity to co-operate* are key factors in the successful functioning of a group. The interest of individual departments and individual job requirements should be of secondary importance in that joint decisions or recommendations should be directed at a higher common goal. It is therefore important when choosing members of consultation groups or teams to pay attention to the individual's co-operation capacities.

It is also crucial that members of work and consultation groups – whether they are representative or expert – are accepted by the rest of the work force, because only then can they exercise influence on the making of decisions and their eventual acceptance and implementation.

4.6.1 Higher-level teams and participative decision making

Higher consultation groups contribute at the level of strategic and organizational decisions. They are concerned with complex problems which can only be solved on the basis of a large amount of information and investigation. For example, a director can be supported by a *permanent* 'committee of long-term planning' which is composed of heads of departments, if necessary supplemented by an external consultant. In addition, a *temporary* task force can be set up to consider decisions concerning product innovation. Such a group would draw up innovation proposals in the framework of the production policy. However, these would also have to be comprehensible to the top management and directors.

In the case of organizational change, participation can also be carried out by the formation of a team. For example, an 'automation steering committee' can be commissioned to set up a new information system or a 'quality team' can address the question of how to make the organization more market-, customer-, and quality-oriented.

4.6.2 Lower level teams and participative decision making

Lower working and consultation groups contribute to operational decisions made at lower levels in the organization. Operational decisions regard the fixing of implementation plans and operational norms – for example, for productivity or sales.

Lower working groups can be set up in order to implement – either partially or fully – the guidelines determined by a 'higher' policy group – for example, in the field of product innovation or automation. Such an operations-directed group can be composed of representatives from the marketing, research and development and production functions.

4.7 THE USE OF EXTERNAL CONSULTANTS

A manager often seeks the advice of an external consultant either when a specific, clearly defined problem needs to be addressed, or when there is a vague feeling that problems exist but they have not yet been identified. Although it is usually the task of management to solve the problems by themselves, they may conclude that problems cannot or will not be solved without external help for some reason. For example:

- The management may not be able to solve the problem because it is *too difficult* or *too time consuming*. Management may wish to take advantage of the consultant's knowledge of the problem and solution possibilities and alternatives based on previous experience. Management may have the ability to solve the problem, but not the time, because of other (more important) activities. The time of the consultant is used instead.
- Management may want a *complete* and *objective* investigation, so the real cause of the problems is brought to light and explained. The *wider view* of the problem at hand is more likely to be supplied by an external consultant than by the organization itself, because the consultant is not involved in the daily course of events which can lead to a certain *narrowing of view*. *Objectivity* is also more difficult if an organization carries out its own internal investigations.
- The *acceptance* of the problem solution by the organization can prove difficult when the problems are solved internally and there are conflicting ideas within the organization. The hiring of an independent consultant overcomes this difficulty.
- The client may not know the *problem*, but can detect the symptoms. The issue is not so much the difficulty of the problem as the ignorance of or unfamiliarity with the problem.
- The client may require *information* which it cannot produce itself. This may involve knowledge of the sector and market data which a consultancy firm with specific knowledge of the sector can supply.
- The client may require a *second opinion* to confirm or reject a point of view. External consultants see things differently from the client as they do not suffer the consequences of 'company blindness'. Such a second opinion often indicates a very radical plan. Such a study would often be commissioned by the board of directors and/or the works council of an organization.
- The client may wish to use the consultant as an *instrument of power* in the solving of problems – that is, the consultant is hired for *organizational–political* reasons. The power of the consultant is often determined by the *influence* exercised by the use of his or her skills. Internal resistance to solutions can only be overcome in some cases once an 'independent person' has considered them. The consultant may only be used to 'deliver' a message which is found to be very tedious by certain members of the organization, or to express a message in different words. Management consultants

have justifiable difficulty with such commissions. Usually, they clearly insist on determining the message (or solution) themselves. In principle, the consultant will not accept an engagement purely on a 'ritual' basis within an internal 'political' game.

- The client may wish to use the consultant to bring a problem to the attention of his or her own organization or the supervisory bodies (for example, board of directors). The consultant should not object to such assignments as they are aware that their advice carries more weight in some situations than that of the management itself.
- The client may not dare or want to take *responsibility*. The management abdicates, or at least appears to abdicate responsibility for a potential risky solution. It may be difficult to find a consultant who is willing to adopt the manager's ideas. If the solution succeeds, the manager can still take the glory; if the solution fails, then the consultant can be blamed. Such commissions usually involve the malfunctioning of 'important members of the organization' and dismissals may form part of the possible solutions.
- A *financier* may seek assurance for debt or credit extension via an independent judgement. The client can use the engagement of a consultant to impress a financier.
- The client may want to *win time* in the process of making a particular decision or may want to *lose* so much time that he or she does not have to implement the measures after all. In both cases, the client is only using the time of the consultant, not the work itself. A self-respecting consultant – if aware of the client's intention – would not be quick to accept such an assignment.
- The client may only want a general, sometime periodic check, or a general *orientation* in relation to the future.
- In certain situations – for example, in case of the sudden departure or death of a manager – the management consultant is asked to support the management in the short term or to fill in temporarily. In some cases, the assignment involves '*turnaround management*' – that is, within a relatively short period of time, through the implementation of all sorts of (often unpopular) measures, moving the organization out of the red or curbing negative developments. The roles of an interim manager and turnaround manager are both at the edge of or even outside the normal professional field of consultants. By becoming part of the organization, they cease to be independent and objective.

SUMMARY

- Decision making is often referred to as the central task of management.
- Decisions, in fact, are the result of a process which begins the moment the information which highlights the problem becomes available, and lasts until a chosen solution is implemented.
- This process involves four steps or phases: identification of the problem; development of alternatives; selection and finally the decision regarding which of the alternatives is the best or optimal one.

continued overleaf

- This process of decision making is influenced by many different factors – for example, the structure of the organization, the quality of the communication and the motivation, involvement and commitment of the members of the organization.
- Once the decision has been made, it is important to proceed carefully and to draw up an initial plan. A number of steps are involved, from words or policy decisions to deeds and specific actions. (Planning and different kinds of plans for different parts of an organization are covered in more detail in Chapter 10.)
- Furthermore, decision making involves 'learning', both by individuals and by organizations, via the observing-judging-designing-applying cycle. Two levels of learning can be distinguished: operational and conceptual learning.
- When organizations are striving for continuity and effectiveness, decisions are based on experiences and expected future experiences.
- Constant change means that on occasions it is necessary to adjust the 'world picture', both of the individual and of the organization, if continuity and effectiveness are to be maintained.

DISCUSSION QUESTIONS

1. In *Management in action* at the beginning of this chapter, Unilever investigated and adjusted the 'systems'. Does this mean Unilever can be described as a 'learning organization'?
2. Is it really necessary in practice to go through all the phases of the decision-making process?
3. 'When everyone in a department has to participate, it costs too much time. It is better if the department manager makes the decision because that's a lot faster.' Discuss this statement.
4. How do the formula E = f(quality × acceptance) and the statement in Question 3 relate to each other?
5. Is there a relation between 'lateral thinking' and 'conceptual learning'?
6. (a) How is it possible that the chairman of Mogren AB (in Exhibit 4.1) can be deluged with information, but is still unable to see what is going wrong?

   (b) How would you advise Mr Bertil Nilsson regarding his reporting system?

Management case study

Decision making and co-operation in a public sector organization

Decision-making processes have to be efficiently and effectively structured. The decisions should be taken at the level at which the necessary information is present, avoiding the unnecessary burdening of other hierarchical levels. In many cases this means that decision making results from informal consultation and deliberation between individuals and departments.

In an institution working in the field of social security, there was a total absence of co-operation between the different departments. The large operational executive department followed its own course; if it required something from the supporting units, this had to be supplied immediately and in accordance with the wishes of the executive department. The support units were very much pre-occupied with maintaining the boundaries of their responsibility and with defending their own interests. Irritation and disagreements between the departments were the result. These cultures were obviously in conflict with one another.

A year earlier, the structure of the organization had been changed and the 'new' structure, in principle, offered a sound basis for co-operation. At the time of the structural change, however, no attention was paid to the required changes in culture and behaviour. When the new director of the organization assigned a temporary manager the task of completing the structural change by introducing procedures for control and the supply of information in the organization, it was decided, after investigation, that certain behavioural changes were required in the project to be implemented. This meant that the project was extended and time was allocated to looking at ways in which desired behaviour could be achieved.

The temporary manager employed a strategy which involved the setting of examples in relationship to a number of areas of desired behavioural change. One of these areas was the co-operation between the departments. A conscious decision was taken that the project group and a number of work groups were to be composed of employees from different departments. During the project, intense co-operation was actively encouraged and the positive results of that co-operation were strongly emphasized.

To reinforce this effect, the responsibility for the making of decisions was, wherever possible, placed with the work groups. In that way, the organization, through the relatively straightforward environment of the project, could familiarize itself with joint decision making at the right level.

In the initial phase of the project, the temporary manager was quite often asked to make a decision about a problem within the working group. Invariably, this manager made sure that the necessary information was present at the level of the work group and then motivated and forced the work group members to take the decisions themselves. Before long, this was no longer necessary, as this form of decision making was adopted first by the work group and then by the rest of the organization.

Source: Adapted from *Bedrijfskundig Vakblad*, December 1993.

CASE QUESTIONS

1. Why was the composition of the project group and the work group so important in this case?
2. Which factors in the initial situation prevented good decision making?
3. Can the organization in this case be referred to as a 'learning organization'?

Chapter 5

Strategy formulation and strategic management

LEARNING OBJECTIVES

After studying this chapter, you should be able to:

- explain the concepts of strategy and strategic management;
- identify the different steps in the process of strategy formulation;
- discuss important issues in the field of strategy formulation;
- understand how strategy formulation takes place and which methods and techniques are used to determine policy;
- indicate the problems which can arise during the implementation of a strategy;
- describe the measures that can enhance the effect of planned actions;
- appreciate that strategy can also be 'discovered'.

Management in action

The MEXX formula for future success

Competition in the clothing industry relies more and more on the different shop formulae rather than the individual brands. MEXX established itself as a strong brand in a short period of time and is working to maintain its position. This is why emphasis is now being put on distribution. The company has engaged in a strategic alliance with three of its direct competitors in order to do battle with the large chains which dominate the clothing industry.

From its humble beginnings in the 1970s, MEXX has grown in the space of 20 years into a multinational company making and distributing clothes for young men and women between 20 and 30 years of age and children from birth to 14 years of age.

MEXX is a successful clothing brand with a substantial reputation. The brand awareness of MEXX among women between 15 and 24 years of age is 80 per cent – a major achievement in a line of business which is highly competitive and where brands are continuously coming and going. The success is even more remarkable given that MEXX is aimed at young people, who are known to experiment a great deal and to switch relatively easily from one brand to another.

The key to the success of MEXX is without doubt the fact that the company was the first clothes manufacturer to bring a complete line to the market. A second factor is the price/performance ratio. MEXX has succeeded in providing affordable quality and keeping up to date with the latest fashions.

The collection is clearly split into three sub-collections:

- the real fashion articles for those who want to be dressed according to the latest fashion;
- the mildly fashionable basic articles ('essentials'), like simple trousers and sweaters';
- a line of 'co-ordinates' – styles which fit together within a theme.

Last, but not least, a consistent marketing communication policy contributed to the success of MEXX. The common thread and main themes of all marketing communication is 'cheerfulness'. In contrast, ads of competitor Benetton in recent years have been confrontational rather than cheerful.

Flighty consumer behaviour

In spite of the totally different communicative approaches of brands like MEXX and Benetton, the average young woman can hardly distinguish between brands like MEXX, Benetton, Esprit and In Wear. In the eyes of the industry experts, Esprit distinguishes itself by more 'basic' and timeless clothing and carries fewer fashionable clothes. MEXX is more fashionable and has more daring items of clothing than Esprit. In Wear is more classic and at a slightly higher price level.

Of course, there are some customers who are fervent MEXX and dress themselves completely in that brand; this does not apply to the majority of customers, however. Eight out of ten young women combine articles from MEXX, with those from In Wear and Esprit.

continued overleaf

Management in action continued

Controlled distribution

One person may buy a pair of MEXX trousers because of their special design; another may buy a pair of Esprit trousers because they fit well and they will go with practically everything. The ultimate decision is very unpredictable. According to M Miel Le Coultre, MEXX Marketing Manager for Northern Europe:

> *The value of brands in the clothing business is higher than you think, based on this unpredictable purchasing behaviour. A known brand gives the security that one is dressed according to the latest fashion. With unknown brands you just have to wait and see. The brand is also a guarantee of quality and indicates something about a certain style. One knows the style of a specific brand.*

Two out of three MEXX customers are women. Given that women are known to combine different brands into one 'outfit' and to buy 'impulsively', the presence in the store is very important. According to Miel Le Coultre: 'In recent years, especially with regard to the presence on the shop floor, a strong brand is an important condition of success.'

The most important goal of MEXX is, therefore, a growth in revenue through controlled distribution. In the coming years, strategy is directed at distribution. MEXX clothing is at the moment distributed via some 9000 speciality clothing stores, which use at least a fifth of the total available store space for the MEXX line. This is not an ideal situation because the independent retail trade is confronted with a high level of change in the clothing retail trade and consumer behaviour. MEXX is threatening to fall behind large chains like Amici and Mac & Maggie as a result, because companies, in contrast to the independent retail trade, in general have a vision of the future.

Competitive field

Working with the many small speciality clothing businesses is not easy. MEXX deals with independent entrepreneurs who accept little interference with their commercial approach. This is in conflict with the desires of MEXX to be able to control its own brand. To guarantee future success, a brand article manufacturer must have the space on the shop floor to make use of different marketing instruments.

According to Miel Le Coultre, there is a further important development:

> *We have a saying: There are wars and there are battles. The issue is to win the war and not the battles. Whether Barcelona or AC Milan wins is not the issue; the issue is whether soccer wins over tennis or another sport. In the clothing business, the issue is less and less the battle between the brands like MEXX and Esprit, but is rather the battle between the 'brand store' on the one hand, and the large chains such as Hennes & Mauritz, Claudia Strater and Amici on the other.*

On this basis, MEXX is going to consolidate its grip on distribution in the coming three years by developing three different franchise formulae:

- Lifestyle Store
- MEXX Youth Box and
- Euro-Concept Store.

Clear formulae

The *Lifestyle Store* is a store in which only MEXX clothes are sold to young women and men. This store formula was introduced in France in 1992 and seemed to be a success there.

With the *MEXX Youth Box*, the company is attempting to tighten its grip on the distribution of kids' clothing. The retail trade for children's clothing is not well developed, concluded Le Coultre:

> *Furthermore, there is no single major professional formula for kids' clothing in our line of business. With the MEXX Youth Box, MEXX established a clearly recognizable franchise formula for children's clothes. We also introduced fashionable articles for babies – a definite gap in the market.*

The *Euro-Concept Store* (a working name; the final name has yet to be determined) is a unique initiative in the clothing business. It is a 'multi-brand' store, in which MEXX, Esprit, In Wear, Sissy-Boy and maybe later even Benetton will be brought together in one store.

The Euro-Concept Store is a response not only to the competition of the large chains, but also to the changing wishes of the European consumers. From market research it appears that consumers who buy clothes tend to prefer larger stores with a wider range. This is why Benetton is disposing of all small stores and opening larger stores.

Miel Le Coultre is convinced of the fact that the Euro-Concept Store has a good future. If brands start operating together, efficiency will be greatly improved. The problem is finding franchisees who have sufficient financial means at their disposal. When the new formula is finalized, MEXX wants to start working with a master-franchisee per country or region. This franchisee will find suitable locations and will take care of arrangements with banks. The master-franchisee will also become the intermediary who will supply all the services for the participating brands to the other franchisees.

Ultimately, the competition between the participating brands in the Euro-Concept Store will continue to take place in the store, just as it did in the old days. That is why higher demands are made of the presentation. At a glance, the consumers should be able to see what is being offered in the store. Consumers are lazy. If they cannot find something easily, then they will leave the store within a few moments. Personnel is also important. According to Miel Le Coultre:

> *The personnel determines the success of the formula. When clients are dissatisfied, in half of the cases, it is because they have not been served or treated well. That is why we have started paying a great deal of attention to training.*

Source: Adapted from Andriesse, F.G. and Holzhauer, F.F.O. (1994) 'MEXX wants to win the battle with new formula', *Tijdschrift voor Marketing*, May, pp 9–12.

INTRODUCTION

This chapter describes how organizations balance their own internal capabilities with the demands of the external environment. The way in which an organization sets its course can be either systematic or intuitive. Strategy can develop more or less according to plan, or it can emerge from actions which the organization undertakes.

Strategic formulation involves a systematic, step-by-step approach to strategy development. *Strategic management* also involves a consideration of how skills and capabilities can be maintained and developed as part of that strategy. We will also cover the resistance which can confront strategic innovations in some organizations.

Every organization – whether it is a shoe factory or a library – is subject to many kinds of environmental forces. Management needs to recognize the influence of these forces and to be aware of what is going on in the external environment. A major rise in the prices of raw materials, the increasing scarcity of labour and the introduction of new technologies are all examples of changes to which management must react.

In Chapter 3, we discussed the influence of certain groups and environmental factors on the functioning and the survival of an organization. To survive, the management of an organization must nurture the relations between the organization and the stakeholders and situations in the 'outside world'. The process by which management gives the *external adaptation* of the organization form and content is referred to as *strategy formulation.* As such strategy formulation is directed solely at the external environment.

The duties of the management of the organization, however, go much further than strategy formulation alone. In addition to tuning into the external environment, management must also *maintain and develop the capabilities of the organization* which are necessary if strategic change is to be realized. Such a process will place certain demands on the organization – for example, the organizational structure may have to be adjusted, new knowledge may have to be developed and/or other management techniques may have to be introduced. This process is called '*strategic management*'.

Strategic management is directed both at the external environment and the internal environment. It is not only concerned with the preparation and the making of strategic choices (that is, strategy formulation), but also with the question of how those choices can be implemented (that is, planning and execution). The implementation of strategic plans can create resistance from those who have to actually execute the strategy. The identification of such resistance should be a part of the strategic formulation process.

In order to be successful in the future, most organizations will need to make choices, especially those of a strategic nature involving external developments. In this respect, organizations expect in the coming years to be increasingly choosing the weapon 'higher quality' over that of 'lower costs'. The battle continues to rage within the company functions of marketing and sales and product development.

Developments in markets and technology (*see* Chapter 3) mean that organizations are now concentrating on their core activities (the most important activities of organization) and are planning to adjust the company value-chain. For example, an increasing proportion of the manufacturing and distribution process is being outsourced, as a result, among others, of the fact that the product life cycle is becoming shorter and shorter and investments must be earned back in an ever shorter period. By contracting out more, an organization is more flexible to sudden changes in market demand and can share some of the increasingly complex problems of business activity – caused by the wider product range – with the suppliers.

In this chapter we examine how these choices arise in relation to future decision making in companies and institutions.

5.1 ● CONDITIONS FOR SUCCESS

The difference between the failure and success of an organization is often its ability (or inability) to react to the wishes of its customers and to achieve this at lower costs or higher quality than other competing organizations.

Strategy determination is the drawing up of a complex series of actions and measurements which can be implemented in order to attain the organization's goals. This is based on the (assumed) external possibilities on the one hand, and on what is feasible internally on the other – that is the organization's capabilities (what it can do) and ambitions (what it wishes to do). This tuning process is depicted in Fig 5.1.

It is obvious that this is not a straightforward, spontaneous, natural process, nor can it be left to take its own course. On the contrary, to arrive at these statements, decisions, actions and measures, a decision-making process must be set up in organizations. This is the process of *strategy formulation*. The first consideration is the handing down of a vision, a mission and objectives and a set of goals for the organization. A clear idea of management intentions is essential to this. Goals will need to develop and change in the light of external developments which are normally also visible internally in the ideas and goals of the organization members.

In spite of the gradual changes in goals, there has to be unity regarding the vision and objectives of the organization. Clarity also needs to exist concerning the methods and resources by which the objectives and goals will be realized and the constraints within which the organization will have to operate. The feasibility of what is desirable and what is possible involves constraints and opportunities regarding personnel, finance, time and other factors.

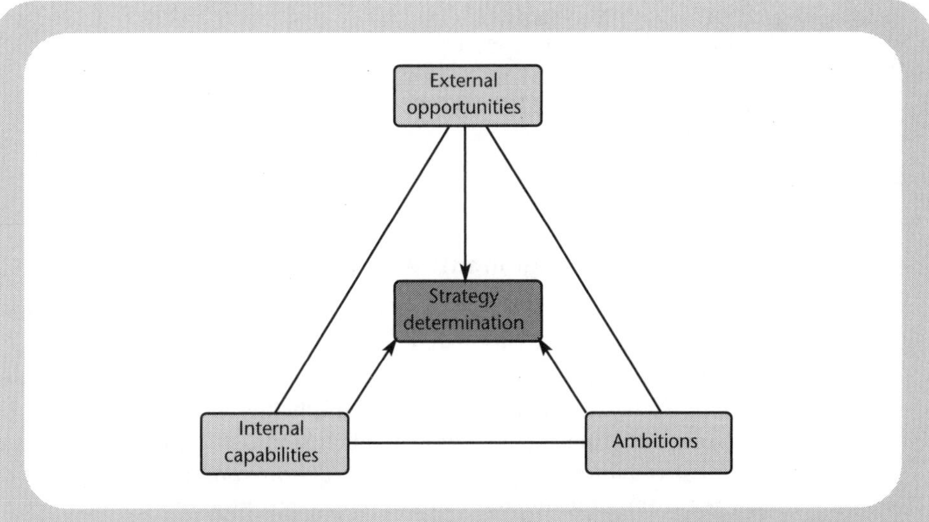

Fig 5.1 ● Strategy determination, resulting from external opportunities, internal capabilities and ambitions

Minicase 5.1

Critical success factors

Internal and external communication is the most important success factor between now and the year 2000. This is the conclusion of 600 directors and managers from Dutch trade and industry who participated in a recent research project.

The top 19 critical success factors, expressed as percentages indicating the relative degree of importance are shown in Table 5.1.

Table 5.1 ● Critical success factors in order of importance

Order	Factor	%
1	Internal and external communication	83
2	Flexibility	82
3	Clear internal mission	77
4	Control of manufacturing process	75
5	Future direction	74
6	Clear picture of the market	68
7	Welfare/well-being of personnel	68
8	Internal information supply	68
9	Education/training	65
10	Innovative capability	65
11	Entrepreneurship	64
12	Ability to change	61
13	Profitability per product	55
14	Managerial development	54
15	Strict personnel selection/recruitment	53
16	Project management	43
17	Staff turnover	43
18	Critical production scale	40
19	Back-to-core business	40

Source: Management Team, 28 November 1994.

5.1.1 Strategic management: a luxury or necessity?

As the environment becomes more dynamic, it becomes more important to pay explicit attention to strategy formulation. It becomes increasingly difficult to gain an insight intuitively into the changing forces and events which influence the organization. Under such circumstances, an implicit environment and market-oriented strategy is obviously inadequate, while explicit strategy formulation yields definite advantages to the organization. A strategy provides *direction for the activities* of the organization; they form a clearer pattern and appear to be more coherent. Co-ordination of the activities is also stimulated.

On the negative side, formulation of a strategy costs time and money which could be used in a more 'directly productive' manner. It can also be the case that once a direction has been chosen, it becomes difficult to deviate from that direction.

Intuition

Intuition is a way of thinking that involves steps which are not all taken consciously and rationally. With regard to the strategy problem, an entrepreneur would take an intuitive approach if he or she saw a gap in the market in which money could be made, and went for that gap without making any analysis of the viability of the project.

There are entrepreneurs who have become very successful with this approach. However, the intuitive approach to business strategy does have boundaries and limitations. There are also examples of entrepreneurs who enjoyed initial success, but who, in the later phases, were confronted with the consequences of not giving sufficient thought to their action in the early phases of a project.

There are two reasons why an intuitive approach cannot offer a lasting solution.

1. As the world outside the organization becomes more complex and dynamic, it becomes more difficult to form an intuitive impression of all relevant developments.
2. The increasing complexity of the activities, applied technologies and other factors within the organization make it more difficult, if not impossible, to manage an organization in an intuitive manner.

Furthermore, it is rarely possible for an intuitive proposal to be discussed with other managers. With increasing dynamics and complexity, it becomes essential for the organization to gather more and more information about its external environment and its internal workings.

Planning

In planning for the long term, there is a basic assumption that past developments will recur in the future. In an increasingly dynamic environment, however, this basic assumption is often questioned.

In strategic planning, there is no assumption that the future is just a continuation of the past. On the contrary, the future will be determined by other forces. Against the background of widespread developments, the management is confronted with the problem of ensuring that the product–market combinations it designs and chooses contribute to the realization of the future objectives of the organization.

It is important not to concentrate on plans to the extent that the implementation of plans is neglected. It too will have its problems.

Strategic control

A strategy that is sensitive to its environment and operations will always have to be supported by changes in the organization's structure and culture and the execution of specific actions. Only then is successful implementation assured.

A strategy is always built on assumptions with regard to future developments. As soon as these assumptions are no longer correct, the plan is of little value. The goal of strategic control is to regularly test whether assumptions/predictions are still in line with actual developments. When the assumptions appear to be incorrect – that is, reality deviates from what was expected – then the plans, the process and the structure will all have to be adjusted. A strategic plan should be capable of adjustment as it is a means to an end, not the end itself.

Minicase 5.2

Philips' open approach to strategy

Philips has undergone almost continuous reorganizations in order to maintain its leading position in the race for cost reduction among manufacturers in the consumer-electronics market.

The choice of product–market combinations is still under discussion. Measures which will have to be taken to ensure the implementation of plans are discussed openly. This means that those who will later be responsible for attaining results, will have been involved in the making of the plans at an early stage.

5.1.2 Strategy at corporate, business and functional levels

Businesses come in all shapes and sizes. There are organizations like Philips, ABB, Daimler Benz and General Electric which have a very diversified range of products and serve a vast number of markets. At the same time, at the other end of the spectrum, there are companies which only have one product which sells in only one market. For both kinds of organization a strategy is required even though its form and the technical problems to be resolved will differ greatly.

The large conglomerates such as General Electric will have to make a choice regarding issues such as activities or 'businesses' which need an injection of funds, activities which need to be consolidated, and perhaps other groups of activities which may even have to be phased out, diversified or sold. An organization with only one activity or business concerns itself with how this activity is to be managed in order to achieve the best results. In both cases, we are referring to the development of strategy at a *business level*, in which the problem is the development of an optimal strategy for the existing activity.

In the larger companies with a wide range of interests, management does not only have to deal with the development of a strategy at a business level, but also has to address the problems regarding the long-term course of the organization as a whole and all the individual businesses that make it up. This is referred to as the development of strategy at a *corporate level*. This often involves a technique called *portfolio analysis* (*see* section 5.2.3).

The relation between strategy at a corporate or group level and strategy at a business level is depicted in Fig 5.2. The foundation of the organization is always based on the translation of the business strategy into the more specific strategic and operational plans at *functional level*.

The term, *diversified enterprise*, does not only apply to large enterprises. In many cases, these are indeed diversified; but diversification also takes place when an organization, regardless of its size, enters a market which is new to the organization, with a product that is also new to the organization and not related to its present product–market activities. In small companies, diversification can result in problems in strategy formulation due to the spreading out of activities.

What is regarded as a balanced package or portfolio of activities depends on the goals of the organization. The portfolio of a company that wants to grow fast will be different to that of a company which is situated in the consolidation stage. In portfolio management it is also necessary to describe in clear terms the contribution each individual activity needs to make to the whole.

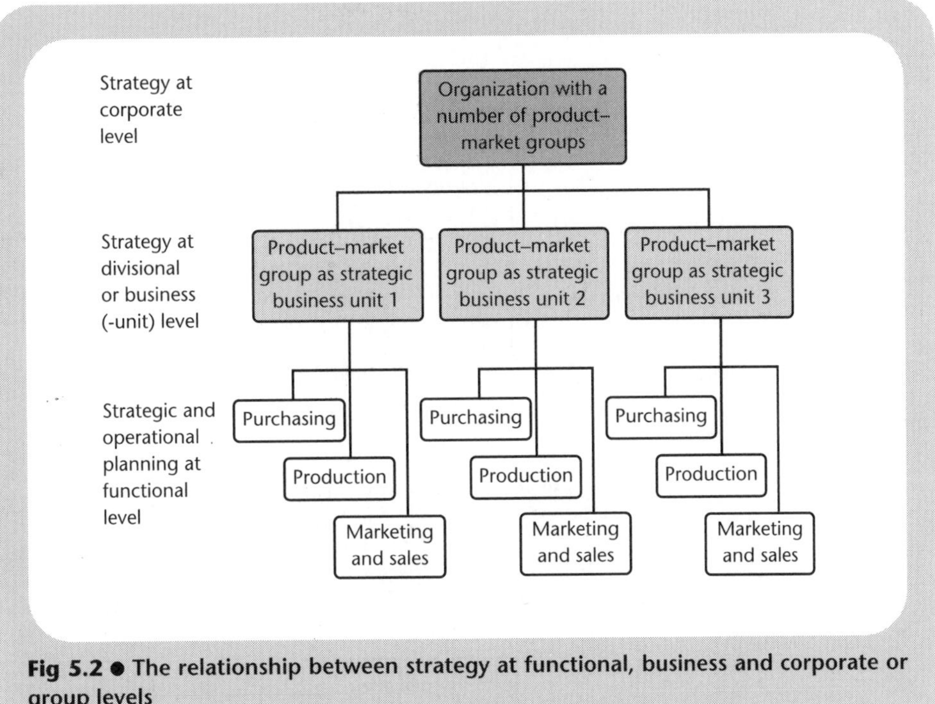

Fig 5.2 ● The relationship between strategy at functional, business and corporate or group levels

For example ...

... the problem can be compared with the tactics in many team sports, such as soccer or hockey. Within the team the attackers, the midfield players, the defenders and the goalkeeper all have different roles. If the team wants to play offensively, then the attackers have to be reinforced; if the team is hoping for a draw or is trying to limit the scale of a defeat, then the defence will have to be reinforced. Furthermore, each player needs to be managed in a different way, depending on his or her personality, task on the field, age and experience.

The performance of an organization – its success or its failure – is closely linked with the strategy, structure and the daily functioning of the organization in a changing environment. In this chapter, we will cover the process of strategy formulation in parallel and sequential steps, before going on to discuss the implementation of the strategic plans. (Organizational considerations will be discussed in greater detail in Chapters 6, 7 and 10.)

5.2 ● THE STRATEGY FORMULATION PROCESS

The definition and resolution of a strategic problem can be a rather complicated process for an organization. It is, however, possible to approach the problem in a structured way. A 'model' that can be useful in strategy formulation is shown in Fig 5.3. The strategic formulation process shown in the figure is followed, albeit with some adjustments, in many organizations. By implementing this procedure, an organization can gain an insight into the developments which are of importance. If necessary, adjustments and/or improvements will be made in existing business policies.

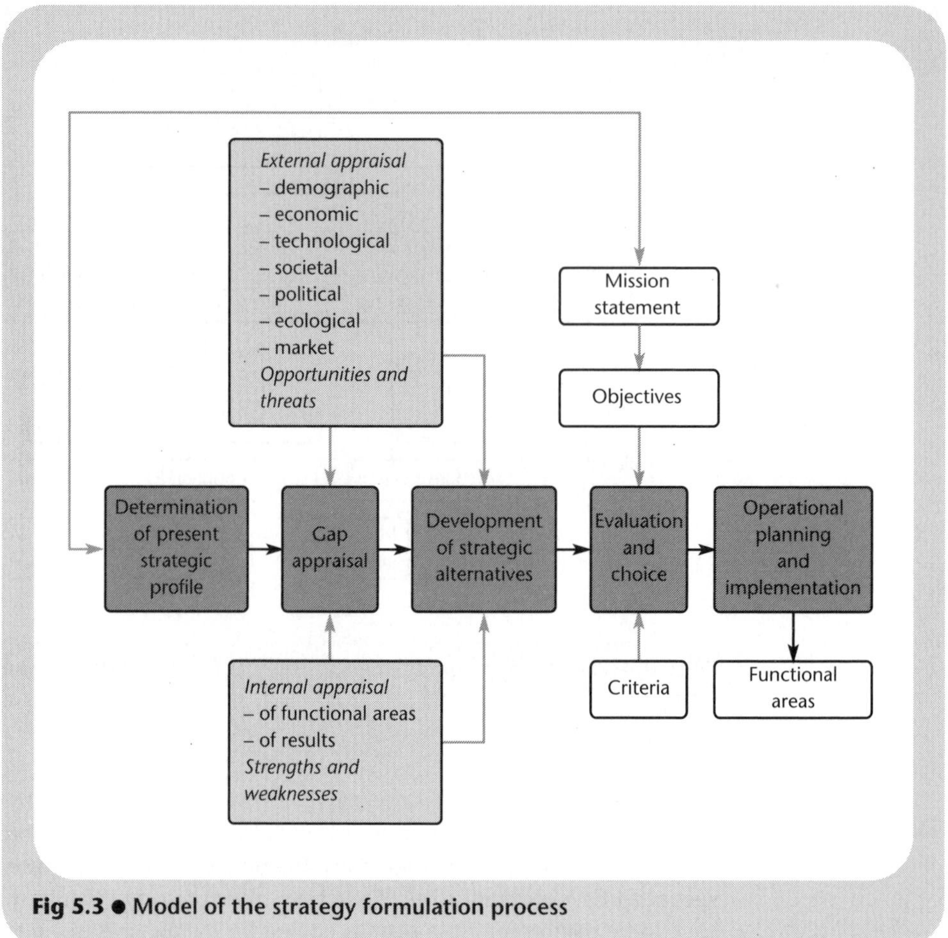

Fig 5.3 ● Model of the strategy formulation process

The process can be divided into the following steps:

1. The *present strategic profile* is determined. The purpose of this is to have a snapshot of where the firm, products and market are at the present time. The present situation will be used as a starting point from which the new strategy will have to be mapped out.

The steps that follow can be implemented in either a parallel form or sequentially.

2. A SWOT analysis is carried out. This comprises an internal appraisal (Strengths and Weaknesses) and an external appraisal (Opportunities and Threats) and highlights the circumstances under which the strategy will be developed.
3. At this point the results of Step 2 are assimilated and the question of whether the survival of the organization is likely to be threatened in the near future can be addressed. The organization can determine whether a strategic gap exists – that is, a discrepancy between what the organization hopes to achieve and what the organization looks like achieving.
4. If there is a gap, alternatives have to be sought to close the gap. Useful information in the search for new opportunities can be retrieved from the results of the external appraisal of the environment and the internal appraisal of strengths and weaknesses.

5. Alternatives and their consequences will be evaluated. These can be tested against existing objectives on the one hand and a number of specific strategic criteria and constraints on the other hand.
6. The best alternative is chosen and this is followed by the translation of the strategic alternatives into plans for the different functional fields, such as purchasing, production, marketing and sales, finance, personnel.

We can now discuss each of these steps in greater detail.

5.2.1 Present strategic profile

The present strategic profile is studied because it reflects the most important characteristics of the present strategy and course, strategic resources and components. In this respect, it plays a useful role in practice in highlighting objectives and goals, areas of current activities, competitive advantages and synergy.

Objectives and goals

It is often difficult to identify the objectives and goals at which the management of the organization is aiming. Sometimes, objectives are expressed in rather general terms, that give little support and direction to the daily events in the organization. It is important to define objectives, goals and targets in economic, technical and social terms.

Economic objectives and goals can be expressed in terms of profit, market share, equity/debt ratios, cost levels, and so on. Management also needs to state how much profit is contemplated and this can then be expressed as a percentage return on equity, for example. If these percentages are not fixed, it is not possible to calculate whether enough profit has been earned. If a profit goal is described as a 'reasonable return for shareholders' it is impossible to determine whether this level has been attained or will be in the future. The consequence is often that actions are only undertaken when there is a loss, by which time it is often too late. Successful enterprises have clear operational norms for returns.

Objectives can also be non-economic in nature. For example, management or the owner might put the independence of the company above all other considerations; some companies only want to make aesthetically justified or environmentally friendly products. These objectives are often the major influence in the development and the ultimate choice of new strategic possibilities. In this respect, the objectives can be viewed as determining the new course to be followed.

Areas of current activities

It is important to determine the fields of activity with which the organization is familiar. Total sales can be split up into product groups, markets, distribution channels, countries, and so on. The possibilities are endless and so it is useful to prioritize the specifications which are the most relevant, as the gathering and compiling of data can take up a great deal of time. It is also worthwhile calculating the profitability of the different areas of activity.

For example ...

... often, surprising new insights result from these analyses. A company can calculate the contribution to profit of the different client categories. One client group may provide 50 per cent more profit per unit of product than the least profitable client group. By selling

10 per cent more to the most profitable clients and less to the low-profit category, the profit can improve spectacularly. The gathering of the numerical data may take several days, but the effect on the profits can be compared with a sales increase of about 50 per cent.

Competitive advantage

A study of the present strategic profile includes a consideration of how the organization thinks it attracts customers to itself in order to gain an advantage over its competitors. There are different ways of winning the competitive battle – for example, by offering the lowest price for the product, or by offering a product (with the services that accompany it) that has a clear 'added value' over what the other suppliers offer in the market. This is best illustrated by considering the strategy of companies like Mercedes Benz and BMW, on the one hand, and companies like Skoda and Lada on the other.

Synergy

Synergy is the advantage (or disadvantage) which arises because two activities are being carried out which complement each other – the so-called 2 + 2 = 5 effect. This effect arises, for example, when a company lets its sales staff sell different products through the same distribution channel.

For example ...

... in some cases, the advantage lies in the development of the product. A number of electronics companies, for example, use a specific technology for a number of product lines (for example, calculators, cash registers, microcomputers). In this way, massive investments in research and development can be spread over a much larger number of end products with resulting cost advantages.

The synergy can also lie in the brand name (for example, Philips) as it might result in the advertisement cost per product sold being lower than in the case of a manufacturer who uses different names.

5.2.2 External appraisal: threats and opportunities

An investigation into the external environment can be carried out from two points of view: total societal environment on the one hand and the specific sector of business on the other. Both points of view can be distinguished, but cannot be separated.

Developments in the societal environment

In section 3.3 we discussed the factors which played an important role in determining the future of the organization. The examples given are not meant to be exhaustive.

Demographic factors

Products and services are ultimately put at the disposal of the population, and as a result the demographic factors, such as the growth, size and composition of the population, are of importance to the organization. For example, a decrease in the birth rate will lead to a reduction in the number of consumers of educational products. This has consequences for the demand for products such as school books, classrooms, and teachers. A decreasing birth rate would also have repercussions for companies such as Nestlé.

The increasing ageing of the population or a lowering of the retirement age will eventually have an influence on the social security system. In addition, the *multicultural* nature of society in many European countries has implications not only for government, but also for private organizations and companies. This relates in particular to education, social and cultural services and the management and realization of participative structures in companies.

Companies should also be aware of population concentrations and changes in them. It is important for the store chains, for example, to follow the drift of the population out of larger cities into the smaller towns so that market share can be maintained.

Economic factors

Economic forces are always an important field of attention for management, both nationally and internationally. It is estimated that within the next 30 years, East Asian countries will increase their share of world production from 15 per cent to 25 per cent. These and other developments mean that international economic negotiations are increasingly important – for example, in the context of the EU or the GATT regulations. In recent years, the negotiations between Japan and western countries regarding restrictions on the Japanese export of cars and electronic supplies got underway. The so-called North–South dialogue between developed and developing countries will have future implications for governments and companies.

For example ...

... the fluctuations in the dollar rate during the past years have had a major influence on the market position of a number of companies. Fokker, for example, carried out its transactions in dollars. The incorrect estimation of the exchange rate resulted in this company's profits decreasing dramatically in the short term and in the long term the sales expectations had to be adjusted.

Technological factors

Technological progress is an essential feature of our time. One could even speak of a new industrial revolution. These forces have left few organizations unaffected. Two important consequences of this progress are the modification of production processes and the launching of innovative new products.

The development of the transistor has had a major influence on the way in which products such as radios, television sets and computers are manufactured. Not only have they changed technically and become more reliable, but they are also a lot cheaper than 10 to 15 years ago.

In this context, we can also point to the developments in the field of communication technology – for example, the rise in commercial satellite television. If this development continues, it will have consequences for both the organizations which currently operate in broadcasting, as well as the organizations, such as newspapers and magazines, which currently receive advertising revenues. Other developments have affected areas such as postal services, telecommunications, and computer manufacturing.

For example ...

... until recently, laser technology was only used in laboratories. This technology is now applied worldwide in consumer products such as compact disk players.

Societal factors

Important societal developments of recent years have included: individualization, assertiveness and consumerism; concern for health and the environment; decrease in the total number of working years; a desire for more comfort; increased importance of paid labour for women; emancipation of second and third generation ethnic minorities; redistribution of tasks in social care between partners; safe sex; etc.

Societal factors are an important element of any investigation of the environment as they can have a profound impact on the organization. These also involve adjustments to the working environment – for example, the tendency towards more participation and co-determination. The higher levels of education have also resulted in fewer people being prepared to do unskilled labour.

Political factors

For enterprises operating in international markets, the political relations in the countries in which they are active, and/or wish to be active, play an important role. Tuning into the economic and political developments is a complex matter. Volkswagen considered the events in Eastern Europe in the 1980s much more promising than did many other western enterprises. Volkswagen developed a very ambitious strategy. To achieve an increase in sales of 25 per cent in three years, Volkswagen invested 50 million DM in the Trabant factory in the former East Germany and the Czech Skoda factories.

Ecological factors

Increasing concern for the environment has led many organizations to establish the environmental 'friendliness' of their products and their packaging. Nowadays it is no longer unusual to read on the packaging of plastic bags that these do not cause any damage during the incineration of refuse.

Developments in the market and sectors

Any study of the forces which influence a particular business sector can be divided into an analysis of competitors and an analysis of the forces which affect the whole sector, including all competitors.

Analysis of competition

Knowing your opponents was already a basic principle of strategy, albeit military strategy, many centuries ago. The Chinese general, Sun Tzu, wrote about this subject around 300 BC. In management literature, the *competitive profile* and *analysis* only recently became a focus of attention (*see* Ansoff (1965) and Porter (1985)). The intensity of rivalry and competition will determine to a great extent the structural opportunity for profit in a particular business sector. The following points should be taken into account:

1. It is important for an organization to ascertain whether its competitors are rash or cautious. A cautious competitor will weigh up the effects of individual actions. A cautious competitor will not plunge into a price war, with eyes tightly closed. Such a competitor may well engage in a price war, but only after ensuring that it will not damage the organization's current position.
2. In situations of slow economic growth, competition often takes on a more intensive nature. This is especially the case when costs rise and sales grow less quickly. This can also be reinforced when such a business sector is characterized by a high level of fixed costs – for example the steel industry and the aerospace industry. Any extra sales will always make a contribution toward covering fixed costs.
3. Competition can become more intense when an organization deals with many different forms of competitor. In the insurance business, for example, regionally based insurance companies compete with both 'direct underwriters' and 'traditional' companies. The different kinds of competitors will have many different cost patterns which will make any analysis of competition less clear.

4. The existence of a withdrawal threshold can also lead to more intensive competition. Withdrawal thresholds can make it more advantageous for a company to keep producing at a loss rather than incurring the costs involved in withdrawing from the market. Withdrawal from a market can also be affected by emotional factors. The leader of a family company is sometimes not prepared to close down the company which was founded by his or her ancestors. Furthermore, the government can prevent the retrenchment of a sector by determining minimal redundancy agreements.
5. Knowledge of individual competitors is also important. The behaviour of a competitor can be determined by its economic and other goals. Some managers are pre-occupied with making high returns, while others feel strongly about maintaining the independence of the organization. A decrease in profits will lead to very different actions in different organizations.
6. The behaviour of competitors is also determined by the kind of strategy which the competitor has pursued in the past. For example, a competitor who has always had the profile of a low sales price company will not be able to change overnight to a strategy based on the quality of the product. Consider, for example, the brands of Yoko and Bang & Olufsen (B&O) in the consumer audio market.
7. The strengths and weaknesses of the organization will also determine the opportunities available to a competitor. A weak financial position will rarely allow large investments in product innovation or process development to take place.

All these factors combine to determine how aggressive or defensive a competitor will be, how and where it is vulnerable, which strategic changes it can carry through and what factors it will react to.

For example ... ...on the basis of an extensive competitive analysis a Swedish company once decided to enter the market for electronic scales (as it concluded its competitors in this market were sleeping), but not that for electronic cash registers (as it concluded that those competitors could not be beaten).

Analysis of the forces which affect industry competition

The competition in an industry is subject to a number of influencing factors (*see* Fig 5.4).

1. *Buyers/Clients*. The influence of the buyers/clients on the degree of competition takes two forms. First of all, the number of final customers will influence sales levels of the product. This will be affected by some of the factors relating to the social environment discussed in section 5.2.2 – for example, a decrease in the birth rate.

   Second, the influence of the buyers/clients depends on the power position which they enjoy relative to the suppliers in the market. The power position can be determined by a great many factors, including the degree of concentration, compared to that of the suppliers.

For example ... ... when we look at the market for insurance, we can see a relatively high degree of concentration in the life insurance market and a relatively low degree of concentration in the accident insurance market. This explains the low profit margins for the accident insurers and the high ones for the life insurers. The suppliers of a quality product often have a much stronger position than suppliers of a product which everyone can make. Think, for example, of the profit figures of Mercedes Benz compared to those of Peugeot and Renault. The buyers of the exclusive brands are impressed by the quality of the products and are prepared to pay a premium for them.

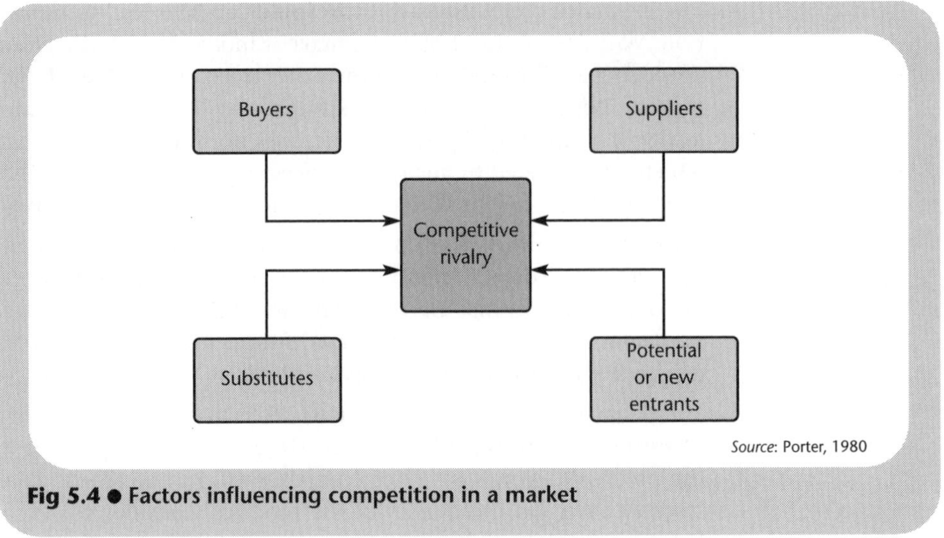

Fig 5.4 ● Factors influencing competition in a market

The size of the purchase amount also plays a part. Research has shown that the profitability of producers of articles with a low unit price is often higher and more stable than the profitability of manufacturers of investment goods. It is not usual (or realistic) to negotiate over the price of a tube of toothpaste at the check out. When negotiating does have a chance of success, this can lead to suppliers being prepared to give price concessions. The supplier's fear of losing the client for good enhances the negotiating power of the client and lowers the sales price and/or leads to a deterioration of the sales conditions from the point of view of the seller.

Recognizing the power of clients is less important in existing markets, as not much can be done to change the situation but it is a major consideration when entering new markets.

2. *Suppliers*. The position with regard to supplier power is similar to that of client power. The manufacturer of a product is now in the position of client for raw materials, components, etc. In a few cases, companies have decided to withdraw from a specific market because the suppliers have had such a strong position that the revenue from the activities would never have exceeded a marginal return.

For example ...

... co-operation on a European scale can be recognized in the food-product retail stores. Ahold (the Netherlands) has entered into a so-called 'strategic alliance' with Argyll (UK) and Casino (France) in the hope of achieving lower purchase prices by joint purchase.

3. *Substitute products or services*. The appearance on the market of products or services which can take over the function of another product often has a negative influence on results. This often happens as a result of technological developments – for example, the ball-point pen (which drove the fountain pen off the market), the quartz watch, the diesel locomotive and more recently the compact disk and the video recorder. The arrival of this kind of product leads in time to a decrease in the demand for the traditional product, which will result in increased competition between the traditional suppliers.

   Studies of the introduction of new products show that it can take five to ten years before a new product strikes the fatal blow to the old products. In part, this can be explained by the slow reactions of clients. The new products often seem to suffer from growing pains, which lull many traditional suppliers into a false sense of security. According to the studies, the fatal blow is only delivered once the perfected products are introduced to the market.

4. *Potential or new entrants*. New entrants into the market lead to the intensification of competition. A larger number of suppliers in the market fights for the same amount of sales. When considering whether new entrants to a market are possible, it is important to identify any barriers to entry – for example, the size of the demanded investment, the access to distribution channels, existing government policy, the advantages of existing suppliers (patents, location, etc.).

   In addition, an organization can consider which companies would want to enter a certain market. The following groups of organizations, although not exhaustive, are worth thinking about:

   - manufacturers from other regions (for example, Japan, Europe, but also regional chain stores that want to grow);
   - suppliers from other segments of the market who want to 'upgrade';
   - manufacturers in 'adjacent' fields (for example, telecommunication and data processing companies).

   Experience shows that many companies underestimate the effects of new entrants to a market.

Concluding remarks

An appraisal of an organization's environment can be divided up into the categories, opportunities and threats. It is often tempting to view a change as a threat. However, if an organization reacts appropriately to such a development in its environment the change can become an opportunity. It is important to consider the positive aspects of a signalled development. Experience shows that what is not seen, often does harm, and what is seen, often has a greater effect than expected.

The external appraisal is concerned with drawing up a total picture of the future situation the company will face. Developments should be highlighted, as should the ways in which they affect each other and are dependent on each other. The combined effect of a number of separate developments is often larger than the 'sum' of the individual effects. Although such information is more difficult to obtain than other data, it is highly recommended that an organization allocates resources to such an analysis.

In conclusion, it is necessary to weigh up the costs and revenues of making a more in-depth analysis. If it is decided, for reasons of cost, to proceed no further with the investigation, the organization should at least try to form a picture of the possible positive and or/negative consequences of specific developments.

5.2.3 Internal appraisal: strengths and weaknesses

Internal appraisal of strengths and weaknesses can be described as a systematic analysis of the characteristics and functioning of an organization at a given moment in time. Such an analysis can relate to a set of circumstances in the past or in the future of the organization carrying out the research or another similar organization.

This appraisal of strengths and weaknesses can be used as the starting point for further decision making and planning in the organization. Such an investigation has two objectives:

1. It highlights the shortcomings or weaknesses in skills and competences which will need to be addressed in the short term if current performance is to be improved.
2. It identifies strengths which can form the basis and give direction to possibilities for further expansion of activities or diversification.

It should be remembered in such an appraisal, however, that the determination of strengths and weaknesses is always a relative judgement. The assessment of strengths and weaknesses can be carried out in two complementary ways: according to functional areas and according to results.

The functional areas approach

A common method of appraising strengths and weaknesses is to examine the major functional areas. This involves an assessment of the skills and resources of the organization, complemented, if necessary, by support and specialist functions which work from other departments.

Table 5.2 is a useful tool in the assessment of strengths and weaknesses. Each of the functional areas is considered and assigned a score ranging from weak to strong.

The calculation of scores can be based on a comparison with competitors and/or a study of the demands of the markets. Such a judgement needs to be based, on the one hand, on opinions and visions, and on the other, on hard, quantitative and financial data. Each functional area can be examined from a number of perspectives. In the following sections we will look at each of the functional areas in more detail and will identify measures of performance.

Product development

Performance considerations include: number of new products per year, new products as a percentage of sales, development costs as a percentage of sales, clarity in direction, know-how of employees and external contacts.

To gain a clear picture, it is useful to gather information not only from the organization itself, but also from customers, suppliers, etc. The organization's own vision that everything is rosy can sometimes be contested by information from customers that competitors are developing many more new products and are doing this more quickly. It is important to remember in relation to this that strengths in an existing market cannot necessarily be transferred to new markets. The innovation of products for the

Table 5.2 ● Rating strengths and weaknesses in functional areas

	Weak	Normal	Strong
Product development			
Purchasing			
Production			
Marketing			
Sales			
Human resources			
Finance			
Management/Organization			

consumer market makes different demands on a product development department, than the adjustment of a product for an existing commercial client.

Purchasing

Performance considerations include: information about suppliers, buying procedures, who decides, spreading of purchases over suppliers, purchase prices and purchase policies.

The relative importance of this department will depend on the extent to which the quality of the purchased raw materials, components or semi-finished goods is crucial to the organization's own product, or the purchase value is a major percentage of total sales revenues. The identification of the goods which constitute a strategically important purchase is crucial.

In recent years, large companies have entered into closer co-operation with suppliers. The suppliers are more directly involved in the operations of the client organization and in return higher demands are made of them with regard to delivery times and quality. As a result, a close relation develops between the manufacturing process of the supplier and that of the client. The purchasing department provides the link between both manufacturing processes and, as a result, is of much greater importance than before. However, in many companies the purchasing function is still considered to be less important than, say, the production or sales functions.

Production

Performance considerations include: layout and routing, ageing of machinery, efficiency, quality, working methods, speed of stock turnover, utilization as percentage of capacity, flexibility of production resources, machinery etc., process automation and quality of personnel.

The above list of performance considerations can easily be expanded further. Comparisons of performance over time can be useful management tools. It is not uncommon for management at a certain point in time to base many of its decisions on fact relating to a situation in the recent past, even though such data may give misleading impressions.

In some cases management considers the application of the most modern and expensive machines to be important, even when the market does not demand such precision or finesse. The price charged cannot reflect the level of precision offered as this is not demanded by the market. The consequence is often that a substantial depreciation component must be included in the cost price which is too high and which, in the end, reduces profitability.

Marketing

Performance considerations include: market knowledge, knowledge of marketing research techniques, sufficient experience, contact with external agencies, degree of external orientation, use of marketing mix components (product, price, place, promotion) and success with product launches.

Marketing is an important function for every business. However, some firms are more marketing oriented than others – for example, those producing branded consumer goods. The relative importance of the marketing function can be determined by comparisons with competitors – for example, with regard to the introduction of new products.

Sales

Performance considerations include: sales per salesperson, sales costs as a percentage of sales, composition of range, administration of order processing, distribution costs, number of contacts per salesperson per day and after-sales service.

For many products, sales and distribution costs are a significant percentage of the sales price. In addition, the actual sales effort is crucial to the survival of a company. An accurate comparison with competitors is often possible. Further information can also be obtained from clients.

Personnel

Performance considerations include: the existence of a personnel department, personnel education/training policy, turnover/absenteeism/illness and reward systems.

Human resources are a crucial factor in the functioning of a company. Many companies state that their personnel is the most important 'factor of production'. It is worth comparing such a statement with hard facts. It often turns out that little money is spent on the 'maintenance' of human resources, few or no training courses are offered, and the levels of absenteeism and staff turnover are high.

Finance

Performance considerations include: cash flow, working capital, equity/debt ratio, loans, liquidity ratios, return ratios.

The financial function can often make an accurate assessment of the actual position of an organization. Many financial publications provide good material for comparison purposes. Business associations in industry sectors and banks gather data which could be useful in such assessments.

Management/Organization

Performance considerations include: planning activities (strategic, organizational, operational, mid-term and short-term), accuracy of budgeting, quality of management information, task and function descriptions and goals per department/manager.

The strengths of the management and the organization are often difficult to assess due to the problems involved in gathering such information. Just because an organization appears to have all the elements of good management listed in the textbooks does not necessarily mean that it is being managed well. Assessing the power, ambition, knowledge and skills of the managers and the employees is an important part of the overall appraisal of a company's performance.

Exhibit 5.1

Swedish workhorse image takes a back seat

Launch of the sporty C70 coupé marks a move up-market for the troubled carmaker

At the Paris Motor Show in September 1996, Volvo pulled the covers off the sleekest, sportiest car it has ever made.

The racy-looking new C70 coupé is the biggest step taken by the Swedish manufacturer in its move away from the boxy workhorses for which it is famous, to a more up-market range competing with the likes of Audi and BMW.

'The design of the C70', says Mr Tuve Johannesson, chief executive of Volvo's car division, 'clearly reflects the new Volvo.'

The high-priced C70 is not a make-or-break model for Volvo. It will be made in small volumes for an exclusive market. But its success or failure will go some way towards showing whether the car division can recover from recent losses and carve out a profitable, independent long-term future.

This has been an issue since Volvo broke off plans to merge with France's Renault in late 1993. It is central to the Volvo group's post-merger strategy of concentrating on its core car and truck making operations. It is a key factor for investors deciding whether Volvo shares, which have fallen from SKr165 a year ago to under SKr150 today, will yield a long-term return on the big investment programme under way at Volvo.

'The risk embodied in the car division is critical, because no-one except the company management professes confidence that Volvo is big enough to survive independently,' wrote Salomon Brothers in a recent report on Volvo.

The task facing Volvo has been clearly illustrated by its results over the past year. A combination of flagging sales and high development costs pushed the car division into the red in the last quarter of 1995 and the first quarter of this year.

In the second quarter, car operations moved back into the black. But a sharp fall in earnings at the truck division caused group operating profits to tumble from SKr4bn to SKr2.3bn ($346.9m) in the first half.

These setbacks were followed this month by reports in the Swedish press – strongly denied by Volvo – of disquiet within the company, and speculation about the position of Mr Sören Gyll, group chief executive.

But Mr Johannesson is adamant the strategy of remodelling the car division is not in question. 'I'm quite sure there are all kinds of opinions, but we in the car company have a strat-

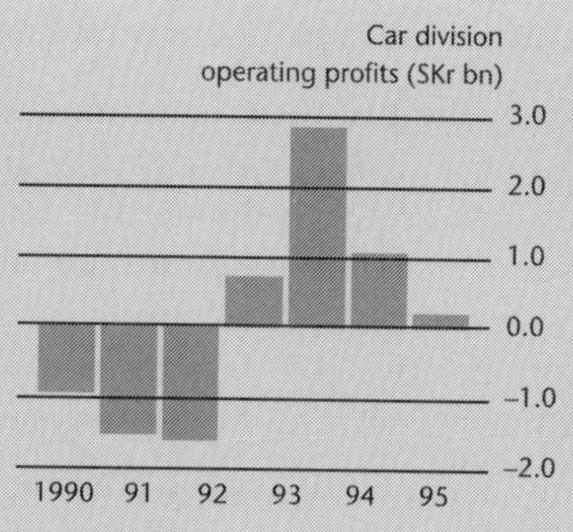

egy and I am convinced that we are unified around that strategy,' he says.

The C70 is one of what Mr Johannesson calls the building blocks of the strategy. The aim is to broaden and upgrade Volvo's narrow product range, and increase output from less than 400,000 now to 500,000 cars a year. Volvo's vulnerability owes much to the high costs that a small-volume manufacturer must bear in development and production.

Volvo is using partnerships to defray some of these costs. The C70 is the result of a joint production venture based in Uddevalla, west Sweden, with TWR, the specialist British sports car company, which will also launch a cabriolet model next year.

An even more important partnership is the NedCar production venture in the Netherlands with Mitsubishi of Japan. Volvo is producing its recently launched S40 and V40 mid-range saloon and estate car models at NedCar on the same production line as the Mitsubishi Carism.

But Volvo is determined to show that it can thrive without being swallowed by one of the world's volume car manufacturers. To this end, the car division is spending most of the group's SKr8bn-a-year investment programme on filling out its model range.

The first big step was the S40/V40 car. It has replaced the old 400-series Volvo, which was losing up to SKr1.5bn a year. The S40/V40 was hit initially by quality and production hiccups, restricting it to an expected 60,000 sales this year. But Mr Johannesson says volumes will rise to 140,000 a year.

The C70 and the cabriolet are spin-offs from the 850, the mainstay of Volvo since its introduction in 1992. The 850, made in Belgium and Sweden, has spawned several versions, including a four-wheel drive model. The 900-series saloons and estate cars complete the current range.

The next development will be a replacement for the 900. But this is expected to be based on a reworked version of the 850 platform, or chassis. Volvo intends to base its wider range of models on two basic platforms in order to cut costs further.

Since taking over the car division a year ago, Mr Johannesson has introduced tough cost controls. He says – without specifying – that he has lowered Volvo's break-even level. Combining the earnings effect of the new cars with these new measures, Salomon Brothers predicts the car division could achieve an operating profit of nearly SKr2bn in 1997.

That would put it well on the way to achieving its long-term goal. But Volvo has little margin for error. Every new model – including the C70 – will have to prove its worth if independence is to be secured.

Source: *Financial Times*, 30 September 1996.

The results approach

The results approach to appraising an organization's strengths and weaknesses concentrates on the financial performance of the different company activities, with particular emphasis on both profit potential and the strategic perspective of each of the activities.

Once again, this appraisal has to be seen in the context of the appraisal of the organization's environment. Attention is particularly focused on the following:

1. *Trends in the results*. The historical pattern of performance is investigated by studying data on measures such as profitability and sales. For large companies with diverse activities, it is useful to divide this detailed analysis into small units – for example, 'business units' – although it is important that when these smaller units are brought together, they form a complete whole. This analysis highlights trends in the results, both positive and negative, and identifies parts of the company activities with performance deviating from the average for the organization.
2. *Sources of profits*. This analysis can be considered as a further development of the analysis of trends. Profitability is analysed from the different perspectives of, for example, products, product groups, geographical areas, sales channels, distribution methods or client groups. Obviously the accuracy of this analysis is highly dependent on the quality of the information which the organization's information system provides. A useful tool for such analysis is the *portfolio analysis*, developed by the Boston Consulting Group, a US-based consultancy firm.

Several tools and techniques can be employed in any analysis of an organization's results. We consider here:

- Portfolio analysis and the product life cycle
- The experience curve
- The product portfolio matrix
- The policy matrix
- Competitor portfolio analysis

Portfolio analysis and the product life cycle

The central financial measure in portfolio analysis is not profit as such, but cash flow (that is, net profit *plus* depreciation). The analysis is also based on each product having a commercial life cycle. If an organization wishes to survive, it must ensure that there are always adequate resources to fund new activities which will eventually replace the older, once profitable activities.

Every product goes through different stages of development – the product life cycle – from its launch on to the market to its withdrawal from that market. At each of these stages, the product will have cash flow and sales patterns, whether measured in units or revenue. The life cycle of some products – for example, iron and steel – is very long, while that of products such as fashion articles and CD singles is very short. The stages of the product life cycle are:

- *Introduction*. The launch of a new product involves an investment in product development and marketing. At this stage it is not clear whether these costs will lead to a successful product. There are as yet no revenues, only expenditure.
- *Growth*. As soon as the product comes on to the market, revenues are received but these are often not sufficient to cover the marketing and other costs. Maintaining quality and reliability is still a priority and will require continued investment.
- *Maturity*. The product has gained a substantial proportion of market share. At this stage revenues should exceed expenditures so that a positive cash flow results.

- *Decline*. In the last stage of the life cycle, it is possible that the revenues are exceeded by expenditures again and cash flow will fall again to zero or may even become negative. At this point it is advisable to withdraw the product from the market. In extreme cases, the company will have to be closed and redundancies made.

A product is only successful when it has a positive total cash flow over the whole life cycle. Figure 5.5 compares the financial life cycle with the commercial life cycle of a product.

The experience curve

Research has shown that there is a relationship between the cumulated level of production and a reduction in costs, which cannot simply be put down to economies of scale. This can result in a decrease of between 20 and 30 per cent in the cost of a product as the accumulated production of that product – that is, the total number of that product produced – is doubled. This relationship is explained by the so-called experience curve or learning curve. An increase in cumulated production is accompanied by the following:

- a higher level of productivity due to technological innovation;
- a higher level of productivity due to the learning of skills from the routine nature of the process;
- economies of scale and specialization; and
- improved product design.

To achieve these possible savings, management will have to pay close attention to cost control. There are two important aspects to the 'experience effect'.

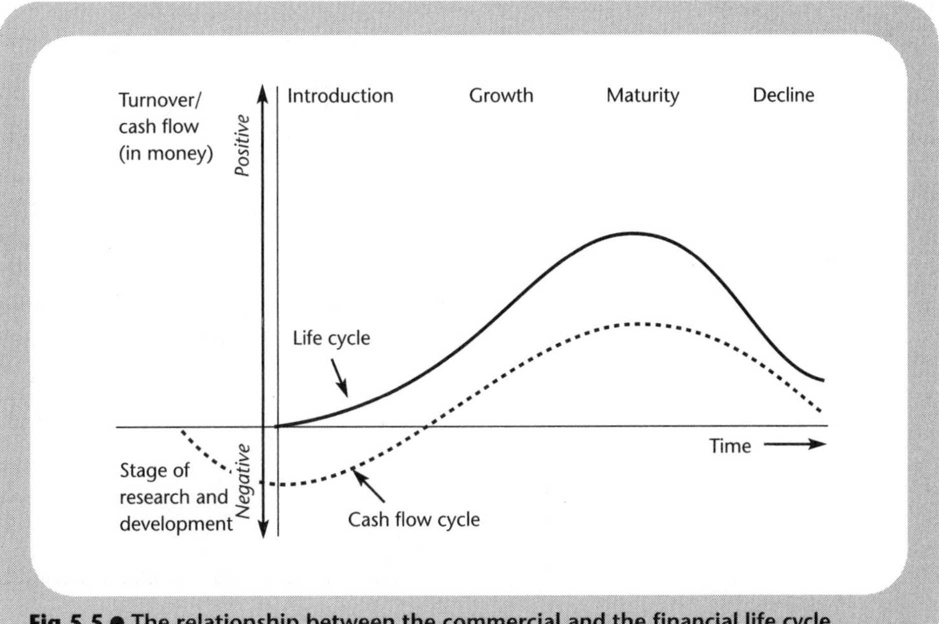

Fig 5.5 ● The relationship between the commercial and the financial life cycle

1. If an organization cannot match the cost savings of a competitor, this will lead to a less favourable cost position, and in turn to a less favourable competitive position.
2. If an organization grows more slowly than a competitor, having started from a comparable position, this will also lead to a less favourable position.

The company with the lowest costs will be able to set the lowest prices in the market. Such a company will in principle obtain the highest sales and as a result the highest profits.

The effect of the experience curve in recent years can be seen in the reduction in price of electronic pocket calculators, compact disk players, personal computers, colour televisions and airline tickets.

An organization's ability to gain market share is also crucial. Its relative market share – that is, its own market share divided by that of its main competitor – will affect its ability to take advantage of the 'experience effect'. The experience effect should result in a better rate of return and cash flow position for the company with the higher market share.

The product portfolio matrix

It is now possible to construct a matrix (*see* Fig 5.6) in which the different activities of an organization can be plotted according to the growth of the market and the relative market share. The boundary between high and low market growth depends on the growth rate of the gross national product. If the growth expectations of the product are higher than this percentage, then the classification of high growth applies. In the reverse case, the classification low growth applies.

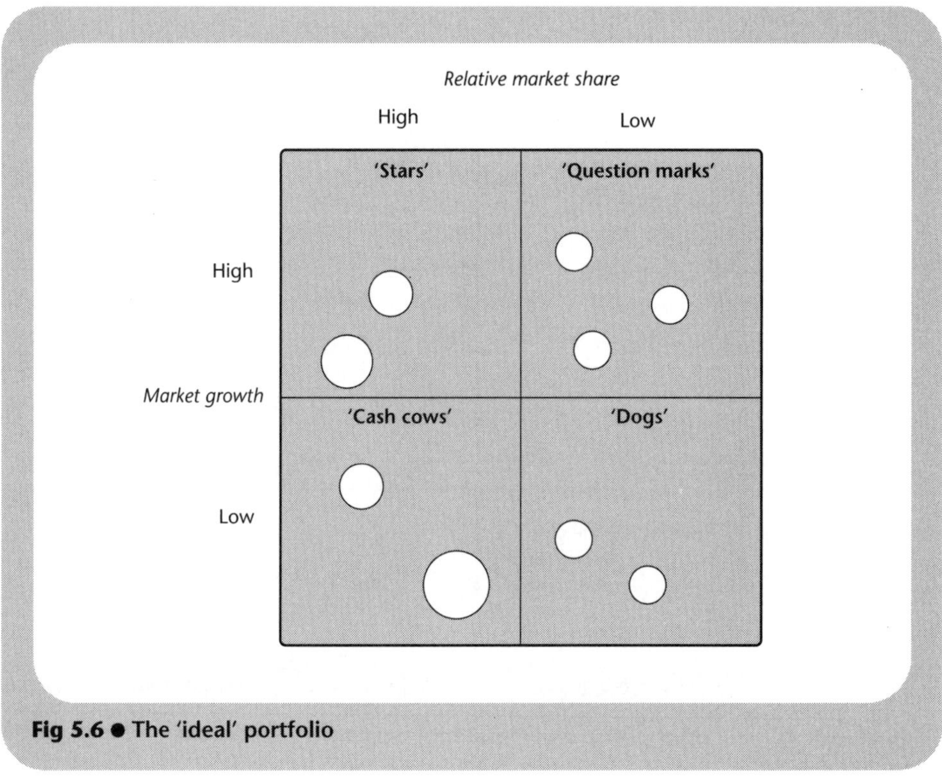

Fig 5.6 ● The 'ideal' portfolio

As can be seen from Fig 5.6, each of the organization's activities appears in one of four categories – stars, question marks, dogs and cash cows. Each of the activities is depicted as a circle – or bubble – in the matrix whereby the diameter of the circle reflects the level of sales. A picture is built up of the current spread of activities and the implications for future cash flow.

Strategically, the financial resources which are earned from activities with low growth and high relative market share (cash cows) should be 'employed' on activities which either have to follow the growth of the market (stars) or have to acquire a larger relative market share (question marks).

Since resources are seldom available to finance all new projects, a choice will have to be made. The activities with a low relative market share and low market growth (dogs) will have to be withdrawn.

It is important for an organization that current and future cash flow is or can be maintained. This means that the organization has to have products and activities which are situated at different stages of their life cycle. Only then can the organization finance its activities on an ongoing basis. A product usually develops from being a 'question mark' via 'star' to 'cash cow' and finally to 'dog'. The 'question marks' and 'stars' can only be developed if the 'cash cows' generate sufficient cash flows (*see* Fig 5.7). When at a certain point in time, an organization only has 'cash cows' and no 'stars' and 'question marks', future cash flows will rarely be assured.

Policy matrix

As an aid to making strategic choices based on a complete picture of activities and future expectations, a policy matrix has been developed (by Shell) from the portfolio

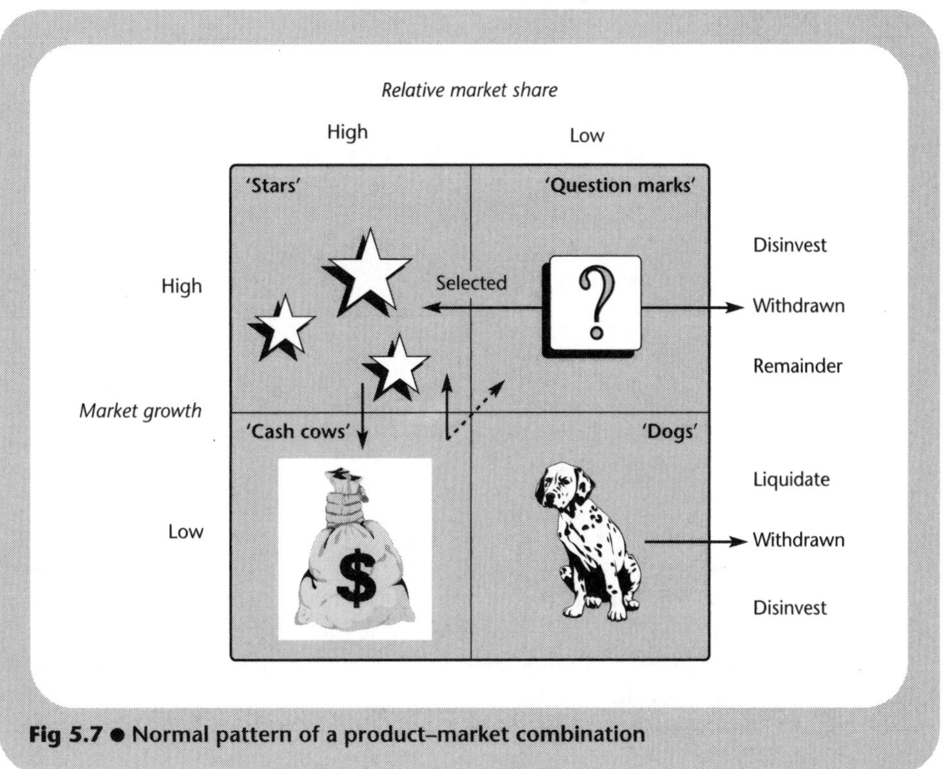

Fig 5.7 ● Normal pattern of a product–market combination

concept already discussed. On the horizontal axis of the policy matrix, we find *'prospects of the sector'* – that is, attractiveness of the industry – and on the vertical axis we find the *'competitive position'* of the organization.

The prospects of the sector are judged on:

- market growth;
- market quality;
- supply of resources;
- environmental influences.

An organization's score for each of these factors depends on a number of components. For example, in market quality, the intensity of the rivalry or competition can be considered, as well as the degree of cyclical vulnerability and the threat of new entrants. The components will vary depending on the particular characteristics of the activities.

To determine the total score with regard to the prospects of the sector, a weighting needs to be applied according to the relative importance of each of the above mentioned factors (market growth, market quality, supply of resources and environmental influences). For each factor, weighting × score will equal the weighted score. The sum of the weighted scores will give the total score for prospects of the sector (*see* Table 5.3).

Table 5.3 ● Factor weighting for policy matrix

Factor	Weighting	×	Score	=	Weighted score
Market growth		×		=	
Market quality		×		=	
Supply of resources		×		=	
Environmental influences		×		=	
Total score				=	

The competitive position of the organization in a specific sector is assessed based on:

- the market share
- characteristics of the product
- research and development.

The total score is calculated using different components, in the same way as that for prospects of the sector. The position of the different activities is ultimately reflected in a matrix (*see* Fig 5.8). Each of the cells gives an indication of which strategy could be followed.

Compared to the product portfolio matrix of the Boston Consulting Group, the policy matrix indicates strategic positions (nine instead of four) and a larger number of strategic options for an activity. The fundamental difference, however, is that in determining the relative positions in the matrix, many more factors must be considered and a high level of judgement is required (analytical, judgemental and strategic) from the managers involved.

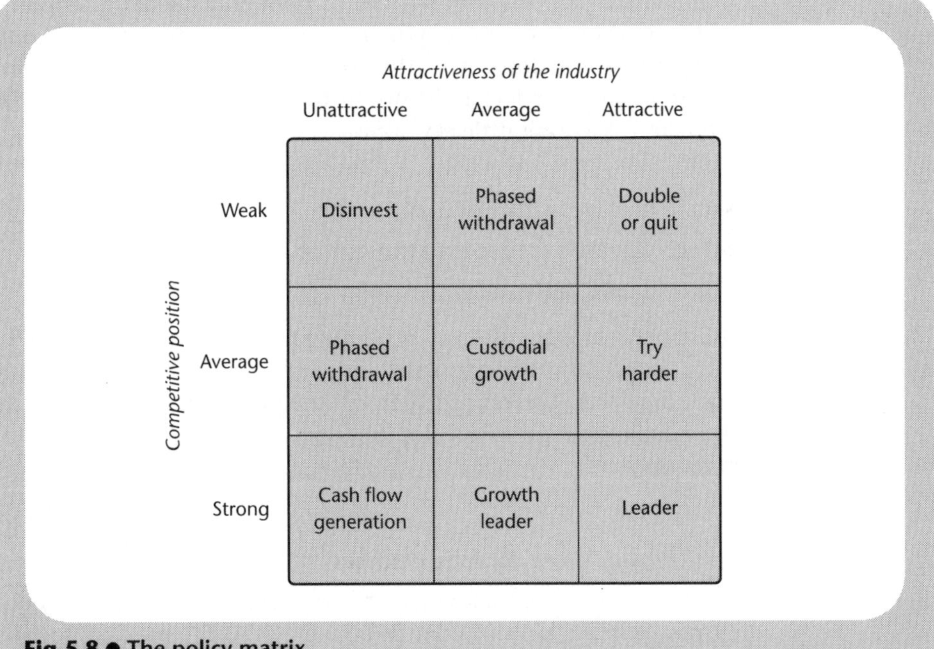

Fig 5.8 ● The policy matrix

Interpretation of current portfolio matrices

At this point it may be useful to study some examples of portfolios and draw some conclusions from them.

From Portfolio A in Fig 5.9 (a policy matrix), it can be concluded that:

- there will be little profit; and
- there will not be adequate internally generated cash flows to finance expansion.

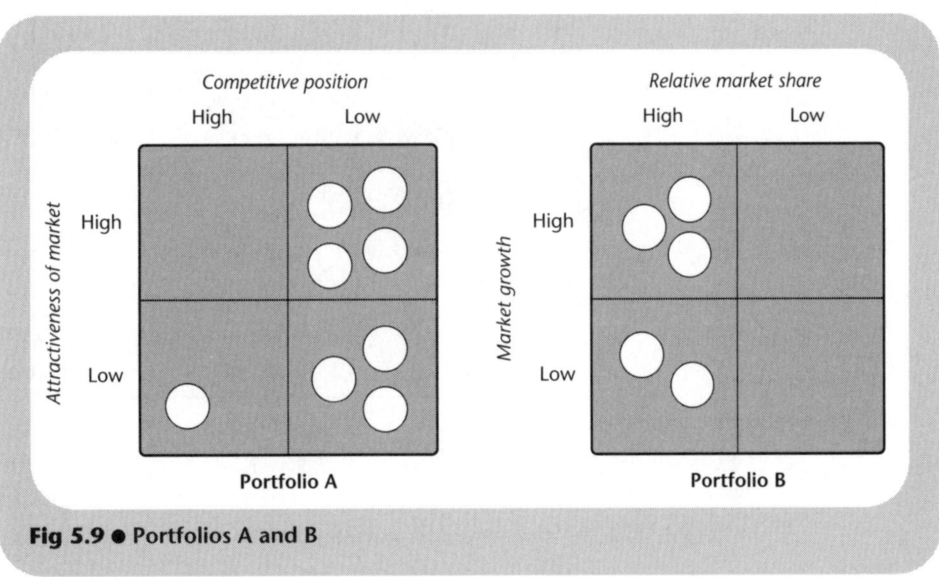

Fig 5.9 ● Portfolios A and B

A substantial proportion of sales stems from growing, attractive markets, which require a high level of investment if the relative market share is to be improved (that is, the competitive position). A further sizeable percentage of sales stems from activities which are unattractive, and thus, in the light of the relative market share, yield little profit and as a result little cash flow.

From Portfolio B in Fig 5.9 (a product portfolio matrix), it can be concluded that:

- cash flow is urgently needed;
- high demands are made of the management; and
- growth and profit are not secure.

Substantial sales are realized in growing markets. This makes heavy financial demands with regard to further growth, and yet relatively few financial resources are being made available. The management of the growth requires a high level of attention as these activities tend to develop by leaps and bounds (for example, the personal computer market).

Constructing future portfolio matrices

It is important to consider how the portfolio matrices will be affected in the future, if current policies are not changed. In Fig 5.10 the present position of a portfolio is

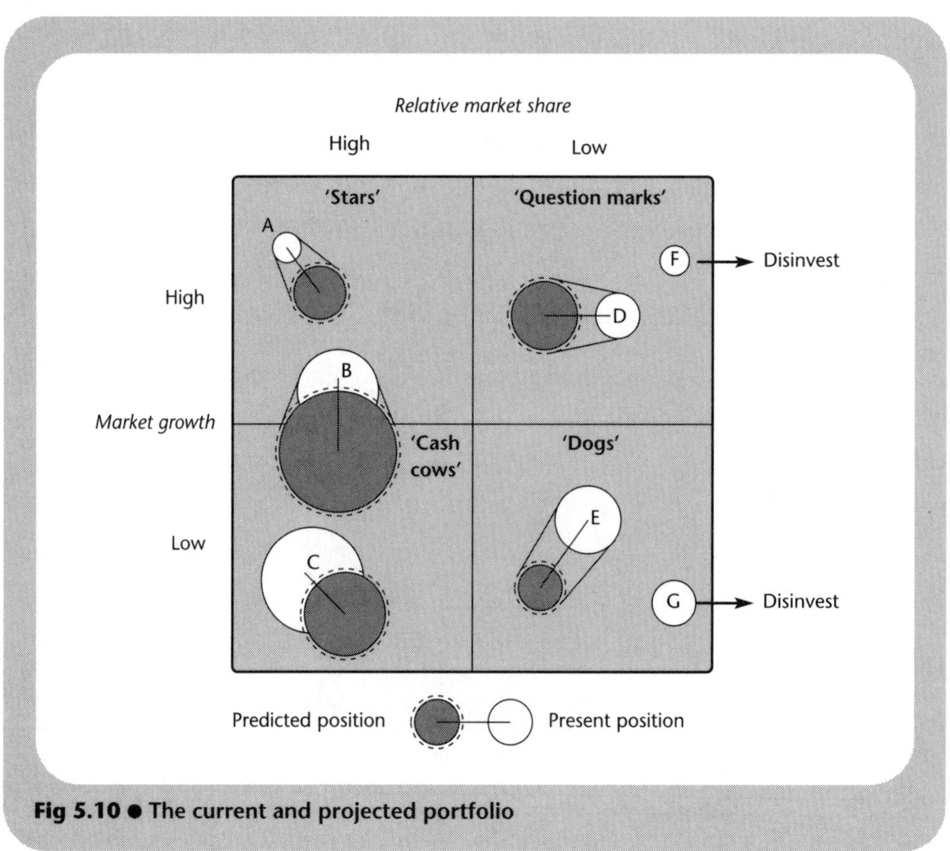

Fig 5.10 ● The current and projected portfolio

developed to show the predicted position of the various elements in *x* years' time. This matrix gives a dynamic picture, whereas earlier matrices gave a static picture.

The information required for the building up of this future picture can be found in the SWOT analysis (strengths, weaknesses, opportunities and threats). By inputting this information into the portfolio analysis, management can make an estimation of the future position. The future picture can then be analysed in the same manner as the present picture. By overlaying the picture of the present with the picture of the future situation, an insight can be gained into the dynamics of the portfolio.

Analysis of the portfolio of the competitors

An application of portfolio analysis which is becoming more popular in recent years is the analysis of the portfolio of competitors. Of course, this portfolio analysis is likely to be less accurate than that of the organization itself, but that does not mean that useful conclusions cannot be derived from it.

For example ...

... suppose that Xerox, the manufacturer of photocopying machines, on the basis of expected growth in the office automation sector, planned to enter the mainframe computer market in competition with IBM. IBM would learn something of Xerox's plans. What could IBM do to avoid or neutralize this threat?

Using the approach of the Boston Consulting Group, the matrix in Fig 5.11 can be drawn up. From this Matrix IBM could conclude that Xerox would have to make a very large investment in order to finance the new activity. The financial resources would have to come from the cash flows of the photocopying machines. IBM could frustrate the

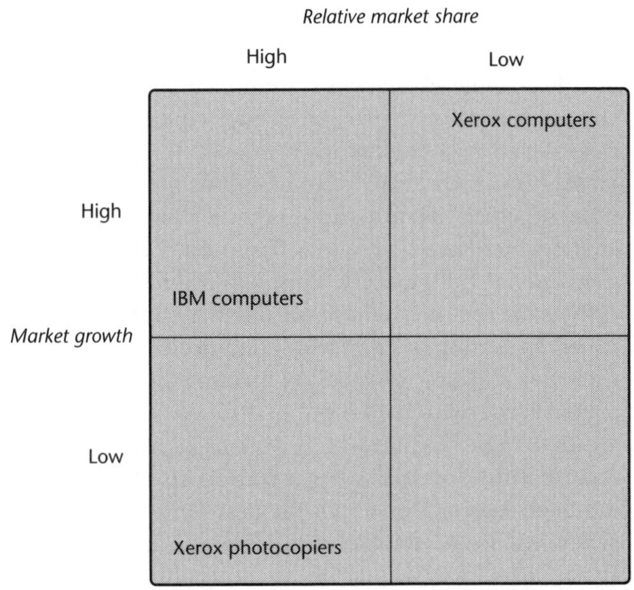

Relative market share (columns: High, Low); *Market growth* (rows: High, Low)

Market growth	High relative market share	Low relative market share
High	IBM computers	Xerox computers
Low	Xerox photocopiers	

Fig 5.11 ● Hypothetical product portfolio matrix showing relative position of IBM and Xerox products

plans of Xerox by putting pressure on the cash flows of Xerox by selling photocopying machines at low prices itself. The required investments of IBM would be relatively low (the machines could be bought from suppliers) and IBM would not necessarily need to make a profit on this activity, because its only purpose would be to protect another activity (computers). Xerox would be in for a very difficult time.

Forming a complete picture

In this final stage of an analysis of an organization's strengths and weaknesses, all the data gathered in the preceding stages, both quantitative and qualitative, needs to be assimilated. In this respect it is helpful to relate the resources assigned to an activity to the results earned from it. This can avoid the possibility of an innovative manager being burdened with the responsibility for a product which has entered the last stage of the life cycle. This manager would be better employed on the development of a promising new activity.

Drawing up the internal appraisal

The assessment of the strengths and weaknesses of an organization can best be conducted by a team of managers from inside the organization. This team should consist of managers from all levels. Experience shows that the position of managers in the company hierarchy affects their opinions, visions and the ways in which they search out answers to problems. If a team is made up of members from a variety of backgrounds, this should limit the distortion of information as far as possible.

It is often useful to discuss an appraisal of strengths and weaknesses with a number of external experts – such as non-executive directors, management consultants and accountants – who know the company well and who can see the company from the perspective of the sector. This discussion will also increase the objectivity of the total picture.

It is possible of course to commission a management consultant to carry out all of the assessment of the strengths and weaknesses. This would maximize objectivity but does have the disadvantage that an external consultant does not always have sufficiently in-depth knowledge of the company and the sector which might lead to a more superficial picture of strengths and weaknesses.

Judgements can be given based on a comparison with competitors and/or the demands of the markets. This judgement needs to be based on both opinions and visions on the one hand, and 'hard', quantitative and financial information on the other. The rating of each of the functional areas can only be given after an analysis of each area and after considering this from a number of aspects.

As in the whole process of strategy formulation, in the appraisal of internal strengths and weaknesses, problems regarding the reliability of information arise. Information about the organization itself is often readily available and reliable, although information about the past sometimes has to be reconstructed. Accuracy and reliability are sometimes compromised due to constraints of time and money. The impact of such inaccuracies on the quality of the final overall picture must be taken into account. The analysis of competitors is fraught with problems of accuracy and reliability. In this case, it is better to consciously work with, for example, optimistic and pessimistic estimations than to pretend information is completely accurate.

5.2.4 Gap appraisal

In the preceding steps of the strategy formulation process, we have determined the current (starting) position through a strategic profile, the expected opportunities and threats, and the organization's strengths and weaknesses. We must now address the question of whether the organization will be able to continue to fulfil its objectives in the coming years? In other words, will there be a strategic gap in the near future between the goals of the organization and the expected reality? This strategic problem is depicted in Fig 5.12.

In considering the possibility of a strategic gap, it is necessary to estimate the results the organization can expect if policies remain unchanged. The projection should determine whether the organization is able to realize its objectives *without the strategy being adjusted*. Of course, this can only happen against the background of the information gathered in the preceding steps of the strategy formulation process.

For example ...

... such a projection can identify the effect of the development of a new market (an opportunity) and not having the services of a strong sales force (a weakness). The effect could be that a goal – for example, a projected rise in sales – will not be attained. Alternatively, entry of a new competitor into a market (a threat) where the organization has a cost disadvantage (a weakness) will lead to the conclusion that unless these is a policy change, results will suffer.

The projected results in the case of unchanged policies can be compared to objectives and goals. From this it will be clear whether a strategic gap exists and whether the

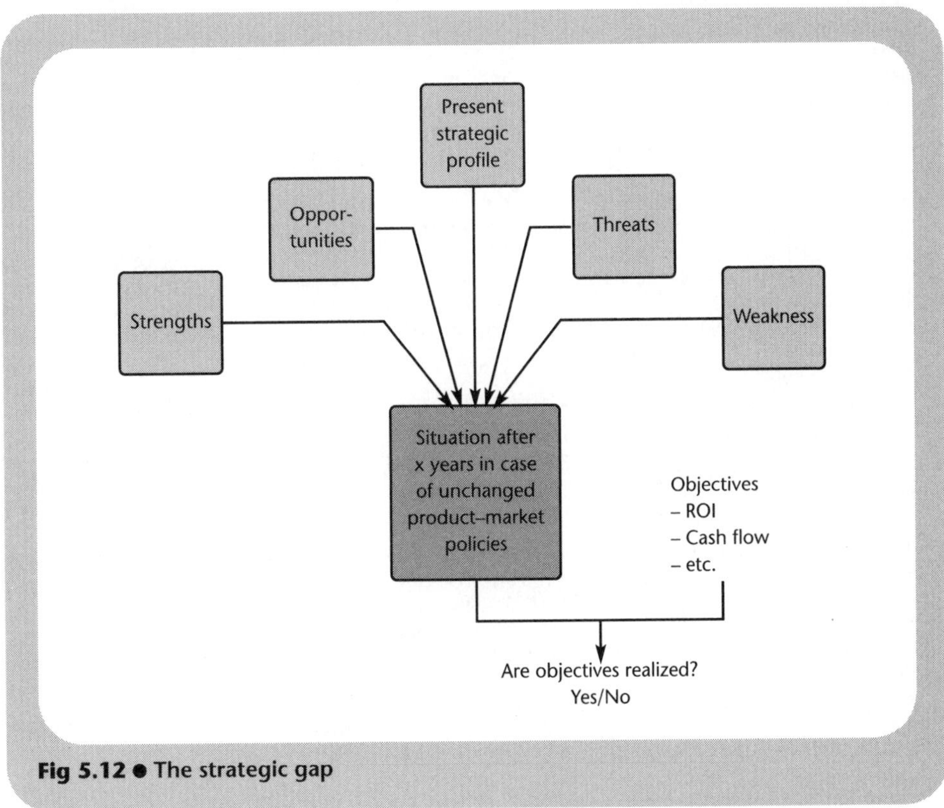

Fig 5.12 ● The strategic gap

company needs to adjust or correct the strategy. In these projections, routine measures such as normal price adjustments are taken into account, but no changes in policy – for example, the introduction of a completely new pricing policy. If it appears that in the future, for example, the return on invested capital or the cash flow will drop to an undesirable level, then alternatives need to be developed in order to close the gap between plans and reality.

Exhibit 5.2

Holderbank single-minded about cement

Switzerland's Holderbank, which has been voted the most respected company in the construction, homebuilding and building materials sector, is well known in the world cement industry as a professional competitor which has never deviated from its simple and successful long-term strategy of being an important participant in all the cement markets in which it competes.

However, visitors to Holderbank's unpretentious headquarters in a small village near Zurich could easily pass by the building without observing that it was the administrative centre for the world's biggest cement company. There are no cement plants in sight and there is no corporate logo advertising Holderbank's sale of more than 50m tonnes a year of cement and its employment of 44,000 people, the vast majority of whom work outside Switzerland.

The history of Holderbank started in a small village of the same name, about 30Km west of Zurich, where the Aargauische Portlandcementfabrik Holderbank-Wildegg was founded in 1912. Two years later, Ernst Schmidheiny bought a stake in the company and began the Schmidheiny family's long association with cement. Today, the family of Thomas Schmidheiny, the chairman and managing director, still controls more than 50 per cent of the company which last year had annual sales of SFr8.3bn ($6.9bn) and earned SFr463m.

Holderbank's emergence as an important multinational owes much to those early years. Even then the Schmidheinys realised that the company's long-term growth could not be secured by depending solely on the domestic Swiss market. The family started investing in overseas cement operations first in neighbouring European countries and in the late 1920s had operations in Egypt and Lebanon.

Over the years, there have been setbacks. Some businesses have been nationalised and the company's fortunes were hit by the problems of the Third World debt crisis in the 1980s. More recently the Mexican economic crisis led to a 25 per cent fall in Mexican cement production and Apasco, Holderbank's Mexican affiliate, saw its earnings collapse from $102m in 1994 to just $17m last year.

These setbacks might have frightened off other companies worried by the stock market's reaction to their exposure. However, Holderbank has always regarded overseas expansion as one of its main strengths and its strong family shareholding has meant that it could afford to be relaxed about the stock market's short term concerns.

When other companies, such as the UK's Blue Circle, were diversifying out of the cement business, Holderbank's diversification took the form of increasing its geographical spread. Today, Switzerland accounts for less than 10 per cent of the group's profits and it is the biggest cement producer in the US and number two in large markets such as Mexico, Brazil, Canada and South Africa. It is very strict about what it regards as its core businesses – cement aggregates, concrete and concrete chemicals – and its diversification is based on geography rather than product. When one market is down another will be up.

Thomas Schmidheiny, who joined the company in 1967 and has been the driving force behind its recent development, says that the cement industry started as a village industry – a small plant serving a couple of villages – and even today it is very much a regional business where dominant market share is the one of the keys to success.

Cement is a commodity product and there are only a limited number of ways that producers can differentiate their products. Quality and services, such as Holderbank's concrete chemicals business, matter. But at the end of the day Holderbank's profitability is very dependent on its pricing power. Consequently, the company's aim is to have market shares of between 30 per cent and 40 per cent in certain well-defined markets. It has sold off plants where its market position is too weak.

Holderbank, in common with other established European producers, has had to contend with increasingly tough competition from eastern Europe. Its reaction has been to attack its cost base, particularly in the area of fuel, and to use its efforts in this area to advance its case as an environmentally sensitive company.

Source: Financial Times, 18 September 1996.

5.2.5 The development of strategic alternatives and options

If the objectives are not being attained, a set of *alternatives* will have to be developed which the organization can employ if it is to survive. The basis for the development of these proposals will be the appraisal of the environment and the internal appraisal of the organization itself.

The first task is to establish what the organization is actually capable of. It may be clear that a strategy gap exists, but it is important now to work out what the company can do to fill that gap.

For example ...

Suppose there is a possibility for a new product in the market (an opportunity). To exploit this opportunity, advanced technical knowledge is necessary (a condition). Unfortunately, the company has been spending little on research (a weak point) and as a result the company can probably not take advantage of this opportunity.

Suppose, in another case, there is an opportunity to realize an increase in sales in a new market area (an opportunity), for example in Germany, which will involve the building up of a dealer network and substantial investment in central distribution facilities (a condition). However, if financial resources are limited (a weak point), this opportunity cannot be utilized in this form. This opportunity could probably be realized in a changed form – for example, by co-operating with another company which has been selling for some time to this market using an existing dealer network. If this company also has some extra financial resources, the sales from this market could be realized and stimulated with so much the more power.

An organization has different growth possibilities. A well-known summary of strategic alternatives is Ansoff's product–market matrix (*see* Fig 5.13).

Market \ Product	*Present*	*New*
Present	Market penetration	Product development
New	Market development	Diversification

Source: After Ansoff, 1965

Fig 5.13 ● The product–market matrix showing strategic alternatives

In this matrix, the different growth possibilities for an organization are plotted. These include:

- *Market penetration* – growth from an existing position through the increase of market share with regard to product or market.
- *Market development* – new markets are sought for the firm's products.
- *Product development* – new products are created to replace current ones.
- *Diversification* – when an organization seeks out both new markets and new products.

We shall now consider each of the strategic alternatives in detail, by dividing them into three groups:

- strategies concerning current product–market activities (market penetration);
- strategies concerning new product–market activities (product development, market development and diversification); and
- strategies concerning phasing out of product–market activities.

Strategies concerning current product–market activities

Strategic alternatives within the framework of the present product–market activities involve the competitive forces which are at work in the company's environment. These forces will already have been determined during the external appraisal of the organization's opportunities and threats at business sector level (*see* section 5.2.2). Possible strategies are:

- competitive strategies (including reduction of competition and improvement of competitive position);
- strategies directed at buyers/clients;
- strategies directed at suppliers;
- strategies directed at substitute products;
- strategies directed at new entrants.

Competitive strategies

These strategies can be divided into two groups: those which *reduce the competition* and those which *improve the competitive position*. In both cases the intended effect is the obtaining of better results.

1. *Competitive reduction*. If the level of competition is reduced, often the intensity of the rivalry decreases and as a result economic results improve. Existing competition can be reduced in a number of ways. The number of competitors in a sector can decrease by means of mergers and takeovers resulting in a lower intensity of competition. A series of mergers or takeovers can also improve the competitive position of the company carrying out the takeover.

For example...

... a foreign company operating in the field of welding took over some welding companies in several European countries. On the one hand, the competition was decreased by this; on the other hand the company's larger size made it possible for research to be carried out which led to improvements in the company's competitive position. The other companies in the sector could not carry out research on product development because of their small size.

In some circumstances, competition can be limited by market agreements. This can be attained by means of cartels, examples of which can be found in areas such as transport (IATA, conferences), banking services (minimum payment conditions, interest rates). In addition a large number of physical goods fall under cartels (for example, bikes).

2. *Position improvement*. The improvement in an organization's competitive position is a much more aggressive option than the reduction in competition. Many alternatives are possible. For example:
   - A company could strive to become the supplier with the *lowest cost price*. For example, Akzo-Nobel strives for the position of 'lowest cost producer' in a number of segments in the fabrics markets. This is referred to as *lowest cost strategy*.

- A company could improve its position by lowering the break-even point. In this way, the company would become less vulnerable to fluctuations in the production volume. A number of the measures used in this area are the same as those used by a supplier with the lowest cost price.
- A company could also reach a better position by clearly distinguishing the product from that of the competitors (*differentiation strategy*). This can be done by strategies such as changing the characteristics of the product, and/or improving the services that go along with the product. For example, the organization can become more in tune with the specific requirements of the customer than its competitors. When the product clearly distinguishes itself from that of the competitor, competition will be based less on pricing policy. Akzo follows this strategy for some of its chemical products. A further example is the small Fiats and small Lancias, which both belong to the same organization and are often also derived from the same technical concept.

Exhibit 5.3

Changing times for Belgium brewers

Like many other national assets, Belgium's beers are little known outside the country.

Only the most dedicated connoisseurs would consider drinking their way through the full range of beers brewed in Belgium. A devotee could try a different brand every day of the year and have 36 left over for a New Year's Eve tasting. No other nation rivals Belgium for varieties of the brew – and yet few Belgian beers are known outside the country.

The traditional strength of the domestic beer market has been a powerful disincentive to exports. Until the late 1980s Belgian brewers concentrated their efforts on winning greater share in their home market. Larger brewers bought up weaker rivals, predominantly family-owned companies that sold up because of disputes over inheritance or because they could not find a successor to the master brewer. The number of independent breweries in Belgium had fallen to 125 by the start of this year from 3,387 at the turn of the century.

Belgian brewers began to look beyond borders when the healthy lifestyle bug, with its encouragement to curb alcohol consumption, hit northern Europe. Domestic beer consumption fell to 115 litres a head in 1989 from 131 litres in 1976, according to the Belgian Brewers' Association, while each Belgian's consumption of mineral water, sodas and fruit juices rose in the same period to 185 litres a year from 119 litres.

The decline in local sales was worrying enough by itself for Belgian brewers. Increasingly, though, they also faced competition in the world market, and particularly Europe, as major continental, US and East Asian players timbered up for the single European market in 1993.

Interbrew is the only Belgian company with the resources to carry the battle for market share beyond Belgian borders. The company is led by José Dedeurwaerder, a Walloon who holds US citizenship and is used to fighting tight corners. He overrode French prejudice against Belgians to rise to second-in-command at Renault, the French state-owned car company where he worked for 30 years, though in 1987 he fell out with its incoming chairman, Raymond Lévy.

When Dedeurwaerder, 59, became chief executive at Interbrew, he set about restructuring the company, closing down some of its smaller breweries to the dismay of the trade unions. However, Interbrew's major competitors had taken similar measures years before.

Dedeurwaerder expects competition in Europe from such giants as Japan's Kirin and Anheuser Busch of the US, the world leader, but believes European competitors pose a greater threat. Although Heineken of the Netherlands is the only European brewery in the global top five in production terms, four of the top five overseas sellers (ranked by their percentage of sales outside their home market) are European. And the current rankings are unlikely to remain static.

European brewers are consolidating their positions ready for the single market onslaught. Carlsberg of Denmark last year set up a joint venture with Allied-Lyons, the UK's fifth-largest brewer, to strengthen its share of the UK market. This April

continued overleaf

Exhibit 2.1 continued

Heineken announced the establishment of a distribution centre in Germany, the market on which all large brewers have set their sights. Germans display the world's greatest thirst for beer, knocking back an average of 142.8 litres of beer each in 1990 against 72 litres in Spain and 23 litres in Italy. 'We will be watching the German market very closely,' Interbrew's Gérard says.

The only beers that are successfully marketed across a wide range of countries and palates are lagers such as Stella Artois. However, as the European lager market becomes increasingly saturated, many industry analysts see a prime growth area in speciality beers, which offer lower-volume – but higher-margin – sales opportunities.

This is good news for Belgium, claimed by the Belgians to be the birthplace of Saint Arnold, patron saint of beer. The kingdom boasts 40 different types and 400 brands; beers made with cherry, mint, raspberries, peaches and herbs; brown beers, white beers, even red beers; *gueuzes*, *krieks* and *lambics*.

Belgian brewers are well versed in fighting their corner with novelty beers and innovative names and packaging. Even the smallest brewers brings out a special brew for Christmas – Stella Artois was originally a Christmas beer. And although Interbrew's star performer is a lager, the company's brands also include Jupiler, Vieux Temps, Hoegaarden Blanche and Grand-Cru, the Forbidden Fruit, Grimbergen and the Mort Subite.

In the meantime, Belgian speciality beers are beginning to find favour with foreigners. In April André Plisnier and his partner Denis Blais opened the UK's first Belgian beer café-restaurant in Hampstead in London. 'The response has been fantastic,' Plisnier says. 'People just can't believe it. Over here beer drinking is just not part of our food culture. We are showing them the delights of Oysters à la Gueuze washed down with a Hoegaarden.' Further afield, Interbrew has sprung its Hoegaarden Blanche and Leffe Blonde on the unsuspecting US public.

'I am proud to say that ours is the most expensive beer in the United States,' Dedeurwaerder said after a pilot launch in California. Interbrew hopes that West Coast citizens will be swayed by the quality and healthy image of its speciality beers and has designed packaging to emphasize these points.

Source: *International Management*, June 1992.

Strategies directed at customers

Sometimes results can be improved over time by developing strategies with regard to the customers. If clients occupy a powerful position, pressure on results will increase.

- In some cases a company may focus on specific segments of the market which offer better profit opportunities. Before this *focus strategy* can be realized, a well considered segmentation of the market must be carried out. Then the profit contributions for each segment need to be calculated. By spreading sales over a greater number of customers, the company becomes less dependent on individual customers and its negotiation position is improved.
- It is sometimes possible for a system to be set up that means that a client will incur high switching costs if suppliers are changed. This can be done, for example, by closely linking manufacturing processes. In the field of order processing, the supplier can provide the customer with a large amount of information through the EDI (Electronic Data Interchange) with regard to sales. This will offer the clients the advantages of better information supply, a higher level of service and lower incidence of mistakes. Switching to another supplier would mean that clients would no longer receive the information or would have to gather the information themselves at high costs.
- A company can improve its negotiation position with regard to the customer if there is a realistic change of *forward integration* – that is a chance that the organization will become involved in distribution or open stores itself.

Strategies directed at suppliers

An organization can adopt a number of strategies in an attempt to improve its position with regard to suppliers.

1. Companies or individuals can come together to make joint purchases. With larger purchase contracts, the transaction costs decrease and the organizations have a stronger position in the purchase market.
2. An organization can use a number of different suppliers in order to prevent becoming too dependent on one. This lack of dependence means that the organization is in a stronger negotiating position.
3. Spreading purchases over a number of suppliers is also recommended as a way of reducing risk. If one of the suppliers has difficulties, then another supplier can perhaps make up the shortfall.
4. The realistic possibility of *backward integration* – that is, a chance that the organization will become involved in the production of supplies – can also influence the negotiation position of the supplier. Companies can also help to establish a new supplier.

It is important to have available as much information as possible on a supplier – for example, financial position, sales, other clients, etc. With this background information, it is often easier to understand and predict the actions of suppliers. In a few cases, this enables an organization and its suppliers to search for solutions to joint problems which suit the circumstances of both parties.

Strategies directed at substitute products

As in the case of new entrants, an organization can only strive to limit the success of substitute products; it is almost impossible to stop a substitute product coming on to the market.

1. To protect itself from the effects of substitute products, the organization should ensure that in the eyes of the customer, the organization's product is giving good value for money. This is also important as a way of protecting against the effects of competitors.
2. Customers often perceive substitute products as having a number of extra attractive features. It is therefore necessary for the qualities of the existing product to be brought to the attention of the buyers. This is sometimes possible by means of (joint) advertising campaigns.
3. An organization can strive for a higher degree of product innovation itself, although this makes heavy demands on the organization with regard to research and development, financial capacity and capabilities.
4. Once the substitute product achieves a good market position, it is sometimes possible for the manufacturer of an existing product to enter into manufacturing or marketing agreements with the producers of the substitute product.

Strategies directed at new entrants

In most cases, there is nothing an organization can do to prevent the arrival of new entrants. It is sometimes possible, however, to make entrance into the market less attractive for newcomers. This effect can be attained in a number of different ways, including:

- If distribution channels are a critical factor for success in the sector, an organization can attempt to link sellers to its brand exclusively. For example, many official car dealers of the well known car brands are not allowed to sell any other or competing brand. As a result, it is difficult for newcomers to build up a dealer network which covers a whole country, which is often a condition for business success.
- It is often advisable to avoid giving too much publicity to high profits as such publicity could make the market more attractive to new entrants. In contrast, when profits are low, publicity will discourage new entrants.
- New suppliers can be excluded from a market through the application of patents. In this way, it is possible to legally prevent the number of competitors from increasing. This will not always be an advantage.

For example ...

... IBM launched a new series of personal computers onto the market in the course of 1992 in order to decrease the competitive pressure of the so-called clones. The expectations of experts was that it would be technically possible to use the software developed for the new IBM on the new generation of clones, even though these are technically different.

- In rare cases, it is possible to influence the process of legislation in such a way that entrance into a market is made almost impossible – for example, by quotas, tariffs or import restrictions. For example, in the US, the Harley-Davidson factory succeeded in having the import tariff on heavy Japanese motors raised from 4.4 per cent to more than 40 per cent.

Strategies concerning new activities

The Ansoff product–market matrix can be used in an organization's search for new activities. New activities can take the form of product development, market development (including internationalization) and diversification.

Minicase 5.1

Heineken introduces German 'cosmopolitan' youth to the 'grand café'

Heineken is going to introduce the *grand café*, which is very popular in the Netherlands, to German cities in an attempt to attract 'open, cosmopolitan thinking young people between 18 and 35 years of age' – Heineken's target group in Germany.

Heineken is teaming up with local distribution companies to set up a grand café in every major city in Germany, and in so doing is prepared for the first time in Germany to grant a loan to the proprietor.

Until 1993, Germans only knew Heineken from holidays abroad, where they often labelled Heineken as the least disgusting of the foreign beers. Back in Germany, many preferred their regional beers. Even though Heineken operated in 150 countries, until 1993 the company did not dare to take on 'the most difficult market in the world'.

Heineken is now sold in 450 restaurants, which either enjoy a very good reputation, or attract the 'right', cosmopolitan clientele. Heineken is sponsoring jazz, sailing, golf and tennis events all over Germany and advertising in cinemas and magazines. Heineken asked readers of local papers in ten large German cities to compile their top ten catering establishments.

In spite of its success in restaurants, Heineken is not yet available in German shops. The company wants to enter the market 'in stocking feet', and first of all wants to establish the image of Heineken as a top brand. Although the brand is available in a select number of licensed outlets, the company does not want Heineken to appear on supermarket shelves before 1998. By 2002, when Heineken will celebrate its first ten years on German soil, the company wants to have gained a 10 per cent share of the German market for import beer and wants to be the major imported brand. This will involve toppling the current number one – the Danish Tuborg – from its throne.

Source: Adapted from *Trouw*, 9 December 1994.

Product development

An organization will try to sell other kinds of products to the existing group of clients by focusing on their other needs. For example, a supplier of everyday stationery like writing paper, cash books, etc. may start to supply word processors and cash registers. Product development can also involve the broadening of the existing range.

Market development

Improved results can also be achieved by starting to service other markets. This can be done both by serving other groups of clients, and by serving new geographical areas. The latter possibility may involve exporting or setting up foreign subsidiaries, but geographical spread is also possible on a national basis – for example by building up a nationwide retail chain, rather than restricting operations to the region from which the firm originates.

In the light of European integration, *internationalization* has come to the fore as a strategic option. Organizations must decide whether they want to operate on an international basis, and, if so, by which means of market penetration strategy and in which countries. Organizations which decide not to 'go international' cannot afford to lose sight of the consequences of this trend toward internationalization, as the nature of competition will change, both internationally and nationally. Three strategies involving internationalization can be distinguished:

- *Internationalization strategy* – in principle, an extension of an export strategy, involving an attempt by the organization to realize an expansion abroad based on its national strategy for the domestic market.
- *Multinational strategy* – an international expansion strategy conducted through local marketing strategies.
- *Globalization strategy* – with organizations determining their competitive strategy from a global (or, for example, European) perspective and making decisions based on the company's positioning within this global market.

Diversification

Diversification is the entering of new markets with products which are new to the organization. Examples of diversified organizations include ITT, Thyssen Bornemisza, Daimler Benz, the Thomson Group, Hanson. Diversification can be very risky, because management may not know the products and the markets sufficiently well to lead the organization through the hard times. *Conglomerate diversification* refers to a situation where an organization is created whose constituent parts are in no way dependent on each other and there is no synergy between the parts.

If there is a relationship between the various new activities – for example, in the technological, manufacturing or marketing field – we speak of *concentric diversification*. In this case synergy can be realized, and the risks are also easier to forecast.

New activities can be added to a portfolio, either through internal development, or through forms of strategic co-operation (mergers, takeovers, alliances). The latter forms can be implemented quite quickly, while leaving other companies to run the risks of internal development. Once developments have proved themselves to be favourable, the company can be taken over.

Exhibit 5.4

Saurer responds to treatment

'Company doctor' Ernst Thomke has turned Swiss group round

When Mr Ernst Thomke, the Swiss 'company doctor', took charge of Saurer just over a year ago, he inherited a famous company which had lost more than SFr100m ($81.1m) in two years. It was also about to relinquish its title as the world's largest maker of sophisticated textile spinning machines.

This week, Saurer reported an operating profit of SFr31m in the first eight months of 1996, against a loss of SFr23m. Mr Thomke announced he was sufficiently pleased with his patient's progress that he was handing day-to-day operating responsibility to Mr Heinrich Fischer, a long-time associate and former executive with Oerlikon-Bührle.

Mr Thomke, 57, who revamped the Swiss watch industry and restructured the Motor Columbus electric utility, wants to spend more time on his biggest challenge – knocking the loss-making Bally shoe business into shape so that it can be floated in a couple of years. By then, he reckons it should be worth SFr1bn–SFr2bn and be attracting the same sort of international interest as this week's flotation of Tag Heuer, the luxury Swiss watch maker.

Oerlikon-Bührle, the conglomerate which owns Bally, is only capitalised at SFr1.4bn, which suggests the market may have reservations about Mr Thomke's bold plans. Nevertheless, Mr Thomke has a strong stock market following, because of his record in rescuing some of Switzerland's most problematic companies.

At Saurer, he appears to have done in one year what bigger Swiss competitors, such as Sulzer, have failed to do in five – namely revive the fortunes of one of the leading textile machinery groups. The turnround is all the more impressive since it has taken place against a background of a relatively weak world market.

Saurer had been dominated by engineers who liked nothing better than designing new prototypes. When Mr Thomke arrived, he found that one-third of the parts of Saurer's machines had been modified. The spare-part business, which was being hit by cheap overseas competition, was subsidising machinery manufacturing. Margins had collapsed in the US, Saurer's biggest market, after a price war with Rieter, a bigger and better-financed Swiss competitor.

Mr Thomke was quick to introduce a clear product and pricing strategy. Instead of producing dozens of new machines, Saurer's engineers now concentrate on adding value to existing models. The spinning machine business, accounting for two-thirds of group sales, has been split into separate profit centres and management attention is being focused on problem areas such as ring spinning and winding machines.

Break-even levels have been cut by nearly half in open-ended rotor spinning machines, the biggest product line. The spare parts business is being expanded aggressively and is expected to become an important source of profits. The wages of the group's Swiss workforce have been cut and more flexible working systems have been introduced.

Switzerland's machine-tool industry was once a world leader, but many companies disappeared because they were unable to compete internationally from a high cost base. Mr Thomke has proved that Swiss textile machinery manufacturers need not follow the machine-tool industry into oblivion.

Source: Financial Times, 27 September 1996.

Strategies concerning phasing out activities

A company can withdraw from an activity in two ways: by shutting down operations (totally or partially) or by selling the activity. The decision to shut down – for example, the closing of a factory – is a very radical one, both in terms of the social impact and the economic consequences. The sale of an activity could involve a third party or the existing management and personnel – referred to as a *management buyout*. Siemens, Philips and Unilever have all been involved with management buyouts in recent years.

5.2.6 The mission statement and criteria for evaluation and choice

Formulating a mission statement

During the strategic planning process, management will have to formulate the areas of activity and main objectives of the organization in a structured form – that is, the *mission of the organization*. A 'mission statement' specifies an organization's vision and direction for the following five to ten years. A mission statement is not changed fundamentally on a year-by-year basis. It comprises information about the nature and the range of the organization's market activities: horizontal, vertical and geographical.

The following questions are addressed during the formulation of a mission statement:

- What do we want to be?
- What is our business? What will our business be?
- Who are our customers? On which customer group do we want to focus?
- In which way do we want to offer a distinguishing and lasting added value to our customers?

These questions may seem straightforward, but an organization's answers must be well considered and well thought out, because to a great extent they determine the results of strategic planning. The mission should not be formulated in terms that are too narrow or too wide: on the one hand, it needs to give clear directions; on the other hand it should not immediately exclude a whole range of strategic alternatives. The mission is also a means of communication for the organization and as such should be succinct and business-like and, most importantly, should engage, commit and motivate its readers.

Criteria for evaluation and choice

In order to make a well considered choice from the alternatives, it is necessary to analyse the expected consequences of each alternative from a number of different perspectives. In this way, both the short-term and long-term consequences can be identified. A specific alternative could have long-term consequences that are very attractive, but at the same time could cause problems in the short term. The reverse could also be the case. It is possible that an alternative could appear desirable, and yet could in practice involve some extremely undesirable consequences. It would be tempting to ignore or underestimate the undesired consequences and instead stress the positive aspects of an idea.

Many of the consequences of a particular strategy can be quantified – for example, market growth, cash flow, etc. However, others, such as environmental consequences or image improvement, are not quantifiable and yet are of great importance. Other criteria which should be kept in mind in the choice of strategic alternatives are:

- consistency in terms of goals;
- consistency in terms of personal values;
- consistency in terms of capabilities;
- the possibility of synergy;
- the degree of risk and uncertainty;
- the degree of flexibility;
- the timing; and
- the change implications.

Consistency in terms of goals

A specific alternative could indeed support the goal of growth in a positive sense, but not the wish of management to maintain a constant ratio between equity and debts. A new activity could demand more financial resources than can be raised by the organization itself, by shareholders or by other financial stakeholders. In such cases, further consideration of goals regarding growth and financial structure will have to take place, or else new alternatives will have to be sought.

Consistency in terms of personal values

The personal ambitions and preferences of top management are of great importance to the realization of a planned development and so consistency between strategy and personal values is a condition for success. A strategy of fast growth which will demand a great deal from the top management, can certainly not be implemented by a group of managers who, first and foremost, value a quiet life.

Recently, the importance of personal values to an organization has been expressed in studies of the so-called *culture of the organization* – that is, a system of values, norms and behavioural patterns which are shared by the employees. In many cases, this value pattern seems to work out very positively when it forms a coherent whole – as was described in the Peters and Waterman book, *In Search of Excellence*. Those authors also signalled that an existing value pattern is not always appropriate for the successful implementation of all plans for new activities.

Consistency in terms of capabilities

The successful execution of a strategy depends for an important part on the *capabilities* of the organization. An organization which chooses the path of product development as a strategy, needs to have a good research and development department at its disposal. If this department is of mediocre quality, then this strategy is doomed to failure. The same holds true if the financial possibilities are too limiting or the capabilities and skills of the managers are not appropriate.

The possibility of synergy

It is important to consider the extent to which new activities can be supported by and profit from the existing activities and capabilities of the organization. When certain advantages can be obtained from the combining of activities this is referred to as *synergy*.

Synergy can result in the following areas:

- *Sales* – when new products can be sold through the existing channels.
- *Production* – when the same machines can be used for the manufacturing of new products.
- *Investment* – when the combination of activities demands lower investments in machinery and inventory, than when individual activities are executed separately.
- *Management* – when the problems which the new activity causes are similar to the problems that have been solved before.
- *Finance* – when cash flow can be allocated and/or utilized by higher yielding related or unrelated activities and in combination gives a higher rate of return.

Synergy can be achieved because the combination of old and new activities involves lower costs and, for example, because time is gained. In certain cases it is very important that a company is first to come to the market with a certain product or service, because the profit margins are still high and are not yet affected by strong competition. Once competition increases, the production synergy might start to become of importance. It is important to establish clearly whether the organization is to be an innovator – in which case the synergy in the initial phase is of paramount importance – or a follower of new developments, in which case production synergy will be more important.

Synergy can also be negative, in the sense that a certain combination can have obvious detrimental effects – for example, companies previously active in industrial markets which decide to also carry consumer goods. The characteristics and the demands of these two markets are so different, that companies which try to conquer the consumer market with an industrial-market approach usually fail dramatically. There is obviously no synergy.

Minicase 5.2

Delayed synergy effects at Akzo Nobel

The advantages of the merger between the Dutch company, Akzo, and the Swedish company, Nobel, have taken longer than expected to be translated into results. The chemical company had counted on receiving a considerable part of the 200 million guilders of synergy effects in 1995. However, according to a member of the management council of Akzo Nobel, this has not happened: 'It will take longer. It is spread over more years. A considerable part of the advantage will only be expressed in the 1996 figures.'

The merger of Akzo and Nobel has had a limited influence on the figures to date. The first results of the merger seem to be coming through now, but it is a slow process. The new company has greater purchasing power and certain cost savings have been made. The head office in Stockholm has been relocated to a less expensive site and has downsized from 65 to 35 people. Work is also proceeding on the changes to brand names, the relocation of distribution centres and the concentration of production activities.

Akzo Nobel has indicated, however, that it wants these synergy advantages to be introduced carefully, one small step at a time.

Source: Adapted from *Het Financieele Dagblad*, May 1995.

Degree of risk and uncertainty

Since strategic decisions often involve the commitment of relatively large amounts of money for long periods of time, it is very important to examine the *degree of risk and uncertainty* which is connected with this sort of decision. Is management willing and able to live with the increased risks and uncertainty? The dilemma is that projects with high profit expectation are often those that involve a higher degree of uncertainty. On the other hand, a company which only has projects with low risk and therefore low profit expectation will rarely enjoy anything other than average economic results.

Degree of flexibility

This refers to the degree to which adjustments can be made to strategy in the light of changing circumstances, possibly as a means of countering uncertainty. When a certain alternative involves high uncertainty with a low degree of flexibility, this is less attractive than when the degree of flexibility is relatively high. In the case of chemical installations, for example, the flexibility is increased if buildings are erected as modules because this means that they can be quickly converted for the production of a different or a changed product, when a planned product does not perform according to plan.

Timing

This is also an important factor in the choice of strategy. First of all, the speed with which management wants to implement the alternative needs to be assessed. High speed means being ahead of the competition, with lower costs in the initial phase. A more gradual execution offers the opportunity to adjust to changing circumstances, although higher costs are incurred. In many lines of business it has proved very difficult for other companies to affect a market position once a company has attained it. The attempt by General Electric and European computer manufacturers to attack the position of IBM in the market for mainframe computers is an example of this. These attempts have led to large losses for the aggressors. However, the highly successful, late entry of IBM into the market for personal computers is an example of how this can be attained – as Apple learned to its cost.

The change implications

The organization must address the question of how much its structure and capabilities will have to be changed in order to execute the new strategy. Organizations cannot change track overnight. The organizational structure often limits the flexibility and manoeuvrability of the organization.

For example ...

... IBM recognized that its existing procedures and structure would become a clear limiting factor in the development of its personal computer business. It solved this problem by setting up a new division with a totally different internal structure to the rest of the company. The approach which was right for the established products was not appropriate for a new, pioneering activity. In the early nineties, the IBM management decided to split up the organization into a number of discrete and independently operated units. The old structure had become too heavy and bureaucratic to cope with the speed of change in the computer market.

Monitoring a strategy

No matter how much thought goes into a strategy, the results are never completely certain in advance. That is why it is always important, after execution, to compare the results of a strategy with the original plan. If the results are disappointing, the causes need to be traced and the strategy needs to be adjusted or corrective actions need to be taken. In some cases, the cause is the strategy itself, if this strategy was not sufficiently based on relevant factors. Competitors may have counter attacks or markets may have reacted differently to expected, or perhaps other unpredictable events occurred. In all these cases, the strategy will have to be adjusted to the new circumstances.

Critical success factors

Before moving on to the actual taking of strategic decisions, the critical success factors (CSF) of each alternative strategy need to be listed (*see* section 2.4.8 and Table 5.1). This is important because it will ensure that the organization is able to make the ultimate strategic choice and to implement this choice successfully. The critical success factors of each alternative can be compared to each other and to the conclusions of the SWOT analysis. This will produce a better picture of:

- the attainability, potential and risks of certain alternatives;
- the actions which will have to be taken to realize certain alternatives;
- the factors which will affect the implementation of the strategy.

Making a choice

Making the final choice is never a simple procedure, due to the dynamic nature of strategic problems. Neither the organization, not its environment is a constant factor; each is a variable which is constantly changing. Strategic problems are characterized by uncertainty, which means that the subjective judgement of the managers involved in the strategy formulation process is of great importance.

5.3 ORGANIZATION OF STRATEGIC PLANNING

A company which wants to introduce strategic planning must address the question of how the process should be organized. In order to provide some insight into this problem, a number of building blocks are suggested in this section.

5.3.1 Forms of strategic planning organization

When strategic planning was in its infancy, this activity was mostly carried out by a small team of specialists who advised, contributed to (often contentiously) or, in a few cases, even determined the strategy. It became clear, however, that of the many plans developed by the bright staff specialists, few were implemented. On the one hand, the plans were not always realistic; on the other hand, the managers who were responsible for the implementation did not appear to be highly motivated.

As a result the committee form of strategic planning organization developed. Line managers at different levels in the organization are supported by one or two planning specialists. Such a committee can, for example, consist of one or two members from the board of directors, the finance director, the controller, some division managers and a few employees chosen for their knowledge and experience on some specific areas which are important to strategy formulation. In this form, specialist knowledge of planning techniques and specialist knowledge of the market, production, etc. sit side by side.

In recent years, a form of strategy organization with greater involvement by line managers has become increasingly common. The making of plans is viewed as a line activity and should not be left to staff specialists. In this form, planning specialists play only a supporting and co-ordinating role.

Exhibit 5.5

Strategic planning

After a decade of US downsizing, Big Thinkers are back in vogue

Many mainstream US consulting firms, including onetime strategy leader BCG, say their strategy business is booming. Meanwhile, a new wave of gurus and consulting firms has emerged. A recent study by the Association of Management Consulting Firms found that executives, consultants, and B-school professors all agree that strategy is now the single most important management issue and will remain so for the next five years.

This wouldn't be management if the new thinking about strategy didn't come with a whole lexicon of new buzzwords. Forget about the value chain, experience curves, stars, and dogs. Now, any enlightened discussion of strategy is likely to include talk of co-evolution and the business ecosystem – creating networks of relationships with customers, suppliers, and rivals to gain greater competitive advantage.

Today's gurus of strategy urge companies to democratize the process – once the sole province of a company's senior officers – by handing strategic planning over to teams of line and staff managers from different disciplines. To keep the planning process close to the realities of markets, today's strategists say it should also include interaction with key customers and suppliers.

Thats also the direction Jack Welch has been moving in ever since he nuked GE's central-planning department. Welch pushed responsibility for strategy down to each of General Electric Co.'s 12 unit heads, who meet every summer with Welch and his top management team for day-long planning sessions. 'The focus is on strategy, both near-term and a four-year look into the future,' says Steven Kerr, vice-president for corporate management development. 'They lay out what they are going to do, what new products they are interested in, and what our competition is doing.'

But there's no one at GE with the title of head of strategic planning.'If you had one, what would such a person do?' asks Kerr. He would require reports. Bound in vinyl, no doubt. Definitely not the way the strategic-planning game is played.

Source: Business Week, 2 September 1996.

5.3.2 The organizational structure

The following elements of the organizational structure are important to the organization of the strategic planning process:

- *The division of labour.* This element of the structure determines the level at which certain types of information are available – for example, with regard to product–market combinations. A functionally structured organization demands a different approach to an organization arranged in divisions (*see* Chapter 6).
- *The degree of centralization/decentralization.* Strategy formulation must link up with the decision-making authorities. This not only involves availability of relevant information, but also the strategic plans (*see* Chapter 7).

5.3.3 The strategic planning cycle

In large organizations with more than one division, the organization of the planning process partly depends on where the main focus of the planning activity lies: in the division (in which case the approach is considered to be 'bottom-up') or with the board of directors (an approach referred to as 'top-down'). Both approaches exist in practice. Many companies use a mixed form, in which intensive interaction takes place between the board of management and the divisional management. The corporate planning staff or the planning specialists should be able to supply and distribute the results of their analyses into economic developments, interest rates, inflation, currency rates, etc.

Regardless of which approach is adopted, the planning cycle should allow the possibility of feedback to the previous steps. However, the strategic planning cycle almost always comes to an end with the formulation of a budget for the coming year: this means that this has to be ready, finalized and authorized before the end of the financial year. The activities in the planning cycle are spread out over the financial year. In many organizations, a timetable with the data for the different steps, will be drawn up with regard to this.

Top-down approach

The planning cycle with a top-down approach is depicted in Fig 5.14.

1. The board of management draws up a planning document in which the expected results from the divisions are laid down.
2. The divisional management converts these into rather general plans and resubmits these to the corporate management.

3/4. The board of management approves these plans and sends them to the divisional management.

5. The individual departments in each division are asked to draw up plans in the functional fields.
6. The plans, along with their financial consequences, are assessed by the divisional management and, if judged appropriate, are sent to the corporate management.
7. The board of management approves these plans.

8/9. The plans are sent to the divisions and functional departments as task assignments and budgets.

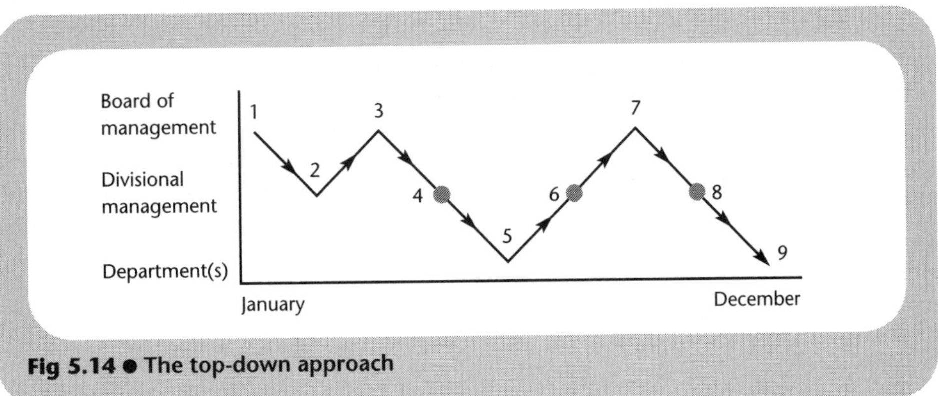

Fig 5.14 ● The top-down approach

In the case of the top-down approach, the initiative is with the top, but there is also a major contribution from the lower levels.

Bottom-up approach

The planning cycle for a bottom-up approach is depicted in Fig 5.15.

1. The different divisions or business units produce plans for the future.

2/3. These are assessed by the corporate management and, perhaps after revision, approved.

4. Divisional management sends the plans to the functional departments for more detailed elaboration and budget preparation.

5/6. These plans and budgets are presented to the divisional management and, after approval, sent to the board of management for approval.

7/8. After approval, the plans and budgets are sent to the divisions and departments in the form of task assignments and budgets.

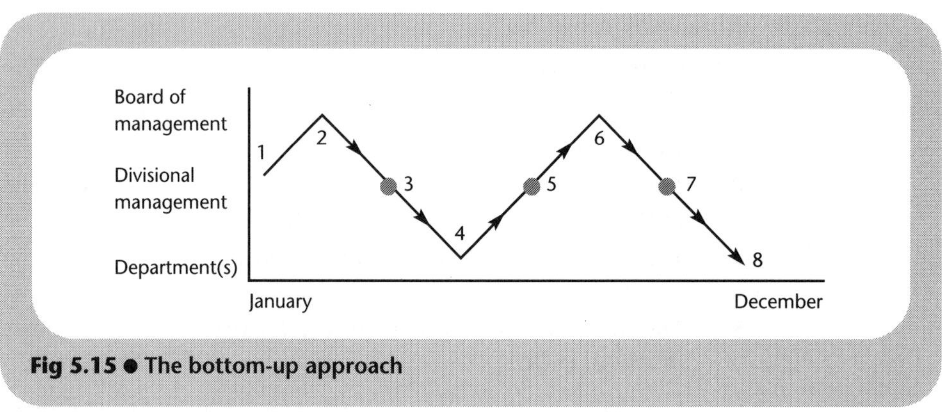

Fig 5.15 ● The bottom-up approach

Although the bottom-up approach offers advantages with regard to the motivation of those involved, there is always a danger that the planning will simply involve extending existing activities into the future. As a result, the possibilities of innovation will be severely limited. In companies where divisional or business unit management are not particularly innovative, are very operationally oriented and have a low strategic capability, the top-down approach should be the preferred form of strategic planning organization.

Figure 5.16 shows, in a somewhat adapted form, the model of strategy formulation described in section 5.2. The adaptation mainly involves the more detailed elaboration of plans for the functional fields. This is further split up into year plans and budgets. The reporting system with regard to implementation and possible feedback, is also indicated. This problem will be covered in more detail in Chapter 10.

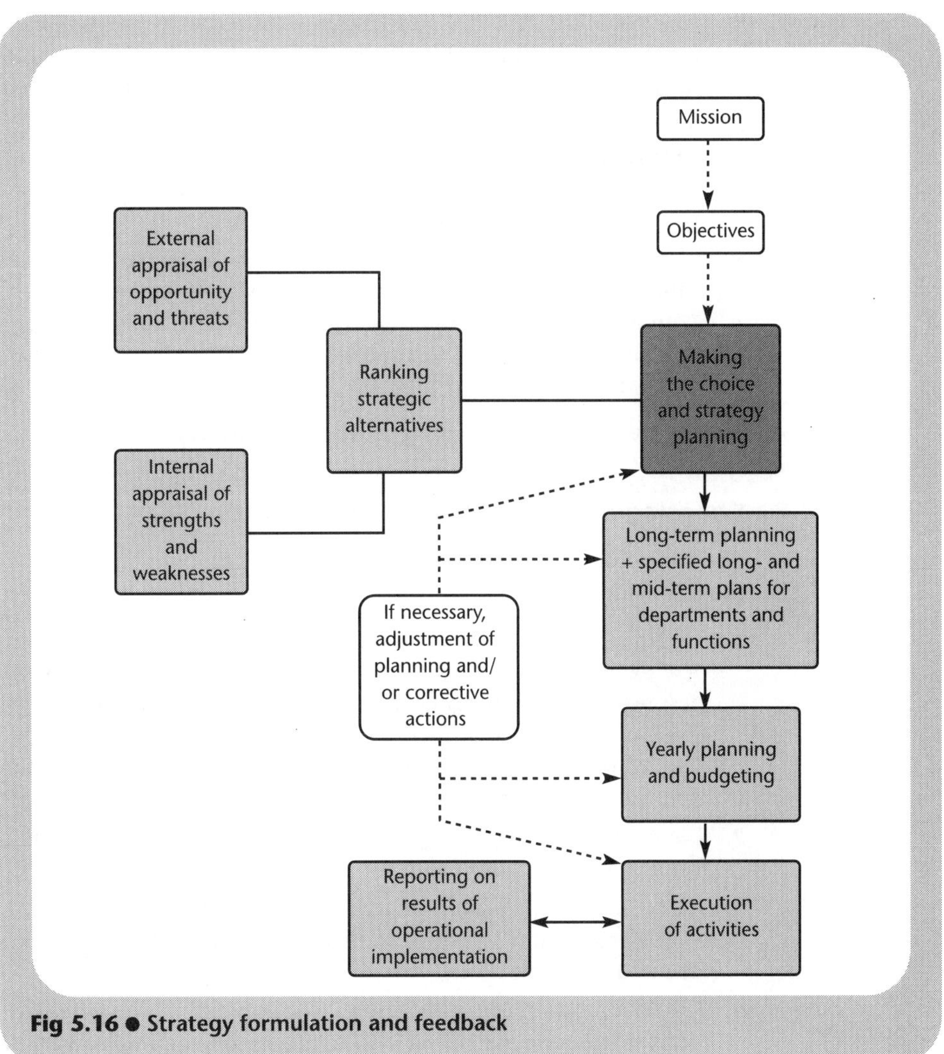

Fig 5.16 ● Strategy formulation and feedback

5.4 ● STRATEGIC CO-OPERATION

In principle it is possible for strategic alternatives to be realized in co-operation with other organizations.

5.4.1 The strategic co-operation decision

When an organization is considering whether it should enter into a co-operative relationship, in principle three factors are of importance:

- *The costs*. When the costs of a strategic alternative are too high for an individual company, it is still possible for the strategy to be implemented jointly with another organization. A higher level of financial resources will then be available, than the organization could have supplied on its own.
- *The risks*. In some cases the risks of the strategy not being successful are too high. The failure of the organization to attain the goal could even endanger its survival. Co-operation would involve spreading the risk.
- *The timing of the introduction of the strategy*. A company may need to implement a strategy quickly in order for it to be successful. If competitors can implement a strategy more quickly, this often means that the organization falls behind – for example, due to higher cost levels (on the experience curve) or of restricted access to distribution channels.

The relative importance of each of these considerations will vary from case to case.

5.4.2 Choosing a form of strategic co-operation

The choice of one form of strategic co-operation over another will be determined by the following factors:

1. *The strategic goals of the organization*. These might include: identifying and accessing new technologies and skills; acquiring knowledge and skills in existing technologies; reacting quickly and effectively to market opportunities; gaining market share quickly; striving for cost price leadership – to name but a few. It is important to determine the strategic goals of a potential partner and to ensure that they do not conflict with the organization's goals.
2. *The market in which the organization operates*. Specific markets often have specific forms of strategic co-operation.
3. *The position in the product–market life cycle*. Certain forms of strategic co-operation will be appropriate for new products and organizations while others will be suitable for mature organizations.
4. *The need for confidentiality*. Strategic co-operation can offer instant access to new technologies and skills, but also carries risks when the organization's own knowledge and skills are shared with a better organized partner.

The partners need to assess the effect the strategic co-operation will have on their businesses and draw up together a co-operation plan in which both the short- and long-term revenues for all parties are described. In the course of the co-operation, the plan will have to be objectively evaluated on a continuous basis and adjusted to prevent potential conflict. Terms for the termination of the agreement should also be settled in advance.

5.4.3 Types of strategic co-operation

Figure 5.17 shows some of the many forms strategic co-operation can take.

The merger

A merger involves two companies joining together as equal partners. Mergers usually mean strategic plans can be implemented more quickly due to the sharing of manufacturing resources, distribution channels, brand names and know-how. Mergers also

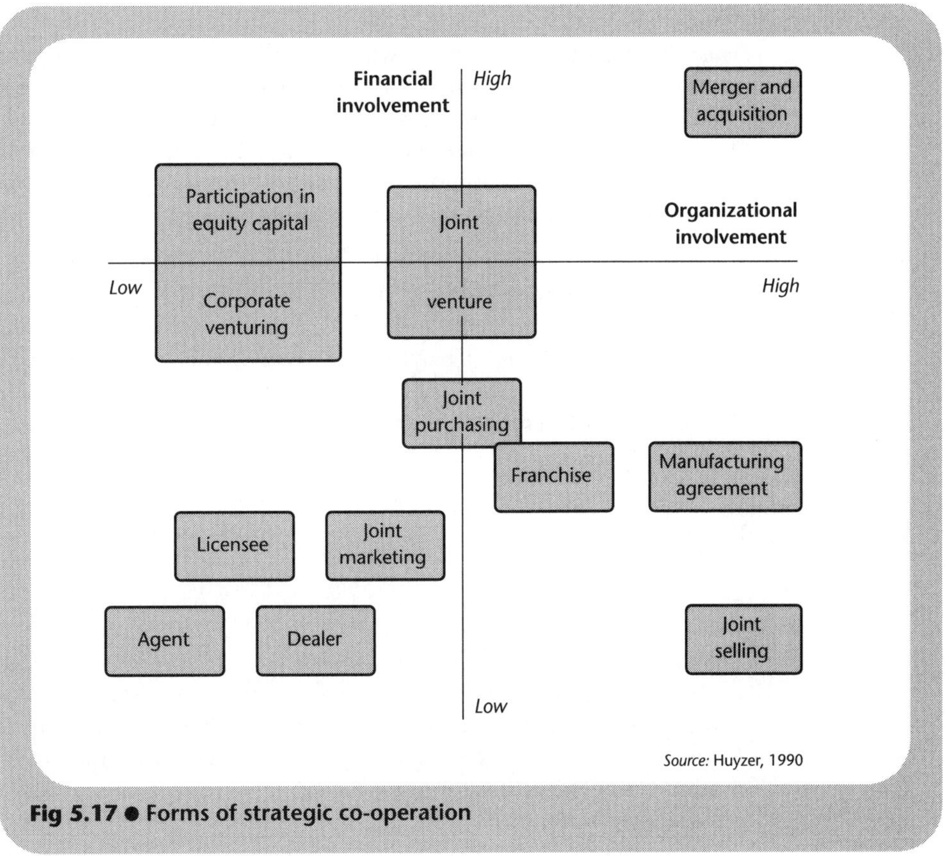

Fig 5.17 ● Forms of strategic co-operation

involve relatively minor financial consequences, involving in most cases a straightforward trading of shares. Disadvantages include the sharing of decision making and the sometimes difficult integration in terms of structure and culture of two companies of equal importance where responsibility is spread over a group structure.

The takeover

A takeover, or acquisition, involves one company buying up another by means of either a friendly or hostile offer. Advantages of acquisition are that complete control is gained over the activities of the acquired firm, and co-operation can go ahead quickly, as long as a good implementation plan has been drawn up in advance. Disadvantages include the effects of domination by the holding company over the acquired firm in terms of financial policies, management, culture and operational procedures.

The joint venture

A joint venture involves two companies deciding to set up a third company together – for example, when Philips and Whirlpool joined forces in the field of household appliances. One advantage of the joint venture form is the access to the knowledge of another company, which would otherwise not be available. In addition, only limited financial resources are required (relative to acquisitions) and risk is shared with another. In some cases, the spreading of control could be a disadvantage.

The strategic alliance

The strategic alliance involves two more or less equivalent companies co-operating on the basis of joint agreements. No new legal entities are set up. The risks are spread and the costs are divided among several partners. Often, the agreements have a closely described goal and they are limited in time. As a result, control problems are less likely. Sometimes, in the longer term, an alliance is set up in the form of a share participation by one of the parties concerned – for example the former link between Rover and Honda.

For example ...

... Sony and Philips have jointly developed a technical standard for the CD player. In preparation for the market launch of the DCC (Digital compact cassette), Philips co-operated with Matsushita Electronic Industries (co-licensee), Polygram for the production software and other suppliers of CDs and other media for the recording of titles on DCC. Contracts were agreed with Tandy for the marketing of the 'hardware' in the US, and with producers of tapes and Matsushita for the 'software'.

Minicase 5.3

The Rolls-Royce–BMW Pact

The strategic alliance between Rolls-Royce and BMW was announced by Vickers, the owner of the famous luxury car.

As a result of the agreement – which signalled the failure of BMW's arch-rival Mercedes to clinch the deal – Rolls-Royce will in future purchase the engines for its new models from BMW. BMW extends its influence in the UK car industry; Rolls-Royce remains independent, and, most importantly, British.

Vickers director, Sir Colin Chandler, declared that the agreement with the German car producer was an 'extremely important development for the company's future prospects'. BMW chief executive, Bernd Pischetsrieder considered the co-operation 'of the two most famous car brands in the world' to be 'a very exciting development'.

Vickers had made it known that it was searching for a foreign partner. The company lacked the financial resources to bear the costs – estimated at about $350 million – of developing a twelve-cylinder engine. The top priority, however, was that Rolls-Royce stayed British. Vickers made it clear that it was not willing to sell its majority share in the last British car producer. Co-operation with BMW allows Rolls-Royce to quickly launch new models onto the market – for example, the Java, a prototype of the new Bentley (the American subsidiary of RR) which had been shown at the Geneva Car Show.

BMW is becoming an important player in the UK market. In January 1994, the Bavarian car company bought the car producer, Rover, from British Aerospace – to the great displeasure of the Japanese company, Honda, who had an interest in Rover and had been behind Rover's rise from the ashes in recent years.

In 1990, BMW decided to work with the British airline-engine manufacturer Rolls-Royce (totally unrelated to the car manufacturer of the same name) to develop jet engines for small and medium-sized aeroplanes of Fokker. The present engines of the Fokker 100 are from Rolls-Royce. Dasa, the former mother company of Fokker and, just like Mercedes, part of Daimler Benz wants to develop new engines for this type of plane itself. Once again, its rival BMW, together with Rolls-Royce, seems to be taking the honours.

Source: Adapted from *Trouw*, 20 December 1994.

Joint manufacturing agreements

In joint manufacturing agreements, an organization works in partnership with a supplier firm to produce a product that meets the desired quality standards and delivery requirements of both companies. This is referred to as *outsourcing*. During this process both partners wish to keep their stocks of raw materials and components at an acceptable level, to improve their competitive positions and to reduce their costs as far as possible. In a certain sense this is a form of *backward integration*, although there is no change in the ownership of either firm. Independence is maintained; interdependence increases. This all implies an intensive, long-lasting relationship that has to be based on mutual trust.

A partner in a joint manufacturing agreement is not just a producer that supplies on the basis of the detailed specifications of the outsourcing company; the partner is preferably also involved in the design, development and production of the product concerned. Joint manufacturing agreements are common mainly in industrial sectors like machinery, metal and synthetic products and also in the electro-technical and rubber industries. However, this type of partnership is also known in the services sector – for example in industries such as cleaning and advertising.

It is important that the supplier has particular expertise in the production of a certain component or a specific product. The quality control system of the supplier needs to be of the highest standard.

The outsourcing company is confronted with a make-or-buy decision. As a rule a joint manufacturing agreement will give the outsourcing company a high level of added value and access to new knowledge and skills.

Specific advantages for the outsourcing company of joint manufacturing agreements include:

- The risks of new investments in technology are shared between the outsourcing organization and its supplier partner.
- The outsourcing company gains the full benefits of the specialization of the supplier partner.
- It is possible to break off the relation with the supplier partner as soon as the product or component is no longer needed. The partnership has a contractual basis; there is no ownership or disinvestment problem.

There are also disadvantages for the outsourcing company:

- The outsourcing organization is dependent on its supplier partner for the supply of important components.
- Problems may arise with big orders, due to the fact that such supplier partners tend to be relatively small companies.
- There is a potential loss of specific knowledge through the supplier partner to a competitor, because of the fact that such companies often work for a network of outsourcing companies.

The supplier partner in the joint manufacturing agreement has the following advantages:

- It is able to focus on specialization.
- It can reduce its business risks by building a network of outsourcing companies which it can serve.
- It limits the possibility of substitution by another supplier.
- It benefits from the knowledge of markets and the experience of the outsourcing company.
- It optimizes the effects of being relatively small and flexible.

Disadvantages to the supplier partner are:

- It has a relatively weak position in negotiations due to the imbalance in power caused by the difference in size of the two companies.
- It has to meet the strict specifications of the outsourcing company, for example in terms of quality or logistical processes.
- It can lose sight of developments in the market at the end of the chain.
- It has to accept the possibility of knowledge and experience flowing away to the outsourcing company.

Outsourcing as a form of strategic co-operation often results in the outsourcing organization reducing investment in productive assets and cutting budgets for product design and research and development. After a certain period of time a relation of dependency will develop due to the fact that the supplier partner is responsible for both product development and the process of manufacturing the product. In the meantime the supplier has learned a great deal about the wishes, needs and requirements of the final user or consumer and has gained experience in the development of the product(s). The introduction onto the market of a competing product by the supplier partner could be realized quite quickly with success assured. In the meantime, the competitive advantage of the outsourcing organization has diminished substantially.

5.5 IMPLEMENTATION OF STRATEGIC PLANS

Implementation of strategic plans involves the drawing up of action plans for the different functional areas and usually also adjustments in the organizational structure and changes in the daily functioning of the organization processes and culture. (Changes in organizational structure are covered in greater detail in Chapters 6, 7 and 8. The functioning of the organization, including the influences on the organizational structure, are covered in more detail in Chapters 9, 10, 11 and 12.)

5.5.1 From overall strategy to functional plans

The translation of strategic plans into functional specifications is depicted in Fig 5.18.

In the light of the multitude of strategic alternatives, it is not possible to lay down a set of simple and unequivocal rules for strategy implementation.

For example ...

... two car manufacturers want to enlarge their share of the market for smaller cars. Manufacturer A strives for sales improvement via a lowest cost strategy, while Manufacturer B strives to attain the same goal via a strategy of product differentiation. The implications for the planning of the functional fields are very different.

In the case of Manufacturer A, attention is focused on the lowering of costs per unit of production. This can be attained, for example, by reducing manufacturing, sales and development costs. Manufacturer B will have to pay more attention to product development and marketing in order to bring the differences in performance compared with the other brands to the attention of the buying public.

These two strategies, which are aiming at the same goal – an increase in sales – make completely different demands on the organization.

The translation of a strategic plan into individual tasks for existing functional fields involves determining which critical core tasks can be derived from the plan. The detailed

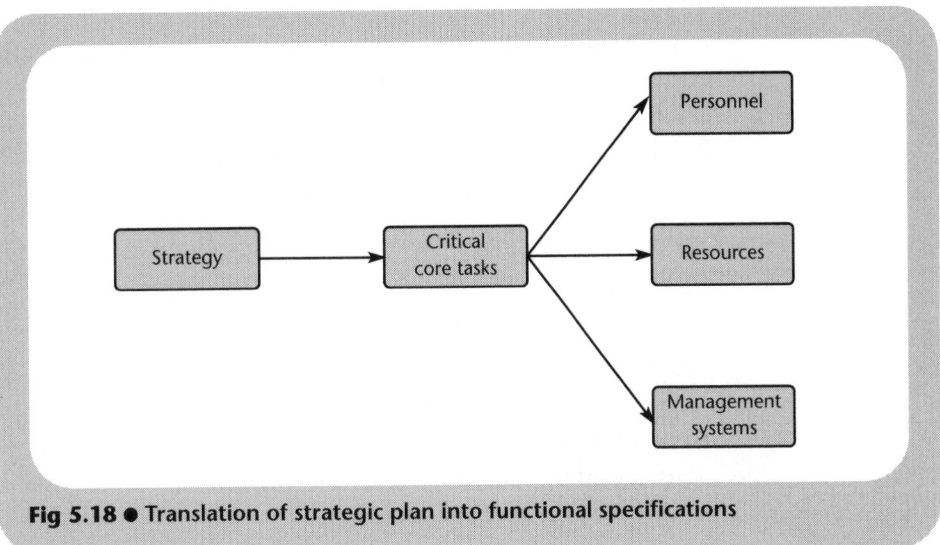

Fig 5.18 ● Translation of strategic plan into functional specifications

plans for functional fields and departments are further subdivided into annual plans and budgets. Implementation and feedback reports then have to be drawn up, as plans are adjusted and appropriate corrective action is taken. (We return to this in Chapter 12.)

Once the critical core tasks have been determined, their consequences must be explored in relation to:

- personnel;
- equipment and machinery;
- the management systems for the units and departments.

The wide range of possible strategies leads in turn to a correspondingly large number of critical core tasks and consequences for personnel, resources and management systems. As a result, the conversion of the strategy into consequences for the functional areas is an activity which makes very heavy demands of management with regard to creativity and insight into the problem.

The translation and specification process is best illustrated using an example. A manufacturer is striving to improve its market position with a low-cost strategy. This strategy demands interventions in the following departments: product development, purchasing, production, marketing and sales.

Product development

Reducing costs for the final products means that the product development department has to obtain better results with the same resources or the same results with fewer resources. This could involve the following core tasks.

- *The selection of promising areas.* The consequence of this will be that fewer projects will be set up, with lower total costs as a result.
- *Research into possibilities for manufacturing under licence.* This could have several outcomes. First, time could be gained if the licence were obtained. Second, the fixed-cost component of product development would be lowered and replaced by a

possible royalty agreement – the amount that has to be paid varying with the sales of the new products. Third, the level of uncertainty in product development is much reduced if the organization buys an existing and possibly well tested process as a result of the licence.

- *The introduction of application-directed working.* Basic research is replaced by the less risky further development of existing products.

These core tasks can have the following consequences:

1. With regard to personnel:
   - education /training of personnel;
   - possible selection of new employees;
   - possible redundancies for present employees;
   - possible moving-on/transfer of employees.
2. With regard to resources:
   - the purchase of new equipment;
   - the withdrawal from use or modification of existing equipment.
3. With regard to management systems and procedures:
   - better production control;
   - assignment of responsibilities and budgets;
   - procedures with regard to engaging in licence contracts.

Purchasing

An overall reduction in costs could mean the introduction of the following core tasks in the purchasing department.

- *Improving insight into market supply.* This could mean that the members of the department will be able to purchase on better terms.
- *Sharper negotiating skills.* Contracts could be closed on better terms than before.
- *Inventory control.* Good inventory control could result in a decrease in the costs linked to this (interest and risk).

These core tasks can have the following consequences:

1. With regard to personnel:
   - training in negotiating;
   - training in structure and keeping documentation;
   - moving on and expansion of personnel.
2. With regard to resources:
   - the documentation of information;
   - the availability of good communication equipment (particularly important for those operating on the world market for raw materials as they need up-to-date information.
3. With regard to management systems and procedures:
   - better co-ordination between production and sales;
   - adjustments to procedures;

- the setting of operational norms;
- budgeting;
- inventory control.

Production

In many sectors of business, the production department is the department which represents the largest part of the cost price. This means that this department can probably also make the largest contribution to the reduction of overall costs. The following core tasks can be mentioned:

- *Reduction of costs and increase in efficiency.* This can be achieved, for example, through the better utilization of machinery, decreasing inventory levels of materials, using semi-finished components, changing layout and routing.
- *Cutting of delivery times.* Although not leading to a direct reduction in costs, the speeding up of delivery times can have an indirect effect on costs.
- *Quality improvement.* This too has an indirect influence on costs: improving quality often means improving production processes resulting in less waste and therefore lower costs.
- *The introduction of shift work.* In capital-intensive companies, this would lead to a more intensive occupation of production capacity.

The core tasks can have the following consequences:

1. With regard to personnel:
   - supplementary training/education;
   - wider and more flexible availability and employability of personnel;
   - changing composition and perhaps size of the workforce;
   - changing of working hours.
2. With regard to resources:
   - replacement or modification of machines;
   - improvement of layout and routing;
   - increase in flexibility;
   - need for working capital.
3. With regard to management systems and procedures:
   - production planning;
   - introduction of work consultation/quality circles;
   - efficiency measurement: control and norms;
   - reward systems.

Marketing

By means of better analysis, the marketing department can make an indirect contribution to keeping costs down. The following core tasks can be mentioned.

- *The analysis of sales patterns.* A detailed analysis of the sales patterns can sometimes mean that production can be scheduled more efficiently. Costs may be high due to inventory levels, but these can be balanced out by a more even occupation of productive resources, which will result in a reduction in unit costs.

- *The analysis of profitability, product–customer groups and distribution channels.* In many companies, this analysis highlights large differences in the profitability of different categories. Tackling this discrepancy can lead both to better margins and to a reduction in manufacturing costs.
- *Use of marketing mix.* Not all elements of the marketing mix – product, price, place and promotion – are of the same importance to the cost price of the product. By investigating the different elements and their effectiveness, a reduction in costs can be attained.

These core tasks have the following consequences:

1. With regard to personnel:
   - the learning of new knowledge;
   - flow and transfer of staff;
   - career development.
2. With regard to resources:
   - documentation;
   - data processing equipment.
3. With regard to management systems and procedures:
   - market research;
   - budgeting;
   - cost/revenue analyses with regard to make-or-buy decisions (outsourcing);
   - role of finance department in analysis.

Sales

The sales department (which includes distribution) can contribute to the reduction in overall costs in many ways. The following core tasks can be mentioned:

- *Increasing sales.* Increased sales with unchanged sales costs will result in sales costs decreasing as a percentage of the cost price. This also affects advertising costs, which for some categories of consumer products form an important part of the sales costs.
- *Reducing distribution costs.* Some kinds of physical distribution are cheaper than others. A well considered choice of system can lead to a reduction in distribution costs.

These core tasks can have the following consequences:

1. With regard to personnel:
   - supplementary training;
   - transferring or changing staff;
   - improvement in instruction.
2. With regard to resources:
   - distribution systems (for example, type of lorry);
   - automation of order processing, EDI.
3. With regard to management systems and procedures:
   - sales planning;
   - sales statistics/visit reports per sales representative;
   - reward system for sales personnel.

Exhibit 5.6

The son also rises at Danone

After earning an engineering degree in Switzerland, Franck Riboud succumbed to a driving passion: to lead the vagabond life of a professional windsurfer. Wisely, his father. Antoine, didn't complain when young Riboud set off for California. Not long afterward, however, Franck got bored and came home to Paris, where he took a trainee job at BSN, the giant French food company then run by his father. Now – 15 years later – the son is succeeding the father as chairman of Groupe Danone, as BSN is now called.

Managing the world's biggest producer of yogurt and cookies is a tall order for 40-year-old Franck Riboud. He will have to show that he deserves the job on account of talent, not his family ties. And that means restoring earnings growth at Danone, which has suffered from weak margins despite a strong stable of such supermarket brands as its namesake yogurt, Lu and Club cookies, Kronenbourg beer, and Evian spring water.

Deals

The complaints of nepotism have already started. His appointment on May 2 reflects a French disease, according to Colette Neuville, a leading French shareholder-rights advocate. 'He may be quite competent,' she says, 'but he had more of a chance than others.' Although the Ribouds own less than 1% of the company, its history is intimately connected to the rise of the father, now 77. Antoine Riboud took a modest bottle manufacturer in 1966 and turned it into a $15 billion food concern. A power in leftist circles, he was a great friend of late French President François Mitterrand.

Young Riboud rejects the carping about his elevation to the company's top spot. Noting that he has risen through a dozen jobs at Danone and knows its products and markets intimately, he insists that 'people should judge me by my ability.'

By most accounts, Riboud has plenty. Jovial and energetic like his father, this youngest of four children has been managing Danone's globalization. With only 15% of its sales generated outside Western Europe – vs. 55% for rival Nestlé – Danone badly needs to tap markets in Asia and Latin America to build economies of scale and offset its mature, cutthroat markets in the European Union.

In recent years, Franck Riboud has guided a global search for acquisitions and joint ventures. This year's crop of deals includes a Chinese venture to produce milk-based drinks, a 33% stake in South Africa's largest dairy company, and a cookie operation in Brazil. On top of its power in yogurt and cookies, Danone is the world's second-largest marketer of mineral water: Nestlé is No. 1. In keeping with a plan to turn its corporate name into a global brand – Nestlé-style – this year the French company will launch a new mineral water, labeled Dannon, in the US (where the brand is spelled differently).

Trouble is, after spending more than $5 billion on global acquisitions in the past five years, Danone has increased its worldwide sales substantially without reaping similar gains in profits (chart). Meanwhile, its European margins have been falling because of weak economies and the growth of house-brand products. Margins are even worse in emerging markets, where Danone is still working with small, inefficient startup ventures.

New captain, old team

Many analysts are betting that Riboud can boost the margins by increasing sales and cutting production costs in new markets. Danone has great savoir faire in brand marketing, says Emmanuel Weyd, a food industry analyst at Standard & Poor's Compustat in Paris. Franck Riboud has also shown that he knows how to cut costs – by engineering plant closings and restructurings in Europe. Those efforts burdened earnings with a $360 million charge last year. The stock price, at $154 on the Paris exchange, is off from a 12-month high of $173 last August. Now, analysts think Danone's European costs are in good shape.

To allay any qualms that the new Danone chairman is lacking in experience, insiders note that his team of seasoned managers won't change – and his father will remain a director. But Franck Riboud's backers insist that he has what it takes. 'He has a vision of the products and is extremely attached to Danone's reputation,' says Michel David-Weill, head of Lazard Frères & Co. and a longtime Riboud adviser. 'For me, the fact that he's his father's son is just chance.' That's surely an overstatement. In any event, Franck Riboud now has the opportunity to prove his mettle.

Source: *Business Week*, 20 May 1996.

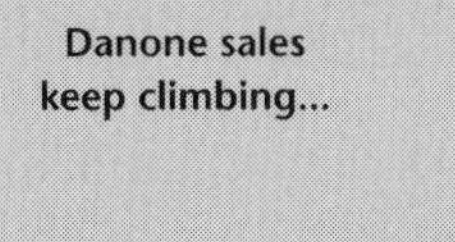

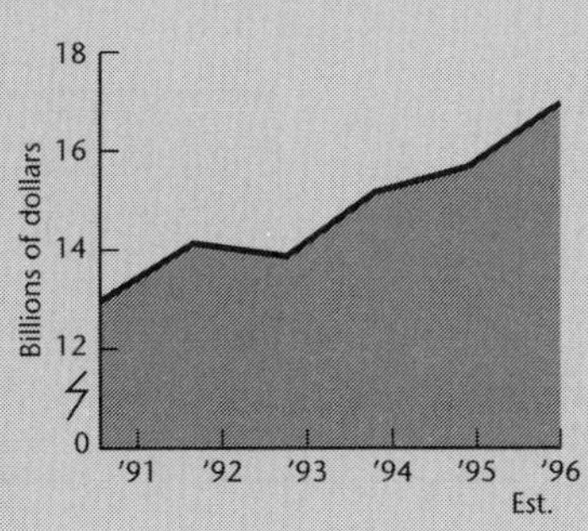

...but its profits are shaky

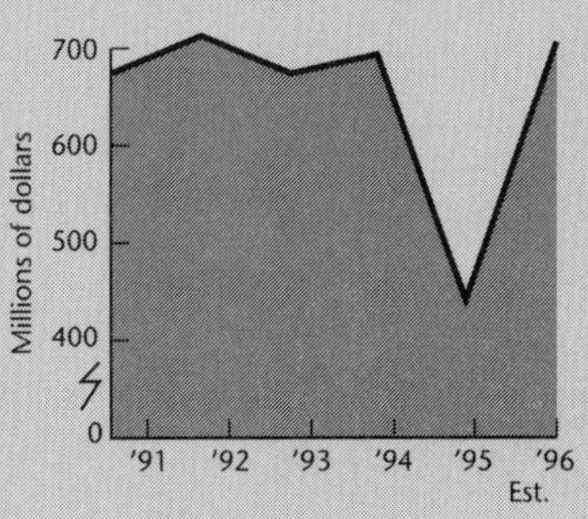

Data: Company reports, BW Estimates

5.5.2 From functional plans to budgets

A frequently used management system is budgeting. Budgeting involves the expression of plans in financial terms. Figure 5.19 shows how this fits into the overall process of translating strategic plans.

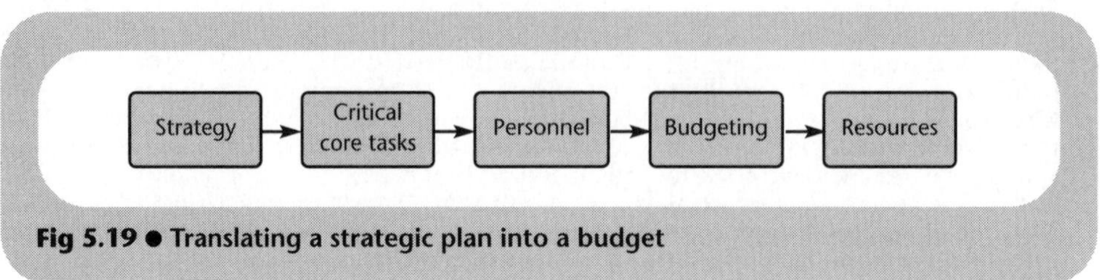

Fig 5.19 ● Translating a strategic plan into a budget

Action plans can be developed from the critical core tasks. The consequences of the core tasks can be used as the basis for the formulation of norms and task assignments. These can be in the form of quality norms (for example, acceptable levels of waste), worked hours per employee, etc. The budget expresses these task assignments in financial terms. In this way, the policy to be executed can be costed and as a result the budget fulfils a communication function. The advantage of using budgets lies in the organization's ability to gauge the success or failure of the implementation of the plan (*see* Fig 5.20).

If a budgeting system is to be used effectively, it has to be clear where the responsibilities for the execution of tasks or the attainment of results lies. For this, a clear organizational structure is necessary, in which responsibilities and the accompanying duties and authorities are determined. (The further elaboration of plans and budgets will be covered in Chapter 10.)

Finally, two points should be particularly noted in relation to the use of budgeting in the implementation of strategic plans. First, an organization needs to be vigilant that norms and goals are not allowed to overrule budgets. Budgeting is not only a

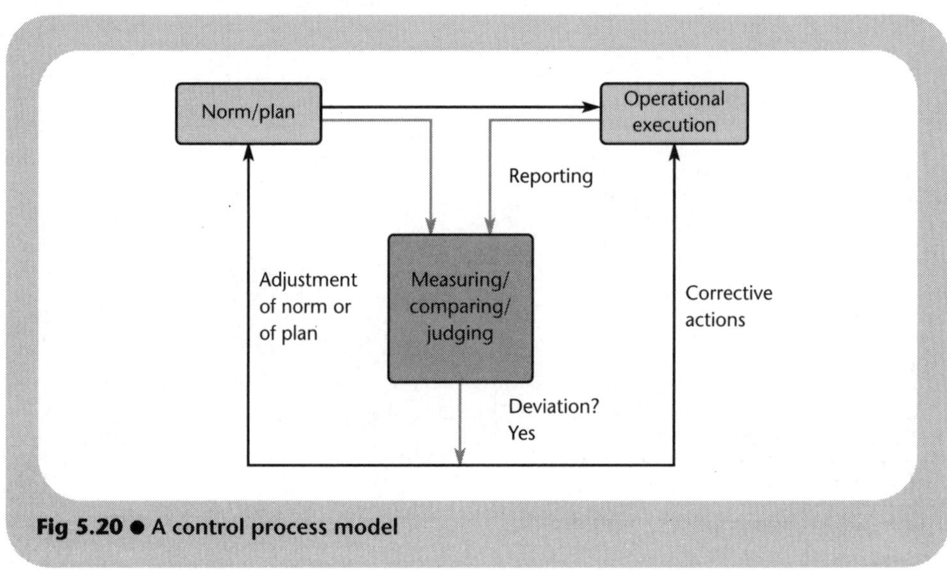

Fig 5.20 ● A control process model

guide to the execution within the functional fields, but also a means of verifying the accuracy of strategic decisions and the assumptions on which these are based. Second, budgets are often determined within the existing organizational structure with existing management and existing influences. As a result, there can be a certain amount of resistance, both implicit and explicit, around the budgeting process.

5.6 ● MANAGING ORGANIZATIONAL RESISTANCE

During the strategic planning process, a choice is made between different alternatives, on the basis of rational consideration. The next logical step in the strategy formulation process is the introduction of the strategy. In practice, a strategy's introduction is often delayed and more expensive than budgeted. This applies as much to product and market development as it does to mergers and takeovers. The reason for this discrepancy is often an inaccurate estimate of the willingness and level of acceptance of the strategy of those involved in its implementation. This resistance to change varies in nature depending on whether it is considered from the perspective of the individual or the perspective of the group.

- *Individual resistance to change* is caused by two groups of factors: *uncertainty* and *personal interests*. Uncertainty is caused when individuals – that is, managers – cannot estimate the importance and the consequences of the changes caused by the strategy. The strategy may involve risks with which the individual has trouble coping. The manager may fear redundancy or may not be able to fulfil the new task.
- On the other hand, a manager may resist a proposed strategy out of well understood self interest. This can be the case when the manager sees his or her position, power, income and status threatened. This can be based on very rational considerations – for example, the manager of a well performing division or business unit who is judged on the level of his or her return, will resist strategies which will result in a decrease in returns.
- *Resistance of groups to change* is usually caused by their common values and norms pattern – that is, their culture – although those rational considerations which hold for the individual can also be at work here. These values and norms can, for example, reinforce the importance of the market approach. This resistance may be based on the quality premium which a group feels it owns. Another possibility is that the group considers that the choice has not been based on the relevant criteria – for example, resistance to environmental and labour market developments. Groups resist strategic changes which threaten the position and the values and norms of the group.

There are three ways in which such resistance can be reduced or eliminated entirely.

1. *Overcoming resistance with the aid of rational arguments*. The person or group who is resisting may not be sufficiently well informed regarding the new strategy and aware of the advantages it brings. Such resistance to implementation can be eliminated by giving information and justification.
2. *Overcoming resistance with behavioural changes*. Resistance sometimes results because the strategic plan is in conflict with the values and norms of those involved. This form of resistance can be overcome by organizing training and education aimed at behavioural changes. The widespread participation of stakeholders in the strategic

formulation process is of importance. This can be done, for example, using the 'bottom-up' approach to the planning cycle (*see* section 5.3.3). In this respect, there is a link between strategy formulation and the 'learning organization' (*see* Chapter 4).

3. *Overcoming resistance with the aid of rewards and punishments, positive encouragement or negative sanctions.* This tactic is especially used with regard to centres of resistance which remain after the application of the above two techniques.

Of course, the attitude of top management with regard to the strategic plans plays a part in all three techniques. The recognizing and the management of the resistance should be a part of the strategy formulation process in anticipation of the implementation of the plans. This process needs to be incorporated into the scheme in Fig 5.16. The problem of resistance needs to be addressed and investigated during the internal appraisal and through the criteria used in the choice of alternatives – particularly with regard to its impact on the criterion of timing.

5.7 ● THE EMERGING STRATEGY

Although it is becoming increasingly common for strategic or business plans to be drawn up because parties in the organization's external environment request them – for example, the bank in the case of a request for investment finance or government institutions in the case of a request for the provision of a subsidy – in many organizations there will be no written explicit strategic plan – the product of a formal procedure. This does not mean that there is no 'strategy' at all, however. On the contrary, the strategy is situated, so to speak, in the head, heart and hands of the entrepreneur who often knows very well what the business should be doing and executes this 'plan' very consistently.

If such a pattern of development is recognizable and slowly comes into existence, this is called *emerging strategy* (Mintzberg, 1987). With hard work and care, this pattern will be refined and actions will be co-ordinated. Strategy will be worked on, in the traditional sense (referred to as '*crafting strategy*' by Mintzberg).

Behind the recognizable pattern of decisions and actions, there is another set of decisions which are taken more or less intuitively or systematically. It therefore becomes more important to look at actual strategy rather than at consciously or dutifully made formal plans, at the real actions rather than the words and well uttered good intentions (which perhaps later do not become reality).

In organizations with an emerging strategy, there may well be a good picture of the environment (in the heads of the people), a form of accepted leadership (intuitive or charismatic) and a rather strong informal organization, in which a stream of contacts can be detected, through which 'strategy' develops and the strategic changes come into being. In this situation, there is usually a good understanding of the forces influencing the organization from the past, in the present and in the near future.

Frequently, however, we see that intuition falls short, so that actions and measures lack consistency. The pattern then becomes more arbitrary and lacks internal order. For example, many possible actions may be started but they are then arbitrarily broken off. In other words, there is no clear direction and the driving forces are at least divided. It is then necessary, in order to set a new course, to introduce a strategic capability, the creation of a detailed vision, the outline of the organization, team building, authority within and outside the organization and some sense of guidance and direction.

Under such circumstances, the insights and methods outlined in section 5.2 would be an appropriate basis for solving the organization's problems.

All this leads us to the conclusion that it is almost impossible for an organization *not* to concern itself with strategy in some shape or form. This applies as much to large companies as it does to small companies, even if they are unable to adopt an explicit and formal approach to the strategy formulation process due to limited resources. The future perspective is no less valid as a result.

SUMMARY

- The central question in strategy formulation is how an organization can ensure its survival by continuously reacting to developments in its external environment in such a way that optimum use is made of its own capabilities. The gaining of a competitive advantage over other suppliers is a key factor in this.
- Explicit strategy formulation gives direction to an organization and is the basis for a stronger coherence between the activities and the components of the organization. This often leads to better results.
- Strategy formulation procedures can vary in depth. Sometimes, an intuitive approach can be recognized and the strategy can be mapped out retrospectively.
- This chapter has covered the definition of strategy and the various approaches, both practical and theoretical, to solving the strategy problems, as they apply to both commercial and not-for-profit organizations.
- The model of strategy formulation was developed and within it the following steps were distinguished.
- *Determining the strategic profile* – objectives, areas of current activities, competitive advantage and synergy.
- *External appraisal of the environment in search of opportunities and threats* – with regard to the societal environment (demographic factors, economic factors, societal factors, technological factors, ecological factors, political factors) and with regard to the analysis of the sector (competition/intensity of rivalry, buyers/clients, suppliers, substitute products, new entrants).
- *Internal appraisal in search of strengths and weaknesses* – an analysis of the functional departments compared to the demands of the market and the performance of the competition. Portfolio analysis is a useful instrument in such an appraisal from the point of view of results. It is not enough simply to gather opinions and visions; they must be supported by 'hard' information. When facts and opinions contradict each other, further analysis is necessary. Not only can an opinion be wrong, but also the information and/or interpretation of it can be incorrect.
- *Determining a strategic gap* – when the goals which are set and expected future results are not in line with each other. On the basis of the present strategic profile and the SWOT analysis an organization can draw conclusions regarding, for example, the position the organization will be in in five years' time.

continued overleaf

- *Drawing up strategic alternatives* – with the aim of closing the strategic gap. Alternatives can lie within or outside present activities or can involve the phasing out of activities. For each of these groups of alternatives, many different forms of strategy can be considered.
- *Evaluating and making a choice from alternatives.* The first step is the determining of the consequences of each alternatives and their testing against the criteria of consistency, synergy, uncertainty/risk/insecurity, flexibility, financial aspects and timing.
- *Translating the choice into plans for functional areas.* Resistance will occur in many cases. Information exchange, education and training are important instruments in the reduction of resistance to strategic change.
- In this way, strategy formulation is seen as a decision-making process in which the decision is taken whether to learn or not to learn new skills and knowledge. This forms the link between this chapter and Chapter 4 which dealt with decision making and creativity.

DISCUSSION QUESTIONS

1. With reference to *Management in action* at the beginning of this chapter, explain why 'distribution' is a particularly important consideration for MEXX in the coming years?
2. 'Strategy formulation costs time and money, so forget it!' Comment on this statement.
3. 'Strategy formulation and competitive analysis are appropriate for commercial organizations, but inappropriate for not-for-profit organizations.' Comment.
4. Your participation in a course of study can be viewed as an organization with a future, in the form of a 'one-man operation'. Your participation in the course is the result of your having studied choice. Did that choice-making process in your case take place explicitly or was it more intuitive?
5. Explain in your own words why Chapters 4 and 5 can be viewed together.
6. (a) Which strategic alternatives are combined to a certain degree in the overall pattern of strategic decisions within Volvo (*see* Exhibit 5.1)?
   (b) What would a portfolio picture of Volvo's product–market activity look like?
   (c) What type of plans are/were part of Volvo's overall strategy concerning partnership or other forms of external co-operation. Which goals do/did these serve?
7. (a) How would you describe the strategy followed by the Belgian company, Interbrew (*see* Exhibit 5.3), and the Swiss company, Holderbank (*see* Exhibit 5.2)?
   (b) What elements are common to these apparently successful strategies?
8. Describe the main characteristics and instruments of the strategy implementation of Danone, by analysing the strategic actions of M Riboud Jr (*see* Exhibit 5.6).

Management case study

Growth strategies at Microsoft

In 1980, computer giant, IBM, approached Microsoft – at that time a small company that had existed for little more than five years – and asked if it could supply an operating system for a personal computer IBM was going to launch. At that moment, Microsoft had nothing to offer, but the director and co-founder, Bill Gates, knew a small software company which had developed a system with the name 'QDOS' – 'Quick and Dirty Operating System'. Microsoft bought the rights for $100,000 and offered IBM the licence. In order not to offend conservative IBM, the name was changed to MS-DOS – Microsoft Disk Operating System.

IBM's personal computer became a great success and MS-DOS became the standard operating system for PCs worldwide.

Microsoft now develops, supplies and supports a wide range of software packages for business, professional and private use. Its most important product lines are operating software (Microsoft Windows, Windows NT and MS-DOS), network products (Microsoft Back Office), programming languages, application programs (for example, Word and Excel) and software for private use.

The $100,000 which Microsoft paid for MS-DOS will probably go down in history as the best investment ever made by a company. Thanks to MS-DOS, Microsoft has grown and become enormously successful. Microsoft has been one of the most profitable companies in the world for some years. In the financial year that ended 30 June 1994, it made a profit of 1.15 billion dollars on a sales total of 4.65 billion dollars. The gross margin (total revenue *minus* product costs) was 83 per cent in 1993.

Its dominance

According to competitors, MS-DOS stands for 'Microsoft Seeks Domination Over Society'. Microsoft has sold more than 100 million copies of MS-DOS – making it the most successful software package in the world. The graphics operating system to succeed MS-DOS, the user-friendly Windows, has also been a great success, selling more than 60 million copies since its introduction in the late 1980s. MS-DOS and Windows together account for a share of approximately 90 per cent of the market for operating software.

In order to stimulate the sales of its own operating software, Microsoft encouraged other companies to develop application software. Thousands of independent software developers did just that, including big names like WordPerfect (text processing programs), Lotus (spreadsheet programs) and Borland (database programs). When Microsoft introduced Windows, the developers of the MS-DOS based programs were forced to adjust their software. At the same time, Microsoft began to compete against them with significant success. Microsoft's text-processing program, Word, is market leader with a worldwide market share of 60 per cent and Lotus 1-2-3 has lost its position as market leader in spreadsheet programs to Microsoft's Excel (65 per cent market share worldwide). Microsoft has entered into direct competition with Borland with its Access program (a Windows-based database).

Many companies could not compete with Microsoft and attempted to fight back via competition legislation. The most significant complaint was that Microsoft had asked computer manufacturers to include Microsoft software as standard with all computers

continued overleaf

Management case study continued

sold. If the companies agreed, they would receive enormous discounts. This meant that it was cheaper for the manufacturers of hardware to simply load all computers with Microsoft software, than installing software in some computers.

Its cost structure

The contribution of application software to the total sales of Microsoft has increased considerably – currently 65 per cent and set to grow further in the years to come. The contribution of operating software to sales is 32 per cent (the remaining 3 per cent of sales being realized in hardware).

The sharply rising share of sales accounted for by application software has major implications for the cost structure of Microsoft. Marketing costs for operating software are modest; the hardware manufacturers knock on the door themselves because the alternative operating software (OS-2 (by IBM) and DOS-7 (by Novell)) have a much less favourable price/performance ratio. With operating software, Microsoft is still in a sellers' market.

With application software, however, things are different. Suppliers of application software far outnumber suppliers of operating software. In most cases, several good alternatives will exist for a particular software package, and as a result marketing costs are much higher. The figures speak for themselves: in 1994 sales costs accounted for around 35 per cent of total costs (rising from 27 per cent in 1990). That percentage will continue to rise. Furthermore, competition in this market is often based on price.

Saturation in traditional markets

The problem is that the business market for application software is starting to show signs of saturation. All the users who really need a text-processing, database or spreadsheet program already have one. Furthermore, in the coming years, no new application is expected on the market which will sell 'like hot cakes'. As a result, according to chief executive, Bill Gates, three quarters of the software sales will involve sales of 'upgrades' to existing clients. This will cause profit margins to decrease from the 1994 levels of 25 per cent to around 15 per cent – a margin which most companies would envy.

In 1993 Microsoft entered the market for networking software – a market dominated by Novell. It introduced 'Windows NT' (the letters NT standing for 'new technology') and hoped to gain a 50 per cent market share. The clients for network software tend to be large companies which make high demands of the service: after all, a network that collapses can practically cripple the whole company. Entering the market for network software meant that Microsoft had to set up a service organization. In this, the company decided to co-operate with third parties.

Consolidation

Microsoft finds itself at a crucial phase in its development. The profit figures give no reason for worry, but it is a fact that profit margins are decreasing, while costs are increasing.

Microsoft set itself the goal of raising profit from 4.5 to 8 million dollars in two years (1995–96). Many an organization would find this ridiculous, but if anyone is able to succeed, it is Microsoft. In order to realize this growth, all four of the growth strategies from the product–market matrix by Ansoff – market penetration, market development, product development and diversification – have to be applied. A functional reorganization has taken place. Sales and marketing were concentrated into three groups which direct themselves to individual users, companies and hardware suppliers. For the first time, the company also has a worldwide marketing strategy.

Market penetration

Market penetration involves increasing sales of existing products in existing markets. Microsoft has been looking at possibilities in the consumer market. Research has shown that during the lifetime of a PC used for business purposes, an average of five software packages will be purchased. For PCs which are used for private use, however, up to 15 packages per year are purchased.

'The problem is that Microsoft has a relatively low consumer profile,' concludes Ingvar Meijers, manager of the end user business unit. 'Everybody knows the name MS-DOS, but far too few consumers know that the letters "MS" stand for Microsoft. This is why a worldwide image campaign has been launched in order to make the name better known, especially to consumers.'

Market development

In market development, new markets are sought for existing products. It is striking that by far the largest part of Microsoft sales is to western markets. Big opportunities for Microsoft lie in the fast growing markets in Asia and the company is making every effort to have its operating programs accepted as standard in that part of the world.

Product development

With the growth strategy of product development, new or improved products are sold in existing markets. Innovation is a continuous process for Microsoft. Many thousands of its employees are occupied daily with improving existing products and developing new products. Microsoft also acquires companies with successful products – for example, its takeover of Intuit for 1.5 billion dollars, the largest purchase in the history of Microsoft. Intuit was prominent in the market for personal finances programs ('electronic banking'). This software was sold under the name 'Quicken'. Microsoft already had software in this field (its 'Money' programs), but sold these to competitor Novell in order to head off possible objections from the American anti-trust authorities. The purchase shows that Microsoft is pragmatically oriented. Intuit had a better product than Microsoft. 'If you can't beat them, buy them,' was the motto. With the purchase of Intuit, Microsoft improved its position in a market with huge potential: many households now have a PC, but very few have the software to make payments via the PC.

Diversification

This is the most risky growth strategy, in that new products are developed for completely new markets. In the coming years, Microsoft want to diversify into multimedia products for the consumer market, because the market for application software for consumers (the 'home market') is set to grow much stronger than that for the business applications.

Microsoft wants to become the market leader in 'edutainment' (educational and entertaining) software on CD-ROM – products in which the software knowledge of the company is combined with image, sound and text on a CD-ROM, which is linked to a PC. Multimedia also means that computer, TV and telephone lines are linked with each other in order to bring new products into the homes of consumers.

Diversification into the multimedia market is a very daring step: although there is agreement that multimedia is the future, nobody yet knows where it is heading. Diversification has important organizational implications for Microsoft. At this moment, the

continued overleaf

Management case study continued

consumer division has a very modest size – of the company's 14,500 employees, only 400 work in this division – but this division is set to grow very quickly. As time is of the essence and in order to limit risks, Microsoft is taking over companies at high speed and engaging in alliances. Microsoft has already acquired a great many licences in relation to, for example, the voices of cartoon figures and famous paintings. In March 1994, the company took over Soft Image, a Canadian enterprise which is market leader in the field of software for animated films. It was involved in the special effects for the film, *Jurassic Park*.

Standards for multimedia?

The ultimate goal of Microsoft is to set a standard for multimedia operating software, just as the company did for MS-DOS and Windows for the PC. It has not yet achieved this, but the intentions of the company are obvious. According to Bill Gates:

> *If you always have to follow the standards and innovations of others, the price is your most important marketing tool. And, in the long term, that is not the basis for the continued existence of a company.*

The company's intentions were further underlined by the announced alliance with Deutsche Bundespost Telecom in the development of multimedia products and services. Microsoft is also in negotiations with other European telecommunication enterprises with the goal of having Windows accepted as the technology behind multimedia.

In contrast to its experiences with operating software, in the field of multimedia the company has encountered strong competition from the very start. For example, Apple, Philips, Motorola, Matsushita and Sony have engaged in a strategic alliance in order to develop products in the multimedia field. IBM is putting all its efforts behind its operating system, OS-2 Warp. The American computer giant still has a score to settle with Microsoft. Its operating system, OS-2, which was considered by many to be technically superior, failed completely because of MS-DOS and Windows. IBM has learned a great deal from Microsoft and will not accept defeat easily.

Source: Adapted from Andriesse, F. (1994) 'Growth strategies at Microsoft', *Tijdschrift voor Marketing*, December, pp 10–14.

CASE QUESTIONS

1. Microsoft's diversification into the 'edutainment' market is rather risky, and as a result Microsoft is quickly taking over companies. In your opinion, will that be a satisfactory means of covering risks?
2. According to Bill Gates: 'If you always have to follow the standards and innovations of others, the price is your most important marketing tool. And, in the long term, that is not the basis for the continued existence of a company.' Do you agree with this?
3. Which strategic alternative does Microsoft use for the consumer market?
4. Which 'risks' do the external and internal stakeholders have in a company that is almost monopolistic (90 per cent of the market)?

Part three

Designing and structuring the organization

Once the objectives, goals and strategy of an organization have been determined (Part two), the next step is to design the structure and the activities of the organization in such a way that these aims will be reached.

In this part of the book, we explore the design of the organizational structure – that is, the framework within which the activities take place. At an organizational level, the structure is influenced by two factors: the diversity of the organization's activities and the extent to which the organization's environment is stable or unstable.

Designing an organization's structure involves both the assignment of decision-making authority at the different management levels (Chapter 6) and the more detailed design of individual departments (Chapter 7). Unless tasks and functions are clearly defined at this stage, there is a chance that employees will end up working at cross-purposes and constantly clashing with each other. We explore the possibility of working in groups as self-managing or autonomous teams, within or on behalf of individual departments.

The structure has to be developed and designed so that it is 'tailor made' for the organization in question, it matches the chosen strategy and it is effective and rewarding for both the individual employees and the organization itself. When circumstances change, the organization may have to change too. This part concludes with a consideration of the processes of organizational change.

Principles of management

Motivating people

Part one • Management and society

Chapter 1
Manager and management

Chapter 2
Management theory and organizational development

Chapter 3
Organizations and environment

Part two • Strategic management and the learning organization

Chapter 4
Decision making and creativity

Chapter 5
Strategy formulation and strategic management

Part three • Designing and structuring the organization

Chapter 6
Designing the organization

Chapter 7
Structuring tasks for groups and individuals

Part four • People at work

Chapter 8
Motivation, work and career

Chapter 9
Leading, motivation and communication

Part five • Planning, control and information management

Chapter 10
Operational planning and control

Chapter 11
Information management and information technology

Chapter 12
Managerial process control: functional processes and process redesign

Chapter 6

Designing the organization

LEARNING OBJECTIVES

After studying this chapter, you should be able to:

- understand the concepts of organizational structure and an organization chart;
- describe how a departmentalized structure matches the organization's activities;
- explain the implications of departmentalization in relation to co-ordination and the centralized and decentralized assignment of authority;
- identify and explain the different organizational structures and systems;
- list the advantages and disadvantages of the different forms of organizational structure with regard to co-ordination requirements;
- describe the growth of an organization in terms of its structural design;
- consider the effects of tall and flat structures on the functioning of organizations.

Management in action

Hoogovens Steel – the elimination of divisional management

Between 1988 and 1995, Hoogovens Steel changed its organizational structure.

Hoogovens Steel is a part of the Hoogovens Group. In 1988, one member of the Group's board of management was responsible for the group's Steel Division.

In the 1988 structure (*see* Fig 6.1), the accent was very much on manufacturing. The structure was designed according to function which meant that relations with the market and the client were of secondary importance. For example, one department within the company could have been supplying steel rims to Dunlop in the UK, while at the same time another department was trying to sell aluminium rims to that same customer. As far as the client (Dunlop) was concerned, there were two 'Hoogovens' from whom two separate articles had to be ordered. Furthermore, the client was visited by two Hoogovens representatives for two versions of the same product.

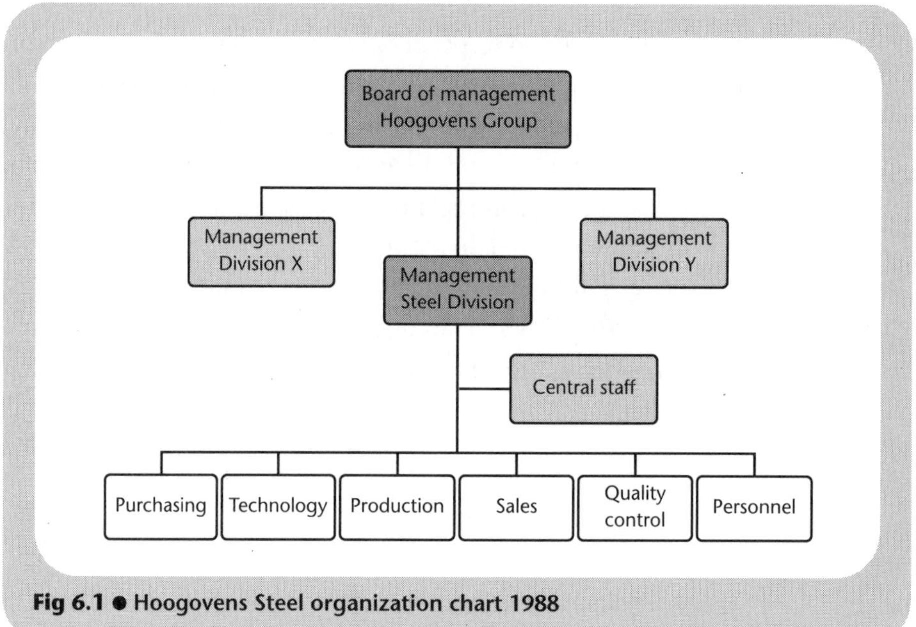

Fig 6.1 ● Hoogovens Steel organization chart 1988

Hoogovens Steel exported more than 80 per cent of its products. Hoogovens Steel's strategy was to decrease its dependency on the European market – both in terms of its sales of final products and its trade cycles. Hoogovens was looking to explore the growth markets outside Europe.

In addition, the organization wanted to exploit a number of opportunities:

- its ability to distinguish itself from its competitors in the eyes of its customers;
- its role, not simply as a supplier of materials, but also as a supplier of solutions to customer problems;

- the increased sophistication and innovation of its product applications development, directed at customers and customers' customers.

The realization of these goals made particular demands on the organization – its employees, its structure and its systems.

- It was important to focus on the activities in which the company wanted to be proactive.
- The advantages of an integrated steel operation had to be maintained at one location.
- The company had to exploit its strengths and the areas at which it excelled.
- The organization had to be ready to anticipate future needs and quickly implement improvements.

In the light of this, the 1988 structure was abandoned and a structure with five units responsible for their own profits was chosen. The units are: flat products, packaging steel, long products, metallurgy and Ymuiden (*see* Fig 6.2). By placing the profit responsibility with these five new units, a more responsive organization has been created which is closer to the market, avoids duplication of effort and is able to make decisions quickly.

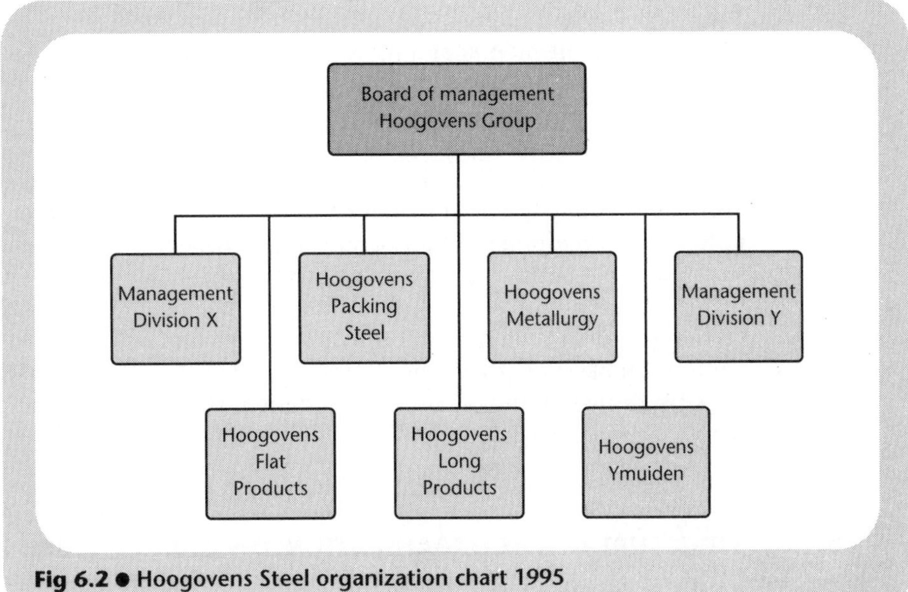

Fig 6.2 ● Hoogovens Steel organization chart 1995

As a result, the management layer of the Steel Division is eliminated. The design of the new organization has direct implications for employment.

Source: Adapted from Dre Grijper, 'Bedrijfskrant Hoogovens Ymuiden', *Noordhollands Dagblad*, 26 November 1994.

INTRODUCTION

In Part two, we considered how the organization has to address the needs of its environment and position itself accordingly, if it is to survive in the long term. The organization now has to consider how it should be designed and structured to give it the best chance of attaining its goals. If the organization structure is inappropriate, the company will not be able to exploit market opportunities to the best of its abilities. Mistakes will be made and goals will not be attained.

In striving to attain the goals it has set itself, an organization must be both efficient and effective. The design of organizational structure has to take into account two factors:

1. *The need for external adaptation.* This involves the adaptation of the organization to the demands of its environment – its markets, society, etc. The organization's goals must be kept in mind and ways of achieving these goals determined.
2. *The need for internal adaptation.* This involves introducing processes and designing the day-to-day workings of the organization which are consistent with the organization's employees, technology and other resources.

In this chapter we consider the structuring of organizations – that is, the designing of a structure that best fits the particular circumstances of a firm or institution. Existing organizational systems and 'old', well tested, organization principles can be used, but the choice of which organizational structure is best will vary from case to case. Key considerations will be:

- choosing the most suitable division of work;
- introducing the most appropriate co-ordination mechanisms;
- assigning decision-making authorities;
- providing a tailor-made communication and consultative structure.

When an organization becomes larger and more complex, the organizational structure needs to be adjusted. This does not happen automatically, however. In this chapter we follow the development of an organization through its changes in operations and structure: from business start-up via a department-based structure to a fully grown or mature organization.

The activities which have to be performed in a firm or institution demand a rational and yet flexible approach to the choice of organizational structure. If operational problems are caused by the organizational design, then the organizational structure will have to be modified accordingly.

6.1 STRUCTURE OF THE ORGANIZATION: DIVISION OF WORK AND CO-ORDINATION

If an organization wants to be effective and efficient, it is important to give careful thought to the way in which the organization should be structured. A firm's structure should be tailor-made to the particular circumstances in which it finds itself. If activities are to run smoothly, they must be channelled. The structure chosen should ensure that the activities of an organization can proceed without arbitrary or unnecessary interruption.

For example ...

... an organization can be compared to a living organism. We would have little use for a 'loose' organ, operating as a separate entity. Only when the working organs combine with other structures to form systems, each fulfilling its particular function according to a division of labour, and a communication system operates between the organs, can a human function effectively. This also applies to an organization.

6.1.1 A definition of organizational structure

The design of an organizational structure and the assessment of an existing organizational structure comprises the following activities:

- the grouping of the activities to be performed into functions, duties and tasks of departments, work groups and individual employees;
- the determining of decision-making authority and relations between departments, work groups and employees in fulfilment of the function and execution of duties and tasks;
- the incorporation of communication channels and the designing of mechanisms, guidelines and procedures in order to attain the necessary transfer of will and co-ordination.

The design of an appropriate structure is therefore concerned both with the *division of labour* and the incorporation of the necessary *co-ordination mechanisms*. With an organization, various combinations of main departments, departments, sub-departments, groups and individual employees can exist, each with its own function within the larger whole. The whole is held together, activated and co-ordinated by establishing links between the individual parts, providing them with appropriate information and by conscious management and leadership. In this way, an organization becomes a whole which is more than the sum of the constituent parts (*see* Fig 6.3). Only then can it work efficiently and effectively.

This co-ordination takes place by means of the consultative structure and channels of communication, which enable the organization to function appropriately by means of frequent exchange of information.

As the necessity for co-operation increases, more and more complex mechanisms will have to be built in in order to enable more intensive co-ordination to take place.

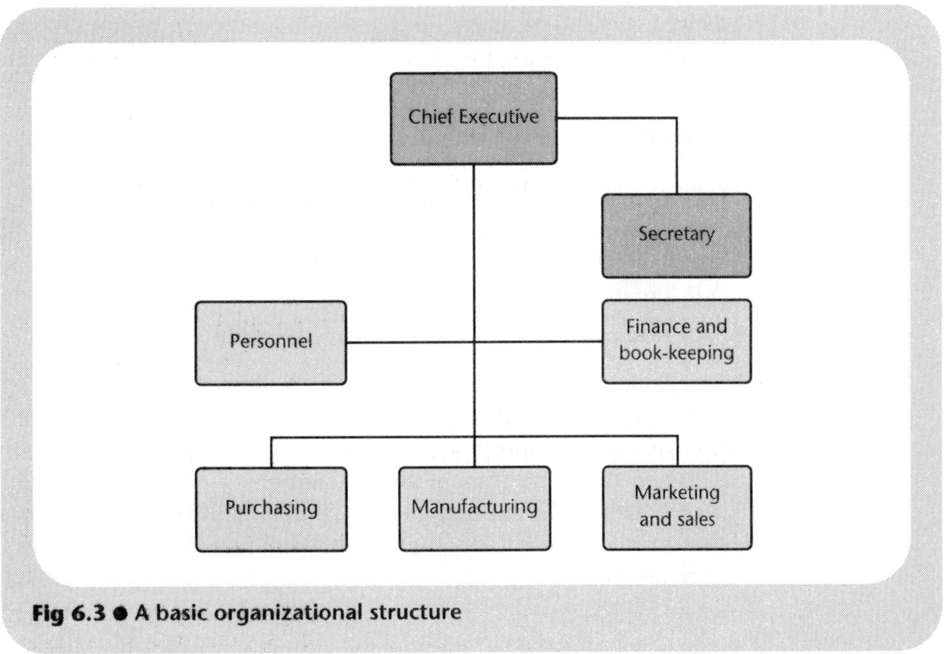

Fig 6.3 ● A basic organizational structure

In the development of an organization from small to large and from simple to complex, the problems of the division of labour and co-ordination must be addressed over and over again. This means that the management must ask itself:

- whether the earlier chosen form of labour division is still the right one;
- whether there is a possible reason for changing the way in which duties and tasks (and their related responsibilities) are delegated or for defining formal relations in a different way;
- whether different or complementary guidelines and procedures are necessary;
- whether changes need to take place in the consultative structure and co-ordinating mechanisms (for example, in the frequency of meetings, composition of working groups, etc.).

A clearly designed structure enables management to stimulate the effective functioning of the organization.

6.1.2 The organization chart and job description

An organization chart, like the one in Fig 6.3, provides insight into the most important characteristics of an organization with regard to:

- the formal *division of tasks and duties*; and
- the formal *authority relations*.

An *organization chart* is an outline of the design of an organizational structure. Precise details with regard to duties, tasks, authorities and relations are not included. When detail is required, in order to clarify the functioning of an organization and to determine the relations between the different positions in an organization, this can be achieved using, for example, *task* or *job descriptions*. Individual roles in an organization are then written out just as they would be for a play. Guidelines and procedures to be followed can also be stated. Job descriptions specify which decisions a functionary is allowed to take, giving insight into the decision-making roles of other functionaries.

6.1.3 Organic and personnel structures

There are two dimensions to setting an organizational structure:

- *The organic structure*. This involves the forming of 'organs' within the organization – that is, main departments, sub-departments, work groups and functions, each fulfilling a particular role in the larger whole.
- *The personnel structure*. This involves the staffing of functions by specific people.

The organic and personnel structures are interrelated in that a well thought out organization structure involves a clear organic structure, in which functions are staffed by employees of an appropriate qualitative level. In practice, this raises the question of the extent to which the present personnel structure in an organization affects the future building up and expansion of an organizational structure. The design of a desired future organic organizational structure can be reflected in a 'blueprint' or 'target structure'.

6.1.4 Formal and informal organization

The *formal organization* is the division of tasks into an official framework established by the management, complemented with job and task descriptions, guidelines and procedures. This often takes the form of charts, procedures, work prescriptions, etc.

In practice, not everything can be anticipated in advance and as a result this formal framework must be supplemented by a set of behavioural rules which will result in the more efficient execution of the roles. In some cases, this may even involve deviating from the rules which were set in the past. This is referred to as *informal organization.*

Informal organization can complement and support the formal organization; alternatively it can also work against the formal organization. Undesirable behaviour can take the form of improper execution of authorities or a too precise interpretation of guidelines and bureaucratic procedures, perhaps resulting in all kinds of delays.

The informal organization works against the formal organization when employees find support from each other and join together to further their own aims. For example, this may occur in the form of an individual or group reduction in productivity (that is, systematic soldiering), resistance to organizational changes or to the setting up of an organizational investigation. This usually involves group action.

For example ...

... informal organization can be said to be harming the formal organization in the following cases:

- Employees with a long term of service come in half an hour late (and possibly leave early).
- A group of employees makes – explicit or implicit – agreements on what it considers a reasonable day's performance.

In the above cases, the informal goals are more important than the formal agreements or the idea of performing as well as possible in order to attain the company's goals. In these cases, the formal organization is harmed.

The role of informal organization can be positive, negative or neutral, depending on the degree to which the informal and formal goals are consistent with each other. If the formal organization is harmed by the informal organization, corrective actions have to be taken. If the formal organization fails to address the problem, this can result in serious delays and problems. After some time, groups will have their own ideas and goals which are inconsistent with those of the formal organization. It is sometimes the case that the formal organization adapts itself to the informal, thus authorizing developments which were not originally meant to happen.

The formal organization maintains itself by means of the power created by authority relations (*see* Chapter 1), structure, agreements, procedures, etc. However, there is a large and important area of activity in which the power of the formal organization cannot be exploited. Regardless of a manager's authority, it is difficult to *force* an employee to carry out a task in a particular way. Little can be achieved without the co-operation of employees.

Informal communication and the creation of informal organizations result in people getting to know one another and meeting outside officially determined relations. These contacts can be used for the good of the organization – for example, to arrange matters quickly. However, these contacts can also be used to spread dissatisfaction with the functioning of the organization.

Informal organization arises spontaneously and is basically always based on personal relations and mutual interdependencies. Where possible, management should try to use the informal organization in a positive way. The power of an organization is determined, to a great extent, by the management's recognition of the existence of an informal organization and its ability to deal with it.

For example ...

... informal organization can be said to be supporting the formal organization in the following cases.

- Employee A intervenes in a work situation involving Employee B, even though he does not have the authority – for example, to avoid danger.
- A manager is passed over by his boss, who gives orders direct to an employee in order to get something done quickly on behalf of a waiting customer.

In times of crisis, situations often occur in which informal aspects of an organization can fulfil a more important role than the formal organization. An informal leader steps forward and takes control.

Effective co-operation cannot be extorted from employees; it must take place on a voluntary and agreed basis. The formal organization can ensure that employees live up to certain agreements and procedures. It is an essential feature of every organization and has an influence on every action. It is therefore important that the informal organization is constantly and critically monitored with the needs of the formal organization in mind.

6.2 VERTICAL AND HORIZONTAL ORGANIZATION DESIGNS

When a division of tasks is being drawn up, the distinction is often made between management tasks and operational tasks – in other words, between planning and doing.

The *vertical* model of organization design involves the division of the organization into a number of layers, expressed in a hierarchy (as we saw in Chapter 1). The layers are:

- top management
- middle management
- front-line management and operational employees.

The division of tasks in a *horizontal* direction involves the conscious grouping of activities into departments and functions. This is called *functionalization* and *departmentalization*. As a result, functions are assigned to individual employees, work groups and sub-departments which are in turn grouped into departments, main functions and support functions. In *horizontal differentiation* (*see* section 6.2.5), groups are formed on the basis of *similarity* of activities; in *internal specialization* (*see* section 6.2.6), groups are formed on the basis of *coherent* activities.

In the company hierarchy (*see* Fig 6.4), each of the layers and each of the functions has its own duties, assignment of tasks and related responsibilities (*see* Chapter 1). The top management has to maintain unity of direction in mission and views and consistency in decision making with regard to the functioning of the departments. In other words, there has to be *unity of direction and control*. Management has to be anchored at all levels of the organization to ensure that there is a consistent view and a common direction in all actions and decision making involving the execution of operational tasks.

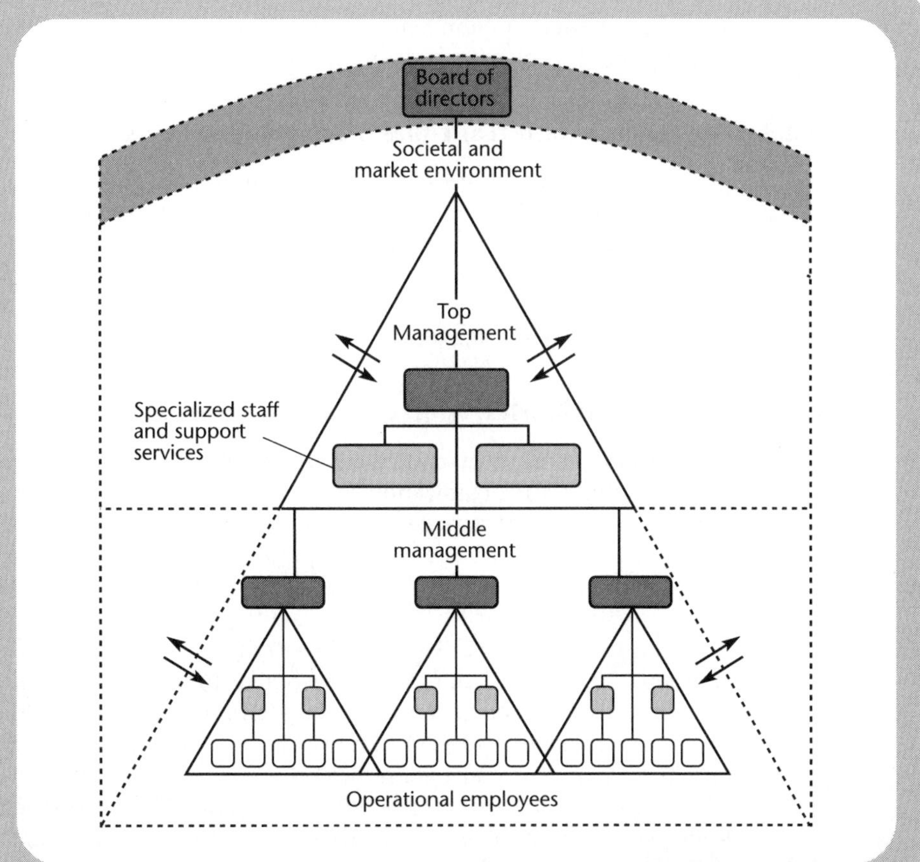

Fig 6.4 ● An organizational structure incorporating both the vertical and horizontal models of task division

6.2.1 Top management tasks

The task of the top management in an organization is to give content to the relation between the organization and its environment – that is, to take the necessary strategic decisions to guarantee the survival of the organization as far as possible. Senior management must carry out the investigations necessary for the implementation of decisions regarding the products or services in relation to markets or customer groups. This will involve both organizational and administrative measures. Middle management will then be in a position to take any further organizational and operational decisions.

6.2.2 Middle management tasks

When a company grows and becomes more complex, a 'new' level of organization will arise due to the fact that a manager can only have a limited number of subordinate employees (*see* the discussion of span of control in Chapter 7). As a result the middle-management level is created (division managers, business unit managers, heads of department, etc.). Middle management has responsibilities both 'to the top' and 'to the bottom' of the organization. It represents the crossing of interests and in a certain sense has a buffer function between the different layers of the organization. It exercises supervision over other employees and, of course, reports to the strategic level above.

6.2.3 Operational and front-line management tasks

The operational employees and the front-line managers have to concentrate on the activities to be executed to attain the target production levels and levels of service. The desired levels of production and quality can be determined by mutual consultation and joint decision making with the employees who execute the operational tasks.

These three management layers were discussed in some detail in Chapter 1. They reflect the classical chain of command or 'hierarchical order' – often referred to as the 'line'.

6.2.4 Tasks of auxiliaries, specialist and support staff

At a certain point, in larger, growing companies and institutions, specialists are recruited. When the organization reaches such a size and problems arise with such frequency, management may decide to bring 'in house' the expertise required to address the specialist and ever more complex problems on aspects of policy and/or execution. When the workload reaches a certain level, it is cheaper for the organization to employ specialists itself, rather than to be constantly using external consultants. When this involves the provision of *specialized knowledge* for the analysis and solution of *policy problems*, the so-called *staff functions* come into being – for example, in the areas of economic research, market research, long-term planning and legislative matters.

It is important that specialist knowledge and techniques are exploited during policy formulation and the preparation for decision making. By employing specialized knowledge, problems can be studied in depth and from different perspectives. Ultimately, this leads to more balanced and better decision making by all layers of the organization.

The employment of specialized staff has to result in the more efficient and more effective working of the whole organization. This can be attained by using specialist knowledge in the improvement of working methods, in planning and control, and also, for example, in the education and training of personnel.

As soon as a company's legal representative or legal department becomes involved in the execution of tasks and the handling of cases, the nature of its function changes. This is no longer a pure consulting or advisory role; there is also an executive element in the fulfilment of tasks. In such a case, the support service element would be considered as 'built in'.

Staff and support services can be incorporated into different levels of the organization. The difference between specialized staff functions and support services lies in the relative scope of the services' authority and not in the specialist knowledge *per se*. The character of a department cannot be determined from its position in an organization chart.

Staff and support functions can be distinguished by considering the following:

- The work of a staff function only influences 'the line'; this will only affect the work of others through the line.
- A staff function provides data or advice – on request or on its own initiative.
- A staff function is not directly involved in any part of the execution of tasks.
- A support function gives compulsory advice to the line and must be consulted before action is or can be taken.
- A support function sometimes executes tasks on behalf of the line.

When the services of specialists in the organization focus on problems of execution in more than one department in the organization, they are referred to as support staff – for example, personnel, administration and finance, maintenance, etc.

For example ...

... a central administration which gives guidelines to the purchasing, production and sales departments about the way in which data has to be processed would be considered a support function. Support staff have the authority to intervene in the functioning of another department with regard to its area of expertise (in our example, administration). A pure staff department does not have this authority (*see* sections 7.5.2 and 7.5.3).

In Fig 6.5, these servicing functions are related to management's constituting tasks (that is, developing strategy, designing an organizational structure and co-ordinating activities (policy-intensive tasks)) and directing tasks (that is, giving orders, motivating employees and controlling and adjusting (operational-execution intensive tasks)).

In some cases, the typing room, reception, security, cafeteria, etc. are counted as support services. These departments are support services in the sense that a service is rendered to other departments in a company or institution. However, specialist knowledge plays a minor role. These departments do indeed conduct a number of defined tasks on behalf of other employees in the organization, but, this does not take the form of specialist or compulsory advice, based on authority and with the aim of improving working methods, planning or education and training. These services can be better described, therefore, as support services rather than support staff.

6.2.5 Internal differentiation

Internal differentiation is the division of work into consecutive phases or steps within a process, based on the nature of the actions which have to be conducted. Such a system, which crosses individual functions or departments, is referred to as a *Functional division*

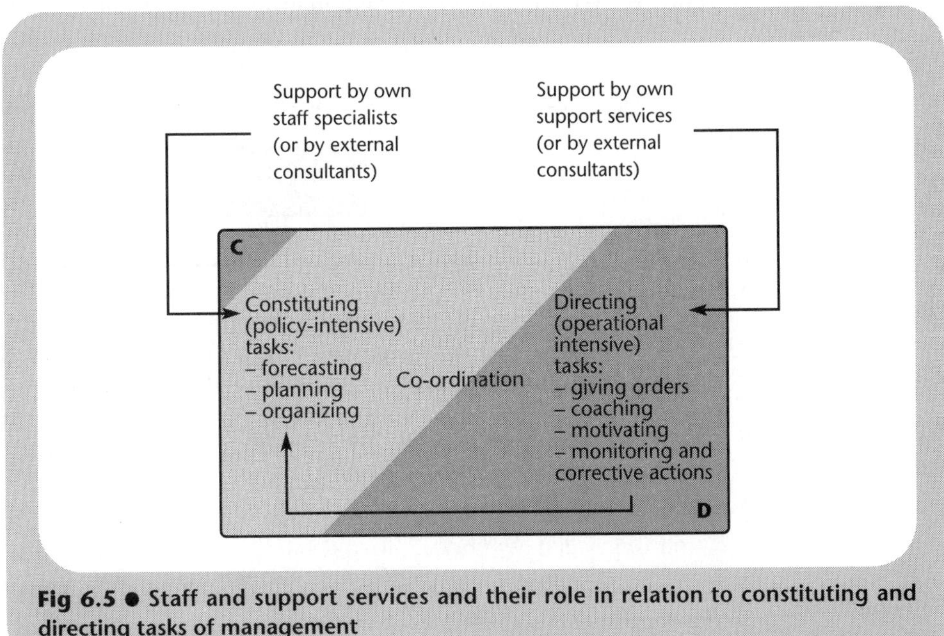

Fig 6.5 ● Staff and support services and their role in relation to constituting and directing tasks of management

of total company activities (the F grouping system). Criteria for the division of processes or actions are, among others:

- required expertise;
- education and training;
- personal skills and characteristics.

Internal differentiation can be applied in many ways. For example:

- the designing of departments or main functions directly under top management (*see* Fig 6.6);
- the designing of sub-departments, for example, within the production department in a furniture factory (*see* Fig 6.7).

One of the drawbacks of internal differentiation is that it breaks down the direct interdependence between the employees working on the individual steps of the process of manufacturing a particular product. The natural 'coherence' of a series of actions

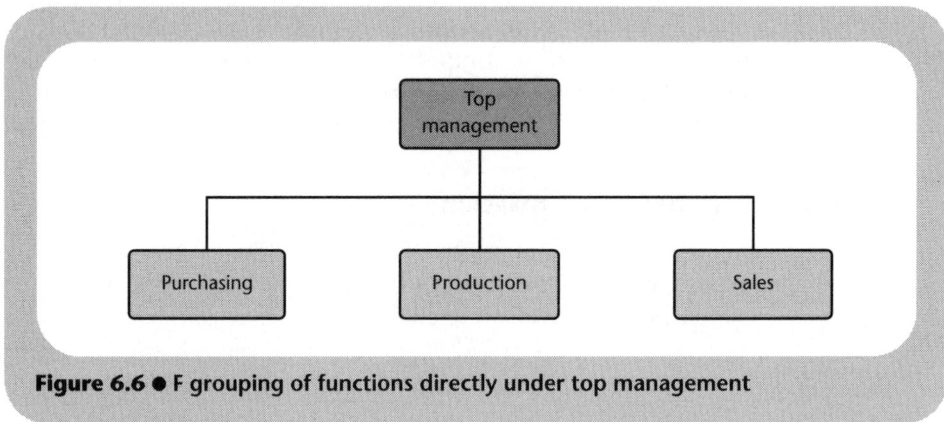

Figure 6.6 ● F grouping of functions directly under top management

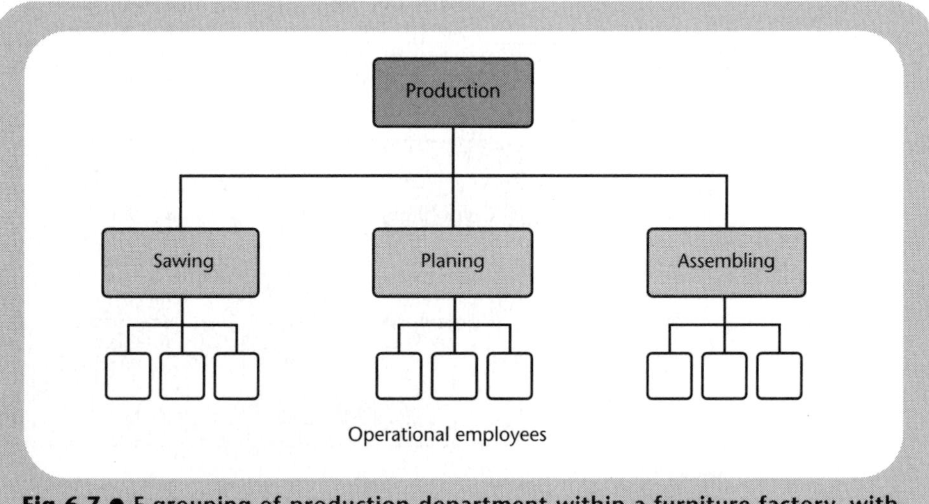

Fig 6.7 ● F grouping of production department within a furniture factory, with sub-departments according to phases of the manufacturing process

which result in the final product is lost. Consultation and planning must be introduced to re-establish this coherence and increase communication between functions, departments and individual employees.

6.2.6 Internal specialization

Internal specialization is the division of labour according to the *common goals* for the actions or functions to be conducted, for products, for a geographical location or for a market segment. The aim of the grouping is *primarily* to achieve *coherence between consecutive actions*. For example, internal product specialization – that is, a P grouping – will draw all actions together which are directed at a single product. The natural coherence between the different activities will be maintained as far as possible in the first instance. Internal specialization according to geographical location is referred to as a G grouping and internal specialization according to market segment is referred to as an M grouping.

Internal specialization can be seen in different applications. For example:

- the designing of departments ('divisions') directly under the board of directors or board of management (*see* Figs 6.8, 6.9 and 6.10);
- the designing of sub-departments within departments (*see* Figs 6.11, 6.12 and 6.13).

In practice, hybrid forms of F, P and M groupings are usually found.

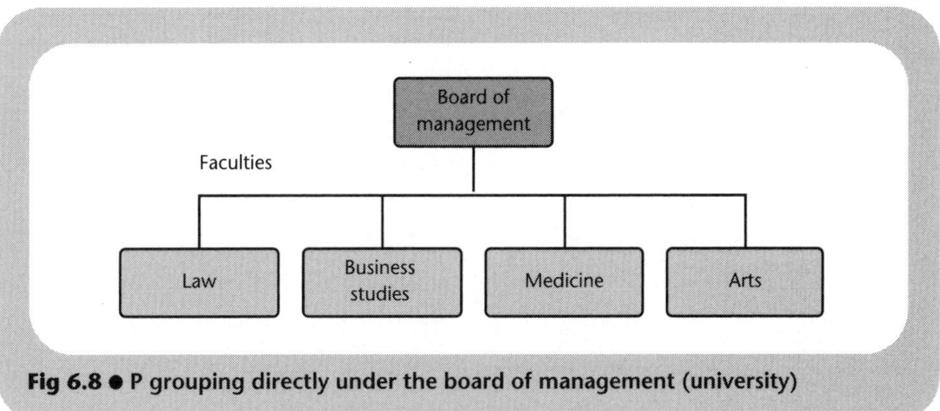

Fig 6.8 • P grouping directly under the board of management (university)

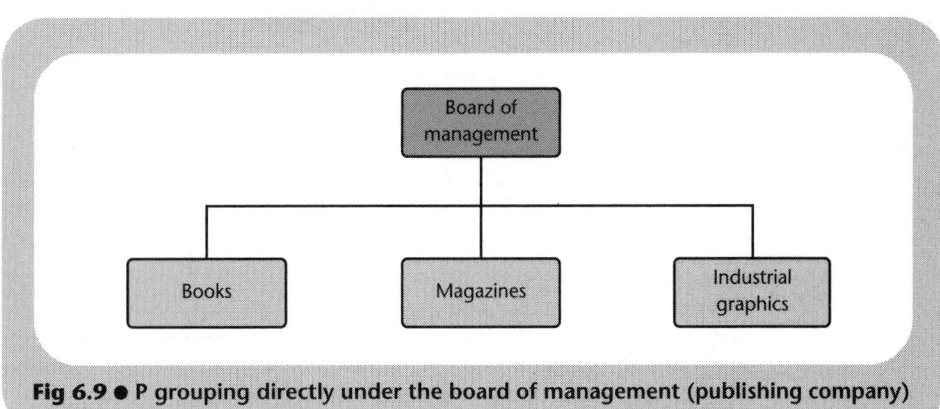

Fig 6.9 • P grouping directly under the board of management (publishing company)

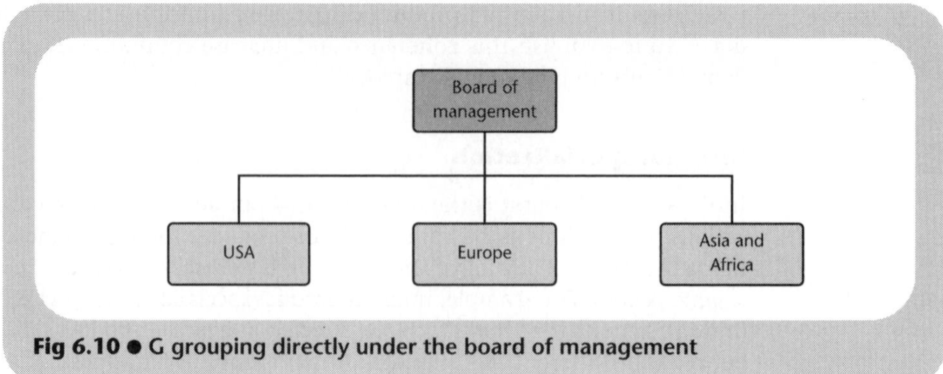

Fig 6.10 ● G grouping directly under the board of management

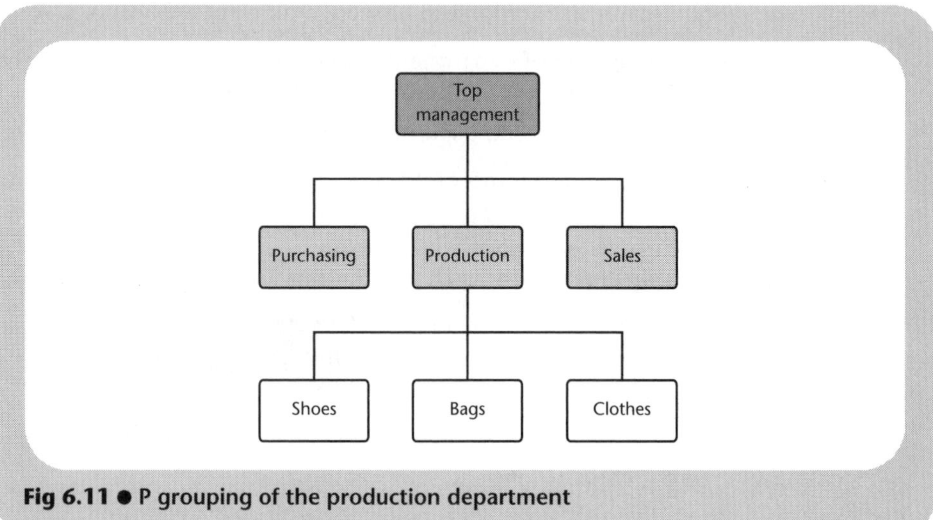

Fig 6.11 ● P grouping of the production department

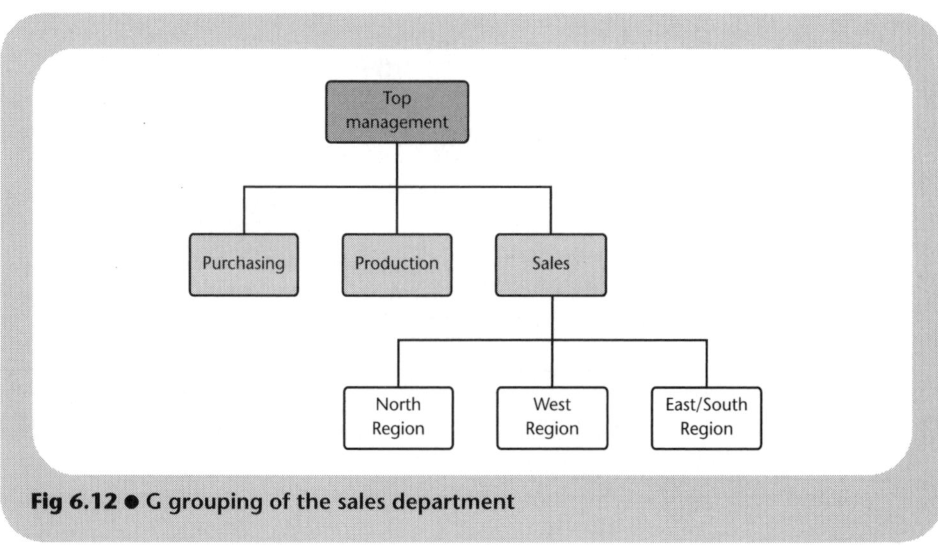

Fig 6.12 ● G grouping of the sales department

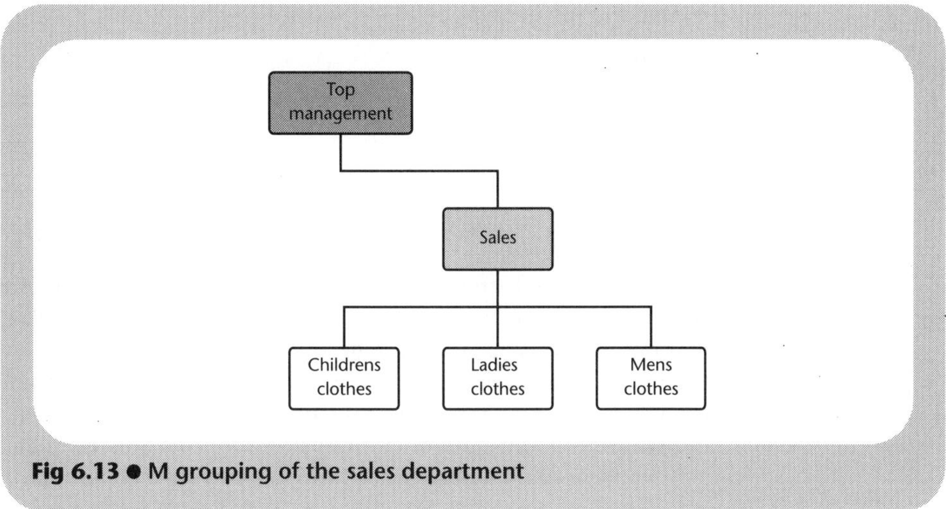

Fig 6.13 ● M grouping of the sales department

6.3 ● THE CHOICE OF ORGANIZATIONAL STRUCTURE

The structure of an organization has three distinct elements:

1. *A form of division of work*. It is possible to divide an organization into:
   - *functions* – for example, purchasing, production, sales;
   - *products* – for example, audio products, medical equipment;
   - *geography* – for example, as per region, province or country;
   - *markets* – for example, domestic users, bulk consumers, consumer products, industrial sectors.

   A grouping into functional departmental areas improves efficiency, but may result in a reduction in flexibility and some interfunctional co-ordination problems. The advantages of the other three possible groupings are a shorter communication line and improved responsiveness to the wishes of the clients. Disadvantages include a higher cost level in some cases and a loss of expertise in the functional aspects of the business and in running the processes.
2. *A degree of centralization or decentralization*. This involves the degree to which the decision-making authority is spread out over the different levels of the organization. A high degree of decentralization often allows the organization to react faster to the changes in the environment. A high degree of centralization leads to greater uniformity in the decisions which are made, and to the top management being better informed about what is going on operationally at the lower levels of the organization.
3. *A system of co-ordination mechanisms*. The co-ordination mechanisms have to ensure that the company's constituent parts work together without any major problems. There is a wide range of co-ordination mechanisms available. As the need for co-operation becomes more intense, more complex mechanisms will have to be incorporated. The following list, arranged in increasing complexity is not exhaustive:

- task and job descriptions;
- plans;
- teams/task forces;
- co-ordinators;
- project groups.

If a new company strategy results in a change in organizational structure, this can mean that the division of work will also have to be changed – for example, from a F(unctional)-oriented structure to a P(roduct)-oriented structure. Adjustments will also need to take place to the degree of centralization or decentralization. Different co-ordination mechanisms may also be required.

As the required co-operation between the departments becomes more intensive, stronger mechanisms have to be built into the organizational structure. For example, in an organization with a F(unctional) structure the launching of products is often a very difficult process because everything has to go via top management. Setting up a team consisting of members from all involved departments can considerably speed up such a project.

6.3.1 Factors affecting choice of structure

The choice of an organizational structure will depend on the particular circumstances the company finds itself in. The choice will be affected by two considerations:

1. *Variety of activities*. If a company makes only one product and sells this to one market, a grouping according to function (purchasing, production, sales) is preferred. If the number of products or the number of markets were to increase, however, and result in an increase in the variety of activities, then that change will have to be processed and reflected in the structure. Sometimes, product groups, business units or divisions can be set up, if size allows. In other situations, the production function can be split up according to product groups; alternatively, the sales function can be split according to market and customer groups.
2. *The nature of the environment*. As more changes occur in the environment, more information will have to be processed by the different organizational levels. This information processing capacity is limited – just like a network of roads which can process the flow of traffic well during the day, but will experience traffic jams at rush-hours. By allowing decisions to be made at a lower level, there is a reduction in the demands on the information processing capacity.

Figure 6.14 brings together two of the elements of an organizational structure – the division of work and the centralization or decentralization of decision-making authority – to reflect the situation with regard to the dynamics of the environment and the variety of activities (for example, in products, markets and geographical areas).

It is important for an organization to be structured in a way that reflects the nature of the organization's activities. For example, the organization's activities may be based around the supply of products to certain key geographical areas; alternatively, the organization may revolve around a number of key product or service ranges. In each case, the division of work must reflect the main focus of the organization's activities – a G structure in the former case, a P structure in the latter – if a coherent whole is to be

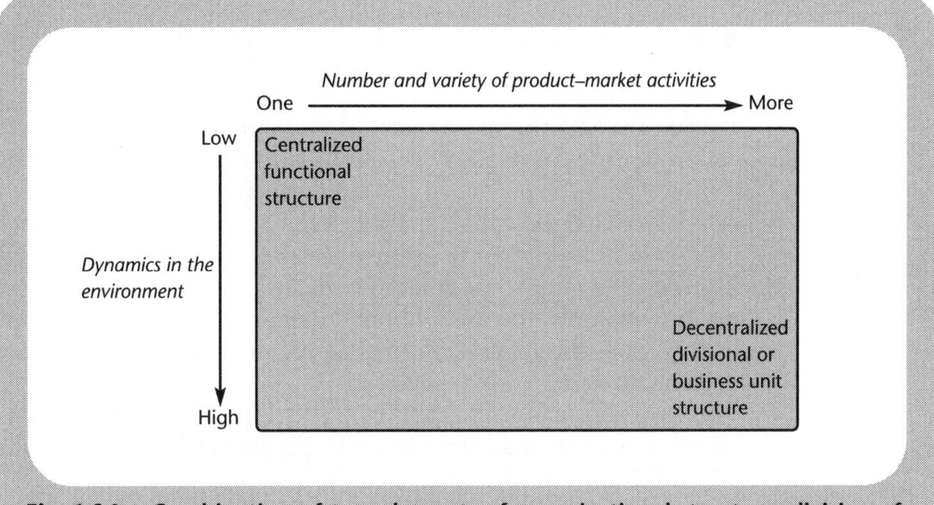

Fig 6.14 ● Combination of two elements of organizational structure: division of work and centralization/decentralization

formed from the individual parts of the organization, from the 'shop floor' to the boardroom. This also applies to organizations whose activities are mostly based around serving a particular market segment (M division) or offering a particular functional field of expertise (F division).

6.3.2 F, P, G and M structures

The 'best' form of labour division for an organization will depend on:

- its size and stage of development;
- the nature of its primary activities; and
- the diversity of its activities.

As the company's activities grow, more employees are recruited for the different functions – production, sales, purchasing, and administration. Within the production department, for example, a more detailed grouping according to the phases of the production process may be introduced. Within the marketing and sales department a more detailed grouping according to geographical areas or possibly individual countries may be chosen. The role of co-ordination for the marketing and sales activities in the different areas or countries then lies with the marketing manager and the sales manager.

Small and medium-sized companies

In small and medium-sized organizations a F(unctional) form of division of work is usually most appropriate, with duties assigned directly from top management. When there are several production locations, for example, these can be arranged as subgroups under one main production function – that is, a G grouping within the production function.

The division of work according to areas or countries – a G grouping – has the following advantages:

- It increases the responsiveness of the organization to local circumstances.
- The results of activities per area are directly visible.
- Short communication lines facilitate effective communication.

This means that the specific factors and circumstances relating to a specific area or country will be given closer consideration in the decision-making process.

However, if the marketing and sales department carries a range of products or articles, a P(roduct) grouping may be preferable. The division of tasks and duties will to a great extent depend on the differences in knowledge, experience and client groups relating to the individual groups of articles. If the articles themselves do not differ too much technically, but are sold to very different client groups (consumers and industrial clients), then possibly a M(arket segment) grouping of the marketing and sales department needs to be considered.

Changes in manufacturing, expertise, experience, distribution channels and customer groups may mean that an earlier grouping may have to be reconsidered.

Medium-sized and large companies

When an organization continues to grow until it is a medium-sized or large company with an increasing number of different, heterogeneous products, a P grouping (directly under the management) may work better than the F grouping used previously. Such a grouping has the major advantage of having the co-ordination of the different operational activities placed one level lower in the organization. The top management is then free to address policy and strategic interests. Such a P(roduct) grouping is often referred to as the creation of divisions or business units. Each product group then has its own management (that is, division management or business unit management) with its own production department, sales department, etc. grouped under that.

If a company is focusing on operating internationally, then, sometimes, a G(eographical) grouping according to country or continent will be introduced under the top management.

We will now review the main options for organizational structure:

- The centralized functional structure (section 6.3.3)
- The decentralized divisional structure (section 6.3.4)
- The decentralized business unit structure (section 6.3.5)
- The project organization (section 6.3.8)
- The matrix organization (section 6.3.9).

6.3.3 The centralized functional structure

In the centralized functional structure, processes or actions are grouped into functional areas according to similarity with regard to expertise, knowledge, abilities, attitudes and skills. In principle, these functional areas – purchasing, sales, production, research and development – are assigned, regardless of the final products to which these activities lead, to functional managers who report to the top management. In this form, concentration and common use (synergy) of professional competences and all other resources are possible when there is a high degree of overlap in the phases of processing a range of final products. In this form, the functional similarities are considered more important than any product, market or geographical links.

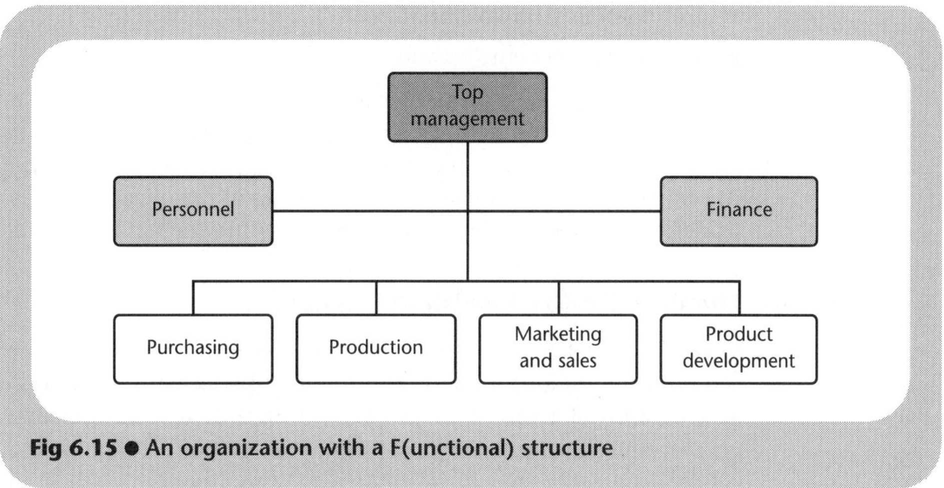

Fig 6.15 ● An organization with a F(unctional) structure

In Fig 6.15, an example is given of a functional organizational structure for a manufacturing company.

The functional structure is optimal when a company wishes to serve one or only a few rather homogeneous product–market combinations as efficiently as possible. The emphasis is on the attaining of advantages of scale and synergy through concentration and utilization of resources within departments. In recent years, however, given the increasing importance of flexibility in product supply, long-term thinking, speed of decision making and innovative capabilities, it is rare for an organization to serve only one or a few product–market combinations. The functional structure is therefore changed to a product- or market-oriented, divisionalized or business unit structure.

In a centralized functional structure, the role of top management is mostly one of co-ordination and the making of product–market decisions. This takes up a great deal of time and attention. The high costs of such a structure must be earned back by means of a high degree of efficiency.

We can summarize the advantages of the functional structure as follows:

- suitable for one or a few product–market combinations;
- central control;
- key activities in departments;
- functional expertise and specialization;
- efficiency created by routine jobs;
- high degree of capacity utilization.

Disadvantages of the functional structure include:

- problems with interfunctional co-ordination;
- problems with lack of market orientation;
- rivalry between various functions;
- over-specialization;
- limited development of internal management capacity;
- profit responsibility only at the top;

- creation of functional empires;
- limited entrepreneurship and innovation.

With the present preference for flat organizations, the functional organization has the disadvantage of offering only a limited possibility for further flattening of the top of the organization, due to the fact that with this structure the top fulfils an important co-ordinating role. However, within functional organizations, it is usually possible to reduce the number of management layers within the ranks of middle management.

6.3.4 The decentralized divisional structure

In the decentralized divisional structure – or strategic business unit (SBU) structure – activities are grouped according to the final performance in terms of product, market, or geographical area. The decentralized divisional structure is appropriate when an organization has an increasing number of different/heterogeneous product–market combinations or geographical areas. The most important goal in this type of organizational structure is improving the responsiveness of the organization to the needs of the different product–market combinations or geographical areas.

Each group of activities is assigned to a product group or to a divisional manager. In this way, managers are not expected to make decisions about products or areas which are unrelated with regard to product technology and marketing activities. The divisional level addresses the issues which are the responsibility of the group under the top management in the F form (*see* Fig 6.15). This means that corporate management can concentrate on strategic planning and control, maintaining the performance level and performance capacity of the divisions. A number of central staff or auxiliary services usually exist in many organizations – finance, corporate strategy, legislative matters, etc. These are not only at the service of the top management, however; they can also be consulted by the divisions.

A divisional structure is shown in Fig 6.16. In this structure, an extra management layer is situated between the business units and the top. Under this divisional layer, different business units are grouped according to related activities.

The main advantage of the divisional structure relates to the realization of synergy in coherent and related activities. The divisions fulfil either the role of consultant or the role of co-ordinator. Relatively high costs are involved in such a structure, and the divisions have the tendency to pull power towards themselves by creating their own, often fast growing, teams of staff. This then leads to an increase in the distance between top management and the shop floor. If this is the case, the advantages of synergy are cancelled out by the higher costs at divisional level.

We can summarize the advantages of the divisional structure as follows:

- enhanced synergy and co-ordination for business units;
- coherence between related activities;
- allocation of capacity based on growth possibilities;
- objective assessment of internal performance by the top;
- good way to structure the business portfolio.

The disadvantages of the divisional structure include:

- extra management layer between the top and the business unit;
- different course for each division;
- difficulties in separating tasks between top, division and business unit;

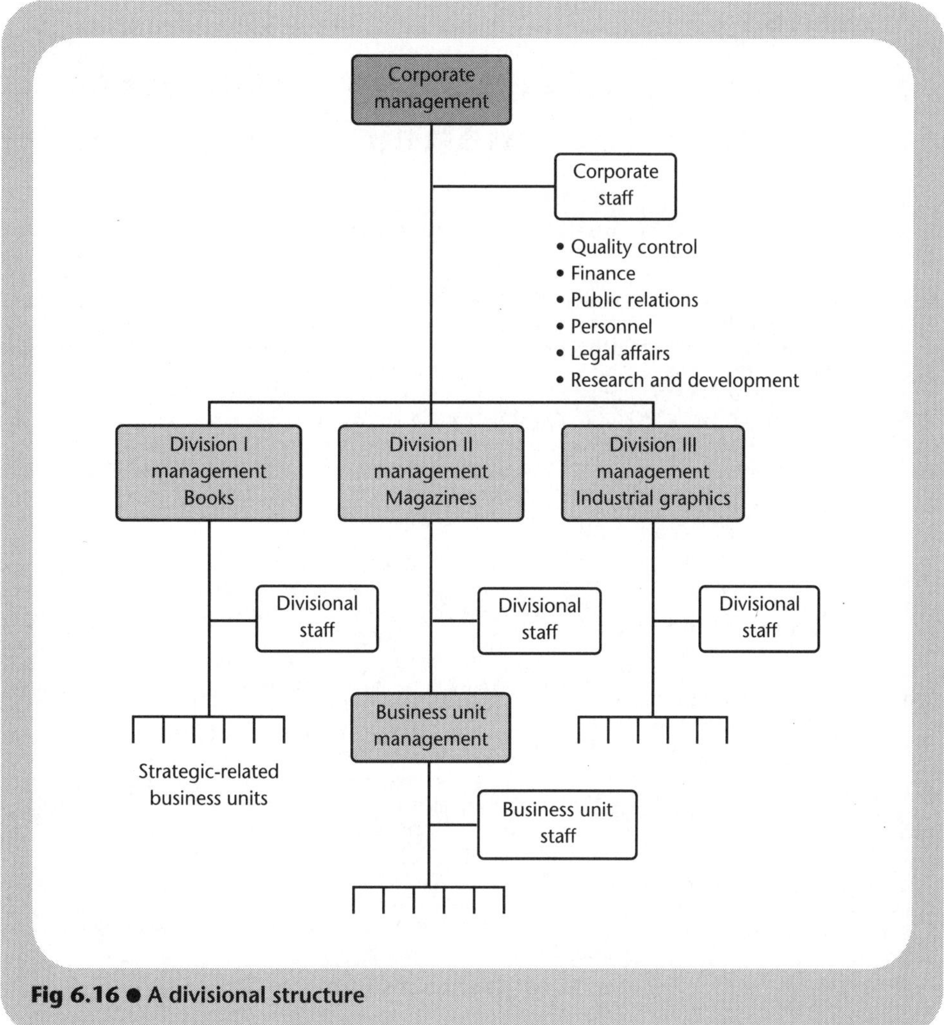

Fig 6.16 ● A divisional structure

- difficulties in assessing responsibility for results;
- top management losing touch with markets;
- duplication of staff functions.

The added value of the divisional level can be reduced in organizations where information technology allows top management to monitor closely the performance of individual business units or where the business unit itself develops a strategic management capacity.

Given the current preference for flat organizational structures, the divisional level has been abandoned in some organizations – for example, Hoogovens Steel at the beginning of this chapter. A condition for further decentralization to business units is, among others, a strong strategic management capacity at business unit level. These business units then have to be fully equipped to cope with their own strategy development. The top operates at a distance and is responsible for providing an explicit overall vision and determining the route the organization has to follow.

Exhibit 6.1

FT

Four core businesses in refocused international financial institution

Credit Suisse, the oldest and most international of the Swiss banks, has a deserved reputation as one of the pioneers of modern Swiss banking. It played a decisive role in financing the industrialisation of Switzerland, including the construction of the Gotthard railway tunnel, and is the only European financial services group with a significant investment banking presence in the US.

However, its recent haphazard growth and acquisition of stand-alone businesses with decentralised managements has resulted in overlapping products and a lack of customer focus.

The purpose of the current restructuring is to change the group from a Swiss bank with international activities into an international financial institution with headquarters and certain core businesses in Switzerland.

Credit Suisse Group, the new holding company, will be refocused into four core businesses, each operating under its own brand name and legally grouped under two separate Swiss banks: Credit Suisse (using the former Swiss Volksbank as a corporate vehicle) and a big new Swiss bank, Credit Suisse First Boston (within the legal framework of the old Credit Suisse).

Functionally, the new Credit Suisse will have two autonomous divisions: Credit Suisse Volksbank (Swiss domestic banking) and worldwide private banking under its existing brand name Credit Suisse Private Banking.

The former will be run by Mr Paul Meier, currently president of Swiss Volksbank, and the latter will be headed by Mr Klaus Jenny, a member of the executive board of Credit Suisse. Bank Hofmann, Clariden Bank and the reorganised Bank Leu will continue as subsidiaries of the holding company but will be managed by the private banking business unit.

Credit Suisse Volksbank will combine the domestic branch networks of Credit Suisse, Swiss Volksbank and Bank Leu.

At present, the group operates a total of 376 branches in Switzerland and there are overlapping facilities in 224 locations. In all these locations, the branches will be amalgamated – resulting in a reduction of 112 branches.

Between 15 and 20 branches will be closed, so the Swiss branch network will shrink by 40 per cent to less than 250 branches after the reorganisation is completed. However, Neue Aargauer Bank, which is the biggest bank in the canton of Aargau, will continue to operate as a full service regional banking subsidiary of Credit Suisse Volksbank.

By far the biggest part of the new Credit Suisse Group will be the enlarged Credit Suisse First Boston, which will be headed by Mr Hans-Ulrig Doerig. This will include two autonomous divisions, Credit Suisse Asset Management, and the corporate and investment banking business, Credit Suisse First Boston.

In essence, the existing international investment banking business of CS First Boston is being merged with the existing international corporate and Swiss investment banking business of Credit Suisse. Credit Suisse Financial Products, a leading player in derivatives and risk management products, will also form part of this unit.

The top management of the new Credit Suisse Group will be strengthened by a number of new appointments to central support functions.

Mr Phillip Colebatch, who will head Credit Suisse Asset Management, will act as interim group chief financial officer until a replacement is found. A new chief risk officer will also be appointed to ensure that the group's strategy towards risk fits in with its corporate objectives. The new management structure will take effect from January 1 next year.

The realignment of the new business units will take place over the next couple of years and by the end of 1998, the new organisation should be in place – with each business unit managing its own infrastructure, accounting system and branch network.

Source: *Financial Times*, 3 July 1996.

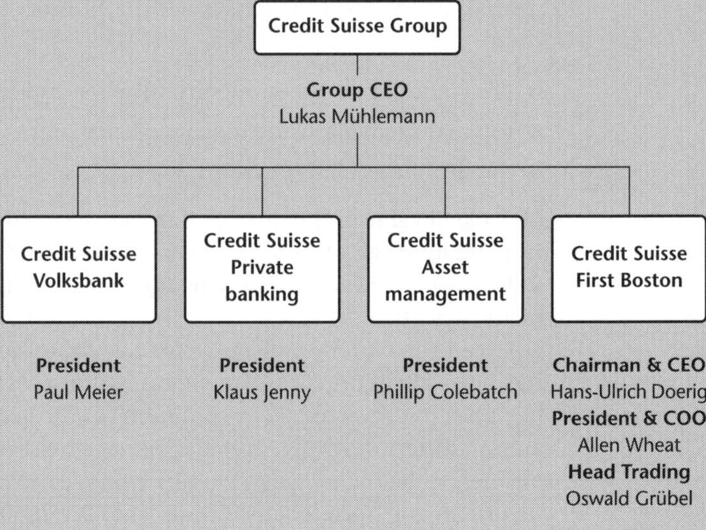

6.3.5 The business unit structure

A business unit structure – or BU structure – is illustrated in Fig 6.17. This structure promotes profit responsibility, decentralization of authority and market orientation. In its purest form, a business unit structure requires business units to be fully equipped with their own service departments.

However, the business unit structure is not without its problems. It keeps top management at a distance from operations and it discourages it from intervening, even though it holds the final responsibility.

The business unit structure presupposes that the business units have a full strategic management capacity.

The concept of the business unit is currently enjoying a certain degree of popularity, although it appears rarely in its purest form, but instead in a somewhat watered down version. Such cases cannot be described as business unit structures in the real sense. When we refer to a business unit structure here, it is the pure form of structure we have in mind.

The advantages of the business unit structure include:

- good opportunity for delegation of responsibility for results;
- strategy remains close to the entrepreneurial environment;

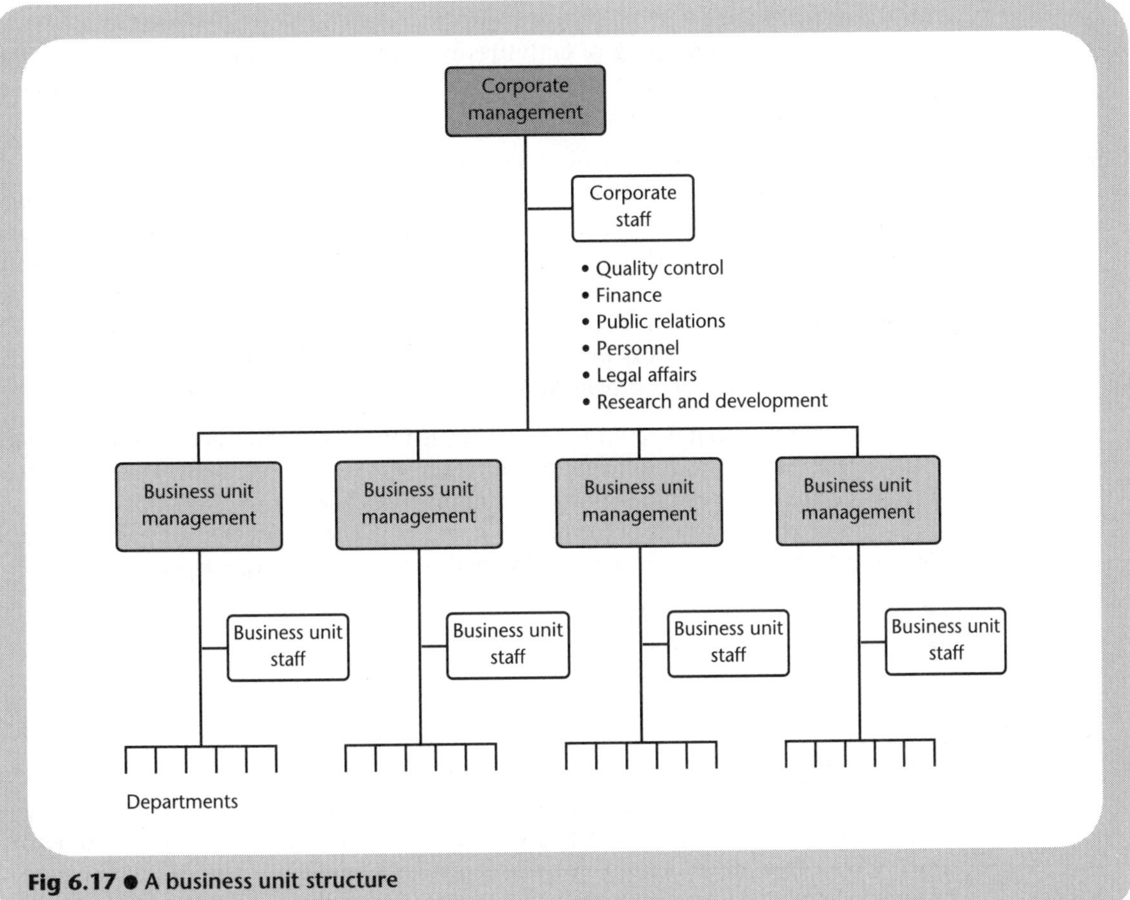

Fig 6.17 ● A business unit structure

- own responsibility for management of processes;
- stimulates entrepreneurship;
- top can concentrate on strategy and portfolio.

Disadvantages include:

- separation of central and decentralized authority;
- rivalry over services and attention of the top;
- autonomy hampers synergy;
- top now dependent on business unit managers;
- duplication of staff functions.

The attraction of synergy did not appeal to one corporate manager: 'Just let the business units compete, as long as they do not pursue a price war. When you wish to attain real synergy, you can merge and integrate the business units.'

6.3.6 Interdependencies and their design solutions

Before continuing with our consideration of the main organizational structures, it is worth considering at this point the relationships and interdependencies which result from the structures we have already discussed, and the problems they create for the organization.

Once a primary grouping of activities is in place, a certain co-ordinating effect occurs automatically for the employees within the organization as it becomes clear who works where in which department.

For example ...

... Phil Curtis, a maintenance mechanic in the production department at Company A, knows that every day he can go directly to the production department in order to commence his job. Every day, when Sharon MacRyan enters the company offices, she also goes directly to her workplace in the purchasing department. Searching for your workplace every morning is not an issue because the organization has made clear its departmentalization. In addition, if Phil wants to speak to Sharon or someone in his own department, then he looks up the number in the internal telephone guide. It can be seen, therefore, that departmentalization stimulates a co-ordinating effect.

What has not yet been determined, however, is the relationships between the different departments and between different employees in the same department. This adjustment involves a number of co-ordination mechanisms. The choice of co-ordination mechanism is determined by the nature of the mutual interdependence between the departments and between the employees involved. We distinguish three types of interdependence:

- 'pooled' interdependence;
- serial or sequential interdependence;
- reciprocal interdependence.

'Pooled' interdependence

In this type of interdependence, an interdependence exists only between 'higher' and 'lower' groups or individuals (that is, vertically). At a horizontal level, between departments, there is no direct dependence: one department cannot influence the daily course of events in another department (although this could be possible indirectly in the long term).

For example ...

... take the MIGROS retail chain. MIGROS-Switzerland – the organization at national level – and the MIGROS branches are, as higher and lower organizational layers, 'pooled' interdependent. The higher organization (MIGROS-Switzerland) exists thanks to the contributions which are made by the lower organizations (the MIGROS branches).

In turn, the MIGROS branches benefit from the fact that they are part of MIGROS-Switzerland, as the national organization offers all kinds of facilities which a branch would not be able to afford itself, if it were an independent store. As parts of a larger organization, for example, the branches can borrow money internally at a lower interest rate than the rate of an external bank.

At the horizontal level, the branches do not tend to affect each other. When light bulbs are sold out in the Basle branch, this does not affect the sales of light bulbs in the Berne or Geneva branches.

This type of interdependence is created when an organization opts for *internal specialization*: a P, G, or M structure. Figure 6.18 illustrates this 'pooled' interdependence.

An appropriate co-ordination mechanism in the case of 'pooled' interdependence is standardization of output per organizational unit. In the case of MIGROS, for example, the national management sets output norms to be realized by local subsidiaries in terms of turnover, profitability and the handling of complaints.

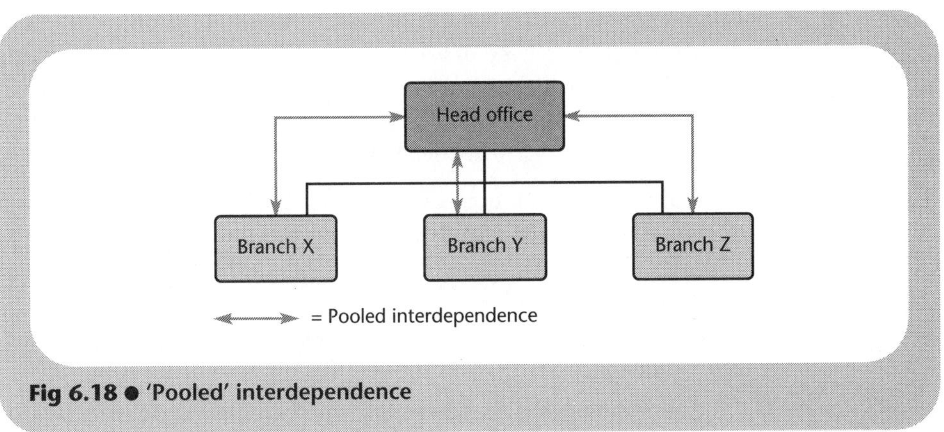

Fig 6.18 ● 'Pooled' interdependence

Serial or sequential interdependence

If an organization opts for *internal differentiation* (F structure), then serial interdependence arises. This is the case with the purchasing–production–sales grouping. The successive phases in the operational process are now directly dependent on each other and as a result it is essential that the order of processing is coherent and fixed. A purchasing activity must take place before production can carry out its activity, and only after that will the sales department be able to start its work.

The scope for disruption is much greater than with 'pooled' interdependence. If the purchasing activities stop, then it is certain that after a while production will have no components and raw materials and that a little later sales representatives will have to go to clients without products. In serial or sequential interdependencies, therefore, the activities have to be more closely co-ordinated than is the case with 'pooled' interdependence and will relate directly to each other. Serial or sequential interdependence is illustrated in Fig 6.19.

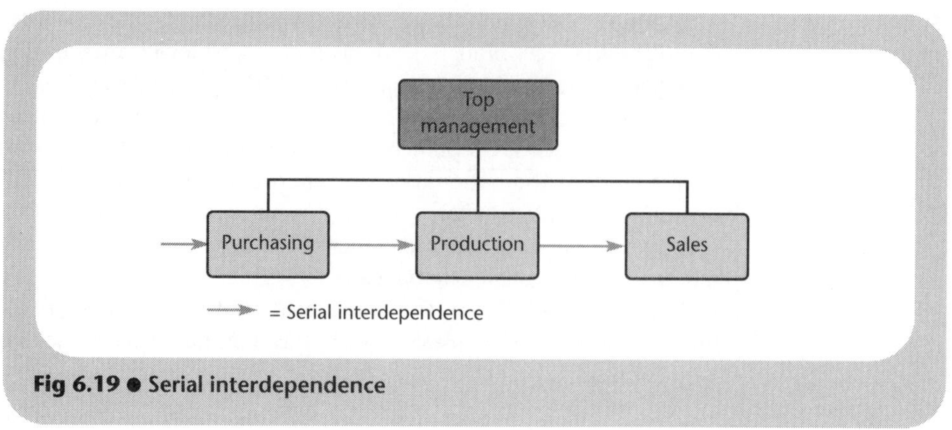

Fig 6.19 ● Serial interdependence

An appropriate co-ordination mechanism for serial interdependence is planning, because of the absolute necessity of the process being coherent and predictable.

Reciprocal interdependence

When there is no fixed order between the different phases of processing or between departments, but these phases or departments are *directly* dependent on each other, can influence each other and can affect each other in the daily course of events, this is referred to as reciprocal interdependence. In short, the output of one department can be the input of every other department.

For example ...

... take the design process of a new model of coffee maker in a company which has an F structure. Research and Development has put an initial idea on paper for the coffee maker. Before this design can come on to the market, however, the input of other departments is required.

- Marketing and sales has to determine whether this model is what the consumer is waiting for.
- Production has to determine whether this model can be produced on existing machines or whether new machines and new techniques have to be purchased/learned.
- Purchasing has to determine whether the required materials can be obtained in the coming years, and to ensure that these materials are not legally forbidden.

Research and Development without doubt needs the reactions of these departments. It is directly dependent. However, it is impossible to predict when the reaction of each department will be received. Nor can the nature of the reaction be predicted (great idea/technically impossible/attainable with some adjustments/no reaction at all). In addition, by the time all the departments have reacted to the first idea, four further versions of the new coffee maker may have been produced. The departments' reactions may result in a further proposal – version six of the design – which will make the round of the departments all over again.

In this kind of situation, there is a high risk of confusion and mistakes – a serious problem in a development process. In such a process, close co-ordination is crucial.

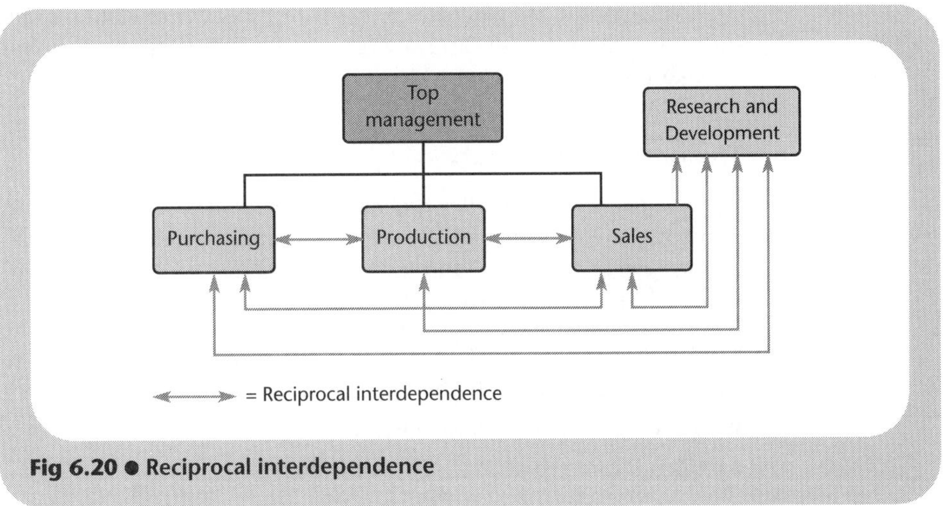

Fig 6.20 ● Reciprocal interdependence

Reciprocal interdependence is illustrated in Fig 6.20. An appropriate co-ordination mechanism in the case of reciprocal interdependence is direct communication via a task force or project group.

6.3.7 The three roles of executive authority

Before we can discuss the project organization and the matrix organization, we must first consider the three roles involved in a manager's authority as these form an important part of these structures.

A manager has the authority to make decisions and within this authority, three partial authority roles can be distinguished.

- *The hierarchical role (the administrative boss).* The manager with this role is responsible for the general running of the department or team. In addition, such a manager takes care of the matters relating to individual employees – for example, evaluation, training or further education, career planning, etc.
- *The operational role (the work boss).* This type of manager decides about the progress of the specific work activities and prioritizes work activities – for example, inserting into the production schedule a rush order which has to be processed quickly.
- *The functional role (the specialist boss).* This manager decides about the way in which the products and services are to be produced and the professional methods, techniques and instruments to be used in the process. An example is the authority of the information and systems control manager to determine that everybody in the organization should use a particular text processing package.

These three roles in executive authority can be given to one person as a manager; this is referred to as 'unity of command'. However, the roles can also be divided among several persons – referred to as 'breaking the unity of command'. It is unity of direction, not unity of command, that is the main concern within an organization. Unity of direction means that the managers do not take conflicting decisions; rather they show employees the clear direction in which the organization has to head.

Having considered the three forms interdependence can take, and the three roles in executive authority, we can now return to our discussion of the most common forms of organizational structure.

6.3.8 The project organization

Project organization implies the splitting up of an organization into semi-autonomous units or project groups which are focused on a particular project – for example, the automation of a financial administration system.

A project can be defined as:

- a whole set of activities
- to be executed by more than one specialist group
- in a temporary co-operative relationship
- which is directed at a clearly specified result
- which needs to be attained within a limited period of time and with limited resources.

Employees from different parts of the organization and different specialist fields are assigned to a project group which then focuses exclusively on the realization of the project. A project manager is appointed. The project manager and the other members of the project group will return to their former roles as soon as the project or a phase of the project has been realized.

The project manager is the operational boss who carries the responsibility for the progress and the prompt realization of the project within the budget limits. The project manager sets priorities, monitors progress, adjusts activities and takes corrective actions, where necessary.

In a firm or institution with a project organization, activities are arranged in two groups:

- *the permanent basic organization*, which can be seen as the reservoir of resources; and
- *the project group*, which can be seen as the executive working unit with a one-off operational task assignment – for example, to develop a new prototype of gasoline engine, to design and build a new hospital, etc.

This division of the organization into two groups is illustrated in Fig 6.21.

Problems in the management of projects

A project-based approach to organizational structure not only brings solutions to existing problems, but also creates new problems.

In practice, the organization of a project will be less than satisfactory when this has not been properly co-ordinated with the basic organization. The basic organization then rejects the 'alien' project organization. As a reaction to this, the project organization starts to organize its own affairs and distances itself from the basic organization. The appointment of senior management to the project groups can help to bring the project group back into the organization and to gain the acceptance of the basic organization.

Almost every organization and every department encounters development problems because of the ever increasing pace of change in the fields of technology and marketing. If top management does not address such developments, many official and non-official groups – sometimes working together, sometimes working in competition – will spring up to attempt to solve the development problems.

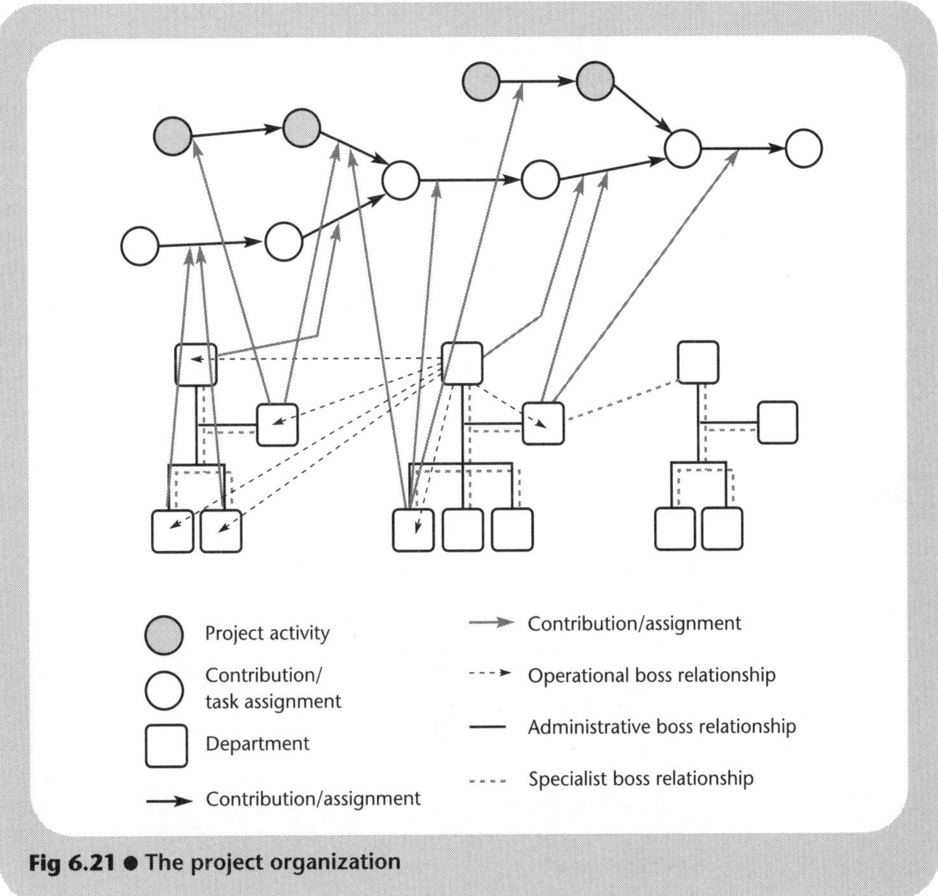

Fig 6.21 ● The project organization

The most common problems of a project-based approach have been categorized, based on the experiences of about 400 project managers from many different organizations, both in the private and public sectors (*see* Table 6.1).

Table 6.1 ● Common problems in project management

Lack of clarity in project philosophy and approach (*philosophy*)	5%
Lack of cohesion and co-ordination (*phasing*)	15%
Exceeding or failing to reach targets with regard to time, money, quality and information (*control*)	19%
Bottlenecks between the project and its environment (especially customers, users and suppliers) (*external structuring*)	22%
Lack of clarity in the internal project structure (*internal structuring*)	6%
Lack of co-operation within the project teams (*co-operation*)	32%
Lack of managerial and social skills and assertiveness of the project manager (*personal quality*)	1%
	100%

Source: Wijnen, Renes and Storm (1984)

In the *matrix organization* (*see* section 6.3.9) authority over operational personnel is shared by the project management and the management of the organizational unit of the basic organization. Here, the deliberation and co-ordination between project management and departmental management are important factors. The project management can assert its authority across fields. The project group is placed across and not alongside the other departments.

In the pure project structure, project managers have three forms of authority at their disposal (hierarchical, operational and functional) which are necessary to control the activities connected to the projects. In other words, project managers have as much authority over their employees as departmental heads have over theirs – that is unity of command in a temporary unit. Project managers may even have a complete executive and staff apparatus at their disposal, while the managers of more permanent departments only have a limited group of employees. In any case, in this structure the

Minicase 6.1

Pink Floyd on tour: a pure project

Pink Floyd on tour. Anno 1994. Volkswagen is the sponsor. The overhead costs amount to the sum of US$600,000 per day.

'Test one two, test one two.' It is time for the last sound check. For the last four days at the Rose Bowl Stadium in Los Angeles, the 200-strong crew has been busy building up the enormous stage set. 700 tonnes of material have been processed. The sky-high speaker towers can blast out 350,000 watts of sound. The stage is crammed with the most advanced laser and computer equipment. At the same moment, in Houston and Dallas, dozens of 'roadies' are busy setting up the stages for the new shows. For the first time in seven years, Pink Floyd is 'on the road again'.

In addition to the 200 crew members, the Floyd tour consists of fifty trucks, eight touring cars, eight cooks (including a dietician) and a few bodyguards. For three months, the band will be touring the United States. After that, it is Europe's turn.

These three months cannot go quickly enough for Jennifer Hurshell, the Volkswagen representative responsible for the execution of the sponsor contract for the European tour. Volkswagen's sponsorship of the European tour of Genesis, Phil Collins' band, some years before, increased car sales by 20,000 units. 'Pink Floyd', according to Jennifer Hurschell, 'is good for double that. Plus, of course, a huge strengthening of image. In addition, both Volkswagen and Pink Floyd built up their image in the sixties. Both partners have always renewed their position over the years by innovating and introducing new technologies.'

At 8.30 on a warm Californian evening, the Rose Bowl slowly fills with rising quadraphonic sounds of rippling streams, twittering birds and croaking frogs. Then there is a sudden explosion as kaleidoscopic laser light floods the stadium, followed by drum rolls and the shrills of the Fender Stratocaster of band leader, David Gilmour. The fathers – the audience is estimated to be 75 per cent male – still remember the songs. Their children are transfixed by the ultimate light show, which no MTV channel, disco or house party could ever offer. Pink Floyd has the most spectacular light show in the world.

'And that', analyses Ms Hurshell, 'is of course the big attraction of Pink Floyd and our deal with the supergroup. Volkswagen and Pink Floyd stand for technical perfection. The 'oldies' treat the music as rock and roll. Their children are mesmerized by the visual spectacle.'

Source: Adapted from *Management Team*, 22 August 1994.

reciprocal interdependence of project management vis-à-vis the permanent department is usually limited to the strategic and sometimes the administrative levels of decision making, and rarely extends to the operational level of decision making.

6.3.8 The matrix organization

An organization may introduce a matrix structure if problems arise which cannot be solved by one department alone (*see* Fig 6.22). Take product development as an example. Product development involves co-operation between the Research and Development department, the marketing department, the production department, as well as a contribution from the finance department in the form of calculations of pay back periods and investments, cost price calculations, etc.

A matrix structure – so-called because of the existence of both horizontal and vertical authority relations – can be created to achieve the required level of co-ordination and co-operation. It is often a combination of a F(unctional) organizational structure and a project structure and/or business unit or divisional structure.

An employee is:

1. a member of a functional department on the basis of his or her expertise; and
2. a member of a project group, operational unit or division in which he or she works on a common development or production task, together with colleagues from other departments, disciplines or units.

The work carried out is decided by the project group; how the work is carried out is assigned by the employee's functional base.

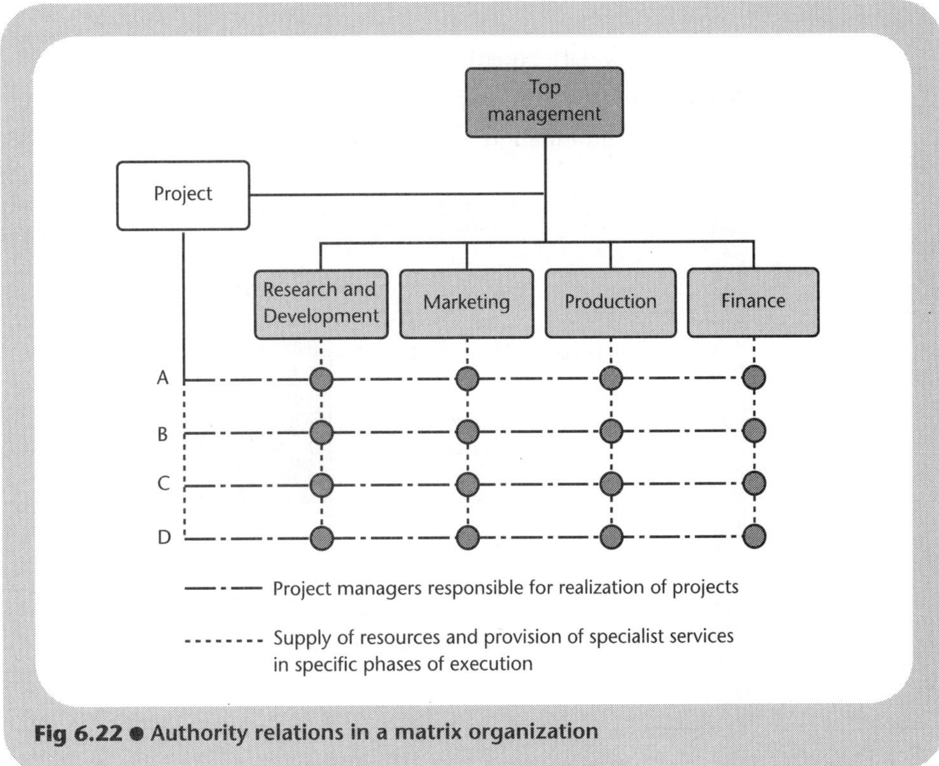

Fig 6.22 ● Authority relations in a matrix organization

In its temporary form, a matrix organization can be seen as a cross between a departmentalized organizational structure and a project organizational structure.

However, if a matrix organization is established on a permanent basis a certain degree of authority is assigned to managers, responsible for a particular product range or client, who then have a dual role with regard to the department line managers. A product manager in a manufacturing company and an account manager in a financial services company are examples of such managers. A matrix organization, therefore, has dual information and reporting relations which can often result in problems relating to the balance of power.

A balance needs to be struck between the interests of the project, on the one hand, and the interests of the individual department on the other. Tensions and possible areas of conflict are created because authorities are not clearly defined. During the execution of the activities, an employee has to report to two different bosses:

- *the functional boss* of the department from which the employee has been temporarily seconded; and
- *the operational boss*, who as project manager is the work boss responsible for the timely, efficient and effective project realization.

This involves, therefore, dual lines of authority, which break the unity of command, and all the attendant consequences. Overcoming these difficulties and creating a balance between the two dimensions of the matrix involve specific skills from both management and employees. Such a balancing mechanism is illustrated in the model developed by Galbraith (1973) shown in Fig 6.23.

A bilateral information and reporting system has to be incorporated so that the project can be monitored and controlled from different areas of responsibility. The quality of co-ordination will depend among other things on the degree to which project group members have:

- the appropriate expertise;
- adequate authority; and
- the right information.

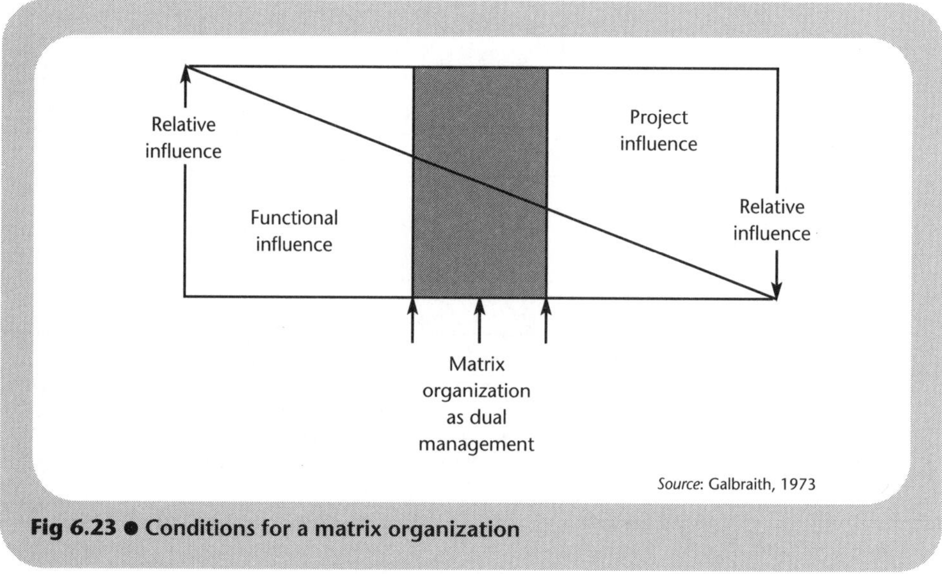

Fig 6.23 ● Conditions for a matrix organization

If these conditions are not met, this will have a negative influence on the effectiveness of the co-ordination effort. In practice, relations will be highly influenced by the quality and skills of the functional and operational managers.

The matrix organization has the following advantages:

- There is a focus on both specialist expertise and operational, execution-oriented co-ordination.
- Consultation and flexibility are directly related to the requirements of the project.
- Teamwork is stimulated.

Disadvantages include:

- The structure is complex and often lacks clarity.
- The optimal organizational balance can be affected easily by personal power relationships.
- A high degree of consultation is required.
- Such a structure demands a high level of effective management at all levels.
- Employees must have organizational skills.
- It is difficult to define authority unambiguously.

A matrix organizational structure is most appropriate in the following situations:

- Joint efforts are required from different disciplines or professional fields.
- The project involves the resolution of complex problems.
- High quality standards are expected.
- A large number of cases of intensive reciprocal interdependence are present.

Projects can also be realized through a matrix-like structure, using a relatively permanent organization as a basic reservoir of resources (*see* section 6.3.8). The required functional expertise is then brought together on a temporary basis in a project organization under the operational authority of a project manager. In cases where projects are the main concern in the production of added value, the most appropriate organizational form is called an '*adhocracy*' (Toffler, 1969; later Keuning/Eppink, 1978; and Mintzberg, 1979).

6.4 ORGANIZATIONAL STRUCTURE IN DEVELOPMENT

In section 2.4, we discussed the growth and development of organizations from the point of view of policy and management factors. We now explore the development of the organization from the point of view of its structure.

As a company or institution becomes larger and more complex, the organization of the different tasks to be fulfilled needs to be adjusted to the new demands of the external environment.

6.4.1 Organizational structure in the start-up phase

When a business has just begun its operations, the organization is usually small, the structure simple. There are only a few primary functions for which employees are hired

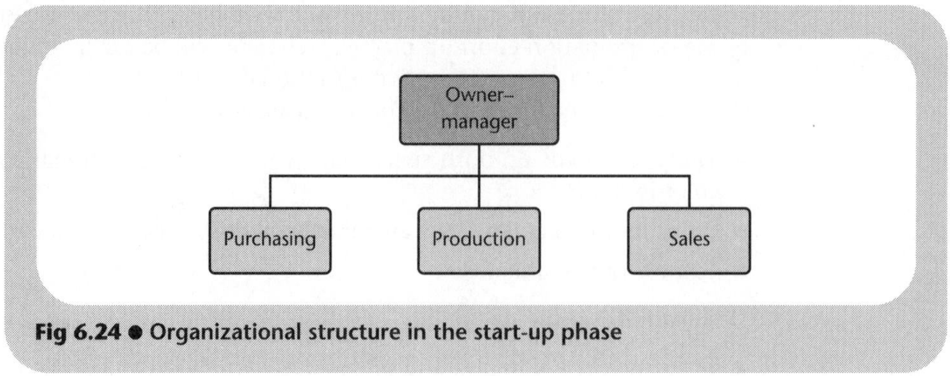

Fig 6.24 ● Organizational structure in the start-up phase

– for example, purchasing, production and sales in an industrial company (*see* Fig 6.24). There is usually only one single product aimed at a limited market in a limited geographical area.

In this first phase of development, the company is still managed by its founder – that is, the person who discovered a gap in a market and decided to set up a business to fill that gap. An employee may be recruited for the performing of operational activities. In other word, this is a *highly centralized functional organization* with a single manufacturing and distribution process.

Such companies are characterized by simple organization, the capacity to influence operations directly and direct and informal communication and working practices. There is little long-term planning and formal prescriptions and procedures are rarely present. Problems are usually solved by 'improvization', often involving the owner–manager – an approach also applied to the marketing of the business. The owner–manager works closely with his or her employees and market, but at the same time occupies a position of authority. There is rarely a management layer directly under the owner–manager. If one exists, it is often a management role fraught with difficulty. The continuity of such a company is therefore not guaranteed without due consideration. Succession is often a problem.

A typical business start-up can be characterized as follows:

- *Structure of the organization*: centralized F form, with a minimal internal division of work.
- *Research and development*: carried out by the owner–manager.
- *Performance measurement*: by personal contact with subjective criteria.
- *Reward/payment*: often unsystematic and paternalistic.
- *Control system*: personal control, with regard to strategic control, design of the organizational structure, and control of the operational processes.
- *Strategic choice*: dependent on the personal aspirations of the owner–manager.

6.4.2 Organizational structure in the growth phase

As a company expands, this growth takes the form of a more detailed subdivision of the organization's primary functions. For example, the sales function may be split into areas or client groups, or the production function into phases in the production process. At the same time some support functions will be created alongside the primary functions (*see* Fig 6.25).

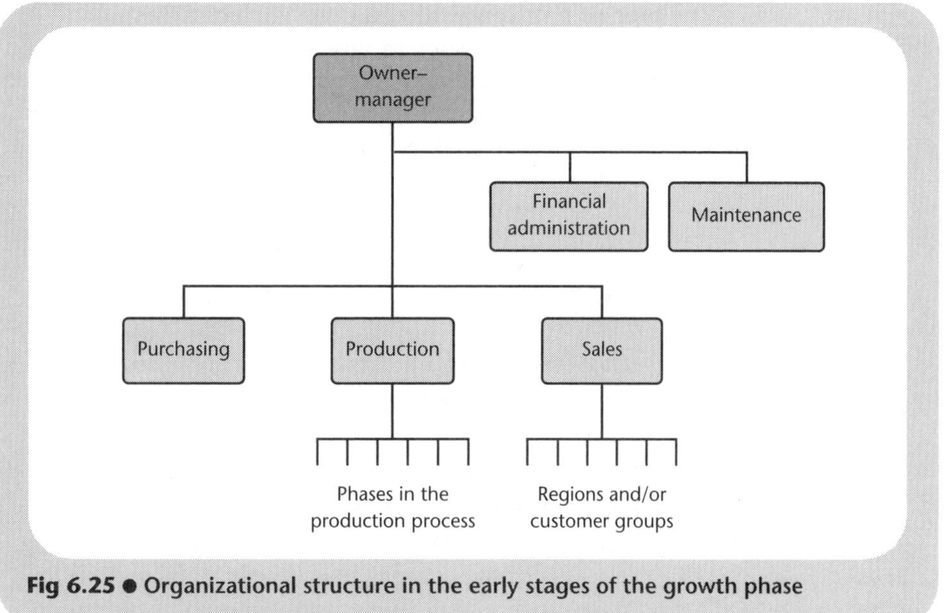

Fig 6.25 ● Organizational structure in the early stages of the growth phase

It is usually necessary at this stage – if the size of the organization allows – for the managerial functions to be supported by specialist departments relating to financial administration, maintenance and so on. Further support and advice in particular fields of specialist and professional expertise can be bought in from external consultants – for example, in the areas of market research, organizational efficiency, administration and automation.

As the organization grows, informal communication and commitment are no longer adequate. The owner–manager must delegate tasks plus attendant authorities to appointed middle managers (for example, a production manager or departmental heads) if the position of the organization in the market is to be consolidated. This new layer of management needs to be incorporated in the growing organization, if it is to survive. At this point, the company will often convert its legal status into that of a private company.

This process of subdivision is then continued. Further growth in sales volume, geographical expansion, market development and vertical integration result in the need for further subdivision of the primary functions. The organization's size allows the recruitment of in-house specialists – for example, in the areas of marketing, planning, research and personnel – who can offer auxiliary support to the management process.

The growth of the business leads to a change in orientation and organization; there has to be a more systematic approach to management and the owner–manager has to adopt a more detached approach to the running of the company. One or more assistant managers may be appointed. A works council and board of directors may be created.

Management needs to be based on a clear division of work and co-ordination. Furthermore, organizational methods and planning techniques need to be introduced. The formal organization will become more important, as will the need for top management to provide a vision and a sense of direction for the organization.

In addition to the creation of new departments, greater demands will be made of existing departments with resulting increases in staff numbers and level of expertise. For example, the finance department will probably be headed up by a controller, rather than a book-keeper.

The support functions will also change in character. In addition to supporting the primary functions, these support functions will take on a policy-influencing and governing role by supplying management information both on request and not. The recently appointed 'in-house' specialists will also make a contribution, although external consultants will still be used when required. The small business has now grown into a *fully departmentalized organization* set up with a *centralized functional structure* under top management (*see* Fig 6.26).

A typical business at the growth stage of development can be characterized as follows:

- *Structure of the organization*: relatively centralized F form, with extensive internal division of work.
- *Research and development*: undertaken by an in-house department, which carries out systematic searches for possibilities for product improvement, product development and process innovation.
- *Performance measurement*: to an increasing degree impersonal and indirect, involving the setting of technical and/or financial criteria.
- *Reward/Payment*: systematic, objective, focusing on commitment and years of service.

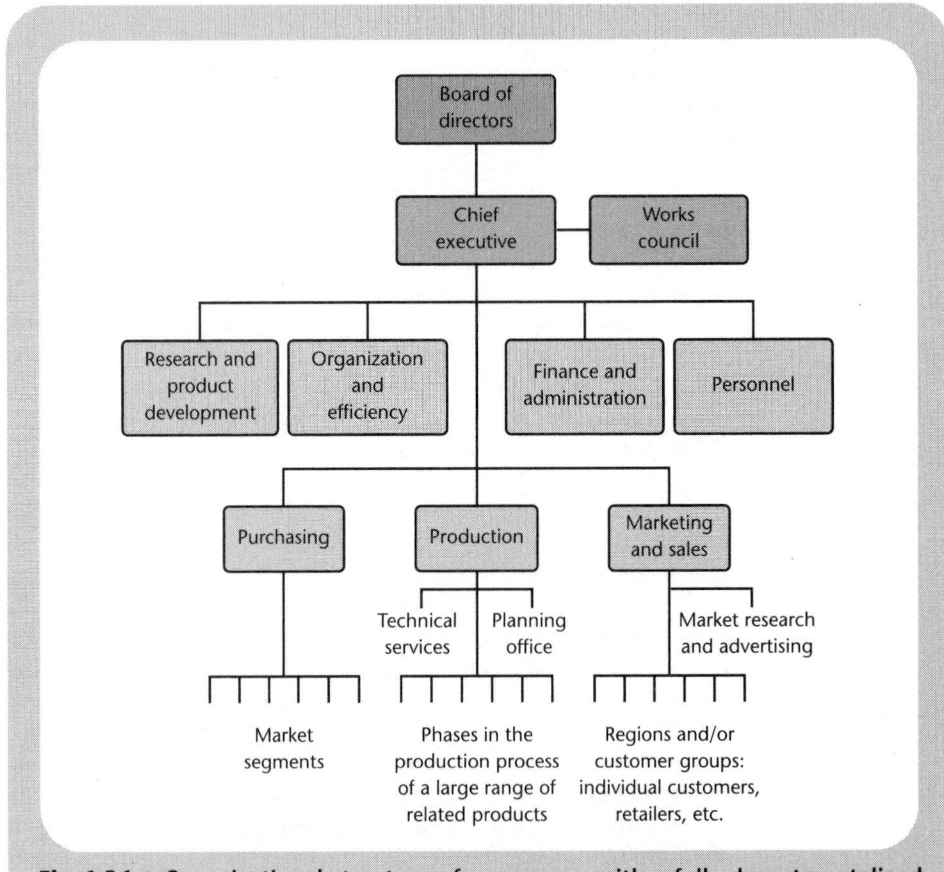

Fig 6.26 ● Organizational structure of a company with a fully departmentalized structure in the later stages of growth

- *Control system*: personal with regard to strategic decision making, but otherwise involving increased delegation of operational decision-making authorities, with control by way of policies, instructions, decision rules and procedures.
- *Strategic choice*: including options such as further vertical integration – forward or backward – increase in market share, expansion via development of related product lines or via related markets.

6.4.3 Organizational structure of full-size and mature company

The departmental structure

As the product range increases in medium-sized and large companies, an organizational structure with a P(roduct) grouping (directly under the top) may work better than the existing F(unctional) grouping. Alternatively, if the main focus of such a company is its international operations or a particular market sector, then a G(eographical) grouping into countries, continents or regions, or a M(arket sector) grouping may be preferred. This would mean that the co-ordination of the different operational activities for a certain group of products or a certain geographical area or market sector could be delegated to a lower level in the organization.

This change would involve a large degree of reorganization. The grouping into primary functions would be abandoned in favour of a grouping into product groups, geographical areas or market sectors; each of these groups would then have its own primary functions.

If a G(eographical) structure is adopted as the basic structure of the organization, a more detailed grouping of the primary functions to product groups can take place, if necessary.

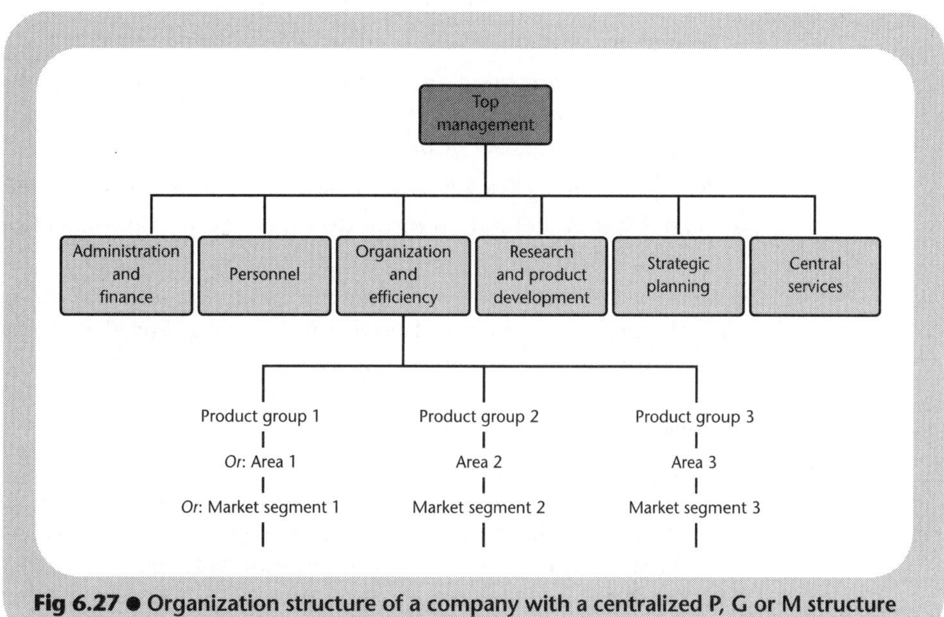

Fig 6.27 ● Organization structure of a company with a centralized P, G or M structure

Often the support services remain attached to top management when a business moves from an F structure to a P, G or M structure, and central staff and support services report directly to the top management. This is referred to as a relatively *centralized departmentalized structure* (*see* Fig 6.27). Top management is now released from the co-ordination of the operational tasks and can occupy itself more with policies and important strategic issues.

The decentralized multi-divisional structure

The product groups will attempt to develop into relatively autonomous units, each with its own people in the central staff and support services, like finance and administration, personnel, product development, etc. In their semi-autonomous operations, their deliberation and decision making, the individual units will have to introduce further delegation and a further spread of decision-making authority (that is, decentralization). This will also be the case with regard to the specialized staff and support services which previously reported to top management. These developments are particularly applicable to organizational and operational decisions (rather than strategic decisions). A number of central services will be maintained, but these will take on more of an advisory, co-ordinating, stimulating and controlling role (*see* Fig 6.28).

A company at this stage of development is referred to as a *decentralized multi-divisional organization*, which is set up directly under the top management along product–market combinations or geographical areas. Growth is effected via diversification to an even wider and more heterogeneous field of activities. The activities are re-grouped into relatively homogenous units, which are accommodated in divisions. These divisions are assisted by their own staff and support services and also by the corporate services which are attached to the top management.

A typical business at this advanced stage of development can be characterized as follows:

- *Structure of the organization*: decentralized divisional form, which is brought about via internal specialization (or grouping of business units).
- *Research and development*: extended to the searching for totally new and other products.
- *Performance measurement*: impersonal, in which, as a result of profit decentralization, financial criteria, such as return on investment (ROI), or market criteria, such as relative market share, can be used.
- *Reward/Payment*: systematic, with reward for top management related to performance.
- *Control system*: delegation of product–market decision-making authorities within existing activities.
- *Strategic choice*: including options such as entrance into and/or withdrawal from particular sectors, allocation of resources to divisions in identified sectors of industry and setting the speed of growth in divisions and of the company as a whole.

The holding company variant

It is important at this point to consider the *holding company* or *financial conglomerate*, which controls a number of business units. Usually, central services are mostly concerned with administrative and financial control, strategy, legal affairs and personnel issues. In the case of the holding company, however, central services have a different role.

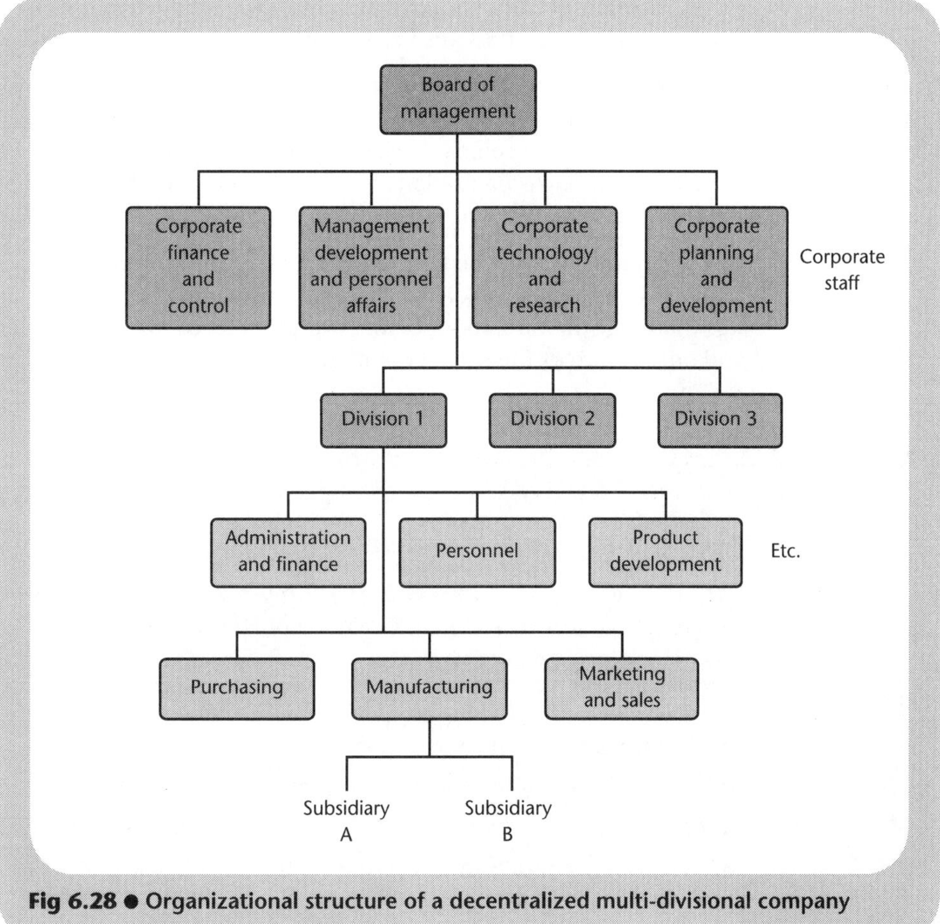

Fig 6.28 ● Organizational structure of a decentralized multi-divisional company

Enterprises which have diversified into a wide field of very different company activities will incorporate these company activities into the company by forming a holding company (the mother) to oversee, co-ordinate and support the activities of the autonomous business units (the daughters). These business units may eventually be grouped again into 'divisions' consisting of business units with a degree of coherence (for example, an 'industrial companies' division).

This holding company then has only a limited supply of central services at its disposal, which are especially focused on the financial control of the organization's activities in the short and long term.

6.5 ● TOWARDS FLATTER ORGANIZATIONS

Influencing the structure of an organization is nothing new. In recent years, however, instead of promoting the development of more complex organizational structures, managers have sought to create 'flatter' organizational structures – that is, to remove some of the management layers. This has resulted in organizations being better able to meet the demands of their external environment, to be more flexible, to improve the job satisfaction of their employees and to raise productivity. Delayering is a structural intervention which offers great scope for improving effectiveness.

For example ...

... companies such as McDonnell-Douglas, IBM, SAS, Chrysler, General Electric and Asea Brown Boveri have all implemented extensive delayering programmes in recent years. At General Motors, a company which has been traditionally strongly hierarchical, experiments with flat organization units are being carried out in the development and production of the Saturn.

This phenomenon may be the beginning of a trend towards increasingly flat organizational structures. It is predicted that within the next 20 years, organizations will have less than half the number of management levels compared with today's counterparts, and only a third of the number of managers.

Minicase 6.2

Seven golden rules of delayering

During the delayering process of Elsevier's top management and the re-organization of the company, Mr Pierre Vinken, Chairman of Elsevier–Reed until 1995, adhered to the following seven golden rules:

- Keep the organization flat.
- Ensure that there is unity within the board of management.
- Appoint a strong Chairman.
- Create a strong team, not in number, but in the quality of the employees.
- Have staff report directly to the Chairman.
- Place the final responsibility for strategy with the Chairman.
- Ensure that members of the board of management are managers with 'front-line' experience.

Before the delayering took place, Elsevier's problems were caused by a lack of competitiveness, insufficient added value and overspending.

According to Mr Vinken: 'The organization had a steering wheel, but this had relatively little effect on the direction of the wheels.' Shorter lines of communication, more direct communication and a faster and improved decision-making process were therefore necessary.

Source: Adapted from Keuning, D. *et al.* (1994) *Delayering Organizations*, Pitman Publishing.

6.5.1 Organizational problems and changes in the environment

Delayering usually takes place in response to bottlenecks within the internal organization created by changes in the external environment (*see* Chapter 3).

1. Consumer behaviour changes very quickly and consumer needs are becoming more diverse. Organizations which operate directly with end users have to be able to respond quickly to market conditions. The individual segments of the market have

to be addressed by different groups within the organization, resulting in the need for a flatter and more decentralized organization.

2. Internationalization and the increase in development costs have resulted in many organizations being merged or taken over. The increased complexity of control creates a move towards decentralization in large companies. Autonomous units are set up, and simultaneously a number of middle and top management levels can be removed.
3. Many organizations acknowledge that nowadays employees are often well educated, highly motivated and able to fulfil broader and more complex functions. An organization with a more flexible division of work, where work is often undertaken by teams, will need fewer managers and organizational levels.
4. The application of information technology in organizations has also resulted in fewer managers and managerial levels being required.

   - The introduction of management information systems and networks has increased the capacity for decentralized decision making.
   - Management information systems allow management to have a central overview.

   First predicted in the early 1970s, the effect of the introduction of information technology is now being felt in every area of business activity.
5. The combined pressures of increasing international competition, on the one hand, and the wider availability of substitute products as a result of information technology, on the other, make it even more important for businesses to keep overhead costs under control by operating as 'lean' an organization as possible, with as few management layers as possible.

6.5.2 Delayering in top and middle management

Delayering can take place at two levels:

- *Delayering of middle management* – for example, at Douglas Aircraft Company.
- *Delayering of top management* – for example, at ABB and General Electric.

Each of the two forms of delayering takes place in response to a different group of organizational problems.

Middle-management problems

Delayering of middle management may take place in response to the following organizational problems:

- weaknesses in market orientation and co-ordination;
- too great a distance between policy making and execution of operations;
- too little entrepreneurship and accountability;
- few chances to develop integral management skills;
- bureaucratic, role-oriented culture.

For many organizations, the hierarchy as a co-ordination mechanism has become too expensive and too slow. Changes in market conditions cannot be translated into action quickly enough. Product development and delivery times are too long. The gap between policy and execution means that the organization is always one step behind and has difficulties in adjusting itself to the changing environment. It can also mean that the enthusiasm for a project developed at the top of the organization is not communicated to the shop floor. Top management is often burdened with co-ordination tasks which could be executed by the less senior management.

Top management problems

Delayering of top management may take place in response to the following organizational problems:

- lack of commitment to the realization of plans;
- difficulties with division of tasks and responsibilities;
- duplication of staff and consultative bodies;
- management keeping each other busy;
- an excessive focus on control;
- delays in decision making.

The process of decentralization often results in the semi-autonomous units created demanding extensive authority and the necessary resources for the realization of their tasks. At the same time, the management and staff immediately above this decentralized layer wish to maintain an overview, co-ordinate and keep control.

Since the decentralized units want to operate as independently as possible, they also create similar management, co-ordination and control functions at the top of their units. The increase in management capacity at this level devalues the added value at the levels directly above.

If the organization is top heavy – that is, there are many layers of senior management – the business units will become frustrated by what they see as constant interference in their activities. Business unit managers will spend too much time 'selling' their projects inside the organization instead of selling them outside the organization.

This may even result in business units competing with each other and perhaps as a result missing out on opportunities for working together. In such organizations, distortion and loss of information are commonplace, decision making is slow and over-complicated and top management is inadequately informed about important developments at business unit level.

Minicase 6.3

The process of delayering at ABB

The process of delayering started right after the merger between the two engineering groups: Asea (Sweden) and Brown Boveri (Switzerland) in August 1987. Mr Percy Barnevik, the CEO of Asea at the time of the merger, chose a fast integral scenario of change. He was the initiator and leader of this process and was keen to keep the period of uncertainty as short as possible. All major changes were undertaken in the first year of this cross-border merger.

After the merger, Mr Barnevik chose a two-step strategy: first, restructuring, then growth.

ABB – Asea Brown Boveri Ltd – is owned in equal parts by Asea AB (Stockholm, Sweden) and BBC Brown Boveri Ltd (Baden, Switzerland). Asea Brown Boveri Ltd (Zurich) is the holding company of the Asea Brown Boveri Group with approximately 1300 companies around the world. ABB is the largest supplier to the world's electricity industry; power generation, distribution and use are its core businesses.

Six or seven years before the merger, Asea had had a matrix structure. BBC had had a geographical structure that had to be converted into a product divisional structure. BBC did not possess an effective matrix organization. In many countries each subsidiary had its own management structure, undertook its own marketing, research and production, thus duplicating costs and dissipating strategy.

The merger created an organization that was top heavy. Mr Barnevik foresaw several bottlenecks and cut drastically the number of headquarters staff. The external motives for delayering were similar to the motives for the merger and are listed below.

External arguments for delayering

- Increasing competition
- Excess capacity in the electrical equipment industry in Europe
- Globalization of markets

Internal arguments for delayering

- Huge headquarters staff with duplication of functions at headquarters
- The need for improved market orientation and customer service
- The aim to achieve technological leadership
- The need for flexibility
- Too long production times
- The need for an improvement in quality
- Poor communication
- Internal competition.

Mr Barnevik's schedule for the reduction of overheads is shown in Table 6.2.

Table 6.2 ● Mr Barnevik's plans for cutting staff numbers

Year 1	*90 % reduction in headquarters staff achieved*
30%	laid off or left
30%	transferred to profit centres
30%	transferred to service centres operating/competing at market prices
leaving 10%	remaining corporate staff
Years 3–4 A further reduction in staff numbers	
Service centres down 50% to 15%	
Profit centres down 33% to 20%	
Corporate centre down 50% to 5%	
Total reduction in staff	
After two rounds of cuts, 60% of staff had been shed, and only 5% remained at the corporate centre.	

Source: Adapted from Keuning, D. *et al.* (1994) *Delayering Organizations*, Pitman Publishing.

6.5.4 Change in organizational structure as a vehicle for change

If an organization wishes to be able to adapt better and more quickly to the changes in the external environment, it has several options to consider. For example:

- It can diversify or begin to operate on a more global level.
- It can undertake quality projects.
- It can set up an education and training programme.
- It can develop a strategy of cost reduction.

Most importantly, however, it can look again at its own management. In most cases, this will lead to changes in tasks, authorities and responsibilities of management – in fact, to changes in the structure of the organization itself.

Delayering involves adapting the structure so that the number of management layers is reduced. This offers new possibilities – a paradox in the eyes of many managers. However, delayering is not just a matter of making cuts. It must be accompanied by a combination of supportive measures, if an effective, flat organization is to be achieved. We will return to this point many times in the course of the following chapters.

SUMMARY

- Once the goals and strategy of an organization have been determined, an appropriate organizational structure has to be designed by management – tailor-made to the particular needs of the organization in question.
- When a business is starting up, the work will be undertaken by the owner–manager, perhaps with a couple of helpers. As soon as the workload picks up and more people are employed, decisions have to be made about the division of work (who does what). This almost always involves the separation of management from operations.
- The division of management and operations means that a number of layers are created in the organization. This makes it necessary for the relative authorities and interdependencies between employees and groups of employees to be determined.
- The choice of an appropriate form of work division will depend on the particular circumstances of the organization. An organizational structure can be built up both vertically and horizontally. The management can choose from a number of options: F(unctional), P(roduct), G(eographical) and M(arket sector).
- An organizational chart depicts an organizational structure and highlights the division of tasks and the assignment of authorities.
- The functioning of an organization can be clarified by job descriptions. These state the employee's authorities, areas of decision making and responsibilities. They also clarify the authority assigned to other people and the decisions which can be taken by other employees.
- There needs to be consideration of the 'informal organization' – that is, the unofficial allocation of authority based on personal prestige rather than a formal position within the organization.

- If the goals of an organization are to be attained, activities at all levels of management and execution need to be co-ordinated and in tune with each other. This is referred to as 'unity of direction'. Unity of direction can be stimulated by using the correct co-ordination mechanisms – for example, standardization of output, planning and consultation.
- Organizational structures come in many forms – for example, the centralized functional organizational structure, the decentralized divisional structure, and the business unit structure – each with its advantages and disadvantages. Divisional organization involves a different way of managing to the centralized functional organizational structure.
- A project organization involves the focusing of management and the organization on a particular set of activities. Project management is concerned with the temporary execution of a whole set of activities which is directed at a specified goal which has to be attained within a limited period of time with a limited supply of resources and people. For effective project management, a number of conditions need to be fulfilled and the relation between the permanent organization and the project organization needs to be clarified.
- A matrix organization involves a combination of a project structure and a departmentalized structure leading to problems of dual control.
- As a company or institution grows and develops from a business start-up to a mature organization, so its organizational structure – its division of work and its management layers – will change.
- Delayering has been a common strategy in recent years. This involves reducing the number of management layers in the organizational structure. The aim of this change is to improve the daily functioning of the organization.

DISCUSSION QUESTIONS

1. With reference to *Management in action* at the beginning of this chapter, explain in your own words how, with the earlier organizational structure, it was possible that two Hoogovens Steels existed in the opinion of the customers.
2. Comment on this statement: 'When an organization supplies many different products or services, an F grouping is the most appropriate division of work.'
3. 'The more management layers in the organization, the more possibilities there are to decentralize.' Comment.
4. 'A product manager in a matrix organization always has both the hierarchical and functional authorities.' Do you agree with this statement?
5. Which of the following statements is the more valid?
   (a) 'Unity of direction is less important within project structures.'
   (b) 'Unity of direction is more difficult to realize within project structures.'
6. What possibilities exist for delayering an organizational structure in a turbulent environment?

Management case study

The development of Recrea Inc.

At the beginning of 1995, Keith Harding and Jack Nicklas looked back with a certain satisfaction at the fast growth of Recrea Inc., a leisure goods supplier, which they had set up in 1989.

Harding and Nicklas had retired in that year from an international consultancy firm and bought their first company – Gereva Inc., a producer of garden sprinklers and other garden supplies. It was exactly what they had been looking for: a producer of consumer products with a good quality reputation, but weak marketing. They felt their education and consultancy experience and their intention to bring aggressive and young management talent into Gereva Inc. would guarantee growth in Europe and a considerable improvement in profitability.

Recrea developed quickly. The formula applied to Gereva Inc. appeared to be successful. The original plans were soon adapted into a wider company concept directed at leisure products.

After the purchase of Gereva Inc., the partners acquired a second enterprise – a small family business in Germany which also made sprinklers. Since the two product lines were the same, this takeover could be easily assimilated into the existing Gereva organization. Six further companies from all over Europe were then purchased in the sector of recreation, garden and sports articles.

Between 1990 and 1992, Recrea Inc. grew fast, with sales rising from US$2.5 million to US$20 million and net profits rising from US$160 000 to US$1 million. 1994 figures showed total sales of US$35 million with a net profit of US$1.8 million. Having started with equity of US$240 000 (share capital) in 1989, with the issue of new shares in 1995, equity had been raised to US$16.2 million. By 1995, Recrea Inc. was composed of eight enterprises, brought together via acquisitions and takeovers, all active in the fields of leisure activities and recreation. The number of employees had also grown considerably.

According to Harding and Nicklas, the acquisitions were part of a well thought out strategy. They were always drawn to enterprises where there was an opportunity to make savings in the operational processes, to increase sales by streamlining the organization and by strengthening the marketing effort, and to rejuvenate and professionalize the management process.

Harding and Nicklas knew growth would create tensions in the organization and were determined not to neglect this even if they themselves were now less involved in the operational control of the business. They consider their success to be founded on having the sales of their product range handled by a single sales organization.

For now, they still see large growth possibilities in the markets for leisure products. Changes in distribution and promotion have strengthened their marketing and sales performance. The retail trade has declined in importance and the chain stores and wholesale trade have improved their positions. As a result, the marketing and sales organization consists of not only the retail trade in many European countries, but also product managers who are responsible for supplying the several buyer groups with specific product information to support the sales force.

Harding and Nicklas are now thinking of expanding into other recreational sectors and activities – namely travel, education and entertainment.

There is no official organization chart at Recrea Inc., but the organization structure is illustrated in Fig 6.29.

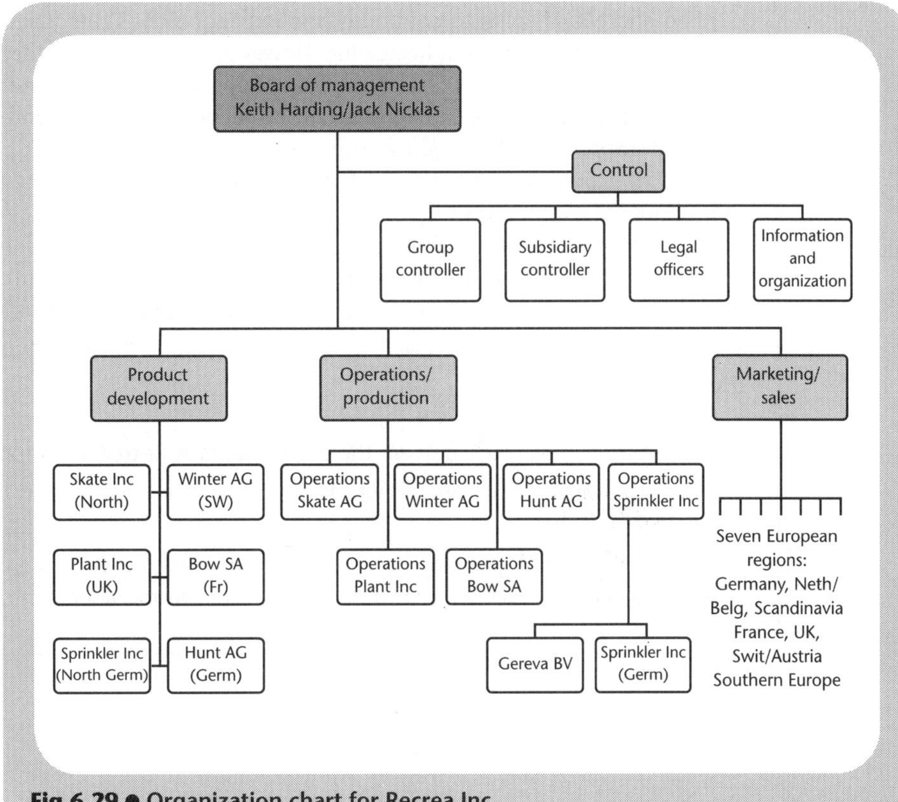

Fig 6.29 ● Organization chart for Recrea Inc.

There are four key functions: marketing/sales, production (operations), product development and control. All subsidiaries and activities are accommodated within that structure. The sales organization has a geographical grouping (into seven countries/regions within Europe) in which every sales person sells the complete product range. Production takes place under the direct supervision of a production manager with responsibility for production quotas and budgets. Product development is decentralized with the exception of sprinklers and garden equipment which are developed at the Gereva site. The control function is highly centralized.

Planning is organized as a complex system of combined actions which work top-down and bottom-up as well as horizontally. The organization has recently noticed some areas of tension which cross functional boundaries, in which informal communication is taking place and employees are in close contact with one another. There is a strong belief in openness in all functions and at all levels.

continued overleaf

Management case study continued

Recrea Inc. has a number of general guidelines, but the annual plan is the most important point of reference. In the case of recurring problems, employees turn to Harding for production/operations and control issues and Nicklas for marketing issues. Harding and Nicklas plan to continue handling acquisitions themselves and as a result determine the future shape of Recrea Inc. However, in recent years, they have been confronted by a steady stream of operational problems which have required their attention. As a result, planning has been neglected in several production lines and there have been regular disruptions to the production process. Product development continues to perform below expectations and the level of innovation in some sectors of the company fall short of that of competitors.

In the interim results for 1994 and the attendant management information, concern was expressed regarding the implications and potential problems in relation to further growth. It was agreed that these issues would be addressed in the near future.

CASE QUESTIONS

1. According to which criterion are the departments at Recrea Inc. structured?
2. Given the variety of activities in which Recrea Inc. is involved, is this the most sensible choice?
3. What other kind of grouping criteria for the departmental structure would you like to recommend to Recrea Inc.? Refer to the issues of centralization and decentralization.

Chapter 7

Structuring tasks for groups and individuals

LEARNING OBJECTIVES

After studying this chapter, you should be able to:

- name and describe the criteria for the design and grouping of operational tasks and functions;
- identify the advantages and disadvantages of different organizational structures in relation to grouping of operational tasks and functions;
- describe the consultative and co-ordination mechanisms needed in order to establish consultative and communication structures within organizations;
- apply important concepts in the design process of an organizational structure;
- name and describe types of change in organizations and the stages in the change processes;
- name and describe different points of view regarding organizational change.

Management in action

Opel creates a new factory out of an old one

Car manufacturer Opel pitches into the old structures: in its main establishment in Russelsheim, Germany, where Adam Opel in 1862 started by making sewing machines and bicycles, the manufacturing structure is being radically brought up to date. It wants to have raised productivity to a globally competitive level by 1997.

Opel has practical experience of new manufacturing methods and techniques which, for the large part, are organized along the same lines as the Japanese. In September 1992, Opel opened a new factory in Eisenach (investment DM 1 billion), which, with regard to efficiency is unequalled in Europe. Complete robotization, the team work and the well thought out logistics make it possible to put together an Opel Astra in 19 hours.

Opel board president David J. Herman now wants to bring the establishment in Russelsheim, where one car still takes 25 hours to output, to the same productivity level. The total costs are DM 700 million – restructuring has to be ready by 1997. 'The giant had become slow and corpulent,' says Herman. 'In 1997, we want to be one of the most productive car factories in the world.'

In order to reach that goal manufacturing is being organized along totally new line's and the spraying department is being brought up to date. The single assembly line for the Omega and the Vectra are being split in two, the pre-assembly (for example, of doors and dash boards) will now take place on the final assembly line, which is itself in the process of change. Since the restructuring is mainly being carried out in current production, Opel has spread out the operation, which started in February 1996, over some years.

Due to the clever replanning of the manufacturing process and materials inflow, the actual work area (currently 1.2 km^2) can be reduced by one-third. The original 1988 warehouse will be closed. The logistics need to be directed at the final assembly line as accurately as possible, and were in close co-operation with the suppliers.

The car engines, for example, which, in the past, were prepared 1.5 km from the final assembly hall, now have to be transported only 150 metres; because of that there are now only 24 engines at any one time in the factory, where in the past there were 1000. Due to these and other measures, the working capital is reduced by 30%. For the employees the new lay-out and the re-routing of the manufacturing process means a new way of working. They not only work in smaller groups than they were used to (about seven instead of twelve as before), but the character of the work has also changed. In the old structure, the groups were responsible for a large number of activities on the line, which they could execute more or less in their own way. In the new set-up their freedom is somewhat reduced. The new groups get a clearly defined task, but keep their freedom to rotate within the group and, in that way, have some variation in their work.

The director of the factory in Russelsheim, Rolf Zimmermann, makes clear, however, that the 'humanization' of the classic assembly line work, by making it wider and more varied in scope, leads to many mistakes and delays.

It is the intention to maintain the central thought behind this working in groups to make use of and stimulate the creativity of the individual employee. It is expected of the employees that, in addition to their assembly job, they also make a contribution to the continuous process of making production more efficient and of better quality. Andreas Oppenheuser, leader of one group, says that the work has become less hectic in the new set-up. 'In the beginning there were some problems with the change to the new way of working, now most are satisfied, there is less stress,' he says. This does not alter the fact that absenteeism in Russelsheim has increased by one-third since the introduction of the new scheme. Factory Director Zimmermann blames the increase on the large number of internal transfers and believes that absenteeism will soon decrease again.

Opel President Herman does not make a secret of the fact that it was by no means self-evident that Opel would decide to update the obsolete factory in Russelsheim. But the good traffic infrastructure (on a rail connection, close to a main road) and the presence of qualified personnel were the decisive arguments to create a new factory out of the old one.

At Opel in Russelsheim in the period 1992/93, 3000 jobs disappeared. Furthermore, Opel suffered the first loss in years in this period (more than DM 500 million) and yet further radical personnel lay offs were not deemed necessary.

In contrast to Volkswagen, where the introduction of a four-day working week meant mass lay offs could be prevented, Opel does not see the point in shortening working time. A four-year company–collective labour contract has been agreed with the personnel, through which the personnel costs could be considerably reduced.

The motto now is: Do more with the same number of people. Director Zimmermann thinks that the market will develop such that the present production of 240,000 cars per year will rise to 330,000 by 1997. New cars from a completely *re*newed factory.

Source: Adapted from *Het Financieele Dagblad*, 9 December 1994.

INTRODUCTION

In the design of an organizational structure, different ways of grouping work can be chosen. This is strongly dependent on the situation as we saw in Chapter 6. In the preceding chapter, the growth and development of organizations was described from the point of view of structuring and changes in organizational structures.

Growth means carrying through changes in organizational structure, even if this involves the experiencing of a crisis. Each phase of development of an organization creates its own problems for which solutions have to be found. If an organization wants to survive it is necessary for it to be able to handle the dynamics of crisis and understand the need for organizational changes.

In designing organizational structure, especially when it comes to the grouping of tasks and the formation of functions for individual employees, individual work groups and departments must be involved. Then decision-making authorities have to be assigned and mutual relationships have to be arranged in order to be able to transfer and communicate the will of the management and to achieve co-ordination.

The design process of an organizational structure always requires a conscious and systematic grouping of activities in tasks and functions which need to be carried out. We will look into these questions in more detail in this Chapter.

7.1 STRUCTURING TASKS AND DESIGN OF FUNCTIONS: CRITERIA

To bring about the different forms of division of work, the grouping of tasks and the design of functions satisfactorily, different criteria apply. In the areas of division of work and design of functions on operational and managerial levels, the organization must systematically examine how and to what degree the different criteria have to be met. The criteria can also be used to examine whether, in an existing situation, the way in which tasks are structured and designed is (still) effective. The criteria may work in different directions and sometimes make contradictory demands since the division of work is influenced by forces which have either a splitting or a combining effect. Sometimes it is desirable to split certain activities off from other activities; it can, however, be desirable to combine activities. In practice, one has to strive for an optimum, where the contradicting points of view balance and match one another.

A function states the common goal of the tasks that have to be carried out. Tasks form the 'technical content' of a function. In the structuring of tasks and the design of functions for individual employees there are two principles to bear in mind:

- see to a fair day's work: from an economical-technical point of view, a reasonable degree of occupation of both people and resources has to be attained;
- see to a worthwhile work package: from a social-psychological point of view, human capabilities have to be used by the contents of the tasks in a satisfying way.

These two starting point principles can be worked out in more detail as criteria that should be applied to the grouping of tasks and the design of functions.

7.1.1 Criteria for the design of operational tasks

With regard to the structuring of tasks and the design of functions on an operational level, the following criteria should be applied.

A fair day's work

The time that someone, via a labour contract, makes available to a company or institution, has to be used as fully as possible and for the best possible operational execution of the activities which have been assigned to him. This holds as much for someone who has a full-time job as for someone who works on a part-time labour contract or in a job share. Here, 'as fully as possible' and 'for the best possible' mean that the necessary effort is to be expected, based on his capabilities. One has to take into account the necessary interruptions for illness and the recuperation. But under normal working circumstances a normal effort or fair or normal minimum performance may be expected of an employee. When insufficient attention is paid to these requirements there will be (quantitative) underutilization (=idling) or (quantitative) overutilization (=overwork) of the present capacity of people and resources.

Worthwhile work package

The criterion of a similar or equivalent task suggest the necessity for such a combination of task-elements that the nature of the activities and the level of the activities which are to be carried out reasonably link to the capabilities of an employee. Similarity of tasks means that the activities are of the same sort or of approximately the same sort. Paying attention to a degree of similarity means that activities are combined which make demands on the same sort of human capabilities and experience. Being employed in the same sort of activities has all the cost advantages of horizontal differentiation (as mentioned in section 6.2.5), but also the disadvantage of monotony. This disadvantage can be eliminated or neutralized to a certain degree by bringing in a degree of variety or a change in the consecutive activities in the tasks to be fulfilled. This can take place by means of horizontal job enlargement (=lengthening the task cycle through expanding the activities on the same qualitative level): for example, not merely sawing but also planing, drilling, etc. It can also be done by job roulation.

Equivalency of tasks means that the activities are of approximately the same qualitative level. Paying attention to a certain degree of equivalency means that activities are combined which make demands on (about) the same level of human capabilities, education, training, abilities and experience. If insufficient attention is paid to this, it will soon be discovered that only a few 'sheep with five legs' appear to exist. Demanding too much and having too high expectations can lead to people reaching a level of incompetence and then becoming stressed. When activities pose too little a demand, the danger of blunting or of qualitative underutilization of human capacities arises. In this respect a certain degree of autonomy and freedom should be given in the planning and operational execution of tasks. This is also called job enrichment (or vertical task enlargement): contact other departments on own initiative, conduct small repairs and maintenance oneself, provide some decision authority in order to control and adjust the speed, the quantity and the quality of work oneself.

Coherence between activities

Besides tuning into the capabilities of the workers in the sequence of tasks, attention has also to be paid to the mutual adjustment of the tasks looking at all the tasks to be fulfilled. These might be executed quite independently from one another, can be sequentially related or may be highly interdependent. This can relate to the consecutive sequence of actions as well as to the related techniques to be used; for example, the fitting and linking of the components in a razor or radio demands successive actions in which different tools are used. In this example, the application of these related techniques could be conducted by one operational employee. This also leads to the necessary variation with regard to the finished product. As soon as techniques and actions start to show greater differences and can no longer be conducted by one employee, the processing cycle becomes shorter and the production activities are split up into phases. This is also dependent on the required knowledge, experience, training and education and personal characteristics of the employee in relation to the sort of activities that are to be carried out. Technology which can be applied in the execution of the tasks also plays a part here.

Work satisfaction

Experiencing a certain degree of work satisfaction is important for each operational or managerial employee. One has to be able to project oneself into the job and be able to identify with the job and the organization. Variation, responsibility and a good working environment, being able to exercise control over the quantity and the quality of the execution of tasks oneself, and work consultation are also important.

In the designing of functions it is important to define the performance to be delivered by an individual employee in his working group or department and to make this requirement visible and explicit. Tasks and authorities determine the responsibilities that result from that. Here a function or job description can serve as an aid.

7.1.2 Extra criteria for the design of managerial tasks

When examining the design of managerial tasks the scope of control of management (=span of control + depth of control) and delegation of tasks are also considered (*see* section 7.4). In short, these points imply that a manager has to be able to manage the people in his responsibility in a responsible way, and should be able to give enough time and attention to consultation and motivation, and to control tasks with regard to his employees. The number of people who can be effectively managed directly (=span of control) and indirectly (=depth of control) is limited and needs to be watched very carefully. The delegation principle implies that the tasks, along with any resultant authority are placed on the relevent hierarchical level, where the consequences of the decisions made can be overseen. The optimal degree of delegation, then, means that on the different levels of management and operational execution right and responsible decisions can be made. Human capacities are then well used and employees carry a responsibility which can also be utilized.

The managerial demand 'unity of direction' needs to be firmly guaranteed, and can be stimulated by co-ordination mechanisms such as procedures, instructions, planning, consultation and so on, which are looked at in more detail in section 7.7.

7.2 P-GROUPING AND F-GROUPING: ADVANTAGES AND DISADVANTAGES

When we look at the advantages and disadvantages of different forms of division of work on the operational level it is useful to place the F(unctional) grouping versus the P(roduct) grouping. We will see the advantages and disadvantages of these two forms of division of work more closely through comparison of the charts in Figs 7.1 and 7.2.

7.2.1 Horizontal differentiation: advantages and disadvantages

The nature of the processes to be conducted is the central issue in the forming of work groups or departments (F-group) according to functional specialisms. In principle, operational workers all do the same sort of work, while the boss, foreman or department chief can be seen as a specialist in that area. For example, saw mill A, planing department B and assembly department C. The overall co-ordination of the production activities is at X, the point at which the phases of the processing come together as separate specialisms and can be overseen. Through these departments then flow components for more products, namely tables, chairs and cupboards. The grouping into functional specialisms is shown in Fig 7.1.

F-grouping advantages

By the concentration of similar processes in departments and sub-departments, advantages arise due to:

- mechanization and purchase of specialized equipment;
- a high degree of utilization of people and machinery;
- the attaining of more skills and routines;

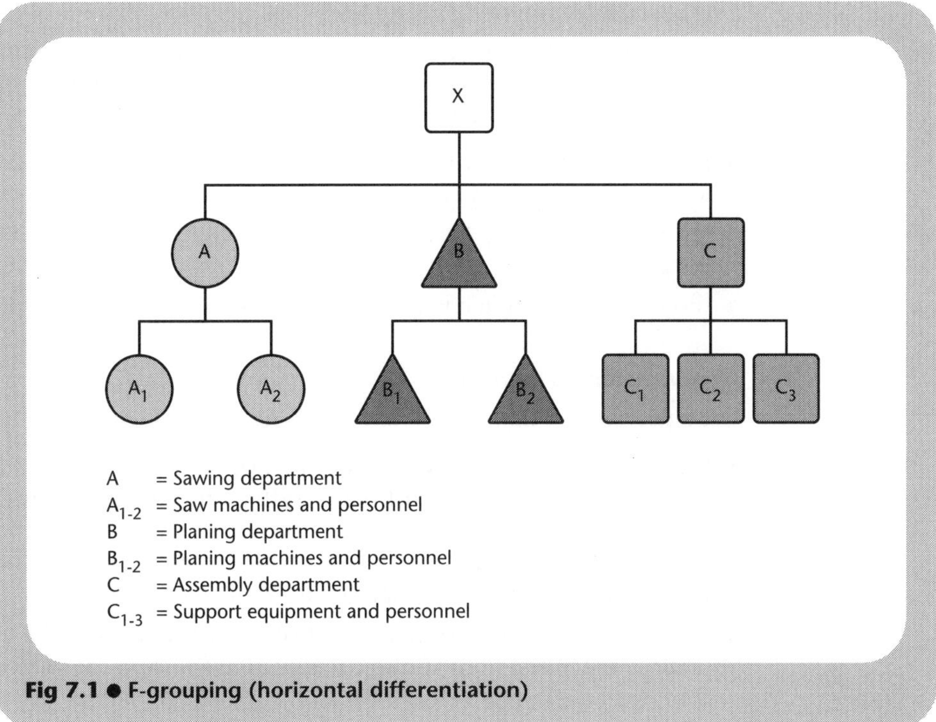

Fig 7.1 ● F-grouping (horizontal differentiation)

- the attaining of expertise and process knowledge in part-operations and processes;
- unity of working attitude and language.

F-grouping disadvantages

The disadvantages that arise from F-grouping are:

- monotony, uniformity and one-sidedness;
- lack of flexibility; due to concentration on one or a few part-operations or processes;
- co-ordination problems, due to breaking the natural coherence in the sequence of processes and operations.

7.2.2 Internal specialization

The central issue in the composed work group (P-group) is the resultant final product. In a production department with, for example, the P-groups chairs, tables and closets, the central issue is those chairs tables and cupboards. Operational employees (or project group members), in direct co-operation, carry out the successive processes. The foreman or department chief can be seen as co-ordinator-general. From this position the different activities are mutually adjusted.

The grouping according to the different final products is depicted in Fig 7.2. The overall co-ordination of the manufacturing activities is located at X as the point from where the different product groups (X1=chairs, X2=tables, X3=cupboards) can be overseen. Per product group, the different necessary technical equipment and the personnel with their differing expertise are assigned to separate manufacturing shops: A. sawing, B. planing, C. assembly.

P-grouping advantages

By bringing together dissimilar processes into one product group and especially by stressing the coherence between the processes as far as the final product is concerned within a product group, advantages arise due to:

- fast flow of products because of a group-like set-up (=product line set-up) of machines and people per product;
- fast problem-solving, because direct product-oriented communication is built into the group;
- short communication channels in case of need for feedback of information.

P-grouping disadvantages

The disadvantages that arise from P-grouping are:

- higher costs, because more resources and equipment are needed and less favourable quantitative proportions exist between the different types of resource: for example, each department has its own sawing machine (3 rather than 2 with F-grouping); so the advantages of scale and the economies of synergy, which arise from only partially using the diversity of capacity utilization, are lost;
- a lower degree of functional expertise in part-processes; the employee does not profit to the fullest from knowledge gained in the different phases of the processes.

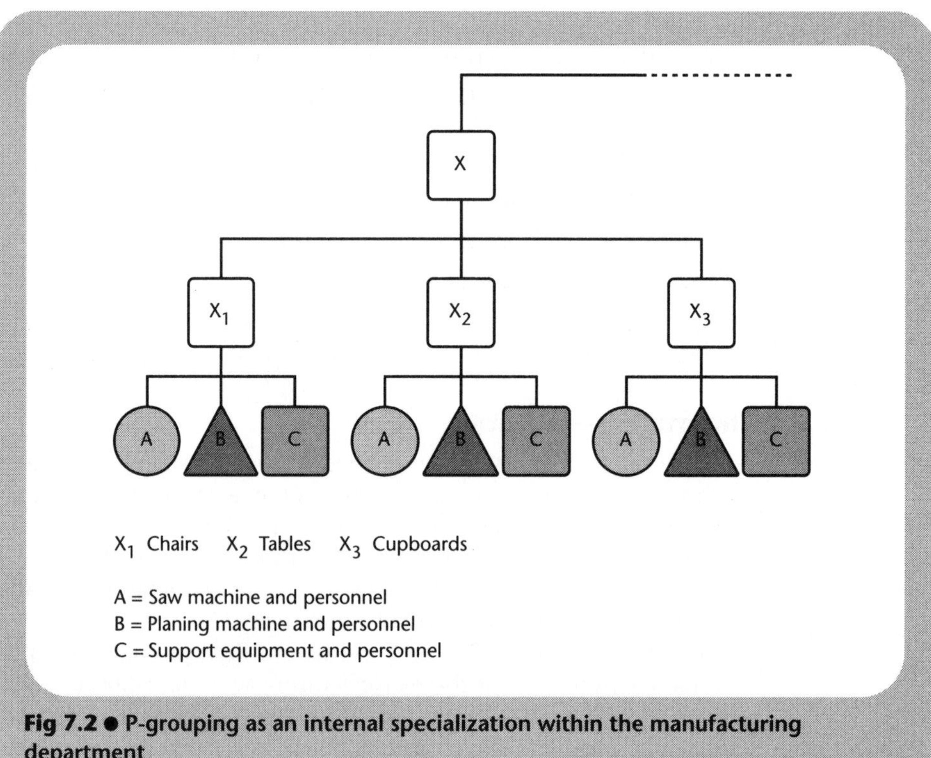

Fig 7.2 ● **P-grouping as an internal specialization within the manufacturing department**

To summarize, then, it can be seen that the technical and economical advantages from shorter delivery times, larger delivery trustability and a higher degree of flexibility are opposed by the higher costs related to need for more resources. And further, that quality and motivational aspects have also to be taken into account.

7.2.3 Ingredients of an effective grouping of tasks and design of functions

There are a number of conditions that can improve job satisfaction. In this respect Lawler (1988) mentions four which should be built in as core dimensions in jobs to be designed. They are:

- variety in the tasks to be carried out;
- autonomy in planning and executing the tasks;
- identification with the tasks to be carried out;
- feedback of both quantitative and qualitative data concerning the way in which tasks were/are carried out.

Alse Herzberg (1968 and 1974) gives a number of specific recommendations. He proposes some ingredients which have to be built in as so-called motivators in functions to be designed. These ingredients are discussed by Herzberg in the framework of strategies to humanize labour. He distinguishes 'orthodox task enrichment' and the 'socio-technical systems design'. The ingredients for an effective design of jobs are relevant in both these approaches, albeit in different ways. Herzberg translates Lawler's four core dimensions into specific recommendations. For an effective design of jobs the following ingredients are important:

- Direct feedback on results of the execution of the work, i.e. not a pre-evaluation, and not through a supervisor, boss or department.
- Client-oriented execution of tasks instead of a boss-oriented task execution. Main concern here is that the external or internal client (e.g. the next working station or department) is satisfied with the performance delivered.
- Being able to gather new knowledge and experience in the work situation, either in a horizontal, or vertical direction and with that the possibility to grow in a psychological sense.
- Being authorized and being able to plan and dispatch the work, being able to take responsibility for self-imposed norms and for the work to be done, instead of being commanded by a superimposed scheme.
- Being able to obtain unique experience, i.e. the worker is free to gather knowledge in and around the organization on other aspects of the job after finishing work, or to transfer knowledge to other employees, etc.
- Self-control regarding resources, so that costs incurred by the organization are kept as low as possible. This will favour the cost consciousness.
- Opening up direct communication possibilities, so that, if problems arise, the worker can spontaneously make contact in a horizontal, lateral or vertical direction, whichever may be useful to problem-solving at that moment.
- Personal accountability. This is the ingredient that gains its presence from all other elements mentioned above.

As designer and builder of the organization a manager has to consider how these recommendations re the grouping of tasks and the design of jobs and functions can be applied, given a specific situation. This achieves its specific aim through job enlargement, job enrichment and to a certain degree through job roulation.

Exhibit 7.1

A glint of change in the gold mines

In the dimly lit mine workings about 3 km below the earth's surface, sweat-drenched black men bend over, wrestling jackhammers and slipsliding on the jagged shards of ore in 100F heat. Here at Level 88 of the Elandsrand Gold Mining Co.'s Carletonville mine, I can understand why critics say South Africa's wealth (for whites only, of course) would not have been mined if not for the surplus of cheap, black labor corralled by apartheid.

The men at Elandsrand, owned by Anglo American Corp. of South Africa, toil in a claustrophobic channel that is just over 1 meter high and tilts at a 24° angle. It is suffused with dust and the thundering roar of drill against rock. Supports called Loadmasters keep the untold weight of earth above from sandwiching what little space there is.

There's no avoiding the squeeze on South African gold mining, however. Overall production dropped to 474 metric tons in 1995, down 56 metric tons from 1994, to the lowest levels since 1957. South Africa supplied 73% of the world's gold in 1979, but the output has declined steadily and today accounts for just 30%.

The mines have shed more than 100,000 jobs since 1990 with employment now totaling about 360,000. Elsewhere in the world, companies are opening surface gold mines that use cost-effective heavy equipment, but here in South Africa, gold is mined the old-fashioned way, by men digging ever deeper into the earth. Miners may spend 45 minutes just getting to the rock face.

Costs are up, too. With higher-grade deposits depleted, companies must mine and process more ore to produce an ounce of gold. During the sanctions era, there was little investment in new mines, and South Africa's protected economy has driven up the costs of everything the mines use, from dynamite to timber. In all, 1995 costs were 36% above the average of the U.S., Canada, and Australia.

Threatened closings

The cost squeeze came to a head in January at the world's largest gold mine, Anglo American Corp.'s Free State Consolidated Gold Mines Ltd. (Freegold) in Welkom, two hours south of Johannesburg. Bobby Godsell, chairman of Anglo American's gold and uranium division, gave mine management and workers an ultimatum: Turn Freegold around or five of the 26 shafts would close, costing 10,000 jobs. An additional six shafts could well follow. The five endangered shafts piled up $11 million in losses for the quarter ended Dec. 31, causing Freegold as a whole to report a $1.6 million loss for the same period.

Despite the negative statistics, South African economists say there is still as much gold underground as has been dug out since the 1886 discovery created Johannesburg, or Egoli, 'the city of gold,' as Zulus can it. It's possible the mining houses could have kept on sending blacks underground in search of it. But apartheid effectively ended in April, 1994, with the election of Nelson Mandela as President, and the new era ended traditional gold mining, as well.

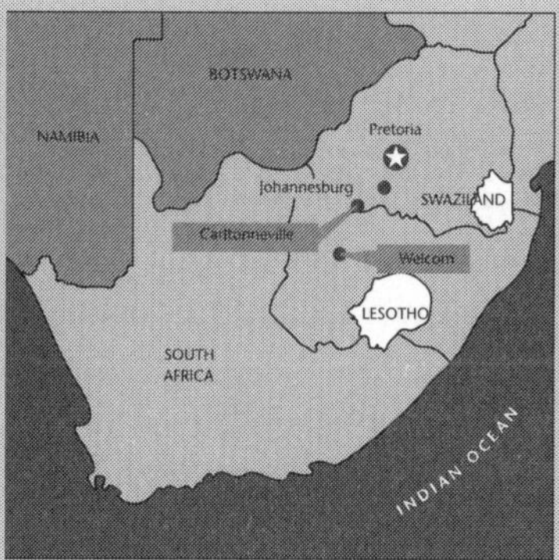

The black miners – laborers actually, because the title 'miner' was long reserved for whites – are now not only bitter but emboldened. Their National Union of Mineworkers, or NUM, is an important ally of Mandela's African National Congress.

Low productivity runs through South African industry, where apartheid protected white workers whatever their abilities and sapped black workers' motivation. The problem is acute in labor intensive gold mining.

Despite working conditions that outsiders might consider barbarous, Elandsrand is a showpiece for mining's new ways. The job hierarchy has been flattened. Workers who once were assigned a single task now train to do all the rock-face jobs, a process called multitasking. Teams of workers jointly plan each day's attack. Blacks are getting adult education and the blasting certificates that make them 'miners.' Still, for blacks to move up, whites will have to move out, and it's not clear how black promotions can be accommodated with the whites in place. That, says Isaac Mthenjane, the black shift boss of the mine section I visited, 'is a topic so sensitive you hardly speak of it.'

Since the changes started 18 months ago, productivity at Elandsrand has outpaced the industry average, and costs are stabilizing. Some blacks now make twice their wages in bonuses, and workers who had not been assigned to teams staged successful strikes so they could join them. Blacks now have hope for advancement. Soweto-born, university-educated Mthenjane, whose job requires him to oversee both black and white miners, ticks off his goals: '...section manager, mine manager.'

Sunday work

Still, there is resistance to change underground. To Letuka Khiba, a Freegold mine worker from Lesotho, new talk about teams and training rings false. 'Multi-tasking' sounds a lot like doing somebody else's work for no more pay, he says, and productivity bonuses, he fears, could mean safety will suffer, no small matter after 41 gold miners died nation-wide in January alone.

'Both sides were locked in a blame psychosis,' says Anglo's gold division spokesman James Duncan. But these days, Freegold's managers and unions are closeted in 'forums,' a consensus-building concept unheard of a few years ago but now entrenched in the new Labor Relations Act. The union has agreed to temporary Sunday work at Freegold, and the ultimatum to turn around the mine may spur permanent change. 'What I want is that whatever stopgap measures we work out at Freegold are a start for overhauling the industry as a whole,' says the union's Motlanthe. That could lead South African gold mining out of the depths.

The innovations at Elandsrand and the crisis at Freegold are being watched not only by other mines but also by the country as a whole. Gold mining produces a quarter of South Africa's foreign exchange and provides huge employment in a country with a 40% jobless rate. Elandsrand's workforce is down to 8,107, from 9,695 in 1994, and a further 30% cut is planned through attrition. Those who remain will be better paid and trained, says Robbie Lazare, Elandsrand's human-resources manager. 'It is all about giving people the skills to man this new organization.' Adds Duncan: 'South African gold mining is South African society in microcosm.' How it changes will be a mirror for the country.

Source: *Business Week*, 29 April 1996.

7.2.4 Job enlargement, job enrichment and job roulation

When a task is experienced as monotonous or if it requires one-sided physical action (with, for example, excessive one-sided burdening of muscles) as a consequence, there are several techniques for making a job more attractive, for example by means of work division, or a different way of assigning tasks.

Job enlargement

Job enlargement (in the horizontal dimension) is the lengthening of the task cycle via expansion of activities on the (qualitative) same level of worker capability. The employee now carries out a larger part of the total sequence of successive actions, hence, the work in an optimal length of a task cycle forms more of 'a (natural) whole'. The traditional structuring principle, where a higher degree of similarity in the sense of 'narrow' task differentiation is being stressed, is partially broken down by this action. The contribution of an individual employee to the whole process evolves a more recognizable character. More insight arises concerning the manufacturing or servicing process and there is also less dependency on the working speed of others. There is more freedom of movement, more latitude.

Job enrichment

Job enrichment (in the vertical dimension) is the addition of 'higher' tasks and the integration of direct and indirect productive tasks, including authority and responsibilities that cohere with the task. Tasks previously carried out by support and staff departments are now, when possible, carried out by the employees themselves. Think of dispatching work and work planning, registration, control, small repairs and maintenance. Essential elements of planning, checking and control can now be added onto the original task.

Job roulation

Job roulation (in the horizontal and, in principle, in the vertical dimension) is the interchanging of fulfilment of tasks. Members of a work group do this from time to time, perhaps according to a fixed scheme, or according to mutual agreements. Through this, the insight into the total process can be enlarged. Insight into the mutual interdependencies of tasks stimulates the sense of being 'all round'. A greater flexibility arises. Status differences are eliminated and unpleasant as well as nice tasks involved in the work are carried out by everyone.

7.2.5 Semi-autonomous work groups

The solution for improvement in the working situation (intrinsic to job content and extrinsic to job environment) can also be found in the re-grouping of tasks in (semi-) autonomous groups into which part-tasks can be integrated. Via such a P-grouping around a natural and rounded-off group task the management role also assumes another character.

A semi-autonomous (P-)work group according to the socio-technical system design of work is characterized by:

- a rounded-off group task;
- the possibility to be able to contact the staff and support services or linked departments independently;
- group members having own discretionary decision authority to regulate speed, quantity and quality themselves;
- a limited size, so that the group members can maintain direct contact with one another and thus can form a 'proper' group.

Minicase 7.1

In many cases, adjustment of technology and the physical work environment is possible. A well-known example of semi-autonomous work groups was the Volvo assembly, in which long assembly lines are completely missing. The 1970s' Kalmar factory was made up of honeycomb-shaped rooms, in which the atmosphere of a small workshop could prevail: production groups of 15–22 members each had their own cafeteria provisions and attention had been paid to colours, large windows and a view onto the natural landscape. Noise levels were similar to those in other offices (important, because deliberation during work was necessary, and the workers had at least to be able to understand one another). In the assembly areas use was made of specially constructed assembly wagons, which made it possible to tilt coach work so that a worker could carry out processes while standing up.

The production group employees independently determined and divided the work and carried out assembly tasks in 20 minute cycles. At the final check the information returned to the group via the feedback system. Within the production group one could mutually interchange tasks (=job roulation). Members of the work group had learned to carry out several tasks.

According to published data this factory and its construction had required an additional 10% in investment. Cost prices were nevertheless considered to be competitive enough to earn back this additional investment. This concept remains in Volvo, and Mercedes Benz and GM have recently installed this design philosophy.

7.2.6 Quality circles

One method for filling in the triangle 'human being – work – organization,' from the job and function aspect with regard to the involvement of people in their own activities, is the so-called quality (control) circles. This Japanese method is also applied in Europe and is directed at the improvement of involvement and the degree of motivation.

Quality circles arose in Japan in the 1950s in Japanese companies that, under the influence of ideas from Deming, Juran and Ishikawa, developed the concept of total quality control. Within companies, and even on the shop floor, work groups ('circles') arose which started analysing and solving the quality problems in their own department, studying techniques of quality control and learning to apply these in their own job. Later, these quality circles started to occupy themselves with manufacturing problems and with analysing other problems in the work place, such as safety, co-operation, communication and so on.

The goal of quality circles is the attainment of improvement in quality in the broadest sense: improvement in the quality of the product or the service, the work methods, the work to be carried out, co-operation and the safety on the job. By making use of quality circles, motivation of employees is increased by involving them in solving the problems in their own work place. Training and education in the use of methods and techniques, and careful planning and guidance in the execution of quality circles are necessary to fulfil the conditions. Application of quality circles not only leads to cost savings but is also generally accompanied by greater involvement and more pleasure in the job.

7.3 ORGANIZATION AND GROUP DESIGN

In the lay-out and the routing of a manufacturing company, there is often a recognizable pattern in the lay-out of the manufacturing equipment: the 'line set-up', the 'functional set-up', or the 'group set-up'. In the 'line set-up' the manufacturing equipment and machinery are set out in a 'production line' in order of the sequence of processes to be carried out; when this is mechanized and mutually linked, an 'assembly line' arises. In the 'functional set-up' the production equipment with the same function are put together and set up in an order which applies to the course of manufacture of most of the products, one after another, for example, the sawing, drilling, assembly and packaging departments. In the 'group set-up' a work group manufactures, through mutual co-operation, a final product, or a rounded-off component which has to be built into the final product, in another department. The group is then a 'mini-factory within the factory'; for example, a group that produces the gearboxes for cars which are built into the car somewhere else in the organization. In a 'processing station' different processes carried out with the manufacturing equipment available there results in the final product, for example, a razor or a component of a car.

Group set-up and division of tasks

In a group set-up, machinery and people are all located in one 'production cell' in order to make a specific component or end product. Within a production cell one can opt for part-processes to be carried out per production employee (F-grouping) and roulation possibilities can be linked in. After a certain time, the manufacturing employee makes changes within the processing station in order to prevent dulling and monotony.

Another possibility is job enlargement: allocating different tasks within the processing station. If, for example, planning tasks, maintenance tasks and quality control are added, one can speak of task enrichment. In such cases, a manufacturing employee can cover all phases of processing up to final product or part-product (P-grouping). And after that continues work, but now on a new product.

7.3.1 Organizing around processes

Figure 7.3 shows how a product or service is arrived at within the functional set-up of an organization.

When servicing several product/market combinations, this leads to more complex management, a large degree of co-ordination, long waiting times and stock and inventory forming. The starting point is maximum utilization of both people and production resources – it is clear that matching activities to one another and the co-ordination involved requires a large management capacity.

By organizing the work around processes instead of around functions, fewer managers are required, and decisions can be made more quickly. Because product/market combinations are at the centre of attention the decentralized responsibility for results increases. This solution may lead to duplication of expensive and unique capacity. However, this disadvantage can be avoided by bundling or grouping this capacity into units. Because these smaller units are, in terms of mutual dependency (Chapter 6), of the nature of 'pooled interdependence', they do not disturb one another too readily in their day-to-day functions. Hence the need for co-ordination is less. The units can be co-ordinated by standardization of output. In essence, by means of organizing around process, the management of processes is being decentralized and simplified.

An important condition for organizing around processes is that the flow of orders does not fluctuate too much. Should this occur one department may end up underutilized, where another is over-occupied at that moment. This situation will require further analysis before a decision is made to change the way in which the company is organized.

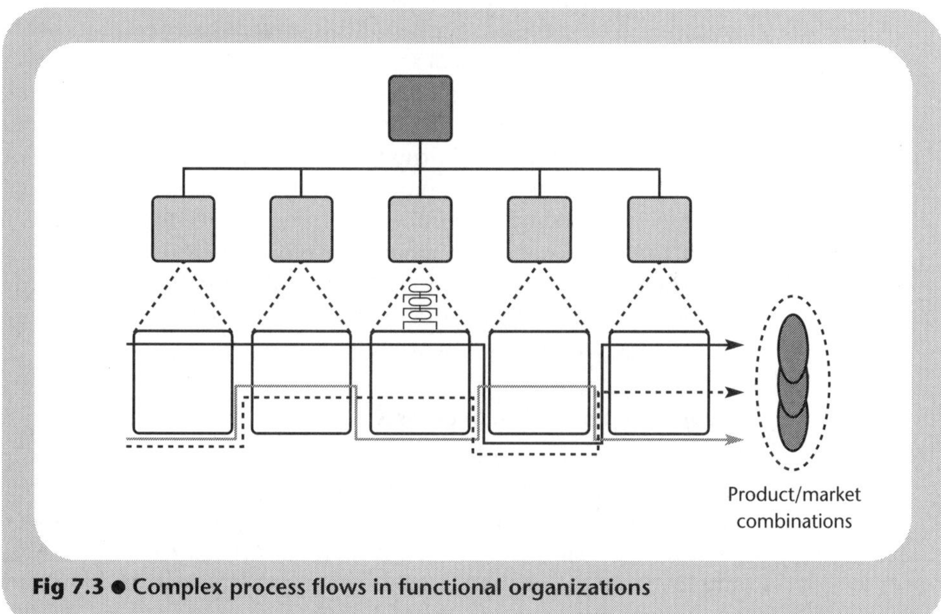

Fig 7.3 ● Complex process flows in functional organizations

By organizing around processes instead of around functions, the managerial complexity is reduced. Advantages are the increase in responsiveness and speed with which market signals are translated into products. There is also less inventory and stock forming and the waiting lines are shorter, which in itself contributes to an improvement in efficiency.

7.3.2 Working in broad task groups

In addition to organizing around processes, it is possible to reduce the need for control within a department responsible for part of a process. Within a department, when the work is split up into different functions, a large amount of planning and co-ordinating capacity is still required at a decentralized level, a disadvantage that can be counteracted by creating broad task groups as this reduces the need for control at a decentralized level, and the number of managers providing leadership to the shop floor is kept to a minimum. Harmonization between these task groups is necessary, taken on by management teams. The role of these management teams is:

- standardization of the output of task groups which execute similar processes; this means that the customer receives similar products or services, independent of which task group it is that realizes these products or services;
- mutual adjustment regarding the assignment of components of the one to the other group (in the case of horizontal differentiation).

Introducing broad task groups may lead to an increase in work satisfaction for interested employees.

The rules of thumb for working with broad task groups are:

- The groups execute the activities as independently as possible. This means that the groups have to have access to regulating capacities and also have to execute preparing, supporting and controlling tasks.
- The members of the group must be able to handle all activities necessary to the process.
- Groups should consist of a minimum of four and a maximum of twenty members.
- Rewards are largely based on abilities within the group tasks.
- Within the group, the co-ordinating role can be fulfilled by members of the group (in rotation).

Minicase 7.2

Working without a boss goes amazingly well.

For some time now, KLM's Technical Service has been working with teams which in time will arrange and organize the work themselves. This already has amazingly good results, one being the implementation of so-called self-regulating teams. 'We see that people are going to feel responsible for their own work in this way.'

Flexibility

Mr Vrieswijk sketches the philosophy which has tempted the Technical Service to call on the flexibility of its employees. Employees are able to impose tasks and responsibilities on

continued overleaf

Minicase continued

themselves and act according to those responsibilities. They are very capable of arranging their own work, can determine the speed and share tasks and responsibilities. A boss who 'puts them to work' is not necessary. But the Technical Service works with self-regulating teams, in which the teams themselves determine how they handle their work: as long as they do the work properly.

'Now there are no rules anymore but guidelines,' says Vrieswijk. 'These give the only constraints which the employees have. Teams do not have bosses but coaches, who stand outside the hierarchy of the organization and have a supporting and stimulating task during the time when the self-controlling teams are implemented. There are also project co-ordinators who take care of the harmonizing and mutual adaptation of the different teams. It is the intention that this task will eventually be handled by the team itself. Each team has a contact who is also the intermediary with those outside the team. The management has to control people and especially be able to listen and communicate well. When you do this right, then you are already on the way to becoming a good manager.

'A self-controlling team is a group of employees which works without a traditional chief and with its own task package,' explains Vrieswijk. 'The team itself is responsible for the end result. Within the team there are sufficient capabilities, instruments and authorities to be able to handle the group tasks. We see that within the teams, people are starting to feel responsible for their work. There is social cohesion. People who in the past kept a low profile are now interacting with their colleagues.

'With self-controlling teams, amazingly good results have been attained,' says Vrieswijk, 'even though they have not all reached the level where they are completely self-controlling. So they do not have their own budget and planning of the work still occurs outside these teams. The number of employees has been reduced by a thousand to 4300,' he sums up. 'In comparison with 1991, the productivity has increased 22%. The middle management has decreased from 600 to 350, and the inventory has been decreased 33%. Here the Boeing 747 has the shortest standing time in the world. When you give people responsibility, they are capable of things which you would not have dared to dream possible.'

'Own' company

'We had one team that did not run well. So we appointed four people as "motors" of the team, and they were allowed to appoint who they wanted in the team. Now the performance of the team is very good. The team functions, as it were, as its own company. Each month it receives an outline of its performance, and you can see the team members have started to self-publicize their own performances.'

Since the organizational turn around in the Technical Service, a lot has changed. The number of formal decision-moments has been reduced dramatically, as has the number of people involved in it. Because of that the maintenance of a plane takes place a lot more efficiently and more quickly than in the past. 'Let me give an example of an electrical problem, for which a hatch had to be opened in the engine,' says Vrieswijk. 'It was usual that the electrician who detected the problem would report it to his boss. He would look for somebody to open the hatch, then would order the electrician to solve the problem. As soon as the problem was solved this was again reported back to the boss. who would order someone else to close the hatch. I know of examples in America in which for simple actions even more people were necessary and which took even more time. Here everything goes much faster now. Within the teams the tasks are telescoped and hence one person controls more than one skill, and so the number of separate specialisms has been reduced from thirteen to six.'

Even though, eventually, the employees will obtain complete responsibility over the operational work, it is not the intention to put all the tasks onto one person's shoulders too swiftly. This should be a gradual process. Teams are not yet up to controlling their own budget. 'You had better introduce it in phases,' suggests Vrieswijk. 'We distinguish three phases: the formation of teams; team members then start to divide tasks themselves and tune their activities into other teams themselves. The control of their own work place is also their own responsibility; then if everything goes well, the teams can become self-regulating. They work as completely independent units within the business unit and even regulate their vacation planning, working hours and work duration.'

Commotion

The process has not gone quite that far yet. The changes caused some commotion in the Technical Service. Soon the first teams appeared to get stuck, because the rest of the organization still worked according to the old rules and procedures. This is why the whole organization has been turned around at once. 'The cultural changes meant an enormous turn around in the thinking especially of management,' says Vrieswijk. 'In the past, the staff services were located in a separate building. These have moved to the production centres. That was an enormous struggle, because the staff considered this step as loss of status. But now, nobody wants it differently anymore. Line managers had to start supporting instead of prescribing. This was harsh for some of them, because management had controlled the organization for decades. Especially in the beginning, too little attention was paid to the human factor. Because of that, our planning was too optimistic. A lot of re-training had to be undertaken in order to familiarize people with all the changes and to take away the resistance to the changes. In an organization which at that moment had more than five thousand employees, this would not happen overnight. It has taken a long time. The consultation with representatives of the work councils ran stiffly. Were we to do it again, then we would do it differently.'

Communication

It is important to keep all employees continuously posted of what is happening within the organization. People who are to be involved and responsible have to have all relevant information at their disposal, and not simply about changes that affect them personally, but also about the things that occur around them.

'That is why communication is vitally important,' says Vrieswijk. 'That is why we involve people from teams as much as possible in the planning that still occurs outside the teams. There is stress laid on that, because we are a company of technocrats. Communication is not in our nature.

'Despite the troubles at the start, the process of allocating responsibilities for the work with the employees is irreversible,' Vrieswijk says.

Source: Adapted from *Bedrijfskundig Vakblad*, July 1994.

7.3.3 Performance management and team structure

From recent motivation literature it appears that feedback and goal setting can have a strong motivational effect on individuals and teams. Based on these principles it is possible to design a system for performance management which supplies the necessary feedback for self-controlling teams. The basic characteristics of this system for performance management are:

- bottom-up development: the team itself sets result areas which they can influence and the accompanying performance indicators; after that, the adjustment to management takes place and consensus arises;
- weighing of the different result areas and accompanying performance indicators, through which an index for the total performance about all result areas becomes available, in addition to data on the performances in separate result areas;
- systematic feedback about attained performance, presented in a clear way; this gives rise to discussion about improvement of performance and improvement of working methods.

7.4 DELEGATION: TASK, AUTHORITY, RESPONSIBILITY AND ACCOUNTABILITY

When a company or institution becomes larger and more personnel are employed it is necessary to face the question: which tasks can be delegated to other employees. This is the delegation problem. An employee, whether a director or a department chief, can only take on a limited number of tasks himself. Because of growth in the company activities and because of the increasing complexity of the problems for management and organization, tasks have to be delegated.

By delegation we mean the delegating of tasks to other employees by an authorized employee. A task is a work activity which needs to be done. The content of a task is formed by the activities which have to be carried out. A given task is, for example, the purchasing of raw material and the keeping of the wage records. In fulfilling the task, many types of activity may have to be carried out, such as making phone calls, typing, filling in forms and so on.

When tasks are being transferred by delegation the necessary authority for handling those tasks also needs to be granted, so that the responsibility for correct handling of those tasks can indeed be carried by those operational employees. By authority we mean the right to take decisions which are necessary for the execution of a task.

Responsibility is the moral obligation to execute a task to one's best ability, as well as the duty to report about the execution of that task. Task, authority and responsibility are intrinsically connected in such a way that the responsibility follows from the delegation and acceptance of tasks and authority. An employee can only be held responsible when, with the delegated tasks, the requisite authority has been granted. One can only carry responsibility when the authority is sufficient. One has to be able to take the initiative to a sufficient degree when this is demanded by the situation and one also has to have sufficient people and resources at one's disposal.

7.4.1 Delegation and 'management by exception'

When operational employees and middle management are strongly motivated to attain the goals of the company or institution with this constraint of freedom of action, one can make use of reporting of exception in the supply of information. Conscious and systematic application of the exception rule can be indicated by the concept of 'management by exception' (MbE). This assumes that, in consultation, boundaries, constraints and operational norms in the task realization are given. If results in the task fulfilment range outside these boundaries, then middle management or the operational employees can readjust themselves and take corrective actions. They are considered to be capable of that, and also have the authority to do so. That is only the 'exceptions' are presented to the management. Consequently, higher management has more time to spend on policy and work creation.

7.5 ORGANIZATIONAL PRINCIPLES: RELATIONS AND AUTHORITIES

There is one basic form that underlies every organizational structure, namely the line organization. Variations on this are possible, for example, the line staff organization and the line organization with specialized support staff services.

7.5.1 Line organization

Line organization: origin

Line organization reflects the managerial and operational functions and assignments of employees on different hierarchical levels. The line organization arises by transferring tasks in a vertical and horizontal direction. Every employee reports to his or her immediate higher manager.

Advantages of line organization

In principle, the major advantages of the line organization are clarity and simplicity. There are no contradictions or contrasts in views and opinions or assignments: the operational employees know exactly what is expected of them, know who their boss is and, therefore, to whom they have to direct themselves and report. Assignments, along with the procedures to be considered, guidelines and instructions, are issued from a fixed point. Supervision and the control of progress in the execution of tasks take place from here, are correcting measures and actions are taken. An additional advantage is that the mutual adjustment and the weighing of different aspects of the activities to be carried out have taken place before assignments are given. The general manager or supervising manager is expected to have an overview of the whole range of activities and to have insight into the different aspects of the work, for example, weighing up of extra production costs involved in producing a short run of a product in order to prevent a halt in sales due to unexpected sell out or in the case of an interesting rush job for an important customer. In the small and relatively simple company, the line organization will work well in this way.

Disadvantages of the line organization

If long, intense consultation or mutual adjustment is necessary between the managerial and operational employees, the 'pure line pattern' may have to be abandoned. If adaptation problems on the line were passed along vertically to the general manager, all communication would move through the hierarchy and the line would soon become overloaded. Likewise, it cannot be assumed that the supervising chiefs indeed do hold the monopoly on

Minicase 7.3

Here is a test which you can use to determine how capable you are of delegation. You should not study the test first: fill in the answers according to your initial reaction.

Tick the column which contains the most correct answer. Only one answer is possible each time: you have to choose.

Test: Can you delegate?	No	Not sure	Yes
1. Do you believe that you do not have personnel at your disposal who can handle the work delegated to them?	☐	☐	☐
2. Within your organization are there detailed job descriptions in which the responsibilities and the authority of each managerial employee are described?	☐	☐	☐
3. Do you prefer to do things yourself rather than delegating, with all the attendant hassle of explaining?	☐	☐	☐
4. Do your employees usually ask for your decision when they have a problem?	☐	☐	☐
5. Are you afraid that subordinates could be a threat to you in your career?	☐	☐	☐
6. Do you know exactly which authority your subordinates should have in order to be able to handle certain assignments?	☐	☐	☐
7. Do you perform a lot of small routine jobs which could be performed just as well by others?	☐	☐	☐
8. Would you be able to handle more work if required?	☐	☐	☐
9. Are you not a little afraid of specialized subordinates who are absolute experts in their field?	☐	☐	☐
10. Is there the possibility for open discussion about certain situations (for example criticism or complaints)?	☐	☐	☐

all aspects of the work qua knowledge and experience. Think of manufacturing technology, material knowledge, cost calculation, administrative procedures, legal matters, and so on. The expertise in specific aspects possibly falls short in some areas. It is then necessary to employ job specialists in these areas. Managers who really are all-rounders are few and far between. Building an organization on the 'sheep with five legs' theory is dangerous. The management has to delegate both tasks, and the relevent authority (*see* section 7.4) and also to employ others when this is necessary. When this does not happen widely enough, the span of control (*see* section 7.8) of management will be only slight.

Line relation and line authority

Via the line relation the manager can exercise his line authority. Line authority is a hierarchical relation or formal authority relation in the sense of a 'command and con-

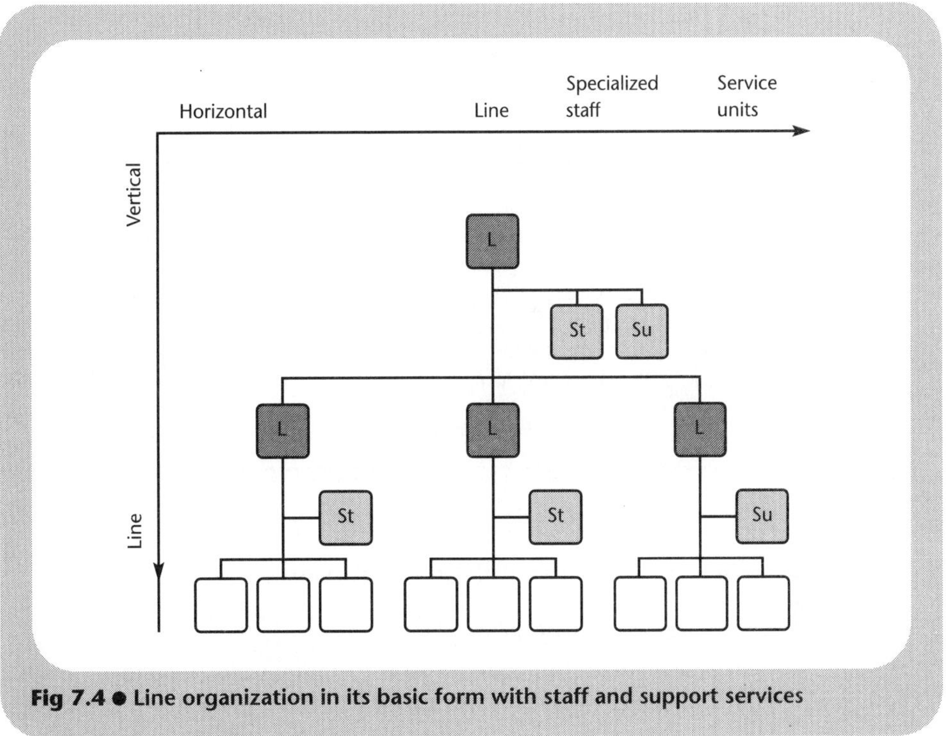

Fig 7.4 ● Line organization in its basic form with staff and support services

trol relation' between manager and subordinate. Via the line, a manager can use his authority to give assignments to an employee. The subordinate has to render account to his manager and has to report to him about the execution of the task, orally or in writing. The manager, in turn, has to exercise direct or indirect control over the execution, so that if necessary, he can interfere, adjust or correct in a timely way.

Line organization: functioning

In its 'pure' form, the principle of 'unity of command' is given shape in the line organization via the line relation. Unity of command means that a subordinate only has one manager, or superior, from whom he receives his orders. From this idea comes the assumption that managers as decision makers on the line are experts in all aspects of managing and carrying out of tasks. They are considered as omniscient in their position and can, without consultation, quickly make correct, careful and optimal decisions. Following on from that, they are the only ones who can give responsible and clear instructions and assignments. The necessary unity in points of view and unity in direction is thereby readily arrived at.

As soon as problems arise in the execution of the task in hand, they have to be submitted to the manager, who then decides what has to be done. Then, should consultation be necessary with employees from other departments, this principle needs to be submitted to and arranged by the overall manager, who has to solve the adaptation problem. By following the vertical line in the organization, the unity in direction is virtually guaranteed.

In the pure form of the line organization, with a strict application of the vertical line relation, there develops clear hierarchical relations between director, department managers and operational employees.

This form of organization, of course, has both its advantages and its disadvantages, and these are schematically depicted in Table 7.1.

Table 7.1 ● Line organization: advantages *v.* disadvantages

Advantages	Disadvantages
1. responsibilities/authority are clear	1. quick overloading of managers
2. control is clear	2. lack of specialism
3. fast decision making	3. fulfillment of managerial functions is difficult because the manager has to become a 'jack of all trades'
4. fast execution of the decisions	4. long lines of communication which can work against desired outcome
5. relationships are clear	

7.5.2 Line and specialized staff organization

Line staff organization: origin

Effective and responsible managing implies that a manager, on a managerial and operational level in the organization, will have to fulfil his policy-oriented tasks well in order to be as effective in his operations-directed tasks. When this does not happen the manager rapidly becomes out of date. The daily problems do not get the attention they really need since they are best solved by means of 'symptom fighting' or by 'fire fighting'. There is no time for problem-solving by reconstituting or delegating tasks. Thus the problems recur. Delivery times are exceeded, people are over-worked, the quality of products or services falls short, market chances are not effectively being used and so on.

When the manager wants to approach this in the right way, a lot of time and attention will be necessary. The larger the organization and the more complex the problems, the more time and attention will be needed for this task. In relatively small companies, with regard to the constituting task in the management, part of the activities is conducted by external experts or consultants. Think, for example, of the activities of accountants with regard to the administration and supply of information, and of external consultants for marketing research.

In larger companies or institutions specialists are recruited from within their own organization. The organization has reached such a size and the problems occur in such frequency that the management needs the relevant expertise in-house, to address problems which are becoming more and more complex with regard to policy and/or execution of tasks. When there is continuous work of this problem-solving nature, it is cheaper to have people in-house rather than making use of external expertise. The accent is now placed on specialistic knowledge regarding analysis and solving of policy problems and the specialized staff functions arise: economic research, market research, long-term planning and legal matters.

Line staff organization: functioning

Staff organs are those which are at the disposal of the board of management or of other managers in a company or institution as consulting or advisory organs. They serve the line manager to whom they are assigned with advice and when necessary, prepare decisions and supply him with information, trace problems and analyse them. They are at the service of the line and have, exclusively, advisory authority. They are specialists on elements of policy and thus have the authority to give asked for or unasked for advice from that specialistic field (legal matters, macro-economic research, market research and so on). A staff relationship in the pure form is limited to being in an advisory capacity. In Fig 7.5, the staff relationships of departments like 'Macro-economic research', 'Organization and efficiency' and 'Marketing research' have been expressed. Making use of specialized staff departments or of individual specialized staff functionaries enables the advantages of the line organization to exist (*see* section 7.5.1) and is further designed to counter some of the disadvantages of the line organization.

Only a line functionary is in the position to convert advice into guidelines, instructions, assignments or orders.

The staff organization is especially directed at eliminating short comings in expertise and skills of the line that could prove to be threatening. However, the line does not need to follow advice made by the staff, since the staff authority is limited to an advisory capacity only. So calling in staff specialists does not change anything about the line pattern along which the instructions and assignment reach employees. But rather, the specialized staff serves as reinforcement of line management. The staff has the time, the knowledge and the skills at its disposal to support the line management with regard to problems which would otherwise, because of pressure of daily circumstances or by lack of specific know-how or lack of time, receive insufficient attention from the line manager.

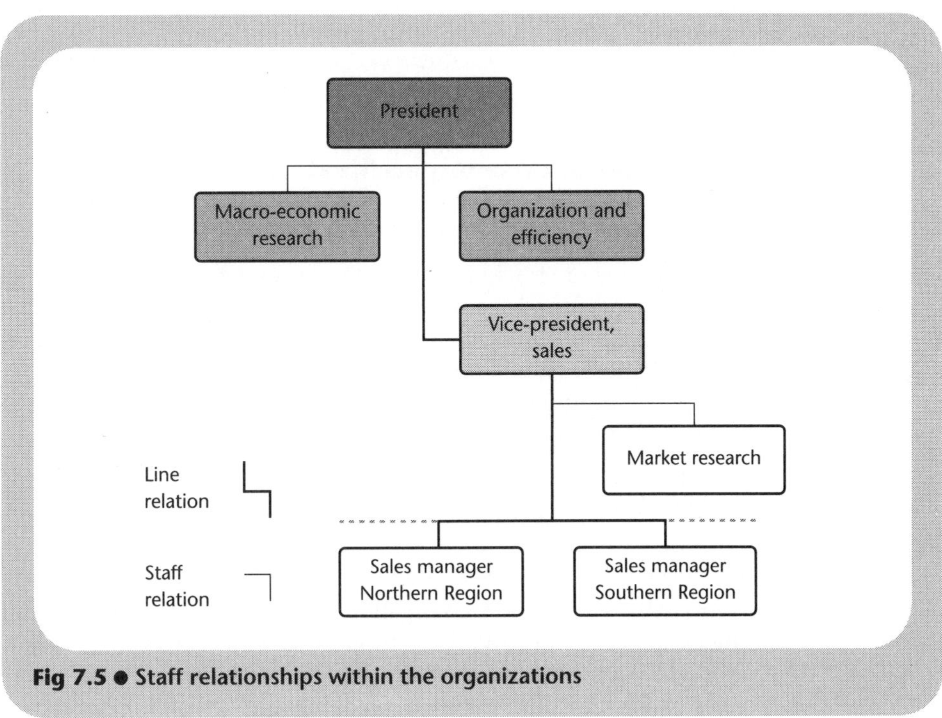

Fig 7.5 ● Staff relationships within the organizations

Line staff organization: advantages and disadvantages

Advantages of the line staff organization are:

- better decisions can be made through practical application of specific knowledge and skills;
- delegating headwork by 'the line' to 'the staff' saves time;
- the scope of control (*see* section 7.8) is enlarged;
- more efficient time spending benefits many other matters.

Possible disadvantages of the line staff organization are:

- too little practical application of specific knowledge and skills may take place;
- contact with the line, and through that with the operational core, may get lost (the so-called 'ivory tower' effect);
- the involvement of specialists costs money;
- by-passing the chief in the line may also occur.

A specialized staff worker needs to prevent being labelled an 'ivory tower worker' or 'theoretically wonderful but practically of little use'. Staff employees have to realize that the decision-making authorities are situated on the line, and thus the approach of staff has to be directed at being accepted through their job specialistic input by the practical and operational thinking managers 'on the line'. Lack of acceptance may lead to lack of involvement since the line is not obliged to use a given piece of advice. When advice is complex and so specialist that the line cannot understand and cannot foresee the consequences, the line will not be likely to adopt such advice. The line manager, as decision maker, does not want to become dependent on the staff, and so it is important that the staff gives sufficient explanation and insight, and sees to it that the line can foresee consequences of decisions reached, because, ultimately, the line has the responsibility for the execution of the tasks involved.

7.5.3 Line organization and specialized support staff

Support staff: origin

When the major concern of the internal servicing of specialistic knowledge involved in the organization is to be directed at the problems of execution in more than one department, the so-called specialized support staff services are required. Personnel, administration and finance, maintenance, and so on.

Specialized support staff are service departments which deliver specialistic services to elements of management and execution of tasks which have a compulsory character, to the other departments or to employees in the line, for example, the departments of Finance and Control, or Personnel.

Specialized support staff: functioning

Contrary to specialized staff organs as such, specialized support staff conduct a part of the execution, hence the term 'support staff'. This relationship is depicted in Fig 7.6. From a specialized support staff, a specific expert area, compulsory directives can be given about the policy to be followed, the way of working or procedure.

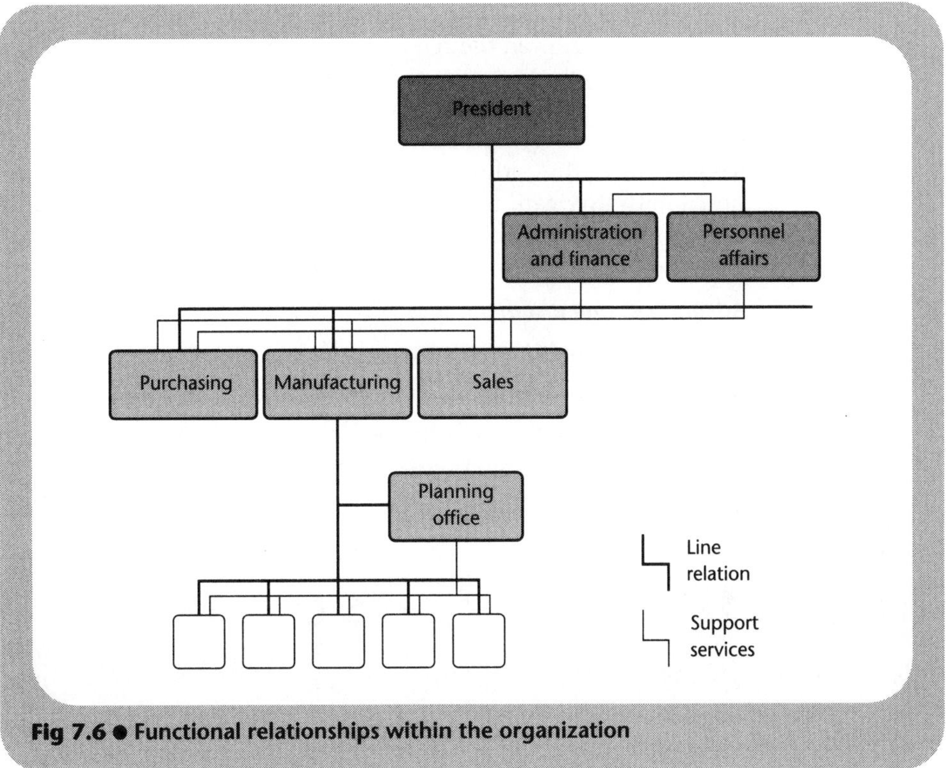

Fig 7.6 ● Functional relationships within the organization

The line, in turn, is obliged to seek compulsory advice from a specialized support staff as soon as problems arise in the line that touch on fields of expertise of the support staff, for example, a discharge problem (via Personnel department), sudden machine stagnation (via Maintenance department), modernization of the manufacturing shop (via the Technical Services), and so on.

A manager with functional authority (*see* section 6.2.7) can then, in a specific specialized field, state how something could be done, not what should be done. Working assignments are given by the line. This holds true for the central administration with regard to the purchase administration. The functional authority or functional relationship is, in many cases, built in between central and decentralized staff services in large companies, for example, between the central Administration and Finance department and the Administration department in a subsidiary or business unit.

Unlike staff organs, then, specialized support staff organs mostly conduct only a part of the execution, or have a controlling task with regard to the line, and functional authority indications are given with regard to the activities of employees who are under line authority of another manager.

Operational employees stand in relationship to several managers, who each can give their ideas on aspects of operational execution. In practice problems may arise through lack of clarity and contradiction. It is important to issue instructions only after lengthy deliberation or consultation, and in a spirit of co-operation. Problems mentioned earlier can be eliminated partially by that.

The functional relation indicates the authority relation between specialized support services and line. Even though a support service is placed outside the line, it can nevertheless give compulsory directives to the line from a specific field of expertise, or can require that the directiveness be compulsory. So-called functional authority can be exercised, that is: indications may be given with regard to the activities of employees who are under the authority of another manager in the line. So a manager with functional authority can, to a limited extent, state how something could be done, but cannot simply say 'do this or that'. Work assignments are given by the line. It is more a question of: 'When this or that is to be done, then it has to be done in this way'.

Advantages and disadvantages

Advantages include the following:

- The required expertise, knowledge and skills are brought in.
- A certain degree of co-ordination, consistency and uniformity can be ensured, for example, in the design of departmental registration systems, the design of forms,

Exhibit 7.2

Has outsourcing gone too far?

It's the corporate rage, but farming out work can cost a company dearly

Call it the growth industry of the Nineties. Outsourcing, endorsed as a cost-cutting measure in recent years by such management gurus as Peter Drucker and Tom Peters, has emerged as the most sweeping trend to hit management since reengineering. In the rush to improve efficiency, Corporate America is going to outsiders to buy ever more products and services that were once made by its own employees. Companies are parceling out everything from mailroom management to customer service, from pieces of human resources departments to manufacturing and distribution. 'We're at the beginning of an explosion,' predicts Scott Hartz, managing partner of Price Waterhouse's consulting group. 'Many of the firms doing more outsourcing aren't troubled corporations trying to save a nickel. They are often the corporate leaders.' About 86% of major corporations now outsource at least some services, up from 58% in 1992 (chart), according to a poll by consultants A.T. Kearney, which surveyed 26 major companies, including American Airlines, DuPont, Exxon, Honda, IBM, and Johnson & Johnson.

But it's a trend that has a decided downside. Outsourcing is a hot button with unions, as GM found when its labor dispute virtually shut down its North American operations. The pay-off from outsourcing, moreover, sometimes falls far short of expectations. One study found the average savings to be around 9%, though consultants often promise gains of 20% to 40%. Another hazard: An errant supplier can delay a key product launch and anger customers. 'You rarely hear about the failures of these contracts, but there are many of them,' says John L. Wyatt, CEO of consultants James Martin & Co.

Such problems, however, have done little to slow the rush to farm out work.

The hype over outsourcing's benefits, however, disguises numerous problems. General Electric Co. stubbed its toe last year when the introduction of a new washing machine was delayed by production problems at a contractor to whom it had farmed out key work. GE only lost three weeks as a result of the glitches, but it could have been worse. Southern Pacific Rail Corp. suffered through myriad computer breakdowns and delays after outsourcing its internal computer network to IBM in 1993.

Some companies have found themselves locked into long-term contracts with outside suppliers that are no longer competitive. Indeed, multimillion-dollar technology-outsourcing contracts are often so complex that companies are hiring consultants at fees as high as $700,000 simply to evaluate the proposals. 'Some companies have outsourced so much staff that they have no choice but to bring in consultants to evaluate and renegotiate deals gone bad,' says Eugene A. Procknow of Deloitte & Touche.

Source: *Business Week*, 1 April 1996.

the setting up of evaluation systems, the ranking of personnel in wage and salary scales, production planning, maintenance activities and so on. The result then is that, in these areas, the same systems and procedures are used throughout the whole organization.

The disadvantages include:

- operational employees are responsible to more than one manager at any one time, each of whom can issue instructions on aspects of execution.
- Unity of command is given up.

Lack of clarity may arise through the existence of contradictions. Specialized support service staff need to maintain sufficient communication with the operational manager about the 'how to act', since they ultimately have the decision-making authority about the 'what and when'.

7.5.4 Communication and design of consultative structure

A manager can give his operational employees the authority to engage in direct contact with sub-ordinates of other managers in order to solve problems. They can brief him later about what they have done in mutual consultation. A form of horizontal contact is built into the line organization, but the hierarchical principle is maintained. The hierarchy (='the line') then can still operate when mutual consultation does not lead to the desired results.

Horizontal relationships

This term implies a consultative relationship between employees on the same hierarchical level, who, by means of direct contact, may lead to a co-ordinated execution of different tasks. For example, consultation is necessary between the Sales and Manufacturing departments to determine delivery times in the case of acceptance of orders . If these employees at the same level in the hierarchy do not reach an agreement after consultation, then the hierarchy can decide via an exception rule, and the commonly shared manager, in this case the board of management, decides. The horizontal relationship can be built in as a fixed element in the design of the consultative structure: it can be institutionalized. The weekly consultation of department heads is another example of horizontal contact.

Lateral (or diagonal) relationships

This term, in contrast to the definition just given for 'horizontal' relationships, implies a consultative relationship between employees on different hierarchical levels or from different departments, who, by direct contact, have to arrive at a suggestion about, or a co-ordinated execution of a mutual task. For example, a committee set up temporarily (or permanently) in order to give advice to management about the salary policy to be followed, product development and so on.

Horizontal and lateral relations as co-ordination mechanisms

In the pure form, we hardly ever see line organization in practice. As soon as horizontal contacts are necessary, and horizontal or lateral consultation between managers is necessary in order to reach co-ordination in management and execution, the pure line pattern is given up, and the horizontal and lateral relationships are placed in the organization as co-ordination mechanism. The hierarchy as co-ordination mechanism would soon become overloaded when all problems occurring on the line would be pushed up vertically to the commonly shared managers. The horizontal and lateral relationships are easy to build into the hierarchy, while at the same time maintaining the hierarchical principle.

Consultative groups

Consultation and participation within a company or institution can take place via consultative or work groups which can be set up as project groups or as committees on higher and also the lower organizational levels, in innovation, automation and organizational change, or, for example, in the field of personnel policy or long-term planning (*see* section 4.6). A committee system emerges within the normal line structure, with specialized staff and support services. Problems with which temporary project groups or permanent committees occupy themselves might concern different types of decision and can be of a policy directed and an operational nature. Depending on the nature of the assignment, the character of the group can differ from advising, co-ordinating, to executive. Similarly, higher consultative groups, lower consultative and work groups can be designed, depending on the decisions which are to be prepared.

Consultative groups are created in order to bundle expertise and information to analyse problems, and to prepare solutions for decisions which are to be made. This leads to improvement in the quality of decisions which are to be made. In addition, in consultation groups the opportunity for participation in decision making is offered. This enlarges the basis of the decisions and leads to improvement in acceptance of results of decisions. These elements of decision making were discussed in Chapter 4.

Work consultation

Besides the consultation which can take place between departments in a company or institution in temporary or in permanent consultation groups on higher and/or lower levels, deliberation between manager and operational employees within the departments has to take place. During the periodical work consultation the problems from the last work period can be discussed. Information can be transferred 'from top to bottom' and vice versa, and work assignments for the coming period can be made. The consultation is direct and takes place between all members of a work group, sub-department or department. In this way operational workers are involved in the decisions which affect their job. By means of this form of consultation and participation, an employee becomes more ready to accept decisions and a higher involvement in the work which is to be conducted can be attained.

7.5.5 Communication and participation

Work consultation is a form of regulated and structured deliberation between managerial and operational employees about all aspects which regard the content and execution of the work, and the work situation. One characteristic of work consultation is that the deliberation is, in general, carried on among the employees themselves and not by means of representation. Work consultation is structured group deliberation. Deliberation between the manager and an individual employee is, therefore, not included in the concept of work consultation. The way in which work consultation is carried out can differ enormously from organization to organization, depending not only on the type of organization (size, nature of the manufacturing process), but also on the culture in the organization (style of leadership and history of participation).

Reasons for the introduction of work consultation are:

- improvement in motivation, involvement and development of employees;
- improvement in the quality of products, services and working methods;
- enlargement of the productivity per employee, per department and for the whole company.

It would appear from these reasons and from the fact that work consultation in 80 per cent of cases is started up by management, that this form of participation and consultation is directed especially at the improvement of the effectiveness and efficiency of the organization and at a growth in work satisfaction. There is a clear 'human relation' vision (*see* section 2.1.2) with regard to participation at the base of this.

It is important that the subjects in the work consultation subscribe to the actual situation of all those involved. The work consultation has to offer a chance to bring up subjects which the employees regard as important. When the management directs itself too much to its own problems and excludes other problems from the consultation, the work consultation will not be granted a long life.

Who should be involved in the consultation? Deliberation with all those who are directly involved in the problems at large is to be preferred over systems of representation or roulation, as are sometimes still found in larger departments. Deliberation and consultation about work and work circumstances is only useful when managers in these deliberations themselves have the authority in these matters. The introduction of work deliberations should be accompanied with the rearranging of authority and responsibilities, to ensure that these are divided over the different levels of the organization. The starting point is that delegation involving as wide a range of authority levels as possible in the organization stimulates an effective, flexible management. It is also a condition for a successful development of work consultation.

Work consultation and management

Special attention is desired for a successful outcome of the work consultation. When the work consultation is not being incorporated into regular decision-making circuits in the organization (*see also* Chapter 4), this quickly leads to the consultation's not being taken serious by employees. In addition it is important to have the introduction of work consultation accompanied by training and education in order to make participants more sensitive to the problems that accompany the development of work consultation.

Work consultation is not an activity which stands on its own within the organization, but it forms a logical link in the total management concept. When a middle manager within the organization has little discretion in making certain decisions or in delegating, those involved will experience the work consultation as senseless and a waste of time. This means that the possibilities for middle management to come to a far-reaching form of work consultation on its own initiative will be constrained. The needs of operational employees are important here. Work consultation can only be successfully introduced when the form and the content of the consultation subscribe to the needs and possibilities of those involved in it. A pre-condition is that a good atmosphere of mutual trust is present. The introduction of work deliberation is no magic formula to mend disturbed labour relations. Further specific requisiter are set out in an immutable agenda and the determination of agreements in decision lists.

Without this kind of formal regulations, the work consultation will soon be reduced to an informal exchange of information, opinions and objections.

The subjects which can come up for discussion during the work consultation are numerous. Many subjects will regard the organization of the work (planning, division of work or working methods) and labour conditions. Work consultation can also be part of the total reward system when in the organization certain reward forms relate to future, and as the unrealized productivity. In all cases, well executed work consultation will be able to contribute to improvement in the organizational climate, because employees are involved in decisions which affect their job. Through this form of consultation and participation, the acceptance of decisions by an employee can be extended.

Conditions

The success of work consultation depends on the following conditions:

- The organization needs the maturity to involve the participation of workers in decision-making processes. This 'maturity' applies to management as well as the operational workers.
- The organization has to implement work consultation as part of a whole package. It can not be introduced in isolation.
- Work consultation has to lead to enlargement in the possibility by operational workers' influence, but is not allowed to undermine the responsibility of the managers.
- Work consultation has to be functional. It has to be directed at the task of the department seen with the context of the work situation *per se*.
- Work consultation has to be seen in relation to the responsibility and authority of employees with regard to their own work situation. Employees who do not feel responsible for what happens in a department will not be able to function in the work consultation process.
- The organization has to be able to adopt the internal changes and developments evoked by work consultation (for example: the adjustment of internal relations, the changing of structures or procedures, the changing of authority relationships).

7.5.6 Substitutes for hierarchy

Middle management fulfils a number of important roles in the line of command and in co-ordination activities. When these roles have been distinguished they can be rendered redundant, making the organization flatter and more efficient. The most important roles of middle management are depicted in Fig 7.7.

There are various possibilities for reducing the role of middle management and for filling its traditional role in the hierarchy. For example, by organizing more around the product/market combinations, by working more in teams or by making better use of information systems. In this way time needed for co-ordinating, planning, measuring and controlling actually decreases.

Substitutes for hierarchy as 'old' vertical directed lines of command and co-ordination provisions are myriad. However, it can be said with almost 100 per cent certainty that hierarchy will never completely disappear. Old and heavy hierarchical connections can, however, be driven back or made redundant by an increasing capacity for self-regulating by employees. For the co-ordinating management level, the policy and strategic task assignments remain, for which, after all, it has been employed.

- Motivating
- Measuring
- Co-ordinating
- Assigning work
- Looking after personnel matters
- Providing expertise
- Setting goals
- Planning
- Linking lines of communication
- Training/coaching
- Providing leadership
- Record keeping

Source: After Lawler, 1988

Fig 7.7 ● Roles of middle management

In Fig 7.8 it can be seen how different organization instruments, managing methods and techniques can reduce or even replace the need for hierarchy. Ways in which to replace hierarchy and reasons for doing so can be summarized by the following:

- Grouping of tasks and design of functions, P-grouping, self-regulating teams, group set-ups and semi-autonomous groups reduce the need for co-ordination and direction from above (by supervising middle managers).
- In computer supported production or data processing systems, operational employees can keep their data and results themselves (instead of staff and controlling line managers).
- Well trained and educated employees can interpret and draw conclusions from financial feedback information themselves. This also works motivationally. Data can even be directed at competitive comparisons in order to stimulate external interest (instead of internal battles and 'passing the buck').
- Reward systems such as profit sharing, performance-based wage systems and rating on merits and productivity also reduce the need for hierarchy. These systems stimulate teamwork and co-operation and improve communication about financial and non-financial performance indicators.
- External and internal customer contact: when business units are co-responsible for their own inputs and outputs, they will, to a large degree, be able/willing to structure and plan their work themselves. This is why units in many cases do not need a chief or boss in the old sense.
- By means of appropriate training (knowledge, skills and problem-handling) of employees, these capacities are to a lesser degree required from a chief/boss or manager. The accent in management tasks is being placed on facilities, careful use of talents and regard to good communication.
- By means of a clear vision and understandable and transferable values, the culture is reinforced; this offers security, standardization of problem solutions and strong teams.
- Accepted leadership instead of formal boss-related behaviour, leads to a higher task maturity (*see* Chapter 9) of employees.

Roles of middle management	Grouping of tasks and design of functions	Data processing systems	Financial information	Record systems	Customer contact	Training	Vision/values	Accepted leadership
Motivating	X		X	X	X	X	X	
Measuring	X	X						X
Co-ordinating	X	X	X	X	X	X	X	X
Assigning work	X							X
Looking after personnel matters	X						X	X
Providing expertise		X				X		X
Selling goods	X	X	X	X	X	X	X	
Planning	X	X	X					
Linking lines of communication	X	X		X			X	
Training/coaching	X	X		X				X
Providing leadership	X							X
Record keeping	X	X						

Source: Adapted from Lawler, 1988

Fig 7.8 ● Substitutes for hierarchy

All these possible substitutes may cause traditional hierarchy to be dismantled still further. A flatter organization is one immediate result of this, since the use of these substitutes is a condition for the effective functioning of flatter organizations.

7.6 ● CENTRALIZATION AND DECENTRALIZATION

An important question which has to be recognized in the design of the organizational structure, is: Where in the organization do which decisions have to be made? According to the answers decision-making authority needs to be granted. It is similarly important to know where in the organization which actions and tasks are to be executed. And in the case of growth in company activities, one will have to recognize which tasks, with their respective authority, can be passed on to other functionaries (=delegation, *see* section 7.4).

Where in the organization this concerns the spreading of formal decision-making authority by means of delegation from top to bottom on the line, one can speak of vertical decentralization. When authority from the line is placed at specialist support service level (section 7.5.3) on areas of co-ordination, planning and control, one can speak of horizontal decentralization.

The degree of concentration or spreading of decision-making authority always has to be taken into consideration together with the following aspects:

- the subject of authority (decision areas such as manufacturing, sales, or finance);
- the directives, guidelines, instructions and procedures concerning the respective subjects in governing, managing and execution; this concerns the degree of freedom and constraint for each decision-making area;
- the phase in the decision-making process in which consultation in policy making, planning or problem-solving is actually taking place.

The question of the degree of concentration or spreading to be preferred cannot simply and unambiguously be answered. A far-reaching freedom in decision making may be unrealistic as far as one area is concerned, whereas it may be possible in another area. To ask permission from head office for every local action will cost too much in time and money. Furthermore it would not be realistic to suppose that head office has sufficient local knowledge. All relevant information, for example concerning local clients, discounts and personnel should be provided to head office without its being allowed to take decisions at local level, as this would hinder adequate reactions and influence the motivation at local level negatively.

As regards several policy aspects, such as pricing and range, production planning, manufacturing techniques, standard costs calculation, salary scales and similar areas, a certain discretionary decision-making authority can be left, while at the same time, constraints can be formulated. As regards other aspects, such as finance, research and development, mergers, acquisitions and major reorganizations, there may be little or no discretionary decision-making authority.

In order to determine where in a company or institution which decisions have to be made, the following questions are some that have to be answered.

- Who has the information at his disposal for making a certain decision, or who can have it at his disposal quickly and easily?
- Who has the capabilities and expertise at his disposal in order to make a correct decision?
- Do urgent decisions have to be taken where they arise in order appropriately to meet the local circumstances?
- Do activities conducted locally have to be co-ordinated carefully with other activities, possibly with activities to be conducted somewhere else?
- How important is the decision?
- How busy and occupied are certain employees who are already eligible for the allocation of authority?
- Are the willingness to take initiatives and the morale improved to a sufficiently worthwhile degree by decentralization?

The answer to these questions gives an indication of the place in the organization where the decision can be taken. There is F-decentralization (in functional decision areas), P(roduct)-decentralization, M(arket)-, or G(eographical)-decentralization, according to the chosen form of work division and assignment of authority.

Urgent and local circumstances, for example, demand spreading the decision authority, that is decentralization. The need for co-ordination and important decisions, however, point in the direction of concentration of decision-making authority at one place in an organization, that is centralization.

With the help of the questions posed above one can try to determine the loci for optimal decision making concerning the subjects in every area of decision making. Decentralization can only take place by preserving 'control' and the centralization of co-ordination authorities concerning centralized policy decisions. In this respect top management will continue to hold its ultimate authority on expansion and diversification, product policy, research and development projects, extending/raising/changing equity capital from shareholders, finance and budgeting, providing external financial information, investment selection, proposing/selecting/appointing board members, remuneration of top management and similar aspects.

From this list one might conclude that only operational decisions are appropriate for decentralization. Lower organizational levels, however, may also contribute substantially to the preparation of centralized policy decisions. The 'bottom up' principle then applies. This is the opposite of the 'top down' approach, in which constraints are superimposed and there is no room for personal initiative or positive contribution from lower level management and operational employees.

Optima for the spread of decision-making authority in different areas are naturally dependent on the economic situation. In an organization which experiences favourable external conditions and positive financial results the reins are loosened and organizational slack may arise in certain areas, for example extra stock, hiring of extra personnel or the purchase of more inventory, all more than strictly necessary. When conditions are less favourable, this organizational slack is cut back. The top management will then give directives to limit the discretionary decision-making authority of the lower management within the organization.

In crisis situations or in situations in which an organization is confronted with a somewhat hostile environment (relative) centralization will have to take place. The more pressure external interest groups or stakeholders put on the organization, the more inclined the organization will be to centralize. The top echelon then is held responsible and needs to be prepared to act quickly, co-ordinatedly and effectively. More than ever before the top will need to be sure that things go as they decide and will need to be kept informed. In certain cases these situations will lead to a relatively strong temporary (re)centralization.

This phenomenon is sometimes called the 'accordion' effect, which indicates a situational or contingent change in the degree of concentration or spread in the decision-making authority, and can be noticed from time to time in the organization's growth and development.

7.6.1 Profit decentralization and divisionalization

In organizations with product–market grouping or a geographical grouping of activities the institutionalization of divisions is possible and it can be combined with profit decentralization.

Divisionalization with profit decentralization can be seen as a specific form of departmentalization. In these cases the organization is divided in divisions which may also be termed 'strategic business units'. In principle divisions or strategic business units are self-sufficient and semi-autonomous.

A division, which itself is usually built up of a number of subsidiaries or 'business units', has, within certain constraints, full profit responsibility for all activities contained within the division.

An important condition for divisionalization is that self-sufficiency or autarchy can be guaranteed. In other words a division should be able to lead its own life and to have its own base of existence, and thus should be sufficiently independent from other units. The sources for its existence have then to be included within the division itself. This also means that the activities of one division have to be totally independent (or at least to a very substantial degree independent) from the activities in other divisions. Between the divisions there will exist a so-called pooled interdependence when this is seen from the top of the organization (*see* section 6.3.6).

Divisions are to a high degree self-responsible for their operational business results and for generating profitable business activities. Most of the time they have only a limited influence on the destination to the profits generated by them. Divisions and subsidiaries or business units render account towards the top by means of their own balance sheet and accounts of profit and loss. Advantages and disadvantages of the divionalized organization and those concerning business unit management are given in sections 6.3.4 and 6.3.5.

Constraints which lead us to speak of semi-autonomous (strategic) business units originate from decision-making areas such as:

- strategy formulation and the determination of objectives and goals in periodical planning and portfolio decisions (*see* sections 5.1.2, 5.2.3, 5.3 and 10.1);
- approval of decisions concerning capital investment in the case of expansion and/or diversification;
- financial planning and budget procedure;
- standard administrative procedures concerning financial information supply, as well as directives for the supply of information on operational tasks;
- selection, remuneration, development and transfer of key personnel in divisions;
- important reorganizations, mergers and/or acquisitions.

There are two angles to the imposition of these types of constraints. On the one hand the top has to retain a sufficient grip on the divisions. The top is responsible for planning and control and has to direct the spotlight onto divisions and/or business units when there are danger signs that might indicate problems to be. On the other hand the top needs to keep a certain reserve in imposing constraints in such a way that the divisional or business unit management can take and realize its own responsibility in a situation of optimal independence and (semi-)autonomy.

7.7 CO-ORDINATION AND INTERNAL ADAPTATION

In putting an organization into operation, it is of great importance to co-ordinate the activities to be carried out. Co-ordinating is directing the different activities at one and the same goal. The activities of employees from different departments have to be conducted in unity. For that reason, activities have to be well co-ordinated and tuned into one another. When the mutual co-operation is not arranged sufficiently well, this leads to a lack of co-ordination. One employee by-passes the other, some jobs get done twice, and some things do not happen at all because the one thought that the other would do it. Everyone does his best within his means, but things still go wrong because of a lack of co-ordination. This kind of problem must be prevented wherever possible.

Co-ordination can be brought about in different ways: in co-ordination the major consideration is directing the different activities at one and the same goal(s). Activities on different levels of operational execution in the organization and in the different departments have to be united. This can be stimulated by as wide a coherence as possible between different activities in the division of work and design of functions (*see* sections 7.1 and 7.2).

Business processes must be matched by the means of issuing assignments and instructions, by taking into account the procedures which have been set forth, along with the standard methods and the given policy guidelines. Here again, the hierarchy is a mechanism of co-ordination. The line can be called in when formulated rules, assignments, instructions or procedures fall short so that decisions can be made concerning the conduct of operational actions, and new instructions.

The official line often runs like this: 'In cases in which the regulation does not provide, the managers decide.'

Policy guidelines and standard methods and procedures

Before we go on to discuss different action plans in Chapter 10, we need to pay attention to the so-called standing plans. In contrast to action plans, which depend on specific situations, standing plans have to be seen as guidelines with a general validity. They influence action plans as well as all other decisions. Standing plans are of three kinds:

1. policy guidelines;
2. standard methods;
3. standard procedures.

Policy guidelines

A policy guideline is a general guideline which indicates what in specific cases should or should not be done. Policy guidelines can concern many subjects. For example, the sales policy: 'We only sell our own brand name.' If a potential client wants to purchase a product from the company in order to bring it onto the market under his brand name, the salesman knows that he cannot accept the order. A policy guideline in the personnel sphere may be that employees who have been employed for five years or more will only be fired in the last instance.

Standard methods

Standard methods can be seen as a refinement and specification of policy guidelines. They give more information about how one should act in certain situations. These methods are usually applied on a lower level in the organization than the policy guidelines. When a policy guideline states, for example, that the wage level of the company has to be the same as that of other companies in the same line of business, the standard method can determine how this has to be calculated.

Standard procedures

A standard procedure is a prescription in which are stated the steps that must be taken in certain situations. These steps are more detailed and specific than in the standard method. It can be prescribed that a warehouse employee must report when minimum stock is reached to the Sales department. This department then uses a certain formula to calculate the amount that has to be reordered.

Standard procedures can be developed for all aspects of the organization, so that it can be prescribed how one has to act in personnel, recruiting or in the making of investments. A procedure is a series of tasks which are connected to one another and which together form a more or less complete whole. The co-ordination can now be stimulated by determining procedures. Procedures direct activities along the correct channels and guarantee mutual adjustment in the decisions to be made. Activities can then proceed 'by the book'.

Standard procedures can be recorded on forms. On these forms different data have to be filled in by employees who execute the actions in a certain procedure. For example, on a form to register the flow through the organization of all important data the following could be involved: the making out of the order form, initials for taking delivery of goods, data about quality control, the warehouse taking deliveries of goods and so on.

In these 'standing plans' – policy guidelines, standard methods and standard procedures – the question remains of how strictly they should be applied. The advantage of this kind of guideline is that a larger uniformity arises in the actions that ensue. A danger is, however, that they are not adjusted in time to changing circumstances. This should be borne in mind when formulating and applying standing plans.

Not everything proceeds by the book

When deviations from the set rules, procedures and instructions occur, or unexpected situations or delays arise, management has to act to come to decisions to make operational actions possible. Or the authority must be given to operational employees so that they can act as they see fit. The management must always still be in a position to take action if the desired result is not attained.

7.8 SCOPE OF MANAGEMENT CONTROL

Each manager can manage only a limited number of activities that are to be executed by others. Managing (=planning + organizing + motivating + supervising) costs time and attention: working time is limited and the managerial capacity itself has limits and so the manager's scope of control is limited.

The manager's scope of control can be described as the number of direct employees the manager can effectively manage, coach and lead, and it will usually follow that the more the number of employees grows, the more the quality of management declines. In addition to 'scope of control', the 'span of control' and the 'depth of control' are also distinguished. Span of control is the number of employees a manager manages directly. When a manager directly manages as many people as possible himself, this has consequences for the organizational structure of the company, which could then be termed 'flat', as is depicted in Fig 7.9.

When the number of employees to be managed is larger than the number the manager can responsibly manage, his scope of control is exceeded, because he will spend insufficient time and attention on the co-ordination of activities, and on the quality of activities – he ends up chasing his own tail. Problems will then occur: delivery times,

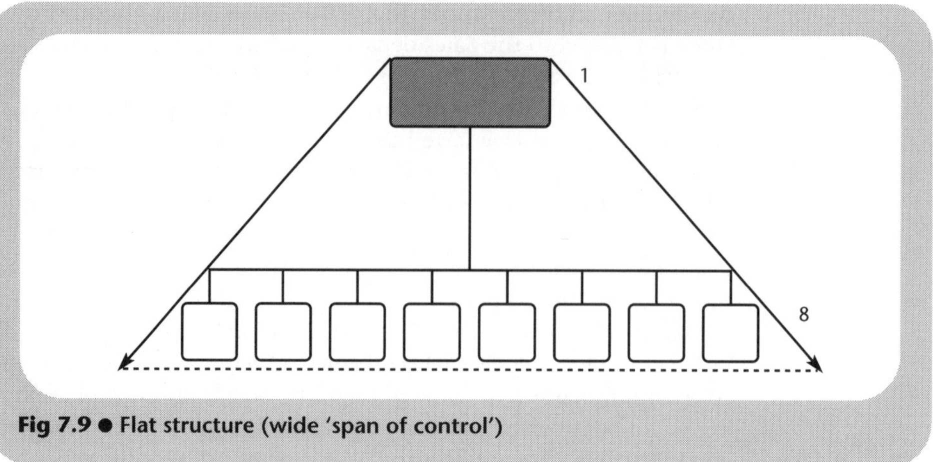

Fig 7.9 ● Flat structure (wide 'span of control')

problems of quality, stress. If a manager does not succeed in keeping a firm grip on the work to be conducted by others, it is possible to appoint one or more employees to whom part of the managerial and supervising tasks are delegated. When these extra managers are called in, a 'tall' or 'steep' organizational structure arises, as shown in Fig 7.10.

It will be obvious that the problem of the scope of management control must be examined in two directions:

- a horizontal direction: the number of employees a manager manages directly, that is the 'span of control';
- a vertical direction, the number of levels that can be effectively managed directly, that is the 'depth of control': how deep does the will of management penetrate into the different levels of the hierarchy.

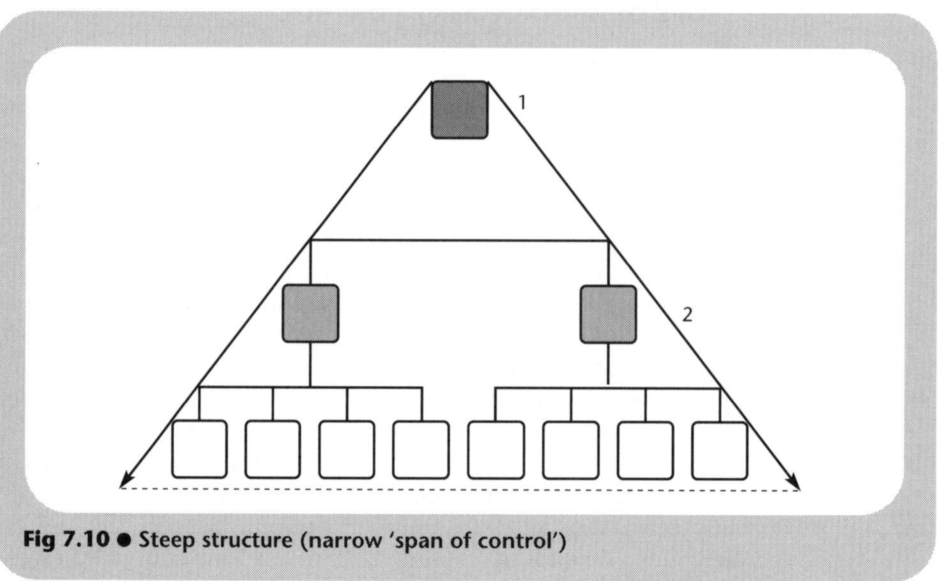

Fig 7.10 ● Steep structure (narrow 'span of control')

7.8.1 Scope of control = span of control + depth of control

The scope of manager control is limited, but, unfortunately there is no formula for working out how the control limiting number of sub-ordinates can be determined. The scope of control varies according to the situation, and depends on the personality of the manager, his willingness to delegate and his ability to have a lot of different things on his plate without losing any of them. The expertise and the time available to the manager also play a role, as well as his ability to associate with people. Willingness on the part of lower managers and operational employees to bear responsibility is very important as is their experience and education.

It is also important to examine whether there are possibilities for the employment of specialized staff and support services. And, in addition to all this, it makes a difference whether the work to be carried out is simple or complex, varied or monotonous, policy intensive or operational.

So it can be seen that as well as the manager and employees, the structure of the organization and the type of work are the chief determinants of the scope of control.

Exhibit 7.3

Delayering and effectiveness

A special study on delayering organizations (Keuning/Opheij, 1994) has described a number of studies into the relationship between the length of hierarchy of the organizational structure and its effectiveness. The results of these studies do not lead to the conclusion that a flat structure is, by definition, more effective than a tall structure. It is, however, possible to draw conclusions for a number of elements of the problem regarding the link between length of hierarchy and effectiveness.

1. The idea that the level of satisfaction of members of an organization is higher in organizations with a flat structure appears to be confirmed in the studies. This seems to apply, in particular, to managers at lower levels and to employees with a 'borderline function', such as salespeople. Unfortunately, no research has been carried out into the satisfaction of, for instance, production employees in tall and flat organizations. At the highest level, tall organizations appear to provide most satisfaction.
2. The effectiveness of flat structures is dependent on the situation. Flat structures are more effective than tall structures in a turbulent environment which is complex and constantly subject to change. In contrast, tall structures are better in a stable environment when information is clear.
3. Effective decision-making requires a certain measure of hierarchy. This appeared from the experimental study by Carzo and Yanouzas, among others. The organizations with a relatively high number of hierarchical levels performed better than their counterparts. The quality of the decision-making process in tall organizations was higher, because decisions were re-evaluated at various levels.

Source: Keuning and Opheij, *Delayering Organisations*, Pitman Publishing, 1994.

7.8.2 Guidelines

If the scope of control is exceeded, different measures can be employed to serve as a solution.

- Delegate more, i.e. delegate even more tasks to other employees where possible with the relevant authority, while still maintaining direct control and correction possibilities; this solution assumes preparedness to delegate (both wanting and being able to) as well as preparedness to bear more responsibility (both wanting and being able to).
- Redistribution of tasks within the existing levels of the organization, i.e. regroup tasks from F- to P-grouping (*see* Figs 7.1 and 7.2), in such a way that the natural coherence of activities is followed and that the necessity to co-ordinate from the top decreases because of a more intrinsic co-ordination.

If these measures are not sufficient, further steps can be taken.

- Call in specialized staff services, in which 'headwork' is delegated and better decisions can be made via the headwork of others; the manager can use the time which then accrues on his own behalf.
- Call in personal staff as 'assistant to'; then delegation of tasks can take place which stimulate optimal organization of the work of the manager; when these activities form a burden, they can be delegated, for example to an executive secretary; this saves work time such that the manager can pay more and better attention to his own necessary activities.
- Call in specialized support services, i.e. make use of expertise of others in the operational elements of management and execution to achieve better co-ordination, better working methods and so on; this then has a direct effect on elements of the executing task, so the manager will need to spend less time on that.

These measures stimulate the development of a flatter structure (Fig 7.11), whereby managers can actually manage more employees in the line effectively.

When these measures are not applied adequately there is another possibility: to expand the organization in a vertical direction, when a relatively tall structure arises (Fig 7.12).

It can therefore be seen that the calling in of more management layers is necessary in order to guarantee sufficient attention on the execution of operational tasks.

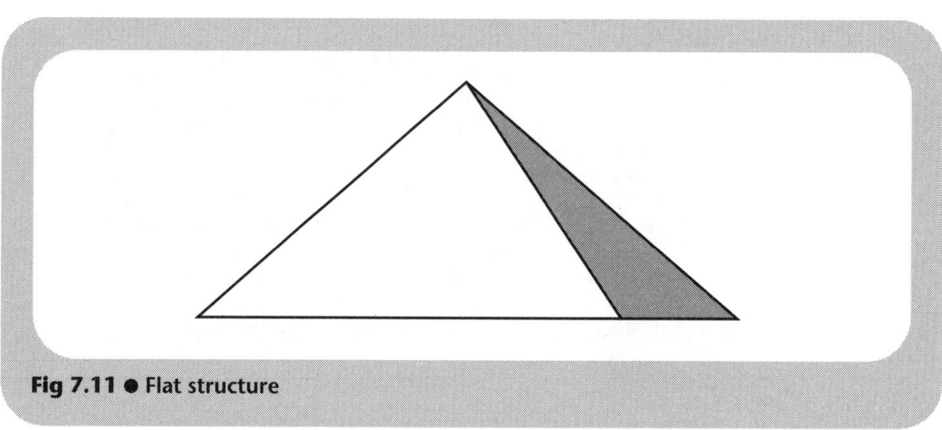

Fig 7.11 ● Flat structure

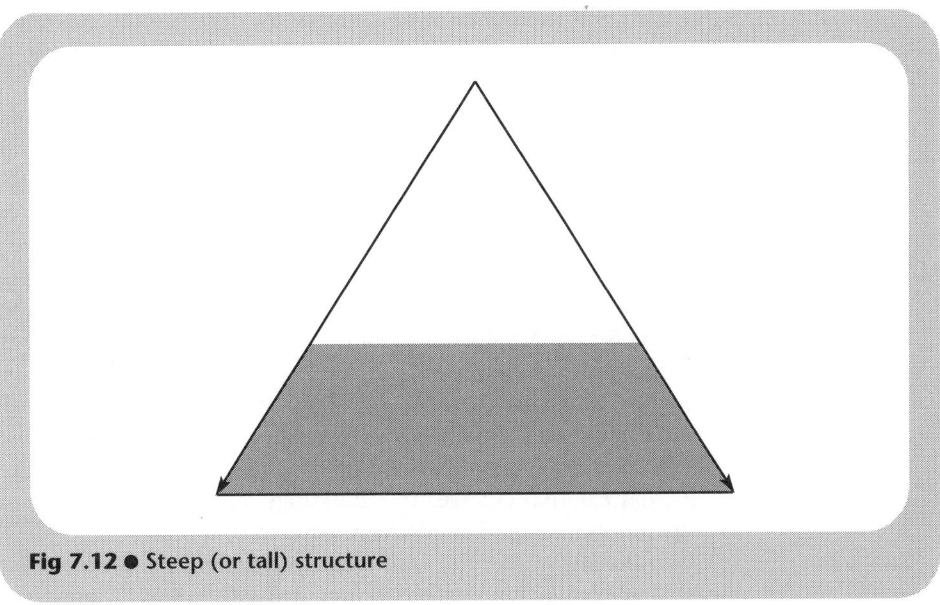

Fig 7.12 ● Steep (or tall) structure

7.9 ORGANIZATION IN DEVELOPMENT: REORGANIZATION AND PLANNING FOR CHANGE

Growth and development of organizations actually means that an organization becomes larger and more complex (*see* section 6.4). Even though the schemes described in this section stop the growth of a new representation of the organization structure, growth and especially development are dynamic processes. In this dynamic process information and energy are exchanged with the internal and external environment, as we have already seen in Chapters 2 and 3, in relationships with customers, unions, banks, groups of employees and managers. The changes which take place do not usually take place overnight. The speed of change can differ, as can the size of the change itself.

The process of change implies necessary uncertainty for those involved, managers and employees, which further means that in the approach to change intrinsic resistance to changes needs to be broken before the new situation arises, and can function effectively.

However, in the dynamics of organization 'crisis' is a more or less necessary condition for the new order and growth and development phase which fits better with the changed internal and external circumstances.

The obverse of this is that organizations often have insufficient energy and vision to renew themselves effectively. In this case it is probably better they be dismantled and abolished. If this seems too radical, then attempt to play for time via various emergency decisions. These may succeed, but more often than not fail, and include: the pumping in of a lot of money and energy from outside, and the purchase or import of external visions and people.

7.9.1 Organizational change: flexibility and capability

To bring about changes in the organization, the capacity for change of the organization on the one hand must be ascertained, with the willingness to change on the other hand. This will then determine whether an organization contains the seeds to grow into a new structure or whether it will start to show the tendency to regression ('back-sliding') (*see* Fig 7.13).

Capability and ability to change depend on the qualitative capacities of the members of the organization, on the knowledge and experience of whom the organization can have at its disposal. The financial and technical possibilities also determine much of what is possible in change and the time span in which this may be possible.

Willingness/preparedness to change depends more on the mentality present in the organization at the moment it decides to change. This willingness to change will be influenced by the degree to which management, possibly with the assistance of an external consultant, succeeds in causing those involved to realize that 'something has to change'.

On the one hand there is, generally speaking, a human resistance to change, because each change involves an element of 'uncertainty' for those involved. On the other hand change is normal and in most cases must occur. For a state of no change means that external changes in technology, markets and environment are not appropriately followed up and are being resisted in other cases.

Given the ability and the willingness to change, one problem with change remains: the kind of change envisaged. Change that coheres with growth can be introduced a lot more easily than change directed at downsizing the organization. Change in organizational structure interferes a lot more deeply than change in the market or in the product/market combination. The most difficult, and also the longest lasting, are those

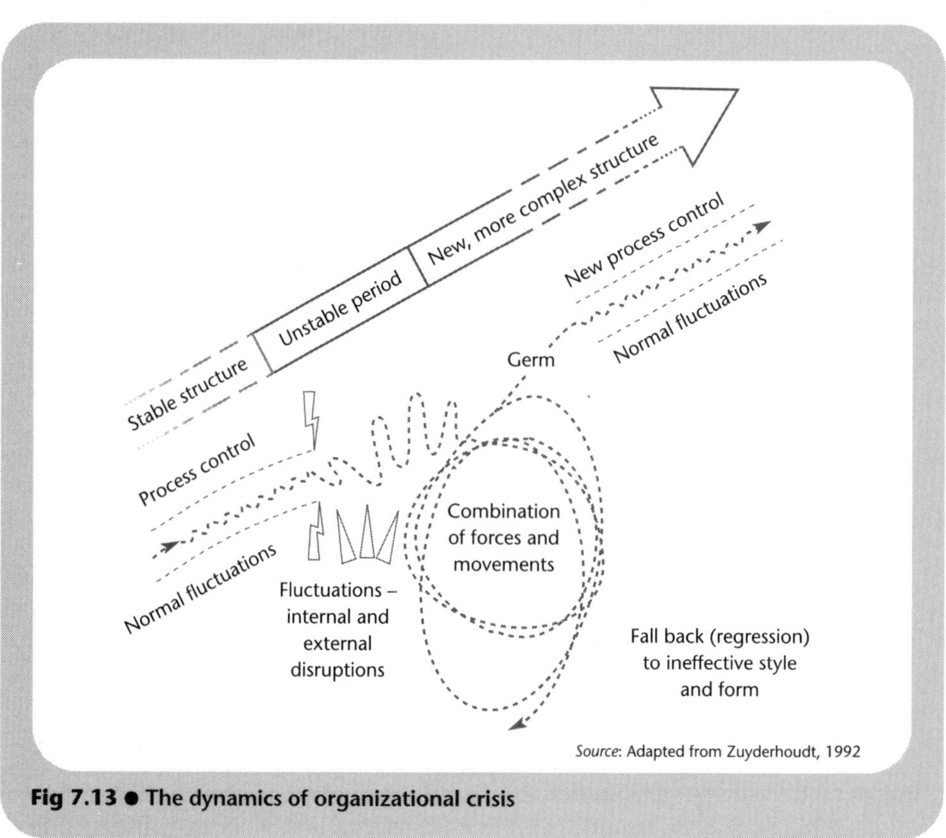

Source: Adapted from Zuyderhoudt, 1992

Fig 7.13 ● The dynamics of organizational crisis

changes which have to do with organizational culture, for here, of course, the style of leadership and the degree of openness will play a role. Sometimes these changes may be accompanied by a change in personnel, which is always difficult and time consuming. Such a change in the organization will always be necessary to arrive at the actual change that is intended (*see* section 9.6).

7.9.2 Organizational change: a process

An organization change process comprises the phenomena that occur in the transition from old to the new way of structuring and the execution of organization policies and the accompanying organizational processes.

Minicase 7.5

Organizations can be seen to 'the mass' of a machine compared to the mechanics. Due to a certain inertia changes do not occur correctly in the plotted direction. Time is necessary in order to bring about a change in the direction of the motion of a 'heavy' body. The more ponderous an organization, the more difficult it will be to set it in motion. In general the smaller organization has an advantage here: compare the time necessary for a course correction of a large tanker to that of a small yacht.

In reorganization an almost incidental and yet in-depth change is involved in trying to attain a desired situation at moment 2 out of a non-desired situation at moment 1. This change is schematically depicted in Fig 7.14.

In essence, transformation is change management; i.e. bringing an organization from an unconscious experience of the situation at T1 to a conscious experience of the new situation at T2. Change does not happen by itself and the change process cannot be left to itself. The variables are complex and the change process needs to be managed.

Transformation assumes a belief in the positive power of the organization and the people in it. As well as change of design of organizations, there is usually an explicit need for the cultural and mental transformation of organizations. This is not often brought about by means of a free transformation, but needs a leadership directed at change.

When the management makes statements about what the organization has to do as opposed to what the organization is able and wants to do, relevant data must be available: impressions, conversations, interviews, internal and external documents, etc. The management may consider the acquisition of this to be its own job, but eventually will have too little time for systematic investigation itself, and then the investigation will be conducted by internal consultants or external management consultants.

7.9.3 Situational factors and penetration of change

As we saw earlier a cultural change interferes more deeply in the organization than does a change in a product/market combination. It can further be seen that where influences from outside can bring about changes within the organization, there are also various changes that can occur intrinsically from within the organization itself. This concerns the degree to which change interferes in an existing structure and/or in behaviour, and refers to a difference in degree of penetration, varying from:

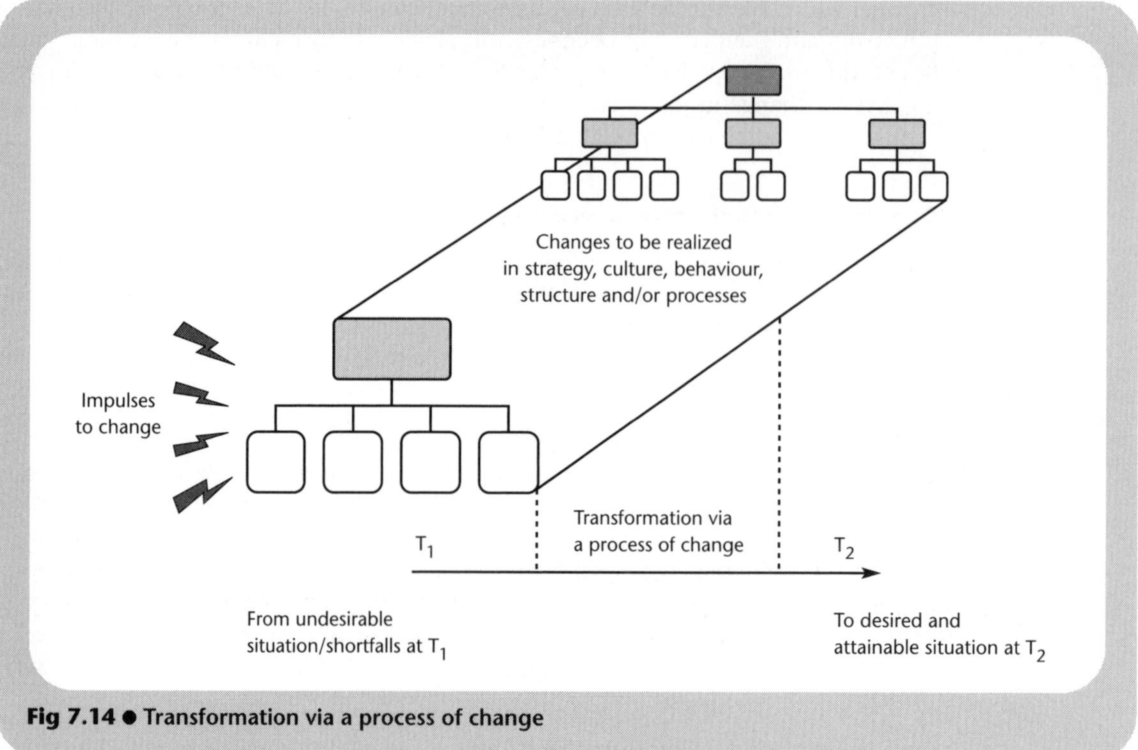

Fig 7.14 ● Transformation via a process of change

- superficial: a techno-organizational change that affects the people only moderately in their position and behaviour, for example, a new form which has to be filled out differently, learning new ways of working and/or a new work process;
- deep: a change in the role or function of one or more people in the company because of which established relation and function patterns are broken; one needs to learn a new role and to show new role behaviour in relation to the new function and also engage in new relationships;
- profound: changes in the behavioural pattern of individuals and/or groups in the organization, because of which one is affected in one's personality characteristics and in one's functioning; in-depth changes are concerned: adjusting to and learning new behavioural rules until these become self-evident in knowledge, skills and manifested behaviour.

7.9.4 Phase model of organizational change

A change process is enacted in five phases starting from a situation of seeming rest.

Phase 0: Organization in situation of seeming rest (quasi-balance)

When an organization is in a situation in which, at superficial observation, no changes seem to be occurring, it is said to be in a state of quasi-balance. External and internal circumstances continuously give rise to changes that engage change process of which one is unconscious. Change may also not be so clearly visible when it is occurring in an informal organization.

Phase 1: Breaking the quasi-balance – the need for change

The quasi-balance is broken when the impulse has such of an intensity that it cannot be ignored. Now the first phase of a conscious and planned change process starts up: namely the experience of the impulses and the consideration of what has to be done next. It becomes obvious that change has to start taking place. In this stage the first contact may be sought with an external consultant.

Phase 2: Preparing the change ('unfreezing')

Now changes in the techno-economic area need to be considered, determined and prepared. There is still a certain degree of incomprehension and misunderstanding about certain behavioural patterns among those involved in the change. In this phase, introduction of a consulting assignment takes place, as well as data collection (for example by interviews and group conversations) and the first propositions for change are being collated. Those involved have to get used to the idea of the coming change and for that reason have to be motivated, then trained and educated. In this phase resistance to change starts to emerge, which means that this phase can last rather a long time. People have to get used to the idea that changes in roles and relations will occur. In this phase there is an 'unfreezing', that is unlearning or deroutinizing of accepted and existing behavioural patterns.

Phase 3: Implementation and shifting ('moving')

During this phase, the necessary changes are carried through and the proposed plan is being realized. This is a phase of discovering and learning new organizational behaviour, the so-called 'moving' phase. Resistance will be noticeable and perceptible. For the individual this is a period of personal experience of the change, and a new role must be learnt. In an immediate crisis, change is quickly 'accepted' and carried through. It is important that change is managed and if necessary redirected by a change manager appointed for that purpose by the organization (possibly by an externally hired interim manager) in co-operation with the Personnel and Organization department.

Phase 4: Consolidation ('refreezing')

The last phase in the change process is the consolidation phase, a phase that is sometimes called integration. This is once more a period of rest, the new is not so new anymore and has even started to become routine. Emotionally the people have acquiesced in the new situation and think that the new situation has advantages over and/or works better than the old situation. There is an adjustment to the new situation. Those involved are not only technically able to work in the changed situation, but also stability has redeveloped. New behavioural programmes and rules have been adopted and things are in order again. This new situation shows only superficial rest since elements for further change in the future are built into the organization. The organization is in a situation of quasi-balance and is now back at phase 0 (*see* Fig 7.15).

So it can be seen that organizing and managing is a continuous process. It is the task of top management to assess the organization as a whole and in its different components (teams, departments, business units, divisions) and adjust it where necessary. In this way organizations change gradually. Seen over a number of years, a lot can have changed, the change process can be seen to have been in operation.

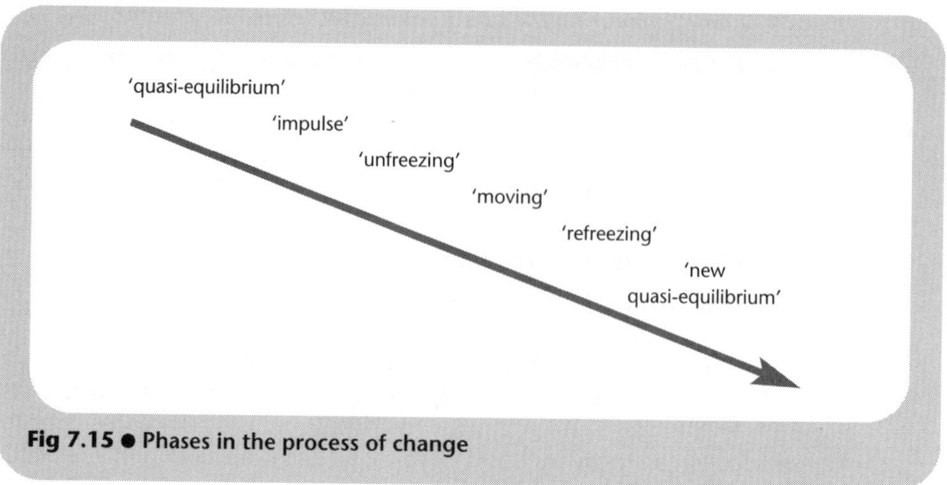

Fig 7.15 ● Phases in the process of change

7.9.5 Methods for realizing change

There are different ways of realizing a change process: it can occur by imposing change through power, by letting the changes take place through a learning process, or by allowing the need for change to be discovered by organization members themselves.

In cases of reorganization as a result of an immediate crisis, often a change imposed by the management team or the board of management will occur (by degree, by replacement or by a structural intervention). The speed of change will be high, the period between phase 1 and phase 3 will be short.

In the learning process approach to organization development the top of the organization has the conception that people are capable of solving their own problems and/or are able to adjust their roles and behavioural patterns. Change in a participative form is brought about via delegated power, for example via a group directed approach and/or by training and education. This approach assumes that sufficient time and resources are available and that problems are on the role and/or behavioural level. The leadership style is democratic or participative and preparedness to change and a strong desire to learn is deemed present in the people involved.

7.9.6 Coping with resistance to change

In every approach to change there must be discussion on the handling of resistance to change. It is, therefore, not unexpected that there are managers who look at and manage change from the resistance perspective. By knowing where the resistance is located, the change agent can adopt his strategy, and, as can be seen in Fig 7.16, opponents can possibly even become advocates.

With this approach, one assumes that every change starts with people who want something (sometimes only for the sake of change). When their ideas are accepted by the early adapters, a critical mass of advocates arises that ensures that the renewing activities are continued. Eventually a number of conservatives will be persuaded to adjust themselves to the change.

This approach also assumes that there will always be a number of unchangeable people. In their turn they can, however, be the initiators of the next renewal. Sometimes the actual development may be hindered by knockdown arguments that block every form of movement. Knockdown arguments are fallacies people use to bring to the fore something they are opposed to.

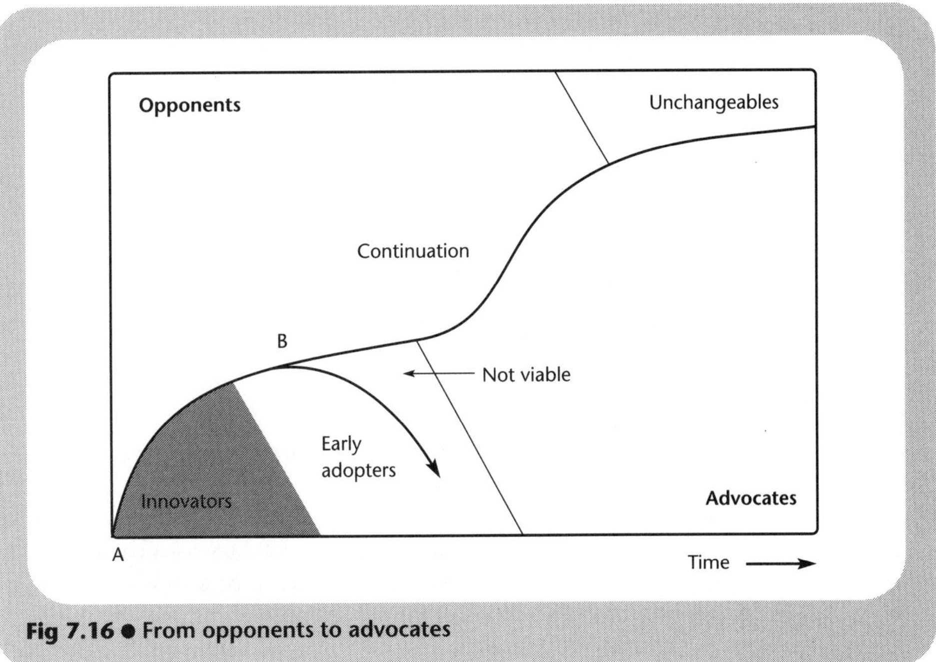

Fig 7.16 ● From opponents to advocates

Resistance is, to a degree, also a valuable phenomenon. It seems to be one of the mechanisms that protects the human being from chaos. Resistance can be seen as the mental activity which is directed at maintaining the existing situation because a certain value is attached to that. However, by holding onto the existing, the development of others and of oneself is, of course, limited severely.

The following activities are necessary to overcome resistance:

- disengaging (unfreezing)
  - recognizing the need to change;
  - investigating which obstacles to change exist;
  - thinking of the direction of change;
- changing (moving)
  - deciding on solutions/changes that can occur throughout the organization simultaneously at all levels;
- stabilizing (freezing)
  - making sure that the change is permanent;
  - making possible for the new situation to be maintained;
  - maintaining the new situation.

7.9.7 Recommendations from practice

In recent research on change within organizations, it has been implied that the degree of changeability of employees is not an insurmountable obstacle in the carrying through of change. Resistance to change does not come from the unchangeable character of the people involved, but rather from lack of understanding about what the change agents want, and why and how they want it. Based on this research, a number of change strategies can be formulated:

- 'put subjects to soak' beforehand, cause no thunder in a clear blue sky;
- clarify the change goals completely, do not sell nicely wrapped vagueness;
- offer participation and possibilities for corrective action, especially where personal matters are concerned;
- carry through change completely and communicate the effects of it by feedback;
- give employees the freedom to expound some of the change plans themselves.

7.9.8 'New' leaders

In order to set the organization in motion or to give form and direction to that motion, new techniques can be helpful. They may be used as a goal in themselves: 'We have never done anything new, let us try something now.' Another reason for applying a new technique is that a lot of new things have been tried already, but without much effect. In this situation, a fashionable hype or a new leader method can be exactly what one has been looking for for so long. Some old and forgotten techniques suddenly come to the fore again, sometimes in a new form. Other techniques are new to some managers because they only notice the technique when they need it. Some of these techniques have a scientific foundation, others may be little more than a slogan – not a concrete solution, but still very appealing.

Minicase 7.6

New management techniques and types – have you made your choice yet?

- flexibilization
- 'just in time' manager
- quality circles
- self-control
- delayering
- business process redesign
- unit management
- management by exception
- virtual organization

7.9.9 Change never ceases

Managers, directors and employees are more or less aware of the fact that there is no definite end point to change, but rather that change is a continuous process in which the points calling for attention are always changing. In Fig 7.17, this process is depicted schematically.

Points that call for attention in the process of change are:

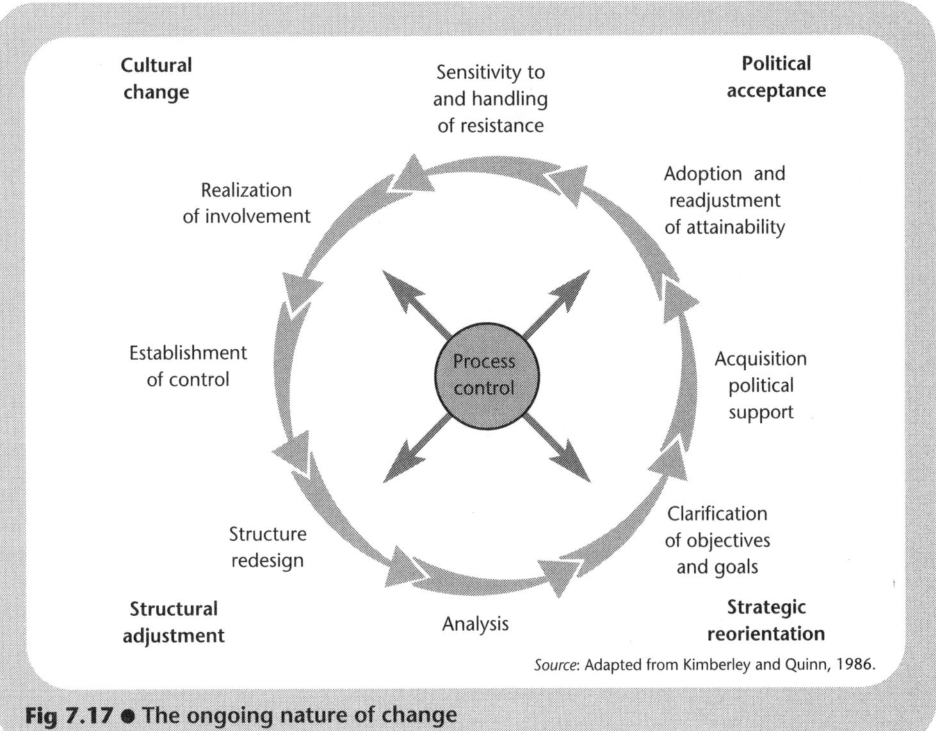

Source: Adapted from Kimberley and Quinn, 1986.

Fig 7.17 ● The ongoing nature of change

- strategic reorientation;
- political acceptance;
- cultural change;
- structural adjustment.

Strategic reorientation

Organizations that want to continue to survive have to react to developments in the market. Fundamental changes occur in a company that asks for fundamental choices, and the internal organization is no longer overtaken by the demands from the external environment. In this situation a financial and organizational analysis is desired, and an analysis of strengths and weaknesses as opposed to opportunities and threats from that external environment.

Minicase 7.7

In a certain company there is a continuous process of strategic reorientation. Without working to a specific plan, the board of directors decides in its regular meeting that it is time for a 'quantum leap'. When the time is right decisions on acquisition or merger are made relatively quickly.

In another company, there is support from a consultancy firm, in which one decides on strategic reorientation over a shorter or longer period.

Political acceptance

Making sharp analyses is but one step; carrying out the outcomes and clarifying new goals is at least as important a step in order to actually be able to carry through the changes. Opponents and advocates group themselves, so it is vital to convince those involved in order to ensure and enable the carrying through of changes. There will, however, always be some fervent opponents left. How should one go to try to persuade these people to change their mind? The process of acceptance is a political one, since the power and persuasive force play an important part. In many cases change only appears to be possible where there is external threat, internal dissatisfaction and a challenging perspective. 'Under pressure, everything becomes fluid', managers and consultants say.

Essential changes cannot be 'ordered per memo'. In order to attain a basis for acceptance, there must be mutual exchange of opinions and common interests, even if this does not seem to be effective.

Changes which aim at eliminating of functions and which lead to change of power bases have to be confirmed with a clear written decision. Then, instantly, the new positions become manifest. The build up of this basis is essential, not only in the grassroots organization itself, but also in the board of directors or supervisory council.

Cultural change

Starting something new implies departure from something old. This is an important point to consider when rethinking existing working methods and contemplating new ways of acting. It must be clear why the existing behavioural norms do not fit with the newly developed goal. The new ways of behaviour have to become inculcated, and a positive picture must exist of the new ways. Descriptions such as 'open', 'honest', 'customer-directed', 'clear' and 'result-directed' are all well and good, but content must be gained by means of example, otherwise they are merely empty words. It can, of course, be seen that not everything from the past is bad: essential values have to be maintained. When one shows oneself to be insensitive to employees' values formed in the past, resistance is only to be expected. Accomplishing new things together is the best way of realizing changes. Co-operating is the means, but not the goal in itself. By co-operating, change ensures a greater chance of success.

When insufficient attention is paid to this process of cultural change, the risk is high that changes in the structure will be frustrated 'via the back door': old ways of acting are resumed in the new structure.

Structural adjustment

In this and the preceding Chapter, we have covered the design and adjustment of the structure. Delayering or delegation, for example, is more than just the designing of a new structure, it is also the implementing and making it work, in itself a process that demands explanation, education, critically following, adjusting and helping.

From Fig 7.18 comes the idea that adjustment of the structure is never a goal in itself, but rather a consequence of other factors. The model seems to indicate that these areas of attention have to be undertaken successively: this is not always the case. The manager who manages the process has to divide his attention between these areas and may find he is occupied with more than one area of attention at any one time. That is why the central point in this model is involvement, direction and control. In order to implement change successfully, attention must be paid to all four subjects mentioned above.

SUMMARY

- In this chapter the different forms of assigning tasks, authority and the consequences of their application have been discussed. The criteria which play a role in the division of work and the grouping of tasks and functions have been extensively covered. 'New' forms have been identified which try to outweigh the advantages of 'old' methods.
- When arranging the structural design consideration needs to be made on whether the people who can be recruited do in fact fit into the designed functions. Reflection must ensue on the design of functions and on the consultative structure for employees, since the structure has to be effective and satisfying for the organization as well as for the employees.
- Examples have been shown of organizational systems of which use is being made in most of the organization creating a new structure. In the functioning of the organization different types of authority emerge, depending on the task assignments which have been assigned to different employees. It makes a difference, therefore whether an employee is situated in a managerial position in the line, or supports the line from a specialized staff position or from a support service. The type of authority assigned and required must always be made clear. This determines the potential for influencing others in their actions and indicates what one is responsible for and what one can be held responsible for by the higher management. The functioning of the line organization, the line staff organization and the line organization with specialized support services have all been examined in some depth.
- The three 'basis' relations, line relation, staff relation and functional relation, have been expanded with the horizontal and diagonal or lateral relation, and shown to be built-in co-ordination mechanisms within the hierarchy.
- Some classical organization principles have been expounded. 'Old' principles still have an effect on the modern organization of companies and institutions as far as the design of functions, delegation, co-ordination, assigning of authorities, and so on, are concerned. 'Old' principles are fulfilled differently and in a more modern way: by means of another type of leadership, by work restructuring, and, at the customer-directed, organizational levels, by means of a strong relation directedness and managing by management teams. Substitutes for hierarchy were also investigated.
- If he wants to delegate, a manager must do it right. There are a number of factors that can hinder optimal delegation. These lie in the personality of the manager, in the personality of the employee, in the structure of the organization and in the nature of the job. Following on from this notion, the problem of the scope of management control was covered. The manager himself has to ascertain whether the employees placed below him can be managed in a responsible way, in the horizontal direction as well as in the vertical direction. When the scope of control is exceeded or threatens to be exceeded, measures need to be taken. Measures to be taken need to be thought through in terms of their effects.
- After the departmentalization and the designing of divisions, the forming of tasks and functions and the assignment of authority, as well as the building-in of co-ordination mechanisms, an organizational structure as design is complete. The structure is the framework within which an organization functions, and changing circumstances within the organization can lead to changes in structure as well as in behaviour. Organizational change can comprise different types of changes, and it occurs in distinct phases. Differences in change approach need to be thought through carefully, and during the process of change management drive plays a central part.

DISCUSSION QUESTIONS

1. With reference to *Management in action* at the beginning of this chapter: How can one refer to the way of grouping tasks and design of functions in the new Open factory?
2. What are the disadvantages of the 'pure' line organization?
3. Is faster and more flexible production more possible with F-grouping or with P-grouping of tasks?
4. What are the conditions necessary for effective functioning of a flatter organization?
5. (a) How does the example of multi-skilling ('A glint of change in the gold mines', *see* p316) compare to such concepts as job enlargement, semi-autonomous teams/work groups, delayering and substitutes for hierarchy?
   (b) What effects of earlier methods of scientific management (*see* Chapter 2, p 55) do you recognize in South Africa? What role do the unions play in this regard?
6. Give your opinion on the following statement: 'Resistance to change is a healthy phenomenon, so – keep it that way!'
7. Do you agree with the following statement: Work consultation is a form of horizontal consultation between departments.
8. Comment on the correlation between resistance in the case of organizational change (Chapter 7), operational and conceptual learning (Chapter 4) and strategy determination (Chapter 5).

Management case study

Engineering a worldwide advance

For Percy Barnevik, the chairman and chief executive of third time overall winner ABB, the Swedish-Swiss engineering group, the biggest challenge is expanding his complex organisation into emerging markets.

What began seven years ago as a push into eastern Europe following the collapse of communism, has mushroomed into a worldwide advance, focused on the former Soviet Union and Asia as well as on eastern Europe. The lessons learned in the early 1990s from investing in factories in Poland and the Czech Republic are now being applied further east, including in Russia, India, China and south-east Asia.

Mr Barnevik says ABB's aim is the 'massive transfer of knowledge from west to east through our product lines ... The group is gravitating eastwards to eastern Europe and east Asia.'

When the expansion into eastern Europe started the company transferred skills to factories in Poland and the Czech Republic from Switzerland, Sweden and Germany. Now it is using Polish and Czech engineers to train staff at newly-acquired businesses in the Ukraine and Russia. Nor does it neglect smaller countries – for example, companies in Norway, Sweden, Denmark and Finland have been entrusted with supporting emerging businesses in Lithuania, Latvia and Estonia, in a Baltic co-operation pact.

The pattern is repeated in Asia. ABB's factory automation plant in Bangalore, India, is being used to train engineers for Thailand and elsewhere in south-east Asia. Responsibility for developing a low voltage apparatus factory in Beijing – a key product in a key country – has been entrusted to managers in Singapore. Staff sent to China are mainly young overseas Chinese, mostly recruited in Singapore and Hong Kong.

Meanwhile, in South America, the large Brazilian operations are used as a base for supplying trained staff to smaller countries and in Africa, South Africa is a base for developing ties with other states.

Mr Barnevik says that without decentralising responsibilities, such transfer of skills would be costly. 'It would be truly expensive if everything had to come through head office. Sending Americans, Swedes, or Germans everywhere would be expensive and less effective since they do not know the culture or the language.'

However, ABB would not be able to achieve this degree of decentralisation if it did not have long experience in running a decentralised operation and a suitable management system.

Mr Barnevik has run the group since its foundation in 1988 by trying to push responsibilities out of head office to individual country and business division managers. When he created the company by merging Asea of Sweden and Switzerland's Brown Boveri he put a strong emphasis on cutting head office staff (*see also* Exhibit 7.3) and decentralising, using methods already used at Asea, which he had run since 1980. But to keep the group from fragmenting Mr Barxievik built a matrix organisation in which managers report to a country manager and to a business area manager.

In the rush to decentralise, the group was broken into more than 60 businesses, but it has since been reorganised into 36 because some of the units were too small and overlapped too much.

Geographical expansion has brought about a rapid increase in country managers from 57 in 1990 to 94 today. There are also nine regional managers covering groups of countries where there is too little business as yet for country managers.

Mr Barnevik says that without the matrix it would have been difficult to expand so quickly. But he argues that the matrix alone does not explain the group's success in spreading to new countries. The solution is mobilising enough skilled people able to bring on staff in newly-emerging economies. Mr Barnevik says: 'One of my big jobs is to strengthen the glue – to make managers feel they are part of a family.' He cultivates 'group-mindedness' and encourages it with praise and bonuses for those who support operations in emerging countries.

Mr Barnevik denies that he shoulders too much of this burden himself. 'People say that. But with every year that passes there are more and more people who are group-minded.'

That conviction stems from the fact that many of the group's most dynamic customers are located outside its traditional home in western Europe. These customers are now driving the group's growth.

Source: *Financial Times*, 18 September 1996.

continued overleaf

Management case study continued

Percy Barnevik passes the baton

Göran Lindahl must push ABB faster into emerging markets

Jetting around the globe assembling and fine-tuning a vast business empire, Percy Barnevik has long seemed like 'a human perpetual motion machine,' as one observer put it. But even the chief of Zurich-based giant ABB Asea Brown Boveri Ltd. seems to have his limits. On Oct.10, 1996 the 55-year-old Barnevik said he would step down after eight years as president and CEO, turning over the reins to longtime sidekick Göran Lindahl. Barnevik will remain as nonexecutive chairman of the maker of power and other heavy equipment. 'All the big acquisitions, the 70-to-80 hour weeks, have been a tremendous strain,' Barnevik said.

What will Barnevik do next? Ruling out seeking another CEO slot, he says he will be a 'discussion partner and coach' for senior management. His easing off at ABB may let him play an even bigger role in the Swedish and European business and political worlds. He chairs a group advising European Union President Jacques Santer on competitiveness and also holds the chairmanships of steelmaker Sandvik and construction giant Skanska as well as that of ABB.

Source: *Business Week*, 28 October 1996.

CASE QUESTIONS

1. How would you understand and explain the functioning of the ABB matrix organization as described by Mr Barnevik in 'Engineering a worldwide advance' (see p358)?
2. What statements about centralization and decentralization would you make in the case of ABB? (In this regard you can use the guidelines and theorectical framework as laid out in sections 7.6 and 7.6.1.)
3. (a) What methods for change would have been used, in your opinion, in ABB's history from 1987?

   (b) What effect regarding the centralization–decentralization issue might the new leader Göran Lindahl have on ABB's further development into emerging markets?

Part four

People at work

Once the strategic position (Part two) of the organization has been determined and the organizational structure designed (Part three), the co-operation of the people within the organization has to realize the whole. In Part four we will look into the 'people' aspect of the organization, the people who work together in this goal-realizing co-operative unit.

In Chapter 8, the motivation of the individual, behaviour in groups and the reward of organization members are discussed in relation with the organization goals. The possibility for individual development is examined, as well as variations on the theme of 'career'. The way employment and development of human capabilities are integrally taken up in an organization's policy is known as 'human resources management'.

In Chapter 9 managing other people is the initial topic. The personal function of the manager is discussed and differences in the style of management are described. Managing means that a manager sometimes has to resolve problems of co-operation and lack of it between organization members – conflict handling and resolution. A manager always operates within an established organizational culture, but can try to change that culture so that it better contributes to the realization of the chosen strategy.

Principles of management

Motivating people

Part one • Management and society

Chapter 1
Manager and management

Chapter 2
Management theory and organizational development

Chapter 3
Organizations and environment

Part two • Strategic management and the learning organization

Chapter 4
Decision making and creativity

Chapter 5
Strategy formulation and strategic management

Part three • Designing and structuring the organization

Chapter 6
Designing the organization

Chapter 7
Structuring tasks for groups and individuals

Part four • People at work

Chapter 8
Motivation, work and career

Chapter 9
Leading, motivation and communication

Part five • Planning, control and information management

Chapter 10
Operational planning and control

Chapter 11
Information management and information technology

Chapter 12
Managerial process control: functional processes and process redesign

Chapter 8

Motivation, work and career

LEARNING OBJECTIVES

After studying this chapter, you should be able to:

- describe the key variables of individual behaviour;
- describe the different aspects of team forming;
- identify some motivation theories;
- explain the relationship between motivation, productivity and design of functions;
- describe the notion of 'empowerment';
- explain the notion of 'human resources management', both in the context of daily activities as well as in relation to the personnel instruments;
- clarify the phases input, throughput and output in relation to the personnel process, including the personnel instruments which are at management's disposal;
- describe different reward systems;
- identify the different concepts of 'management development'.

Management in action

Close the personnel department?

'Without being provocative, when I meet line managers I say to them that they should close the personnel department,' says Arne Olsson, director of corporate staff management resources at electrical engineering company ABB. 'If they did that they would be forced as a line manger to be involved directly with personnel matters. Line managers are the real personnel manager.'

Olsson's comment touches a raw nerve among personnel and human resources managers. They suffer from what one consultant describes as a 'continual neurosis' over the value of their expertise – and the current wave of corporate change, restructuring and 'delayering' is doing nothing to soothe their nerves.

Most large companies are in no doubt that people are their greatest asset. As the concept of 'the knowledge-based company' comes nearer to reality, staff qualifications, training and motivation will be increasingly vital to future growth. This applies even in traditional industries such as food. 'I believe that quality of staff will be one of the most important factors in keeping a competitive edge in the years to come,' said Helmut Maucher, chairman and chief executive of Nestlé, in a recent address to the Kellogg School of Management in the US.

If human resources professionals are a corporation's experts on managing its greatest asset, why are they worried? First, as Olsson indicates, if people are a company's prime resource, then it is line managers who must bear responsibility for them. They alone are in a position to make key decisions, while human resources managers tend to be handed the resulting problems without having the power to solve them. This explains why, in some of Europe's most prosperous countries, human resources can have such an apparently low status – and no status at all in some companies that seen to prosper without a personnel function.

According to a survey of 11 countries conducted by a group of nine European business schools and the accounting and consultancy firm Price Waterhouse, the human resources head is represented on the main board in 87% of large Swedish companies, but in only 19% of German companies and 18% of Italian companies. In no more than half the enterprises in any country are human resources involved from the outset in the formulation of corporate strategy.

Source: *International Management*, April 1994.

INTRODUCTION

In organizations oriented on market and society, new wishes constantly arise and higher demands are made – on the one hand by customers, on the other by the employees of an organization. The effectiveness of an organization demands flexibility, motivation, involvement, creativity and innovative ability. Employees value interesting work, more responsibility, participation, discretionary decision making and a tailor-made reward. Modern human resources management requires that all these elements be included in a consistent common policy (sections 8.7 and 8.8). The statement that the human factor in organizations has become 'the' important factor, is in itself, however, an insufficient basis for operating effectively. For success, one also needs to understand the behaviour of the individual organization members in order to influence and direct that behaviour in such a way that the organizational goals can be attained more readily. Insight into individual behaviour forms the starting point, therefore some notions from psychology are examined, then we turn our attention to the behaviour of groups in an organization (sections 8.3 and 8.4), and motivation (sections 8.5 and 8.6). There is a close examination of the relationship between design of functions, productivity and motivation, important since the content and structure of a function can influence an employee's effort.

8.1 ● KEY VARIABLES IN INDIVIDUAL BEHAVIOUR

In a model derived from Robbins (Fig 8.1), it can be seen that an individual enters an organization with a relatively fixed number of values and attitudes, and an established personality. The perception of the working environment is of influence on the degree of motivation and on what somebody learns at and from his job and also of influence on the behaviour of the employee. Talent has been added to the model in order to show that behaviour is influenced by talent and skills at the moment of entry into an organization. Seen by itself, however, talent is not a key variable of behaviour and so is not separately clarified. With this model, Robbins gives an extensive explanation that has been summarized briefly here.

8.1.1 Values

Values reflect basic convictions, which mean for the individual or for society as a whole, certain behaviour or a certain situation is preferred over the opposite behaviour or situation. They reflect someone's personal ideas about what is good and/or desirable or bad and/or undesirable.

Value systems give mutual priority to values, and therefore they reflect the relative interest an individual attaches to such values as freedom, pleasure, self-respect, honesty, obedience, equality, etc. Everyone distinguishes values and those values influence attitudes and behaviour because they are stable and, usually, long lasting.

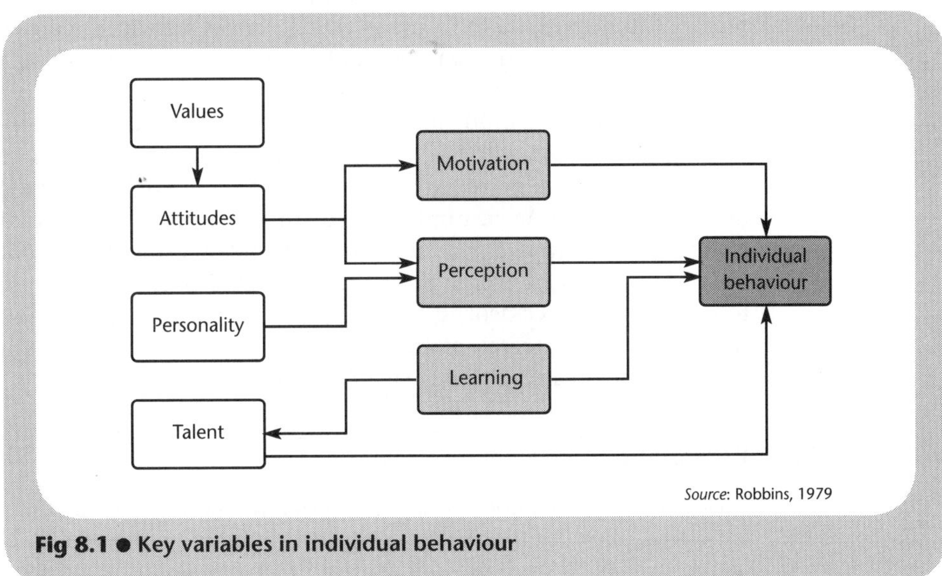

Fig 8.1 ● Key variables in individual behaviour

Minicase 8.1

Based on their values people can be grouped, the value scale itself (levels 1–7) reflecting the value hierarchies of its designer.

Level 1: reactive. These people are unconscious of the fact that they and others are human. They react to basic physiological needs. Rare in organizations. The best example of this type is a new-born baby.

Level 2: tribal thinking. Characteristic of this type is the high degree of dependency. There is a strong influence of tradition, and authorities exercise a lot of power.

Level 3: egocentric. These people believe in pure individualism. They are aggressive and egoistic and react mainly to power.

Level 4: conforming. These people have a low tolerance of ambiguity, have trouble accepting people with other values and want everybody else to adopt their values.

Level 5: manipulative. These people try to attain their goal by manipulating people and things. They are materialistically oriented and try actively to attain higher status and recognition.

Level 6: sociocentric. These people find it more important to associate well with other people and to be liked, than to progress. They hate manipulation, materialism and conformism.

Level 7: existential. These people are very tolerant of ambiguity and of people with other values. They are distinct opponents of inflexibility, restrictive policy, status symbols and the arbitrary use of authority.

Source: Hierarchy of seven values and life styles (derived from Graves, 1970).

8.1.2 Attitudes

Attitudes are judgements about things, people or events, in a positive or a negative sense. Attitudes are not the same as values. Values are wider, more comprising. An attitude is more specific. Human beings have thousands of attitudes, of which the most important for an organization are: job satisfaction (attitude with regard to the job), involvement (degree of identification with the job), and dedication (degree of loyalty to and identification with the organization). One of the most important aspects of attitudes is that people strive for *consistency*. The theory of *cognitive dissonance* states that human beings try to minimize the dissonance between contradicting images. An example of cognitive dissonance would be: 'Management is an obligatory subject in my education' and 'I do not think that management is a nice subject.' Someone's wish to reduce dissonance depends on the importance of the elements which cause the dissonance, on the degree of influence which someone believes he has over those elements and on any advantage which comes from dissonance.

8.1.3 Personality

Personality is the combination of psychological characteristics used to classify individuals. The following four personality attributes are used to define behaviour in more detail: locus of control, authoritarianism, Machiavellianism and risk acceptance.

Minicase 8.2

Personnel in the banking and insurance sectors, especially the 'front office' personnel, need to possess a certain attitude in accordance with the market orientation and the drive for quality of service. This can be initially handled via recruitment and selection of personnel, and in addition should be a subject of training. The service attitude is divided in three groups:

1. technical knowledge of content (professional knowledge and skills);
2. associating with clients and quality of service;
3. working in teams.

One can speak of an internal 'locus of control' when people believe that they can control their own destiny. People who think that whatever happens is by accident or luck work from an external 'locus of control'. It has been shown that employees who are to a high degree driven externally, alienate from their work sooner and are less involved in their work than more internally driven people.

One can speak of authoritarianism when someone thinks that status and power differences belong in an organization. Authoritarian-oriented people are intellectually rigid, are quick in judging others, have respect for higher placed persons, exploit lower placed colleagues, are suspicious and are resistant to change.

Machiavellianism is closely related to authoritarianism. Someone who is strongly Machiavellian-oriented is pragmatic, keeps an emotional distance and believes that the end justifies the means.

People who have high risk acceptance make decisions more quickly and based on less information than people who tend to take little risk.

Individuals vary widely in their personality and that is also true for jobs and functions. The 'theory of personalities' states that the job satisfaction of an employee, and his tendency to change jobs, depends on the degree to which his personality is in harmony with his working environment.

8.1.4 Motivation

In manufacturing and service areas, motivation of personnel is of decisive importance. Motivation is for a large part derived from the meaningfulness offered by the organization. Motivation is the will to do something, and is influenced by the degree in which certain behaviour can satisfy the needs of an individual. A need is seen as an observed physiological or psychological lack due to which a certain something is appealing. This motivation process is depicted in Fig 8.2. Motivated employees can be seen simultaneously to put themselves under pressure, and to start activities to reduce this pressure.

One of the widest known motivation theories is based on the so-called 'hierarchy of needs' by Maslow. The hypothesis is that every individual has a hierarchy of five basic needs (*see* section 8.5.1 and Fig 8.5). When one need has been satisfied, the next comes to the fore. So a need which has been sufficiently satisfied, no longer works in

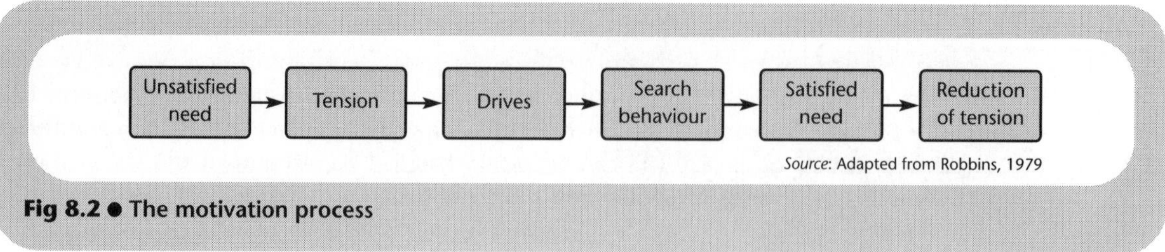

Fig 8.2 ● The motivation process

the motivation process. Social needs and the need for respect and self-actualization belong to a higher order and can be satisfied by the human being itself. Other theories on motivation may examine one aspect of motivation or more.

Some of these theories will now be discussed briefly, so that some points for further attention can be derived.

The theory of the three needs states that there are three incentives or needs in work: the need for performance, the need for power and the need for affiliation. Organization members do not, however, form a homogeneous group: they not only differ in their needs, but also in their attitudes, personality and in other important personal variables. These differences need to be taken into account in the design of functions and the assigning of tasks and functions.

The goal theory stresses that intentions, expressed as goals, can be an important source of labour motivation. In this respect it holds that specific and complex goals improve performance more than simple and generally formulated goals. Further, attention must be paid to the degree of participation in the determination of goals and the provision of feedback information about the realization of these goals.

The equity theory states that employees weigh the 'input' and the 'outcome' of their work against one another and compare the results to those of the categories of reference: if people think that their input/outcome ratio is unbalanced in comparison to that of others, tension arises, and since people strive for justification, this tension works in motivating the employee.

The expectancy theory assumes that the power which drives behaviour in a certain direction depends on the power of the expectation that certain behaviour will lead to a certain outcome and on the degree to which that outcome is valued by the individual. There are three variables in this theory: attractiveness, the relationship between results and reward and the relationship between effort and result. These three variables will have to be met if the individual is to be strongly motivated. In section 8.5.3 a more detailed explanation of the expectancy theory is under scrutiny.

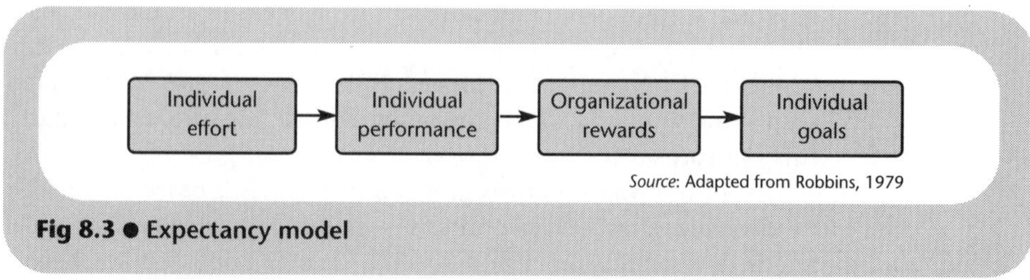

Fig 8.3 ● Expectancy model

8.1.5 Perception

Perception is the process in which individuals interpret sensory impressions, so that they can assign meaning to the environment. Research into perception has shown time and again that when individuals observe the same thing each interprets it differently. A number of factors contributes to perception and may sometimes disturb an earlier determined 'image'. These factors may lie within the observer, in the object which is being observed or in the context of the situation in which the perceiving takes place.

People judge one another continuously, and because they do not absorb everything they see, they select. Selective perception allows the human being to place others quickly, but carries the risk of an incorrect image being formed. It is easier, therefore, to judge others when it is assumed that they are like the observer. These assumed similarities lead to the judgement of others depending more on the person who observes than on those observed. This leads to stereotyping when someone is judged based on the perception of the group to which he belongs.

An impression of someone based on only one characteristic gives rise to the so-called 'halo-effect'. The one characteristic then influences the judging of other characteristics. For example, if an employee inspires confidence and is trustworthy, there is a tendency to judge his other characteristics positively.

8.1.6 Learning

Almost all human behaviour has been learned. When an organization wants to explain, predict or control human behaviour in all its complexity, it must understand how human beings learn. In Chapter 4 we saw that learning is every more or less permanent change in behaviour based on experience obtained. In section 4.5 we extensively discussed the learning of individuals and the learning organization. For more detailed coverage of the last key variable, refer back to Chapter 4.

8.2 THE EMPLOYEE OF THE FUTURE AND CHANGING WORK BEHAVIOUR

Making work and getting people to co-operate within an organization in the realization of organizational goals will remain a management task of prime importance in the future. Organizational goals will be formulated from interaction with the employees and with the environment. This requires other patterns and other leadership styles within the organization than were, in the past, expected. Possibilities will have to be created for development, initiative and entrepreneurship on all levels. This is in line with the higher education level of the employee, and is consistent with the wish to bear more responsibility oneself.

8.2.1 Organizational context and the changing organization

In recent research into changes in employees' wishes and the consequences of that for management, the following is signalled with regard to the 'new' employee. Changes which were signalled deal especially with the increased work pressure, higher educational demands and individualization. The demands made on the people increase, the number of jobs in the office decreases and because of individual performance planning, the sense of compulsion to perform increases. Work is taken home, study is undertaken at home and there are meetings outside work hours. The importance of going on courses and gaining certificates increases. New employees are better educated. Performing well is in itself not sufficient enough anymore for a higher position on the function scale. Respect for older employees with long service time and experience decreases. Higher functions become more difficult to attain for home-grown workers; these go to trainees and other more educated people 'from outside'.

The orientation shifts from the team onto the individual, loyalty is under pressure, internal entrepreneurship becomes the central issue and attaining of 'own targets' becomes over important. This is a further consequence of horizontal differentiation (F-grouping).

The reaction of most people involved in this will be a mix of acceptance and resistance. One individual may become convinced of the strategy to be followed and is prepared to devote himself to this. Another thinks, however, that the 'changes have gone too fast' and that too little attention has been paid to the interests of the individual employee. Yet another, ambitious, experiences the new demands as a challenge and sees possibilities for a career improvement.

Minicase 8.3

In a bank where such an experience has been observed there is a small group which actually dropped out. The employees concerned are averse to all changes and do not feel like 'letting themselves go crazy' any longer. These people – in their early thirties with at least ten years' service – are situated at the top of their ability and they get burned out. There are not a lot of possibilities left within the bank, and outside the bank nobody is prepared to see them: 'Sir, I am already over thirty; who wants me now?'

The problems of the older employee do not start at forty-plus.

A large group at best tries to keep up with the changes. This group is well motivated, but gets into difficulties because of the increased pressure: in addition to a full-time job, these people also have to run a household. They get stuck between work pressure and work motivation on the one hand and their domestic responsibilities on the other. They are also a little anxious: 'The work poses more and more demands, impinges on my spare time, but what do I actually get back from it?'

Only a few young employees are not really bothered by this; they have never known differently.

Source: de Korte and Bolweg 1994.

8.2.2 Opinions on good middle management

The opinions about good management are unequivocal. The manager has to give his attention to his people, must value the employee as a human being and be able to listen well. He has to keep them informed, involve them in policy, give them responsibility and make them enthusiastic. He has to give compliments and appraisal, back his employees up, be clear and honest, divide tasks well and be able to co-operate when necessary.

A bad manager pays attention to production, does not keep his people informed, keeps them dangling and pushes off work. Favouring 'what comes from outside' and bad education and coaching are also flaws.

When good managers are running operations, the employees are enthusiastic about their job, the job is challenging and varied, with the chance to climb and with educational programmes to be attended. There is an open, informal culture, more than enough opportunities for initiative and the organization is flat and only slightly hierarchical. The managers are aware of the fact that changes in strategy make other greater demands on the employees. In recruiting new employees a new employee–profile is sought: young, ambitious, well educated, self-confident and full of initiative. Older employees also have to start to show this kind of behaviour. There is only limited room for people of the old school. There is a choice: adapt to the new demands or search for something else.

A survey of the 'new' employee concluded: ' ... the new employees are an obvious consequence of a new recruiting and selection policy of the organization and in part of the developments which were "reinforced" by the employer. Existing social cultures are broken up and it is not unthinkable that as a consequence, existing employees assume an attitude which is similar to that of the new employee. Spontaneous development has been sparked by the new employees, reinforced by management. One can certainly not speak of autonomous development in the present work population.'

8.3 ● GROUPS AND THE ORGANIZATION

Organizations as co-operative units comprise individuals who, within departmentals, mostly have their own task which has to be conducted. The 'phenomenon' group in organizations has its own specific characteristics. A group in the psychological sense is formed by a number of people, who are in contact with each other, who are conscious of each other and consider themselves to be a group. As a consequence, the size of a group is determined by the possibility of mutual contact and mutual consciousness. Thus formulated, any arbitrary number of people is not a group simply *per se*. Only if there is the interaction and the awareness of each other does notion come into effect. A work group, a committee, a sub-department, other informal relationships within an organization all satisfy the demands of the notion.

Different groups can be distinguished in an organization:

- formal groups:
  - permanent: board of management, work group, committee;
  - temporary: 'task force' for problem-solving, a project group, a committee;
- informal groups: arise from the place of employment and the nature of the job in combination with the needs of people for social contact, companionship, acknowledgment; this informal group forming can serve as a supplement to the formal organization.

Informal groups can have different manifest forms:

- horizontal group: informal interaction between operational employees, between managerial employees or between other organization members who have more or less the same rank and are employed in more or less the same field;
- vertical group: a group which is composed of members of different levels in one specific department. These groups usually form a key function in the upward and downward directed communication. One employee knows another from before or is regularly in work contact;

- mixed group: a group of which the members originate from different ranks, from different departments and from different geographical areas. This is, for example, the group that arises in the fulfilment of specific functions not yet taken care of within the organization, e.g. the maintenance of equipment. This is also the group which champions a specific common interest, to which too little attention is paid in the formal organization.

Informal organizations may arise spontaneously and rest on personal relationships and mutual dependency. There is often mutual emotional support and a positive supplementary function of the informal organization in the form of a useful and complementary communication network. A formal group, just like an informal group, can provide a number of psychological functions:

- the possibility of satisfying the sense of belonging as a human need, need for companionship, affinity and support;
- a way to develop, enlarge or confirm an identity and self-respect;
- a way to confirm or test the reality standard of points of view; for example, how others see the boss;
- a means to enlarge security or to exercise power with regard to a common 'enemy' or source of threat;
- a means to get done work which should actually be conducted by other members of the group.

Thus it can be seen that most groups have a formal as well as an informal function. They provide for the needs of both the organization and individual members. Groups, be they formal or informal, influence the behaviour of individuals. Groups put pressure on individuals with regard to behaviour which is to be learned, which means that individuals usually conform to group habits and standards. The individual who does not wish to adapt, is under increased pressure and may be placed outside the group (sometimes with physical violence) or is treated as deviant and an outcast.

From a managerial position, these functions of the group need to be recognized in order to deploy them in a positive sense. In cases of resistance these functions can be used to great advantage. Key figures from certain groups can be approached via preliminary consultations to explore how proposals will be received, and what adjustment of plans may be necessary. Important group members in committees can stimulate a certain degree of involvement at a very early stage.

8.3.1 Organization, group and individual: goals and conflicts of interest

Within organizations conflicts of interest are actually built in. It is expected of every work group or individual that these perform their job as well as possible and devote themselves to their own departmental interests. There is also a 'battle' over the available built-in resources, while everyone expects to be rewarded for effort taken. These forms of conflicts of interest, which are built in by the way of division of tasks and functions, can be seen as 'functional' conflicts of interest. However, as soon as these conflicts do not make a positive contribution to the functioning of a part of an organization, these conflicts of interest become dysfunctional and damaging.

Smooth functioning of an organization can be served by functional organizational conflict. Conflicts of interest and disagreement are, to a certain degree, desired in order to search for and to find the best solution or to stimulate the delivering of the best performance. This demands openness, exchange of information and opinions and mutual trust in case of problem-solving. Contradictions become damaging, however, as soon as they become a goal in themselves and escalate, since information will be held back and there will be mutual distrust.

The goals of the organization are, of course, determined by people. Organizations do not have goals originating from themselves. These are set by individual people or by groups involved in the weal and woe of the organization or department. A goal indicates a desired result or a situation to be attained. Usually an organization has more than one goal at any one time. Every organization, every department and every individual employee has specific personal goals with their own specific results to be attained. In all contradictions between the different interests there is at least one common interest, namely the preservation and continuation of the organization, for the survival of this source enables all to realize at least a part of their own interest. For that reason something has to be sacrificed. But something is gained in return. It may be difficult to come to a decision in an organization, for example, in case of reorganization, relocation of a subsidiary, closure of a company department. Differences in interests, feelings and experiences may play a part in this. A formal voting procedure can be introduced, but this is not always advisable. A common form of solution is the compromise. Agreement is reached because everyone drops some part of his demands, wishes and desires. In fact the original difference remains and it cannot be ruled out that it returns later. It is best to strive for a 'new solution', in which everyone can find satisfaction and because of which the original contradiction is eliminated. Often the time is lacking for this, and also just as often the will, so that in many cases the 'solution' arises by means of domination of the minority over a majority, or arises by the closure of a compromise (*see* section 9.5).

8.3.2 Group behaviour and productivity

People in groups behave differently than when they are alone. Furthermore, the behaviour of individuals in groups is more than the sum of the behaviour of the individuals separately. We have defined a group as two or more mutually dependent individuals interacting together and consciously considering themselves to be a group. Groups can be formal as well as informal. The most general reason to participate in a group is related to the needs for security, status, self-actualization, power, and sense of belonging and to attain the determined goals.

The behaviour of a group can be explained and predicted with the help of the three so-called 'contingency' variables: individual personality characteristics, group size, and the degree of heterogeneity between group members. Heterogeneous groups work more efficiently than do homogeneous. There is a positive relationship between general characteristics which are judged positively in western culture and productivity, morale and mutual solidarity of the group. Groups of odd numbers, which are large enough to receive a variety of inputs, yet small enough to control the dominance of individual group members, resist the forming of sub-groups and prevent a long decision time, are those that generally function best.

Group cohesion and productivity

The degree to which group members feel attracted to one another, and underwrite the goals of the group, is called cohesion. This can be influenced by factors such as time spent together, the way of initiation into the group, group size, external threat and previous successes. Research shows that groups with a higher degree of cohesion often are more effective (*see* Fig 8.4).

Coincidence of group goals and the organization's goals	Cohesion: High	Cohesion: Low
High	Large increase in productivity	Slight increase in productivity
Low	Decrease in productivity	No significant effect on productivity

Fig 8.4 ● Relationship between cohesion and productivity

Where the relationship is more complex, a high degree of cohesion may not always be positive. In the first place, a high degree of cohesion is a cause as well as a consequence of high productivity. In the second place, the relationship between cohesion and productivity depends on the degree to which the attitude of the group coincides with the formal goals or with the goals of the total organization of which the group is a part.

8.4 THE POWER OF TEAMS

Teams can deliver high performance levels for a long time when a number of prior conditions have been met. Structural frameworks (clear task and clear assignment of authority), 'human resource' frameworks (a quantitatively and qualitatively sufficient staffing and reasonable rewards), the political framework (sufficient power and influence) and symbolic frameworks need to be examined here. The symbolic frameworks, especially with regard to the bringing in and maintaining of a common and binding culture, usually receive scant attention.

Elements of the symbolic framework around a group which has to deliver a high performance can be found in special thresholds built in for entrance into a group, and in the diversity within the group. Other elements which can stimulate a close cohesion are: an own language, leadership through 'role model' or exemplary behaviour, humour and play for discharge and stimulation of creativity, the development of an own culture through rituals and ceremonies (*see* sections 1.7 and 9.6).

8.4.1 Interacting forces

In the management of groups, four frameworks can be distinguished to drive at a more effective group performance:

- The structural framework emphasizes rationality, efficiency, planning and policy. Structure-directed managers value analysis and data, keep track of end results, give clear

Exhibit 8.1

Transnational teams, communication and decision making

Many transnational teams must communicate and make decisions across vast geographic distances. Geographic distance can be both an advantage and a disadvantage. For example, some companies have capitalized on differences across time zones to accelerate the product development process. Texas Instruments divided a mobile telephone R&D team among locations in California, France, and Japan. The results of each day's work were transmitted electronically to the group in the next time zone so that the total team could work 24 hours a day.

Conversely, large geographic distances between members of a transnational team can aggravate the difficulties of assembling an integrated, cohesive work group. A feeling of 'out of sight, out of mind' can be harmful to a team that must process a lot of information to accomplish its task.

Transnational teams therefore make heavy use of telephones, voice mail, e-mail, and fax machines, and members must agree on how those communications devices should be co-ordinated and prioritized. Some teams use teleconferencing and videoconferencing, but those communication modes have not been adopted extensively.

Source: Snow, *et al.* 'Use transnational teams to globalise your company', *Organisational Dynamics*, Spring 1996.

instructions and hold people responsible for the results. They try to solve organizational problems by developing other policies and new methods – or by restructuring.

- The 'human resource' framework directs itself at the interaction between the needs of the individual and those of the organization. 'Human resource'-directed managers value human relationships and feelings: their striving is directed at managing by passing down facilities and possibilities. When problems arise, they prefer to solve these by means of participation and training.
- The political framework emphasizes the conflicts between different groups and interests with regard to scarce resources. Politically directed managers are advocates and negotiators who spend a large part of their time on the development of networks, the bringing about of coalitions, the building up of a power base and the making of compromises. They consider conflicts a source of energy and not as a cause for concern.
- The symbolic framework sees a chaotic universe in which meaning and predictability are constructed societally and in which facts are not objective but open for interpretation. Symbolically oriented managers pay a lot of attention to myths, rituals, ceremonies, stories and other forms of symbolism. When something goes wrong, they try to formulate a new story or return to the cherished values.

All four of the frameworks are of equal importance, since each determines an essential part of the organizational reality. Research into effective groups shows that each framework can make a contribution. In the 1960s and 70s, authors such as Douglas McGregor and Rensis Likert (compare to section 2.2.2) presented a series of recipes for successful teamwork. They stated that a clear goal, open communication, shared leadership and a pleasant informal atmosphere were characteristics of a successful team.

In more recent research (Hackman, 1990) into groups and teams in different sorts of organizations, the researchers found both structural and human resources variables which were essential for the effectiveness of groups. Groups with clear structure and a clear time limit had much better results than groups that did not. A general recipe for failure was: burden the group with a vague goal, variable time limits and unclear criteria, and then order the team to 'work out the details'. Other groups had little chance from the start because they lacked resources. Sometimes the bottleneck was the lack of the necessary expertise among the group members or the lack of the essential organizational coherence. Other times, the group had unclear or insufficient authority and mandate. Hackman and his colleagues also came to the conclusion that the history of the group was very important. Groups which had started out right and had early successes, often developed a self-maintaining process in which they functioned ever better. In groups which had an unfavourable start, bad functioning often became a negative routine. When they tried to liberate themselves from this, they drifted off even further.

Exhibit 8.2

Transnational team cultures

In many transnational teams, three powerful cultures operate simultaneously. The most obvious cultural characteristics (to an outsider) are those associated with a particular nationality: language, gestures, modes of dress, and so on. In addition, corporate culture affects team dynamics.

Last, some teams have a very strong occupational culture.

National Culture
An individual's orientation toward:

- universalism v. particularism
- analyzing v. integrating
- individualism v. communitarianism
- inner-directedness v. outer-directedness
- time as sequence v. time as synchronization
- achieved status v. ascribed status
- equality v. hierarchy

Corporate Culture
A particular company's:

- values
- rituals
- heroes
- symbols

Occupational Culture
A given occupation's:

- analytical paradigm
- work norms and practices
- code of ethics
- jargon

How should transnational teams address culture-laden issues such as group norms, language, and styles of communication and leadership? In other words, how can a 'multinational' team become a 'transnational' team – a group of people whose effective interpersonal relationships recognize and integrate cultural differences? One way to build such a team is the approach used by MacGregor Navire, a subsidiary company of Finland's Kone Corporation.

MacGregor Navire, a small company of approximately 900 employees, is the global market leader in shipboard cargohandling equipment. It was created more than ten years ago by the merger of two companies, one Finnish and the other British. The company must enable a Norwegian shipbuilder, for example, to design cargohandling equipment in Norway, build it in Taiwan, and service it in South America. Hence, although it is a small firm, MacGregor Navire has all of the core elements of a 'boundaryless' international organization.

The CEO of the newly merged company hand-picked his executive team of five managers, all of whom he knew and trusted and who shared his vision of where the company should be headed. Because he allowed each of them to choose where to live, the team is spread across Finland, Denmark, Sweden, and England. Each executive is multilingual, but team members speak in English during their weekly teleconference. Every month the team meets at one of the company's divisional headquarters and spends the next day with the managers of that division. The team leader encourages all team members to be part of every discussion, whether it is within their specific field of expertise or not. However, the roles and responsibilities for implementation are kept very clear so that interaction on a day-to-day basis across geographic distances is unnecessary. Above all else, the team emphasizes high performance goals for all members.

Source: Snow, *et al.* 'Use transnational teams to globalise your company', *Organisational Dynamics*, Spring 1996.

8.4.2 Symbolic approach

In these important and useful reports all too often little attention is paid to matters such as power and conflict, because of which groups are often hindered from performing at a high level. Even more striking is that only rarely are symbolic elements – charisma, character, enchantment – touched upon, and these also form part of the core of exceptional performances. Managers try to let teams work better, but often the political and symbolic matters are what they trip on, meaning their efforts come to nothing. From research it would appear that managers in the public as well as in the private sector have a tendency to act too much on the structural and the 'human resources' perspective and make too little use of the political and the symbolic approach. The first mentioned concepts often help to be a better manager, but not to become a better leader. In recent research the structural framework is especially linked to effectiveness as a manager, but the symbolic framework is the best predictor of effective leadership. Symbolic thinking is subtle and complex. It rests much more on intuition and sensitivity than on analysis and linear thinking. For that reason, managers often experience it as incomprehensible, elusive or mysterious. But it touches upon the core of matters such as meaning and trust which are not covered in the other perspectives.

Basic principles of an effective group

From research into effective groups, basic principles of the symbolic approach can be derived which can contribute to the success of a team. These are as follows:

1. It is important how someone becomes a member of the team.
2. Diversity brings a team ahead of the competition.
3. Not orders, but example behaviour keeps the team together.
4. An own language stimulates cohesion and involvement.
5. Stories contain history and values and supply the team with an identity.
6. Humour and play discharge tension and stimulate creativity.
7. Rituals and ceremonies rejuvenate the spirit and strengthen values.
8. The contribution of participants in the informal culture is not relative to their formal role.
9. Inspiration is the real secret of successful teams.

It is inevitable that managers, together with their employees, are responsible for budgeting and end result. They also have to react to personal needs, legal prescriptions and economic pressure. Team forming, however, is the creation of a bond between people connected by trust and the culture they share. Top performances arise when the team gets 'the spirit'.

8.5 MOTIVATION: A BETTER LOOK

A high resulting performance from the labour force cannot be extorted. This means that in the realizing of an organization's goals, the willingness of other people to work to this end has to be relied on. In order to discover what that willingness is based on, one cannot but examine more closely what motivates people to do (or not to do) certain things.

By motivation we mean: the totality of reasons and motives which move the human being to do things or to do things in one way rather than another. In principle there is a conscious and an unconscious motive behind every human action: a rational or emotional impulse which works on the will and urges it to activity. Motivating then is adapting to the needs of the other person in order to ensure for oneself a willingness necessary to attain the set goals.

The notion of motivation has changed in interpretation since Maslow demonstrated that people are characterized by a diversity of needs. This is particularly true for people employed in the organization as a 'goal realizing co-operative unit'. A consequence of this is that contemporary demands are made to the circumstances under which work is being carried out. The organization which is tuned exclusively into adapting to the material needs of the employee requires a thorough revision, as those material circumstances are not the only ones in which the employees are interested.

8.5.1 Contributions from psychology

To date nobody has succeeded in presenting the 'mystery' human being in such a way that has led to a complete understanding of oneself or other people. This means that the human factor in the organization is still unique, and is likely to remain so. So far, few theories have been promulgated which say something about the various influencing possibilities of different categories of people. In present management a base must be found for the development of styles of leadership and the development of organizational methods and techniques which can lead to optimization of results.

In quoting a number of psychologists it becomes obvious that every researcher has his own approach, everyone searches in his own way for certain relationships and laws. When one places different theories next to each other they are seen generally to overlap and/or complement.

Sigmund Freud (1856–1939)

One of the best known psychologists and creator of many important theories in psychology must be Sigmund Freud. He is praised by many, reviled by others. He declared that the largest part of our actions springs from the unconscious. According to Freud the conscious is so limited it compares to the visible tip of the iceberg: this then also means that the human being hardly knows what motivates him, what moves him to do something or not to do something.

Freud's theories strike home because of the tracing back of behavioural patterns to experiences during childhood. According to him, the outlines of human behaviour are determined by the fifth year of life, and after that, only minor deviations occur. Instincts and reacting to stimulus from the environment are decisive in this process. How important these instincts really are Freud emphasizes in an interesting statement: these instinct-originated behaviourial patterns hold a kind of primitive power, and continuously keep asking for satisfaction as if the question of survival is under discussion.

The child, who from youngest childhood is used to the fact that others satisfy its instinctive needs, has to learn that the environment is no longer at its service, and that in time the environment will make demands to it. On the acceptance of these demands hangs the degree to which the child develops to become independent and mature. All these matters, and also experience the child has gained in the fields of praise and punishment, play an important part in the motivational processes that develop later. The example of others on which the child models itself cannot be left out of consideration.

Exhibit 8.3

Austria – a strong Uncertainty Avoidance country

We do not know to what extent Austrian culture has changed since Freud's time, but evidence suggests that cultural patterns change very slowly. It is, therefore, not likely to have been much different from today's culture. The most striking thing about present-day Austrian culture is that it combines a fairly high Uncertainty Avoidance with a very low Power Distance. Somehow the combination of high Uncertainty Avoidance with high Power Distance is more comfortable (we find this in Japan and in all Latin and Mediterranean countries). Having a powerful superior whom we can both praise and blame is one way of satisfying a strong need for avoiding uncertainty. The Austrian culture, however (together with the German, Swiss, Israeli, and Finnish cultures) cannot rely on an external boss to absorb its uncertainty. Thus Freud's superego acts naturally as an inner uncertainty-absorbing device, an internalized boss. For strong Uncertainty Avoidance countries like Austria, working hard is caused by an inner urge – it is a way of relieving stress. The Austrian superego is reinforced by the country's relatively low level of Individualism. The inner feeling of obligation to society plays a much stronger role in Austria than in the United States. The ultrahigh Individualism of the United States leads to a need to explain every act in terms of self-interest, and expectancy theories of motivation do provide this explanation – we always do something *because* we expect to obtain the satisfaction of some need.

Source: From *Transnational Management* by Bartlett and Ghoshal, (1992).

Alfred Adler (1870–1937)

Alfred Adler, a contemporary of Freud, also delves deeply into the experiences of childhood. The power motive is particularly emphasized. By power Adler means: the aptitude to make others behave in the way one wants them to (manipulation). He points at the screaming and unwilling behaviour of toddlers in order to force others to do something. Adler does not imply a striving for absolute power, but rather a striving towards the elimination of a certain degree of helplessness, any of these signs remain clearly visible in the behaviour of adults. In the case of managers this might happen when, lacking sufficient personal effectiveness, they reach for power means. Adler develops from this assertion the well known theory on inferiority complexes and how to compensate for them.

Robert W. White

The classic theories of Freud and Adler have been adjusted substantially by later psychologists. Robert W. White, especially, thinks the approach of the human being as a 'collection of instincts' much too simplistic. According to him the urge of the human being to get to know its environment cannot go by unexamined. Where Freud assumes comfort-seeking instincts and Adler emphasizes the striving for power, White seeks a solution in the need to get to know the environment. The human being wants to actively make things happen rather than passively wait for them to happen. The desires to explore and to control the environment he calls the competence motive.

In the case of a child this is already visible when it explores the environment with its fingers. Gradually, a child gets to know its potential. It will depend on its experiences with this whether the child will later face the future optimistically, in the understanding that it will come a long way with common sense and perseverance, or whether it will hesitatingly let situations come towards it. In practising craftsmanship or being a professional, White sees an extension of this competence motive. He implies that job and function are, as paid labour, areas in which the human being will be able to prove himself.

Stanley Schachter

Stanley Schachter concerned himself with the problem of why some human beings are considerably more social than others. He reaches the conclusion that the affiliation motive, the searching for affection, does not emerge as strongly in all people. Schachter discovered that the human being, in searching for affection, lets itself be led by several things: these may be more impersonal things, money, favours, security; it may be that they crave affection. From this Schachter comes to the conclusion that human being let themselves be led by what others think about them. This idea can be used to explain the unpopularity of new ideas, and the power of the informal organization. Freely translated, it also means that many people do something in this way or in that way because also others want it that way.

David MacClelland

David MacClelland emphasizes three motives: the need for achievement, the need for power and the need for affiliation. MacClelland's studies have made clear that striving for success and performance motivate certain people more strongly than money. Here money is seen as the benchmark of success. Stated differently, the salary determines how important someone is, not the luxury car. That is the manifestation of the organization where the driver of the car works. It is obvious to all that the organization thinks highly of him by giving him, through the means of a high salary, the opportunity to buy a luxury car.

Abraham Maslow

The ideas of Abraham Maslow have been saved to last since in the area of motivation theory, Maslow is the most quoted expert. His theories offer most of the starting points for practice. In *Motivation and Personality* (1954), Maslow explains a certain hierarchy of human needs. He distinguishes five and makes these visible by categorizing them in a pyramid (Fig 8.5).

- Needs of a physiological nature (food, drink, clothing, shelter and so on) fulfilled by wage, salary, government payments.
- Needs of safety and security (protection against threats of an economical and physical nature) fulfilled by pay, retirement plans, social security/insurance policies.
- Need for love and social acceptance (affection, companionship, belonging, acknowledgment by family, friends, neighbours, and colleagues) fulfilled by work which offers people a possibility to obtain and maintain the acknowledgment and acceptance.
- Need for esteem and appreciation (esteem, respect and status) fulfilled by importance of the job, title, promotion and so on.
- Need for self-actualization (the need to fulfil one's own potential) fulfilled by growth and development possibilities in the job, being able to deliver creative performances, the bearing of responsibility.

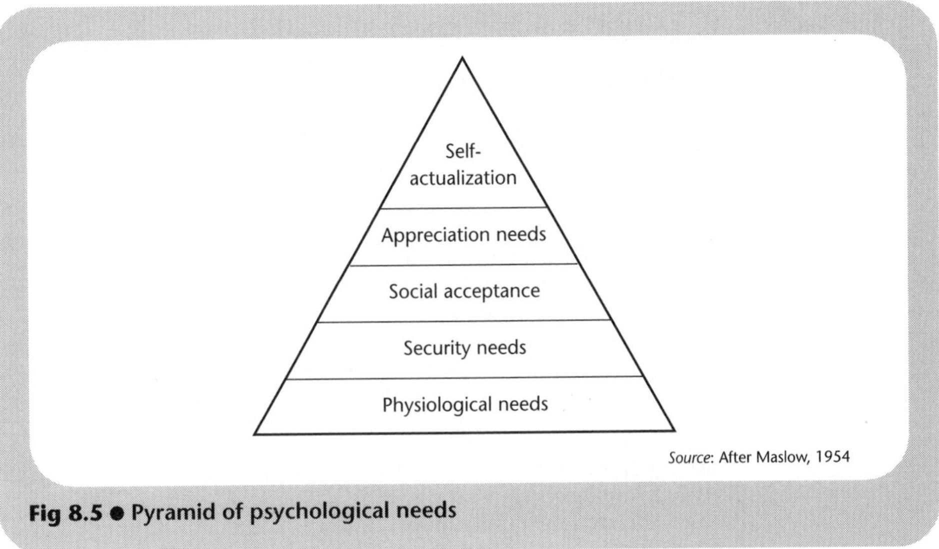

Fig 8.5 ● Pyramid of psychological needs

This pyramid of needs is based on two assumptions:

- the human being is a 'wanting animal' and without taking into consideration his position or rank he always wants more and/or something different;
- satisfied needs no longer form effective stimuli and do not or hardly ever urge any further change in behaviour.

In the interpretation of this hierarchy of needs, it is important to know that all the needs mentioned are latently present simultaneously in a human being: i.e. the satisfaction of one need leads only later to the other arising. Each of the needs always plays a part, while different needs can work as 'motivation' at the same time. Thus, these need to be fulfilled on a level acceptable for the person. In practice, it is often the case that the ability to satisfy a higher need totally only gets 'space' to arise when the lower need has been substantially satisfied.

8.5.2 Management by motivation

What do these theoretical insights mean for managing, and for motivating people in the labour organization? Here 'management by motivation' comes into play. In this respect it is important to determine how these different needs play a role in different people in their willingness to achieve and deliver performances in their job. It also has to be determined which stimuli have to be used in order to evoke this work behaviour. These stimuli will have to be used in the management of people, depending on the persons and situations encountered.

Satisfaction of the needs indicated by Maslow can be realized by:

- money (material needs: level 1 and 2);
- a say in things and involvement (level 3 and 4);
- a certain degree of autonomy or independence (level 5).

As a human being grows to maturity, the need for experiencing respect increases, implying both respect for others and self-respect. The same is true for the need for self-

Exhibit 8.4

Motivation and national cultures

One practical outcome of presenting motivation theories is the movement toward humanization of work – an attempt to make work more intrinsically interesting to the workers. There are two main currents in humanization of work – one, developed in the United States and called *job enrichment*, aims at restructuring individual jobs. A chief proponent of job enrichment is Frederick Herzberg. The other current, developed in Europe and applied mainly in Sweden and Norway, aims at restructuring work into group work – forming, for example, such semiautonomous teams as those seen in the experiments at Volvo. Why the difference in approaches? What is seen as a 'human' job depends on a society's prevailing model of humankind. In a more masculine society like the United States, humanization takes the form of masculinization, allowing individual performance. In the more feminine societies of Sweden and Norway, humanization takes the form of feminization – it is a means toward more wholesome interpersonal relationships in its deemphasis of interindividual competition.

Source: From *Transnational Management*, by Bartlett and Ghoshal (1992).

actualization. Both needs function as motivator. From this the following conclusions can be formulated.

- People have different need and motivation patterns with regard to their job. A central need, however, is the desire to be able to deploy their own capabilities.
- This urge, though present in everyone, requires fulfilment in different ways, and it depends on the relationship between this desire and other personal needs such as safety, independence, power, and affection.
- The need to be able to deploy own capability can probably be best used by the bringing about of clear coherence between people, work and organization.
- The need to be able to deploy own capability remains, even when a certain level has been reached. In that case a different, or higher goal must be set.

In the practice of management it is wise, on these grounds, to start from the principle that every human being has needs of different natures, but in all of them the emphasis must be placed on the potential for growth and the development of the human being.

8.5.3 Vroom's motivation theory: path–goal model

With this theory, Vroom assumes that behaviour is instrumental in attaining something. In other words, the human being acts to attain a certain goal. Vroom does not go into what motivates a human being internally or what a human being strives for, the accent is not put on the process and the events are enacted. In section 8.1.4, 'motivation' was defined. Vroom comes to a somewhat modified definition. For Vroom, motivation is: 'a process which heads the choice which is made by people between alternative forms of voluntary activity.'

How is the strength of someone's work motivation to be measured? Different elements play a part:

- the preference to attain a particular result;
- the expectation of attaining that goal at own pace;
- the expectation of receiving a reward.

The strength of the motivation can then be seen as the product of the strength of someone's preference for a particular result and someone's expectation of attaining a goal at own pace and of receiving a reward.

$$\textbf{Motivation} = \textbf{Preference} \times \textbf{Expectation}$$

Vroom's motivation theory makes a clear relation between motivation, productivity and satisfaction. Productivity is not a goal in itself, although it can be seen as a goal by someone in order to enlarge his income, which is instrumental in attaining a higher status by, for example, buying a certain type of car. Then his effort can be seen as instrumental for that enhancement of status. Instrumentality is explained as a person's idea about the relationship between his need and the reward. When an employee sees higher productivity as a way to attain one or more of his personal goals, then he will be inclined to higher production. When he sees lower productivity as a mean for his goal, he will produce less. This theory then states that people will be motivated to higher productivity when they:

- feel that they can be highly productive and so can influence the speed and the quality themselves;
- are aware of a number of positive outcomes linked to high production and realize that not the same outcome is linked to good as to bad work and so know that higher and lower productivity will not be rewarded in the same way.

8.5.4 Practical implications

Vroom's motivation theory attempts to describe what moves people to do or not to do something. This applies to organizations with regard to paid labour as well as in other areas. A number of practical recommendations can be made to make the theory more specific, because a manager has the task to move employees to deploy themselves for intended productivity: that can only be done when it is clear to him what drives the employees he manages.

The following recommendations can be derived from the theory.

- Recognize the needs of employees and activate those needs towards results in which they have a say or on which they can have some influence. Managers must see to it that employees really do have influence on results to be attained, and are involved in the formulation of those results.
- Try actively to link the desired outcomes to the attaining of work results. This applies in two respects: in the first place, make clear that there is a link between the income of the employee and the results achieved, the 'weight' of the function and so on; in the second place, make clear that the non-material outcomes also depend

on results. The image of the department, the image of the profession within which one works, and so on, will also depend on the work results.

- Make a detailed and careful analysis of the way in which results are to be best attained. Make this easier by supervising and giving direction. Not only does the goal have to be clear, but also the way in which the goal is attained has to be clear to the employees. Involve the employees here also, so that the relationship between outcome and effort is permanently recognized as a motivator.
- By means of consultation reach an expression of expectation. In this way employees get a better grip on their own affairs. They also realize that they can make a contribution to a common goal.
- Eliminate impediments which block the way to the goal. Provide an adequate system for supply and conveyance of resources and raw materials. Prevent or eliminate frustration by preparing people for changes in time. This also helps make a permanent link between product and effort.
- Create the potential for the creation of personal satisfaction. Do this by, for example, building in the following elements into the job and link them to agreed performances:
  - variation;
  - autonomy;
  - identification;
  - feedback and information.

By using these recommendations human being and organization can be better matched because mutual needs and expectations have been clarified.

8.5.5 Design of functions, productivity and motivation

The content and structure of managerial and operational functions can influence the effort of employees. The design of functions implies the way in which tasks are combined into functions. Functions differ, for example, in the degree of routine, the use of varied skills, the following of procedures, the freedom in way of working, independence. When it comes to the case of the design of functions, there is an old assumption that a high degree of task specialization offers many economical advantages. Narrow task specialization has led to many functions being dull for employees, can lead to stress, and offer little meaning. New methods of assigning tasks and design of functions are used to enlarge the quality of the work as well as the productivity of employees.

Possibilities with regard to the design of functions for individuals concern:

- job roulation: the horizontal or vertical changing of tasks; via work consultation one can circulate reasonably quickly;
- job enlargement: the horizontal enlargement of functions; enlargement of task span and lengthening of task cycle;
- job enrichment: the vertical enlargement of functions; enlargement of depth of tasks.

For groups, the following design possibilities are available:

- integrated teams: task enlargement at group level;
- semi-autonomous groups: task enrichment at group level;
- quality circles: a group of employees with shared responsibility in a certain area to solve the quality problems there.

The so-called task–characteristic model indicates five characteristics of functions by which the design of a function can be analysed (see Fig 8.6). The model also provides insight into the mutual interrelation of the five characteristics and predicts their influence on productivity, motivation and satisfaction.

Explanation of the most important task characteristics

There are five task characteristics that should be taken into consideration.

- Variation in skills: the degree to which a function comprises different activities for which different skills and talents are necessary.
- Task identity: the degree to which a job demands that a total, identifiable piece of work is completed.
- Task interest: the degree to which a function influences the life and work of others.
- Autonomy: the degree to which a function provides discretion/freedom, independence and the right to influence the planning of work and operational procedures.
- Feedback: the degree to which the activities to be conducted signal direct and clear information about the effectiveness of the performances delivered.

When broad task groups are designed, employee satisfaction can increase. Changes on the work floor may be accompanied by delayering of the organization, where the number of hierarchical layers is reduced and the lines are shortened, and the design of tasks and functions is occurring as a substitute for hierarchy (section 7.6).

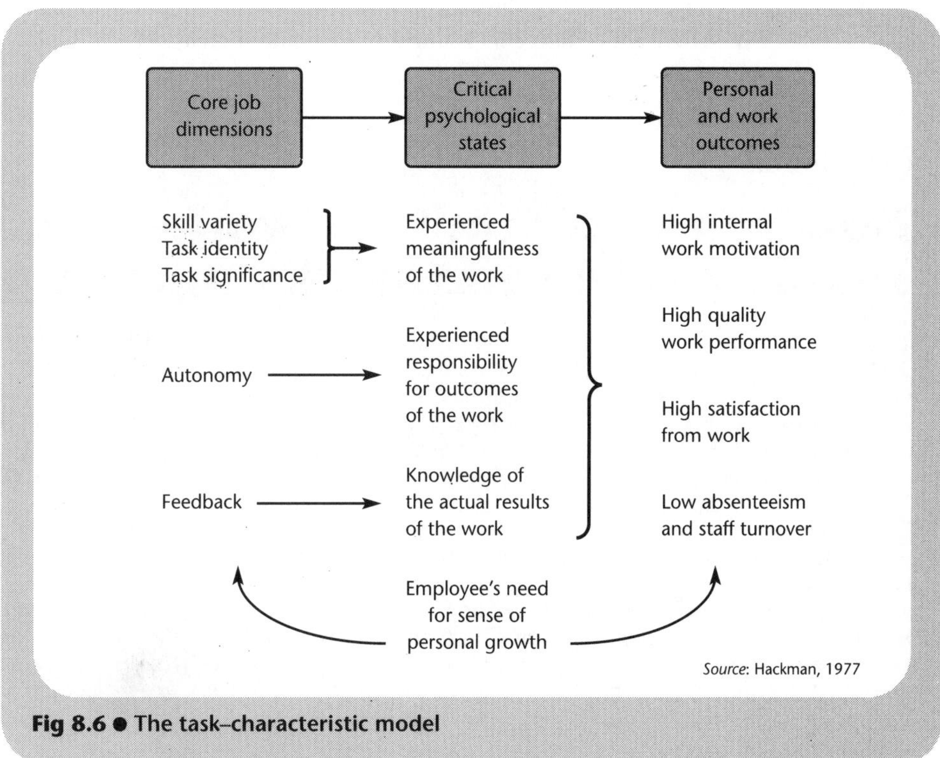

Fig 8.6 ● The task–characteristic model

8.6 ● EMPOWERMENT

The notion 'empowerment' will arise within an organization in a period characterized by delayering, cost cutting and overhead reduction, recession and lay offs – organizations realize that they have to work on 'revitalization'. Empowerment intends to realize new energy and new possibilities by:

- influencing positively the behaviour, the motivation and the effort of employees;
- enlarging effectiveness and flexibility.

Organization theorists, practising managers and management consultants seldom agree but on this point they do: empowerment can help organizations in their battle to compete for the favour of the client, in the need to be flexible, and of course also to work more efficiently.

Empowerment as a form of self-management comprises:

- independently set goals and decisions made within given constraints;
- responsibility for own performance, in quantity as well as in quality;
- effective, co-operation that is flexible, efficient, customer oriented and creative.

The notion of empowerment came to Europe from the USA in the late 1980s. What is so new about this notion, when for decades 'delegation', 'semi-autonomy', 'self-development', 'self-control', and 'motivation' have all been bandied about. The 'new' notion, empowerment, consists of three elements.

1. Two parties are involved.
2. Delegation takes place.
3. There are certain effects, most particularly increase of effort.

Exhibit 8.5

How can uncommitted workers in a small firm be successfully motivated?

Luigi Cappa was beginning to wonder what had made him give up a smoothly running job in New York to tackle what had turned out to be a baffling problem in southern Italy.

He was a US citizen, and if he had stayed with his company he might have had a seat on the board within two years.

Then an uncle in Turin, in northern Italy, had written to Cappa, imploring him to come and run his printing plant near Palermo in Sicily, which produced transfer designs and other specialized printing, some of it for export.

Cappa was 28 years old, unmarried and ambitious. The offer had appealed to him in several ways.

First, there was the chance to be his own boss immediately. Second, there was the challenge, as Cappa saw it, of bringing US know-how to the Italian family firm. Third, there was the satisfaction of returning as a man of some authority to the country where his own father had been born.

He was a believer in scientific management. He also believed that people everywhere are basically alike and will respond in about the same way to the carrot of cash rewards and the stick of firm leadership.

After only a few months in Palermo he knew differently. Cappa's uncle had set up the plant five years previously with the active encouragement of the Italian government. But the 300-strong labour force still had no loyalty to the company from the north. The workers still dreamed of orange groves rather than production targets.

Indeed, on one occasion Cappa had found a worker blissfully cleaning equipment from one of the printing machines in an orange grove near the plant. When he had ordered him back into the plant the man had looked astonished and replied: 'Why should I work inside when I can do my job here?'

Productivity was very low. When Cappa had visited a local barber, who knew that he worked in the printing plant but did not know he was the boss, the man had said: 'Sir, can you get me a job with the printing company so that I no longer have to work?'

As Cappa walked round the plant he saw plenty of modern machines. He also saw a workforce that yearned to be out in the sun, and wondered how he could get his employees to change their attitudes.

First, he tried using his personal appeal as an American-Italian. That did not work. He would have been more successful, he ruefully admitted to himself, had he been born in Palermo.

He instituted production committees, which were supposed to generate their own ideas of improving productivity. He worked at them very hard but they too were a dismal failure.

When managers sat on the committees the workers seemed struck dumb, failing to produce constructive ideas. Then, when Cappa gave the committees more autonomy to run their own affairs, their members used the time allocated for their meetings to leave the factory and take a siesta outside.

Cappa decided that a bonus system relating pay directly to output was the only solution. At first the union opposed this, saying it was the kind of piecework they had been fighting against. Then, to Cappa's surprise, they gave in. He thought he had won a victory.

If so, it was a hollow one. The workers began demanding the bonus as a right, whether or not they had worked extra hours or produced more. When Cappa refused to pay, the workers went on strike.

Cappa felt that he was dealing with forces beyond his control, with people who, although Italian, he could not fully understand.

'They just don't seem to want to participate,' he wrote to a friend in New York. 'If you give them the chance to run their own affairs, they take advantage of it. If you offer them a carrot, they eat half your arm as well. And if you wave a stick, they strike.'

He could advise his uncle to concentrate production in Turin and get rid of the Palermo plant. But then he would have to return to the US without a job and with a feeling of defeat.

Alternatively, Cappa could find a way of motivating his workers. But *how*, he asked himself for the thousandth time.

Source: International Management, May 1978.

8.6.1 Empowerment: a new way to manage people

It is essential to realize that empowerment in the framework of organizational knowledge is concerned with a special way of managing employees. How do we use the human potential in the organization and how do we deploy this in such a way that organization goals are optimally attained?

- Managing in its narrowest form can be the classical 'giving of an order', i.e. two parties are involved.
- Managing can also take place in a situation in which there is conscious delegation.
- Empowerment as a form of management involves a form of interaction in which, when delegation is included, an increase of effort is striven for and there is total development of the others within an organization as a co-operative unit.

In Maslow's terms, empowerment meets the higher needs that people wish to realize during their existence, namely the need for self-actualization and the need for recognition. Practically seen, this means that, through empowerment, business units, groups and employees are enabled to function independently, with some form of 'control' only at a distance. A form of self-control by the employees is being aimed for. The current interest in empowerment indicates that the situation is apparently unsatisfactory in that respect, and that something has to be done about it.

Empowerment means that people are enabled more to do their job independently than in the past. Not because this is easy for management, but because empowerment disengages positive forces and energy and may lead to higher efficiency and effectiveness, and greater innovative and creative abilities. One condition for this is, however, that the potential of the employees needs to be better exploited than in the past.

8.6.2 Empowerment: an attractive concept for young and old

It is sometimes observed that it is especially the young, highly educated employees who are attracted to companies where there is a climate evoked by decentralization, debureaucratization, downsizing, privatization and customer orientation.

This kind of company characterizes itself in the following ways:

- it has a flat structure with short lines of communication;
- it gives room to creativity;
- it delegates responsibility;
- it does not have a strict hierarchical structure but is much more based on informal co-operation and communication;
- it is more directed at the individual;
- it sees innovation with the accompanying changes as important;
- it contributes to the development of the employees themselves.

However, it has become clear that these kinds of company characteristics are not only attractive to young employees, older generations often value a climate which is characterized by these elements. If employees who are used to other circumstances are to be enabled to do their job more independently, and if they are to be empowered to make their own decisions, it is vital that the employees have the knowledge and resources at their disposal to be able to carry out their work. So in addition to their being involved in the decision-making process, empowerment, as far as employees are concerned, involves a relationship with transfer of knowledge, with being informed.

Employees have (and indeed want) to:

- be informed on all important matters within the organization;
- understand the decisions of management; what is more, they have to be able to participate in, rather than simply being able to exercise influence on, the decision-making processes;
- be able to make contributions with ideas they consider necessary for the processes of change;
- participate in policy making;
- use the most modern technologies and methods, through which a contribution is also made to their own individual development.

It is important that the ability to change, renew and innovate are guaranteed and, of course, here the structure of the organization plays a part. Structure is, however, only an instrument, one of the tools used to design and set up the organization so that tasks can optimally be executed. Few hierarchical layers fit in that structure and there is usually an important role for project management. Given these strictures, the functional organization needs to be able to adapt quickly to changing circumstances.

The organization has to be mobile and flexible with regard to the continuously changing circumstances. Important processes for the departments can best be mapped out separately and solved in separate, often ad hoc groups. It is best to arrive at a situation in which the necessary adaptations from the organization itself are deployed (*see* section 6.5).

Minicase 8.4

The elderly, the pluses

Employees aged 50 or 55-plus are often considered privileged compared to their younger colleagues. The older employee may be more expensive in wage costs, but there are benefits in return.

- His knowledge and experience are worth their weight in gold.
- His social abilities are often greater.
- He is more stress resistant and has more stomach for the business than younger employees.
- He inspires more trust than younger employees.
- At the age of 55 the employee has the productivity of a 35 year old, and the ability to learn remains stable up to the age of 60.
- Older people are more careful, cause fewer work-related accidents and have low rates of absenteeism.

8.7 THE NEW CONTEXT FOR HUMAN TALENT DEVELOPMENT AND HUMAN RESOURCES MANAGEMENT

In the market-oriented organization, new expectations constantly arise, new demands are constantly made. On the one hand by clients, on the other by employees, in the industrial as well as in the services sector. Success in the product/market environment is, to a large degree, determined by flexibility, motivation, involvement, creativity and innovative ability. For their part, employees value more interesting work, more consultation and participation and tailor-made rewards. In industry (which is 70 per cent internally provided services) and in the services sector if this is predominantly a 'people's business', a well thought through personnel policy (in terms of marketing, manufacturing and purchase) is necessary. This involves 'human talent development' and 'human resources management'.

8.7.1 New demands and other constraints: the changing organization

Looking more closely at the adjusting organization, a number of impulses can be seen for the elaboration of HRM in the organization's policy.

1. Pluriformity in the labour package.
2. Qualification demands on employees.

3. A flat organizational structure.
4. Culture as a binding factor.
5. Boundary crossing approach.

Pluriformity in the labour package

Initiative and entrepreneurship, coming from creativity and flexibility, need to be stimulated. This requires a rethink of the existing appraisal and reward system to make necessary adjustments to changing circumstances possible. Present labour conditions have many characteristics of a care structure, which has developed in relation to the employees. They are often the result of negotiations against a background of a justified division of needs and equal treatment. Reward systems, based on appraisal of functions, and an uniform package of primary and secondary labour conditions are characteristics of this. Such a structure has a curbing rather than a stimulating influence on entrepreneurship, flexibility and mobility.

The rethink of the system could involve greater take up of individuals' wishes, capabilities and ambitions. The background to this is equal treatment and justified distribution according to performance. A package of facilities could be developed by means of which both managers and employees have the potential to affect the judgement of quality and growth capacities. The package could include:

- reward based on developed capabilities, efforts and performances;
- 'cafeteria system', that is, the employees compose their reward menu themselves: for example, a lower wage, more days off; work longer, retire at 72 (*see* section 8.9.5);
- certain 'incentives' which are linked to the attained result;
- level of the reward based not only on the description of a function, but also in terms of qualities demanded for the organization.

Qualification demands on employees

It has already been stressed that other demands will be made on employees: knowledge and job specialization will lose their relevance for wide categories, although they will remain necessary for the exercise of time and place linked functions. Experience is, however, subject to strong erosion, as seen by changes which occur in work due to technological influence. Orientation on information systems demands other knowledge and skills and these will also have to be kept up with. So it is important that employees learn to handle the potential that information technology offers, knows how to combine information from different disciplines and, based on that, arrive independently at well considered decisions. This demands an analytical intellectual capacity, a higher general level of education and the ability to react to direct environmental changes.

A number of qualitative demands have to be made on employees and management, given the changes to be expected in the future, demands which make it possible to face the uncertain future optimistically. Characteristics such as internal entrepreneurship, creativity, innovative ability and responsiveness are called for. This means developing learning ability, one's own qualities and capabilities further, and there has to be a willingness constantly present to adjust the knowledge anew. One-off professional training for a career is a thing of the past. Internal mobility will be a basic principle since it widens both knowledge and skills. This requires a willingness for geographical and functional mobility, even when this does not lead automatically to personal improvement in position in the organization.

This last point can only occur in a company culture where there is trust in the objectivity of judgement, in which employees feel safe, are not considered as disposable and know that their interest and that of the organization are parallel. It also involves supervision and effort of management in transfer of employees.

A flat organizational structure

Adequate reaction to rapid changes not only makes demands on the employee, but also on the organization. Self-conscious, entrepreneurial employees who are full of initiative, will not be able to develop within a large-scale, centrally managed organizational structure and thus, the reaction to change will be insufficiently smooth and flexible. With regard to organizational structuring there will be more certain degree of structuring rather than firm structures, leaving room for self-accomplishment of the tasks in the framework of visible company goals.

A network of relative autonomous units can be seen within the organization as a whole. Responsibility for quality, vision and directness concerning the end result, involvement in the total process within one's own sub-system from input through to output are essential characteristics for such structures. A flat, decentralized structure with short decision lines is appropriate, one that has to meet the desire of employees to bear responsibility (*see* Fig 8.7).

Tasks, authority and responsibilities have to be delineated in such a way that they do not hinder employees' further development, but rather stimulate it. Intimately connected to that is the need for employees to be responsible for their own decisions and to be charged for that. The need for rapid reaction to charged circumstances, offering new product varieties within existing markets or the opening of new markets do not

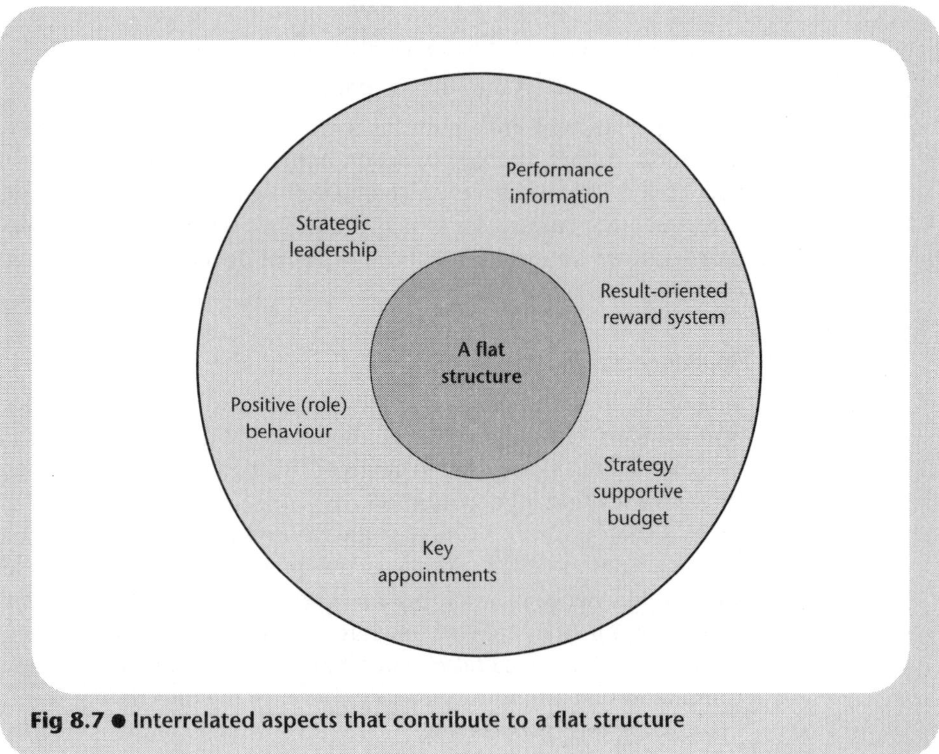

Fig 8.7 ● Interrelated aspects that contribute to a flat structure

accord with slow decision-making processes. Operational freedom should be as wide as possible within a well considered strategic framework. This delayering process is to a large extent supported by new information technology, and also makes possible other communication patterns.

When the structure is changed by reducing the number of management layers, it does not automatically follow as a consequence that decision-making runs faster, that energy is more directed at entrepreneurship or that more attention is paid to the needs of the customers. Use needs to be made, therefore, of several other instruments to increase the effect of the change in structure. Carrying through change involves enhancing or supporting measures for effective delayering.

Culture as a binding factor

The culture within the organization will have to breathe a spirit of openness, offer possibilities and chances to anyone suitable for that who feels called upon to bear greater and/or different responsibilities. The danger of relatively autonomous units is that the tie with the totality of the organization can be lost, that employees represent only a part of the whole and start lacking the psychological and emotional bond with the total organization. This demands a reflection on that basic philosophy: there is a pressing need to maintain or create a sense of unity to remove the 'them and us' mentality.

The so-called corporate identity of the organization is then of vital importance, and must be more than merely a house-style – the corporate identity is, rather, an organizational culture in which employees can identify themselves in the philosophy of their organization. This demands an organizational climate in which everyone:

- is aware of clearly formulated organizational goals;
- trusts in the validity of those goals;
- recognizes his own tasks as a contribution to the goals;
- wants to put effort into the realization of the end result.

The importance of cross-cultural theories for managers who have to operate in an unfamiliar culture, training based on home-country theories is of very limited use and may even do more harm than good. Of more importance is a thorough familiarization with the other culture, for which the organization can use the services of specialized cross-cultural training institutes – or it can develop its own program by using host-country personnel as teachers.

Boundary crossing approach

One of the most important qualities necessary to cope with a quickly changing world is a boundary crossing capability. By involving the environment in one's own activities, one can react promptly to change. This boundary crossing approach is an issue on three levels within an organization.

On a strategic level it concerns the environment which affects the organization and the organization which influences the environment through its services and societal added value, hence maintaining a feeling for outside events is essential. Society, industrial life and politics are very much interwoven. Company activities in the direction of political parties, consultation on employers' level in the direction of the employee, consultation on an industry or sector level in the direction of regular education are all examples of this interweaving.

On an organizational level the manager finds himself at the crossroads of company activities and needs to involve the environment in his policy intentions and activities. He needs to have boundary crossing capabilities himself to tackle the quality of service, customer orientation or willingness to serve. There is, further, a quality demand being made to think and act in an interdisciplinary and multi-cultural way (and concerning aspects of organizational change).

On the operational level the effectiveness of the organization as a whole is to a large degree determined by the way in which the individual employee is capable of communicating with the environment: external clients in addition to the internal clients, or system of the clients. The shift of responsibility onto operational units which, in direct interaction with one another, address and solve problems, or as in service companies, the shift from back office to front office, will supply almost every employee with openings to engage intensively with the environment, and especially with the client.

Practical management case 8.1

Boundary crossing capability

Multi-cultural organizational development

Providing services to people from another culture, or employing them does not mean necessarily that the organization is multi-cultural. It does, however, mean that one is working on the process to grow from a mono-ethnical and mono-cultural organization to a multi-cultural organization. This usually happens in the first place by building up a multi-ethnic personnel file and by an organization's subsidiaries already having or wanting to develop an intake of people from several cultures.

The process towards a multi-cultural organization involves three different phases.

- A mono-cultural company starts from the idea that 'the way we do things is the only way'. It is a common type of start and, as such, it leads to the exclusion of others.
- In the next phase, the idea is that 'the way we do things is best'. This type is also quite common.
- In the multi-cultural labour organization, the idea forms that 'a combination of the ways in which we and they do it may, in fact, yield the most'.

A model

This model starts with the whole organization as a system and with a clear vision of a multi-cultural organization as a labour organization which, in a coherent way, works on:

- the personnel file with quantitative and qualitative goals, including representation on all functional levels and function based on equality;
- the culture established by all employees not only the majority;
- learning to appreciate diversity, so that people can use and develop their individual capacities;
- a proportional division of all formal and informal sources of power within the organization, including board, working council, formal and informal deliberations;
- product development and services on behalf of a multi-cultural customer or client file;
- making a contribution to the multi-cultural perspective of society;
- involving of minority groups in the realization of all these goals.

continued overleaf

Practical management case continued

The model has three distinct phases, with a particular organization type with specific characteristics belonging to every phase. Analysis can also be made on a departmental level, or of different components of the personnel instruments.

Phase 1: Mono-cultural

Etnocentricity and xenophobia leads to the conscious exclusion of people who are different from the majority. Under external pressure, for example, government policy, demographics or pressure groups, someone 'different' from the majority is taken into the work force. This person, let's call her Alibi Ali, serves as proof that discrimination does not exist. The appointed token function requires that she assimilates into the mono-culture, but this form of assimilation leads to suffocation of qualities.

Phase 2: Anti-discrimination

The management has to make a conscious strategic choice to anticipate external developments, and events within the organization. Commitment is essential, as is a clear vision of the final goal, the goal from which one anticipates specific developments. At this stage the characteristics of the organization have changed, and involve:

- intake on the lowest function level;
- people being seen as representatives of a certain group and not as individuals, eventually leading to a loss of 'human resources';
- the diversity not recognized yet, the idea of the melting pot overrules;
- structure and culture are not being up for discussion;
- conflicts, overt and covert;
- there not being a so-called 'critical mass';
- the share of a minority group in a labour organization being so large that members of it feel at ease and are able to help in shaping further changes;
- a demand for conformity;
- a premium on higher positions.

In labour organizations, specific policy directed at run down groups, are often neither well supported nor embedded in the total personnel or organization policy. A long-term vision is rarely the starting point, an eventual goal which one wants to attain with the organization. In many cases, this leads to an insufficient base in the organization to resistance and failure. The majority believes itself left to its fate, with no advantage from the policy and possibly experiences only disadvantages. Situations can arise in which the established personnel believe the quality of people taken on thus by means of positive action is lower.

Many organizations remain in this phase, in a positive action cycle. The failure of the new person is still blamed on her. This negative way of thinking can only be broken by making a conscious choice to address the organizational culture and structure.

Phase 3: Multi-cultural

To eliminate structural barriers for minority groups in the organization, screening is necessary and the examination of management policy, culture, structure, procedures, technology and the product and service supply. People can and have to be seen as individuals to make use of the advantages of diversity and to minimize the disadvantages. Learning to appreciate diversity with the help of training sessions, searching for alternative management approaches and discussion of the dominant mono-culture are key factors in the phase. Finally, the organization will have changed, the dominant mono-culture replaced by a dominant heterogeneous culture with diversity in values, norms and ways of working. The organization has become a learning organization and, because of that, can handle all kinds of changes in the environment.

Source: Adapted from *Personeelsbeleid jrg. 30*, No. 11, 1994.

8.7.2 Talent development: some practical implications

Application of talent development in practice asks for a number of matters to be taken into consideration. First, a system of contracting and coaching needs to exist. Contracting and coaching must offer insight into the need for development of the employee, in the light of the demands from the organization as well as in the light of his own career. Contracting and coaching result in a programme of demands for 'talent development', and indicate individual and collective learning needs. Application of talent development based on contracting and coaching requires the presence of four factors.

- The willingness of managers and employees to work with the approach of contracting and coaching, whereby conditions are created in which to talk about the development of talent in an open and mutually obliging way.
- Open communication about performances and talents in the organization, in the form of mission, goals, and strategy discussion. Having done this it is clear for everyone in the organization what the expected performances are and how talents can be deployed to that end.
- A simple set-up and approach of the formal 'instruments': performance judgement, potential prognosis, and contracting talk. In this way discussion on the development and tracking of talents is not disturbed by more complex systems. In this way, the instruments remain a means in to the end of 'talent development' and do not become the end in themselves.
- The capacity of the managers to work with the approach of contracting and coaching. The organization has an obligation to stimulate the development of talents of the employees. Managers have to be capable of working with the instruments necessary for that purpose, especially contracting and coaching.

The foundation for 'talent development' has thus been laid. Managers and employees have next to search for suitable forms for 'talent development' to take. The application of forms which involve coaching and mentoring deserve priority because these provide the employees with a deeper insight into their function and because they teach employees to learn. By frequent use of these forms, the use of others such as education, training and instruction is already embedded in desired personal development.

8.7.3. Developing and managing organizational competencies

Organizational competencies describe firm specific resources and capabilities that enable the organization to develop, choose and implement value enhancing strategies, and include all firm specific assets, knowledge, skills and capabilities embedded in the organization's structure, technology, processes and interpersonal relationships.

Turner and Crawford (1994) use four types of competencies at organizational level.

- Personal and firm specific competencies: the knowledge and skills in systems and processes which are embedded in people, technologies and structures.
- Management competencies: the direction, development, motivation, administration and integration of the organization's performance.
- Operational and renewing competencies: the capability to meet and tackle present and future problems and challenges.
- Basic and distinctive competencies: the aspects that give the organization an advantage over their competitors, which are built from unique combinations of elementary competencies.

Throughout the application of performance management it can be seen that an organization is going to perform better. Goals are set within a strategic framework, outcomes are constantly measured and used to strengthen or adapt activities, performance is rewarded and the management constantly gives feedback through information systems.

A more in-depth look at the four types of competencies might bring up strengths and weaknesses, especially where the combination or mix and the balance are concerned. A number of competencies are found particularly in functional units, whereas the basic and renewing competencies are usually seen to be working beyond and across functional departments.

Good coaching by management is an essential factor. Managers and semi-independent employees can make or break one another. Managers have to enlarge the capacity to learn and strengthen the reflective side of the work, so that teams are able to look critically at their performance and thereby to look for more effective ways of doing the job.

The development of knowledge or competence of semi-autonomous teams can be directed effectively by means that may have little to do with further education and training. Learning may arise specifically out of the work that has to be done, so that further education first takes place on an ad hoc basis, triggered by deficiencies or challenges which arise from the work to be done. Coaching is important certainly, but within this context it remains a rather mysterious activity.

What makes a manager a good leader? Effective leaders use different styles of leadership, but they are always capable of combining or matching the daily work with the organizational goals. In coaching management is the axis that matches individual capabilities with the organizational tasks. The manager nevertheless stands on the line: at crucial moments the results might appear to be dependent on the collectivity and on individual 'stars'. Coaching has to grow from within and requires long-term orientation, which might be contradictory to flexibility and short-term direct results or performance.

It is the same story when it comes to building competencies on the organizational level. The relationship between investment and returns is clearer in the case of material than in the case of firm competencies. The development and maintenance of these competencies does not pay off in the short term, so the urge to invest in them might be correspondingly hesitant. Registration of competencies at different levels in an organization can be useful to find out which are lacking, or whether they correspond with those required by the customers and the quality standards to be met. Knowledge has to be judged not only on its contents, but also on the applicability and span of application. Learning processes in organizations are both social and collective. Working on projects, rising to challenges and providing for continuous flow might be better and more effective learning strategies than those methods based on the search for deficiencies.

Managing core competencies

Thinking about competencies is stimulated by two key factors. The first stresses that maintaining and improving the capability of an organization to perform is a central strategic activity for the realization of competitive advantage. The second concerns the idea of the learning organization and refers to the need for the knowledge of individual employees to be embedded in the organization as a whole.

Hamel and Prahalad (1994) refer to the dubious existence of big corporations such as IBM, Philips, Daimler-Benz and Boeing, which for years have held a solid position in their markets, but yet which also seemed to forget to keep their eyes on the market of tomorrow. Innovation and renewal are key terms here. But innovation and renewal also require a different look at the internal organization and especially when it concerns the creation of competitive advantage. A prerequisite for this is that organizations learn to bundle their core competencies.

In contrast to traditional concepts the resource-based perspective on organizations stresses the internal resources of a firm more than the market as such. One key question that arises from this perspective is how competitive advantage can be gained and, more particularly, how a sustainable advantage can be realized.

Competitive advantage arises from this way of thinking when a firm implements a value-creating strategy that is not simultaneously being implemented by any current or potential competitors. This is only possible when there are differences between organizations regarding their available resources (heterogenity), especially where these resources are not completely mobile. If all necessary resources were the same for every organization (homogeneity) and could be used freely by everyone because of their mobility, a competitive advantage based on resources could never arise. Any resource that might show a certain advantage could be used by competitors, imitated or could be taken over in one way or another.

To gain sustainable competitive advantage resources have to meet certain conditions. Resources should:

- add value to the organization;
- be unique or scarce;
- be difficult to imitate;
- be hard to substitute by other resources;
- be applicable in many fields.

It is clear that human potential can be a source of sustainable advantage, in addition to such things as a unique technology or an advanced information system. This is even more relevant where the human potential is important for the strategy of the organization, and where it possesses unique knowledge systems and skills which cannot be learned simply or substituted by machine or computer. The personnel factor then is essential for maintaining a position of strategic advantage. Of primary concern is keeping this advantage by advanced forms of management. Knowing and exploiting core competencies is extremely important in formulating organizational strategies. Hamel and Prahalad think in terms of 'strategic fit', the fit between changes in strategy and potential of the organization. In their view core competencies are 'the collective learning in the organization, especially how to coordinate diverse production skills and integrate multiple streams of technologies'.

8.8 ● HUMAN RESOURCES DEVELOPMENT: AN INTEGRAL CONCEPT AND A SET OF INSTRUMENTS

The human resources within an organization comprises the way in which personnel are selected, hired, educated, developed, promoted, salaried, fired and retired. This decision area covers the wide area of human relations, for which behavioural science and technical administrative background have both developed systems and methods. Human resources management (HRM) aims to be a concept and a set of instruments to realize the ultimate organization goals (*see* Fig 8.8). HRM starts from the basis of the strategy of an organization and the structure demanded by that, function demands and culture, and thus needs to be an integral part of the total management process.

In order to control human potential, management has a large number of instruments at its disposal. The different components of HRM and the relationship between these components, in which the ultimate performance is seen as a dependent variable, are shown in the HRM cycle (Fig 8.9).

It has to be stated clearly that in the content of HRM, employees are seen as the source of all prosperity in which the organization wants to invest. It is not so much capital in a financial sense, but rather the quality of the 'human capital' which determines the success of the organization. Quality implies not only the notion in the

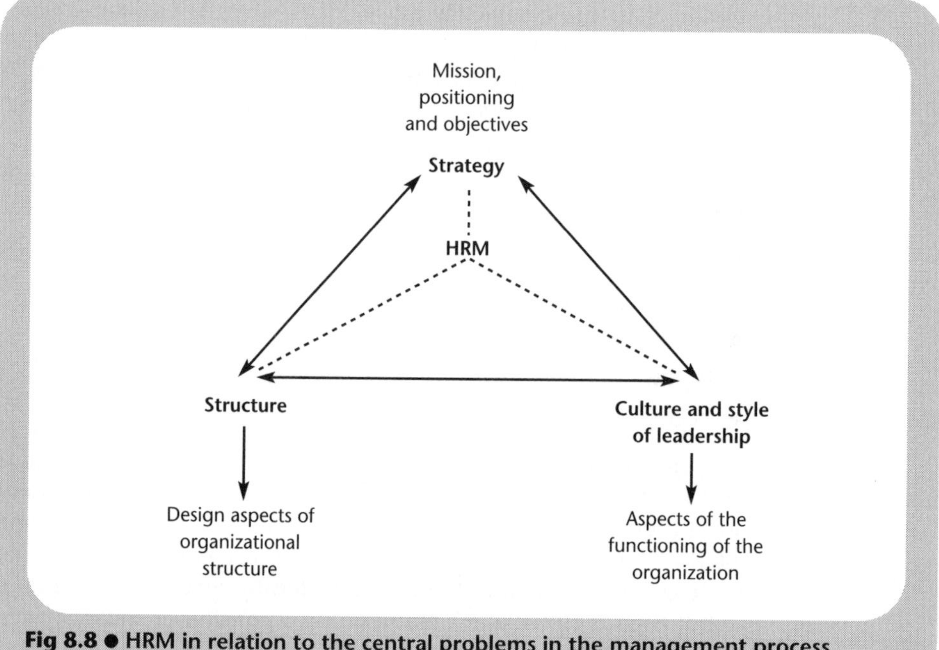

Fig 8.8 ● HRM in relation to the central problems in the management process

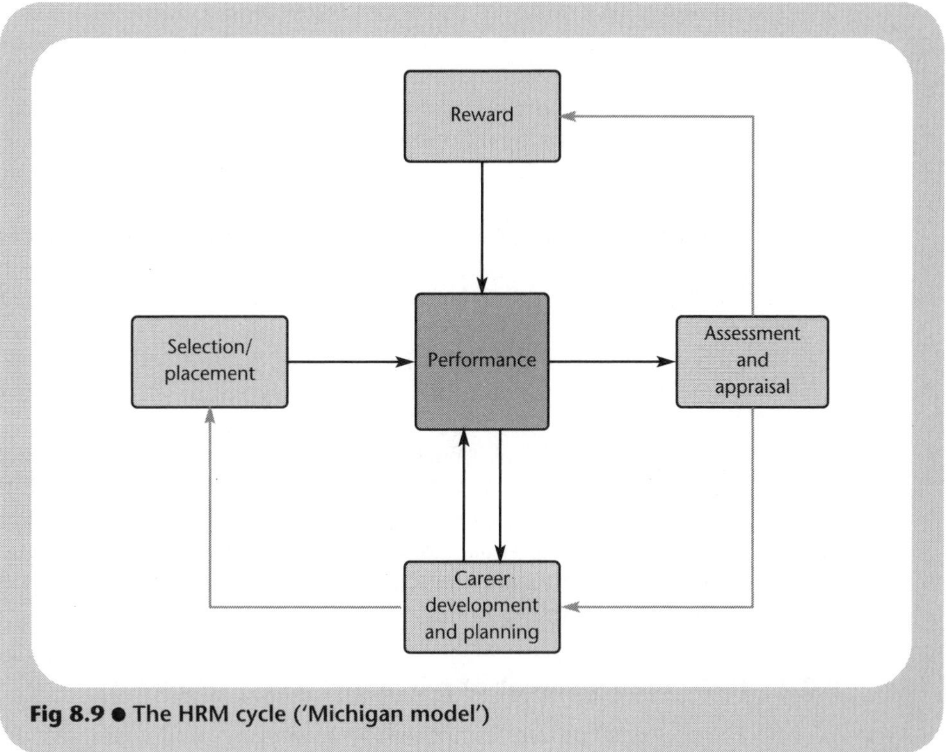

Fig 8.9 ● The HRM cycle ('Michigan model')

narrow sense: the level of knowledge and skills, and especially the way in which these are structured into the organizational relationships and the way in which these can be brought to validity at the service of the organization. Rewards, training and non-material rewards are instruments at the service of management to control that. In directing human potential facilities have to be created which give room for development of initiatives and ideas. A connection, a mutual engagement between the realization of the general organization goals and specific career development is aspired to by the individual employee as his personal goal.

8.8.1 HRM: characteristics

HRM displays three important characteristics.

1. An approach is made to labour as a source of inspiration, action and result.
2. The employee has room to exercise influence.
3. The social policy is integrated in the organization policy.

In the foreground of HRM material and non-material conditions are created to motivate and stimulate employees to take initiatives themselves, directed at the organization goals, and in agreement with their own ambitions. The employee then becomes a co-determining participant in career planning, active and responsible for his job and his career himself. He can expect support from the organization in the development which he sees for himself in direct relation to the realization of the organizational goals and within his capabilities.

Employees who act as co-controlling potential can make an essential contribution to the customer-oriented functioning of the organization, as the organization will be able to react more quickly to change and be able to attain its goals more effectively. To achieve this the organizational culture will have to be open to small, relatively autonomous operating units and should not stand in the way of internal entrepreneurship. The relationship between social policy and organization policy will demand further integration.

In traditional notions, social policy was reduced to a package of labour conditions, this could easily mean that new organization policy breaks down having disregarded human potential: insufficient preparation on changing tasks, little identification with organizational goals and resistance to change. On top of that developments in issues such as labour morale, social legislation, agreements on labour time reductions, employment planning and education make their influence felt on organizational policy to an increasing degree.

Using HRM, external influences can be processed as well as possible within the organization and external development can be influenced through the organizational needs where possible. Organizational goals, aspiration and development potential of employees are all of equal standing in the organization and because of this organizational relationships must be created whereby aspiration, creativity and operational alertness can be shown to full advantage.

8.8.2 HRM: management of personnel and instruments

The personnel process comprises the quantitative and qualitative determination of the personnel needs, the recruiting, selecting and appointing of personnel as well as the determination of labour conditions and the educating, judging and promoting of personnel and the co-determining of the working climate, transfer, retirement, and firing of individual members of staff. The personnel process is directly related to the other organizational processes, but has an integrating and supporting function.

Human resources management assumes the use of an integrated and coherent system of personnel management and personnel development instruments and systems. Within the system of personnel management, the managing of intake, flow and departure of employees are central issues. In each of these three phases, management has a number of instruments at its disposal to carry out management of personnel. In order to conduct integrated personnel management it is important to tune the personnel instruments from the different phases well. Managing the departure of employees is just as important as managing the intake and flow. In the case of flow, there is both vertical flow to higher functions and horizontal flow to other functions at an equal organizational level.

Top management will have to fill in these different phases of the personnel process from strategy, desired structure and desired organizational culture. It is assumed that management obeys the rules and laws which serve as legal protection of the employees, leaving sufficient room for his own way of acting with regard to the employees (*see* Chapters 2 and 7). This in turn means a social policy can be formulated and carried out. The operational activities which arise from this are known as personnel work.

Personnel work stands for all activities executed by personnel functionaries, including activities which have to do with the execution of social insurance legislation, application of the labour laws, handling of legislation in the field of the safety, health and welfare of employees, application of legislation on participation (for example, on works councils).

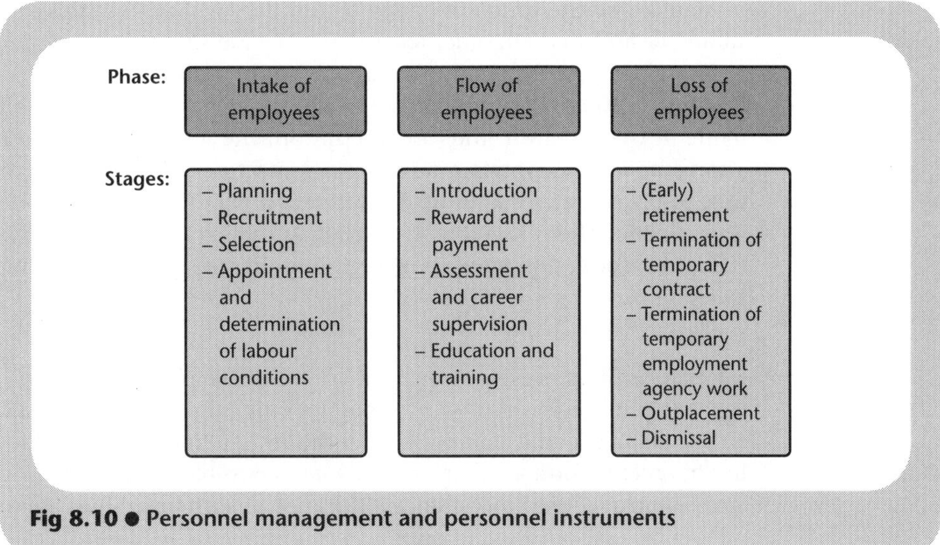

Fig 8.10 ● Personnel management and personnel instruments

Intake: activities before and at entrance into the office

First there is a prognosis of the personnel need and planning. From the department plans and long-term development plans of the organization can be derived how large the need is for particular kinds of managerial and operational employees over time. It will be necessary to analyse the present personnel file and the future personnel needs more closely. When this is offset against future plans it can be derived to what extent external recruitment has to take place and when, and then estimates can be made on the need for internal recruitment and promotion.

In personnel planning there are factors of influence needed to be taken into account: for example, labour times, holiday, labour time reduction, available budget, absenteeism, turnover, absenteeism due to internal or external education and so on. In the short- and middle–long-term planning these factors must be processed into the figures. Furthermore the planning (per department) is co-determined by the customers' orders, production capacity and any occurring rush orders. If, for example, there is a high level of absenteeism, more people need to appear on the books than the job actually calls for.

Recruitment

Recruitment involves enlisting certain candidates for certain functions. The personnel department will often recruit employees for 'lower' functions via certain standard procedures, preferably in consultation with the department where the employees will find their work place. The recruiting of 'higher' managerial staff for key functions in the organization or of top management often does not take place through the personnel department. External firms or 'head hunters' may be called in which advise management or the board of directors.

An important document in the preparation of a recruitment procedure is the job description. A job description provides possible candidates for the function with information about what has to be done in that function. In a personnel ad which is drawn up, it is important to lift function relevant matters from the job description and translate these as specifically as possible into function demands. This means that it has to be stated how the function has to be fulfilled, what the individual should know and should be able to do in order to carry out the job successfully.

In a good personnel ad, in addition to the name and nature of the company or institution, the location and size of the organization there should also appear: the name of the function, the job description, the job demands and labour conditions. The name and telephone number of a contact person need to be mentioned and it is wise to provide candidates with information about the application procedure and the way in which they should reply (including closing date). All this provides an applicant with the information which enables him or her to submit a meaningful application.

Selection

Selection is the process by which the most suitable person is chosen from those who are eligible. 'Suitable' in this instance does not only imply professional skills, but also personality factors. A candidate may be, after the first interview, subjected to a psycho-technical test in order to form as complete a picture as possible of the person. Such a test is considered only part of the process since it does not, as such, offer 'hard' guarantees.

Tools in case of selection are:

- data from the past: education, work experience, reasons for change of job and so on;
- interviews: in a conversation a better impression of someone can be formed, explanation of the earlier supplied data is asked for and so on;
- tests:
  - intelligence test: aimed at measuring the learning capacities and the general development of the candidate;
  - performance test: aimed at testing the professional skill of the applicant and investigation into problem-solving and decision-making ability based on simulated or real situations;
  - job test: testing someone's use of professional language, ability to handle tools and so on;
  - aptitude test: the emphasis is placed on investigation into the capacity to learn specific requirements of the job;
  - personality test: research is carried out into the personal characteristics of the applicant.

All these combined do not offer an absolutely sure way of getting the right candidate in the right place, although they certainly provide some help and support.

The availability of function relevant knowledge and skills is of importance in the selection procedure, so it can be determined whether candidate A knows more than candidate B, or if candidate B is more skilled than candidate A, and so on. By this stage it is more or less known whether a candidate has the qualities to perform well in a function and so will be able to conduct a reasonable minimum performance in this type of work. The departmental management will have to be able to rely on this knowledge and skill. It is also important to test notions to do with task fulfilment. Differences in notions about task fulfilment will in general lead to conflict. It is therefore wise to find out in advance whether people can engage in fruitful co-operation. In order to be able to choose meaningfully, candidates have to be compared based on standards which have been set in advance. This means in a function relevant knowledge area, all candidates take the professional skill test in the same practice situation, or that they take a standard psychological test. References may also be required and/or work history is checked out. In the case of applications for government positions, several countries require a 'statement about public behaviour' to be sent in. A medical test often belongs to the procedure as a standard element. The personnel selection interview is the final opportunity for getting extra information and for giving a judgement about more or less equal candidates. In many cases this is done by a recruitment and selection committee that then has to reach a decision as to the most suitable candidate.

Recruitment and selection of employees is not regulated by law, although attempts have been made to develop certain codes of conduct. It might be obvious that an organization has a lot of freedom in determining how it goes about recruiting new employees. Care in handling the interests of the organization and of applicants is, of course, one of the first priorities.

Appointment and determination of labour conditions

A suitable system of labour conditions, comprising a system of reward and payment, is of course one requirement of a good personnel policy. Labour conditions can include holiday arrangements, arrangement of work and rest times, retirement regulations and other secondary labour conditions such as travel and cost reimbursements and so on. Reward and payment are important components of the labour conditions. Special attention is paid to reward in section 8.9.

Generally speaking higher management functions are still rarely filled by women. This is changing, however. Gradually, more young graduate women are being taken into the trainee programmes of large organizations. In order to make a career possible for them a number of organizations are taking measures which can stimulate their uptake. Pregnancy leave, job sharing, child care, re-entering and so on are all measures that improve the chance of females within the workforce.

Job sharing is labour which is set between fixed times for a fixed number of hours a week/month. In middle and higher functions, few are offered for job sharing. Job sharing is the term applied when two people share one job, and is becoming increasingly widespread.

Job sharing is higher functions often requires that one needs to be working full time. Sharing responsibility between employees in the same managerial function can, in practice, be a source of disagreement and confusion. This can be prevented, however, by deliberation between managers and agreement about the approach and style of leadership, good work planning, stimulation of exchange of employees and so on. Resistance may also linger in the psychological field and in the prevailing notion in the work culture, where it may be common still to be of the opinion that someone who wants to maintain himself in a higher function can only do this when he works full time. For many who have to work full time, it is often difficult to endure that someone who spends less time at work still has greater influence in that organization. This may be accepted in directors, consultants in special services and similar, but it still remains little known among employees in normal line relations.

Flow: activities during employment

The activities during employment start with the introduction of the new employee, at the moment that he or she enters the organization. A good introduction is important for motivation in the job, and determines the first impression of the organization. The goal of a good introduction procedure is:

- show the new employee what he or she will mean to the organization;
- meeting colleagues and managers with whom he or she will co-operate in the fulfilment of the function;
- making clear what is expected of the new employee in the fulfilment of the function within the department and in the organization as a whole.

During the introduction, a new employee will be given the chance to get to know the nature/peculiarities of the organization. This is important in order to teach the new employee behaviour which suits the culture of the organization and the department. The new employee has to feel at ease to be able to work productively. Introduction in the organization may be taken care of by someone from the personnel department, by way of a general introduction, making the acquaintance of the organizational culture and management personnel, covering house rules and a tour through the organization. The departmental introduction is the responsibility of the concerned departmental head and is taken care of by him or by one of his immediate colleagues. The departmental introduction forms the bridge to learning the ropes. After acquaintance has been made with new colleagues and management and it has been explained how one works in the department and which role has been intended for the new employee, the actual working/learning the ropes begins. Learning the ropes means learning to execute the task to be fulfilled in the way which is usual in the department. Learning the ropes is important because new employees are often judged after only a short period of time. New employees have to be able to show their qualities in a responsible way with regard to the function demands. In a good training programme three components are, therefore, important:

- choosing the tasks in the programme;
- spreading these tasks over the training period;
- supervising, controlling and correcting the carrying out of the task.

Assessment and career supervision

The feedback of information about expectations created earlier in employment, as well as information about expectation or desires which are present in the employee, is in the area of career coaching during the period one is employed in the organization. Coaching is directed at the individual employee to offer him or her information and the provision to develop further his or her capabilities. Assessment of someone's function in the organization is a mutual exchange of thoughts about that function. This means that periodically attention is paid to how a function is being fulfilled, the strong and weak points of an employee and what changes are possible and desired. An assessment discussion can lead to a better insight into the employee's own potential and his development potential within the organization. Assessment gets a meaningful followup if it is followed by regular work discussions with the manager or with other department employees about work, results, progress, problems and such topics. A followup can ensure that the contents of the function are described more precisely and that clear task agreements are made. The desires of the employees must be tuned into the function which is to be fulfilled and the tasks which have to be carried out. Differences between function fulfilment and the exercising of function requirements can lead to adjustment of the task package, the possibility of promotion, placement in another function, further education and so on.

In the assessment of personnel in discussion form, three types of assessment can be distinguished:

- performance assessment: directed at making statements from which derives performances an employee delivered in the past;
- potential assessment: directed at making statements about the development potential of the employee in his knowledge and skills in the future;
- mutation assessment: directed at providing insight into the question of whether an employee can function as well in another function at the same level, or even perhaps perform even better.

Besides the assessment discussion, job evaluation or performance appraisal can be distinguished.

Job evaluation is not an assessment method as such but is, rather, a discussion based on events in the work carried out in the past. It especially effects the way of actual functioning which is then discussed by an employee and his chief. Problems and bottlenecks are discussed, as well as possible solutions which can be found together. In such a conversation the following can come under discussion: the circumstances under which the function is conducted, possibilities for task enlargement and career prospects. Emphasis is, however, placed on matters that did not occur as they were supposed to, and there can then follow a mutual discussion as to how future problems can be handled. Agreement must be reached. In a followup conversation can be discussed to what extent the agreement has led to improvement in the functioning. If it appears that the work still cannot be done properly because the right resources are missing, other actions will have to be taken. A job evaluation is open in character and makes demands on the style of management, considering that this conversation is concerned with exchange of information, improvement in communication, stimulation and development of employees and at further function and organization development.

Demotion and function relief

Demotion is a lowering in rank and involves the removal from a higher to a lower function. Demotion can be a policy instrument in the personnel sphere to offer possibilities to personnel members in management (including members of the management team or the board of management) who have been employed by the company for many years to encourage them to take a step back when approaching retirement. Demotion can increase willingness on the part of managers to take formal measures with regard to employees.

The tendency to accept a function at a lower level increases as we grow older. The tendency to reduce effort follows in the same way, while the will to work harder in order to be promoted yet again is also less pronounced among older managers.

When younger managers look for another job they find higher positions usually limited to the older managers. The tendency to accept demotion increases under those circumstances. It is a different story when accompanied by a 'lower' function name or title, where an aggressive reaction may occur, without clear relation to age or management level.

If someone has to choose between working in another function with 10 per cent salary cut or early retirement with 40 per cent salary cut, 70 per cent of managers over 55 years of age have been found to opt for another function. Spare time seems attractive only at a reasonable distance.

A completely open demotion is more easily accepted when the employee is older. If not handed out with care or not chosen voluntarily, demotion is, of course, more than just a step lower on the hierarchical ladder: it is then degradation and is accompanied by negative psychological consequences for the person involved.

If demotion is experienced as degradation and this feeling is reinforced, employees will feel badly treated. They will react bitterly and depict the organization an insecure place to work. However, an open atmosphere can be created around demotion, giving information about future possibilities and/or by means of *outplacement* help can be given regarding a new function somewhere else, and transfer can be overseen. In demotion, in which degradation is felt to play a part, it is especially important not to increase the pressure caused by lowering salary. The salary problem is a critical point in demotion. Even if someone can adjust to loss of status and power, a decrease in income remains a bitter reality. Rules of thumb which can be used are: see to it that the employee keeps his salary, perhaps at a frozen level and try to adjust the salary to the salary scale of a lower level in a creative way. All these steps can contribute to demotion's being made an element within the organization culture.

Demotion can form a function relief for older employees. A career, during the natural lifecycle of employees, follows a rising and falling curve. This last point is not yet a matter of course in western culture. Via demotion policy negative consequences can be reduced by making it possible to step aside or step back within the organization, sometimes in a staff function, sometimes via job sharing.

Flexible retirement is another step on this road. Flexible retirement is a system of retirement in which the retirement date is not fixed on the year in which the employee turns 65, but one in which the employee gets to make the choice to work for a shorter period or for a longer one. Through this system justice can be done to the diverging vitality of different employees. If the atmosphere around demotion is open and sincere and a respected board or management member asks for demotion for personal reasons and wants to withdraw from an important function, for example, at the age of 55, then the demotion policy is more easily accepted in the organization. What is important here is that there is clarity about the age limit and that no exceptions are to be made.

Education and training

Within the personnel function, education and training are also important. For the individual employee this is particularly important for promotion prospects. Education and training usually have a professional technical and an organizational aspect, and are concerned with learning within a department and offering of orientation possibilities in the organization or the providing of insight into growth potential of people in the organization. Education and training can differ from professional technical education in a classroom in a company school, a training by actual exercising of a function ('training on the job') in the organization, to enlargement of the general professional skills and general development or preparation for a managerial position in the organization. In the last case attention will have to be paid to: associating with people as individuals and handling of groups, questions of cost control, insight into the workings of the organizational structure and so on. Often used training methods here are lectures, instruction, discussions, case studies and similar.

Management development

A special place is reserved in the notion of management development for future management. Young managers have to be educated, on the one hand by systematic coaching by older managers, on the other by having them externally educated and trained. Management development will always be strongly determined by the level of young managers and by the level they will attain in time. Systematic management development can take place within a personnel department, at the level the highest management of the organization actually concerns itself with. In fact, management development is the responsibility of the highest management because through it the succession of present management at different organizational levels is being arranged.

Young, future, promising managers who have been selected to go through a special education programme with the fulfilment of future top functions in mind and who, because of that may receive preferential treatment, are sometimes referred to as 'crown princes'. In large organizations first a reservoir of potential managers has to be created, for example through the recruiting of trainees. Once selected and the reservoir for education and training is being maintained, it is often thought that from this 'nursery' (*see* section 8.10) some real 'toppers' will emerge. This label can, however, also work to the disadvantage of those involved. The goal of management development is to provide the right qualitative and quantitative occupation of managerial functions in the organization. Management development comprises a determination of the need for future management (in numbers and quality), registration of the interest of present managerial employees, registration of the functioning of individual managers (by assessment and function discussions) and career planning and management education plans.

So, on the one hand, in making plans one takes into account the wishes and capabilities of the people while, on the other hand, it is important to know what the organization needs in order to stay in the throes of societal developments.

Departure: activities at the end of employment

In planning for the middle–long and long term with regard to the composition of the personnel file, account must be taken not only of the function to be filled, but also of the available people in terms of age and education for the exercise of those functions. The composition will have to be reviewed anew every year. Vacancies can arise through retirement, discharge, replacement or death. Vacancies can sometimes be filled by internal promotion, but in other cases, recruitment of new personnel has to take place.

If vacancies are indicated and new function demands are formulated in time, they can be filled by aimed education of the present personnel. Sometimes, however, downsizing may be necessary. This can be the consequence of demand reduction or of structural causes, perhaps from mechanization or automation. Downsizing can be tackled by natural turnover, labour time reduction, and by early retirement. Here the age structure of the entire personnel must be examined. Careful monitoring of voluntary early retirement and preparation for that moment of retirement and for the ensuing period of relative inactivity after a long, often laborious work life all play an important part in this process.

Outplacement is a whole series of activities/services, both internal and external to the company, that exist to help someone who has been given notice find another job outside the organization, but preferably affiliated with the previous employment. The cause of this is found in the working of the so-called 'Peter principle', based on the experience that an employee promoted to higher and more demanding functions based on the good performances from a previous function does not appear to suffice

Exhibit 8.6

Cultural traditions in management development

There is no established one best way of tackling management development. Focusing on the development of those persons with high potential, we observe different traditions in different organizations. We have labeled these with national stereotypes – the Japanese model, the Latin European approach, the Germanic tradition, and the Anglo-Dutch model. There is great diversity in American patterns. Some American firms are 'Latin' in their approach, while other European firms follow the Japanese pattern.

The Japanese Model

The model that emerged in large companies like Matsushita, Sanyo, and Nissan after the Second World War is based on the recruitment of elite cohorts and a competition, a tournament of elimination, leading the winners into senior positions. The educational system in Japan is a progressive filtering of elite achievers, and it is from the select few at Tokyo and other top universities that high-potential individuals are recruited. Manacement potential is thus identified on a person's entry into the company.

The Japanese system is highly competitive, where widely held beliefs about Japanese lifelong employment and seniority-based promotion are distorted clichés of the reality. Most firms apply the system to their foreign subsidiaries, and if the shop-floor climate of Japanese factories abroad has a favorable public image, the managerial development system tends to be viewed as alien. Western managers do not have this patience or long-term orientation, and Japanese firms have found it difficult to recruit local managerial talent in other countries (this has been described as the 'Achilles heel' of Japanese management practices in an era of globalization).

Fig A Elite cohort approach: the 'Japanese' model

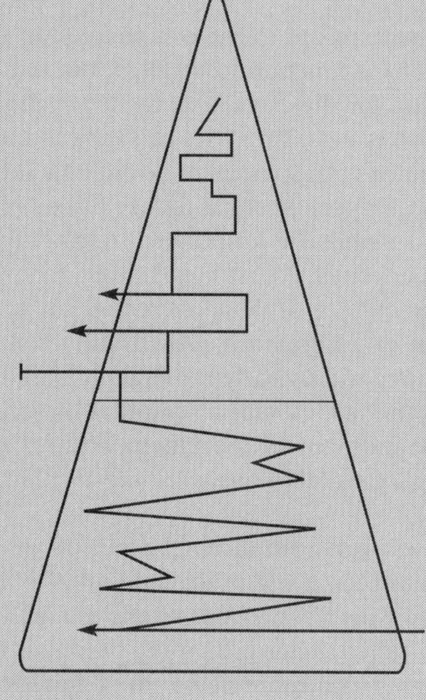

Potential development – time-scheduled tournament:

- unequal opportunity; good jobs to the best
- four to five years in a job, seven or eight years up or out
- comparison with cohort peers
- multifunctional mobility, technical-functional track for minority

Potential identification – managed elite trial:

- elite pool or cohort recruitment
- recruitment for long-term careers
- job rotation, intensive training, mentoring
- regular performance monitoring
- equal opportunity

The Latin Model

It is the structure of management development in Latin Europe that most approximates that of the Japanese, though without the systematic tracking of cohorts. Taking France as an example, selection of potential top managers also takes place at entry, mostly on the basis of elite educational qualifications. Studies have shown that the graduates of the three top 'Grandes écoles' (the elite engineering schools) who chose an industrial career had a 90 percent probability of landing up as president of a company. The only open question was the size and importance of the company.

The career progression of these individuals is a tournament as in Japan, though one that is more political and without systematic norms. It is a competitive struggle of achievement, selling of oneself, and building alliances that is captured by the social game theory of the French sociologist Michel Crozier, though subtly combined with the camaraderie of association with a mafia of fellow peers.

The Germanic Model

The Germanic tradition (embracing to some extent Switzerland and certain Scandinavian and Dutch firms) is different, characterized by formal apprenticeship

Fig B Elite political approach: the 'Latin' model

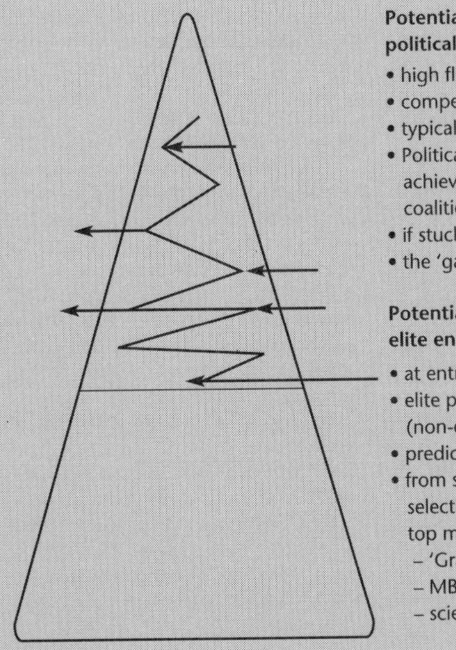

Potential development – political tournament:

- high fliers
- competition and collaboration
- typically multifunctional
- Political process (visible achievements get sponsors, coalitions, read signals)
- if stuck, move out and on
- the 'gamesman'

Potential identification – elite entry, no trial:

- at entry
- elite pool recruitment (non-cohort)
- predictive qualities
- from schools specialized in selecting and preparing future top managers
  - 'Grandes écoles'
  - MBAs
  - scientific PhDs

Fig C Functional approach: the 'Germanic' model

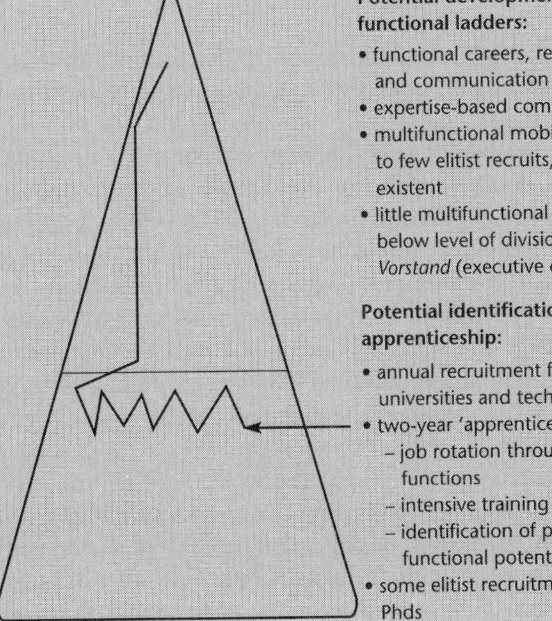

Potential development – functional ladders:

- functional careers, relationships, and communication
- expertise-based competition
- multifunctional mobility limited to few elitist recruits, or non-existent
- little multifunctional contact below level of division heads and *Vorstand* (executive committee)

Potential identification – apprenticeship:

- annual recruitment from universities and technical schools
- two-year 'apprenticeship' trial
  - job rotation through most functions
  - intensive training
  - identification of person's functional potential and talents
- some elitist recruitment, mostly of Phds

and greater attachment to expertise-based functional career paths. Apprenticeship is a well-rooted Germanic tradition for skilled and blue-collar employees: a two- to five-year period of on-the-job training, courses on company practices and policies, and training in partnership with local technical or trade schools. However, even graduates undergo a two-year apprenticeship, a period of job rotation through the enterprise accompanied by training.

For those with the depth of education that is provided by a doctoral diploma in particular, this may ultimately lead into a board-level position where the disadvantages of the functional orientation are balanced by a collegiate sharing of responsibility.

But just as there are two industrial Japans – the former Zaibatsu concerns of international renown and the lesser firms – so there are two Germanies, that of the large established firms and that of the smaller-sized companies; and two Frances, that of the establishment and that of the self-made entrepreneurs. Also in Germany certain individuals find the functional or technical orientation of big business to be unattractive, leaving for positions in smaller companies (the *Mittelstand*) where responsibilities are more generalist in nature.

The Anglo-Dutch Model

The generalist notion of management development is most rooted in the Anglo-Saxon cultures, and in some Dutch firms, joined more recently by the Scandinavians. If there is a model for transnational firms, this approximates it. Entry is less elitist, with most graduates being recruited locally for specific technical or functional jobs. During the early career years (about the first eight years at ICI), these graduates are expected to perform and climb in their functional hierarchies.

continued overleaf

Exhibit 8.6 continued

Fig D Managed development approach: the 'Anglo-Dutch MNC' model

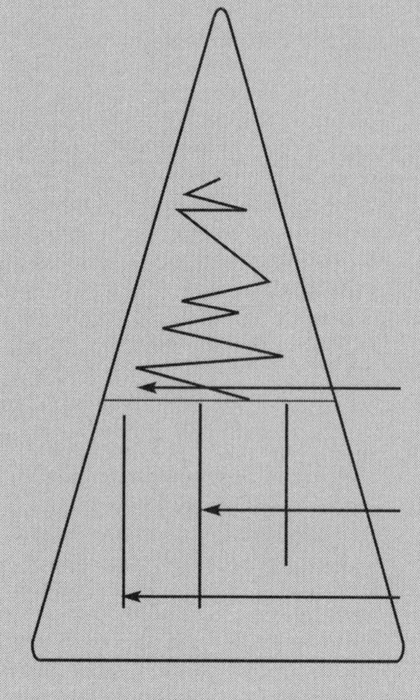

Potential development – managed potential development:
- careful monitoring of high potentials by management review committees
- review to match up performance and potential with short- and long-term job development requirements
- Importance of management development staff (reporting in Europe to GM/CEO)

Potential identification – unmanaged functional trial:
- little elite recruitment
- decentralized recruitment for technical or functional jobs
- five to seven years' trial
- no corporate monitoring
- problem of internal 'potential identification' via assessments assement centres, indicators
- possible complementary recruitment of high potentials

Around the age of 30, after these testing years, the human resource management problem is to identify those individuals who have potential (a concept that is difficult to operationalize. Since Japanese-style systematic performance appraisal is less traditional, companies resort to a variety of devices for the identification of potential. For some US firms, the MBA diploma has become an entry ticket into the high-potential development ladder, thus leading toward the elitist entry pattern of Japanese and Latin companies. Other firms have invested in assessment centers: two- to three-day simulations of managerial situations where the performance and qualities of aspirants can be observed and evaluated by psychologists and trained managers. Most firms, however, rely to a greater or lesser degree on the collective judgment of senior managers in the particular subsidiary.

Source: From *Transnational Management* by Bartlett and Ghoshal (1992).

because he had already reached his level of competence in that previous function. So there is a natural tendency within organizations to allow employees to grow to their level of incompetence.

Outplacement offices take up the task to take care of and accompany the respected people on their way to a new job. This often involves employees from higher and middle management. Besides the job itself, their status and esteem among friends and family is under pressure. When everything goes as it should, outplacement starts even before the people involved know that discharge hangs over their heads. In the first contacts between an organization and an outplacement office agreements are reached about the way in which the involved employee will be accompanied, how payment is to be arranged, and so on. Then follows the moment at which the discharge is announced, directly after which the outplacement process proper can commence.

Controlling the personnel process is part of the managing process that has, at policy level as well as at operational level, to obtain meaning. Giving meaning to the personnel function is one of the responsibilities of top management of a company or institution. Tasks which belong to this can be delegated to the personnel department. The execution of part of the operational work can be delegated to managers on the line in departments in co-operation with the personnel department. The assessment of an employee, for example, takes place in the department by the department chief, while the assessment system and the accompanying procedure are designed and monitored by the personnel department.

8.9 PAYMENT SYSTEMS AND SALARY STRUCTURES

The types of rewards which can be given to managerial and operational employees in organizations are more varied than is generally assumed. The direct rewards are clear cut. But there are also indirect reimbursements and non-financial rewards. In Fig 8.11, different types of rewards are depicted (Robbins, 1979, p. 365). All these kinds of rewards can be divided over individuals, groups and organizations.

Intrinsic forms of reward come from the work itself and are the express result of work satisfaction. Extrinsic forms of reward can be subdivided into direct reimbursements, indirect reimbursement and non-financial rewards. An employee expects the direct and indirect reimbursements to be in accordance with his contribution to the organization and also that they relate to the reimbursements of other employees with similar qualities and results. The non-financial rewards quickly form a reservoir of wishes which the organization can possibly fulfil. They are only limited by the innovative capacities of managers and possibilities to give the rewards people in the organization desire and which managers have at their disposal.

8.9.1 Payment: performance or merit orientation

Most theorists agree that a reward system has to be based on merit, but what that actually means is debatable. Merit, therefore, is only one of the many factors which determine the eventual reward.

Other factors from which criteria can be derived, are:

- performance;
- effort;
- seniority;
- professional skill;
- degree of difficulty of the work;
- judgement capability.

In a group or organization, the payment or reward problem is almost always experienced as a question of fairness. This asks for openness around systems, for deliberation with and participation of employees. Preventing dissatisfaction and social unrest appears to be of greater importance than the extra impulse which radiates from a differential performance reward (*see* section 9.4).

In most countries, reward of an employee is the result of the application of three or four different principles. In working these out, however, large differences occur, not only between countries but also between company sectors and within a company between categories of personnel.

Important for the determination of the reward size is the value of the function (or the weight of the function). In this first principle it is the qualifications that are necessary for the job and how much is to be paid for those on the labour market. In determining the functional salary, for which guidelines have usually been included in the collective labour contracts, one can take into account internal considerations.

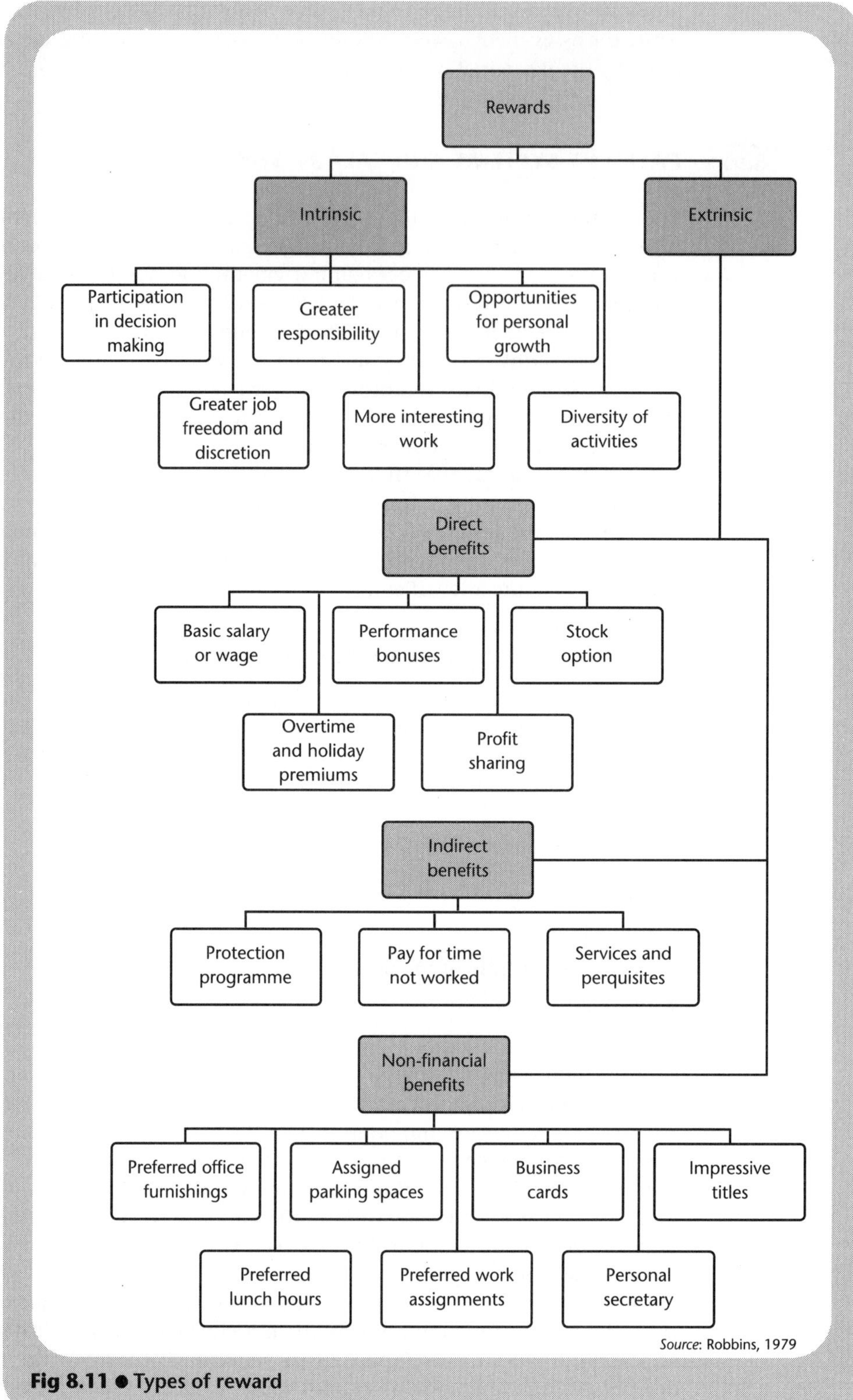

Source: Robbins, 1979

Fig 8.11 ● Types of reward

In cases of reward according to performance, a bonus or premium is paid for performances which exceed a certain norm or standard. A structural salary increase may be granted: the fixed salary then increases with one or several steps along the salary scale under consideration.

Another principle concerns secondary labour conditions. Social security does not play such a large role here, but rather additional provisions which have been agreed on per company and/or sector. These provisions may include, for example, additional retirement insurance, health insurance or life insurance. Here also large differences within an organization can exist.

In conclusion, tertiary labour conditions need to be mentioned: these apply to several categories of personnel. A wide variety of reimbursements is included, for example, car mileage (or a company car), telephone use, and memberships of clubs. Cafeteria subsidies, compensation for mortgage interest, or favourable saving arrangements are also included which in some sectors of industry may apply to all employees.

8.9.2 Opportunism or system?

In many small and middle-sized companies there may be opportunistic determination of salaries paid. Here payment is an estimate by the employer of the amount which he would have to pay to the employee in order to prevent him from leaving the company. Age, company loyalty and such aspects all play a part. Systematic attention is not paid to comparison of salaries within and outside the company, however.

'Streamlining of subjectivity' is preferred in order to avoid a sense of discrepancy between employees' salaries. Through a form of valuation of functions salary groups and scales can be designed. This of course applies for functions of which content and nature of tasks to be carried out can reasonably be determined, and also for higher company functions, in which someone is able to design his function himself.

8.9.3 Choice of payment system

By choosing a particular payment system, a particular labour behaviour is evoked. So it is important to examine the motives on which the choice of system is based. In the choice of payment system attention will have to be paid to the following factors:

- demanded precision of the job;
- influence over the job;
- measurability of performance;
- individual or group work;
- style of leadership;
- nature of the manufacturing: piece, mass, serial production;
- size of the organization;
- number of performance norms.

The functional salary comprises the basic amount for an employee which is further determined by bonuses for seniority, merit and other factors. In the payment of a wage or salary account must also be made of the legal requirements for social security and income tax. Personal reward is also brought about by choosing a particular payment system (Fig 8.12).

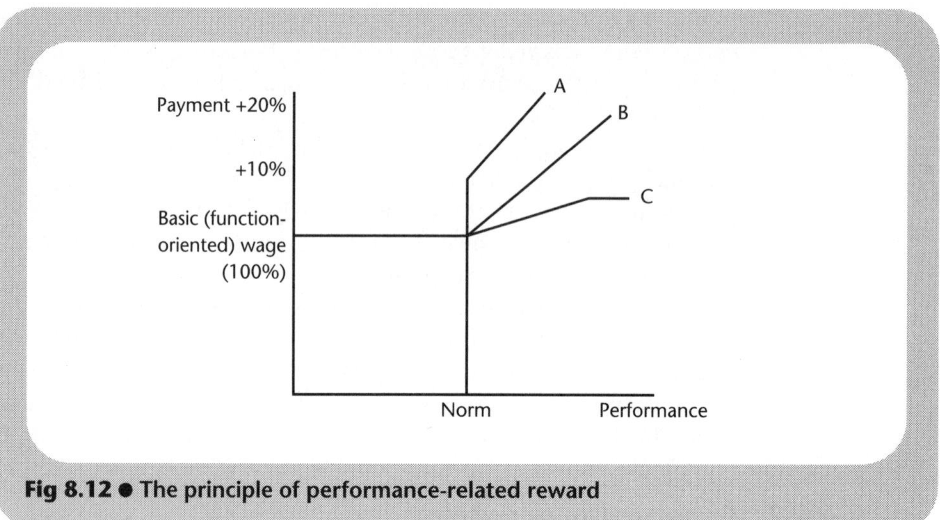

Fig 8.12 ● The principle of performance-related reward

8.9.4 Payment on performance

The principle of payment on performance requires on the one hand that it be determined what a normal and fair performance is, that is: a performance which, under average circumstances, can be delivered by suitable personnel members (selected, educated, with the necessary experience) and with a normal effort. An increasing amount of research is being carried out in order to try to determine what a normal fair day's performance is. On the other hand, payment on performance also involves the link of performance to a premium. It is already the case that attaining the normal performance involves a premium being given. The premium may only apply to performances which are better than the norm. Essential in each system of payment on performance is that the performance identified is relevant to the core activities and is clearly alterable by the personnel member concerned.

It is important that the chosen payment system meets the following demands.

- The elements should be alterable by the employee.
- Both employer and employee should have an economic interest in there being a positive influence of the employee on the elements.
- The elements have to be measurable objectively.

In new technologies and in modern organizational structures alike, the emphasis is increasingly placed on groups, or even larger units. This means that a shift of emphasis will take place from the application of individual payment of performance to that of group payment on performance. This is referred to as profit sharing, when part of the annual profit of the organization is set at the disposal of the employees. Profit sharing is not an independent payment system, but can be regarded as an addition to other systems. One attractive element of profit sharing is that it can create a bond between the employees and the organization in which they are employed. A problem is that the stimulus for delivery of higher performances which radiates from it is not very large.

8.9.5 'Cafeteria' plan

The cafeteria plan is not a system which determines the level of the payment, but rather a plan which offers employees the opportunity to structure the total payment package in such a way that best associates with personal needs. Personnel members in this system have little or no influence over the secondary and tertiary labour conditions which apply to them. It means that almost everyone deals with some conditions which are not valued, or of which one is not even informed (because the employer, for example, pays the premium for it). By the same token, certain other conditions are indeed attractive, but are not part of the package. That is why the plan intends to give the personnel members choice possibilities in the field of:

- duration of working day and/or working week;
- length of holiday;
- level of pension contribution;
- early retirement;
- health insurance package.

8.9.6 Incidental payments

A common complaint is that the practice of the payment policy is very inflexible. Managers want to have the opportunity directly to show their appreciation of personnel members, individual or as a group, in a financial respect, when extraordinary efforts or results have be delivered. That is why in several organizations other forms of incidental payments have been introduced, including:

- offers of lunch;
- dinner for two;
- attending an expensive congress.

8.9.7 Bonuses

In many organizations bonuses are determined and paid at the end of the year (= 13th month). In many cases this bonus is based on fixed agreements determined in advance and the size of the company profit is not relevant. Bonuses for higher personnel do not usually have this same agreement and the yearly royalties are strongly linked to the degree of economic success. The bonus then becomes a variable component of the labour income: it is determined each year anew. The size of bonus usually depends on the level of one's function in the company and on the influence one is believed to exercise on the attained company result.

8.9.8 Top management salary

In a private or public company, the board of management has the final responsibility for salary policy within the organization. The income of the members of the board of management is determined by the board of directors or supervisory council. In cases in which the directors are at the same time the owners of the organization many kinds of financial and fiscal motives determine the board income. In determining the income of a managing director several aspects play a part, for example company size, company profit, geographical spread. A link between attained results and payment seems to be an important factor in this regard, as are honouring the job and respect for the man or woman who carries out this job.

8.10 ● CAREERS AND MANAGEMENT DEVELOPMENT

Career development needs to be integrally linked to career planning: set up a career plan with the employee, implement those decisions and in conclusion, evaluate the decisions made in the past. Career plans regard specific people and specific functions within the organization, as opposed to personnel planning for groups and categories of functions. A dialogue between the organization and its employees is the lynch pin in career planning and the resultant career plan is the tangible outcome of the tuning of the individual's needs to those of the organization. The process of career development is therefore a coincidence of structural-organizational and individual aspects, as is shown in Fig 8.13.

In practice there are three forms of application of management development systems which more or less meet the demanded MD goal, namely: an appropriate

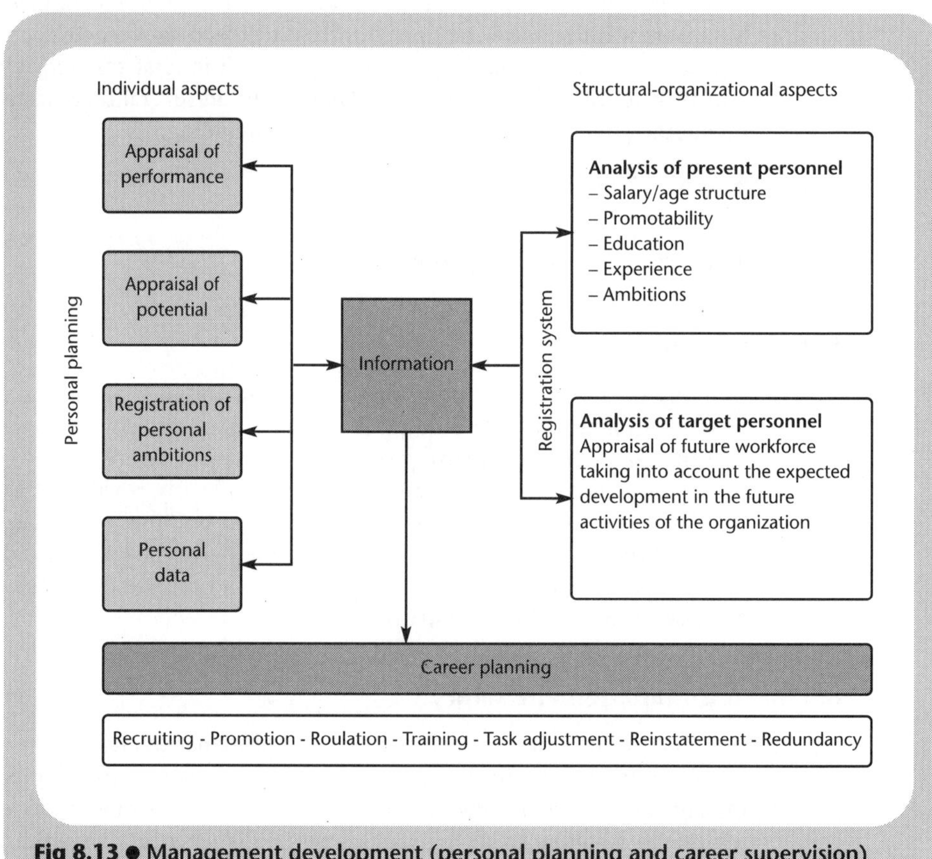

Fig 8.13 ● Management development (personal planning and career supervision)

operating management both now and in the future. The different systems can be placed on a scale, on one side of which lies the formalistic, and on the other side the ad hoc MD system. Somewhere in between stands the nursery model (otherwise known as the fish pond model).

8.10.1 The formalistic MD system

From the moment a new graduate enters a company until approximately six years later, it is clear what happens to him or her. This pre-determined path comprises a minimum of three functions and a fixed education programme. After the first phase of six years it is usual that a well considered choice of line or staff function is made. Further possibilities in the progress of the career depend on the individual and the organization (Fig 8.14).

As a consequence of strict planning an education and training path can be determined in great detail. The first six years especially are directed at broader development and the development of skills. In the second phase the involved people may obtain their first managerial experience.

8.10.2 The fish pond model

It can be seen from Fig 8.15 that the first two or three years are particularly important. A new graduate is taken into the organization as a management trainee. The big difference from the previous model is that these trainees are often appointed over the regular formation. As in the first phase they do not fulfil a particular function, but they occupy themselves with projects at different points within the organization. Just as in the previous model, the traineeship tries to realize growth towards a line or staff function.

Because a trainee contributes to different projects within the organization, in a short period of time he or she gets to know the organization well in different places. This traineeship offers time and space to explore self-potential in the organization. All these factors in combination with the capabilities of the individual, lead to a very satisfactory selection method for organization as well as individual.

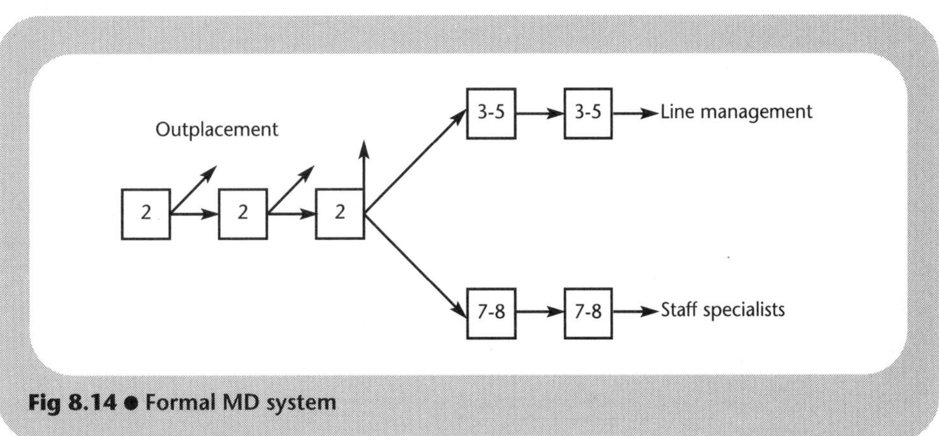

Fig 8.14 ● Formal MD system

8.10.3 The ad hoc MD system

In reality there is no such thing as an absolutely ad hoc MD system. As soon as a management vacancy occurs, it is filled. Every organization has contingency plans should anything happen unexpectedly to the managing director. Organizations with a well worked out MD system are regularly confronted with the possibility of hiring someone from outside. There are unpredictable aspects within even the most advanced systems in respect of people.

8.10.4 The career path in flat organizations: horizontal promotion

The tall pyramidal structure is increasingly giving way to the flat organization. In a flat organization, every component of the organization is complete and operates as independently as possible.

The pyramid flourishes at the thought that the human being at the top is a better kind of person who can cope with tasks of more complexity. The staff think, the top decides and the rest execute. The reality differs.

The manager in a flat organization finds himself to an increasing degree confronted with the question: 'What actually is my added value?' Fortunately for him increasing attention is being paid to the drawbacks of the top positions: too intense a focus on vertical steps up the ladder actually hinders one's development. A manager who wants to stay in the race has to be flexible, and is able, for example, to side step or set up a business for him/herself. In the past everyone wanted up in the hierarchy; nowadays more seek a solution in the horizontal direction. Status and salary are no longer decisive; quality and pleasure in the work are.

In the case of delayering of middle management, internal replacement of employees can be a constructive solution, for example, by means of mobility officers, have to develop an eye for the hidden skills of managers and personnel and for alternative career possibilities.

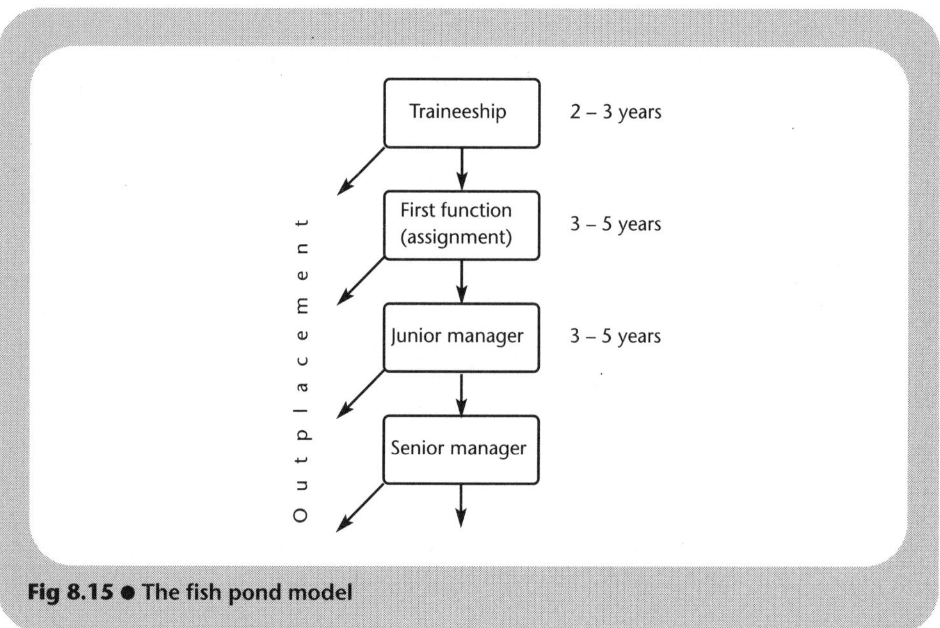

Fig 8.15 ● The fish pond model

For employees in a flatter structure steps up the career ladder, which were traditionally linked to the concept of hierarchy, no longer exist in the same form. Flatter organizations have a tendency to ignore the human need for hierarchy. In this situation it is possible to motivate employees without the traditional promotion perspective. Recent notions on human resources management (HRM) suggest that promotion can indeed be important, but that acknowledgment of performance, self-motivation, interesting experiences, more challenging assignments and the ability to carry them out are found to be more important. The rise up the ladder, titles, being the boss and the feeling gained from that belong more in the background in this perspective. In addition to vertical promotion, we can also think in terms of horizontal promotion. Horizontal promotion, in terms of progress, is to be translated into learning new skills, executing more interesting and challenging assignments: aspects which nowadays are not necessarily linked to the climbing of a vertical ladder.

Flatter organizations demand substantially different HRM concepts. Where this condition is not met and where strongly traditional notions concerning organization, management and control remain in the forefront, hindrance could well be created to the delayering of the organization.

SUMMARY

- Within organizations people must co-operate. To a certain degree organization members are prepared to make a contribution to the organization in exchange for rewards. This leads to the theme of motivation. Different factors appear to be of influence on individual behaviour: the so-called key variables.
- Groups function within the organization. Formal and informal groups can be distinguished. With regard to the forming of teams, the following frameworks can be distinguished: the structural, the human resources, the political and the symbolic framework.
- Different contributions have emerged from psychology for the explanation of individual motivation, such as Maslow's hierarchy of needs theory and Vroom's instrumentality theory. The coherence between motivation, productivity and function design is mapped out by means of the task characteristic model.
- A new form of directing employees is 'empowerment' with which, as well as an increase in motivation, improvement of effectiveness and flexibility go hand in hand.
- Within the framework of the new context in which the development of capabilities and talent of employees is a necessity, there is a need for human resources management (HRM). HRM starts from the strategy of an organization and its structure and culture. HRM thus needs to be an integral part of the management process.
- The management of the personnel process is mapped out by means of the phases of intake, flow and departure. The personnel instruments that deal with these are: recruitment and selection, assessment and career supervision, demotion and function relief, management development, retirement, discharge and outplacement.

continued overleaf

- Valuing the effort of employees involves the reward and payment problem. Different payment systems which can be used are: functional wage, payment on performance, multi-factor payment, group payment, profit sharing and the so-called cafeteria plan. The choice of a reward system implies a certain labour behaviour. A reward system has to be experienced as fair by all those involved. One can build payment systems based on the principles of equal treatment and justified payment according to needs, and equal treatment and justified payment according to performance.
- Given developments outside and inside organizations, it is to be expected that in the future, career prospects will tend to involve horizontal growth and promotion rather than the traditional vertical 'career ladder'.

DISCUSSION QUESTIONS

1. With reference to *Management in action* at the beginning of this chapter: What is your opinion on Arne Olsson's suggestion to line managers to 'close the personnel department'?
2. Of the theories on individual motivation covered in this chapter, which appeals to you most? Which of the theories, if different, do you think most relevant?
3. In your opinion, what is the difference, if any, between 'human resources management' and 'personnel work'?
4. (a) What are the similarities and differences between delegation and empowerment?
   (b) Does empowerment offer the solution to Luigi Cappa's problem of successfully motivating workers in a small firm? (Exhibit 8.6)
   (c) How would you handle his problem?
5. Give your opinion on the following statement concerning two instruments of human resources management: 'Management development and horizontal careers are mutually exclusive.'
6. How would you, as an employee, prefer to be rewarded: via a functional wage, payment for performance, or profit sharing? Does each system still have its distinct disadvantages?

Management case study

Making the grades

A staff appraisal system is demanded even though pay rates lack logic

'You can lead a horse to water but you can't make it drink,' Hendrick Lubbers says resignedly. The Dutchman is manager of human resources at Generation Cinque (GC), a pan-European consortium formed in an attempt to match US and Japanese companies in the development of 'smart' computers that can think and talk. He wants to apply the management disciplines which worked so well at the international oil company from which he was recruited.

However, gaining the full co-operation of the disparate nationalities and specialists at GC is more difficult than he imagined. The crunch comes when Paul Masson, the general manager, asks him to give priority to installing an appraisal system. 'That's precisely what I have been doing,' Lubbers replies patiently. 'But may I remind you that you rejected my suggestion that everyone be on the same payroll, within generously wide salary bands, as the precondition of meaningful appraisal?'

About 20% of GC's staff have been seconded to the consortium from their parent companies at their former, or slightly higher, salaries. Another 20%, who have been working for the same companies under contract, have been released from those contracts and encouraged to negotiate their own with GC.

The other 60% of employees have been hired by GC direct, and most are paid considerably less than the seconded and contracted people. Masson, while conceding that this patchwork recruitment is unfortunate, insists that to change it now would be disruptive. Nevertheless, he wants appraisals to go ahead.

'What is the point, when it means next to nothing in terms of remuneration?' one department head complains. 'I have two seconded men who are earning more than their supervisors.' Other managers object to the very idea of systematic appraisal. 'It's typical of the Anglo-American approach,' Lubbers hears an Italian manager say. 'They expect me to spend hours with each of the 15 people reporting to me, grading them from A to E when I know what their strengths and weaknesses are. And half of them will not be here long anyway.'

When Lubbers perseveres with appraisals, using the forms that elicited a 95% response at his former company, only 10% are returned by his deadline. Many are inconsistent. Thus some managers are loath to equate a C rating with 'satisfactory', grading most people as B, while others are harsher.

'It's a mess,' Lubbers admits to a friend. 'Should I dig in my heels and flatly refuse to go ahead with appraisal without a rethink of employment policy?'

Source: *International Management*, December 1992.

CASE QUESTIONS

1. Do you think it would be possible to carry out a staff appraisal without first reforming the chaotic pay structure?
2. In your opinion, what conditions must exist if a staff appraisal system is to work?

Chapter 9

Leading, motivation and communication

LEARNING OBJECTIVES

After studying this chapter, you should be able to:

- describe the concepts 'leading', 'managing' and 'entrepreneuring' and explain the different factors in leadership;
- describe the effects of different styles of leadership;
- explain the coherence between situational factors and leadership;
- identify different sources of influence and explain certain factors in the exercise of power and authority;
- identify and describe different factors in communication between people;
- describe and explain different styles of conflict resolution;
- describe and explain the typology of organization cultures according to Harrison;
- explain the coherence between leadership and influence in an organizational culture;
- apply the terms from this chapter in a practical case setting.

Management in action

Search for inner values

Brian Bacon (41) has a pure, analytical atmosphere to him and around him hangs the sweet smell of success. Bacon is president and owner of advertisement firm IPC World Strategic Marketing. He is one of the modern 'change agents' who direct the activities of Ford, Motorola, Shell and Citicorp. A big boy among the big boys. And an important observer of the economic and societal developments with which each manager is confronted sooner or later.

Bacon is remarkably open about the way in which he has obtained his by now famous insights. 'A few years ago, my brother and I had a marketing consultancy firm. We earned so much money that between us we owned seven houses in seven different countries. Cars, swimming pools, planes, women. You name it, we had it all. Surrounded by everything which I thought I should own, I was looking around me depressed, seated on the terrace of my house at Kreta with a glass of champagne in my hand. Desperately seeking for new challenges. Which countries had I not seen yet? Which large lines of industry had not consulted me yet? It sounds sentimental, but at that moment something snapped inside. Looking back, I realize that I had started an internal journey. Searching for internal values.'

Bacon is one of the internationally acknowledged apostles who disseminate the necessity for so-called self-management. He is convinced of the fact that it is not the contents of the annual report or the vigorously handled costs and personnel reductions that determine the success of a company. 'The crisis with which western countries are confronted is not just a triple dip of the economy, but more particularly a crisis of the ideas which form the basis of the economic process.'

What does this imply?
Bacon: 'Many companies perpetuate the notion that everything has already been done to control perpetuate costs and to reduce personnel and to ensure that the quality of the products is more competitive. Despite that the production sometimes lags 25% behind that of companies in the Pacific, and the market share also declines. Something is very wrong with the western approach it seems to me. Logic and economic rationalism seem to have had their day. The aggressive approach does not work anymore and has a decreasing effect. Western managers who still venture on optimistic predictions are naive and acting dangerously in my opinion. They have lost contact with the reality of the new economic order and base their expectations on experiences from the past. Well, that past need to be closed. Now the fact of daring to seem insecure and not becoming rigid is relevant. Industrial life needs a totally different approach in order to be able to make it. For the time being, lasting and solid growth is no longer part of your world.'

Why not?
Bacon: 'Because the flow of thought of the western manager, politician and civil servant is subject to a certain degree of mental pollution. Now that needs are greater, businesslike behaviour does not always adjust as intuitively to the new assignments. And the consequence of that is that the thinking does not flow free and unhindered from care. The competition in the fast developing countries and the threat that radiates from that, has a paralyzing effect on both thinking and doing. Nothing is sure and predictable anymore. An end has definitely come to the illusion of the feasible society. The western

continued overleaf

Management in action continued

manager has to realize that he and his company are part of a larger whole: the whole of the world. He is becoming more and more dependent on developments on the other side of the globe. We now have to start looking at the world as an organic whole, in which every country and every company will start playing a role which contributes to the fact that in this way a better balance arises between the continents and between poor and rich. Working harder, better products or smarter sales techniques do not help anymore. On the contrary. The emphasis will have to be shifted from competitive to strategic and characteristic advantages.'

What do you understand by strategic advantages?

Bacon: 'The western manager is often directed at toughness and expansion. His strategies are often the result of a calculated technical nature. Until recently, he did not need other instruments. Because of that, his emotional life and especially his empathy did not need to develop itself. It was not necessary, he would sell anyway. Where empathy is concerned, the average western manager does not know what he does not know, nor indeed what he should know. Even more important, he does not feel what he does not feel, and indeed should feel. This puts him at an enormous disadvantage in comparison to competitors from other cultures, in which more emphasis is traditionally placed on intuition. Those competitors are engaged in matching their specific, more non-material skills, to western knowledge and approach. With good results, I might add. In contacts and negotiations with Asian colleagues and clients, the western manager falls short. He has little feeling for cultural and human characteristics. His bluntness is the consequence of the systematic pollution of his thinking and his poor ability to draw critical conclusions with the attendant consequences in his way of acting. Because of that, his strategic ability leaves much to be desired. The result can be directly traced in the annual figures of the past years, of the present, or of the near future. So it is important for every western manager to first rethink his own identity and sensitivity for the identity and the sensitivity of others. And to do that, he should go not to the outside world, but into his own internal world.'

Can you give an example?

Bacon: 'A few years ago, we consulted a large company, the size of, lets say, Philips, which had to delayer and downsize massively. We reduced the number of employees by forty percent and flattened the organization from twelve to five levels. In the first instance, we were satisfied, till we noticed that the new core group had difficulties with the new responsibilities. The stress level had risen enormously. When I brought that to the attention of the president of the board of management, he referred me to the company medical officer. He in turn described to me the results of an investigation into the measurable health of those involved. They appeared to have as much adrenaline in their blood as soldiers have before they go into battle. All members of the group had lost sight of their function. There was fear and compartmentalization in their thinking. Chaos was rife. We had not attained anything lasting with our reorganization. On the contrary. We had gone totally wrong in the emotional field. In the heads of remaining personnel, fear had taken the place of motivation and inspiration. And that fear consumed all their energy and narrowed their view on whatever form of strategic acting came into sight.'

How can a development like that be prevented?

Bacon: 'In the past few years, there has been fear for the future in the west – a strategic chaos. Many managers struggle with the question of whether they should let the company make a step forward or fall back on their core activities. They are becoming more and more innovative in the battle for the maintenance of their competitive advantage. And that is what is important. Difficulties arise concerning the difference between business and societal ethics. They lose the view on their ethnical boundaries. They behave more and more like generals who let their front soldiers fight a meaningless battle. They are "human doings" instead of "human beings". The solution to this problem lies in the human, the spiritual field if you wish'.

That sounds rather way out. Are you talking about the psychical aspects of human acting?

Bacon: 'Yes and no. In the company in which I learnt this lesson of modern life about the new problems of managers, managers were not able to change themselves just like that. They had too little contact with their emotional potential and an enormous gap in the development of their coping tools. I realize that such an observation is not very helpful. Yet there's the rub. Feeling, just like intellect or talent, is a tool that is present in a rudimentary form in everybody. But feeling, also like intellect and talent, needs to be developed. Having empathy is not necessarily an innate and individual gift, it is the fruit of instinctive observations and a lot of thinking. Not only about the behaviour and reactions of others, but also about one's own behaviour and reactions. When I exchanged thoughts about this with the management of the earlier mentioned company, one of the members of the board of management reacted very honestly by saying: "Of course we have to work much more empathetically, but we do not even do that with our own children."'

Brian Bacon: 'The fact that they had doubts about their authoritarian attitude was hopeful. They realized that, nowadays, you cannot manage anymore when you are not able to indulge yourself in the emotional sense in your employees and your clients. And internal growth and development of instinct are necessary for that. That acknowledgment was a kind of turnround in their thinking and feeling. We started searching mutually for coaching in a more psychological form of introspection about self-functioning. We ended up at Brahma Kumaris, a spiritual university in India with a large number of establishments in western countries. We chose them because we noticed that this institute, managed by women, does not demand any form of religious or other sort of devotion. Their approach and methods concentrate on the rational demands of everyday reality. Management starts from the fact that all human beings on earth have a right to spiritual development. We have been cooperating for many years now and have achieved many good things in several companies both large and small. With the help of tested reflection techniques even diehards seem to be able to temper their aggressive approach and to transfer this into a "warmer" attitude to life. In conversation they start to focus on the functioning of the internal mechanisms by which they observe and estimate situations. The employees of the university urge them to ask themselves essentially different questions. They are brought into the mood to enter into that direct confrontation with themselves: Why do I always want to act as the boss? Why do I always want to be right? Why am I such a bad loser? They give the answer themselves. And in this way get a better view of their own function and after that of the function of their company in society. The results are stunning. In the first place because of the greatly improved climate, and after that in the company results. Managers and employees learn to trust themselves and one another again, and once more get pleasure from doing their job. All energy can now once again be directed at the challenges which this "brave new world" offers us.'

Source: Adapted from Oppenheim, A., 'Search for inner values', in *Elan*, May 1994.

INTRODUCTION

In an organization – as a co-operative working relationship between people – the human being is the most important resource. It is the art of managing to deploy this resource well. Managing people also comprises, in addition to making work arrangements and passing down constraints and instructions, motivating the co-operation and directing others in their actions and aiming working behaviour at the goals of the organization.

Managing people occurs in a process of interaction between leader and immediate subordinate. So it is important to give careful thought to the way in which a leader conceives his task with regard to his subordinates as colleagues. In each style of leadership, a certain idea of the leader resounds with regard to his notion about motivation of employees.

Besides 'style of leadership' and 'leadership' as such, it is here also important to give careful thought to the problems of conflict resolution and influence over the organizational culture. In influencing communication and the exercise of authority and power will come up for discussion.

Before covering these subjects, it is necessary to agree on what is being meant by 'leading'. This leads us briefly into the discussion about differences between an entrepreneur, a manager and a leader.

9.1 LEADING, MANAGING AND ENTREPRENEURSHIP

A managerial functionary spends a large part of his time on directing his employees. On top of that he also supports his employees in a practical sense in the execution of tasks. This is 'leading'. Then there is management: by management we mean the process which leads to the determination of a strategic course for the organization as a whole and the organizational and communicative structure of the total organization, tuned into the organization goals.

Management then is the whole of the activities directed at an effective and efficient set of goals and the execution of these goals through directed actions within an organization. Management is a more complex notion than 'leading' in the narrow sense, since leading is more influencing the organizational, and work behaviour of employees, based on personal contact.

Besides the notions 'leading' and 'management', the notion 'entrepreneur' may be put up for discussion separately. This emphasizes that looking for and making use of opportunities is of importance and that, by being aware of the outside world, one formulates specific goals and executes those goals (and also of course takes risks). In this sense entrepreneurship regards the searching for challenges, the finding of new combinations, the initiating of actions and the taking of calculated risks. An entrepreneur sees problems as a challenge rather than as a hindrance. He or she will not only wait for chances to occur, but also knows that chances can be created. Hereby a notion is developed which is patently applicable in private business, but can also be used in the world of not-for-profit organizations, such as hospitals and (privatized) government organizations.

9.1.1 Entrepreneurship

Entrepreneurship then is the whole of the thoughts, the mentality and the actions that direct themselves at the conscious acceptance of risks in the offering of products and services, often with the apparent intention to make a profit. It also comprises the gift to search for possibilities for the better or different and 'new' use of available resources and ideas of people.

In principle, entrepreneurship can be found at every level in the organization. Searching for possibilities to do something new for others has to do with external clients as much as internal colleagues, who have to work on with the results of the predecessor surrounding them. In any case entrepreneurship is an important condition for the survival of the organization in the future. When board rooms or management teams stop the conscious acceptance of risks in attempts to create new services, products or markets, this is the first step toward an organizational culture in which initiative is no longer appreciated.

Reasoned in the most pure form, 'entrepreneurship' can be exercised without interaction between the entrepreneur and others. If other people become necessary, for example in order to shape or execute ideas, then leadership, organization and management are also being called in to take their part.

9.1.2 Leadership

Leadership involves the creation of a common feeling of direction with the employees. It involves inspiring and involving. An accurate definition of leadership is difficult, but good leadership is really phenomenal when experienced. In the first place, leadership is the bridging of entrepreneurial plans and their execution. Here, leadership is directed at employees and at obtaining their commitment.

Minicase 9.1

So, theoretically seen, one can be an entrepreneur without paying attention to people. Experience teaches us that some entrepreneurs do indeed adopt this attitude. These soloists do not involve employees and others who have an interest in the actions of the organization. They do not want to and are not able to let others share in their intentions in the emotional sense. One should not expect any enthusiasm from them. Stated differently, such entrepreneurs lack leadership in the sense that they lack the power of creating a common sense for direction for the employees.

9.1.3 Management

In the classical sense managing means making it possible for other people to be able to and to want to execute activities directed at the goals. In this classical notion, important management activities are: 'plan' (research, drawing up of plans), 'do' (arranging, co-ordinating, giving assignments, creating conditions), 'check' (testing, measuring, controlling), and 'action' (reviewing, adjusting).

As a list, these activities still say little about what a manager really does, but they do give an indication of the picture of managers' work. Managers themselves often associate their work with notions like chaos, communicating, disciplining employees, cleaning up and removing obstacles along the road.

Where entrepreneurship is directed at conscious acceptance of risks and finding new combinations and where leadership implies goal-directed motivation of employees, managing occupies itself with the 'how' question. More specifically, how to manage people and other resources most effectively to achieve optimum efficiency.

Minicase 9.2

Vitality: body and mind

'Vitality is a subject that, especially in the world of entrepreneurship, is more current than ever,' states Roy Martina, physician, world champion karate expert and vitality trainer. 'More and more people fall between two stools because changes go too fast. All securities that existed in the past around career, have been thrown overboard in no time. Savings, mergers, reorganization, increased competition, stress, performance pressure, the disappearing of management layers. People have to adjust themselves to those changes. That takes a lot of energy. And because of that vitality is of such high importance. Vitality is a surplus of energy in order to pull through moments of strong stress increase without any problems. Only really vital people can handle those changes.'

Here we are expressly thinking in terms of the revitalizing of companies. According to Roy Martina, having vitality is of importance especially for managerial functionaries. The most vital in the company determines the direction of the team. The only way to attain that is by example behaviour. The fact is that the top man must convey his vision in such a way that the whole team gets inspired. 'When a middle manager is more vital than the director, strange situations can arise.'

In the slipstream of the managerial importance of vitality of entrepreneurs, Roy also indicates that the value of life especially becomes more and more important. 'No longer do only material things count. Matters like private life and spare time also start to play an ever more important part. The issue is, however, that the majority of managers come home exhausted and lack the energy to make something out of that life. So, for them, vitality is particularly necessary.'

The big question is then, assuming that fitness is indeed that ultimate acid test for people, as Roy argues it is, how can people go through life at their most vital. According to Martina it all revolves around energy. 'The concern is to waste as little energy as possible and generate as much energy as possible.'

The two most important energy wasters, Martina argues, are digestion and stress. The acquisition of energy starts at night, when the body regenerates. All weak cells are then replaced by new, powerful cells. Decay, hence loss of energy, starts when that recovery process is frustrated. Martina: 'That happens when too much energy is spent on digestion processes by too high a food intake or by bad food combinations. Also, when too much energy is spent on stress, the body cannot recover sufficiently. It is ironic to note that people who are as right as rain and vital, need two hours less sleep because the body needs less energy to remove waste matters. In the morning, that process of detoxification continues at full strength. That is why drinking coffee in the morning is so bad. It frustrates the process in which the body is busy trying to regain strength. So that is the first loss of energy of the day.'

But that is not the only thing. Stress, or the lack of vitality of the mind, also comes up for discussion. Martina: 'Vitality is for sure also between the ears. As I mentioned, stress is an important energy waster. An optimist is ill less often, recovers faster and lives longer than a worrier or a pessimist. Our way of thinking has an enormous influence on our well-being. When we want to change the quality of our life by increasing our vitality, then we have to start by changing the quality of our thinking.'

An important lesson for managers is, according to Martina, that they learn to cope with stress. 'Leaders have to learn to let go of things which they cannot change. They have to commit themselves four hundred percent to the matters which they can actually influence. That saves energy.'

Roy Martina's ten commandments for lasting vitality

- Give yourself the gift of vital breathing. Most people have a shortage of oxygen because of wrong breathing and are less vital because of it. Breathing in deeply ten times three times a day helps.
- Give yourself the gift of living water and living food. The body needs a lot of water. So eat a lot of water-rich food and drink eight to ten glasses of pure water a day. Water detoxifies the body.
- Give yourself the gift of aerobic power. By exercises the oxygen production is increased. Endurance and fitness increase.
- Give yourself the gift of maximum food (*see* 'Food directory').
- Give yourself the gift of a directed mind. Stress is a bad advisor for the body. The new conviction should be that there is always a solution. Having a challenging future is very important.
- Give yourself the gift of structural support. Sufficient rest, sufficient sunlight, relaxation (sauna, massage) and when necessary chiropractic help.
- Make use of oil and fats.
- Reduce the use of dairy produce. Milk is unjustifiably labelled as healthy.
- Reduce sour products. (Among others sugar, vinegar, salt, tobacco, alcohol, coffee and non-fresh fruit juices.)
- Reduce the percentage of animal proteins in food. Animal proteins have been found to be a contributary factor in many diseases of the immune system.

Food directory

In the morning, begin with a breakfast of fresh fruit and eat fruit only until lunch time. Fruit has a high percentage of water, detoxifies, takes little energy to digest and, on top of that, supplies a lot of energy. Limit coffee and tea in the morning and possibly replace with water. A few glasses of water in the morning sees to an efficient removal of waste material. Light lunch in the afternoon, especially if an important meeting follows. Digesting a heavy lunch takes a lot of energy and makes people lazy and sleepy. A good combination of food is essential.

- Combine proteins and carbohydrates as little as possible.
- Green salad is always good.
- Fat blocks the digestion of proteins; a salad of raw vegetables neutralizes this effect.
- Drink before the meal rather than afterwards.
- Fats and oils combine well with carbohydrates and vegetables.
- Proteins combine well with vegetables.
- Fruit should always be eaten separately.
- Do not eat just before going to bed; it takes a lot of energy.
- Do not over-eat and do not eat because of stress.

Source: Buitenhuis, R., 'When a manager is more vital than the director, strange situations arise, in *Elan*, December 1994.

'The manager of the future' is the one who has the capacity to get things done for and by the people, who gives the direction for that, and who creates reasons internally and externally, and can adjust when circumstances change or when activities do not work out as meant and directed. Here we recognize traditional management functions such as planning, organizing, co-ordinating, commanding, controlling and adjusting. Within the more complex notion of management, in the rest of this Chapter, emphasis is placed on elements in managing such as leadership, motivating, influencing culture and behaviour, communication and conflict resolution.

Minicase 9.3

John Sculley (President of the Board of Management of Apple computers) about leadership and management: 'In my eyes, leadership is concerned with vision, ideas and determination of direction. It has more to do with inspiring people with regard to direction and goals than with seeing to it that everything goes right in the daily course of affairs. You cannot lead when you are not able to disengage more than just your own capabilities. You should be able to inspire people to actions without chasing them with a check-list – that is no leadership, only administrative management.'

9.1.4 The paradox of 'management leadership'

The traditional manager – in the role of lonely decision maker, untouchable expert or almighty boss – does not exist any longer. The new manager is much more a leader, a coach, someone who makes it possible for others to do their job. That automatically means the modern manager is no longer the centre of attention: he is assessed on his ability to determine the general strategy in order to have it executed by 'his' people. In other words: the individual success of the new manager coheres closely with the success of his team. This turnround in the approach of the management task is not surprising. For some time companies have been saying that people were the most important asset. Until now it was just words. Present developments, however, force companies to suit the action to those words.

Different types of leadership

Leadership is an essential and integral component of good management. Managers who do not lead will not succeed in fulfilling their function as manager. Management without leadership dimensions is reduced to sheer administrative control. Organizations which are managed without leadership generally perform badly: they are bureaucratic, inefficient and have low responsiveness.

The essential points of this notion are shown in Fig 9.1. The variety comes from three distinct but complementary ways of apprehending leadership: supervisory leadership (the hands), organizational leadership (the head) and inspiring leadership (the heart).

Inspiring leadership is the most universal concept of the three. It is unique insofar that it, by definition, excludes the use of force of authority. In the case of the other two concepts the contrary applies – it is possible to apply force to the application of them, and indeed use of force of authority is not at all uncommon.

The notion holds that all three types of leadership are essential components of good management. Further that the two organization-specific types form an integral component of management as such, whether or not they are considered as being types of leadership. Without these types management is nothing more than administrative control. In this way administrative control and the complementary leadership activities form the core components of management. Inspiring leadership can be seen as something separate: it excludes the use of power as means of coercion and of authority and can also take place outside the organization. Without this form of leadership the possibility remains open for core management activities to be exercised in an autocratic or, at best, a bureaucratic way.

That is why inspiring leadership is considered an essential component of good management, even though, strictly speaking, it is perhaps not necessarily a component of management. It is through the application of inspiring leadership to the leadership aspects of management that the concept of 'transforming' leadership takes on an organizational meaning.

Management is more than administrative control

Modern organizations have arisen as an instrument to make large groups of people co-operate effectively. In organizations people co-operate in different and sometimes complex tasks to make cars, for example, or to supply banking services, or to produce computer software. The administrative skills necessary successfully to lead such organizations, including planning, organizing and control, are described as 'management'. Not for nothing is the most eminent English management title MBA – Master of Business Administration.

But management comprises more than that, as shown in Fig 9.1. When the management concept must comprise the necessary activities in order successfully to lead a large organization, it needs to be considered within two dimensions. In one dimension, management concerns the relationship between the organization and its environment. In the other dimension, management deals with getting things done through other people in the organization.

Management mix

Nicholls (1993) is applied to all the information in Fig 9.1, we see that leadership in its different aspects is an integral component of management as such, as well as an essential ingredient of good management.

Organizational and supervisory leadership, which can only be exercised within an organization, are further integral components of management. Without these leadership aspects, the manager is merely an administrator, a position that can quickly drift off in bureaucracy, that does not react to changes and has no feeling for people.

Inspiring/inspirational leadership can, on the contrary, be exercised outside the organization and is, because of this quality not an integral component of management itself. But because it is a counter-force to autocracy, it is essential for good management. The application of it on the management aspects of leadership makes them transforming in nature.

So if we return to our initial question (section 9.1): Do managers differ from leaders? Are organizations managed too much and led too little? The answer is both yes and no, a paradox! Yes, in the sense that universally inspiring leadership is used too little in order to make the leadership aspects of management transforming. No, in the sense that the leadership which is said to be lacking, is in fact a component of management itself.

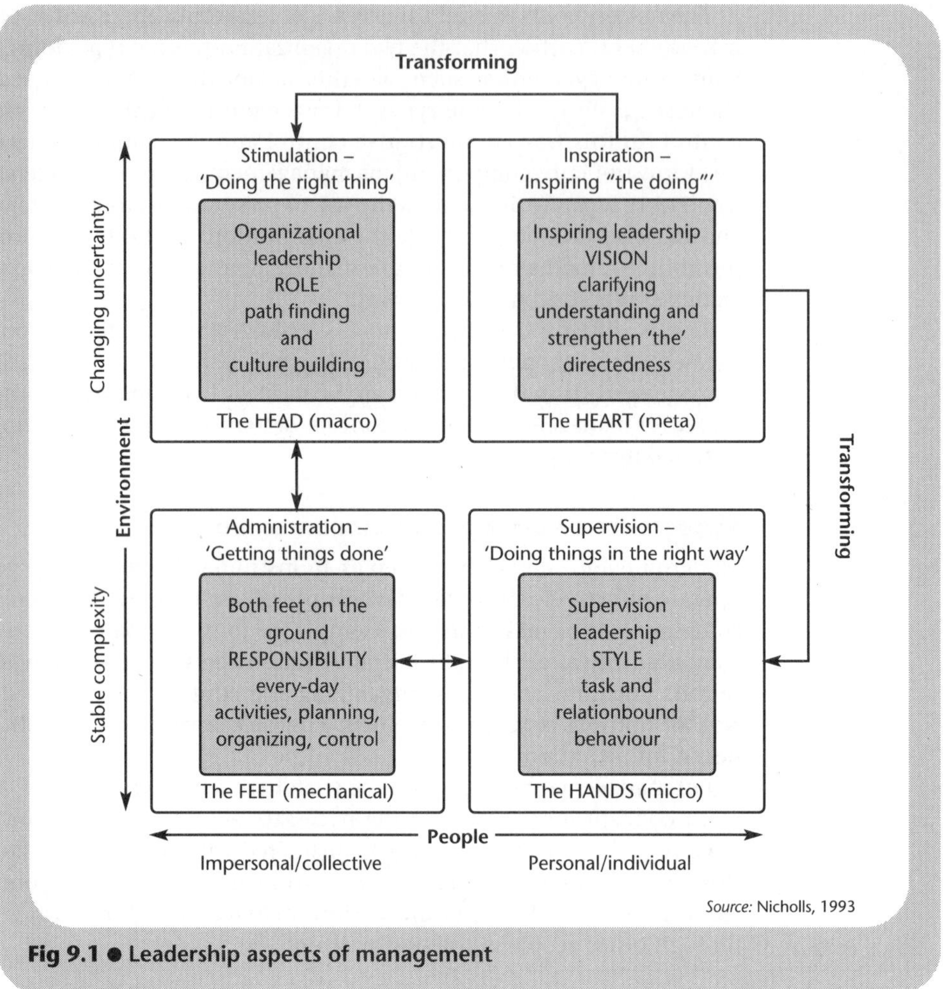

Fig 9.1 ● Leadership aspects of management

When this management–leadership is lacking, that does not indicate over-management, but rather bad or incomplete management. Not too much management but too little!

So, when we consider management more closely, it appears that managers are also necessarily leaders in two respects – organizational and supervisory. This means that they complement administrative control with the two aspects of management–leadership. On top of that, the best managers become transforming by inspiring 'the doing' through inspirational leadership.

Briefly summarized: managers who disregard the management aspects of leadership both organizational and supervisory, reduce themselves to administrators, when the addition of the universal inspirational aspect makes their management–leadership of a transforming nature.

Drawing up of weekly/monthly plans, or filling in planning schemes in order to see to it that available capacities are occupied as optimally as possible, is a component of management, and as such, does not involve leadership. The deployment of the human resources is a totally different matter. The productivity of people is to a high degree continuously determined by their motivation (*see* Chapter 8).

In leadership a certain charisma is indispensable, being able to be a source of inspiration for other people, for employees of the company or the institution. Here the element of charm also involves offering a possibility for identification to others.

Added to the social intelligence and the ability of a leader are also added the ability to be pleasant and at the same time keep a distance. The capacity for relativity and to be able to put things in perspective are asked from leaders (for example, to put earlier successes in the past) and a willingness to learn from the past and not linger on it or complacently to think that everything is under control.

9.2 ● MANAGERS AND THEIR MOTIVATION

From research directed at practice, Maccoby (1988) has distinguished five types of managers:

- the expert manager;
- the helpful manager;
- the protective manager;
- the entrepreneurial manager;
- the developing manager.

In Fig 9.2 a brief description of these five types of managers is depicted.

Motives	Types of manager				
	Expert	Helpful	Protecting	Entrepreneuring	Developing
Positive	• delegates • takes risks • decides quickly • is directed towards efficiency	• cares for people • has ideals • co-operates well • starts from the positive in people	• coaches • protects values • creates loyalty • removes obstacles	• thinks holistically • tries and experiments • has vision • is enthusiastic	• creates opportunities for others • has humour • has real interest • builds teams
Negative	• takes risks • knows everything better • lusts after power	• over-estimates himself • makes others dependent • is idealistic • is a coward • is naïve	• creates we/they relations • creates followers • avoids conflicts	• is utopian • manipulates • is intolerant • forces his own ways and thoughts onto others	• is uncertain • is inconstant • cares too much for himself

Fig 9.2 ● Types of manager and their manifestation as affected by positive and negative motives

The expert manager is someone who strives, in his own work, for professional characteristics and skills as well as for technical perfection. The most eminent motive of this type is wanting to be capable. They are often managers who emphasize rules and procedures. In a negative respect they can develop into rigid bureaucrats. Typical examples of this category are in the medical staff of hospitals and in the management of other professional service organizations.

The helpful manager is strong in creating team spirit and a sense of unity. He has idealism and his most eminent motive is belonging somewhere. This type is especially supportive and occupied with people and can be found in care-oriented professions, in education, in R&D organizations and in staff services as 'right hand man'. In the negative sense this type may develop itself into a naive softy.

For the protective manager, to manage means more especially supervising and protecting individuals and the organization as a whole. Their most important motive is wanting to survive, and they require loyalty and openness from their employees. In negative sense, they can develop into suspicious, self-righteous people. Organizations with a relatively large number of protective managers are found in government and monopolistic companies.

Entrepreneurial managers are often good at thinking out and executing new or renewed ideas. Their strongest motive is wanting to play. They do not consider the organization as an immutable, but rather as a playing field on which something new can be done time and again. This type occurs in all organizations, but when an entrepreneurial manager is not given the room he needs, he does not stay long. The negative side is like a blind gambler who takes too great a risk with himself and with all who depend on him.

Development-oriented managers are facilitators by nature. In principle, they consider people equal and they like giving their employees new chances. They are good at building motivated teams. Their most powerful motive is integrity and wanting to be upright. They can be found in all kinds of organizations, but especially in organizations which are in motion. When there is insufficient motion, they will bring it in or leave. In a negative sense they can develop into narcissists.

9.2.1 Characteristics of good managers

Separate from these types of managers and their motives, we can arrive at a list of characteristics which managers have to meet to be successful (*see* Table 9.1). Not every arbitrary characteristic mentioned can simply be developed in a human being who wants to become a manager, or respectively a leader. We keep hearing the statement that leaders and managers are born and not made, that some human characteristics are formed in the first years of life and get the chance to be expressed and strengthened during childhood. Work on optimism: courage and tact: other behavioural characteristics can still develop at a later age.

When the important element of leadership in the management of organization is concerned, as far as the development of leadership goes, a number of resources can be used. Training, the acquiring of experience for example. Conscious acquisition, grouping and evaluating of all kinds of experiences is a meaningful activity. Becoming conscious of unconscious experiences and situations in managing is important here. This means that one starts seeing consequences that arise from one's own actions and which characteristics these come from.

Table 9.1 ● Fourteen characteristics of 'successful' managers

A successful manager	
• is loyal	• is optimistic
• likes people	• is courageous
• looks across the borders	• has managerial power
• is tactful	• is especially trustworthy
• is honest	• has ambition
• is consequent	• is modest
• has self-confidence	• is a teacher

Source: After Tracy, 1989

9.2.2 Managers and styles of leadership

Of modern managers who contribute to the future of many organizations it is demanded they associate with other employees skillfully. Besides that they have to understand the primary process of an organization well. In managing, a manager – whether director, team leader, department chief or foreman – is in direct contact with his employees. It is then the task of the manager to influence the behaviour of employees in such a way that organizational goals are attained as well as possible. The way of acting or rather the style of leadership is seen as an important factor especially when it comes to associating with other people. It then concerns making other people deliver that performance for which

Exhibit 9.1

Leadership and national cultures

In the United States a current of leadership theories has developed. What these theories have in common is that they all advocate participation in the manager's decisions by his/her subordinates (participative management); however, the initiative toward participation is supposed to be taken by the manager. In a worldwide perspective, we can understand these theories from the middle position of the United States on the Power Distance side. Had the culture been one of larger Power Distance, we could have expected more 'Machiavellian' theories of leadership. In fact, in the management literature of another country with a larger Power Distance index score, France, there is little concern with participative management American style, but great concern with who has the power. However, in countries with smaller Power Distances than the United States (Sweden, Norway, Germany, Israel), there is considerable sympathy for models of management in which even the initiatives are taken by the subordinates (forms of industrial democracy) and with which there's little sympathy in the United States. In the approaches toward 'industrial democracy' taken in these countries, we notice their differences on the second dimension, Uncertainty Avoidance. In weak Uncertainty Avoidance countries like Sweden, industrial democracy was started in the form of local experiments and only later was given a legislative framework. In strong Uncertainty Avoidance countries like Germany, industrial democracy was brought about by legislation first and then had to be brought alive in the organizations (*Mitbestimmung*). (*See also* in section 2.3).

Source: From *Transnational Management*, by Bartlett and Ghoshal (1992).

the organization was created. It is, of course, important that a manager can and wants to manage. In addition to this, social communicative skills, observing, listening, having conversations and handling conflicts, are of importance. It is required of managers that they develop a style which suits themselves, their motives, capacities and behaviour, as well as the demands of the employees and situations in the organization where they are employed. There is not one single best style of leadership. Rather, different factors are involved in making it possible for other people to do their work in a meaningful way and influencing all this in a direction favourable for the organization.

9.3 ● LEADERSHIP AND STYLES OF LEADERSHIP

In an organization, one first and foremost works with people. The way a manager acts, or rather his or her style of leadership, is of great importance as an influencing factor. In this section, attention is paid to this aspect. The social aspect in leadership refers to direct intercourse with people, as well as the attitude (*see* Chapter 8) with which this takes place.

The art of managing also includes preventing such tensions in and between employees that they are hindered in their functioning. Fear of managers, cringing, docile and nervous behaviour are symptoms of wrong management. So insight into one's own way of managing and understanding the way a manager should manage is of importance. From the position of manager it holds that it is of importance to have insight into factors which determine the behaviour of employees, in order to be able to handle this behaviour better.

Leading is influencing the behaviour of employees based on personal contact. This influencing takes place by means of a combination of directing and task-oriented behaviour and supporting or relation-directed behaviour. Leading in organizations can be further characterized by the formal basis on which it takes place. The organization has given the manager the authority to supply employees with assignments. In order to manage, someone is needed who can, may and will take initiative and employees are necessary who are prepared to execute the activities which come from that initiative and who let themselves be influenced by, for example, directives, model behaviour and assignments, but who also act through respect and affection for the manager.

It is of course important here to give careful thought to the way in which a leader takes up his task with regard to his subordinates as immediate colleagues. Namely, in each way of managing and style of leadership a certain notion of the leader resounds about motivation of employees. Two notions can be distinguished which are both to be found in practice: autocratic leadership and participative leadership.

9.3.1 Autocratic leadership

Autocratic (*auto*=self, *cratos*=governance) leaders manage accompanied by stringent directives and assignments, exercising control and threatening with sanctions. This last measure is, to a certain degree, based on a feeling of fear of the employees. When an employee does not act in accordance with the wishes of his manager, this results in a form of punishment for him or her: a lower reward, a reprimand, a fine or, perhaps worsened promotion chances. Autocratic people believe that the employees can be directed only in this way towards the organizational goals. Money is seen as an important spur to be used to force employees to performances.

The idea of this type of leader is that this is the way to see to it that goals are attained. In this way of managing, subordinates will be little involved in the course of affairs in the organization or in the department where they work. Of course, here too, in this way of managing the personal characteristics of the leader play a part. This type of leader is usually task-oriented and instrumental with regard to his employees in attaining goals. Besides notions about and experiences with other people in their working behaviour the personality of the leader is co-determining in this. It may be that managers who behave autocratically and use the hard hand are insecure themselves about their success and so operate from their own insecurity.

Exhibit 9.2

Leadership, national cultures and Power Distance

In practice, the adaptation of managers to higher Power Distance environments does not seem to present too many problems. Although this is an unpopular message – one seldom professed in management development courses – managers moving to a larger Power Distance culture soon learn that they have to behave more autocratically in order to be effective, and tend to do so; this is borne out by the colonial history of most Western countries. But it is interesting that the Western ex-colonial power with the highest Power Distance norm – France – seems to be most appreciated by its former colonies and seems to maintain the best post-colonial relationships with most of them. This suggests that subordinates in a large Power Distance culture feel even more comfortable with superiors who are real autocrats than with those whose assumed autocratic stance is out of national character.

The operation of a manager in an environment with a Power Distance norm lower than his or her own is more problematic. US managers tend to find it difficult to collaborate wholeheartedly in the 'industrial democracy' processes of such countries as Sweden, Germany, and even the Netherlands. US citizens tend to consider their country as the example of democracy, and find it difficult to accept that other countries might wish to develop forms of democracy for which they feel no need and that make major inroads upon managers' (or leaders') prerogatives. However, the very idea of management prerogatives is not accepted in very low Power Distance countries.

Source: From *Transnational Management*, by Bartlett and Ghoshal (1992).

9.3.2 Participative leadership

Participative leadership indicates a very different notion about the role of a manager. A participative leader starts from the fact that the goals of the employees and those of the organization are not contradictory. Rather; they can be brought into accord with each other.

A participative leader strives to give room to participation in his department. The vertical relations are then seen rather as consultative relations in which a contribution from below may be made. One will also strive for the creation of team spirit in departments and in work groups in the stimulation of mutual co-operation.

This type of leader is more people-oriented in the attaining of goals. The participative way of managing lets the employees take part in what is going on in the department. By involving them and by stimulating co-operation, thinking alongside and co-organizing, participative leadership is directed at influencing the results in a positive sense.

9.3.3 Theory X and Y (McGregor, 1960)

McGregor has stated that each form of managing can be brought back to a certain notion of a leader concerning the motivation of his subordinates. He distinguishes between contradicting notions which, as such, can be found in practice.

'Theory X' (McGregor, 1960)

The first notion is framed as 'Theory X' and rests on three assumptions:

- The average human being has an adversity towards work, and because of that
- has to be forced to performance, and
- shuns bearing responsibility.

Leaders who start from this notion will usually show an authoritarian or autocratic style of leadership as seen in section 9.3.1, because, in their opinion, this way of managing is the only way possible for goals to be attained. This way of managing will often go with force, control and punishment, which is expressed by the concept of management by direction and control.

They believe that only in this way can employees be directed towards organization goals. A contribution from the subordinates will then not be asked. The consequence can be that employees themselves start behaving according to the 'Theory X' assumptions, as if this theory were true. This pattern can only be broken if the notion is perpetuated that the 'Theory X' image of the human being and its nature is in fact not true.

'Theory Y' (McGregor, 1960)

'Theory Y' is based on a completely different notion of human nature. The theory rests on these assumptions:

- Work is just as natural as rest.
- The human being is prepared to bear responsibility.
- Every human being is a source of creativity.
- Money is not the only impulse to work; the need for self-actualization also plays a role.

From this can be derived that the goals of the individual and the organization are not contradictory, but indeed can be brought into accord. This leads to a way of managing which is also expressed as management by integration and self-control, a way of managing that can be practiced by the application of management by objectives (MbO) (*see* section 10.3.3).

It will be obvious that in the case of leadership according to this notion, a participative style is favoured. Participative leadership basically implies another role of the leader. The role of the leader which starts from the integration principle (that is integration of interests of individual employees and those of the organization) can be described as follows:

- He supports his subordinates.
- He trusts their integrity and ability.
- He has high expectation of their performance level.
- He provides a good education for the tasks to be carried out.
- He helps those who perform below the norm.

9.3.4 'Linking pin' structure (Likert, 1961)

The starting points mentioned at the end of the previous section are processed into the notions 'supportive leadership' and 'overlapping groups'. Within these notions, such a type of leader strives for the transformation of his department into a group by making use of participation. In this vision, he is then the leader of the group. But the leader is also himself still a member of an overhead group of managers. Between these layers the leader fulfils the role of 'linking pin'. This has been schematically depicted in Fig 9.3.

In this set-up, which organizationally shows a linear structure, one can speak of groups that overlap in the person of the 'linking pin'. By means of this construction, the wishes and ideas of the lowest levels in the organization can reach the highest level. Even though the structure is said to be linear, this set-up shows a remarkable variation. The vertical relationship, instead of travelling along the traditional command relationship path, have become consultative. There has been 'horizontalization' of the line relationship.

In Likert's notion, leadership in this 'linking pin' structure is based on positive expectations which the managerial and operational employees have of each other (compare 'Theory Y' of McGregor).

9.3.5 Development of leadership

In order to determine which type of leader one will need in the future, it is important to understand the direction of organizational development and the direction of instrumental and social leadership development. Here, two movements are obvious:

1. the development of improvisation to planning;
2. the development of commanding from above to consultation.

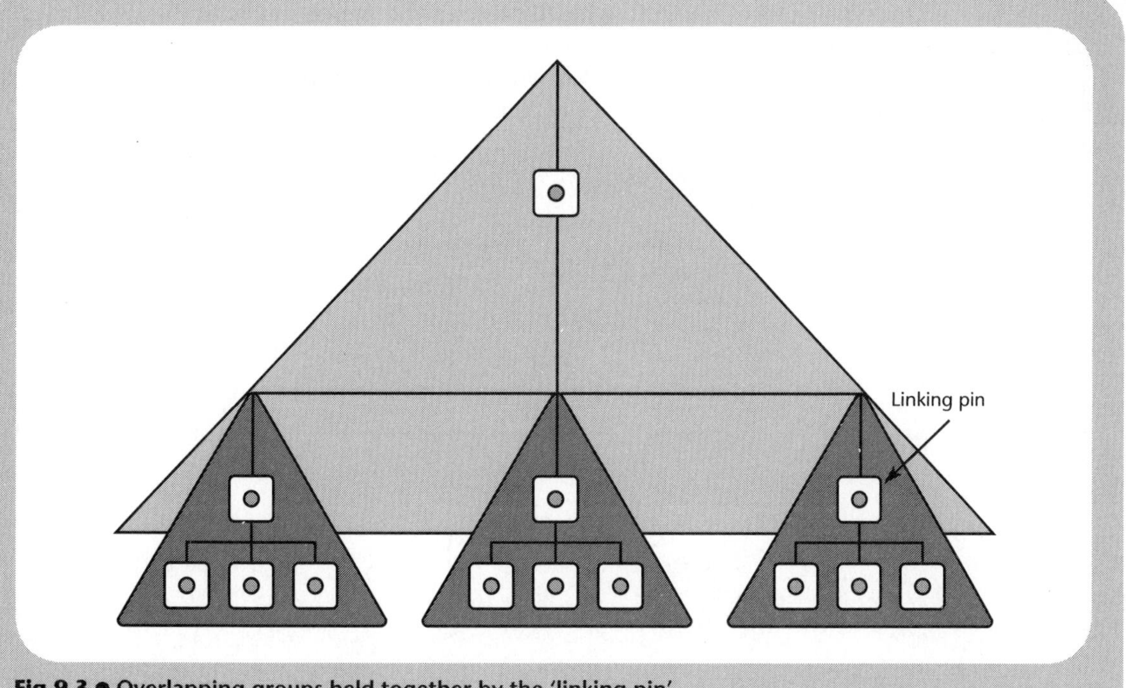

Fig 9.3 ● Overlapping groups held together by the 'linking pin'

The development of improvisation to planning generally contains three phases. First, one adapts onself, then one tries to stay ahead of development, and next one tries, via planning, to control development to a certain degree.

Willingness blindly to accept authority from above has definitely been broken. It is obvious that the tendency towards democracy makes totally different demands on the social leadership. The way to get people to accept decisions is by consultation in advance and in time and by asking them to think alongside. These directions are depicted in Fig 9.4.

Based on Fig 9.4, a four-way category of leaders can be built up.

The authoritarian–improvising type: the autocrat

This type does everything based on insight and personal authority. Here intuition plays a clear part. In this type, one may encounter brilliant people who, especially in the pioneer phase, can lead the group they manage to great successes. A disadvantage of this type is, however, that too little is left to other people, a consequence being that skilled people walk away and that the lower (or middle) management generally stays weak. Succession is a problem on its own, because beneath the top a vacuum often arises. Characteristics of the style of leadership of the autocrat are especially that:

- strict obedience is demanded of employees;
- the contacts are very detailed and critical;
- communication is one way;
- everything happens in a real 'me' style.

The authoritarian–structure type: the bureaucrat

This type arranges everything based on rules and prescriptions. Authority is based on strict ordering. Hardly anything comes of consultation, often from lack of nerve. This style can have a paralyzing effect on employees and the organization. Contacts are avoided, because of which a lack of communication arises.

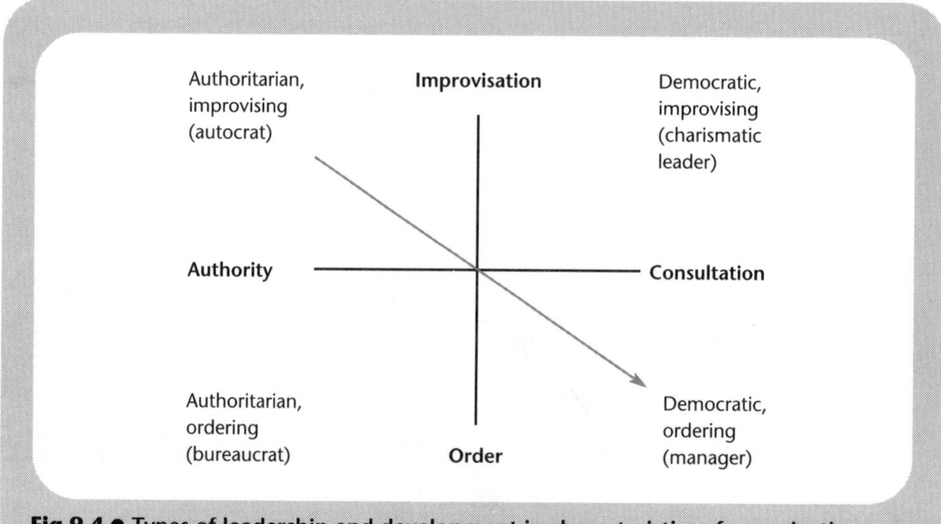

Fig 9.4 ● Types of leadership and development in characteristics of organization

The democratic–improvising type: the charismatic leader

This 'inspired' leader is often depicted as the most ideal type. He inspires his employees by consultation and intellectual improvisation. There is, perhaps, one negative effect in the case of this style of leadership: the relationship is very much that of 'father and son'. Another disadvantage is that because of the presence of the improvisation talent little is definite and many decisions are put off to the last moment. This brings uncertainty and sometimes even chaos.

The democratic–structure type: the manager of the future

The advantages this type has for the organization is clear. There is a high quality of instrumental and social leadership. There is structure and consultation. But the dangers of this type of leadership must not be underestimated. A shortage of alertness and decision-making capacity are latent. Despite that risk, this type seems to be most in accord with what modern society and the organization of the future asks as a leader.

9.3.6 Styles of leadership: different approaches

In the first, classical approach to leadership, special attention was paid to the characteristics of a leader. With the help of these, it was determined which characteristics distinguish the good leader from the bad. Attention was paid to issues such as:

- physical characteristics: research has shown that leaders generally are taller than those they manage;
- personality characteristics: other research shows that good leaders have more self-confidence and take more initiative than bad ones; good leaders also appear to have more understanding for what their employees thought and felt than less effective leaders;
- intellectual characteristics: research show that good leaders generally appear more intellectual than less capable leaders.

This approach directs itself exclusively upon the personality of the leader. Personality is seen then as the total of someone's qualities, characteristics and traits. Using this approach, if the one who manages is compared to a non-managing functionary, the manager is more socially-oriented, shows more initiative, pushes more, has more self-confidence and has greater adaptability and wider verbal skills.

One of the disadvantages of the personality approach is that it appears that management cannot be learned by those who do not meet the demanded characteristics, and unfortunately there are few who possess them all. It is also paramount to remember that leading is a process of interaction between leader and subordinate, and equal weight must be placed on both sides in that interaction. In the later, modern approach a lot of attention is thus paid to the relation between leader and employee as well as to the style of leadership.

Employees, task characteristics, superiors, colleagues and the organizational culture itself all influence the style of leadership. Employees can adjust themselves to the way of leadership, an adjustment which is dictated by their experience with other managers (habituation), their own values and norms and their own ability and willingness to execute a task. In this way, therefore, employees directly influence the style of leadership.

The characteristics of the task to be executed by the employees (routine work, amount of uncertainty and so on) are also of influence on the style of leadership. So it can be observed that in many organizations more eminent work is being conducted, because of which employees to an increasing degree obtain the characteristics of professionals: relatively autonomous thinking, using craftsmanship and problem-solving capacity in the realization of the goals of the organization as well as their personal goals. If employees who are able to execute their work relatively autonomously have to be managed, it is to be expected that good working circumstances are arranged, that a contribution is made to the creation of an inspiring working climate and that attention is paid to the work culture. Where the work consists of repeating tasks, with a high degree of standardization and clear operational rules, the management task is especially pertinent in explaining those rules, in seeing to it that materials and people are in the right place at the right time and in giving personal attention.

The behaviour of superiors is also of influence. By giving rewards and promotion, they influence the behaviour of those who report to them. On top of that they must also often function as a role model. Superiors are especially determining factors because of the amount of influence they can delegate to their managerial employees, for having power is one of the conditions to be able to manage.

Furthermore, the style of leadership has to be in accord with the style of the organization. The manager has to exercise his influence within the cultural borders of the organization. That is the functioning in an organization may be subject to a large number of unwritten notions about what is and what is not done. For example, the desired distance between manager and employee, being on familiar terms or not, the accessibility, approachability of the manager and the degree of necessary consultation between management and employees. Stated bluntly: the organizational culture is concerned (*see* section 9.6.1).

Practical management case 9.1

Burned out

The burnout syndrome causes tens of victims yearly among top managers. Companies can do something against that.

It happens that managers are good at managing a company, but keep a less appropriate tight rein on themselves. Each year, numbers of top managers burn out, suffer a form of extreme exhaustion. The exact number is not known. Often they disappear from the stage quietly. For health reasons, as one calls it euphemistically. 'Burnout' is a real health problem. It fits onto the list of heart and vascular diseases and stress, phenomena which are often accompanied by high work pressure and neglect of health. Apart from the social misery in the case of burnout, it is a waste of money and human talent. It costs a lot of money in supervision to patch up burned out managers. More often than not he is not available for the old functions. In the best scenario, he returns at another level: it is mostly the case that he does not return at all.

Five stages

The notion of burnout is often confused with overwork or stress. Burnout is a medically acknowledged phenomenon, the last of five stages of overburdening. Too great a work pressure results first in tiredness. This leads to health problems, like head, back, or stomach ache, sleeplessness and high blood pressure. The following stage is exhaustion, followed by collapse. If overburdening persists, then burnout follows. Managers with the longest endurance and the greatest sense of responsibility are the most liable.

It is a phenomenon which occurs less in boards of management than in the layers below. The highest managers are relatively free to map out their own time. People beneath them have a heavy responsibility, but not the greatest latitude.

Burned out managers take on average a year to recover. Sometimes it may take five years before someone is his old self again. Age, duration and intensity of the overburdening and personality structure determine the rehabilitation process. Recovery depends on the depth of the burn and the will to change.

About twenty percent remain damaged, physically or psychically. Some people will never be capable of returning to managerial positions. In extreme cases, a burned out manager remains a wreck.

Signals

Often the problem only becomes manifest when it is too late. Managers can hide the fact that they are on their way to total exhaustion for a long time. Signals can be recognized. Right up to the fatal moment, managers in the danger zone work at high speed, even though little comes from their work. Often they behave like automata. Sometimes they act in a euphoric way. But they also have a glazed expression in their eyes, and sometimes the eyes are even blank. Their family suffers in silence. But they always deny categorically that there are problems. People close to these managers see it coming ahead of time, however. But nobody dares to say anything because it concerns higher management.

Fighting

Even though burnout seems to have the character of something huge and inevitable, companies can fight this successfully. Individual attention to employees can eliminate overburdening and prevent the fatal consequences. The instruments are there. Programmes exist, directed especially at higher management, which thoroughly screen the physical and psychical condition, map out bottlenecks and give advice to prevent or fight the disease as a consequence of work pressure and unhealthy habits.

There are companies that have included the maintenance of vitality in their managers in their policy. They try to make their managers conscious of their physical and psychical condition. In performance reviews they are asked which task they think they can cope with in the period to come. Based on that, a strategic plan for carrying out the tasks is made. The striving of companies for efficiency, higher productivity and cost control has a high price tag. Carefully selected and educated personnel are subject to erosion. Without a counterweight, this wear continues undiminished. A policy against absenteeism alone falls short as an instrument. Managers should not be stimulated individually to better performances. They should, to an increasing degree, also be protected individually against the undesired consequences of that stimulus.

Waste of talent

- Increasing numbers of managers are burned out.
- Only some succeed in returning to the old post.
- Burnout is a waste of human talent.
- Individual attention and supervision at an early stage prevent a lot of misery.

Source: *FEM*, 16 April 1994 (adapted).

Style of leadership: contingent on the situation and person

It is not possible to make absolute statements about one best and most effective style of leadership. Some research shows situations in which employees prefer an autocratic style of leadership. This preference may be encountered where employees conduct typically individualistic work in which very little contact with colleagues is necessary, truck driving for instance.

There is not one style of leadership which everywhere will always lead to the best results. One should also not lose sight of the fact that the personality of the leader plays a part. In a nutshell: the most desired style of leadership is one that must suit somebody.

9.3.7 Situational leadership (Hersey and Blanchard, 1986)

The idea of situational leadership is further developed, among others, by Hersey and Blanchard. In their theory, the demanded style of leadership depends on the degree of task maturity of employees. Task maturity means being able to take responsibility for a certain task in a specific situation. The degree of task maturity then depends on the capability and the willingness of the employee. The capability can be measured on the knowledge, experience and the skill of someone to conduct a specific task. The willingness depends on the self-confidence, the devotion and the motivation of the involved employee.

Hersey and Blanchard distinguish four levels of task maturity.

- M1: incapable and not willing or insecure.
- M2: incapable and willing or sufficient confidence.
- M3: capable and not willing or insecure.
- M4: capable and willing or full of self-confidence.

The manager can bring the employee to better performances through guidance and support. Guidance involves determining results to be attained, organizing the work, setting of time limits and checking the delivered performances. Guidance has the character of one-way traffic: the manager explains and determines what needs to be done. Guidance is task-oriented. Support first of all concerns the delivery of support, communication, stimulating co-operation and giving feedback. Support is communication in two directions and is relation-oriented.

Depending on the degree of guidance and support four styles of leadership can be distinguished.

- Style 1: telling (S1). In the case of this style, there is a lot of guidance but only little support. The manager prescribes the goals and roles, gives detailed instruction and closely supervises the conducting of tasks.
- Style 2: selling (S2). In the case of this style, there is both a lot of guidance and a lot of support. The manager explains the intention of the instructions and goals, tries to determine the emotions of the employees with regard to decisions and listens to their ideas and suggestions.
- Style 3: participating (S3). In the case of this style there is a lot of support but only little guidance. This style of leadership is characterized by managers who take decisions together with their employees, and by active listening, support and encouragement, make the fulfilment of the tasks by the employees easier.
- Style 4: delegating (S4). In the case of this style there is both little support and little guidance. Working in this style, managers let their employees take care of the operational and support functions themselves and the responsibility for making and realizing decisions is left totally to the employees.

Hersey and Blanchard state that the leadership has to be in accord with the task maturity of the employee. This link is depicted in Fig 9.5.

It is the task of the manager to see to it that the task maturity, or capability level of the employees is enlarged. By means of guidance and support based on authority and power, the employees become more capable: the manager will always need to adjust his style of leadership to the increasing capability of his employees. That is why the effective manager does not have a uniform style of leadership for all employees, but uses a style tuned to the degree of capability of the individual employee.

The development of people is the key to an effective organization in the long term. If task maturity of employees in an organization increases, managers will be able to delegate more to employees. For managers this means that they get more time for new challenges and tasks.

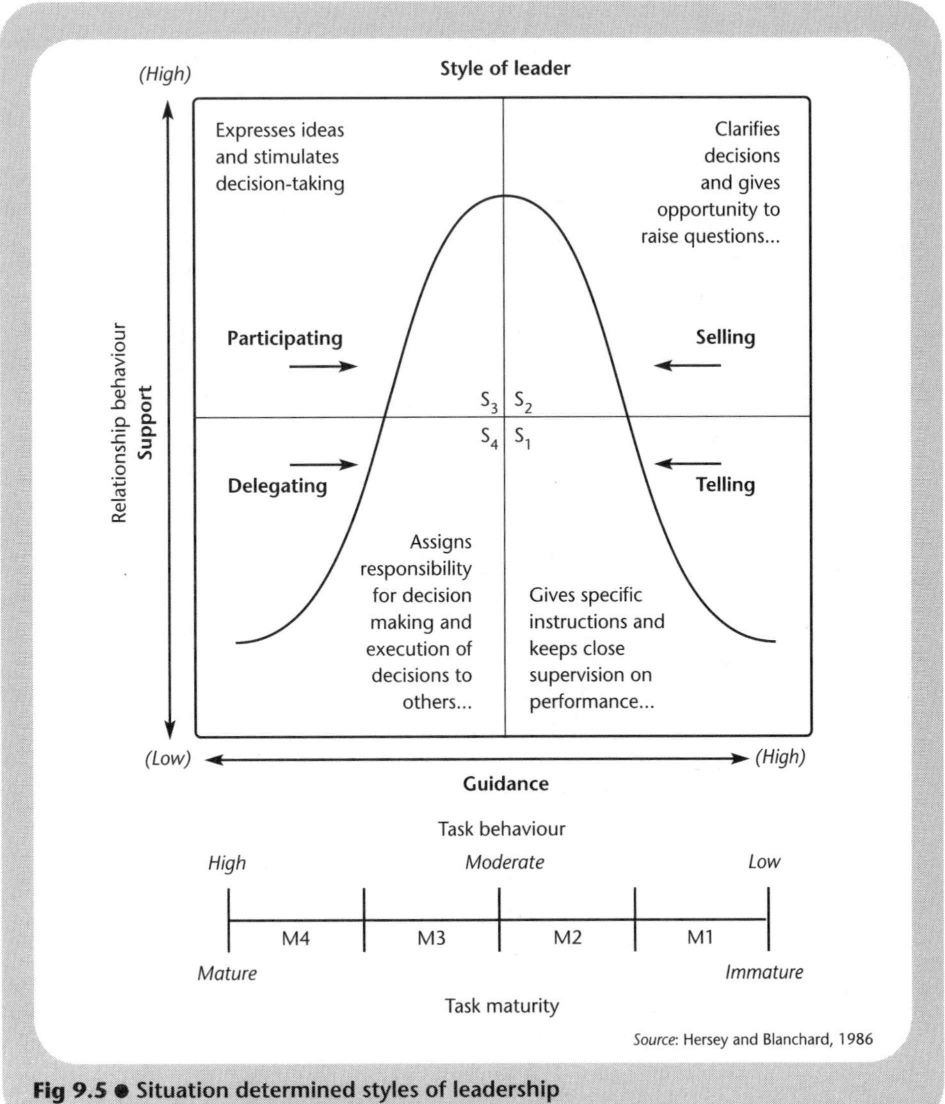

Source: Hersey and Blanchard, 1986

Fig 9.5 ● Situation determined styles of leadership

Minicase 9.3

Hunt the leader: the consequences of modern management styles

PTT Telecom

Nowadays the chief at PTT Telecom remains out of the frame as much as possible and employees have direct contact with one another, a horizontal way of working. It is not difficult to imagine that because of this the roles of chief and manager change dramatically.

Middle management already had the tendency to resist, now it is situated between two fires: on one side there is the top, positive about the proposed changes, on the other, employees see their own responsibilities increase. Middle management has no other option than to co-operate.

Apart from that all managers, irrespective, have to re-apply for a management function. It is clear that a considerable number, an estimated third, would have to be dropped because of the decrease in the number of hierarchical layers. Their livelihood is not at stake, those dropped end up in non-managing functions or are deployed into special projects. Despite all of this it is not a sinecure. The higher functions are made vacant nationally, lower management functions are filled in by the regions. The selection method is very simple: people who are in principle considered, are invited for a chat with a selection team in which one question is raised: How do you picture your task? From the answer it would automatically become clear to what extent the candidate could picture him/herself as a 'people manager', someone who could manage the method of horizontal process-oriented working which has been introduced.

Managers need to clarify how they picture their added value and what they can mean to their 'internal' clients – in most cases this means the district and regions.

9.4 ● INFLUENCING HUMAN BEHAVIOUR

Managing people involves, in addition to giving orders, assignments and instructions, motivating employees and directing them, in their actions and working behaviour, towards the goals of the organization. Managing people takes place as a process of interaction between leader and immediate co-workers. The way this happens depends on the way in which a leader conceives his task with regard to his workers. In the style of leadership a certain notion of the leader resounds concerning the motivation of his employees.

Particular in this is that employees in labour organizations more or less voluntarily accept an authority relationship via an exchange process and are prepared and willing to adjust personal goals to a certain degree. In order to attain this, organizations offer different material and non-material incentives or rewards to people in order to bring them into motion and to evoke work behaviour. So for the contribution to the organizational goal they get an incentive. In exchange for this reward they have to be willing to conduct work, adopt loyalty and bring their personal goals into accord with or perhaps even subordinate them to the organizational goals to be mutually strived for. What remains most vital here is that, through work consultation, these goals can be influenced by the employees themselves.

9.4.1 Motivation of others

Managers can contribute to the success of their employees by expecting good performances from them and by making it possible for them to deliver these. One point of view which should be added to this is thinking from 'co-workership': what actually drives an employee and what does an employee do in order to realize his ambitions and intentions? In other words, being motivated and wanting to be motivated is involved. As already covered in Chapter 8, motivating means the totality of motives active in a human being at a certain moment. A motive is a rational and emotional impulse that affects the will and stimulates the human being to activity. So having insight into someone's motivation provides an answer to the question of what creates in him or her a certain behaviour. Here, the degree to which different motives are active at a certain moment in a certain situation can be brought into relation with the strength of different motives or stimuli. Starting from the thought that different people are motivated by different factors, it can also mean that what is a motivating working environment for one does not appeal to the next in the same way. There will always be people who consider work as a source of income or social contact. In organizational theory, however, we start from the fact that a lot of people always want more from their work situation and working time, and that they often look for work whose contents are in accord with their own capacities and development. Included in this is a certain belief in people. It makes quite a difference whether a vision of the human being and notions about motivating start from the assumption that people are lazy, stupid, uninterested, untrustworthy, incapable and unwilling, or from an opposite, optimistic notion about the human being and his behaviour. In 'Theory Y', McGregor confirms his belief that people are creative, sensible, interested, trustworthy, helpful and well willing.

The risk that a 'Theory X' manager incurs is that the starting points of the theory will confirm themselves by his behaviour in a vicious circle. People will behave in accordance with the way in which they are treated. They get little freedom and independency, are being controlled and punished, because of which they start behaving dependently. Instead of developing mature task behaviour, they will behave childishly in their work.

The 'Theory Y' manager, in contrast, creates conditions within which people can develop in their work. People will then always see to it themselves that they become motivated.

The manager who is capable of his job can contribute to the success of employees and to their motivation by expecting good performances and by using the bad experiences to learn from. Managers and employees need to be in agreement then about what good and bad performances are. To be able to adjust in time, it is also necessary that employees and manager regularly, formally or informally, go through the progress of task fulfilment. Here it is important to show satisfaction in cases of good performance, and strive for improvement as in a learning situation in cases of shortfalls. There is always the need to adapt to motives which guide people in a certain direction.

Managing assumes one understands this as it stands, but in addition it assumes that someone, being a manager, is capable of giving direction to that in his style of leadership. As soon as this comes up for discussion, there is talk of use of power and exercise of authority, with which conscious influencing occurs to direct work behaviour at attainment of organization goals.

Exhibit 9.3

Subordinateship for three levels of Power Distance

Small Power Distance	Medium Power Distance (USA)	Large Power Distance
Subordinates have weak dependence needs.	Subordinates have medium dependence needs	Subordinates have strong dependance needs.
Superiors have weak depedance needs toward their superiors.	Superiors have medium dependance needs toward their superiors.	Superiors have strong dependence needs toward their superiors.
Subordinates expect superiors to consult them and may rebel or strike if superiors are not seen as staying within their legitimate role.	Subordinates expect superiors to consult them but will accept autocratic behaviour as well.	Subordinates expect superiors to act autocratically.
Ideal superior to most is a loyal democrat.	Ideal superior to most is a resource democrat.	Ideal superior to most is a benevolent autocrat or paternalist.
Laws and rules apply to all and privileges for superiors are not considered acceptable.	Laws and rules apply to all, but a certain level of privileges for superiors is considered normal.	Everybody expects superiors to enjoy privileges; laws and rules differ for superiors and subordinates.
Status symbols are frowned upon and will easily come under attack from subordinates.	Status symbols for superiors contribute moderately to their authority and will be accepted by subordinates.	Status symbols are very important and contribute strongly to the superior's authority with the subordinates.

Source: From *Transnational Management* by Bartlett and Ghoshal (1992).

9.4.2 Influencing behaviour: different sources of power and authority

A director who has to lead an organization to the goals or a department chief who wants to attain his departmental goals, has to make use of possibilities to let employees do or leave what fits within the intended framework. In other words, managers, whether they are work group leader, department chiefs or directors, have to be able to influence the behaviour of their employees in the direction desired by them. To do this they have five sources of influence at their disposal.

- Reward or positive sanction. When the actions of an employee are in accord with the assignments or wishes of the chief, this leads to reward. The reward can take different forms: a compliment, a new challenging task, or money, as in the case of payment of performance.
- Punishment or negative sanction. This source of influence is actually based on the fear of the subordinate. When an employee does not act according to the wishes of the chief, this can result in a scolding, passing by the employee in the distribution of 'nice jobs', ignoring his opinion in work consultation, less chance for an extra allowance and even decreasing promotion chances.
- The function as such. This source of influence is based on the functional and hierarchical place the manager has in the organization. A president can, based on his function, exercise more influence than a division manager or a department chief.

- Expertise. Acceptance of directives and assignments by subordinates increases when they are more convinced of the fact that the manager has more knowledge and experience at his disposal.
- Identification. Influence can also be based on identification of the subordinate with his manager. This often depends on the degree to which the manager possesses a certain charisma.

Power and authority

The five sources of influence can be divided further into two groups. The first group, reward, punishment and function, coheres with the position the leader takes in the organization. He derives his authority from these formal sources of influence. The second group, expertise and identification, coheres with the manager as a person, including his personality and characteristics. All formal and informal sources of influence count in the case of use of power.

When power and authority coincide an optimal situation arises. This means that the formal authority a manager has based on his position is experienced by his subordinates as correct and is valued positively. Authority comes from the formal position and because of that is known as positional power. Power involves making dominant the values or goals one strives for. A situation which deviates from the optimum is one in which an informal leadership exists that does not support the formal leadership.

Besides forms of informal exercise of power which relate positively to the formal organization and so work in a supporting way, it can happen that the exercise of power leads to a reduction in production (incidental or systematic soldiering), a strike or work to the rule. A group can make a front, exercise power by collectively taking a stand by, for example, resisting a reorganization. These forms of informal behaviour turn against the intention of the organization.

Minicase 9.4

The actual power relationships in an organization can deviate from the formal organizational structure and the formal definition of authorities. In this way, an assistant can in fact have more influence than his chief. This is the case when he or she, without having the authority at his/her disposal, knows how to associate with people in the department, so that he or she, in opposition to the chief, gets all kinds of things done.

Handling power and authority (= using sources of influence)

In order to function well as leader in an organization or as participant in processes of decision making and to get the things done for which one can be held responsible, it is important to use the previously mentioned five sources of influence wisely.

In the case of positional power (also called formal or legitimate power) the power which flows from the position an employee fulfils within the organization is examined. People do something for someone else because they think that it is allowed to do so. Based on the position held in the organization the right is obtained for access to all kinds of networks: membership of committees, steering committees and so on. This right of access does not only lead to more information, it also makes people more reachable. The position the employee holds may also lead to a direct say in resources such as personnel formation, money, equipment and such. The most appealing forms of positional power are the authority to inflict punishment and grant rewards. Power can also be based on being allowed to divide, or hold back desirable resources such as promotion, time, pleasant work, parking tickets, equipment, trips and congresses. It is obvious that these sources of power only have power when others value them as such. The value of positional power does not only depend on the importance the employee attaches to reward or punishment. Just as important is the degree to which the organization that created the position is flexible with the resources.

Personal power or personal prestige is granted to someone based on who he or she is not on the function someone fulfils. Thus a person can get something done by others because they respect him, for example, based on his knowledge, personality or experience. Personal power can also be based on the need of an employee to belong to or to identify himself with someone and to see that person as an example. The manager/leader of the future will depend predominantly on these person-oriented sources of power, as is said time and again.

Even though the notion of power often has a negative sound to it in daily use, we need to realize that a manager without power and influence cannot live up to his responsibility. In this sense power is a resource that allows the organization to attain its goals. Which is why each manager needs to handle his own power consciously and conscientiously. In order to realize the goals of the organization, he is, per definition, dependent on others. However he also has to take care not to become unnecessarily dependent on others.

Power is (Kotter, 1982) obtained and maintained by:

- having at one's disposal tangible resources on which others depend; then, the manager can by means of assigning or not assigning of those resources, influence someone else in his behaviour;
- having at one's disposal information and control of information channels; the power of experts is in a large extent based on this ('knowledge is power');
- developing positive relationships with others; these can be based on developing a feeling of obligation, building up a professional reputation, aiming for a higher degree of identification or uniting in a sense of dependence.

To the five sources of influence mentioned, based on someone's position and on his personality, we now add information power and connection power: having at one's disposal information and access to other people and/or information. For completeness we can add physical power as the archetype of power exercise, namely the power of physical strength. In the modern labour organization, however, this is unlikely to be a source of someone's individual power.

From their function as person, effective managers handle power very consciously. In their relationship to others, they leave little to chance. In order to understand the functioning of an organization, it is necessary to know the power and authority relationships. A sharp eye is needed for this, especially when things have to be done, when obstacles need to be removed and so on. Who has the influence and who has to be approached to get something done? All together then it is being able to use and being able to handle the following sources of power (*see* Fig 9.6).

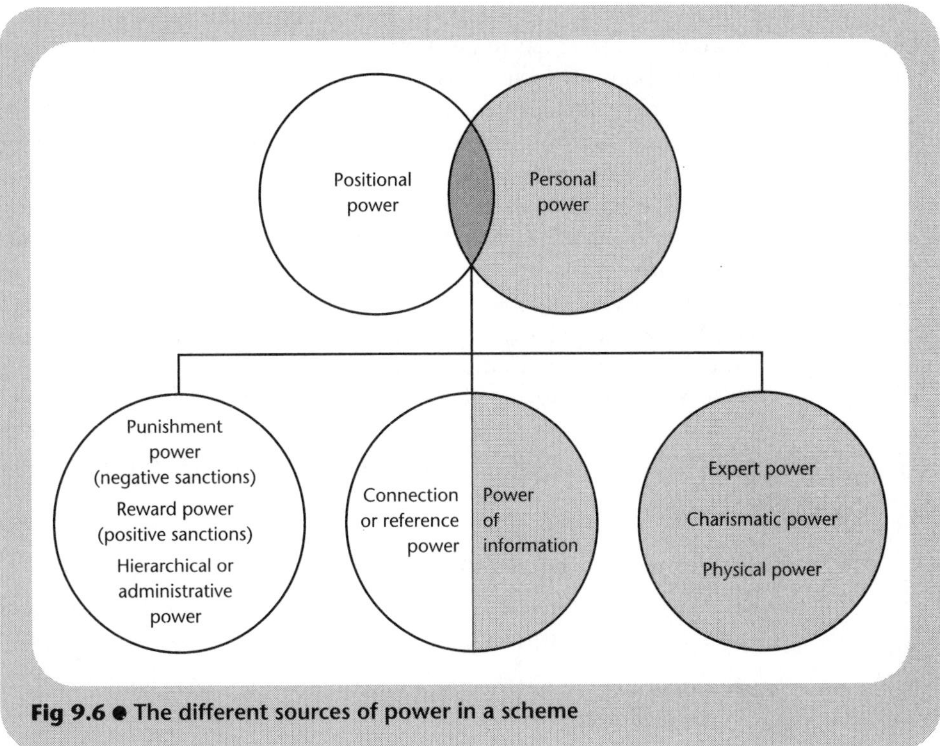

Fig 9.6 ● The different sources of power in a scheme

Managing with power

In his book *Managing with Power* (Pfeffer, 1992) Jeffrey Pfeffer states how the effective handling of political processes in organizations requires a perspective on management which stresses the development and execution of power. The power perspective offered by Pfeffer consists of seven prescriptive steps, directed at the individual manager.

- Determine what your goals are, what has to be attained.
- Make a diagnosis of patterns of power and interdependence, determine which persons and parties are influential and of importance for the attainment of your own goals.
- Keep track of what points of view other people and parties express, what opinions they have and how they might react to propositions from your side.
- Determine which sources of power other people and parties have and which of those sources can be activated in relevant situations.
- Determine what sources of power are at your own disposal and how you can develop your sources of power further.
- Determine which power strategies and tactics are most appropriate in which situation and what strategies might follow.
- Choose an appropriate strategy on the basis of the other six steps in order to attain your goals.

As Morgan (1986) stated in his book on images or metaphors of organizations one can understand an organization well only when one uses different ways of looking at the phenomenon of organization. The conceptualization of an organization from the perspective of power has many advantages. Power and influence are basic characteristics of organizations. By focusing attention on the power processes the myth of organizational rationality is broken. One comes to realize that apparently rational things like goals, structures, technologies, management styles and so on, have a political dimension which is co-determing and sometimes decisive for the functioning of the organization. But there are also disadvantages in using this perspective. Good management also requires trust. When looking at events in and around an organization in terms of power, influence, rivalry and conflict, one encounters the danger of an extremely suspicious, cynical and paranoid perception of reality. By only looking at hidden agendas, manipulation, intrigues, strategic behaviour and political games, suspicion is nurtured and events in and around the organization are politicized. This might lead to a situation where the power perspective is no longer used as a means of understanding reality better, but only as an instrument to realize self-interest. In this respect 'Managing with Power' offers enough Macchiavellian tips to play the power game with no holds barred.

Power: power relation and power distance

The concepts of authority and power have been described as bound by function and person. To summarize:

- authorities are assigned to a function by the organization (= the role to be played in the organization);
- the manager derives authority from his function (= formal authority);
- the way in which a manager puts his function bound authority into practice determines for employees the experience (either positive or negative) authority exercised (= power) by the manager as a person.

Power concerns to a certain degree being able to determine or being able to give direction to the behaviour of another. Exercise of power is the actual determining of the behaviour of others to a certain degree or giving of direction to the behaviour of others.

In the case of the exercise of power between individuals it holds that the more powerful person determines to a greater degree the behaviour of the less powerful person than vice versa. So a power relationship is one of inequality. The degree of inequality in power between a less powerful person or group (P) and a more powerful person or group (A) is called power distance (*see* Fig 9.7).

In exercising formal power one person (P) follows another (A: the leader), because he thinks that he should do that due to the respective positions A and P hold in the organization.

Expertise power is when the leader (A) according to a person (P) possesses a larger ability or more relevant information than P himself possesses. P further assumes that A is prepared to use this larger knowledge honestly.

Identification power is when a person (P) experiences that he and the leader (A) are one of a kind: that is why he is also more liable to be influenced by the other. P may even consciously or not try to set A up as an example for himself. P identifies himself with A in both thinking and doing. This influence relation occurs frequently, even though it is sometimes considered less suitable and may even be denied. A charismatic leader may sometimes deny having this power over his followers and will ignore the negative effects of too little criticism of over-compliant employees.

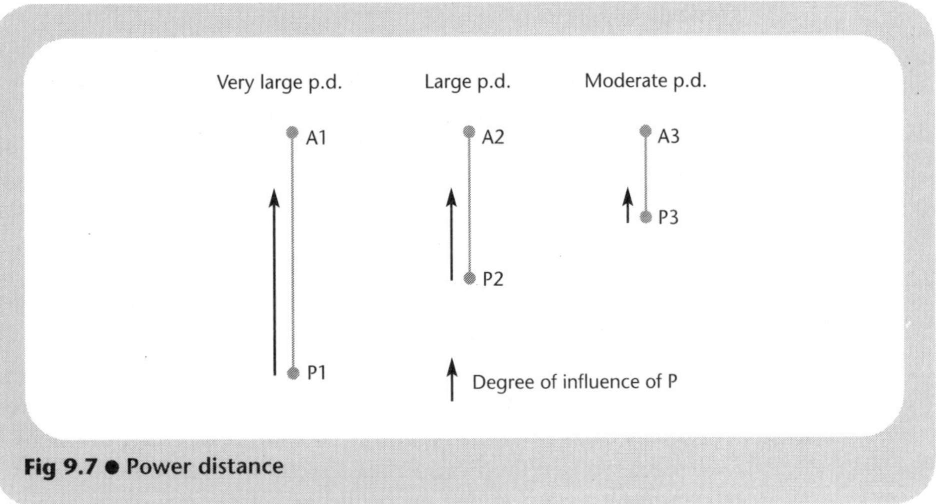

Fig 9.7 ● Power distance

'Non'-power

In addition to the forms and expressions of power and power exercise mentioned already, the quality of power is also co-determined by convincing directedness or open argumentation in the relation between A and P. This is known as 'non-power', and can be summed up by following statements.

- When he and I do not agree on what has to be done each of us has an equal chance of having one's opinion accepted.
- He lets himself be convinced of my point of view if I come up with better arguments than he does.
- His people do what he says willingly because he explains why something has to be done.

The contents of communication more often than not determine the outcome of the influencing process. The one (A) and the other (P) are each as willing to let himself be convinced (non-power relationship). This comes into play in all forms of democratic deliberation, starting from the principle of equality.

Influence upward and influence outward

The influence a manager has within the organization and outside his own organizational unit can be summarized in the following statements.

- He has a lot of influence on what happens in the levels above him.
- He is listened to by the top management.

Expert power and identification power are, in addition to convincing power, important in this situation; while sanction power and formal power are of limited importance of course.

Influence outward indicates the influence which someone has outside his own organization, and can be expressed in the following statements.

- He sees to it that certain important things outside the organization can be realized.
- He has a lot of influence in relationships with people outside his own organization.

Findings from research

In crisis situations, a leadership with large power distance becomes manifest, especially in terms of his expert power distance combined with sanction power and formal power. In non-crisis situations, mild leadership appears to dominate, with a small power distance between leader and employee, and convincing processes in open argumentation and personal relations. The harder, more powerful leadership is likewise valued more as good leadership in crisis; in non-crisis situations the mild, small power distance leadership is judged correct.

9.4.3 Interpersonal communication

Influencing behaviour through deliberation, consultation, participation and co-decision making demands intensive and good communication. Conveying information, receiving signals from the organization and transmitting decisions in the organization take place via communication processes. So communication is vital. Without good communication, intended outcomes of decisions are not attained or the decisions themselves do not come about.

In an organization not only do exchanges of facts and data take place, but also of thoughts, feelings and wishes. In other words, a lot of communication. Communication includes all activities through which information, that is facts, data, wishes, feelings and thoughts, are transmitted to or are discovered by other people. Communication can be seen as a process which engages a number of successive steps between a 'sender' and a 'receiver' via a 'communication channel'. Good communication is two-way traffic. After reception and interpretation of a 'message', feedback has to take place for the receiver to be able to test the translation of the intention of the sender of the message. This is shown in Fig 9.8.

In personal conversations and in meetings, non-verbal communication also plays a part. So in such situations a state of absolute non-communication does not exist.

Aspects of communication

The process of communication between sender and receiver (according to van Thun) has four aspects: the sender shares information in content (the business-like aspect),

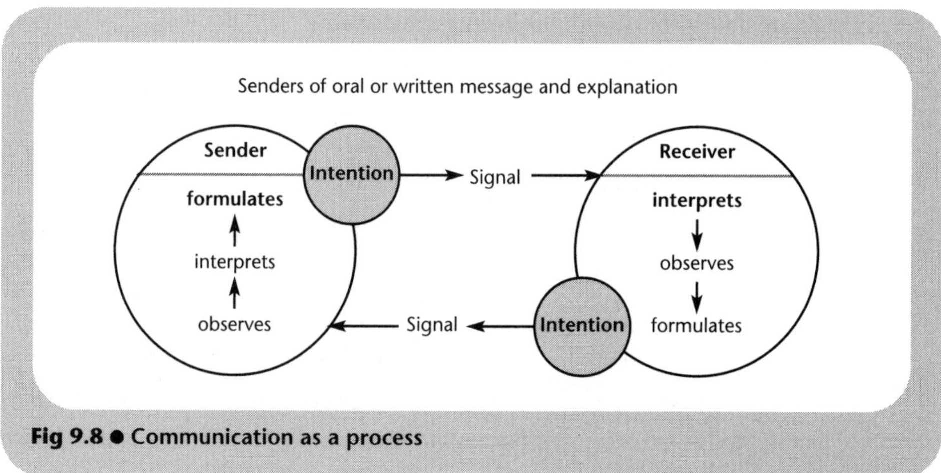

Fig 9.8 ● Communication as a process

and shows what he thinks important or relevant (the expressive aspect), thereby, by means of words, but especially non-verbally, makes clear what his relationship to the receiver is (the relational aspect) and tries to influence the thinking, doing, or feeling of the receiver (the appealing aspect). What makes the communication process so fascinating but simultaneously so complicated is that the receiver is free to choose those aspects of the sent out signals he wants to react to. Here, for ease, we assume that he has been able and is willing to observe the four component parts of the signal (Fig 9.9).

Depending on the situation, the relevant history of the themes under discussion, the experience in its relationship with the sender and the sender's state of mind, character, education and so on, the receiver will tend to observe and interpret one communication aspect more closely than another.

In a general sense for each of the four aspects it holds that the more noticeable the different aspects are and the more discussable, the more effectively the concerned aspects can be communicated. For the business-like aspect this implies simplicity in style, short sentences, common words, clear structure and an attractive presentation and so on will stimulate the noticeability and intended interpretation.

With regard to the expressive aspect (whether or not consciously sent information about the sender) is that the less one fears expressing oneself and the greater the need to be honest and open in goals, the smaller is the chance that the three other aspects will be observed in the wrong way. Thinking that one can communicate with someone else without also giving away something about oneself is an illusion: that the other person does not always want to or is not able to observe the expressive aspect is a different matter.

In the relational aspect (the personal relationship which the sender at that moment wishes to have with the receiver) it holds that this is especially communicated by non-verbal signals (intonation, physical distance, posture). In general it can be stated that high emotional involvement of the sender makes it difficult for the receiver to receive the business-like aspect objectively and completely.

In the appealing or inviting aspect the exercise of influence on the thinking, doing, and feeling of the receiver is at the forefront, transmitted signals can contain explicit and hidden invitations for interpretation.

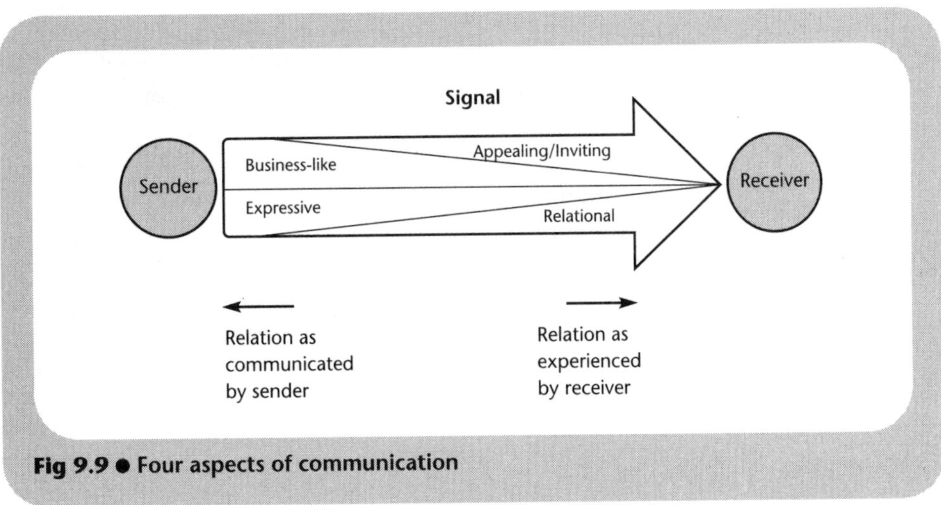

Fig 9.9 ● Four aspects of communication

Communication and influencing factors

In addition to information which rests on systematic processing of internal and external organizational data, good communication is of the highest importance for decision making. In the meantime mistakes can be made in communication between people in the organization. Communication between people in the organization is also influenced by all aspects of human behaviour, for example not being able to listen well, frustration etc. The lack of good open communication channels can have a negative effect. In some cases, communication channels in an organization are blocked because someone does not agree with a message or does not take any notice of it. Censoring and the conscious or unconscious reshaping of messages can also cause problems.

Effective communication assumes, as we have already seen, two-way traffic and demands a willingness to listen as well as a willingness to speak. Many organization members be they high or low in the organization:

- listen insufficiently;
- pay too little attention to misunderstandings that can possibly present themselves;
- formulate sloppy or little thought out responses.

In the process of communication, in order to prevent these mistakes, one has to be prepared to 'step into the shoes of the receiver' to understand the ear and the language of the receiver of the message and the feelings that may be used to explain the message. The other's view on a message is of course a determinant of his reaction. In other words, the art is then to formulate a message in such a way that it is received and explained with the same intention it was originally sent out with. Often, however, distortion occurs. This happens for many reasons, including:

- environmental factors, e.g. noise in a factory hall or geographical distance between subsidiaries and establishments;
- human factors, in which intellectual factors (memory, forgetfulness, not recognizing a 'line' in a story, not being able to 'read between the lines') as well as emotional factors, e.g. fear, frustration, prejudice etc. can play a part.

Besides the formal communication which takes place in an organization in the prescribed way, according to the formal planning system, the budget procedure, function description, guidelines and procedures, there is also a lot communicated in an informal way. This complements the formal organization and is also a means of reaction to unexpected events. Formal organization and formal communication are of course necessary. The real power of the organization, however, lies in the positive power of the informal organization and informal communication.

Types of communication and choice of communication channel

It is of great importance for conveying a message and to ensure that that message gets delivered, to pay the necessary attention to choice of form in which the communication should take place. This choice will depend on the goal the sender wants to attain. One can, for example, make use of oral or written communication. Oral communication occurs in a direct conversation between two functionaries or in a meeting of department heads, in work consultation in the department, in meetings between members of the working council and the board or in the case of an oral report.

Written communication and communication via digitalized information carriers occur in an exchange of letters via electronic mail or messages on a screen, in a newsletter, via announcements on a notice board, in a personnel ad, in a written task assignment, in a written report or in an annual report. One advantage of written communication is that messages can be conveyed in multiples. Data can be issued at the same time to different departments, can be saved, sent back etc. In oral communication an immediate explanation can be given when necessary.

Communication occurs in different directions: vertical communication is conveying of will of management to lower managerial and operational levels, by means of task assignments, instructions or via communication of planning via functional plans in departmental budgets for the coming period and in the opposite direction via determination and reporting of the operational employees to management about results attained in the execution. Addresses by management to inform the personnel are included here, for example via a speech or a briefing, a lecture from a company functionary or in the discussions of the works council; horizontal communication takes place in consultation between chiefs or executive functionaries from different departments about order acceptance, delivery times etc.

Lateral (or diagonal) communication takes place in teams or groups and in committees composed of people from different departments or different hierarchical levels (*see* section 7.5).

Communication structures

In addition to the meeting style of a team chairman or the style of leadership of the department chief, the structure of the communication lines influences the way in which people solve problems. These communication structures are recognizable within an organization (Fig 9.10). In research (Leavitt, 1957) into communication structures the 'wheel structure', the 'chain structure', the 'circle structure' and the 'open network structure' can be readily identified as viable structures within the organization.

The wheel structure can be seen when a chief has four subordinates who report only to him. The chain structure shows a similarity with hierarchy, while the circle and open network structure look similar to horizontal and lateral consultation.

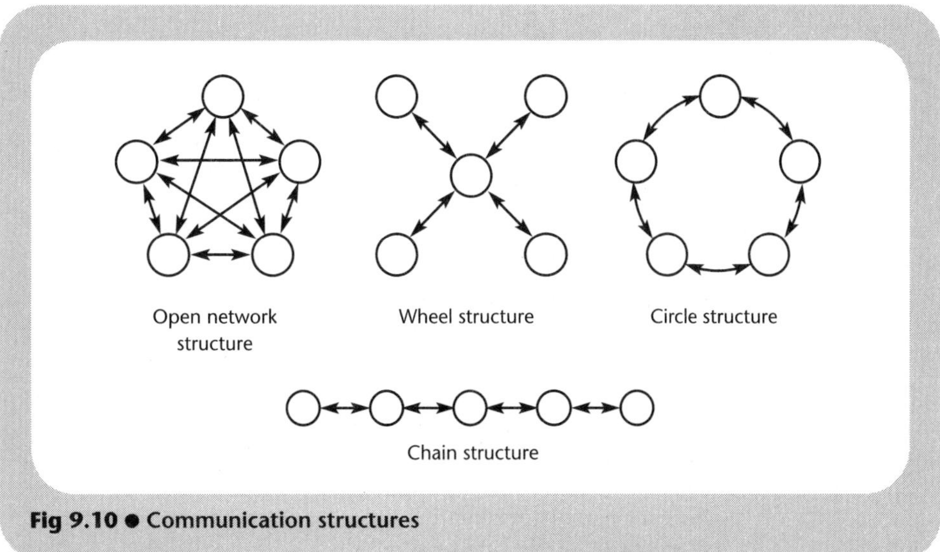

Fig 9.10 ● Communication structures

The effectiveness of the different forms can be judged based on factors such as speed of solution, number of mistakes, number of messages sent and satisfaction of the participants. From research it appears that the wheel structure leads to the shortest solution time and the smallest number of messages, but also to the least satisfaction. So while this form has clear advantages on the efficiency side, the disadvantages of it lie in the field of human satisfaction. The circle structure requires the most time, demands a lot of messages and makes the most mistakes, but, in contrast, provides the most satisfaction in the work. The chain structure lies in between. The open network structure attains the same effectiveness as the wheel structure, but only after a much longer period. The satisfaction is then also higher. It is noticeable that, after some time, the open network structure almost always starts to show some aspects of hierarchy.

9.5 ● STYLES OF LEADERSHIP AND CONFLICT RESOLUTION

When people co-operate, one can speak of differences in notions, goals and interests, since it is characteristic that every human being has his own individual needs and emotions, for example, tensions at home can penetrate the working situation. Earlier research showed that the middle manager spends about 26 per cent of his time on conflict resolution. The expectation then was that this would demand a larger amount of time in the 1990s and in the future.

In situations where interests/goals of two people or of management and work group are contradictory there are different possibilities for handling that conflict. The approach will depend strongly on one's own involvement in the problem, one's own power, the degree to which one is a 'doormat' and/or the degree in which one is willing and prepared to give the other the freedom in problem-solving. Organizations show certain characteristics in given styles of conflict as can be seen in Fig 9.11.

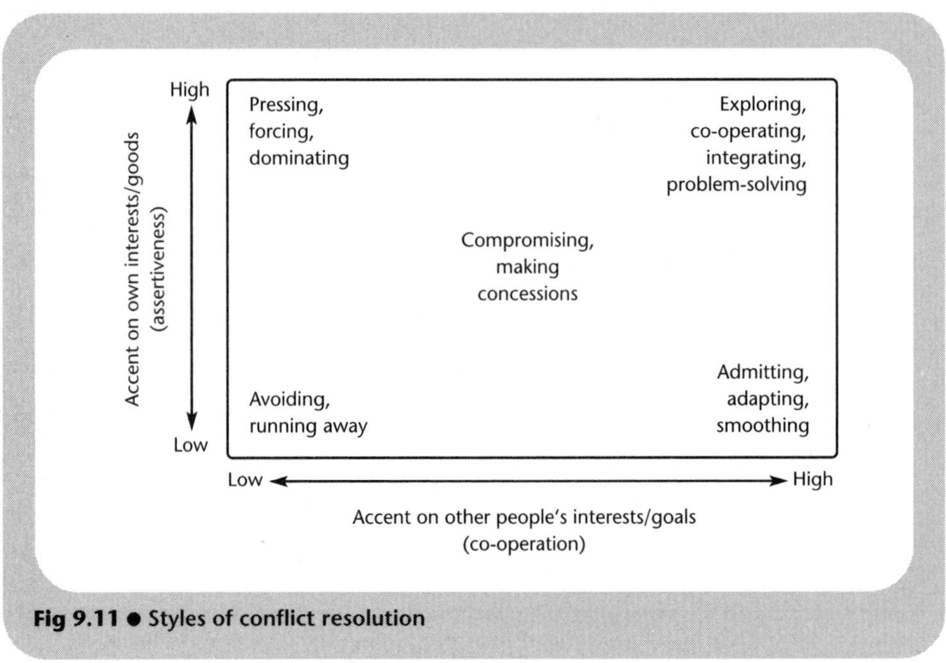

Fig 9.11 ● Styles of conflict resolution

Suppressing/forcing

If confrontations are the order of the day, if there is a lot to fight about, a hard line in conflicts, an 'all or nothing' attitude, power plays an important part. Someone who follows this style strives for his own interests at the expense of those of others. The conflict situation is a matter of win or lose and mutual interests are considered contradictory and mutually exclusive. This style is oriented towards power: one's own goal has to be attained and to do that, one makes use of or makes threats with all possible power resources whenever they may lead to a win situation.

This style is recognizable in the following characteristics:

- being insistent;
- suppressing contradictions;
- threatening behaviour, even involving use of violence;
- following the hard line;
- overruling opinions of others.

This means that a conflict is never solved properly. Open or indirect resistance may arise and in the process of co-operation something will definitely go wrong with the motivation of the one on whom the will of the other is imposed. In the mutual relationship and communication lines this will be extremely noticeable.

There are some situations in which this style can be used:

- in crisis situations;
- in situations in which interests are vital and one definitely has right on one's side;
- in situations in which unpopular measures have to be taken.

Avoiding/running away

Formal, hierarchically oriented conflicts are avoided rather than openly discussed to cover possible problems. Someone who possesses this style strives neither for his own interests, nor for the interests of others. There is indifference towards mutual relationships. When contradictions arise, one pulls back, figuratively or literally speaking. One avoids taking on board points of view that could lead to controversy.

This style is recognizable in various behaviours:

- by acting dumb;
- by handling delicate subjects with a joke, i.e. by running away from them;
- by postponing the sensitive subject to a 'more suitable moment'.

This again means that the conflict is never really solved. One spares the other and everyone goes his own way.

There are situations in which this method of conflict handling can be followed:

- in situations where a 'cooling off' period is necessary;
- in cases in which more information has to be gathered first;
- when the subject is not important enough to enter into immediate conflict about it.

Admitting/adapting

A human-oriented attitude, involving mainly professional employees (*see* section 9.6), is an attempt to solve conflict in a mutual fashion. In this situation one's own interests are neglected in order to satisfy those of others. Conflicts are prevented by stimulating an harmonious atmosphere and friendly relations.

This style is recognizable by:

- avoiding painful subjects;
- handling controversial subjects so abstractly and generally that everyone can agree;
- soothing minds quickly when something conflicting appears;
- only taking up the subjects on which all agree.

In a situation of this type conflicts of interest do not penetrate the organizational armour: this is not conflict solving either.

A style like this can be used in situations in which:

- saving harmony is important;
- building up 'credit' is important to be able later on to handle important subjects;
- fighting is more harmful.

Exhibit 9.4

Should managers resist cost reductions to maintain morale?

The first time that Marcel Dupré set eyes on François Petain he had a sense of foreboding. Like Cassius in Shakespear's play *Julius Caesar* Petain had a 'lean and hungry look,' Dupré thought.

This adverse reaction was reinforced when Petain, at the first executive meeting after his arrival to head the gears division of Duval et Cie, a large manufacturer of industrial machinery, said that he wanted Dupré to implement immediately a comprehensive cost-cutting programme.

His brief from corporate management in Paris, Petain announced, was to ensure that the division not only met but exceeded its profit targets. Costs had been getting out of hand and there would have to be severe pruning to ensure future growth.

Dupré, who had been plant manager at the division's only factory for five years, and who himself had ambitions to become divisional chief, had heard it all before.

In the recession of 1974, another divisional head provided by headquarters, Michel Leblanc, had wielded an axe fiercely. Managers had been sacked and the plant's administrative, maintenance and quality control departments had been decimated. The plant manager of the day had been prematurely retired and Dupré had been appointed in his place, having previously served as deputy manager.

Leblanc had headed the division for exactly 16 months, in which time he had produced impressive-looking profits at the expense of truncated departments and shattered morale. He had returned to Paris, and a seat on the board, like a victorious general.

Dupré had learned to steer a precarious course between going along with Leblanc and ameliorating the effects of some of his policies. He strongly believed in positive motivation and a contented work-force. But he had not been moved up to fill Leblanc's shoes. Instead, another outsider had been brought in and Dupré had found himself serving his third boss within two years.

As plant manager, Dupré had borne the brunt of the havoc caused by Leblanc's purging and cost-cutting. Slowly he had restored to the work-force a sense of harmony and purpose. The economic upturn had also helped the plant to produce results acceptable to headquarters.

Then had come the latest upset. There had been a power struggle in Paris in which Leblanc had been the loser. He had resigned. Within a month, his successor as divisional head also left.

Petain, who had started life as a management consultant, arrived in the division as the latest chief. It was rumoured that he was the company president's personal nominee.

As Dupré listened to Petain at the executive meeting, it was like being back in 1974. 'I don't want any more hirings ... one secretary for every three managers ... look at your departments and tell me within a week where cuts can be made ... we are going to produce real profits in this outfit.'

Worse was to follow. Petain made it plain to Dupré that his past performance as plant manager counted for nothing so far as he was concerned. 'You have to prove yourself with me, now,' he said. 'I judge a man on today's performance, not yesterday's.'

Dupré soon found that Petain was incapable of real delegation. Not content with weekly reports on inventory, labour turnover, absenteeism, production and sales, he demanded day-by-day verbal updating.

A ceaseless flow of memos emanated from the divisional office, down the corridor from Dupré's own modest room. For example, although the plant's order book was full, Petain sent a message suggesting that all overtime should be abolished as a cost-cutting exercise. When Dupré pointed out that shipments would then fall behind, Petain replied: 'That is *your* problem.'

The most deeply felt blow, however, and the one which convinced Dupré that things could not go on as they were, was when Petain asked about the dance that Dupré proposed to give to all employees at the grandest ballroom in town.

Dupré explained that the dance had been promised as reward for a special effort in meeting an emergency order. 'You must cancel it,' Petain said. 'I simply cannot sanction that kind of expense at this time. I couldn't justify it to Paris.'

Dupré left the other man's office seething. He unburdened himself to Jacques Gabin, the personnel manager. Gabin had worked with Dupré to restore morale in the plant and was a friend as well as a subordinate.

'Your problem, Marcel,' Gabin said, 'is that you don't have a friend at head-quarters. You're a first-rate production expert and an able administrator. You go about motivating people in the right way. But your record in selling yourself and your ideas to the top is dismal. You deserve to be division manager, yet all these people keep getting appointed over your head.'

'I know,' Dupré said. 'But it's a bit late to start trying to win friends in Paris. Anyway, that's not my style. I don't want to resign. That would really be giving in to Petain. But if I allow him to cancel the dance and push through all his other measures, this plant will really go downhill. And it won't be Petain but myself who will get the blame.'

Then he said to Gabin: 'Tell me, what would you do?'

Source: *International Management*, February 1980.

Looking for compromises/making concessions

Democratically oriented, innovations are made worse in order to compromise, there is an emphasis on sharing and co-operating. In this situation, an interim solution is looked for in which each party can find something of its own point of view. It does not necessarily lead to finding the best qualitative solution either, but rather finding the most fair, acceptable, attainable solution for both parties. Looking for compromises means making concessions and sharing the differences.

This style can be recognized in negotiations where it is a matter of giving and taking; finding a common denominator in the points of view is then of utmost importance.

Handling conflict like this can be used when:

- a rupture cannot be risked because goals are important for both parties;
- temporary measures have to be taken under pressure of time;
- force is not an option.

Exploring/co-operating

New ideas are handed out, there is the possibility to experiment, other directions for solution are researched and tried out, there is a large measure of freedom and creativity. Of vital importance now is:

- direct and open communication: openly discuss the business and emotional aspects of the contradiction;

- the mutual analysis of underlying causes;
- uttering emotions and images which the one has of the other;
- clearing up misunderstandings.

The problem-solving directed at negotiating means that a real solution is being sought to the problem, one that is acceptable to both parties. Contradictions are now permanently solved and all parties feel involved in the result.

This style of conflict resolution necessarily takes time and energy. In situations which risk involvement, in which learning is important, in which disturbed relations have to be restored, this style will – given that time and energy – be able to work out a solution positively. Here, creativity too has a good chance.

9.5.1 Conflict as a process

In the case of less authoritarian leadership and more participation in the decision making other conflicts will naturally come up. The organizational culture determines to a large degree how this is handled.

A conflict is the process in which A consciously attempts to frustrate B by means of a form of obstruction in attaining his goals or being watchful of his interests. The process can be modelled in four phases (Fig 9.12):

1. potential resistance;
2. awareness and personification;
3. behaviour;
4. consequences.

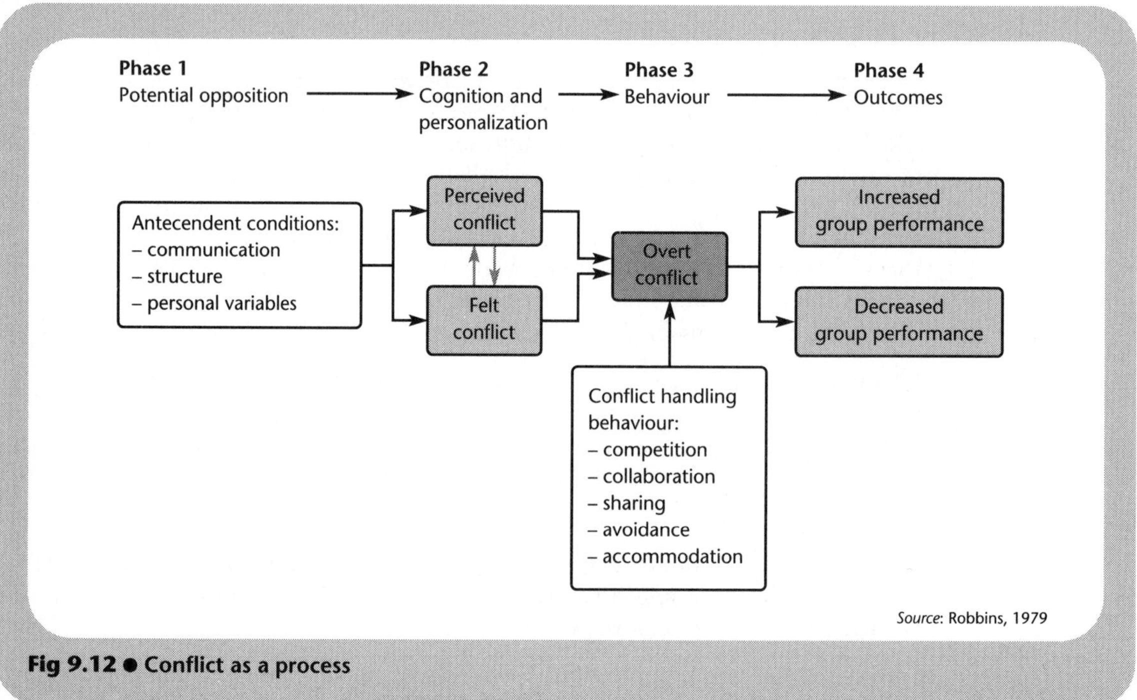

Fig 9.12 ● Conflict as a process

The first phase in the process is the presence of circumstances through which conflicts can arise. These conditions belong in the category of communication, structure or personal variables. When the circumstances in phase 1 evoke frustrations, potential contradictions become reality in the second phase. The existing conditions only lead to conflicts when one or more of the involved are affected by it and become conscious of the conflict. In phase 3, there is open conflict. Those involved now have to start negotiating in order to handle the conflict.

Starting from these two dimensions: co-operative (the degree to which someone tries to meet the need of the other) and assertive (the degree to which a party tries to fulfil his own needs), there are, as we have seen, five possible forms of conflict handling: forcing (or competition), co-operating (or collaboration), avoidance, adjusting (or accommodation) and making compromises (or sharing).

The interchange between open conflict behaviour and conflict handling behaviour has its consequences. These can be functional, that is, that the conflict has led to improved group performances. But if the consequences are dysfunctional performance will suffer.

9.5.2 The best style is a situation style

The 'best' style for handling conflicts does not exist. They all depend on, among other things, the role one fulfils in one's professional life. Project leaders, people who have to act as innovator, will in general be served best by an exploring style and people who handle the chairman's hammer will be better using a more compromise-seeking role. Furthermore, most people will have a more mixed method than has been described in the various schemes.

Exhibit 9.5

Organizational conflict and national cultures

On a research project (at INSEAD) MBA students from Germany, Great Britain, and France were asked to write their own diagnosis and solution for a small case study of an organizational problem – a conflict in one company between the sales and product development departments. The majority of the French referred the problem to the next higher authority (the president of the company); the Germans attributed it to the lack of a written policy, and proposed establishing one; the British attributed it to a lack of interpersonal communication, to be cure by some kind of group training.

The conclusion was that the 'implicit model' of the organization for most French was a pyramid (both centralized and formal); for most Germans, a well-oiled machine (formalized but not centralized); and for most British, a village market (neither formalized nor centralized). What is missing is an 'implicit model' for four Asian countries, including India. The family (centralized, but not formalized) is placed in this quadrant as the 'implicit model' of the organization. Indian organizations tend to be formalized as far as relationships between people go (this is related to Power Distance), but not as far as workflow goes (this is Uncertainty Avoidance).

Source: Adapted from *Transnational Management* by Bartlett and Ghoshal (1992).

The same holds true for organizations: not all organizations have a strongly expressed style of conflict handling. Most organizations actually possess a mixed form of these styles. The reason an organization should fix on a style of conflict resolution lies in the fact that it can then exploit the possibilities involved. It can then indicate enlargements of style that will be stimulating for the further functioning of the organization.

9.6 ● ORGANIZATION, STYLES OF LEADERSHIP AND ORGANIZATIONAL CULTURE

Organizational culture can be defined as the common understanding of the members of the organization about how things are enacted in their organization daily. It concerns all the written and unwritten rules which channel and shape the social intercourse between the employees of the organization, as well as the intercourse with customers, suppliers and other parties in the external environment. The organization expresses itself in house style, logos, company cars, uniforms, buildings, portraits, myths and stories, celebrations of a jubilee, use of language, style of meetings, etc. These are all expressions of culture. In essence, however, it is not the expressions themselves that are important, but rather the meaning the organization members attach to them. The expressions of culture in symbols, heroes and rituals point to and are rooted in deeper values and norms, which also form the heart of the organizational culture. These can be present strongly and are then present in many organization members. One can, however, also speak of inconsistent and even conflicting value patterns: this is then a weak culture. This occurs, for example, where different subcultures in and between departments clash.

Values unconsciously determine human behaviour. In organizations this can lead to a community in which one thinks of 'good or bad' in terms of what suits or does not suit the organization, from a 'we do that this way here', 'we think that is important' mentality. So the basic principles and values form the 'inside' of the culture, while the symbols lie mostly on the 'outside'. Thus symbols are the things which are most easy to change: a new logo, a new house style, new slogans. Changing 'heroes' means

Minicase 9.5

In a company where women usually stop working after they had a child, a woman tells her boss that she is pregnant. Without any discussion about whether the woman should leave the company, the chief sounds another employee out as to whether she is interested in the vacancy which, as the chief expects, will arise. The cultural meaning given to 'motherhood' in this company is linked to 'not carrying out paid labour anymore'. The chief believes this to be a situation with no alternatives, and acts on this cultural meaning.

The woman indeed resigns, even though she would have preferred to keep working. However, that is not possible because in her function there are no possibilities for part-time work; and even if she had wanted to keep working full-time, no suitable child care could have been tuned into the second shift. So the structure is in agreement with the cultural meaning which excludes other options, such as working while also taking care of children. The woman, with her decision, re-affirms the current cultural meaning.

Source: M & O, January 1995.

bringing new people to the fore, appointing them in key positions and letting them fulfil important roles in the organization. Changing rituals demands that the current people are involved in the new situations and that meaning is giving to their new role.

9.6.1 Influencing organizational culture and leadership

Often a crisis caused by external influences is necessary to come to an effective influencing of the organization culture. A crisis means that an organization is off balance and under those circumstances there is a task for management – perhaps via a new leader – to develop a new common understanding, a new culture. The management can also consciously choose to be the cause of the crisis.

Leadership is necessary to shape and influence the organizational culture. At the same time we need to realize that management, in a certain sense, is or can become a prisoner of the prevailing culture. Of course leaders have their eras and in the growth and course of development of an organization now and then new leadership is demanded. So it is possible, within an organization, to change style by influencing the culture. To do this the organization needs to answer two important questions.

- 'How do we typify ourselves and how do we associate with one another in our organization?'
- 'What would we want to be and how would we want to associate with one another?'

Culture diagnosis

In determining the organizational culture, one can make use of the culture types distinguished by Harrison (1986) (*see* Fig 9.13). This classification also distinguishes between two dimensions. First of all the degree of co-operation: this is the degree to which the organization members co-operate with each other during the daily execution of the processes. In an extreme case it may be that none or hardly any consultation is necessary between employees (everyone works alone); in the other extreme one continuously co-operates in a team relationship. The second dimension is the degree of spread of power in the organization. When there is a large spread, there is no clear power centre and decentralization will often be the case. Where there is a small spread of power, most decisions will be taken at the top of the organization.

Role culture

In the case of role culture one can speak of a small spread of power (centralization) and of a low degree of co-operation. One expects of the other to live up to rules and procedures developed in the past by higher management. New problems are solved with great difficulty because they fall outside the framework of existing procedures.

In a role culture, one will seek the solution to new problems in the development of new procedures. In such cases there is rather a learning of new routines than conceptual learning (*see* section 5.5).

Persons' culture

In the case of the persons' culture, the spread of power is great (decentralization). Many organization members in all sorts of places in the organization take multiple decisions, and the degree of co-operation is low. The organization members work individually.

Minicase 9.6

Examples of organizations with a persons' culture:

Hospitals where the doctor receives the patients individually during consulting hours, the school where the teacher is in front of the class on his own and the lawyers' firm where one lawyer serves his clients individually.

Power culture

In the case of power culture one can speak of a small spread of power (centralization) and of a high degree of co-operation. This type of culture occurs a lot in small pioneer companies, where one co-operates intensively in an informal atmosphere and calls everyone by their first name, except 'Mr X' and 'Ms Y', the pioneers/founders of the company.

Task culture

The task culture characterizes itself by a high spread of power (decentralization) and a high degree of co-operation between the organization members.

There are different way in which to influence the culture of an organization. A direct way of influencing culture is to change personnel in key positions. Drawing in new people with other backgrounds and experiences can have an important influence on the culture of the organization (Fig 9.13).

Another slower method is to discuss in teams the present style and the desirable style, maybe with some external coaching. Here team training and work conferences can be an important instrument, or intervention. A condition of this method is that in the teams several departments and functional levels are represented.

Examples of culture interventions are:

- adjusting the style of leadership;
- changing key personnel;
- 'team training or conferences', in which as many departments and functional levels as possible are involved.

In some cases these changes in culture are only really meaningful after a change in organizational structure. In an organization in which no or perhaps a bad task definition is present and in which there is a large overlap in the responsibilities and authorities, more clarity has to come into the structure. Only after that is it possible, by means of cultural interventions, to try to change the style of leadership and conflict resolution.

Minicase 9.7

Task culture is typical of organizations that work with temporary project groups composed of employees originating from different departments and several specialties: project organization and the matrix organization (*see* sections 6.3.7 and 6.3.8).

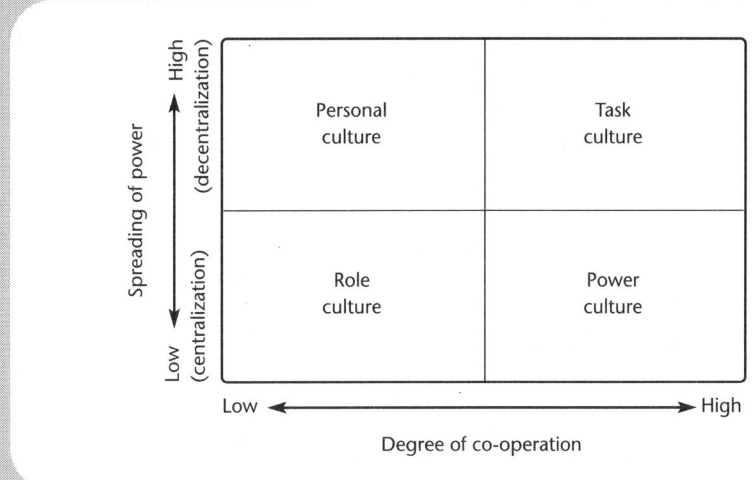

Fig 9.13 ● Typology of organizational cultures (derived from Harrison)

Exhibit 9.6

El Corte Inglés, Spanish retail group

Big towns in Spain have four landmarks: the cathedral, the city hall, the bullring – and the Corte Inglés store. Spaniards spend a lot more of their time in the fourth landmark than in the other three put together – perhaps explaining why it is Spain's most admired company.

With a turnover in its last financial year of Pta1,015bn ($2bn) and net profits of Pta33.5bn, El Corte Inglés is by far the largest privately-owned business in Spain, and with the biggest marketing budget in the country, dominates domestic advertising and ensures total awareness of its presence.

For many Spaniards, the chain's large department stores constitute one of the main reference points in their lives. The Corte Inglés is the first choice for about-to-be-weds when they draw up their wedding gift list. Likely as not the chain's travel department will organise their honeymoon and its interior decorating unit will advise on the fittings of their new home.

An important part of the Corte Inglés business formula is to provide virtually every consumer product. The same large store contains high fashion and basic household goods, high-tech equipment and groceries. It is a large emporium strategy that sells right across the social scale. The tested formula of selling everything to everybody, with a fast delivery service and a money-back guarantee, is peculiar to Spain and it has built tremendous customer loyalty.

There is probably better value elsewhere and better quality as well, but the Cortes Inglés combination of quality and value is firmly imprinted on the minds of domestic consumers. The strength of this perception, together with the extraordinary range of customer services and the availability of goods, is one explanation for the store chain's success.

Another is its extraordinary promotional energy. Every year is punctuated by a succession of special thematic weeks in which the Corte Inglés stores promote the products of a given country or sector, or, as in the case of its Spring and Autumn fashion promotions, the change of a season.

Sales at the Cortes Inglés are media events and so are its Christmas decorations. Children are drawn to Cortes Inglés stores at Christmas like moths to a light bulb because several stores around the country set up mini amusement parks in adjacent plazas.

No Spaniard is ever very far from the Corte Inglés. Last year the company bought a rival domestic chain, Galerias Preciados, adding a further 23 large stores to the 32 it already operated and establishing itself in 13 cities where it was not previously present.

The acquisition was in itself testimony to the Corte Inglés' financial muscle – a strength that

continued overleaf

Exhibit 9.6 continued

is all the more remarkable because the 60-year old business has always financed development out of its own reserves.

The Corte Inglés paid Pta30bn for Galerias Preciados in June last year and spent a further Pta50bn revamping its rival's stores in order to relaunch them under its own logo in time for the Christmas buying spree six months later. Ownership of Galerias had changed hands six times since the late 1970s and, with its management adrift, it had run up accumulated losses of Pta39bn since 1989.

With Galerias under its belt the Corte Inglés has gained more than an increased market share. The takeover has now allowed it to experiment with specialised stores in big cities such as Madrid, Barcelona and Valencia where both chains formerly competed, often with big stores on the same street.

Although the Corte Inglés will maintain its giant emporium formula in most of its large stores it intends to move into market segmentation, as developed by US retailers such as Toys Я Us and known in the retail industry as 'category killers'.

The Corte Inglés is no stranger to specialisation and it is a nimble follower of retail trends. The company has built up a unit called Hipercor with 12 large out-of-town sites spread around the country to compete with the main hypermarket groups.

The final factor behind the success of the Corte Inglés is tight management and a pronounced corporate culture. The company is owned by a foundation that was set by its creator Mr Ramón Areces, who returned in the 1930s with enough savings from a spell in Cuba as a youth to open a small drapery shop in Madrid.

Since the death of the publicity-shy Mr Areces in 1989, the company is run by his no-less-reclusive nephew, Mr Isidoro Alvárez.

The Corte Inglés prides itself on the continual training programmes, fringe benefits and incentive schemes that it provides for its more than 50,000 staff. Most of the company's executives have worked their way up from the sales floor.

Source: *Financial Times*, 18 September 1996.

9.6.2 Influencing organizational culture: instruments

Conscious influence on the organizational culture is, in general, however, not easy to bring about. People have the tendency to hold onto safe behaviour and often show resistance to change. If an effective influence of culture can be envisaged, the measures used have to form a consistent whole. If this is not the case confusion will arise among the employees and the so-called new culture will come across as untenable to, for example, customers and other external stakeholders.

Important instruments in the influencing of organizational culture can be divided into two groups:

Direct working mechanisms are:

- new appointments in key positions;
- criteria with relation to recruitment, selection, promotion, retirement and exclusion;
- introduction and training of new employees, e.g. through in-company training;
- important matters for the attention of top management;
- reaction of top management to critical events;
- model behaviour;
- criteria for assigning rewards and status.

Indirect working mechanisms are:

- design and structure of the organization;
- systems and procedures;
- design of buildings and interior;
- stories and myths;
- formal declaration of policies.

Exhibit 9.7

Organizational change and national cultures

It is tempting to view the task of managing change as one of sketching alternative chart structures by moving boxes and redrawing lines. Such a view loses sight of the real organization behind those structural representations. The boxes that are casually shifted around represent people with abilities, motivations, and interests, not just formal positions with specified roles. The lines that are redrawn are not just formal reporting channels, but interpersonal relationships that may have taken years to develop. As a result, forcing changes in organizational process and management mentality by altering the formal structure can have a high cost. The new relationships defined in the reorganized structure will often take months to establish at the most basic level, and a year or more to become truly effective. Developing new individual attitudes and behaviours will take even longer, since many employees will be frustrated, alienated, or simply unequal to the new job requirements.

Most European and Japanese companies tend to adopt a very different approach in managing organizational change. Top management in these companies consciously uses personnel assignments as an important mechanism of organizational change. Building on the informal relationships that dominated their earlier management processes, European companies use assignments and transfers to forge interpersonal links, build organizational cohesion, and develop policy consistency. Such mechanisms are at least as important as structural change for developing their desired international processes.

Japanese companies place enormous emphasis on socializing the individual into the organization and shaping his or her attitudes to conform with overall corporate values. Organizational change in these companies is often driven more by intensive education programs than by reconfigurations of structure or systems.

Source: From *Transnational Management* by Bartlett and Ghoshal (1992).

SUMMARY

- In the process of leadership it is vital that the capabilities of people are used optimally, and attention must be paid to how people think and how they act.
- First of all the concepts of leadership, managing and entrepreneuring were covered. Inspiration, vision, creating the right conditions and daring to take risks are essential elements of managing in the present day. Motives and characteristics of managers were looked at, with special attention paid to styles of leadership and situational leadership.
- Influencing human behaviour and resources used was covered extensively. Handling of power and authority are central issues here. In influencing of behaviour special attention has to be paid to communication.
- When people co-operate different notions, goals and interests play a part, and for management, conflict resolution is involved.
- In the realization of changes in the organization and putting into motion human potential, an understanding of the culture in organizations is essential. One can try to influence the prevailing culture with direct and indirect working instruments and in that way, try to influence inculcated behaviour in a more desired direction.

DISCUSSION QUESTIONS

1. With reference to *Management in action* at the beginning of this chapter: Do you agree with Bacon's diagnosis or vision with regard to western management and future global developments? What is your opinion about the 'solution' Bacon recommends for the future manager?
2. Which of McGregor's theories, Theory X or Theory Y, would you use if you had to manage?
3. How do Hersey and Blanchard describe 'task maturity'?
4. What is your opinion on the statement: Informal groups always work within the communication structure of the 'circle'?
5. Formulate your opinion on the following: Due to the division of labour, organizations have in-built conflicts. The best conflict handling method is to discontinue the organization.
6. (a) How should Marcel Dupré (Exhibit 9.4), as manager, resist cost reductions in order to maintain morale?

   (b) How would you handle this problem?
7. If, according to the external and/or internal stakeholders, there is said to be management failure with an organization, it can happen that 'heads have to roll'. Is this a direct or indirect working mechanism in influencing organizational culture?

Management case study

Semco-style 'natural entrepreneuring': no management

The inspiring story of the most spectacular workplace in the world
Ricardo Semler (34) is Brazil's most eccentric businessman. His management book has been published in 14 languages in 134 countries. What is so special about Ricardo Semler? Little in itself, except that he has his own unique idea about managing a company, and that is: 'no management'.

Employees determine their own salary, every half year they subject their self-chosen chief to a function conversation, paint their workplace in the colours they like and come to work when they feel like it. Abuse? No', says Semler. 'At first, the employees of course chose the nicest chief, but when they want to attain their production quotas and profit share, the most competent is naturally chosen. People do not need a manager to choose their chief; leaders stand out by themselves.'

Semler's philosophy sounds simple: when you want creative employees, do not entangle them into a straitjacket of rules. You have to treat them like adults. Only when you inflict all kinds of rules on them, e.g. reduction in salary due to lateness or frisking at the gate to prevent theft, they will start behaving like children and seeing how far they can go.

In this anti-parternalistic situation, the employees are asked to set up their own production quota themselves, in which they can arrange their own time. Overtime does not exist anymore at Semco. In the meantime, the employees get involved in the design and the sales plans on their own initiative, according to Semler. The bookkeeping has also strongly been simplified. 'Everyone bluffed at meetings and pretended to know every detail. We have eliminated all kinds of codes and initials, which were "highly essential" in the past. Now each manager has to make an estimate of the sales, costs and profit of his department at the end of every month. By comparing that to the official figures, you can see whether a manager has insight,' adds Semler.

In the twelve years that Ricardo Semler has been at the top, the company (a producer of washing machines, cooling units, pumps) has been through an impressive development, if we believe the figures in his book. Despite the Brazilian economy with its high inflation, the sales have grown with a factor of 6, production is seven times greater than at the beginning of the 1980s and the profit is five fold what it was. The company grew from 100 to 830 employees and now comprises six factories.

Whenever the company experienced less flourishing times and a factory had to be closed, the personnel took a surprising step: they turned in 30% of salary paid their own meals and gave up the travel cost reimbursement. The cleaners, doormen and the cafeteria personnel could go home and their work was done from then on by the other personnel. 'The employees had economized so drastically that after one month their factory made a profit,' says Semler. In cases where sackings are really necessary the group decides who has to go and this is decided as 'socially' as possible: someone at the age of 30 goes out rather than an employee of 45 with seven children and an ill wife.

The principle that middle and higher management within Semco determine their own salary works smoothly, states Semler. 'Everyone knows what the rest earn, so you think twice before asking an outrageous sum.' His newest invention in the wage field: introduction of the risk salary, for whoever wants it. When things go badly, the employee gets 25% less; in a good year he gets 25% more.

Ricardo Semler has his own ideas about efficiency too

'In the hall of our head office, a normal office building with storey of steel and glass, there is a counter but no receptionist. It is the first sign that something is different about us. We do not have receptionists. We do not think they are necessary, even though we have so many visitors. We do not have secretaries or personal assistants either. We do not want to burden our wage costs with unsatisfying, dead-end jobs. Everyone at Semco, even the top manager, meets his guests himself, makes his own photocopies, sends his faxes, types his letter and dials phone numbers himself. We do not have a separate cafeteria for management and parking occurs according to the rule: first come, first served. All that is part and parcel of running a "natural company". At Semco we have eliminated all unnecessary extras and privileges which are good for the ego but bad for results, and which only distract everyone from the actual task of the company: producing, selling, invoicing and so on.'

Everything within Semco seems idyllic, even though the game rooms and the plants between the machines make one think of the 60s. Higher placed employees are allowed to stay home for a few weeks or even a few months once a year in order 'to think' or 'to do something inspiring'. Democracy is in every aspect. 'I want everyone at Semco to be able to take care of himself. The company is organized in such a way – well, for us that might not be the correct word – that it does not depend too much on a certain person. It gives me a sense of pride that, during my longer trips, I was given a different room twice – and each time was a smaller one. My role is that of catalyst. I try to create a context in which others take decisions. Success means that I do not have to take them myself.'

continued overleaf

Management case study continued

Stress?

'At Semco we try to prevent stress. No, we do not have ping pong tables or a fitness room. Of course, stress will never disappear completely, we all worry about profit and other things at times. But we have eliminated the artificial stress, about arriving too late and so on.'

Does something ever go completely wrong? Is everything really like paradise within Semco?

'There are sometimes disappointments,' admits Semler. One of his frustrations is the failure of the anti-discrimination programme in the company. 'This is still too much imposed from above. Now we have to determine how many people from minority groups become chief, the employees and those involved have to choose that for themselves.' It is a matter of persistence, thinks the president. Semco-style is a kind of a mission. A belief that it has to be done in that way and not differently. And just as with the mission of the church, many of our ideas have been cast aside and set up again from scratch. The managers, for example, had to really get used to losing their authority. They mixed up authority and bossiness, wanted to be able to punish subordinates for making a mess of things. Now they cannot play boss anymore and have to call on other talents to be able to feel their power.

Some people have called the Semco philosophy socialist. 'Nonsense,' says Semler. 'What we prove is that participation does not mean bosses lose power. What we undo is the blind, irrational exercise of authority which indermines productivity. We love it that our employees take care of themselves, make decisions themselves. This means that they are involved in their work and their company, and we all profit from that.

'In the restructuring of Semco,' continuous Semler, 'we have taken the best elements from many systems. From capitalism we derive the ideas of personal freedom, individualism and competition. From the theory, and not the practice, of socialism we have learned to eschew greed and to share information and power. From the Japanese we have learned the value of flexibility, even though we do not have an affinity for their family-like bonds within the company and their automatic honouring of the elderly. We want people to progress because of their abilities, not because they are so old already or so co-operative. Our manufacturing people, for example, can start work in the morning somewhere between seven and nine o'clock. It is their choice, not ours.' But when one wants to start at seven o'clock and a teammate decides not to come until nine o'clock? That would mess up the whole production, would not it? 'That is what we were afraid of too, and so we set up a work group in order to mediate in case of possible problems. Up to now, the group has not been called into action yet. Our employees understood that production would suffer if they did not tune their work times into each other – and so that is what they did. At Semco, we even prefer not to think in terms of employee and boss. We had rather speak of employees and co-ordinators. And we like to see that everyone is in contact with everybody else, not considering the function. In the offices, we have mixed the purchase and the design department, so that everyone sits together, close to the work floor. The idea is that we all can learn from each other.

'Some managers still worry about production cells. If we left the organization of the factory to the employees, they thought, we would never allow them to instal equipment which would cost labour places. But our people knew how important labour saving equipment was for our competitive position, and more than once, a company committee has pleaded for a new machine which we needed according to them even at the expense of some jobs.

'Besides that, the people in our cells tended to take up more and more of the management of the production process themselves. Take quality control. In the past, in every unit we had a separate department for the inspection of products. But in the course of time, our manufacturing employees took over this task, so that we could eliminate jobs. The employees also recruited new members from their group – or eliminated members from their group. Nowadays if someone wants to become a mechanic at Semco, he has a conversation with a group of mechanics, not with a director, and that is the worst that can happen to him, because he perhaps can fool a manager, but he will not succeed with people who know all about the profession and may even become his colleagues.

'Sometimes, "cells" take longer in making a product than would be the case with a traditional assembly line. But still our delivery times have become shorter. And then there are all those departments for quality control which we do not need anymore. But, and this is the most important thing,' the people in our "cells" clearly have a more interesting job than those who have to execute mechanical clusters of tasks the whole day. And because of the "cells" people get closer to each other, so that the processes in our factory are much more detailed and tuned into each other. This has translated itself in higher productivity. With the "cells", our inventory levels have decreased to a ridiculous level and each year we can do with less storage room. Some of our "cells" sell their complete inventory seventeen times per year, while the line of business has a sales speed of a little more than three. '"What do the chiefs think of all this?" I am often asked. Well, we do not have as many as in the past. The most influence employees have on their work and the larger say in policy, the smaller the need for chiefs. We have reduced our staff department – which provides our production units with legal, administrative and marketing advice – by more than 75%. We do not even have an Automation or Education Department anymore. Everyone is responsible for his own work and so we can do without a Quality Control Department. We have taken a very close look at ourselves and then reduced the bureaucracy from twelve management layers to three, and designed a new structure: the traditional, limiting company pyramid as replaced by a system of concentric circles.

'We have also changed the way in which departments deal with each other. When one does not want to purchase services from the other, it is free to get these outside the company. By that threat of competition we all stay alert. For a short time we have been encouraging our employees to start up their own company – we rent them Semco equipment at favourable prices. Of course we buy from our late employees, but they are free to sell to others as well, even to Semco's competitors. By means of this programme we are leaner and more flexible, and we have total control over our livelihood. It makes entrepreneurs of employees.

'This is of course an extreme case, but we try to maximize the possibilities and minimize the supervision for everyone at Semco. Not that people do not have to render account. Before people are hired or appointed in a managerial function, they are questioned closely and approval or disapproval is sought from everyone who has to work for them. And every six months, managers are assessed by their subordinates. Everyone can express their experiences.' Does this mean that employees can fire their chief? 'That seems to be case to me, because when someone always scores badly, he usually ends up leaving Semco – one way or the other.'

continued overleaf

Management case study continued

Ricardo Semler still spends only 30% of his time on Semco. The rest of the time he writes a column in a weekly paper, he is board member of a political party and he attends courses in golf and Chinese. At least two months of the year Semler travels. He does not leave a number. 'I do not call in either. People who can always be reached everywhere, are afraid that another person can do their job. And when nobody calls during their holiday, deep in their heart they are disappointed.'

CASE QUESTIONS

1. In what way is the 'management leadership paradox' applicable to Ricardo Semler?
2. In terms of McGregor, what image of mankind is behind the Semco style?
3. Would you want to work at Semco as a middle manager?
4. Of which type of organizational culture, in terms of Harrison, can one speak in the Semco organization?
5. In what way do the style of leadership and the organizational structure at Semco contribute to the realization of the demands made to the organization in the areas of effectiveness, flexibility, continuity, clarity, efficiency and satisfaction?

Part five

Planning, control and information management

After the long-term course of action has been determined (Part two), the fitting organizational structure been developed (Part three) and the employees as well as the managers have been motivated to work (Part four), it all has to be monitored as to how much the daily work does indeed contribute to the long-term course.

In Part five we will cover management, control of and information to do with the processes in organizations, based on the strategy that there is a long-term plan. In order to know whether an organization is indeed on course, instruments and techniques have to be developed to make clear the effects of daily efforts. Techniques which come under discussion here are: budgeting, management by objectives, network planning and instruments such as ratios (Chapter 10).

Because of the large influence on organizations and the fast developments in automation and information technology (IT), separate attention is paid to information management in Chapter 11.

Automation projects have to fit in with the information planning, which, in turn, has to fit within the information policy of an organization. Attention will be directed to failure factors in automation projects, since applications of advanced information technologies will have strategic and organizational consequences. In Chapter 12 we will cover the process approach of the activities in organizations and the process control. In this aspect, quality control, care for the environment and logistic control and management will be raised for discussion.

Organizing is the grouping of processes into a certain structure. This structure is a tool or an instrument to facilitate processes. If the structure no longer suffices and blocks processes, then a redesign of the processes may be necessary and as a consequence adaptation and change to organizational structure. Process comes first, structures have to facilitate: this is known as business process re-engineering (BPR).

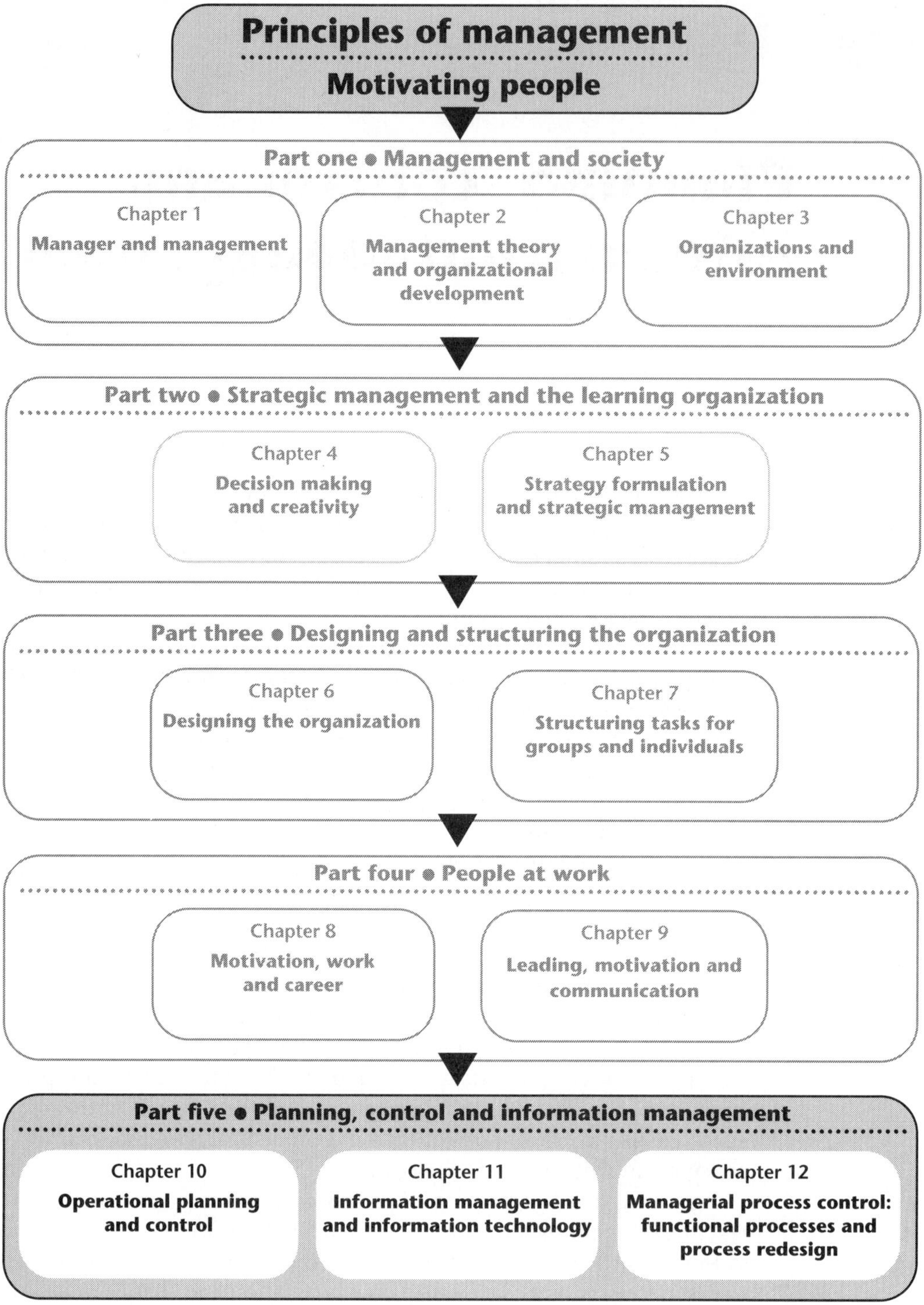

Principles of management

Motivating people

Part one • Management and society

Chapter 1
Manager and management

Chapter 2
Management theory and organizational development

Chapter 3
Organizations and environment

Part two • Strategic management and the learning organization

Chapter 4
Decision making and creativity

Chapter 5
Strategy formulation and strategic management

Part three • Designing and structuring the organization

Chapter 6
Designing the organization

Chapter 7
Structuring tasks for groups and individuals

Part four • People at work

Chapter 8
Motivation, work and career

Chapter 9
Leading, motivation and communication

Part five • Planning, control and information management

Chapter 10
Operational planning and control

Chapter 11
Information management and information technology

Chapter 12
Managerial process control: functional processes and process redesign

Chapter 10

Operational planning and control

LEARNING OBJECTIVES

After studying this chapter, you should be able to:

- give a definition of planning;
- explain the relationship between planning and budgeting;
- state the relationship between management, budgeting and management by objectives;
- explain the goal, structure and working of network planning;
- state the differences between financial and non-financial ratios;
- explain the concepts of integral quality management and benchmarking in their different aspects;
- state some specifics of management control in not-for-profit organizations

Management in action

Tendency to more intensive use of non-financial ratios

Relying exclusively on financial ratios does not suffice anymore. Top management needs to have a continuous view of all its employees' performances. Directing with 'non-financial performance measurement'.

'Measuring is knowing', says Bill Bosman, president of a Danish transportation company. Besides the classic financial ratios, this sturdy general director uses tens of non-financial indicators to manage his expedition firm. More than thirty years ago he started on his own, with one truck which he drove himself. Now the firm has 550 employees, sales of ECU 75 million and ten subsidiaries over the world.

'An important advantage of non-financial data is that they are available much sooner,' explains Bosman. 'Three days after the end of the month, I already have the non-financial figures. The financial figures do not come until six weeks later. So, in this way you can react much earlier. I use the first group to estimate the course of affairs as quickly as possible, the financial ratios for the finishing touch.'

Three years ago, Bosman started with 'performance measurement' – what boils down to the more intensive use of non-financial directing variables. The cause of this was the ISO9002 certification of his Dutch subsidiary. This happened at the instigation of the American computer firm Digital, an important client. At that point the notion of 'total quality management' was introduced and all kinds of thoughts about measuring and control systems in respect of quality.

Bosman has done his quality homework well. Nowadays he also drives for the British manufacturing subsidiary of Toyota, and soon also for Mazda. On a 'just in time' basis, components are picked up from suppliers on the European mainland and delivered to the Japanese car factories in the United Kingdom. Japanese industrial companies have a world name when quality control and the related application of measuring and regulating systems are concerned – and in the field, Toyota is supposed to be the finest.

'Yet, at the heart of it, the Toyota approach is very simple,' assures the frank entrepreneur. 'What they are very good at is thinking about their goals thoroughly in advance. They record this on paper and with that I, as service provider, have clear starting-points which are especially fit for testing. We first drive every new route for Toyota with an empty truck. So you do not start doing things off the cuff.'

Everywhere along the route, measurement points have been built in. As soon as the chauffeur passes such a point, he reports the office by means of his car phone. In that way the operational management can directly intervene when irregularities occur. Besides these time data, the quality of the load, documents and internal communication are measured daily and systematically reported in the information system.

The monthly computer printout yields a wheelbarrowful of paper which, on the management side, is summarized on one sheet of paper. 'I am only interested in outlines and the things which have gone wrong,' says Bosman. 'I do not need to know that nineteen out of twenty times things go as they are supposed to, I need to know about that one time when the truck has not been on time. And it interests me particularly why that has happened and how we can prevent it in the future.'

What does 'performance measurement' eventually yield? 'Cost reduction! It costs money, but it also yields money. And satisfied customers,' answers the logistic service provider.

More and more managers, just like Bill Bosman, have come to the conclusion that, in the assessment of the performance of a firm, the profit figure or other financial control variables, such as return on investments, are not enough. Financial data often concern the past, but that does not suffice anymore now that changes overtake one another more quickly than in the past.

Source: *Elan*, May 1994 (adapted).

INTRODUCTION

When the different strategic possibilities in an organization have been weighed and a choice has been made, this choice will have to be worked out further in different operational plans for marketing and sales, manufacturing, servicing, personnel, finance etc. The continuation of the model of strategic decision making (*see* Fig 4.3), with regard to operational planning and the execution of functional plans, looks very different now and is depicted in Fig 10.1.

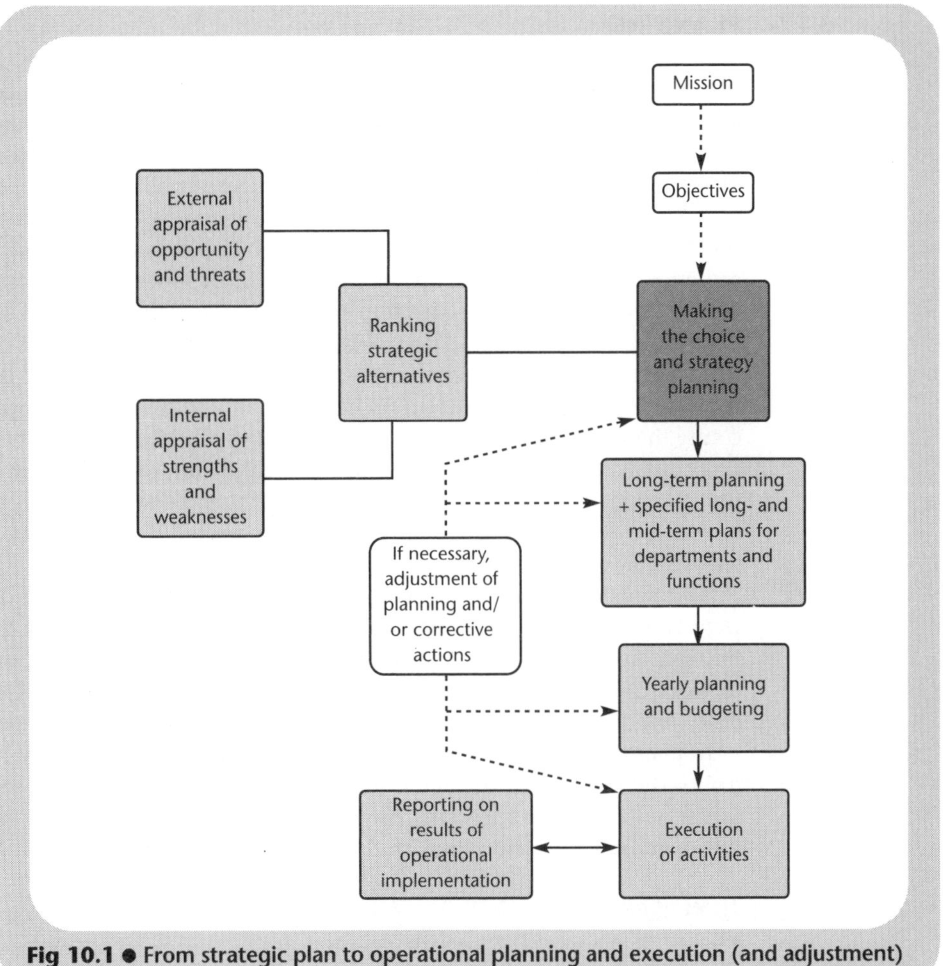

Fig 10.1 ● From strategic plan to operational planning and execution (and adjustment)

As a responsible manager in an existing company or as starter in a new company, it is necessary to think in advance about what is going to be done, how it will be done, where the activities will be conducted, etc. In other words: the direction for the coming period has to be determined and beacons have to be set out along the route to be followed. People and resources can then be steered in a certain direction. This gives the necessary structure to managing company activities. One then not only knows what one wants, but one also indicates the ways along which, and the resources with which these goals can be attained.

However, matters cannot be left to the mercy of policy intentions and words. These have to be transmitted into specific actions. In doing this, it is good to examine whether the things one had in mind are attained and whether in the execution one really does what was agreed on.

In order to come to an effective execution, it makes sense to work out strategic plans, determined from organization policies, in operational plans for the shorter term. There are, as they say, more ways to skin a cat. In an organization it is good, however, to make a choice in advance in a specific direction and after that, choose a way to follow in the first few years and set out this way in specific actions and results to be attained in the short term. The longer the period, the less detailed the plans can be. In the meantime if chances occur or circumstances change, it is then of course possible to adjust the plans.

10.1 PLANNING

Planning is the systematic preparation and attuning of decisions aimed at the realizing of goals in the future. Planning precedes the acting. In planning, management has to look forward and based on that set out tasks for the execution. In making operational plans it has to be determined what has to be manufactured and sold, where this will take place, how this will occur, when this will occur, how much has to be made and finally who will do this with what resources. By means of good operational planning control is kept on activities to be conducted. One has a grip on things. Effects of developments which are to be expected have been considered in advance in the plans and the execution of the activities has been well thought through. By means of planning, activities have been regulated in advance and tuned into each other. In this way planning serves to control the course of the activities. During the execution, should new and unexpected developments occur, of course the planning needs to be adjusted. In any case plans need to be based on sufficient and trustworthy data with regard to the future. One can then take decisions based on that. During the operational phase planning must be kept up with and will eventually have to be adjusted. Only in the case of unexpected developments, 'force majeur' and sudden new possibilities is there cause to review the plans drastically.

All forms of planning regard future activities, in the long, middle–long, or short term and so precede the actual acting. In this respect regulation of the necessary activities and also co-ordination of the actions to be conducted are examined. For one has to work in one direction: that means that on all levels of execution there has to be unity in point of view and unity of direction. Here, planning is the pre-eminent tool.

In planning, besides regulating future actions and co-ordinating of all that, the control of the progress of the activities is concerned. Comparison of the planned and the actual outcomes can then give rise for the need to take additional, and perhaps corrective operational decisions and/or the adjustment of the operational norms.

Types of planning

Besides planning the future development of a company or institution as a whole, in the form of a corporate plan or strategic plan, planning is also necessary for the different functional areas in the form of partial planning for the functional departments in the organization.

The character of corporate planning is rather broad, is directed at the longer term and more particularly provides for the necessary adjustments and investments in buildings, machines, equipment and people.

Planning for the different functional areas in the form of partial planning for the functional departments in the organization is directed first of all at the operational planning in the shorter term. This planning specifies the direction given in the strategic plan and is detailed to the different functional areas in the organization. Examples of this are: a marketing and sales plan, a manufacturing plan and a research and product development plan (*see* sections 10.1.2–10.1.7).

Controlling processes by planning

All forms of planning consist of the following three basic elements:

- information;
- norms;
- plans.

Information

Planning rests on the systematic processing of external and internal data. Without data, there is nothing to plan. In policy making and planning in the long term, on the one side financial data and information concerning developments and trends from the societal environment are required. On the other side information as a result of the internal appraisal of the organization regards the organization itself. The more planning regards the specific and detailed daily execution of actions, the more the internal information becomes important. The quality of the planning then especially depends on the quality, trustworthiness and survey ability of the information from within the company itself, as well as on the speed in which this information can be supplied. The quality of information processing and internal information provision is of decisive importance here.

Norms

Norms are guidelines, prescriptions etc. which indicate the constraints within which one has to act. Norms specify the way of acting, method or procedure which in the execution of tasks has always to be considered. These norms can consider the organization as a whole, can be meant for a certain functional area or can refer to a specific activity.

Plans

Plans describe the goals of the organization or indeed of the departments to be attained; they determine the measures necessary to attain these goals; they indicate the personnel and financial resources necessary to attain these goals; and in conclusion they indicate the period or the horizon in which the set goals have to be attained. A plan can be seen as the result of planning as an activity.

Planning to functional areas and departments

Plans which have to be drawn up for the different functional areas or departments, concern the functional areas including:

- marketing and sales;
- manufacturing/servicing;
- product development;
- finance;
- personnel;
- purchasing.

In other words, there is no function or department in an organization for which planning is impossible. For the primary processes as well as for supporting activities goals can be specified and measures can be determined to attain these goals. The coping stone of this is always operational planning in the short term and budgeting as a financial translation of the operational plans.

10.1.1 Marketing and planning of sales

On the one hand, marketing and sales planning comprises the determination of the markets to which an organization directs itself, and on the other the way in which these markets will be approached. This concerns the so-called marketing mix or 4 Ps: the Products which one wants to bring out, the areas and places where one wants to direct oneself by Placement and distribution, the way in which Promotion through advertising and sales efforts will be approached and the determination of the Price of the product or the products. The marketing and sales plan will have to contain statements about:

- sales and sales growth;
- market share;
- demands of profitability;
- product itself and development;
- distribution channels;
- price;
- promotion of the product.

In all these aspects, a long-term vision as well as a short-term plan for the first and even the second year, will have to be developed.

Exhibit 10.1

Snowboard crazy

How Europe's ski makers are fighting back

In the past few years, snowboarding has gone from being a curiosity practiced largely in the US to a medal event at the 1998 Winter Olympics in Japan. Although snowboarding is nowhere near as big as skiing, participation is growing globally at a yearly rate of more than 30%, according to Minneapolis brokerage Dain Bosworth Inc., with snowboards and gear generating estimated wholesale revenues of more than $600 million for 1995–96.

Now snowboard fever has hit the Continent full force, and it's pitting small upstart US snowboard companies against old-line ski manufacturers, most of them European. That's because the high crossover rate from skiing to snowboarding is eating into the already soft sales of the ski industry. 'The snowboard market is cannibalizing the Alpine ski market,' says Anne Marie Berrette, general secretary of the French ski giant Salomon. Austrian ski giant Völkl's sales have been flat for the past two years, and Salomon expects its sales to shrink 8% this year. The Innsbruck-based International Snowboard Federation estimates that worldwide sales of snowboards – at an average of $325 a board – will hit more than 1.2 million in the 1995–96 season, up from 540,000 in 1994–95. At the same time, brokerage Hambrecht & Quist says worldwide sales of skis – at about $265 a pair – have dropped from 6.2 million pairs in 1993–94 to about 5.3 million in 1995–96.

Völkl minority

To survive the American onslaught, Old World ski companies are coming out with their own flashy boards. But they are finding it difficult to appeal to the kids such as Liddiker who are fueling the snowboard craze. Indeed, young 'riders' have written off a good many brands that make the skis their parents use – and ski manufacturers realize that. Völkl doesn't dare come out with its own board, although it has been the snowboard manufacturer for hot-selling US brands Sims and Santa Cruz for the past two years. 'Snowboarders want to be different,' says Völkl Chief Executive Franz K. Julen. 'They don't want a snowboard that says Völkl all over it.'

Völkl isn't the only ski company hawking its snowboards undercover. Atomic Austria, now a unit of the Finnish holding company Amer Group Ltd., began making snowboards under the Oxygen label three years ago. And Dynastar, a Rossignol subsidiary, recently acquired US snowboard company Original Sin.

The big ski makers already have worldwide distribution networks in place and advanced ski-making technology to help them race against US-made snowboards. But they are still weak on marketing. 'It's not enough to have great R&D and a lot of money to invest,' says Dennis Jenson, director of marketing at industry leader Burton Snowboards. 'You've got to be in tune with youth culture.' Unlike ski manufacturers, the leading players in the snowboard industry make more than 30% of their revenues from selling grungy apparel and accessories such as funky goggles. Ride Snowboard Co. even markets a line of condoms called Safe Ride.

However, the battle isn't just between hip snowboard brands and staid ski labels. There are dozens of garage-shop companies with average annual sales of less than $5 million, and analysts say the business is ripe for a shake-out. 'A lot of the smaller guys are going to fall off the hill as consumers start choosing the more sophisticated and quality name brands,' says Chad A. Jacobs, an analyst at New York's Ladenburg, Thalmann & Co.

As the competition heats up, the winning brands will be those with a strong presence in the US and in the key Japanese and European markets. Building a variety of boards – from racing to acrobatic – will be important, too. And, of course, it will probably help a company's image if it does not become boardmaker-of-choice for the old fogeys of the slopes. You know, the 35-year-olds.

Source: Business Week, 8 April 1996.

10.1.2 Manufacturing planning/planning of services

With the strategic plan as a base, with regard to the manufacturing further steps can be taken which require a further detailing of the plans.

Capacity planning

The first step is determining the size of the necessary capacity, based on sales expectation with regard to the totality of new products. In this respect, one should not only think of buildings and machines, but also of people. This last resource is especially important when further education or supplementary training has to take place before new recruits as opposed to existing personnel will be available. If sales expectations are not very sure, it is desirable to build in the necessary flexibility in this planning. This can be done, for example, by setting up a relatively small capacity which has expansion possibilities. Capacity planning is still quite broad in nature.

Production planning

As soon as capacity has been realized, it is necessary to analyse how the order flow fits into the capacity. In other words, one needs to examine how the capacity will be occupied. From this, one can, in the case of over- or under-utilization, decide on certain new measures, for example, in the case of overutilization the recruiting of temporary employees or the use of overtime. In the case of underutilization one can try to fill up the capacity by extra sales efforts, strengthened possibly by temporary discounts.

From production level planning, information also emerges about the purchase function. This especially counts in companies that make one product or only a small variety of products. In companies with a large variety of products, it is better to take the incoming individual orders as a basis for the purchase of materials or components.

Delivery planning

If production planning gives an idea of utilized capacity, delivery planning intends to give further detail on this, in the sense that it determines when raw materials and tools have to be in certain departments or machine groups.

In this form of planning, problems come up with regard to the most effective way an order can be followed through the manufacturing departments and the processing times which are allowed. In this respect, this is also known as work planning.

Detailed order and machine planning

In this stage, the work is divided over the machines and/or over different people. This is the last phase before actual manufacture. In this relation one can speak of work distribution or 'dispatching'. Depending on the kind of manufacture, this form of planning will be done by the planning room or by the department chief. In capital intensive companies with series or mass production the planning room will play an especially important part.

A necessary supplement to the last two planning phases particularly is control, the goal of which is to determine whether the activities run according to plan. Reality then confronts the plan. If reality deviates from the plan, corrective action will have to be taken. It is self-evident that this demands timely processing of information. In planning and operational control, tools such as planning charts can be used. Planning and control are of importance for every organization. A planning system running well in the short term, which, in an industrial organization, is set up by the planning department, is not only directed at attaining a higher degree of efficiency, but also at better service to clients; for example with regard to given delivery times.

10.1.3 Product development planning

In order to prevent misunderstandings, it must be stressed that the notion of product is conceived here in a broad sense. Planning for new services has to be taken into account.

In the first place product development needs to be conceived as an exploration of new possibilities. Next all or a number of those possibilities can be worked out and judged on their merits for the organization. After this an analysis needs to be made of the economic aspects of the product idea, after which the chosen alternative is developed into a complete product and can be manufactured. This product has then to be tested, and finally it can be brought onto the market. Even though these steps seem obvious, in the development and bringing of new products to market, a lot can go wrong. Only a fraction of the number of ideas for new products (about one in forty) ends up as successful products.

It is self-evident that in this phase good co-ordination of both new and existing marketing efforts are a first demand for success. A product needs to be tuned into the desires of the client as finely as possible.

10.1.4 Financial planning

When it comes to financial planning, a number of aspects need to be looked at more closely, such as the debt and equity structure, the assigning of financial resources to different investment projects and the control of working capital. Financial needs in the long term worry organizations particularly in times of high inflation and high interest rates. Where there is moderate or slight profitability, equity capital grows insufficiently to finance all needs that arise from the growth of inventories and accounts receivable.

Sometimes this can even go so far that a negative leverage effect comes about, which only serves to intensify the problems further.

The answer to questions such as: 'Do assets (the building, the machinery) have to be financed or leased?', or: 'What policy of dividend payment has to be followed?', are within the remit of financial planning. Here, one can make use of investment selection methods, techniques concerning control of working capital, optimization of funding etc.

10.1.5 Personnel planning

By means of personnel planning, an organization tries to obtain insight into the question: 'What quantitative and qualitative consequences does the chosen strategy have for the structure of the personnel?' When activities are extended, a lack of sufficient and appropriate trained personnel can hinder the execution of the strategy severely. In the case of a planned phasing out of the activities, it will have to be examined as early as possible how this can be realized with as little social suffering as possible.

Personnel planning regards the short term (perhaps only weeks or months), and the outcome of the planning will have consequences especially for the recruitment or the sacking of personnel. Recruitment also comprises recruiting personnel on a temporary basis.

The longer the term becomes which the personnel planning affects (a year or longer), the more the complexity increases. The cause of this is that many aspects are of influence here: intake, flow of personnel, career development, management development, training and further education, promotions, work structuring, organizational change, etc.

In personnel planning, specific content must be given to social policy and to the goals which have been formulated for that reason. (Compare 'human resources management' in Chapter 8.)

10.1.6 Purchasing and material resources planning

A field to which less attention is usually paid is that of material resources planning. It is the task of material resources planning to see to the purchase of necessary materials: of the right quality, in the right quantity, at the right moment, for the right price, from the right supplier(s), and the delivering of these goods to the right place.

Because of the scarcity and therefore the increasing expense of a number of raw materials and a worsened competitive and profit position, the purchase function is becoming even more important. Usually this means a search for alternative suppliers and a replacement of raw materials. Within the framework of material resources planning, problems such as the degree to which work can and may be outsourced are contained.

In larger, divisionalized companies, in which cross-deliveries can take place, this is expressed in guidelines which limit the freedom of the divisions. They are, for example, not allowed to purchase from third parties materials produced within the company. Here also the problem arises of transfer pricing and determination of internal pricing systems.

10.2 FROM PLANNING TO BUDGETING

When the policy to be conducted has been determined and then fixed in plans, the framework and the conditions are created within which the execution of actions will have to take place. It then needs to be examined, from month to month, from week to week and from day to day (via planning in the short term), how one can make use of existing possibilities and available resources in the best way possible. So when important decisions in the long-term planning have been determined with regard to the profit level to be attained, the market share, the product assortment, the production resources etc., in the short-term planning, these have to be translated into task assignments. One has to make the best use of the possibilities present now and here also the people and resources available now have to be used as well as possible. The long term then gives the framework within which operational plans in the short term, for example, for the coming year, have to be drawn up. Short-term planning is task specific/prescriptive and needs to be executed in the immediate period.

Short-term planning is operational planning and specifically states, in task assignments, what has to be done by whom, when, with the aid of what resources, in what quantities. When these task assignments are translated in financial terms, we speak of budgets (*see* section 10.2.1). Short-term planning usually takes place on a department level. The department chief, a boss of a sub-department or a group leader is often burdened with this. So in this stage, as well as the work, resources are also assigned.

One of the goals of a profit organization is make a profit. In a not-for-profit organization, for example the public utilities, one of the goals is the delivery of a service at a certain tariff or at the lowest possible cost. That is why in every organization the management always needs to control costs and revenues. This can actually only be done well when before the operational phase of the activities one has planned well and when operational control of the execution occurs as a matter of course.

With the help of budgeting and planning one can try to control the activities as well as possible. The broader context (the organization strategy) has been outlined in the strategic plan. Now the broad policy lines have to be worked out in more detail in operational plans for the short term. For that purpose an organization plan needs to be drawn up for departments and responsible employees. In these plans it is stated what one expects of departments and of the employees working there.

As soon as these plans are translated into financial consequences, we speak of budgeting. So budgeting is planning translated into sums of money. With the help of budgeting, in terms of costs, expense, revenues and income one wants to see what the organizational results are in the coming period, expressed in money. If a plan is task specific, a budget (i.e. a formal plan expressed in terms of money) also has a task-specific function. Here, the management hands out task assignments, expressed in sums of money, to sales, manufacturing, purchase etc., which in mutual coherence, have to realize the organizational goals together.

10.2.1 Budgeting and setting norms and targets

Budgeting is nothing more than planning translated into sums of money. Money is the only common denominator into which all activities in the organization can be translated. This is because planning must always have a financial aspect: budgeting is a logical consequence of planning. Just like planning, budgeting has an active character.

Budgeting always comprises a certain task assignment. Budgets are performance norms expressed in money terms. When everything is right, norms meet several requirements. Norms, just like plans, have to be based on investigation into the future. A plan based on inaccurate and insufficient information can never lead to good results. A good plan then needs to be quantified, for example in terms of necessary machine time, hours of personnel and associated costs. Norms also need to be attainable. It makes no sense to assign something which cannot be realized as this is a waste of motivation. The best seem to be norms which are seen as an attainable challenge. These stimulate to effort without the feeling that one really has to strain oneself to the maximum. Norms which are set at a too low level do not form a challenge either and will in time also have a de-motivating effect.

A last but not unimportant requirement is that the norms are measurable. When this is not the case, it will become hard if not impossible to control the operational execution of tasks. This requirement, however, stems from the demand that a plan has to be quantified. Budgeting is the pre-eminent tool to live up to these requirements. Thus there is a close relation between the planning process and the budget procedure.

A question which can be asked is whether budgets have to be 'fixed' or if they can be 'variable'. Fixed budgets can be applied when the utilization of capacity can be determined. A variable budget, on the contrary, can be recommended when the utilization of capacity shows a rather strong fluctuation. In all cases, the company results depend on the utilization of capacity. In an organization, operational employees can be involved in drawing up department plans and budgets in many cases. When one has assisted in drawing up goals to be attained and the norms oneself, this can work in a motivating and stimulating way in the execution of plans. Cost reductions may come about by means of employees' budgeting.

Differences between actual and budgeted outcomes always have to be subject to closer analysis. Measuring and control precede the budget analysis (respectively the differences or result analysis) before this assessment can take place. In business terms we speak of 'post-calculation' when the periodical comparison of allowed costs to actual costs is undertaken. As soon as the difference (i.e. the budget result) exceeds the zone of tolerance, it needs to be analysed more closely before any adjustment is made. For budget verification, the information book-keeping system needs to deliver the required data.

The causes of differences can be very different in nature, and before adjustment can take place, it is important to recognize these causes. When the causes of differences lie outside the organization, for example in stagnating sales or calculated price increase of raw materials into sales price, the chief of the final assembly department cannot be held responsible for the increase in stock of the final product.

10.2.2 Budgeting as a management tool

Seen in this way, budgeting is first and for all an important tool for management. By means of budgeting, planning is translated into money terms as daily task assignment for employees in different functional departments.

Marketing and sales: the sales plan is translated to results which have to be realized in total and to separate product groups in terms of sales to be attained, sales results to be attained and sales costs to be spent. In this relationship, direct cost budgets can be drawn up for, for example advertising, sales promotion and representatives. In the marketing and sales sphere, to monitor activities and results, one can work with index figures for sales per client and per representative, per area, average order amount, sales costs per order.

Manufacturing: the manufacturing plan is, by means of a budget, translated into the different components of the manufacturing costs: raw material, labour and machines; from production costs in total to types of products and product series etc. To monitor activities, one can work here with quality norms and productivity norms, for example, measured per machine, per man hour.

Purchasing: in order to secure a quick execution of company activities, inventories of raw materials and components usually have to be purchased. Sufficient inventory has to be present to execute orders. Here delivery times almost always have to be taken into account. In many cases account needs to be taken of seasonal fluctuations. The nature and duration of the manufacturing process are closely aligned with the purchase of materials, components, installations and other durable production resources to be budgeted for in sums of money and to be fixed or determined in purchasing budgets and capital investments.

Research and development: in this type of budget, statements are made about the allowed amounts for improvement or development of new products or new production methods. The course of the activities can be followed in costs per development hour, investments and other costs per development activity.

Financing: Here the statement of results for the coming years is drawn up and profit and loss account and cash flows projections are determined. The cash or liquidity planning serves for the determination of needs or surpluses that will arise in the coming period with regard to financial resources to state which extra financial resources have to be drawn in or how the surplus of resources can be invested (either in the short or the longer term).

Personnel: in the personnel budget, statements about wages, salaries, social securities etc. are determined. Here too sums of money are made available, for example, for education and training, company social care and other costs of the personnel policy. In this sphere it is important not only to work with indexes or ratios for wages and other personnel costs, but also with ratios which regard absenteeism, turnover etc. In the annual reports on this issue an increasing amount of information is required.

The specification of tasks in activities of different functional departments need to be tuned into each other. This also needs to be expressed in the financial translation of the performances to be delivered by the department. Budgeting, in other words, is also a tool for co-ordination with the intention that the departments and employees work in the same direction, namely in the direction of the organizational goals. The unity of direction can be strengthened by this.

Drawing up budgets demands that functions and tasks of departments and employees are clearly determined. Linked to that it has to be clear who has the authority over what in a department and along which lines accountability needs to be rendered. In accordance with the authorized budgets, one is empowered to take decisions and to run up expenses.

Coherence between budgets

The departmental budgets can be divided further into operational and capital budgets. Operational budgets regard the daily activities, expressed in costs and revenues. Capital budgets come from the desire to change the level of balance posts decisively. We can think in terms of inventories, accounts receivable, accounts payable and of investments in land and buildings.

Both kinds of budgets result in a liquidity budget, where the financial consequences of all plans come together. Based on a provisional liquidity budget it can, for example, be determined whether a planned investment can be financed out of the normal cash flows. When this is not possible, one will have to search for other sources of finance and when these cannot be found, the intended investment will possibly have to be dropped.

The coherence between the various budgets has been depicted schematically in Fig 10.2. The different budgets can be summarized in an analogous coherence as a so-called general or master budget. This is discussed further in the next section.

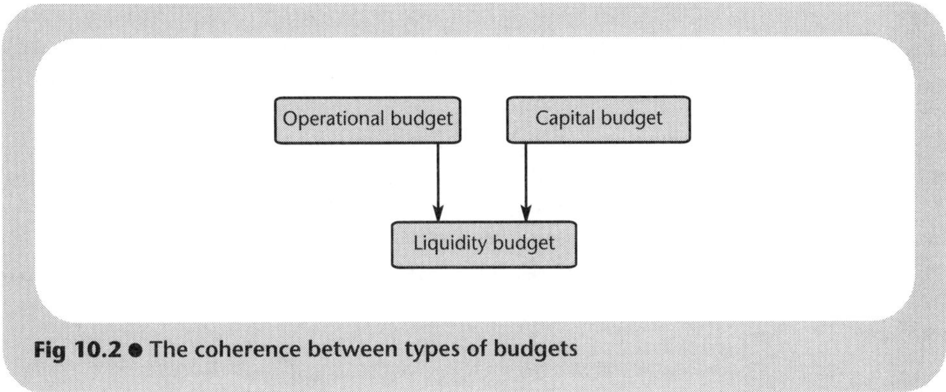

Fig 10.2 ● The coherence between types of budgets

10.2.3 Budgeting and the general (or master) budget

We have seen that by means of budgeting, a task specifying financial budget for the total activities of the organization is composed. For the different functional departments the partial budgets follow from this for the coming year. Partial budgets form a financial translation of the intended activity programmes of different functional areas. These are looked at in mutual coherence and tuned into each other, and reflect the task specifications which have to be realized next.

A year is the usual time horizon in drawing up budgets. With regard to the term envisaged, one can, however, also make use of rolling of shifting budget periods (a so-called revolving budget). For the initial period, the budget has a task-specific character, while the drawing up of figures for the next period (for example, per quarter of a year) has an orientating character. With the revolving budget method one builds in flexibility, and at the same time continuity is intended and for the next period it is already stated what costs and revenues are expected respectively for what sums of money in the next period mandate will have to be given to employees.

In this way budgeting is a tool which gives management the possibility to control different organizational processes, in advance as well as afterwards. Budgeting is a pre-eminent tool in order to determine results to be attained, because of which a good possibility is offered for control, adjustment and corrective actions.

The budgets which have been drawn up for different functional departments can be summarized in the so-called general or master budget. From this summarized budget the profit and loss account for the coming budget year can be derived. In the general or master budget the task-specific income cost and/or expenditure budgets from the departments are processed. In the general budget expenditures are included which require liquidity or cash resources: e.g. payment of wages and salary.

In the general budget, costs are also included which do not require expenditures as yet, but for which in the future cash resources will have to be cleared. This includes such things as depreciation, provision for maintenance and so on. Interest cost of credits, accounts receivable, inventories and other company resources are also part of the summarizing company budget. This is necessary in order to determine a fair business result from an economic point of view.

So the general or master budget of an industrial company can be composed, for example, from the sales budget, the manufacturing budget, the purchase budget, the personnel budget and the capital investment budget. From this result the cash forecast and the forecast of cash needs. Based on this, a projection of the balance and profit/loss account for a next period can be composed.

The coherence between the different partial budgets and the general budget as the basis for the forecasted balance and profit/loss account results has been depicted schematically in Fig 10.3. In order to be able to do this, one has to know the relationships between the different departments in the organization and the degree to which they can make use of each others' services. When one knows these relationships, it is possible to determine costs expected for the budget year.

10.2.4 Functions of budgeting

A budget is a summary of a plan which is translated into sums of money. A particular employee can be rendered responsible for a budget. Sometimes the term estimation is used instead of budget, though strictly seen, this notion has a different meaning: it is more an estimate of costs and revenues which, seen in itself does not have a task-specific character as does a budget. In having a task-specific character, budgeting fulfils four functions.

First of all, budgeting forms a reflection on the future, on the policy to be conducted and the actions to be undertaken to realize the policy. This function of the budget flows from the goal in its place in the total planning process in the organization. By

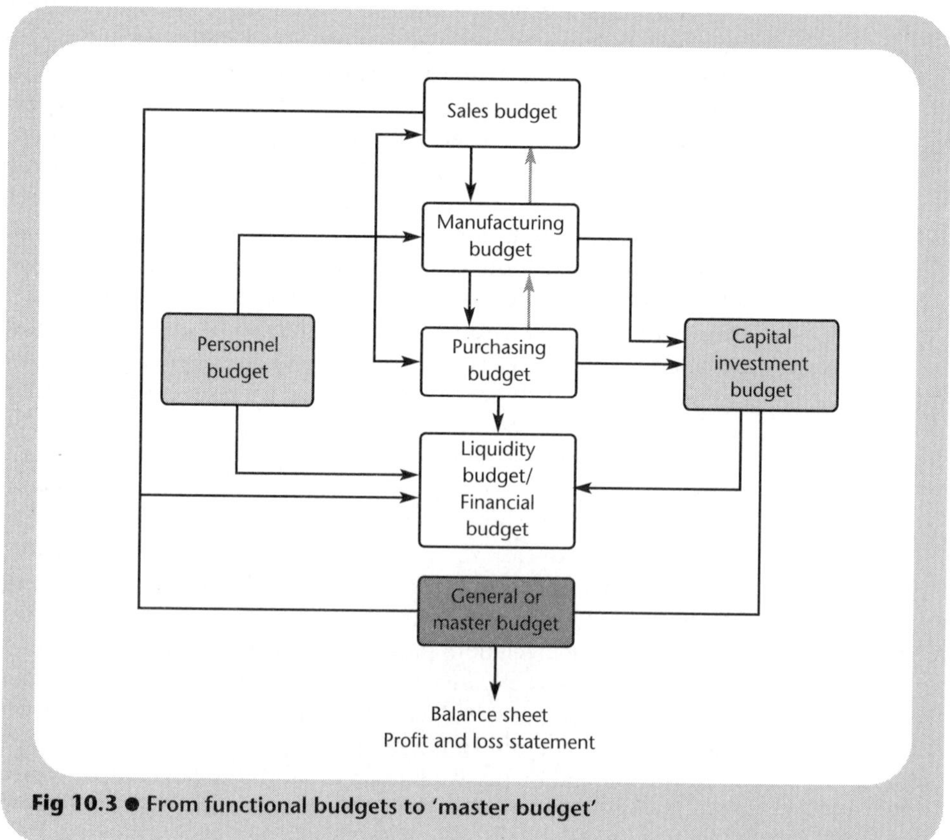

Fig 10.3 ● From functional budgets to 'master budget'

means of budgeting activities in an organization are tuned into each other and in mutual coherence activity programmes arise.

In the second place a budget is a tool for transferring the broader organizational policy to lower levels in the organization. By means of budgets, task assignments are given to different employees. Higher management then grants them the authority to make decisions independently and to conduct actions demanded for the execution of task assignments within the constraints of the approved budget. In other words, a budget is an instrument of communication. Often management will, however, already involve the lower levels in the preparation of plans, so that the communication function is two way. With this policy transfer the possibility is there to give task assignments to different employees by means of budgets which have to be covered by the appropriate authority of the employees.

Besides being a tool to transmit the strategy and policy to responsible employees, budgeting, in the third place, is an instrument to motivate these employees to conduct tasks as well as possible. Often the higher management will already involve the lower levels in the preparation of the budgets, then based on the budget, they can be held accountable about the execution. A budget states what is expected. A responsible employee will thus try to attain this task specification. In the case that he or she succeeds in this, there is reason for satisfaction; if he or she does not succeed, the reasons have to be given.

In the fourth place for higher management and employers themselves, the budget is a tool to test the execution of plans. Budgeting allows for the appraisal of performances of departments afterwards. This is of great importance because one obtains insight into the 'why' when plans have not been realized. This can sometimes be the consequence of external factors, for example, decreasing demand for a certain product. Sometimes it is the consequence of internal causes, for example, inefficiently working or a loss of raw materials. Based on such a conclusion, one can then try to improve the organization or to buy better raw materials. Comparison between financial plan and outcome generally speaking has to lead to corrective actions and measures (*see* Fig 10.4). In some cases improvement in execution will be recommended. In others, perhaps the norm will have to be adapted. Adaptations have to be carefully tuned into budgets which have been drawn up for other functional departments.

From these four functions it can be seen that the budgeting process supplies the organization with the possibility to control business processes, in advance as well as afterwards. Budgeting is a pre-eminent tool to determine the results to be attained, and thus it presents a good possibility for control, adjustment and/or corrective actions.

10.2.5 Conditions for effective budgeting

Even though budgeting clearly has financial-technical aspects, effectively budgeting can only be introduced when a number of conditions have been met.

Support from top management

Support from the top is a 'must'. Besides being a technique, budgeting is more particularly a philosophy of managing. No single technique can successfully be applied without the acceptance of the notions or thoughts which form the basis of it. Budgeting demands that top management be prepared and willing to delegate and hence replace a part of the decision-making authority to a lower level in the organization.

There has to be a clear organizational structure

In the case of budgeting, every employee gets the responsibility for executing certain tasks or for attaining certain results. These have to be clearly assigned in the organizational structure, with regard also to authorities. Control is not possible otherwise.

The budget system has to be a part of the total planning system

In detail the budgets state which activities have to be undertaken in the coming year and which sums of money are allowed for that. So budgets clearly have to connect to the company strategy and policy. The budget system provides the possibility to co-ordinate the different activities in the short term.

Responsibility for the budget system has to be determined

Even though budgeting eventually falls under the responsibility of top management, supervision of the budgeting process in larger organizations will often be delegated to the manager of the Administration and Finance Department, or to the controller. This department sees to the collecting and transmitting of information which the different employees need.

The use of business or economic jargon has to be limited

Even though budgets are drawn up in financial terms, these still have to remain understandable for the involved employees. With regard to use of language, budgets are not allowed to be too far off the daily world of the employee. When this is the case, budgeting is no longer 'a tool of management'. In other words, budgeting has to stay an understandable tool in order to be able to keep managing with it.

Clear goals and norms have to be determined

Goals are the base of the budget. When goals and norms are not clear, it will not be possible to translate them well into sums of money. Comparing the execution to the norms afterwards is not as meaningful either.

Need for participation in the development, drawing up and use of budgets

Few people like to be watched, and budgeting is a technique and tool which does involve this function. In order to prevent sabotage of the system, it is necessary to involve the organization members in drawing up the budgets. Through this involvement information on which the budgets are based is as good and complete as possible. In addition, the organization members will be better motivated because they are involved themselves in determining the goals. They will then also start to see the budget more as a challenge than as a threat.

When all these conditions are met, an organization possesses not only a management tool which can follow and control the execution of plans, but also a good basis for developing managerial function on all levels in the organization.

10.3 ● MANAGEMENT OF OPERATIONS

In organizations one wants to ensure that all activities/operations are directed towards goals. That is why it is necessary to develop strategic plans further into action plans for functional areas. For departments, goals can be set which, when large organizations are concerned, have to be split up further in sub-goals. To attain these goals, certain employees are made responsible and accountable.

In order to control the process of goal realization, one needs both during and after the execution to examine whether everything is going according to plan. When deviations arise, an adjustment will have to take place, so that the execution is either adjusted, or the set norms are adjusted by corrective actions. The control process or the control cycle is schematically depicted in Fig 10.4.

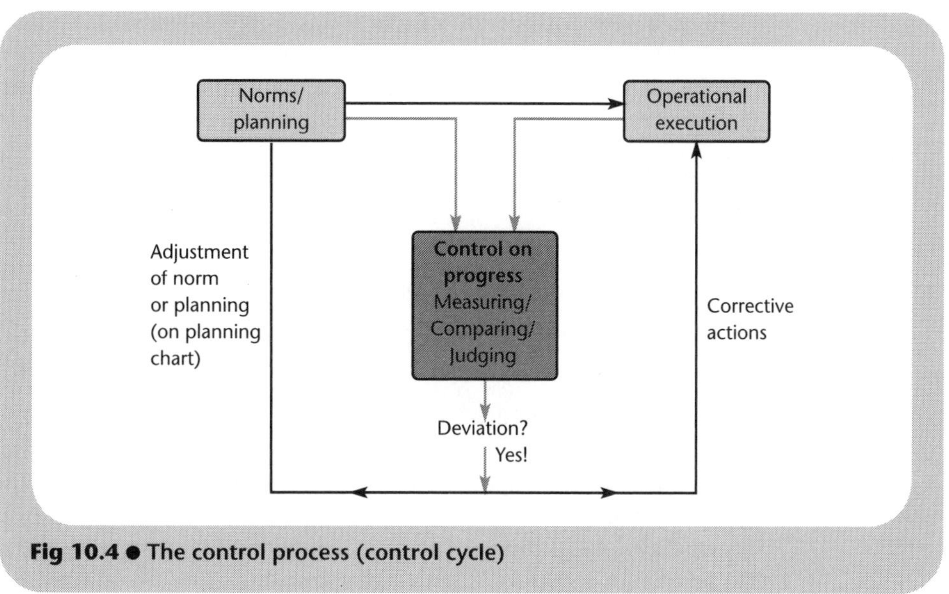

Fig 10.4 ● The control process (control cycle)

In management a control circle arises in the case of budgeting such as the one discussed in section 10.2. Deviations between allowed and actual costs are pinpointed. Then an examination occurs into how correction or adjustment can take place. When deviations exceed a certain level of tolerance, one has to intervene and adjustments have to take place, either in actions and/or norms. Within the tolerance level, the process can proceed with no further intervention.

In the development of a departmental plan and the determination of operational norms, employees are often involved. This can work towards motivation and stimulation and enlarges the acceptance by employees of management plans

10.3.1 Control: systematic grip on activities

Control of activities/operations demands that execution takes place only if one has first planned well, and also control of progress in the execution has to occur. In this way, planning, execution and monitoring all lead to control of the organizational processes. Systematic control involves five activities, namely:

1. setting operational norms (via planning);
2. giving task assignments and instructions;
3. monitoring and measuring the execution (i.e. collecting data about actual performance during the execution);
4. comparing the execution to the planning (according to budget or planning chart) and the given assignments and instructions and stating and analysing of causes or possible differences;
5. taking of adjusting measures with regard to planning and/or execution (for example: longer working hours, another dispatch of work; this leads to changes in norms and/or in planning on the planning chart and/or to new task assignments which are to be given out).

Monitoring and control of progress serve to determine possible deviations, when there will be timely notification of where and when deficits, disadvantages, standstills or overruns occur with regard to the budgets and the planned machine time (according to the planning chart). Deviations of actual costs, revenues or spent time with regard to the planned costs, revenues or times can arise through:

- late replenishing of materials, components, etc;
- bad materials;
- absenteeism;
- machine standstill because of defects;
- low level of motivation;
- falling demand.

The quality of the products or services will also have to be monitored. Sometimes quality control is part of the production department. In other cases, it is a separate department in the organization, so that it can operate more independently from the production department.

Quality control can take place by conducting random tests and testing the product to set quality demands. Based on that an adjustment can take place, either in the product design or in the actual production activities to make better products in the future.

Via administrative procedures, control of the manufacturing activities needs to be made possible. Data about used materials, worked hours, disruptions and so on have to be presented in an orderly way to be able quickly to form an idea of the progress of affairs in this department. Financial administration has to supply employees with information in such a way that decisions in departments can be made based on that. In a certain sense, the supply of information is the nerve system through which all company functions are linked. For example, signals have to be passed on that suppliers have to be paid, debtors exhorted, that sales per client lags behind expectations, that cost budgets are exceeded, that calculations have to be adjusted. In order to do this timely information processing is demanded (*see also* Chapter 11).

To stay informed of progress, different tools can be used. Sometimes deviations are registered by means of direct control. More often, however, control is indirect and deviations are determined afterwards. As long as deviations lie within a certain zone of tolerance, the decision-making authority for adjustment can be delegated to operational employees. When these terms are exceeded, adjustment needs to take place.

Conscious and systematic application of the exception rule is called 'management by exception' (MbE). In this situation, a manager only has exceptions presented to him. The most important goal of this way of working is to relief the manager of a large amount of the routine information, so that he or she can pay more attention to the more important tasks and problems. Good employees can very often solve their own problems themselves when they are given more trust and freedom in their function to do that.

Adjusting the operational norms or department plans is never an isolated event. This almost always has consequences for other departments or phases of processing. It therefore must always happen in mutual consultation. Deviations have to be carefully tuned into operational norms or plans drawn up for other processes; that is why they need to be authorized by the management. This occurs preferably in consultation with the employees who are involved in the execution. Here, one needs to render account to valid procedures, and existing plans, accepted standard methods and given policy guidelines (*see* section 7.7.1).

10.3.2 Giving orders

A plan can only be executed when management takes charge in the control for this by giving task assignments, instructions or orders. A task assignment is an order to conduct certain activities or attain certain results. In the last instance, the executive has greater freedom to act than in the first instance. Two aspects in giving task assignments can be determined:

- the way in which the task order is given;
- the type of task order.

Task assignment: oral or written

We can distinguish oral and written task assignments. Both have advantages and disadvantages. That is why it is necessary to examine both well before a choice is made. The advantages of the oral task assignment are: speed, simplicity and prevention of a pile of papers. The most important disadvantage is the danger of a wrong interpretation. In the case of a task assignment the execution of which occurs over a long period of time, it can happen that when the result comes to be judged, it is not clear what order was exactly given. This is especially the case when the execution shows a negative deviation. The written task assignment has the advantage of safe possibilities for later control. In addition to that, it can be multiplied and given to more involved employees at the same time. A written task assignment needs to be carefully formulated. Disadvantages here are the pile of papers and not being able to give an explanation directly this is desired.

The form chosen will depend on the specific situation. A frequently occurring task order will usually be given orally and a complex task assignment will preferably be given in written form.

Task assignment: simple or multiple

The choice of the type of task assignment is important. We can distinguish simple and multiple task assignments.

A *simple task assignment* is an order for a certain result. The employee is free to determine for himself how he executes the order. So he can develop initiative, since only the result is being judged.

In the case of a *multiple task assignment*, coercive indications are given about how the task has to be executed. For example, which procedures or steps have to be followed or who should be given feedback information. Here the initiative of the operational employee is reduced. The more critical moments stated, the more limited is the possibility for taking the initiative.

Instructions

The execution of tasks can also be arranged in a way other than by a task assignment, namely through an instruction. An instruction is a total of *general guidelines* which have to be considered in the execution of tasks.

An instruction needs to be considered as the complement of a task assignment. It is clear that the added value of an instruction is largest when it is complement to a simple task order. For there exists here in principle the greatest need to limit the taking of initiative. To keep instructions updated it is necessary to examine whether they are really being followed or not.

Instructions have to be reviewed continuously when the situation asks for it. When an instruction appears to be partially superseded, it is better to skip the irrelevant part than to allow this part not to be followed through. If that is allowed, the danger exists that those involved also start neglecting the relevant issues.

10.3.3 Management by objectives

A special way to formulate orders on core issues in the process of management, is developed under the term 'management by objectives' (MbO). The concept of managing by objectives comprises more than the giving of orders alone. This management technique is especially directed at the improvement of the total performance of the organization, and the philosophy and the way this works technically will now be examined briefly.

The central thought of 'management by objectives' is that the manager and the employee come to a clear formulation of the function and the most important results to be attained by them mutually and individually in the coming period based on mutual consultation to determine and develop goals. These are called the key results and they are preferably determined in such a way that they are measurable. In addition one determines dates in between on which progress is tested. This method is based on the basic thought expressed in 'Theory Y' of McGregor (*see* section 9.3.3).

The manager and the employee involved in the consultation will depend on their level in the organization, but it is clear that different hierarchical levels have to be well matched. In an ideal situation, a hierarchy of objectives should arise with long-term goals on the top and derived from that, more specific goals and targets on each level and for each employee, each lower goal making a contribution to the next higher goal. So 'management by objectives' is directed at stimulating, and respectively improving, the unity of direction in the organization.

Since employees are enabled to bring their own ideas and wishes into the consultation, it may be expected that the goals of the individual and those of the organization are better matched. This is a favourable condition for improving the motivation and collective effort of organization members.

Exhibit 10.2

MBO and national cultures in terms of Hofstede's culture dimensions

MBO presupposes

- that subordinates are sufficiently independent to negotiate meaningfully with the boss (not-too-large Power Distance)
- that both are willing to take risks (weak Uncertainty Avoidance)
- that performance is seen as important by both (high Masculinity).

In a book of case studies about MBO in Germany, Ian R.G. Ferguson states that 'MBO has acquired a different flavour in the German-speaking area, not least because in these countries the societal and political pressure toward increasing the value of man in the organization on the right to co-determination has become quite clear. Thence, MBO has been transliterated into Management by joint Goal Setting (Führung durch Zielvereinbarung).' Ferguson's view of MBO fits the ideological needs of the German-speaking countries of the moment. The case studies in his book show elaborate formal systems with extensive ideological justification; the stress on team objectives is quite strong, which is in line with the lower individualism in these countries.

The other area in which specific information on MBO is available is France. MBO was first introduced in France in the early 1960s, but it became extremely popular for a time after the 1968 student revolt. People expected that this new technique would lead to the long-overdue democratization of organizations. Instead of DPO (Direction par Objectifs), the French name for MBO became DPPO (Direction Participative par Objectifs). So in France, too, societal developments affected the MBO system. However, DPPO remained, in general, as much a vain slogan as did Liberté, Egalité, Fraternité (Freedom, Equality, Brotherhood) after the 1789 revolt. G. Franck wrote in 1973, 'I think that the career of DPPO is terminated, or rather that it has never started, and it won't ever start as long as we continue in France our tendency to confound ideology and reality.' In a postscript to Franck's article, the editors of *Le Management* write: 'French blue- and white-collar workers, lower-level and higher-level managers, and "patrons" all belong to the same cultural system which maintains dependency relations from level to level. Only the deviants really dislike this system. The hierarchical structure protects against anxiety; DPO, however, generates anxiety.'

The reason for the anxiety in the French cultural context is that MBO presupposes a depersonalized authority in the form of internalized objectives; but French people, from their early childhood onward, are accustomed to large Power Distances, to an authority that is highly personalized. And in spite of all attempts to introduce Anglo-Saxon management methods, French superiors do not easily decentralize and do not stop short-circuiting intermediate hierarchical levels, nor do French subordinates expect them to.

Source: From *Transnational Management* by Bartlett and Ghoshal, (1992).

'Management by objectives' in steps

In Fig 10.5 we have summarized the steps involved. From this it appears that the individual as well as the management plays a role. The management has to see to optimal circumstances on the basis of which the individual can realize his or her personal goals.

Determining of key result and performance norms

First it is determined which core results are decisive for the effectiveness of the employee and it is then stated what performance level has to be attained. This analysis results in a description of the performance to be expected.

In the case of performance norms, one distinguishes between quantitative and qualitative norms. It is highly desirable to set as many quantitative norms as possible. By doing this, the possibility of comparing the norm and attained results improves considerably. This makes it possible to discuss deviations in objective terms, and

Minicase 10.1

In an American investigation researching the degree of agreement between managers and subordinates about results to be attained by them, it appeared that agreement existed in only 10% of researched cases. In 40%, there was tantamount to total disagreement.

misunderstanding about interpretation of attained results is almost excluded. But of course it is not always possible to set purely quantitative norms. Yet there are often quantitative measurable indicators used to review certain results. The turnover and absenteeism percentage of a department are, for example, objectively measurable and they give at least an impression of the morale, working climate or work satisfaction within that department.

Drawing up action plans

The following step consists of two complementary steps, namely the drawing up of a personal action plan of the employee to attain set results and an action plan of management – directed at eliminating environmental factors which hinder the employee in attaining his or her goals.

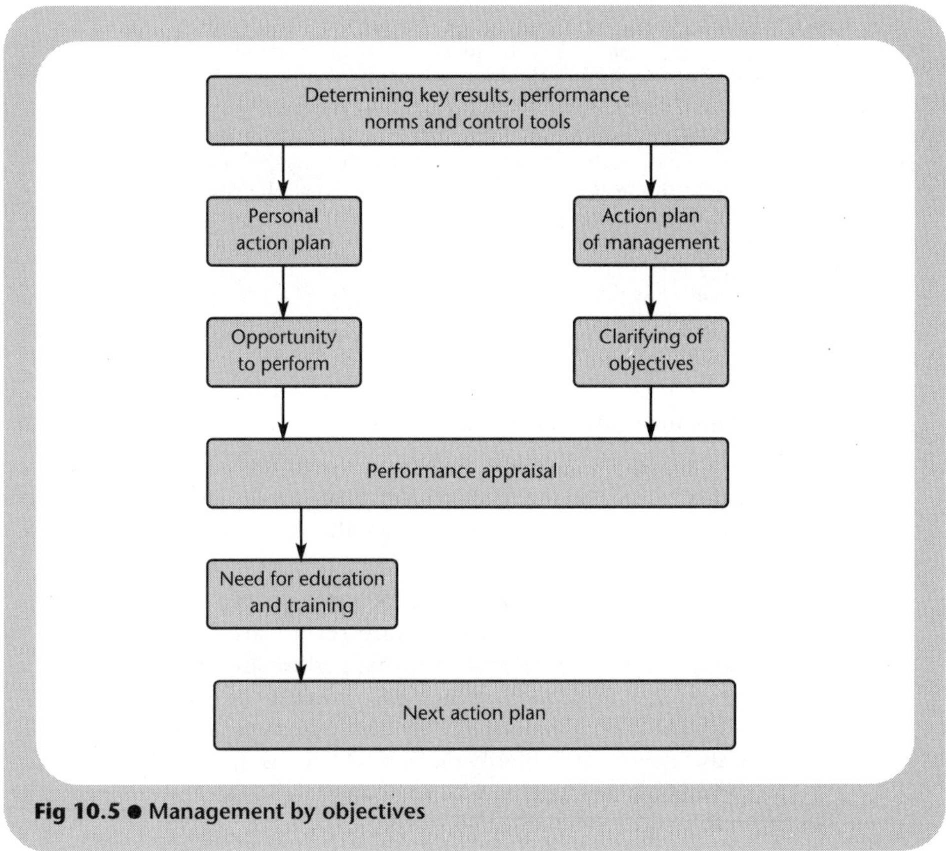

Fig 10.5 ● Management by objectives

In the personal action plan, measure can be included to eliminate bottlenecks, for example, in organizing, division of work or co-ordination. If the employee does not have sufficient authority to be able to attain the norm, management will have to acknowledge the authority increase or adjust the norm. Management needs to ensure that the employee can work under optimal circumstances.

Execution of the personal action plan
After the personal action plan has been made, the employee has to realize it. In this situation it is the task of management to clarify goals continuously, the short- and middle-term as well as the long-term goals.

Performance appraisal
After a pre-determined period, results attained are compared to the norms. Here too the question arises as to the causes of possible deviations and wishes the employee has in the area of further education and training. New performance norms for the following period will have to be determined. After that the steps progress as has been previously described. Action plans are adjusted. There is a repeating cycle which undertaken step-wise.

Advantages of 'management by objectives'

For both manager and involved employee, management by objectives has a number of obvious advantages. For the manager, MbO of course has the advantage that it motivates subordinates to work on core results. The formulating of that creates favourable conditions for delegation, management by exception and performance appraisal. Furthermore, MbO supplies a framework for supervision, coaching and also for the building up of a good personal relationship between managers and subordinates.

The co-worker participates in the determination of core results, and because of that not only knows what is expected of him, but also will accept the norms sooner. The results attained can continuously be compared to the agreed norms. In conclusion, the current conditions can influence those within which one has to perform in future by bringing up hindering factors for discussion.

One expects of a smooth running system of management by objectives that morale will improve and productivity in the organization will increase.

10.4 PRODUCTION PLANNING: METHODS AND TECHNIQUES

In planning and control different methods and techniques, such as planning charts, Gantt charts and optimization techniques can be used. Application of priority rules can contribute to shortened waiting times and because of that to improvement in delivery times.

10.4.1 Planning charts

In order to attain a high degree of efficiency and to offer a good service to clients, it is necessary that information is at one's disposal in an easy and well-organized way. Based on that decisions can be made about the utilization of people and machines, about the sequence of processes, orders, rush orders etc. In this area planning charts can serve well.

A good planning system makes promises and agreements visible and in a well-organized way shows the sequence of activities, the decisions on people and resources and capacity still available, for example, by means of order planning, machine planning and the planning of people or groups or shifts. This may prevent late delivery of orders or machine standstill due to late delivery of materials. The situation of the flow of orders becomes visible at a glance.

By means of coloured slips, for example, per order number and per working week, the production time and the kind of process is indicated, and the planned production time can, per day (via the date line), be set off against the actual progress per order. Deviations are indicated with a progress signal: for example, 'delay' with a red triangle, 'on schedule' no indication and 'ahead of schedule' with a blue triangle. This can be indicated on an 'old fashioned' wall-hanging planning chart with plug-in signals, or on a screen via an automated system. There are various 'electronic planning charts': Optimal Plan, Timeline, Plantrac are some of these.

An early version of the planning chart is the so-called Gantt chart. The layout of that is shown in Fig 10.6. On a Gantt chart, information is registered permanently, replanning can be done more simply on a planning chart than with the help of a Gantt chart. This last method, however, is cheaper. Of course computers are becoming cheaper, and more attractive, and replanning and optimization problems can be achieved more quickly than ever before.

In small organizations, the methods are often used by the production manager himself. In the case of further growth however, the management may shift to the introduction of a planning room which then conducts work preparation, dispatching, routing, etc., and planning and production control.

Minicase 10.2

When machine planning, the degree of utilization of different machines is immediately visible. This is indicated per type of machine or part of the day. With coloured strips the occupation of each machine in machine time is indicated. With a progress signal, deviations in date line can be indicated.

A hospital can, with the help of a planning chart, map out occupation of beds or a villa-renting company the rental planning.

10.4.2 Inventory control

Manufacturing companies usually hold inventories in the form of raw materials, half products and final products, thereby serving different goals. First of all, fluctuations in the demand can be met. It is possible to profit from scale advantages in production and purchase. Some estimates indicate that 25 per cent of the balance total exists in inventory. Thus, costs linked to the holding of inventory can be considerable: think of the necessary space, lost interest, the risk of ageing, decay or theft, the necessity for administration, etc. Most often, the total inventory costs lie around the 15 per cent mark. It is self-evident that organizations will try to keep their storage costs as low as possible.

10.4.3 Optimal ordering

One of the methods to reduce inventory costs is through the use of optimal ordering size. The result of this method implies that the amount of goods ordered is such that the ordering costs and the costs of keeping the inventory are as low as possible.

The more one orders, the more the costs per unit product decreases. In other words placing an order costs a fixed amount of money which is independent of materials ordered. Conversely it will be obvious that the more one orders, the more the costs linked to holding the inventory will increase.

When the demand curve, the period between ordering and delivering, the ordering costs and the inventory costs are known, one can with the help of a formula (the so-called Camp formula) calculate the optimal ordering size. Since the demand curve and the ordering term can never be predicted with absolute certainty, there is also the need to hold a 'safety' inventory.

10.4.4 MRP (Materials Requirement Planning)

MRP is a method which is directed not only at the reduction of the inventory, but also at the making of production plans. The MRP approach starts with predicting demand for the product. Based on this prediction, a so-called 'master production schedule' is drawn up in which the amount of the goods to be produced is stated. With the help of a specification of the necessary components for every product (the 'bill of materials'), it is determined how many components of which type are needed for production in a certain period. After comparing this with the 'inventory status record', which states the present inventory per component, the reserved amounts for production of other orders, ordering time and ordered amounts, it is calculated how much of the different components have to be reordered.

Based on this predicted need, the materials are, as it were, pushed into the production departments. This is, in fact, known as the 'push' system.

10.4.5 Just in time

'Just in time' (JIT), the system which was first applied in Japan by Toyota at the beginning of the 1970s, is well known by now. This approach starts from orders which have come in. Based on those orders, a production scheme is drawn up in which orders for every department in the links in the production process, and those of internal clients, are included. Based on the principle of the 'pull' system, orders are given at the output side by the internal customer (client or next department). In the case of short production times one can then work with extremely low inventories. Such a system is also called a *kanban* system.

A JIT system poses heavy demands on the organization and its suppliers. Supplied components have to meet the set quality demands without exception. Every mistake can lead to stagnation of production. Suppliers need to be located in the direct environment of the organization: 'Toyota City' exists, a complex comprising the factory and its suppliers. Besides that one needs to build up a trustworthy file of suppliers: disruptions there lead to disruptions in the home factory. In this system it is vital that the personnel are very disciplined. Every co-ordination mistake can disrupt production. The system has hardly any slack or zone of tolerance to withstand mistakes with.

In Europe and in the USA, companies are increasingly introducing the JIT system. The experiences are promising: inventories decrease strongly – Volvo in Sint-Truiden, Belgium, succeeded in bringing inventories back to 40 per cent of the previous level in a short time. However, the set demands can not always be met in the short term. Suppliers are rarely prepared and able to relocate their company to the immediate environs of their clients. The lay-out of factories causes problems, too. Suppliers experience difficulties delivering their products directly to the required location.

10.4.6 Reducing waiting times

One of the causes of low machine return or low labour productivity is that at a particular moment no order is available to process (machine or worker stands still). In order to overcome this difficulty, the standstill of the capacity sources, one can try to plan in such a way that the capacity never stands still. This disallowing standstill due to lack of orders can in practice only be realized when sufficient orders are always ready to be processed, in which one needs to render account to all sorts of situations, such as sudden cancellation of a complete order during manufacture. In order to prevent machine standstill, another order has to be waiting for processing at all times.

Reduction of waiting times can be realized by means of the following measure.

- Increase of capacity. Through this, the degree of utilization or occupation of the capacity will decrease, but waiting time shortens. When one shortens the waiting time in the manufacturing process, i.e. less work in progress, this will generally influence the flow time in a favourable way. When one thinks of increasing the capacity, one will have to weigh the costs of that against savings in work in progress.
- Concentrating the same sort of processes. In waiting time language: letting several 'counters' or 'stations' do the same work. In a post office, for example, this leads to shorter than average waiting times.
- Favouring a more gradual issuing of work orders in the manufacturing process. This alone will shorten waiting time.
- Application of priority rules. Giving out orders according to determined priorities and capacities which are to be used. Priority rules can for example be:
  - small jobs first;
  - first in, first out (FIFO): round off the 'oldest' orders first.

10.5 CONTROL OF TIME: PROJECT AND NETWORK PLANNING

The planning forms described above can be grouped under the term 'period planning'. In fact, they are included in the planning for a certain period in one department and not primarily on the coherence between different functional departments. A form of planning which does pay attention to this is project or network planning. Project and network planning is applied especially in the case of large, one-off activities. In the case of large construction projects and mapping out of mergers, this form of planning can render good results.

The objective of network planning is the determination of total necessary flow time for completion of a project and possible shortening of this flow time. A network gives an overview with regard to the totality of a project and gives insight into the complex interrelationships between the various activities of a project.

Network planning involves a number of steps. First of all it is necessary to determine what actions or activities have to be conducted. Next the coherence between them and the coercive order of the activities has to be determined. These can then be drawn in a relation diagram or network (Fig 10.6).

In Fig 10.8, only the logical coherence between the successive activities is given, without the time element playing a role. In order to build this in, an estimation of the necessary time per activity needs to be made. After filling in the necessary time per activity, the schedule looks like Fig 10.7.

From Fig 10.7 the flow and completion time can now be calculated and the earliest possible moment at which the project can be completed can be determined. It appears that, in the case sketched in Fig 10.8, this is after fifteen time units, i.e. 8+5+2=15, via activities b, d, g. Every other order in the scheme thus leads to a shorter time. The path via b, d, g is called the critical path and determines the earliest moment at which the project can be completed.

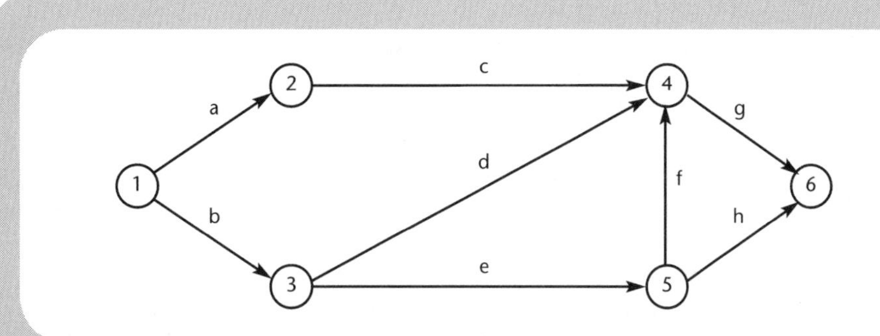

Fig 10.6 ● Relationship diagram or network

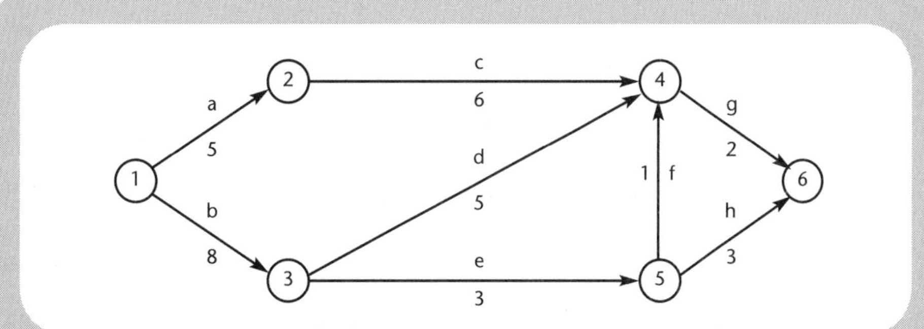

Fig 10.7 ● Relationship diagram or network with time estimates

Network, critical path and slack

In order to draw up the network of a project, use is usually made of two symbols, namely of:

1. an arrow: the arrow represents an activity; the length of the arrow and the angle at which this is drawn do not have any meaning; of importance is only the mutual coherence of the arrows;
2. a circle: the circle is placed at the beginning and end of every arrow and functions as a junction or milestone; a junction is only reached when the activities of all the arrows that end up in that junction are completed; an activity can only start when the milestone where the arrow starts from is reached; in other words, the next activity can only start when all preceding activities have been completed.

When the network has been drawn, one needs to determine the duration per activity in order to determine the total duration of the project. The path along which the total project duration is determined is the 'critical path', and this indicates those activities that are determining for the total project duration: acceleration or delay of one of those activities immediately and directly influences the completion time of the project.

Activities not situated on the critical path have a certain latitude or slack. In order to determine this slack, it is established:

- when at the earliest one can start with the activity (earliest moment);
- when at the latest one can start with the activity without endangering total project duration (latest moment).

To indicate the slack the circles which indicate the milestones are used. These are divided into three parts, as shown in Fig 10.8. At the left top the earliest moment is indicated, at the right top the latest moment. In the bottom half the number of the junction is indicated.

The slack per junction is determined by comparing the figure indicated at the left top to the figure at the right top: the difference is the slack time at that junction. For the calculation of the latest moment milestone needs to have been reached not to endanger the total project duration, one always starts from the end of the project and works back to the beginning. It is determined at each junction the longest time needed in order to attain the junction.

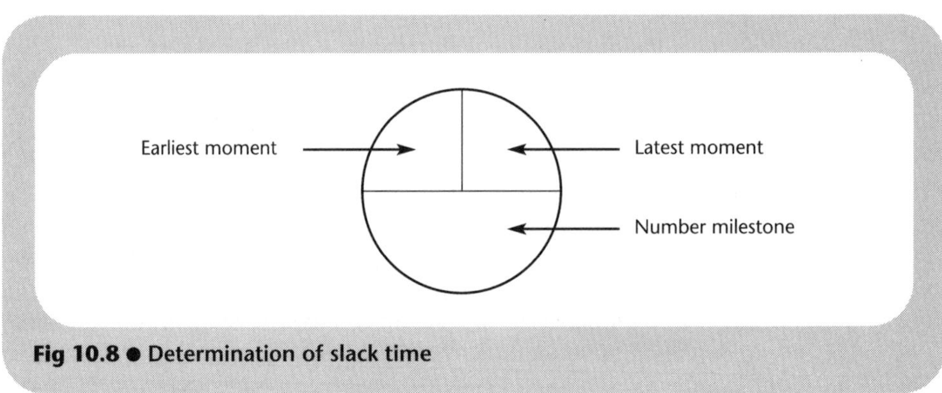

Fig 10.8 ● Determination of slack time

Network analysis: PERT and CPM

Network analysis is a technique for planning the execution of usually large and complex works. Control of time (and costs) is the result of application of this planning technique. As PERT (Program Evaluation and Review Technique) this technique was applied in the 1950s in the development of weapons systems. At the same time in the chemical industry, the so-called 'critical path' method was developed, also known as CPM (Critical Path Method). In PERT one works with milestones to be attained and one also renders account to uncertainties in the estimations of the duration. Via PERT–cost, a relationship is made between durations and costs, by means of which attention is directed at control of time as well as at control of costs. Cost–price/time relationships are also included in the planning by this stage.

The network can be used to take decisions with regard to the further course during the execution. Take, for example, the case that after execution of activities a, b and c it appears that for several reasons delays can be expected in the case of the activities d and e. The network can then be used to make a number of analyses and to come to a decision with regard to the way to be followed further. By means of reviewed time estimations and a possible earlier finish to activities a and b, the critical path may now take another course; the minimum completion time becomes, for example, 17 months; now a problem can arise if a contract has been drawn up in which both delivery date and a fine clause have been included should the date be exceeded. The question is then which actions can now be undertaken in order to be able still to meet contractual obligations and the costs of these extra efforts. These then need to be weighed against the imposed fine. The problem directs itself now at searching for possibilities to shorten the critical path to 2 months. When no other considerations play a part, one will opt for the combination of measures which involves the lowest costs in this shortening of the critical path.

10.6 QUALITY CONTROL AND TOTAL QUALITY MANAGEMENT

The introduction of quality programmes demands first of all the creation of an understanding for quality care, then the creation of conditions for a new work attitude, and only after that, can work behaviour really change and acquire a more permanent character via continuation of the 'new' work behaviour.

In striving for integral quality care, a better process control can be attained: mistakes are signalled more quickly and structures can thus be addressed. The people at the machines are closest to the production process and thus fulfil a central role the controlling that process. Quality care leads almost certainly to delegation of more tasks and to more responsibility for the operational employees. Their capabilities and skills are also better used than before. Management has to see to it that people on the work floor get the tools required to be able to execute the new, more responsible tasks in the way they should. Departments should here be able to make demands on internal relationships, that is, to supplying departments and employees. They, in their turn, need to satisfy their clients from other departments. The same holds with regard to external relationship: suppliers and clients. In this, the involvement of employees is decisive.

Once decided then, in regular work consultation or in new consultation structures, it has to be arranged how delegation of tasks and authority will be shaped further, and how the coherence between departments will be given a new shape actually to be able to bear the increased responsibility. A 'flatter' organization structure, flexibilization or multi-availability of employees, changes in rewards and payment systems, changing labour circumstances and contents then become matters for closer attention.

Quality care demands cultural change

Quality care in many organizations has only limited success since in practice insufficient attention is given to the organizational structure. According to 'quality gurus', people must get more involved in the organization. Working without mistakes (zero fault) must be seen as a new personal challenge. Motivation must increase and absenteeism has to be reduced. Employees have to be creative and flexible, always prepared to think about possible improvements: and often without any extra money. In one case, people may be asked to take part in quality circles and in other, innovation directed consultations in their leisure time.

Participative management, a leadership style which can work to increase quality, is hard to realize overnight. Few managers have the courage to dive into their own heart and utter self-criticism, for, in many company cultures, managers who ask the employees questions are considered to be incompetent, and people who are used to authoritarian leadership, mistrust a managing director who used not to be visible and who now spends half his day on the shop floor.

10.6.1 Quality management: 14 points of attention

Fourteen points of attention have been developed to stimulate attention towards quality care.

1. See to consistency in company goals with regard to improvement of production, the products, the whole system and the servicing, as well as to a plan to be competitive and as a company to survive successfully ('management by objectives').
2. Accept this philosophy. We live in a new economic era. We can no longer accept that deliveries are made late or that bad work is produced.
3. Abolish mass inspection. In place of this require statistical proof that quality is built in, so that no mass inspection is necessary. Place the responsibility for quality with the manufacturing departments themselves.
4. Do not buy based on price considerations alone. Require a statistical quality guarantee and eliminate suppliers who cannot give such guarantees. Reduce the number of suppliers, but build up an optimal relationship with the remaining ones.
5. Track problems in all parts of the organization and improve these.
6. Apply modern training techniques in the company.
7. Work on a modern method of supervision on production employees. The accent in the responsibility of bosses and chiefs needs to lie on quality, not on amounts of goods produced. React immediately when mistakes and other short-comings, statistically backed up, are reported.
8. Eliminate fear in people so everyone dares to express himself and can work optimally.
9. Banish barriers between departments. The people in research, development, sales, administration, service and manufacturing have to co-operate as a team.
10. Work with quantitative targets with regard to productivity, but, in doing that, supply the right methods and tools.

11. Abolish work norms which imply target figures.
12. In all areas stress the element of professional pride and craftsmanship.
13. Set up a powerful and effective programme of education and training.
14. Create a management structure which is directed at the powerful striving for and living up to the preceding thirteen points.

10.6.2 Problems in introducing integral or total quality management

A number of bottlenecks in the introduction of integral quality care appears to come forward from research. These are in the areas of:

- top management;
- middle management;
- the employees;

Exhibit 10.3

Components sector 'declining' – Volkswagen chief hits at standards

Volkswagen, Europe's largest vehicles group, wants to nearly triple its annual spending on motor components in the UK to £1.5bn ($2.34bn) within the next three years, more than double that of Toyota or Honda. But it claims it is being frustrated by the UK components industry's 'poor and in many cases declining quality and productivity.'

In a performance analysis of 170 UK suppliers, in the industry publication Automotive Sourcing, only 11 per cent were given A-ratings and classified as fit to become a supplier to the German group.

The verdict by Mr Frans Boot, the VW executive charged with procuring UK supplies, on the majority of UK manufacturers contrasts with praise from Mercedes-Benz and BMW, which recently announced substantial components contracts with British suppliers.

BMW has just awarded a £17m contract for Midlands-based Automotive Products to supply BMW with high-technology fly wheels, while Mercedes-Benz has given a £15m contract to supply gearbox shafts for its forthcoming 'A-Class' small car to Unipart Industries of Crawley.

Mr Boot, while acknowledging Unipart and some other leading UK suppliers as exceptions, said poor quality and productivity in the rest of the sector meant Volkswagen would fall far short of its target of lifting its UK components 'spend' by £400m this year to £950m.

'Instead, it will rise by only £100m to £650m. Yet Volkswagen really wants to spend this money. It is right in principle that Volkswagen should balance the 6 per cent of its sales it makes in the UK, with raising its UK parts purchases to 6 per cent of its total spend worldwide. Currently the figure is only 2.5 per cent.'

Mr Boot criticised under-investment by industry and short-termism by financial institutions as factors. He also condemned as largely misguided an initiative by the Society of Motor Manufacturers and Traders (SMMT), backed by the Department of Trade and Industry, under which Japanese engineers are to be brought to the UK to help raise standards.

Most of the UK sector's business lay within Europe. 'UK suppliers must look to the Continent and do what Continental operations like Volkswagen require. There should be much more emphasis on creating engineers and in long-term planning. In Germany at the heads of companies we are all engineers.'

Mr Ernie Thompson, chief executive of the SMMT, said the UK industry was 'pretty patchy; we've got some very good components companies who are already winning a great deal of business with Japanese and German manufacturers. But there are also an awful lot whose performance has got to be improved.'

Source: Financial Times, 27 September, 1996.

- the organizational structure;
- the information systems;
- the goals and plans.

Top management

Top management succeeds insufficiently in translating the 'quality' thought into specific action plans. For the employees it remains a concept with many empty slogans. There is also often a lack of unity within the management team with regard to the quality problem. Not everyone can or wants to identify himself with this and actually give quality care the highest priority. Besides that there is uncertainty with regard to its personal consequences of its introduction. For authoritarian management, the new style is threatening and insufficient time is set aside for quality care.

Middle management

When an organization deals with a 'no change' middle management insufficiently convinced of the importance of quality care, the introduction of the process can easily stagnate and even stall. Confronting middle management with top-down imposed goals, in which there is no room for one's own translations and interpretations, will certainly not enlarge the chance of success of the process.

Employees

There is a lack of operational quality definitions. So quality is insufficiently recognized and made visible. Because of this, the employees can give insufficient feedback about delivered performances. Within many companies there is a traditional relationship between boss and subordinate, and the employees are to a lesser degree involved in their work and are not motivated actually to make quality care a success.

The organizational structure

Maintaining the existing, often functional hierarchical organizational structures clashes with the thought of integral quality care. Existing organizational structures characterize themselves by a far-reaching splitting up of regulating and operational tasks.

The information systems

Information systems often only supply financial information such as sales data, expenses, profit figures etc. and not the information required to arrive at quality improvement.

The goals and plans

Quality goals and plans are often discussed to an insufficient degree with lower levels in the organization.

Quality management can be of strategic importance. In this approach to management and organizational problems, three goals are aimed at simultaneously: higher quality, higher productivity and optimal involvement of employees.

10.6.3 Deming: measurement and control

In the approach of American statistician William Edward Deming (1982 and 1986) regarding quality control, statistics are a very important tool.

A dogmatic approach based on such a simple model can cause a lot of damage if applied in the wrong place, especially as the system is recommended as generally applicable. Statistics is not something to be applied just like that. It is a tool used in order to analyse a process. Apart from this the statistical working out of problems can become difficult when certain factors start influencing each other. So by the wrong application of statistics, wrong conclusions can be arrived at. Even more important is the fundamental application of the technique. Where does one place measuring points so that one receives meaningful information?

Minicase 10.3

The seven ingredients of Deming's 'statistical recipe'

1. Diagram of cause and effect, also called fish bone or Ishihakwa diagram. Along a horizontal axis, on sloping axes, all factors are set forth which are of importance for a certain manufacturing process, and, where relevant, the mutual relationship.

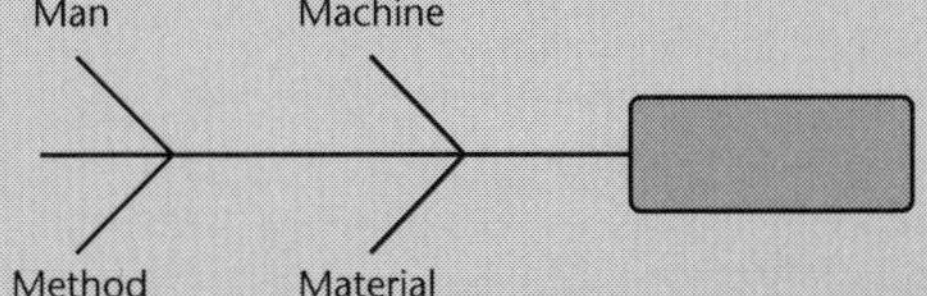

2. Line diagram, the most simple and the most used graphical representation of a development in time; the X-axis is the time axis and the Y-axis is quantity to be measured.

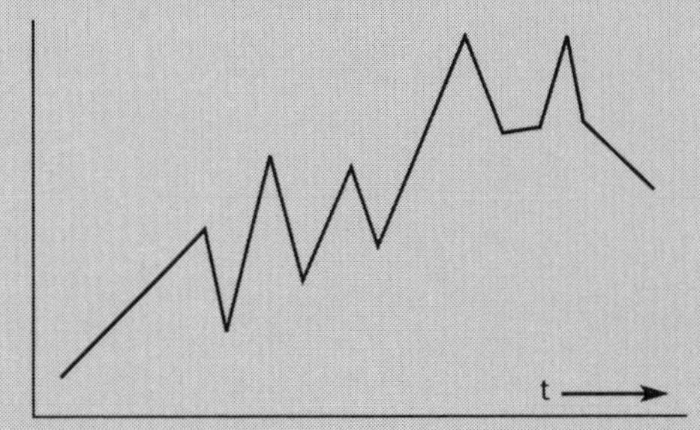

3. Control chart. In principle, this also is a line diagram but it also contains an indication of the top, and bottom limit and the median. This is more for the short term, while the production employee can directly see whether production meets demands.

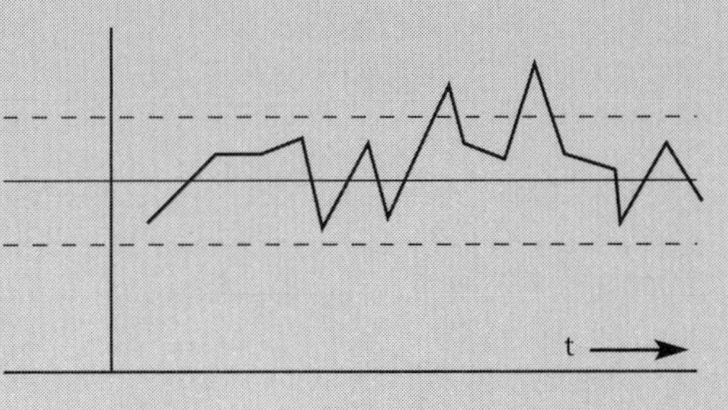

continued overleaf

Minicase continued

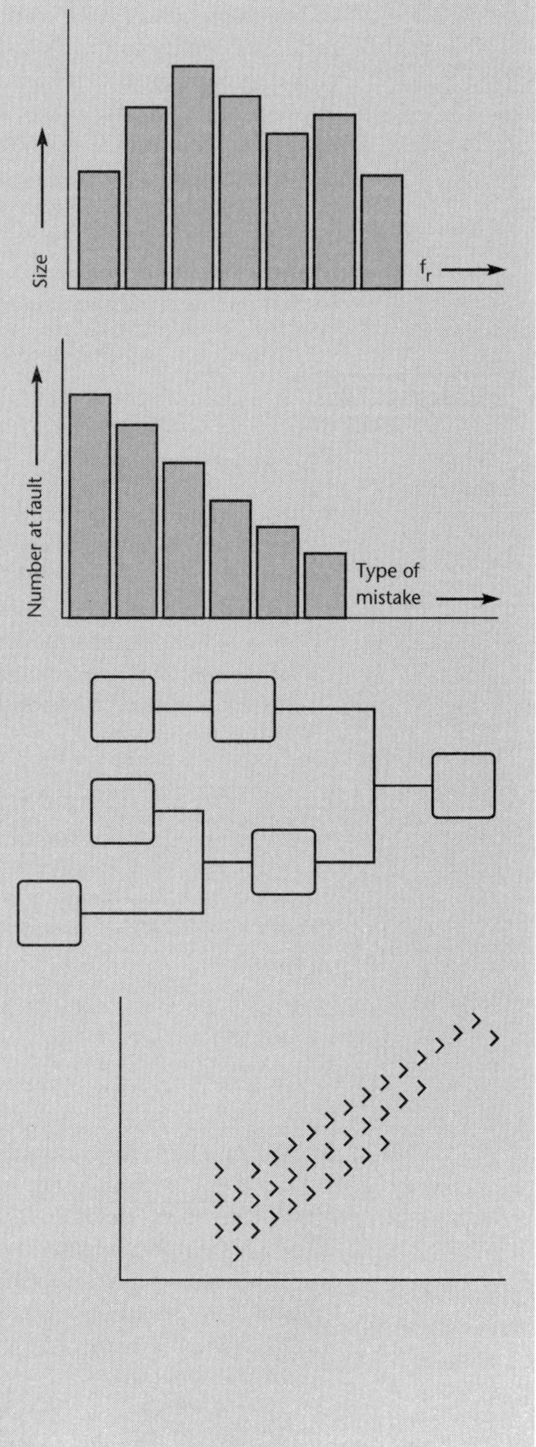

4. Histogram, a simple form of a bar chart, in which along the vertical axis the frequency of a certain phenomenon is set forth and along the horizontal axis the size of those same phenomena.

5. Paretogram. In fact this is a block diagram, in which the cubes are placed in sequence of size. Along the horizontal axis one can display a series of causes and mistakes for the accompanying cube.

6. Flow diagram, a kind of graphical map, in which the course and the size of each separate production flow in the total company process is made visible.

7. Spread diagram, also called scatter diagram. Here along the vertical axis the exact size of products made on the line, including the deviations of specification, are for example indicated. For every unit produced a point is placed at the point which corresponds to the produced size and the operational speed at that moment, and after placing fifty or a hundred points, the relationship between the speed and the correct dimensioning can be read off from the form and density of the scattered points in the diagram.

10.7 BENCHMARKING: LEARNING THROUGH COMPARISON

In answer to the problems in the ever more intense competitive battle in national and international markets, prominent American companies have taken a series of initiatives to improve their strategic and operational performances and results. One of those strategic management techniques is 'benchmarking', systematic comparison of company performance. In America notably Xerox, Ford, Eastman Kodak, General Motors, Motorola, AT&T and Du Pont are active in this area. It is said of Xerox that this is the first American company systematically to introduce benchmarking for the company as a whole. Japanese companies are already well known for the use they are able to make of competitors' products. In this way, they find weak spots in American companies and conquer strong positions in different sectors or businesses such as steel, cars, microchips and consumer electronics.

Benchmarking is the continuing process of measuring products, services and methods and procedures in which results are confronted with those of the toughest competitors, or of companies acknowledged as sector leaders.

This process of measuring and comparing has to be continuous and systematic in order to be able to identify 'best practices' and methods in the sector or line of business and to be able to discover how these performance levels can be realized. Information obtained in such a way is used to determine goals and strategies. Benchmarking can be applied to almost all functional areas of the organization, such as manufacturing and marketing, but also for support functions, for example 'human resources management', accounting and management information systems.

Successful companies use company comparisons to strengthen their own creativity. They learn what their competitors do, but also develop a vision of what clients want, a critical factor in the formulation of a competitive strategy. It will be obvious that both points of view are necessary. Information about client needs connected to the best practices in the line of business improves the ability of the company to adapt to market circumstances.

10.7.1 Types of benchmarking

There are three main sorts of benchmarking:

1. strategic;
2. operational;
3. management.

Strategic benchmarking comprises the comparison of different company strategies in order to identify the elements of a successful strategy.

Operational benchmarking concentrates on the relative costs, product characteristics and product positioning, in order to find ways which improve the cost position and/or enlarge the differentiation of the products. Company components to be compared depend on the function to be analysed. For example, if technical development and process functions are to be regarded, then the analysis can direct itself at the efficiency of the design process. Cost effectiveness can be the central issue for manufacturing, distribution and sales activities.

Benchmarking of the management exists of an analysis of supporting services. For almost every supporting service external comparisons can be made such as P&O and HRM functions, marketing planning, management information systems, logistics and order processing.

10.7.2 Benchmarking as a process

The benchmarking procedure comprises five steps:

1. identifying functions to be compared;
2. selecting companies with superior performances and/or results;
3. collecting and analysing data;
4. determining performance or result goals;
5. implementing plans and monitoring results.

Identifying functions to be compared

Elements for which benchmarking can be executed include: cost price per unit, turnover in sales, number of times the service is requested, satisfaction of clients. Every function within the organization provides or produces a certain product, which can be a physical good, an order or a service. Benchmarking can direct itself, for example, at the outcomes of activities, and also further at procedures, processes and methods, in other words: at the factors which determine the cost levels to be attained, service levels etc.

In general, benchmarking will be executed for activities which are of essential importance for the build up of a competitive advantage. So a company such as Xerox, which is interested in production costs, will wish to make comparisons for activities which have an important or growing share in the costs. Methods such as the 'value chain analysis' (Porter, 1985) (*see* section 12.3) can be used for the determination of key activities.

Selecting companies with superior performances and/or results

The competitor or the leading company in the sector or line of business (business-to-business or direct competitors for product or service) is the first candidate eligible for comparison. But benchmarking can also be executed with prominent companies or organizations in general, not considering the specific areas in which they are active.

For example ...

When, for example, the Business Systems Logistic and Distribution function from Xerox was looking for ways to improve productivity further, it took as benchmarking standard L.L.Bean, the mail order company known for its effective and efficient storage and distribution activities. This Xerox component also used other non-competitors for systematic comparison of order collection procedures and automated inventory control.

Collecting and analysing data

Data about competitors can be collected in many ways. The analysis should be based on a complete insight into and knowledge of existing processes of one's own organization and of the organization used as benchmark. The collected data have to be aggragated about the processes, procedures and practices and may not exclusively regard results.

Comparison of one's own functions with the best executed function ('best practices') somewhere else brings a possible performance gap to light.

When the analysis indicates that the organization itself performs better than the comparison organization, then the assignment becomes the identification of ways in which to maintain that superior position.

For example ... Xerox, for example, used public sources, consultants, personal contact with leading companies, knowledge and insights of their own employees and questionnaires which were filled in by students of business schools. Xerox also sent a team to L.L. Bean's establishments.

Determining performance or result goals

The results of the analysis have to be communicated in a clear way to all levels in the organization. Employees have to have sufficient time to evaluate the outcomes of the benchmarking process. They will agree more readily with performance levels and procedures, practices and processes to be introduced to realize the goals to be improved if this is done. Performance goals and the selected best practices have to be processed in the functional, operational and company plans.

Minicase 10.4

After application of 'competitive benchmarking', Xerox was able to reduce the production costs by 50 per cent, to reduce the cycles of product development by 25 per cent and to enlarge the wage per employee by 20 per cent. The percentage of mistake-free copying machines from Xerox increased from 91 to 99.95.

Xerox succeeded in obtaining impressive results and in 1989 the company received the prestigious Malcolm Baldridge National Quality Award, the counterpart of the most sought after decoration in Japan, the Deming Prize. The company is convinced absolutely that company comparison with competitors and involvement of employees are the keys to success with regard to quality and competitive ability.

Xerox now requires that benchmark analyses are included in strategic and operational plans.

Organizations benchmarked by Xerox in terms of products, processes and practices

Areas compared	Benchmark organizations
Manufacturing activities	Fuji-Xerox
Quality management	Toyota Komatsu
Factoring and collection	American Express
Research and production development	American Telephone and Telegraph (AT&T) Hewlett-Packard
Automated inventory control	American Hospital Supply
Distribution	L.L. Bean, Inc. Hershey Foods Mary Kay Cosmetics
Systems of employees' ideas and propositions	Milliken Carpet
Lay-out and routing on work floor	Ford Motor Company Cummins Engineering
Marketing, participative management, involvement of employees	Procter & Gamble
Quality improvement	Florida Power and Light
Implementation of strategy	Texas Instruments
Automation	Deere and Company

Implementating plans and monitoring results

Application of the benchmark method implies that one measures and evaluates periodically the degree to which the indicated goals have been attained. Corrective measures have to be taken when performances remain behind the goals. In order to render account to changes in the competitive environment, provisions also have to be built in to rematch measures and ways of measuring and to actualize perceptions with regard to the clients. Such an approach makes it possible to attain a balance in attention for competitors and clients and reduces the danger of selective attention and simplification. Progress has to be reported, so that feedback is stimulated which is necessary for the implementation of a plan. This feedback can also be useful in the gathering of new performance goals.

10.7.3 Benchmarking: advantages and constraints

The process of benchmarking is a method for bringing changes into motion. This method provides standards with regard to requirements and expectations of clients and impels employees to thinking in terms of competitive force. It often makes the employees more conscious of costs and results of the products and services of the organization. The process also stimulates looking outside the borders of one's own organization for solutions of problems and comparing and putting into perspective of the company results.

When company comparisons are used only to equal and imitate the performances of the competitor, a superior position can never be attained. This leads at most to short-term success, and innovative employees are then restrained in their actions.

Benchmarking certainly goes further than the 'usual' analysis of 'strengths and weaknesses' in the strategy formulation process (*see* section 4.2.3). In strategic partnership and co-makership, the Strengths, Weaknesses, Opportunities and Threats (SWOT) analysis is insufficient. In the case of strategic partnership, in one's own organization the best practices have to be used and always aimed for. When this is not done, the basis of the co-operative relationship is shaken; new partners will be sought who do know how to attain the highest standards.

So benchmarking is a method used to compare an activity, function or process of an organization with 'best practices' of other organizations, so that one's own activity can always be improved based on that comparison. Benchmarking assumes in its principle sense the learning attitude of organizations and of the people there employed.

10.8 RATIOS: A VEHICLE OF CONTROL

A management tool used in the control process, is formed by ratios. Ratios serve to obtain insight into complex situations and not to control and direct processes as such.

Management must be able to have at its disposal as many trustworthy figures as possible, rather than unfounded stories. The method of ratios forces as exact a formulation and systemization as possible and because of that contributes significantly to problem signalling.

The size and complexity of the information the manager has to base management of the organization on, makes it inevitable that work with quantifications in the form of ratios, statistics and so on is carried out.

Ratios are the figures between two (in our case business-economic) phenomena, from which one can sketch the situation in one or another respect of the company or institution. The goal of such ratios is to describe a certain aspect of the performance of an organization. In part an impression of the return or the risk is gained, but often too the measuring of activities themselves is involved, in order to determine whether the organization makes efficient use of available resources and whether it is effective in attaining set goals.

10.8.1 Types of ratio

In addition to their application to a single company or institution, ratios can also be determined for a total line of business or group of businesses. A number of ratios are in general rather commonly used, and every organization needs to develop its own, because specific circumstances hold for every organization. In Fig 10.9, an overview is shown of a number of frequently used ratios.

For its own situation, every organization will have to determine what the content is of the ratios. When this is decided, it must next be asked to what degree the ratios will apply to a general situation, and also to a partial situation. So one can, for example, apply the ratios with regard to costs, manufacture and personnel in general, but also to the cost categories to be distinguished or product groups or personnel categories. In Fig 10.10, a selection of important ratios has been included from a series of often used ratios. These are grouped according to different aspects of management which are important (taken from the subjects mentioned in Fig 10.9). Every individual organization must choose its own ratios.

This series of ratios is a choice from available ratios (or ratios to be developed), of which in standard overviews more than 120 can quickly be found.

Financial management
Debt to assets (leverage)
Liquidity
Return on net worth
Gross operating margin
Productivity of assets

Investment ratios
Earnings per share
Price/earnings
Dividend yield

Commercial
Market share
Turnover utilization
Product mix
Sales representatives
Customers
Stock turnover
Collecting
Debtors
Purchasing

Manufacturing
Inventory turnover
Production costs

Efficiency
Productivity
Cost per product group
Cost turnover
Added value
Cost control

Personnel
Composition of personnel
Productivity
Turnover
Wages and salaries

Fig 10.9 ● 'Standard' ratios categorized by subject

Liquidity	Current ratio (CR)	Current assets (CA) / Current liabilities (CL)
	Acid test	Liquid assets (LA) / Current liabilities (CL)
	Working capital (WC)	Current assets – current liabilities
Solvency/leverage	Debt to total assets	Total debt / Total assets
	Interest cover	Profit before taxes + interest + charges / Interest charges
Profitability	Return on Equity (RoE)	Profit after tax / Equity
	Return on Net Assets (RoNA)	Profits before interest and tax / Net assets
	Gross operating margin	Gross operating profit / Sales
	Net operating margin	Net operating profit / Sales
Activity (financial/non-financial)	Net assets turnover	Sales / Net assets
	Stock or inventory turnover	Sales / Inventory or stock
	Average collection period	Receivables / Sales per day
	Market share	Sales own company / Total sales in the industry
	Sales – development	Sales this period / Sales basis period
	– per customer	Sales / Number of customers
	Product mix – innovation	Sales new products / Sales
		Number of new products / Number of elimated products
	– results	Sales per product group / Total sales
		Sales / Number of sales representatives
	Product costs	Total production costs / Number of products
		Production costs product group / Total production costs
	Productivity of personnel	Gross profit / Number of employees (per category)
		Absenteeism days / Total productive days
		Number of employees resigned / Average number of employees

Fig 10.10 ● A selection of financial status, performance, activity and investment ratios

Investment	Earnings per share	$\frac{\text{Profit after tax}}{\text{Number of ordinary shares}}$
	Price/earnings ratio	$\frac{\text{Share price}}{\text{Earnings per share}}$
	Dividend – yield	$\frac{\text{Dividend per share for one year}}{\text{Share price (at start of year)}}$
	– cover	$\frac{\text{Earnings per share}}{\text{Dividend per share for one year}}$

Fig 10.10 ● continued

Exhibit 10.4

Are profits shakier than they look?

Slowing cash flows may be a sign of widespread trouble

Most cash flow sleuths looking for companies in trouble begin with operating cash flow. But cash flow specialists at Ernst Institutional Research in Boston have gone a step further.

Using a technique known as dual cash flow analysis, which compares the cash a company is getting from operations with cash coming from its balance sheet, they can often spot signs of deteriorating fundamentals well before traditional cash flow analysts can. 'If we see a fall in operating cash flow, paired with an abrupt shift in the way a company manages its balance sheet, that's a sign that management sees trouble ahead,' says Ernst President Jeffrey D. Fotta, whose tiny firm provides research to the likes of Fidelity Investments, Signet Banking, and other major institutions.

One recent success: By watching the buildup in capital expenditures and inventories throughout the semiconductor industry even as many companies were logging falling OCF, Ernst warned clients away from chipmaker stocks in mid-1995, well before recent earnings problems surfaced.

How does dual cash flow analysis work? The biggest difference between dual and standard cash flow analysis is in how the numbers are defined. Unlike conventional measures, Ernst counts changes in accounts payable and receivable as part of balance sheet cash flow rather than operating cash flow.

That's because those numbers can be massaged: Management has lots of leeway in stretching out payments or speeding collection of its receivables when its returns from sales start to slow down. 'Management only has so many levers to pull when they hit trouble,' says Fotta. 'It's the first place they turn for cash.'

Using those reworked numbers, Ernst then creates a number comparing operating cash flow with balance sheet cash, which it calls dual cash flow. When dual cash flow is positive, that means a company is meeting its cash needs from operations. When dual cash flow turns negative, the company is turning to debt or other balance sheet maneuvers for the cash it needs. That may be sustainable in the short term – or in periods of strong growth – but it can't last forever.

A Jeff Fotta tip sheet

By comparing cash flow from operations with cash from the balance sheet, Jeffrey Fotta's 'dual cash flow' model may spot problems months before they show up in earnings or in conventional operating cash flow analysis.

Favourable companies:

- BellSouth
- The Gap
- Intel
- Tidewater
- Nike
- Toys 'Я' Us
- Microsoft
- Hasbro

Unfavourable companies:

- General Motors
- Merck
- Nucor
- United Technologies
- Hewlett-Packard
- IBM
- AlliedSignal
- Alcoa

Favourable industries:

- beverages
- pharmaceuticals
- oil

Unfavourable industries:

- autos
- paper
- semiconductors
- steel

Data: Ernst Institutional Research.

Source: Business Week, 5 August 1996.

10.8.2 Ratios and periodic registration

In the set-up of Fig 10.11, room has been left for periodic registration of the outcomes of a ratio, by means of which the development of the ratios can be followed in time. Two columns have been reserved to fill in a certain norm value, by means of which an immediate comparison between the actual attained value and the norm value is possible. These two columns can also be used to include the value of ratios of comparable organizations, so, to the extent an external comparison of the ratios become possible, one can similarly attach the same value to the notions included in the ratios. When such an external comparison is possible, the use of ratios will be more productive and meaningful.

	Development of ratio in time					Normal level	
	Basis situation per:	Situation per:	Situation per:	Situation per:	Situation per:	Normal level	Standardized level
Current ratio (CR)							
Acid test							
Working capital (WC)							
Debt to total assets							
Interest cover							
Return on equity (RoE)							
Return on Net Assets (RoNA)							
Gross operating margin							
Net operating margin							
Net assets turnover							
Stock or inventory turnover							
Average collection period							
Market share							
Sales – development – per customer							
Product mix – innovation – results							
Product costs							
Productivity and personnel							
Earnings per share							
Price/earnings ratio							
Dividend – yield – cover							

Fig 10.11 ● Ratios: periodic registration and trends

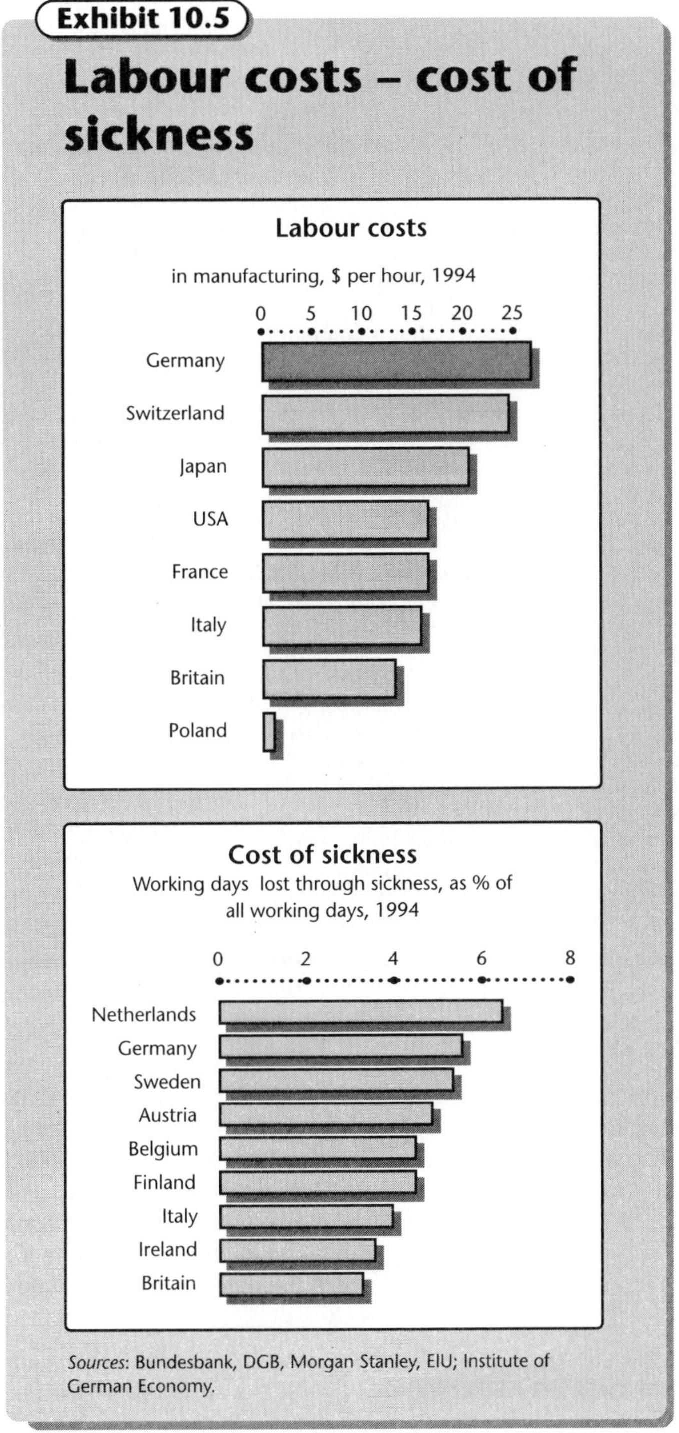
Exhibit 10.5
Labour costs – cost of sickness
Labour costs
in manufacturing, $ per hour, 1994
0 5 10 15 20 25
Germany
Switzerland
Japan
USA
France
Italy
Britain
Poland
Cost of sickness
Working days lost through sickness, as % of all working days, 1994
0 2 4 6 8
Netherlands
Germany
Sweden
Austria
Belgium
Finland
Italy
Ireland
Britain
Sources: Bundesbank, DGB, Morgan Stanley, EIU; Institute of German Economy.

Exhibit 10.6

Currency crisis

Sales at European subsidiaries have increased, but so has working capital

Earl Wade, chief financial officer of US-based Global Electronics, has been concerned for some months at the quality of working capital being sucked into the group's European operations. Global has expanded rapidly in the past few years through acquisition. It has manufacturing operations in 11 countries supplying 18 sales and distribution networks with safety monitoring equipment for heavy lift cranes, oil exploration and other industries. From a mere 5%, European sales now account for more than 20% of group turnover, and are expected to rise to 30% in two years.

To rationalize the structure, management has focused on the fashionable 'centres of manufacturing excellence' in four countries, with a hub-and-spoke distribution system based on three countries. Performance is now nicely on target – except, that is, for the increase, rather than the expected cut, in working capital.

Wade takes a closer look. Unused to European conditions, he is careful not to jump to conclusions, but is none the less surprised to find that each factory and distribution outlet has retained its own banking arrangements, with, in all, 12 different banks. He further finds that Global is a net borrower in four countries, although cash balances are available elsewhere, albeit under local control.

The solution seems obvious, but what propels him into action are the strains in Europe's exchange rate mechanism. A recent sudden surge in the dollar cut the value of some European earnings – not what shareholders want to hear. There might not be much he can do about that, he muses, but when he realizes the group is heading for dollar losses on accounts receivable and the surplus cash denominated in European currencies, he draws up a plan to centralize all cash management and currency management – and books his trip to Europe.

He calls a meeting with the country heads of four principal operations to outline his reasoning. To his surprise, three of them vehemently oppose the idea. They say it would dilute their accountability (which is measured in dollars) and that they would have to carry the overhead. Two product lines in particular are in sensitive markets where local markets need maximum freedom. In any case, they say, the turmoil in foreign exchange markets is temporary.

Uncharacteristically, Wade does not know which way to turn. He believes strongly in direct accountability, but he has a duty to protect dollar earnings and shareholders' funds. A solution is needed urgently.

Source: International Management, April 1993.

10.8.3 Industry ratios

The interpretation of the ratios demands a certain amount of attention. One cannot speak of an absolute, for all organizations holding norm values. Per sector or line of business, special circumstances can hold which have to be understood before meaning can be attached to a ratio. In many countries, periodic research results appear containing the outcomes of ratio calculations which regard a large number of companies in different lines of business or industries. Through these, the possibility arises of comparing the outcomes of one's own organization to the averages in that sector or line of business.

10.9 PERFORMANCE MEASUREMENT: FINANCIAL AND NON-FINANCIAL INDICATORS

The measuring of the execution, or review and comparison of the outcomes of that with the set norms, is called checking. This notion should not be confused with the broader notion of 'control, for control comprises checking, adjustment and corrective actions. This section is about checking, reviewing, monitoring or inspecting.

The first question in the case of monitoring and checking is who carries it out. This may be the task of the manager of the department concerned. If he gives the order, is he at the same time also the right person to examine the outcome of it? This is by far not always so. Sometimes checking/inspecting is such a specialistic matter that it has to be executed by a separate department, e.g. in the case of chemical or pharmaceutical products. In order to be able to determine whether these meet the required specifications, extensive lab tests must first be conducted. Additionally it may happen that the manager, because of a lack of time, has to leave inspection to an assistant or a special supervisory department which has been added to his own department. In many manufacturing companies the planning office is charged with the efficiency check on work. Because adjustment is in principle a task of the department manager and an operational unit, supervision, inspecting and checking preferably need to take place as close to this manager and unit as possible.

10.9.1 'Traditional' performance measurement

How and what has to be monitored and supervised strongly depend on the kind of department one wants to supervise. Here distinction is made of the degree to which input and output for an organizational unit can be more easily related. Distinguishable here are:

- standard cost centres;
- revenue centres;
- discretionary/expense centres;
- profit centres;
- investment centres.

Relating input and output is easiest in the case of standard cost centres and most difficult in the case of investment centres. In the case of standard cost centres, for example, manufacturing departments, this is quite easy: the goal of monitoring is the control of costs. Outcome of the calculation 'number of units of product' is multiplied by 'standard costs per unit product' and can be compared with the actual expenses.

In the case of revenue centres, for example, sales departments, the relationship between revenues and costs is less simple. An important factor here is price setting. Starting from fixed prices, for these departments actual costs and revenues can be placed opposite budgeted costs and revenues. In the case of changes in pricing policy, the relationship is even more difficult to make.

It is more difficult again to determine the relationship for the expense centres, since it is difficult to determine output. Examples of expense centres are staff and research departments. Here it is important to indicate clearly the direction of the activities and to confront the actual expenses with budgets. Strict cost control is, however, not always the best way of supervising results, because here also it is more than pure quantitative considerations that play a part. In a research department, for example, a certain extra expense can enlarge the effectiveness and the striving to keep costs as low as possible might work out the wrong way.

When one creates profit centres, that is, departments for which a profit figure can be calculated, extra problems arise. In companies with different divisions, the following problems arise: inter-company transactions, intra-company transactions and transfer prices between divisions and the pricing and paying for services which are delivered to divisions by central staff or service departments.

Investment centres are cases where not only the profit per centre is measured, but also the size of investments per centre. It is self-evident that here the system of measuring will be even more complex than in case of the profit centres.

New developments and limitations of 'traditional' performance measures

The nature of entrepreneuring and competition has been changing recently (*see* Chapters 3 and 4). Quality, innovation, speed and service become just as essential as costs. These factors are, however, rarely expressed in existing internal and external reports and performance measurements, and yet the importance of them is often undervalued. It is also becoming increasingly apparent that the organizational measuring system has a strong influence on the behaviour of managers and employees. Also the notion is growing that traditional financial measurements such as 'return on investments' (ROI) and 'profit per share' can give misleading signals with regard to continuous progress and innovation, while that is currently what is being demanded in the competitive environment. 'Traditional' indicators may realize improvement in the short term, while these actions have a negative long-term effect. This is the case, for example, with quarterly reports: managers tend to postpone necessary actions because that influences the quarterly figures negatively. Besides that, long-term effects of the execution of those actions are not expressed in the report. It is also the case that traditional financial measurements are mostly meant to satisfy the obligations of external reporting. Even though this is very important, they are not developed to help management improve effectiveness and efficiency of the total organization. They analyse results from the past, not the factors which will determine future performance and effectiveness.

The limitations of the traditional indicators include the following characteristics.

- They are mainly financially oriented and because of that indirect.
- They are mostly reactive, not proactive, 'backward looking' instead of 'forward looking'.
- They insufficiently support the relationship between the strategy of the organization and the operational execution of activities. The consequence is a gap between what is being measured and the things in which an organization has to perform well in the face of the competition.
- When they do not specifically match the strategy, they can supply irrelevant or misleading information, or worse, encourage behaviour which undermines the 'result' of the strategic goals.
- They often come from financial external reporting, in which mostly principles of precaution are preferred. On top of that performances are influenced too strongly by principles of valuing assets and liabilities.
- 'Bottom line' measurements (like profitability) come too late for half-course corrections and recovering/repairing actions.
- They are often directed at profit maximization in itself.
- They are mostly directed at short-term results.
- Mostly they do not work in a motivating way, or stimulate to learn from; on the contrary they are often seen as a way to 'punish'.
- They often do not distinguish between value adding and non-value adding activities.
- Often use is made of too many measurements, because of which the survey ability decreases.

Changes	1960s	1990s
Entrepreneurial climate	Product driven 'sellers' market'	Market driven 'buyers' market'
Processes	Simple	Complex
'Product range'	Limited	Wide and varied
Production size	Mass production with high conversion costs	Series/piece production with low conversion costs
Costs	Low fixed costs, high labour costs	High fixed costs, low labour costs
Lifecycle	Long	Short
Competition	Regional	Worldwide, global
Clients	Quickly satisfied	Very demanding

Fig 10.12 ● Internal and external developments

The idea of the limitations of traditional performance measurement is reinforced even by the fact that performances are observed in different dimensions.

- Performances like these are measured on the shop floor, in numbers, costs, delivery and completion times etc.
- Performances like these are judged with the aid of the management information system (including consolidation and the stress on financial quantities).
- Performances like these are experienced (an instinctive, but important dimension in the weal and woe of a company: culture, climate for co-operation, creativity and learning ability).
- Performances like these are struggled for on the basis of the vision and strategy at the organizational level.

In many organizations, these dimensions are insufficiently related or controlled in relation to one another. For modern organizations it is necessary to communicate better, be faster and especially be more flexible. For markets become more turbulent and competition becomes more intense (*see* Fig 10.12). When the dimensions mentioned do match well, this helps organizations to function better in strongly changing market circumstances.

Managers need to realize that one single measurement cannot supply a clear image with regard to a performance goal or the critical areas of an organization.

It is of vital importance to measure the factors which are determining for the future effectiveness of the organization, as this is the underlying 'health' of the organization. In order to be able to measure that from more than one point of view, it is necessary for financial as well as non-financial indicators to be integrated, so that a more balanced picture arises of attained performances. In order to enable managers to direct their attention at the right areas it is important that the non-financial indicators obtain the same status as the financial indicators. If this is not the case, managers will tend to lose on quality, client satisfaction and innovation.

Minicase 10.5

Modern performance management can be compared to the meters and lights on the dashboard of a racing car. The complex task of driving at speed while not damaging the car demands that the driver has detailed information at his disposal about many different aspects of the car and the race: the speed, level of fuel, oil pressure, temperature of the engine, condition of the tyres, position in the race, and other indicators which summarize the present and future environment. Dependence on one instrument can prove fatal. The same can in principle be said about the complexity of managing a modern organization: management must be enabled to look at performance from different points of view at the same time.

10.9.2 Non-financial indicators

Non-financial measurements have to be based on the organizational strategy. Furthermore, one has to execute key measurements with regard to manufacturing, marketing, customer satisfaction and R&D results. A limited number of goals have to be set which the organization, the divisions and units will attain in the long term. This means that managers have to put less stress on short-term measurements such as 'return on investment' and 'net profit'. Short-term financial measurements will have to be replaced by or complemented with a number of non-financial measurements which provide better 'targets' and predictions for the long-term goals of an organization.

Measurements have to be developed to help the management and not exclusively to prepare financial messages. Simply put, non-financial measurements, directed at internal processes, customer satisfaction, improvement and innovative activities of the organization, need to form the basis of the financial performances in the future by means of operational indicators. This forward directed process is very important when market circumstances change.

Demands for 'renewed' performance measurement

Four main rules can be formulated for renewed performance measurements.

1. Understand and know the critical success factors of the organization.
2. Relate performance measurements to the objectives and goals of the organization.
3. Only measure factors which can be influenced/controlled.
4. Set goals ('targets') which are attainable.

Critical Success Factors (CSFs)

Critical Success Factors are factors of decisive importance for the success of the organization. Critical Success Factors concern company functions that deserve the permanent attention of management. Experience teaches that three to eight factors are determining for the success or failure of an organization.

Based on the internal and external strengths and weaknesses of the organization, as well as opportunities and threats which come from its relationship with the environment (competition), the organization determines its goals and so develops its strategy. Based on that strategy, the critical success factors are determined. CSFs are determined by management which also indicates its information need.

Minicase 10.6

GE values

The American company General Electric Plastics (sales: US$80 billion, 200,000 employees), produces, among other things, light bulbs, jet engines, medical systems and plastics. This company has developed non-financial ratios based on used quality norms. Top management has made the demand to divisions and business units that in all aspects of the enterprise they have to be number one in the world. To that end GE values have been developed. All employees are tested on them. We can speak of a 360° assessment, that is: everyone's functioning is scrutinized and assessed by superiors, colleagues and subordinates and compared to the starting-points expressed in the GE values.

1. **Vision.** Every employer has to be able to put into words a clear, simple and realistic goal aimed at a customer-directed vision.
2. **Accountability.** Every employee is responsible for the definition of his own aggressive goals. Independently he takes decisions in order to realize those goals, with preservation of integrity.
3. **Excellence.** Every employee needs to have a passion in order to strive for perfection and has to hate bureaucracy.
4. **Empowerment.** Every employee has to have sufficient self-confidence to stimulate other employees and to break the borders between departments.
5. **Teamwork.** The management has to be able to coach teams.
6. **Receptive for change.** Every employee has to stimulate change and get satisfaction out of that. Changes have to be seen as a chance and not as a threat.
7. **Energy and speed.** Having the energy to stimulate others to exploit the advantages of speed in the competitive battle.

The testing to the above mentioned non-financial ratios leads to an organization with the following three characteristics: speed, simplicity and self-confidence.

Source: *Elan*, May 1994 (adapted)

One can distinguish different groups of CSFs deriving from different environmental sources.

1. The structure of the concerned line of business.
2. The position of the organization in the line of business.
3. Socio-economic relationships.
4. Specific circumstances.

Furthermore, it can be said that CSFs are only determined on a strategic level. Since internal reports are directed not only at the strategic level, but also at other management levels, so-called critical factors (Cfs) are distinguishable. Cfs do not apply to the organization as a whole, but to specific business units, departments etc. Cfs can often be derived from the CSFs.

Anthony *et al*. (1992) state that the 'financial performance' is the final result of management decisions and actions. Effective 'management control' should thus not only be occupied with the final results, but also with the processes and the resources themselves. For this purpose, non-financial information is necessary. Here, the critical success factors come into the picture or rather the 'key variables', as they are referred to by Anthony et al. A 'key variable' displays the following characteristics.

- It is important in the explaining of success or failure of the company.
- It is mobile and can change quickly.
- Those changes are unpredictable.
- It is important that in the event of an essential change, quick action is possible.
- It can be measured directly or indirectly.

Besides 'key variables' one can also distinguish 'exception variables'. These are not, frequently reported, like the 'key variables', but only when their behaviour goes beyond certain limits (they can be compared to alarm lights on the instrument panel of a plane, which only light up when something is going wrong. This is in contrast to instruments which have to be read continuously).

The 'key variables' differ per sector or line of business, varying from 'productive hours/available hours' in an accounting firm to 'the sold kw' in a power plant.

Exhibit 10.7

Norway's Statoil is trolling as fast as it can

It needs foreign fields to offset declining domestic production

When Harald Norvik took the top job at Norway's state-owned oil company in 1987, he wondered at the time 'if I was the winner or the loser.' With huge cost overruns, management turmoil, and plummeting morale, Statoil was a mess. But Norvik, a former deputy energy minister, skillfully used his understanding of Norwegian politics to cut government interference and chop $400 million in operating costs. Results have improved: On Feb. 22, Statoil reported pretax profits for 1995 of $2.1 billion on sales of $13.6 billion. In contrast, losses in 1987 approached $236 million. 'I now see I was the winner,' Norvik says.

But Norvik, 49, can't relax. He must maintain his winning ways in the face of a serious problem: declining production at Statoil's biggest fields. The company has revealed that last year its oil output fell for the first time ever, contributing to a 7% drop in overall earnings from 1994. Because of shrinking reserves, production from its three North Sea 'elephants' – industry jargon for massive oil fields – should decline by 1998 to one-half the 1994 level, when they contributed 74% of Statoil's production. 'It will be very hard for them to replace those reserves. The management is under pressure,' says Douglas Montgomery, oil analyst at Edinburgh-based Wood Mackenzie.

Norvik has to find a solution because to a large degree Norway's welfare state – one of the world's most lavish – depends on Statoil's ability to pump and sell oil. The energy industry accounts for 13% of government revenues, which go to support generous pensions, health care, and education for Norway's 4.3 million people. Statoil is responsible for 60% of Norway's total production of 3.1 million barrels per day.

To avert a crisis, Norvik has spent much of this decade scouring the earth for new fields of oil and gas. His goal: build Statoil's non-Norwegian production from 2% of its total output now to one-third by 2005. To that end, Norvik, an economist by training, has become a dealmaker. There's a joint venture with British Petroleum Co. to explore in West Africa, Southeast Asia, and the former Soviet Union. After two years of arduous negotiations, a consortium including Statoil/BP is close to an agreement that will allow transmission of early oil production out of Azerbaijan. The partners have also discovered a major natural-gas field off Vietnam. And despite pressure from human-rights groups, they continue to look for more oil off Nigeria. In January, Statoil acquired Aran Energy Plc, an Irish oil company with promising offshore acreage, for $315 million.

Skeptics Norvik figures that his plan to boost profits is well under way. Besides the overseas ventures and the development of smaller Norwegian fields with new technology, Statoil also expects to get an enormous lift from natural gas. It could overtake oil in importance for Norway and Statoil by 2020, thanks to the country's massive Troll offshore field.

But some analysts aren't so sure of Norvik's latest efforts, which in 1995 alone cost $945 million. 'The question is whether they have paid too much' to realize their overseas ambitions, says Erik Storelv, analyst at Enskilda Securities in Oslo. Montgomery figures many of Statoil's overseas projects won't mature until after 2000, and while selling gas helps offset the decrease in oil production, gas doesn't have the same margins as oil.

Norvik also has downstream problems. Because of a surplus of refining capacity in Europe, profits at Statoil's refining business plummeted last year. Yearend results weren't helped by a 40% construction cost overrun on the new Kalundborg (Denmark) refinery.

Norvik says the company can only keep pushing while also cutting costs. It plans, for example, to continue expanding its profitable retail gas business in the Baltic region, Germany, and Ireland. Borealis, Statoil's petrochemical joint venture with Finland's Neste, will expand into Asia. Borealis reported big profits last year – but will have to battle through a projected slump in petrochemicals in 1996.

It's tough enough keeping shareholders happy, especially in a business as volatile as energy. Keeping a government and its citizens content can be even tougher. In some ways, the true test of Norvik's skills is just beginning.

Source: Business Week, 18 March 1996.

10.9.3 The balanced business scorecard: a new way of internal reporting

The 'Balanced Business Scorecard' is developed in order to help management map out performances. The inducement to their development was the necessity for companies and institutions to adapt better to the quickly changing circumstances in which they have to compete. Better products have to be brought onto the market more quickly and must meet the individual wishes of the customer. The structure and functioning of organizations changes thoroughly because of that. But the traditional performance measurement is still based on old organizational structures and thus also has to change.

The basic thought behind the 'Balanced Business Scorecard' is looking at the delivered performances from four important perspectives.

1. Customer perspective.
2. Company processes.
4. Organizational learning processes.
5. Financial perspective.

In other words: the 'Balanced Business Scorecard' looks at the organization from four points of view.

1. How do the customers see us?
2. In what do we have to excel?
3. How can we continue to improve and create added value?
4. How do we look at the shareholders?

Goals are determined for each of these points of view. These goals then have to be translated in CSFs and divided over the four above mentioned points of view. In order to prevent an abundance of information, per point of view only a few measurements have to be used. In that way management is forced to direct itself at the most critical factors.

The 'scorecard' protects the organization from sub-optimization: by presenting everything in one report, it is prevented that management stresses one aspect too much while the other aspects are 'forgotten'.

The points of view of the Balanced Business Scorecard

The point of view of the customer: How do the customers see us?
The interests of the customer generally break down into four categories: time and being in time, quality, performance and service and the price. For each of these categories indicators can be drawn up, for time, for example, the 'leadtime': how much time passes between placing an order and the delivery of it. And in order to measure the performance, for example, in the area of price, one would have to conduct periodical investigation into the prices which competitors ask for the same products. It also needs to be examined whether one's own measurements are in agreement with the wishes of the customer: what the customer thinks is a good delivery time also has to be the measurement the organization uses.

The internal point of view: In what do we have to excel?
This is actually an internal translation of the customer perspective: what needs to be done within the organization in order to meet the expectations of the customer. Eventually, good sales performances are derived from the processes and decisions of the organization itself. An example of this is the employing of account managers, so that every client has a fixed point of reference within the organization.

The point of view of innovation and gathering knowledge: How can we continue to improve and create added value?
In the preceding points of view, parameters are set which are considered to be the most important for the success of the organization. But the goals keep changing, fierce competition sees to it that companies have to improve their existing products continuously and have to be capable of introducing new products. Only when one is capable of that, can one supply added value to the clients, improve the internal efficiency and eventually enlarge the value of the organization for the shareholders. One possible measure in this regard is the percentage which expresses the degree to which new products are part of total sales.

The financial point of view: How do we look at the shareholders?
In this respect it is examined whether the organizational strategy contributes to the improvement of the bottom line to a sufficient degree: the net profit after taxes. Typical goals are profitability, growth and shareholders' value. In a 'scorecard' relation, however, the financial point of view is considered to be the least interesting: too directed at the short term, too directed at the past, unable to estimate the future value of the present investments. One could even surmise that when operational measures are all 'on green', financial measures will also indicate good values. This goes way too far however: an exact balance between financial and operational measures is important to realize a representative 'scorecard'.

Internal reporting

It appears that the introduction of the 'scorecard' means a change in the thinking about internal reporting. Not only does the financial controller draw up the ratios, but the whole management team is involved.

In the traditional internal reporting and performance measurement, 'control' was the central issue. One examined whether the employees had actually undertaken the actions they were supposed to have. In the 'scorecard', however, strategy and vision are the central issues and then control. The 'scorecard' presents goals and holds the employee responsible for them. This new approach fits into the current nature of entrepreneuring and co-operating: scale enlargement, speed and services, co-operation, ever continuing innovation and teamwork. By combining the four areas of attention, many of the interrelationships are better understood by management. The management is forced to look from all four points of view and put this way, also look further than their own department. The most important contribution of the 'scorecard' is perhaps that one directs oneself at the future instead of at the past.

10.9.4 A dilemma in operations measurement

A dilemma, which occurs in the measuring of the execution, is that of timeliness versus accuracy. When deviations are signalled between norm and execution, it is of importance that these come to the light in time. In this way negative effects can be kept within limits. The speed with which one reports, however, can itself have a number of negative effects on the accuracy, because of which it is less possible to conduct trustworthy analyses. The answer to the question of whether a report should be fast or accurate, depends on the goals which are set. For total assessment of a situation, an accurate report is demanded. For activities which ask for rapid adjustment, more value of course needs to be given to timeliness. Based on these considerations, a manager will have to make his own choice.

10.9.5 Management control in non-profit organizations

In this aspect, we pay attention to the 'management control' problem in not-for-profit organizations: organizations in the area of welfare, health, education and culture. On a number of issues, the 'management control' problem in these organizations can be compared to those of discretionary/expense centres in profit organizations. Think of the non-monetary valuation ability of output and the comparison between costs and results. These organizations additionally have characteristics which make this problem even more difficult. So a not-for-profit organization often has a monopoly position with respect to a client (for example, a hospital with respect to a patient), while there also is no market price against which one can offset the costs. Besides that in not-for-profit organizations 'professionals' are predominantly employed, with their own, sometimes divergent value patterns and a specific know-how, on which management sometimes has little grip. In conclusion, in the management of such organizations several societal interest groups may be represented, all of which try to realize their own goals.

For the control of not-for-profit organizations it is highly important that there is agreement about the goals, not only on an abstract level, but also in terms of rendering services which have to be carried out, target groups which have to be served and size of the servicing. Besides that one needs to strive for clear and preferably quantifiable norms for the 'production process': the delivered performance and the quality of that. So the social services of a village or in a town can indicate how many requests an employee has to handle per day or per week. One condition is that one knows the effect of this on quality, respectively on the customer. This last matter is difficult to measure. In not-for-profit organization those involved (politicians, customers and professional service providers) will have to try to come to generally accepted norms which offer a possibility for the solution of the quality problem.

10.10 CONTROL: ADAPTATION AND CORRECTIVE ACTIONS

When, from the review and monitoring of performances, it appears that deviations occur between norm and execution, the manager is faced with the choice of adjusting the norm or the execution of actions. In essence, here is the start of a decision cycle that was discussed in Chapter 4. The gap has already been determined by then. Now the manager must answer the question how he is to close the gap. For this purpose, the cause of the deviation first needs to be determined. The approach to that is the key to effective problem-solving. One is not cured by just fighting the symptom.

As a rule it can be proposed that the norm has to be adjusted when the deviation is caused by structural deviations in the circumstances. When, for example, it appears that exports to a certain country have decreased because of extra heavy tariffs on the import, it makes little sense to increase export efforts. The Sales Department will have to draw up a new norm for that country. Besides that one needs to search for possibilities to compensate for lost sales. Correction or adjustment of operations is recommended when deviations are caused by *accidental circumstances*. If sales have decreased because of the temporary advertising campaign of a competitor, this deviation from the plans can be fought with an extra effort in the sales area, for example, by a temporary price cut or extra advertising. In that case, it would not be right to accept the lower sales and take this as a norm for the future.

A corrective system is often seen as a cybernetic system. Known examples of this are thermostats and self-adjusting brakes. For the design of an organizational system of adjustment it is important that one is conscious of the differences with a cybernetic system. This might stop one applying the design rules which hold for a thermostat to an organization. A decisive difference is that in an organization one deals with people, with all their needs, wishes and characteristics. In the structure of a control system one certainly needs to render account to this. No human being reacts like a machine. The person who turns the thermostat to another temperature does not meet any resistance from this piece of equipment. Changing a reward or performance measurement system, however, can never be arranged as simply. More is involved in that. To start with it will have to be clarified to those involved why a change in the system is necessary (*see* Part four). Besides that it is necessary that they experience those changes as desired and meaningful. The effectiveness of change increases even more when they get the chance to participate in the design of the new system.

One always has to conceive of a deviation from the norm as an impulse through which the decision-making process has to be put into motion. The manager then has to examine which decisions he has to make and take them. For adjustment can affect policy (*see* Part two) as well as operational execution (*see* Part five) and structure (*see* Part three). Adjustment measurements therefore always need to be taken in coherence. We have covered indications for these measurements earlier in this book.

SUMMARY

- Planning is the activity directed at matching decisions to be able to realize formulated goals. We have discussed several plans and have indicated the relationship between planning and budgeting. In this Chapter different planning techniques and methods in order to clarify processes have been covered. We have paid closer attention to the aspects of budgeting as a 'tool of management'.
- For an organization, budgets are the performance norms expressed in money. Besides budgets, in order to obtain insight into complex situations and in order to control and direct processes, one can use appraisal of company performances and ratios. In one-off activities, project and network planning can be used. For the control of the flow of goods, we can distinguish 'push' and 'pull' systems.
- Once activities are under way, they should not be left to their own devices. Monitoring of the execution of the actions, and examining whether the desired action has arisen, are of importance. When necessary adjustment and corrective action can be taken. In measuring the execution, 'new' non-financial ratios have become important, in addition to the 'traditional' ratios. The traditional financial ratios are more oriented at the past; the non-financial ratios are more directed at the future effectiveness of the organization.
- The use of non-financial ratios takes place in the case of statistical techniques used in the framework of total quality management. Besides that, non-financial ratios are important in the case of benchmarking, an approach to processes in which factors are traced which influence the present and future effectiveness of organizations. Adjustment can take place after analysis and evaluation of measurement results. Managers can then adjust by deciding via a creative search and design process: change the course (*see* Part two), change the organizational structure (*see* Part three) or conduct the operational execution differently (*see* Part five). Considering that an organization is a co-operative relationship of people, a manager will always have to be able to explain a corrective decision to others. This is in order to motivate the external (*see* Part one) as well as the internal (*see* Part four) stakeholders to continue their contribution to the organization.

DISCUSSION QUESTIONS

1. With reference to *Management in action* at the beginning of this chapter: What is the role of financial compared to non-financial ratios in Bosman's company at present?
2. Suppose you have to formulate a strategic plan for an organization. How would you make use of project planning in this respect?
3. Why should a clear organizational structure be a condition for budgeting?
4. Can you explain research findings that autocratically oriented managers experience integral quality management as a threat?
5. Give your opinion on the following statement:

   'Benchmarking means analyzing your competitor.'

6. Do you agree with the following statement: 'Management by objectives is only suitable for drawing up departmental and personal goals for a certain period but is not the right instrument for the evaluation and possible adjustment of activities.'
7. (a) Taking into account that local managers' freedom of manoeuvre must be balanced against group interest, what would you suggest Earl Wade do in the 'Currency Crisis' case (*see* page 520)?

   (b) What can be done about the banking mechanisms in the various European time zones as far as Global Electronics is concerned? Where is the best location for a possible centralized treasury for Global?
8 (a) What would you define as Critical Success Factors (CSFs) relating to Norway's Statoil company (page 526)?

   (b) How would you group these factors to get a balanced picture based on internal (and external) factors?

Management case study

Performance indicators for a chocolate producer

Quality, delivering trustworthiness and short completion times are three requirements modern companies need to meet. Actions for improvement are the consequence. But how does one measure whether efforts have the desired result? Performance Indicators (PIs) are a meaningful tool, as appears from the following example from practice. It involves a chocolate factory 'somewhere' in Europe.

The chocolate factory started as part of a family company in the 1920s. The company is presently part of an international concern with subsidiaries in several western European countries. It specializes in industrial chocolate, the raw material for 'chocolatiers', candy manufacturers and confectioners. In the course of the years different types have been developed, in accordance with the demands of industrial users, not only in Europe, but also in the USA and Japan. At the moment the programme comprises about 400 kinds of chocolate.

Manufacturing process

Cocoa beans are supplied in gunny sacks from tropical countries such as the Ivory Coast, Ghana, Indonesia and Brazil. They are stored on pallets in a cool warehouse. The manufacturing process involves the following steps.

- *Mixing.* Sacks with beans of different origin, each with their typical characteristics, are emptied by hand into a pouring funnel. The mixture determines the eventual taste of the chocolate and so is carefully chosen. After this step the process continues completely automatically.
- *Cleaning.* The raw beans are sifted and ventilated. Foreign material, such as stones and heavy metal objects are eliminated.
- *Roasting.* This is critical since the eventual aroma depends on very carefully arranged roasting times and temperatures.
- *Breaking.* Cocoa beans have a hard shell. After breaking, the shells and cocoa beans are separated, and cocoa dust is eliminated.
- *Grinding.* Pen mills shatter the cores. Because of this, the cocoa butter comes out and a liquid mass forms.

- *Mixing.* With special moulders the ingredients, including sugar and milk powder, are mixed into the cocoa mass.
- *Fine rolling.* To obtain a very fine chocolate, the small parts are rolled between steel cylinders located very close together and which turn at an ever-increasing speed.
- *Conchering.* This is a mechanical process. A high temperature is needed to derive small amounts of moisture and volatile sour aromas from the chocolate mass.
- *Pouring.* After having been brought to the right temperature, the chocolate mass is poured into forms for customers who desire their chocolate in block form. There are also customers who receive liquid chocolate per tank lorry.
- *Trembling.* The filled forms are led over vibrators to allow the air bulbs to escape and to divide the chocolate evenly.
- *Cooling.* Cooling tunnels with accurate temperature control see to a perfect crystallization of the cocoa butter.

The first eight steps together form the 'cocoa preparation', while the last three steps are called 'perfect manufacturing'.

Assignment

As is the case in so many companies, the chocolate factory needs to strain to maintain and if possible, improve market position. The company has a position of respect among the worldwide competition but management and employees are aware of the fact that alertness is demanded. So continuous improvement in company affairs is a generally accepted goal, and a lot of effort is directed at that. Gradually this created the need for a tool with which the effect of such efforts could be measured. Management understood that performance indicators are such a measure: 'In order to be able to evaluate and follow up our efficiency, effectiveness and service (internal as well as external) in the different departments, we urgently need relevant indicators.'

An external consultant was asked to help with the introduction of performance indicators in manufacturing, and in two operational departments (cocoa preparation and production of couverture) and in two supporting groups (production planning and maintenance).

Operational execution

In mutual agreement with the client, i.e. the technical manager of the chocolate factory, a four-day lasting program was drawn up for middle management of the involved departments. This program comprised five parts.

- *General introduction.* Plenary meeting. Introduction by the client. Lecture by the consultant about the sense and nonsense of PI (Performance Indicators). Examples from practice. Discussion.
- *Group work.* Brainstorming, choice of PI. Definitions. Necessary data.
- *Reporting.* Plenary feedback of the group work.
- *Mutual tuning of outcomes.* Discussion. Eliminating of differences in definitions.
- *Drawing up of action plans for implementation.* What has to be done? Who does it? Who co-ordinates it? When should it be ready? Agreements/Arrangements.

Mission

Mission and company culture came up for discussion during the introduction on the first morning. It was stated that the goal of the firm is: 'To be the most successful in the

continued overleaf

Management case study continued

industrial chocolate market, achieving recognition as the ultimate supplier by maintaining leadership in quality of people, service, products, expertise, profitability and excellence of execution.'

Group work

The participants were divided in advance into four groups of about ten persons by the client. In each group there were not only employees from the department for which the PI were meant, but also representatives of their 'suppliers' and 'clients'. In the group work different phases can also be distinguished. Phase 1 was individual, the other phases were executed by the group as a whole.

- *Phase 1. Brainstorming.* Uncensored and unstructured generating of possible candidates for the list of PIs.
- *Phase 2. Regulating.* Mutually eliminating double ideas and grouping of candidate–PI which relate to each other. Thinking of a name for each of the group's PIs.
- *Phase 3. Priority setting.* Discussion of the weight of the found candidate–PI, followed by a regulating with decreasing importance for assessing the performance of the department. In that, the company mission sometimes served as guideline.
- *Phase 4. Choice.* In those groups in which the preceding steps yielded more than ten PIs, discussion and critical investigation into different candidates led to a choice of ten or fewer.
- *Phase 5. Definitions.* For each of the remaining PIs, it was written down exactly what was meant. The group also determined a formula for the calculation.
- *Phase 6. Input data.* From the definitions and formulae followed a list of necessary data. Which do we already have? Where are they? How can we measure the missing quantities and where can this best be done? After sometimes heavy discussion, these questions were also answered.
- *Phase 7. Preparation of presentation.* Answering the question how and by whom the found PIs would be made known in the plenary meeting. Most of the time, the leader of the department was chosen which was central in the group.

Conclusion

In the late afternoon of the fourth day, each group presented the outcome of the group work to its colleagues. After that discussion and comparison of definitions followed. This was necessary because some PIs were put on the list by more than one group. A definition with general validity was then the result. It was also discussed which data were necessary, which were already available and for which a measurement would have to be drawn up. Here, it appeared, not unexpectedly, that one department possesses data the other needs for its PI. Thus a system of indicators arose which was valid for the whole company.

General and industry specific indicators

The chosen PIs are partly of general nature and partly very specific for the chocolate industry. Some in the general category are:

- delivering trustworthiness;
- return/profitability of production;

- efficiency: number of necessary man hours per ton of product;
- strategic inventories;
- quality of raw materials (with regard to the norms);
- absenteeism;
- hygiene;
- environmental taxes.

Specific for the chocolate industry is the measurement of the fluidity of the cocoa mass at many points in the process, as well as the texture, the fineness of the chocolate.

Action plan and evaluation

Drawing up an action plan was an important element of the afternoon meeting. What has to be done? Who does it? When to start, when ready? For implementation that plan gave the 'time schedule'. In conclusion, at the request of the consultant, all participants filled out an evaluation form, the goal of which was insight into the opinion of the participants about the programme offered. A programme for choosing PIs is also subject to improvement.

Valuable remarks after the sessions

The distinction between external and internal indicators was experienced as meaningful.

Rather than allowing the participants to generate individual candidate–PIs, one would have preferred to do that together. That prevents duplications and opens possibilities of inspiring one another. A quicker route to meaningful PIs is the consequence.

It is desirable that the coach of the group process has knowledge of the company processes.

It is meaningful to try to generate one figure from the chosen PIs which is representative for the 'health' of the company.

Implementation

Since September 1991, the employees of the respective departments of the chocolate factory have been occupied with the introducing of the chosen PIs as a tool to follow the course of affairs in their department. Depending on the department, these are reported weekly or monthly. The communication occurs right down to the factory floor. Within the company all information is available to everyone. The organization calls the implementation 'very successful', but prefers to give no further comment or examples to the outside world.

Useful

Performance indicators are a useful tool in management because they visualize the course of affairs, make it discussable and improvable. When well motivated, a group of employees can quickly find meaningful and well defined PIs. Such a group should not be larger than ten or twelve people. Active involvement of company management is a necessary condition for that motivation.

It is essential to include representatives of the 'clients' and of the 'suppliers' in the group besides the key figures of a department.

Often, more data are available than one thinks, but they are present somewhere else, and perhaps spread around in the organization.

continued overleaf

Management case study continued

CASE QUESTIONS

1. Why would 'the mission' have come up for discussion in the development of the indicators?
2. Where can one speak of operational plans in this case?
3. Where in this case do you recognize coherence between elements from theory about decision making (Chapter 4), consultation groups (Chapter 7) and performance indicators (Chapter 10)?

Chapter 11

Information management and information technology

LEARNING OBJECTIVES

After studying this chapter, you should be able to:

- describe the notions of 'information' and 'data';
- describe different kinds of information;
- explain the relationship between management information and functional information systems;
- describe the content of different functional information systems with regard to different aspects;
- describe goals of information planning;
- clarify failure factors of automation (and lessons which have to be learned from that);
- state three directions of strategic applications of information technology;
- state three organizational consequences of working with information technology.

Management in action

FT

Successful retailers compete on value, not merely on price

In-store IT systems were once confined to clever cash registers. Now retailers seek ways to enhance customer-response and monitor purchasing patterns.

Back in the 1980s when scanning systems and electronic point-of-sale (EPoS) were still a novelty, retailers' use of information technology tended to involve counting things – goods sold, money taken, or items left on the shelf.

Today, the technological emphasis has shifted: instead of 'things', preoccupation is with people – tracking shoppers as they enter the store, monitoring customers' purchasing patterns or giving them the technology to do it all themselves.

The retail pundits talk of 'customer-facing' systems or 'efficient consumer response' while 'point-of-service' is replacing 'point-of-sale' and 'supply chain' is giving way to 'demand chain' in the retail vocabulary.

In today's increasingly competitive high street, many retailers have realised that keen prices or promotional 'loyalty' schemes are simply not enough: to differentiate themselves from the rest of the pack takes something extra.

As Dr Leonard Berry, the JC Penney Professor of Retailing Studies at Texas A & M University and one of North America's leading retail gurus argues, there is one question that all retailers should regularly ask themselves when it comes to considering their future success. It is quite simply: 'If our company were to disappear from the landscape overnight, would customers really miss us?'

Those store directors who can honestly answer 'yes', he suggests, are the ones where customer service levels are highest, rather than where prices are lowest.

'Retailers with a future compete on value, not solely on price,' says Dr Berry. 'Price is price, but value is the total experience.'

That 'total experience' is being enhanced by an assortment of leading-edge technologies that can range from use of radio systems for interrogating back-office computers and solving shoppers' queries on the shop floor, to the slick use of interactive media (in-store or in the home) to encourage repeat store visits and purchases.

In supermarkets, 'self-scanning', where shoppers scan their own purchases rather than waiting for a checkout operator to do so, is seen not so much as a means of reducing staff as an improved customer service.

Safeway's 'Shop and Go' service – which uses hand-held scanners from Symbol Technologies, originally developed with the Dutch chain, Albert Heijn (part of the Ahold group) – is being rolled out to more than 60 stores.

'The system has considerable appeal to our target markets,' says marketing director, Roger Partington, 'especially young families for whom time is at a premium.'

It is these customers for whom waiting in line at the checkout – with its tempting array of sweets and novelties – can be especially gruelling. Somerfield, Waitrose and Superquinn in Ireland are among a growing number of retail chains piloting similar customer-operated systems.

Self-scanning systems had been trialled – unsuccessfully – more than 10 years ago, but it is only now as customers become familiar with high-tech systems that the concept seems to have taken off.

It has been much the same with multimedia which first had an airing back in the early-1980s using cumbersome 12 inch video disks. Numerous schemes have been tested since then and most have failed: notable exceptions include Florsheim's shoe-selling kiosks in the USA or the Zanussi information boxes for white goods in the UK.

As with self-scanning, interactive media now seems to be gaining popular acceptance. In the US, consumer electronics retailer Best Buy has equipped stores with a dozen interactive kiosks offering information on some 65 000 CDs, 12 000 videos and 2 000 software packages as a valued alternative to more conventional shop assistants; meanwhile, Crate & Barrel has an easy-to-use application for purchasers: an interactive wedding list.

Elsewhere, there are now numerous wine selection systems and recipe kiosks, as well as applications aimed at the next generation of shoppers: typical is Daewoo – attacking the European market without a conventional network of car dealers – which has a children's 'design a car' kiosk to keep the little ones amused while the parents concentrate on buying the real version through a neighbouring kiosk.

Many observers see these experiments as a simple stepping stone to selling direct to the home via interactive television or the World Wide Web – although even here not all experiments have been successful.

Michael Rollens, president of the New Media Network in the US is not alone in his critical opinion of current electronic shopping. He suggests that most 'break the basic rules of retailing' with their limited merchandise ranges, erratic delivery and poorly thought-through concepts.

Many early entrants in the home shopping arena, such as Time Warner's Dream Shop, have already gone out of business, while others – such as IBM's World Avenue, comprising 20 retail 'stops' and e-Shop Plaza, which has just been bought by Microsoft, are proving extremely slow to really take off.

'In general, the Internet is not a very exciting place to go shopping,' says Mr Rollens. Such high profile developments apart, much of the customer emphasis of 'retail IT' is concerned with fast identification of – and response to – changing patterns of demand.

Bill Gilmour, retail partner at Coopers and Lybrand, the management consultants, shows how 'exploiting the data' can drive better business performance. He points to a formula: "Customer traffic" multiplied by "customer activity" equals sales, which when multiplied by gross margin gives you bottom-line profitability.'

Loyalty cards are helping to boost what analysts call 'frequency of shop', especially in the food retailing sector. But in-store technology comes into play long before any purchases are made by measuring 'customer traffic' using infra-red or video-tracking systems to monitor shoppers' movements, identifying 'cold spots' in the store and helping to ensure adequate staffing levels in service-critical areas.

IT systems sort out 'customer activity' helping to classify shoppers by 'type of purchase' (categories include the 'beauty conscious', 'pet lovers', 'sentimental', 'casual drinker', 'sports conscious' and 'new families') and promoting goods that will appeal to them while in that frame of mind by product juxtapositions or related discount offers.

'Using these techniques,' he says, 'you don't need to know anything personal about the individual, just the mode of shopping they're in.'

The new customer-focussed world is thus one of data warehousing, shopping basket analysis and of seamless systems' integration so that store managers can access just about anything from anywhere. On the shop floor, this can mean electronic penpads to communicate with remote systems to solve ad hoc queries, while for merchandisers it can mean digital cameras and laptop computers. A typical user is the C&A subsidiary, Hamells, which has installed a fully-integrated Windows application from Business Developments which allows its buyers to use digital cameras to input images of their latest selections.

From overseas buying trips, these images can be transmitted to colleagues back home for comment. Alternatively, they can be stored in the system and then used to create merchandising ideas for display staff or provide new product training presentations for staff – all to be ultimately transmitted to the PC-based, EPoS tills in branches.

'We see this as an important range development tool,' says operations manager, Mike Randle, 'as buyers will be able to develop merchandise moods more easily.

'If we can send pictures of new lines and display recommendations to the branch staff before the goods arrive in store, then it helps to create more interest about the products and will also encourage them to alert good customers about expected styles' – yet another way for IT innovation to add to that total 'service offer'.

Source: *Financial Times*, 2 October 1996.

INTRODUCTION

Good decision making, tuning strategic decisions into each other, the specific and more detailed functional plans, and the control of the different organizational processes are only possible when readable and trustworthy information becomes available in time. In other words, controlling processes is not possible without good information processing and a trustworthy supply of information in the organization.

The supply of information fulfils the function the nervous system fulfils in the human organism, so to speak. For that purpose, all parts are linked to a whole which is integrated, so that one can also react in mutual interrelatedness.

All reporting about a product, material supply and the personnel supply, therefore, have to match in order to support the functioning of the people in the organization and the functioning of the company processes. This stresses the importance of good information management. Information management can be described simply as the management of information activities. These activities are of importance in two ways: on the one hand, information is important for employees and management in order to be able to take well considered decisions; on the other, information itself is often also the input of the servicing process or the manufacturing process. Here, information management has a two-sided character as depicted in Fig 11.1.

The general notion of 'information management', then, comprises not only the management of the information flow, but also the supply of information on behalf of management.

In this Chapter, we first pay attention to different aspects of information and after that to management information and functional information systems. From the point of view of information planning and automation closer attention is paid to the question of how supply of information can be optimally matched with the needs of the organization. Finally we discuss the role of information technology (IT) in organizations.

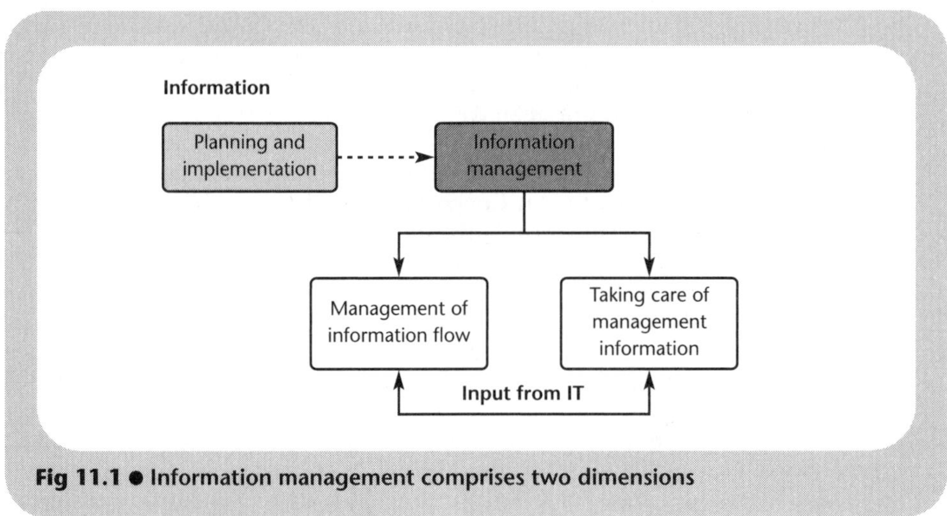

Fig 11.1 ● Information management comprises two dimensions

11.1 ● INFORMATION AND CONTROL

The notions of 'data' and 'information' are not the same as that of 'contents'. For a good understanding it is important to distinguish these from each other.

By information we mean ordered data based on certain criteria or points of view. So information consists of meaningful combinations of data. A datum is any notion with a meaning, for example a number, a figure, a letter or a word. When information is needed the available data have to be processed.

Defined in this way data only become information when they have a relevant meaning for people. Employees may receive thick computer printouts with an enormous amount of figures and other data which are not clarified in any way, or which are not understood, or not presented in the right way. Because of this such data offer limited or no information.

In principle, four aspects can be recognized in 'data'.

1. The syntactic aspect. The syntax determines the rules one may have at one's disposal in order to use the data. When one deviates from this syntax, a disruption can occur in transmitting the data. This is known as a syntactic disruption.
2. The semantic aspect. The semantics concern the meaning of data. In the exchange of data, sender and receiver will have to attach the same meaning to these data. When this condition is not met, then one speaks of a semantic problem.
3. The pragmatic aspect. This aspect concerns the effect which those data have on the behaviour of the receiver. When this effect is different from that intended by the sender of the data, one speaks of pragmatic disruption.
4. The technical aspect. This means the way in which the data are determined, processed and transported. Here the technical medium with which the data are handled is under discussion.

Minicase 11.1

The four aspects of a word

An example to clarify the distinction between the four aspects: the syntax regards the grammar, the correct spelling of a word, for example, the word 'imediately'. Here, this word has not been written down correctly with regard to the syntax. The disruption in the grammar (=syntax) is so slight, however, that the 'meaning' (=semantics) can still be traced. One recognizes the word 'immediately' in it. The pragmatic aspect of the deliberately incorrectly written word is the explanation of the four aspects of information to the reader via a wrong spelling. The fourth, technical aspect regards the way in which the word 'immediately' is sent: in this case via a book.

In the framework of the processing of data as regards supply of information it is also of importance, for a good understanding, to keep distinguishing these four aspects of data. By doing that, data can really be seen from different points of view and disruptions can also be explained as they arise from different causes.

Information is an 'economic good'. It is goal-oriented knowledge. Reality is indicated by information. Information is demanded for decisions and reflects these and the consequences of them. Seen from another point of view, information is a 'scarce' good: it provides a certain utility, is brought about with the use of scarce resources and, so, has value. As far as information is traded on the market, one pays the price. Furthermore, information can be seen as a production factor, as product or as part of a product.

Information on management side can come available in 'different' forms, for example as text, image, and/or spoken word.

In the execution of all kinds of tasks, employees have to take decisions. Formal information is provided according to certain rules. These rules regard the content, the presentation, the frequency and the time of supply of information, for example balance of assets and liabilities, profit and loss statement, surveys of debtors and receivables or inventory lists. Besides this formal information, employees also make use of informal information such as scribbling lists and remarks in their notebooks. To an extent this is caused by the fact that they think formal information does not completely provide all their information needs. This in itself is caused by the fact that it is impossible to save and process all information according to fixed procedures. In the organization, however, if one relies more on 'own' informal information than on formal information, something is wrong with the information provision in that organization.

Formal information (structured information) such as balance sheets, reports of assessment conversations, etc., informal information (unstructured information) from intuition, rumours in the lobby, emotions and experiences, all contribute to decision making. Formal information is provided via information systems and administrative processes. Information, both formal and informal, also comes from other employees and/or sources outside the organization.

Strategic information is information which supports the process of policy making and formulation in an organization in the longer term. This information comes from external and internal sources, but is hard to predict. That is why it is also important to keep possibilities open and as such to use these opportunities to gather and provide ad hoc information. The goal of tactical information is to compare planning data to actual attained results. When deviations occur corrective actions need to be taken. Tactical information is especially directed at middle management in support of the management of operational employees based on, for example, weekly surveys of receivables and/or debtors, cost surveys, sales figures, production lists, recruitment data, surveys of utilization of machinery etc.

Operational information is information on the daily execution of activities and, as such, regards details of the operational company processes. Characteristic is the routine progressing according to fixed procedures and rules. This information goes to different departments on different levels in the organization and often also to persons or institutions outside the company or institution.

In the sphere of the supply of internal information, a management team, in order to be able to make decisions, needs to have insight in, for example, the development of results of the past months in order to see whether this comes close to the budget, they will have to know the order portfolio or the work in progress, the development of cash flow, the development of inventory. It is possible also that a board, to be able to make an investment decision that needs to take into account the purchase of a new machine, wants to have insight into the cost price, the sales expected increase and so on.

Information about delivery times, data on amounts receivable, inventories of raw materials and final products, quality and quantity of the production, utilization of the manufacturing resources is of importance to the Sales and Production Departments when accepting new orders.

To determine the information need in the organization and to determine the form and the frequency of the information and how it will become available, it is necessary to know who is allowed to take what decisions and where in the company.

The information need and information provision which is to be based on that, in combination with the level in an organization, is presented in a so-called 'information triangle'. Strategic information, for example, demands aggregation and separation of information originating from operational and tactical level and will be presented in summarizing surveys with other time intervals and with the consequences in the longer term in mind (*see* Fig 11.2).

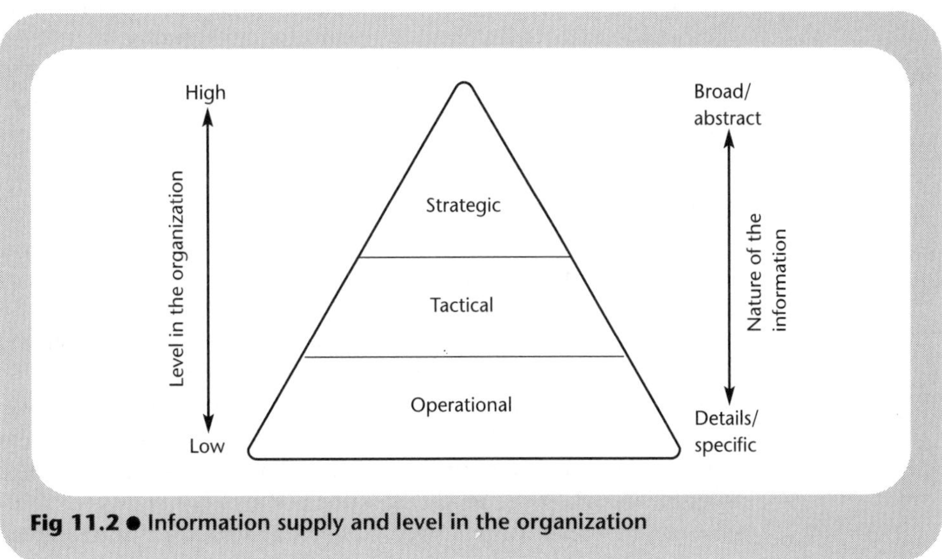

Fig 11.2 ● Information supply and level in the organization

11.1.1 Measuring, checking, information and control

A necessary supplement to plans is continual control over the progress of the processes, the aim of which is to determine whether the continuing activities in the execution are going according to plan. Reality is then confronted with the plan. In the case of deviation between the two, corrective actions will have to be taken. It is self-evident that this demands timely information processing. In section 11.1.2, we will pay separate attention to the process of signalling and monitoring.

Some reasons for internal control

Control is necessary because people and systems are liable to error. Often things can be carried out better or differently from how at first seemed possible, or a judgement may turn out to be not totally correct. So it is always important to remain informed about the actual course of affairs.

In addition, delegation (*see* Chapter 7) makes control necessary, for one needs to be convinced that the execution of tasks takes place properly. Only then can the execution itself be delegated to others. For this reason internal control takes place in a company or institution on behalf of the management. It is important to choose the right measuring points and to determine effective norms. Only then will comparison between norm and reality provide management with meaningful and required control information. Internal control is directed at controlling the processes engaged within an organization. Without conscious supervision, control is not possible in any way.

In order to remain informed of the progress of the execution, a managerial or operational employee can use different methods. Sometimes deviation can be determined by direct control or observation. Often, however, there is indirect supervision when deviations are determined afterwards through a report about the execution or the present state of affairs.

Supervision can be directed at the examination: either whether one has acted according to the given authority; or whether the execution of assignments has been correct and efficient; or whether activities have undergone sufficient progress; or whether the right norms in time, quantities and quality have been used. So it can be seen that the control function directs itself especially at the actual company activities. Review and examination can be further directed at decisions made, at the material values present in the company (in money and/or in goods) and at the registration.

From supervision to control

Supervision is limited to the check of actual reality to the norms set. Besides the setting of norms and making plans for the execution of activities, control also comprises the necessity to adjust and/or correct the execution and being able to adjust the planning. So control is a notion wider than merely checking, reviewing, monitoring or supervision. Control means having a grip on ongoing affairs.

Decision-making authorities with regard to adjustment of execution can, in many cases, be left to operational employees, as long as the deviations remain within certain limits or zones of tolerance (*see* section 10.3). This is certainly the case in simple task assignments, when the result indicated is the only one expected of the execution, for example, by means of a budget. As soon as these limits are exceeded, however, it is necessary that adjustment of deviations with respect to norms takes place in consultation between managerial and operational employees. A deviation in a plan or in an operational norm can only be brought in by a manager authorized to do so or in the last resort by the management team or board.

Supervisor, controller and production planner

In middle sized and large companies, in the matter of business economics, the board is itself supported by a functionary called the 'controller'. In small organizations, this functionary may be called the 'head of administration and book-keeping'. As advisor to the management team and managing director, a controller occupies himself with planning and budgeting, audits and reviews, interpreting and analysing deviations between actual results and norms in the planning, recommendations and advice to the board of management. Besides all that the controller often manages the Department of Financial Administration in the organization. The controller becomes, as it were, the business-economic 'conscience' of the organization.

The 'business-technical' conscience is the head of the planning department in manufacturing or production function. This functionary also occupies himself with planning, the review and monitoring, interpreting and analysing of deviations and making recommendations. In the hierarchy this functionary is the closest colleague of the head of the manufacturing department. In the framework of signalling (*see* section 11.1.2) via the technical planning department many important data become available.

In a number of cases, the management team also lets itself be informed directly by the head of the production/technical planning department. When, for example, the quality and quantity of products and services are concerned, the management team can inform itself about this by means of a periodical report. In that way, one can then form one's own opinion about the performance of the manufacturing department, for example expressed in quality, quantities and time.

Information management and the information manager

The 'old' book-keeping and financial registration functions have developed such that we can see (especially in large organizations) a fourfold rise in the splitting of tasks and hiring of specialists, namely the controller function, the treasury function, the tax planning function and the information management function.

Involvement of information technology in companies and institutions takes on an ever more important meaning, with not only consequences for processes and organizational forms, but also with consequences for products and competitive position, when at the highest level in the organization functionaries are hired who are assigned with information management: an information manager who reports to the financial director, or sometimes an information director.

An information director is seen particularly in large and/or information intensive organizations: banks, insurance companies, and government ministries and services. In those cases, using the possibilities which information technology offers is often of strategic importance, since the need for information is great, the importance of information systems themselves is great and a lot of application of information technology is necessary.

In many companies and institutions, an information manager is assigned with the co-ordination of the provision of information in different functional areas. Sometimes the information manager is positioned next to the EDP manager (electronic data processing manager) who, as technical expert, is assigned to the co-ordination of the purchase of equipment and programs, the design of systems and the control of the computer centre. The functions of the information manager and EDP manager overlap when, from the technical point of view, information products and information services are offered which adapt even better to the information need in functional areas in the different company departments.

11.1.2 Internal reports (reviewing, monitoring and signalling)

Internal reporting is the system of providing internal information in a company or institution which, at different levels and in different departments, provides the management with directed and timely information for supervision and adjustment of planning and execution of current company activities. Company budgeting and budget control, planning via the planning charts and planning software in any case form a basis of internal reporting. Besides that data can become available in another way. In addition to book-keeping, for example, data can be supplied about material use, quality, personnel utilization, course of orders and order portfolio. Besides data expressed in terms of money, data in terms of quality or quantity will supply closer insight into the course of affairs in the organization or in a department. With a certain frequency (daily/weekly/monthly), these data thus need to be available in surveyable form in order, if necessary, to be able to take corrective action in time (*see* section 10.10). If, for example, signals come through that the sales per client are falling, or cost budgets are exceeded, or that calculations do not appear to be attainable, adjustment in the planning and/or corrective action in execution is demanded. In this way, internal reporting forms an important tool in the systematic control of planned activities.

11.1.3 Information and book-keeping

Information provision then is certainly more than book-keeping. Book-keeping is static in nature. This is, however, an element which should not be missed and which has to be used in order to provide signals for the management, for example for adjustment of sales, production, or purchase activities. A contribution also has to be made to the setting up of the planning and the company and departmental budgets.

Information provision is especially directed at determining possible activities in the future: investments, recruitment of personnel, development of new products, drawing in of financial resources. Besides that information provision is directed at following and adjusting present company activities: exceeding costs, absenteeism, numbers of produced and sold products, machine return, and so on.

Finally, information has to be supplied to the external stakeholders, such as shareholders and the bank, and to the internal stakeholders about profitability (return), solvability, liquidity and the important developments in the sector or line of business and so on. This takes place by means of the published profit and loss statement, balance sheets and the report of the board, via the annual report, by announcements to the works council and by periodical external financial messages, for example in quarterly reports.

Brought together as one figure, a pyramid arises linking the management level, decision areas and aspects of management (*see* Fig 11.3).

Within each information system which is set up, handling of these data takes place. In this process, the following activities can be distinguished:

- collecting;
- transforming;
- communicating;
- changing;
- analysing;
- organizing;
- storing;
- searching.

The goal of these activities is threefold.

1. The bridging of time. When an invoice is sent to a client on a certain date, and a statement a month later, the data on the original invoice have to be mentioned in the statement.
2. The bridging of distance. All establishments within a company have to have the inventory data at their disposal when an article is not in stock at the establishment itself.
3. The bridging of access to information. More or less complex information must be made available in order to draw conclusions based on it. From an inventory registration reports can be drawn up in order to plan future inventory levels. Too large an inventory means greater use of working capital. Too small an inventory means, however, that one cannot deliver in time.

At places where a decision has to be made timely, directed and trustworthy information needs to be available and with a certain frequency in surveyable form or can be

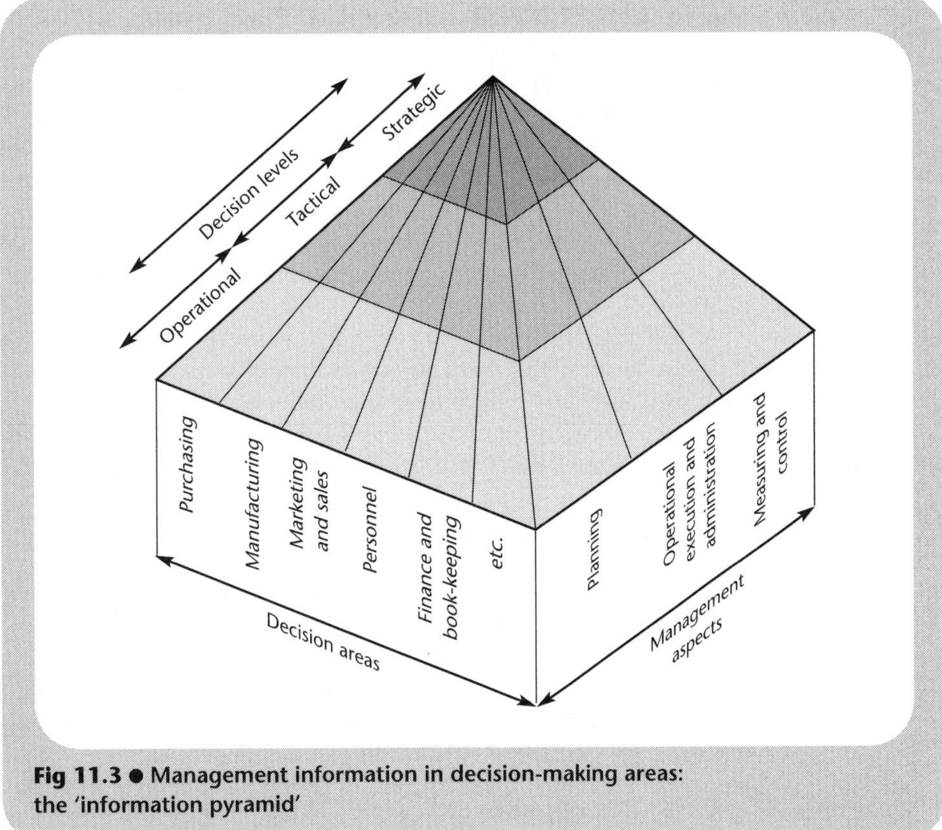

Fig 11.3 ● Management information in decision-making areas: the 'information pyramid'

called up at any arbitrary moment, if this is necessary. Requirements for supply of information regard timeliness, completeness, correctness and continuity.

In the structure of the supply of information it is also necessary to know the loci or points of decision in the organization. Here, it is also necessary to map out the channel along which information and communication in the company travel.

If information has to fulfil a need, it should be:

- problem oriented, that is, connected to the problems to be handled at the point of decision;
- current;
- simple and not liable to overexplanation;
- easy to obtain.

Tools for this include pre-printed forms, readable and surveyable statistical surveys. Data can be processed and presented by computer or on screen or in another way but is still available for presentation in the hand. It is wise, however, to bear in mind that there is a distinction between essential information (information which is vital for the work – 'need to know' information) and information in the 'rather interesting but not really important' category ('good to know' information).

11.2 MANAGEMENT INFORMATION AND FUNCTIONAL INFORMATION SYSTEMS

Besides information to do with the administration of company resources, information systems also have to deliver information for the sake of planning in an organization, for example, long-term prognosis on return of investments, or a representation of the development in a certain sector of the labour market. In the case of more short-term oriented information, this might include, for example, a survey of personnel costs and data about quality control; oriented at departments, for example, prediction of sales per product, per country, per market segment, production planning for the following month and inventory control, credit control of clients, surveys of training programmes of employees.

At the different levels in a company or institution, in the case of functionaries in different departments, three aspects in their task assignments have to be recognized. At their own level and within their own functional decision-making area this concerns: planning, execution of tasks, administration of company resources including reviews and checks afterwards. These aspects together form the 'control cycle'.

11.2.1 External reports and information

The external information supply from an organization is oriented at reporting to or at direct communication with groups and agencies outside the organization. It involves the annual report (*see* section 3.5), and quarterly report to shareholders, providing insight to the bank on the financial position of the company (balance sheet and profit and loss statement) in order to be able to negotiate credit facilities. This might also regard, for example, the provision of data on sales, cost development etc. to organizations of employers or sectoral organizations, or providing data on wages, sales, profits and so on to the taxation authorities in relation to payment of social securities and taxes.

11.2.2 Information supply and information needs

For the design of a management information system within an organization, two steps are important.

1. Determination of the information need. When one wants to determine what function the information will have to fulfil, it first needs to be clear what goals are served. For more information on this see the functional processes which are described in Chapter 12.
2. The supply of information as such. For healthy functioning of an organization, one should not only know the kind of information needed and its frequency, but also in what format managers need the information presented in their work in the organization.

For this purpose one has to know where in the organization the loci or points of decision are located and the issues about which decisions are taken at these points of decision.

11.2.3 Functional information systems (FIS)

Figure 11.3 shows, in relation to an organization, a 'federation' of functional information systems. On the one hand, the word 'federation' reflects the coherence between parts and on the other, the relative independence of the different functional company parts. The contents of FISs can be indicated as follows.

Minicase 11.2

For the supply of information it makes quite a difference whether, for example, at a certain point in the company policy decisions are made (for example about an investment in one of the foreign establishments), or operational decisions are taken (for example with regard to the choice of whether machine 90I will be involved with the product type 12A or 15C), or whether that information serves for the control of the manufacturing process or for the operational execution of assignments and reporting about it. In the first case, for example, information is needed about the economic and societal developments in that country; in the last case, an overview per product has to be available about the state of affairs with regard to the use of materials, production time, quality control and such. The second case demands insight into machine and personnel utilization, the course of orders, stock of final products, inventory in raw materials etc.

FIS–Purchase

Together with information given in Chapters 5, 10 and 12, this involves the following.

Strategic planning:
policy choice purchase markets;
policy choice with regard to the fact as to whether or not inventories are held;
policy choice distribution methods.

Tactical planning:
determining purchase conditions;
quota reservations with suppliers;
determination of inventory control variables;
determination of degree of service (total percentage of non/negative sales).

Operational management:
inventory control raw materials, components or parts, half fabrics (among which emballage), final product in total and per location;
analysis turnover, age, decay and dead stock, taking corrective measurements;
accounts payable registration, monitoring timely payments and realization of discounts;
accounts receivable registration, monitoring credit level, special collection measurements;
monitoring of delivery times of the purchases and sales.

Transactions:
purchase orders and calls;
purchase invoices;
sending announcement;
receiving and issuing of goods;
payment to suppliers;
transactions on futures markets;
sales orders and calls;
sending messages and documents;
final product storage and issuing;
sales invoices;
collecting from clients.

Definition problems arise from the specification of the above given contents. For example, in FIS Production, material calls and production announcements are mentioned. These are related to the Purchase (or logistic) function, including issuing goods, respectively final product storage. In the FIS Finance and registration, for example, cash/liquidity levels are registered. These can be seen in interrelation with transactions in the logistic events which directly influence the cash position, namely through payments to suppliers and collecting from clients.

FIS Production

Together with information given in Chapters 5, 10 and 12, this involves the following.

Strategic planning: long-term capacity prognosis/planning; policy choice new production technologies; new production organization and product innovation.

Tactical planning: utilization planning per production phase; choice of suppliers; documentation production process: routing, norm uses, to be used; support materials into sort and time occupation and norm times in man hours; determination of size of series, completion times, waiting times and levels of demanded inventories; assessment of effectiveness or manufacturing processes based on the analysis of production reports; determination of expansion and replacement investments in machinery.

Operational management: detail planning, work preparation and work dispatching; efficiency control: manufacturing reporting, analysis of actual uses and of actual occupation of materials based on norms and budgets.

Transactions: production assignments, assembly assignments; production announcements; material calls; material use announcements; man and machine hour registration; refuge reports; work-in-progress announcements.

Manufacturing means the processing of raw materials, components, materials or half fabrics to final products or services. When companies have diversified and/or geographically spread manufacturing activities, it is also important to express the 'intercompany' traffic in the system. The final product of one production unit then serves as raw material or as half fabric for another unit within the larger concern.

FIS Marketing and Sales

Together with information given in Chapters 5, 10 and 12, this involves the following.

Strategic planning: developments at sales markets; level of geographical spread, fashion/taste/need/trends;

	price developments; own and potential clients/customer file: composition, purchase power; technology, innovation aimed at competitors.
Tactical planning:	middle- long- and short-term market analysis compared with demand analysis; acquisition, sales promotion/stimulation; sales and comparable activities: absolute data, comparable figures, ratios, analysis; commercial results, market share.
Operational management:	allowable categories of clients; credibility prescriptions; payment and delivery conditions; price determination compared with price prescriptions; discount facilities; availability compared with deliverability of product or service: delivery or production term, reservations, order level; possibilities/norms for complementing inventory/capacity.
Transactions:	delivery contracts, production assignment or servicing request; original data concerning clients, products and services; data concerning used credit, contingency inventory, schedule or agenda room.

Minicase 11.3

Help, my data have disappeared ...

Automation? You should leave that to the experts. This is true, as long as everything goes according to plan. When you leave too much to others it can cost you dearly in cases of calamities. The continuation in automation has, in many cases, become a synonym for the continuation of the organization. So top management is and remains responsible.

Fire broke out in the office of a technical wholesale house, because of which the total administration, including the computers and their programs and files, was lost. Something general had been said about making back-up files, but no detail had been filled out, and no company management control was exercised on the back-up procedure. So there were no current inventory and order lists, no overview of accounts receivable and payable, no correspondence and internal reports – nothing was left.

To build up a decent administration from scratch took two months, not taking into consideration all the other inconveniences fire brings in its wake. Two months in which the commercial activities of the company were, necessarily, slow. The creditors were the easiest to trace: they announced themselves, because when something like this happens to a company, you never know ...

Dependency

Companies have become dependent on automation. Calamities in this area are marked in the annual figures. In the most severe cases, the continuation of the company is in danger. So there is an important reason to make the risk as small as possible.

continued overleaf

Minicase continued

A lot of companies are burgled. Automation equipment is placed high on the list of the thief. When a pc is stolen, all its data, on the hard disk, often representing a multiple of the value of the hardware, are taken along with it. In the case of fire, comparable risks occur: if the computer goes up, the data are lost too. Did you know, for instance, that data in a file can be damaged beyond repair when exposed to a temperature of only 55°C?

Continuation plan

An entrepreneur can be insured against fire and theft. But the loss of computer files is a non-insurable risk. That is why making back-up copies, at a frequency adjusted to the needs of the individual company, is the most important precaution which can be taken in every automation situation. But this measure should be part of a total continuation plan which comprises all aspects of the company automation. Here, four main areas can be distinguished:

1. the hardware;
2. the software, to be subdivided into system software, application software (applications) and supporting software;
3. the data, to be subdivided into internally produced data and datastreams from the outside;
4. the personnel.

A good continuation plan is based on risk analysis. This is not a simple matter, since there are quite a few situations, in different degrees of seriousness, in which the continuity of the automation is threatened. It is important that one learns to think about the 'what ... if ...' scenario.

Hardware

Hardware problems seem to be the most easily solvable. You can always buy a new pc and the accompanying equipment. But it is not that simple. The problem of software immediately pops up: in many new computers operations software has already been installed, but is it the same program, the same version the personnel are used to? Furthermore, it is useful to determine how your hardware is configurated and where exactly the components of that configuration can be bought. Even when it is only slightly different from before, problems can occur that might lead to stagnation in your automation.

Software

On the one hand software consists of standard programs, and on the other of applications which have been designed especially for one company. Here again distinction is made between independent programs written to the specification of a company, and tailorrmade work applications because of which the standard program serves as a platform.

Standard programs have to be configurated for a specific user situation, however, but they are relatively easy to replace; even so it is advisable to store official standard packages in such a place that in case of calamity they are directly at hand. For tailormade software which is unique, this holds to a greater degree. Process software not being available in time can mean a complete production process comes to a standstill for quite some time.

Data

There is one basic requirement in the case of datafiles which rises over everything, namely that back-up copies need to be made and saved somewhere else than within the company. When back-up copies are stored somewhere else in the building and the whole building burns down, you still have a problem. It makes sense to include a frequent printout of important lists in procedure beside the back-ups. This could be extended to include inventory files, a list with open entries (accounts receivable), client data, piece lists etc.

Together with the necessary cards and forms to be filled in by hand, these can see to it that, in case of calamity, the most important activities can be continued. In short, a kind of 'sleeping' manual shadow procedure.

Back-up procedure needs to be determined in detail with the inclusion of frequency, method followed, back-up file name, the place where copies are stored and the persons responsible. For this one can make use of the services of companies specialized in the continuity of automation.

It appears that the data traffic from, to and within many companies has almost become uncontrollable. Data are withdrawn from external databases, personnel members work at home and take the result of their work to the work place on disk, salesmen and maintenance engineers gather data while on the road via their laptop and send them to the company via a modem, and there are many other ways in which data are added to and/or retrieved from the company system.

The risk of viruses and undesired electronic peekers who snoop around in your system from the outside are unthinkable. Certainly good and trustworthy protection constructions are possible, but it has become a virtual competition between company automators who minimize the risk as well as possible and the hackers and virus inventors who bring their automation genius into battle to break through that protection. Companies that do not want to run too high a risk, will every now and then have to hire external experts.

The least management can do is to determine and implement within the organization rules and procedures for responsible data traffic.

People

Whether everything eventually occurs in the most desirable way, depends on the people involved in the automation. In a department of automation a lot of expertise should be present, but this may never result in a knowledge monopoly. You cannot make back-up copies from people, but a board needs to see to it that the principle 'nobody is indispensable' also holds for the automation personnel. Continuity in automation means especially continuity in people. The risk is too high to leave to coincidence what exactly should happen if your head automation person is overnight not available anymore.

Continuity via escrow

Every entrepreneur knows that a good relationship with the software supplier is essential. For he has delivered the programs by means of which complex administrative and production processes can unroll efficiently and undisturbed; he maintains those packages and expands them.

When an organization has trouble with its software, this has to be solved quickly. But when the software supplier falls short or, even worse, goes bankrupt? In that case the organization concerned has to be able to manage.

A so-called escrow agreement provides in such cases: it comes down to the fact that the supplier deposits the source codes of the programs which have been developed by him with a third party. When situations occur which are described in the escrow agreement, this third party makes the source codes available with the accompanying documentation and software to the user of the software.

Source: *BIZZ-Missers*, November 1994 (adapted).

FIS Personnel

Together with information given in Chapters 5, 8, 10 and 12, this involves the following.

Strategic planning:	information recruiting policy; information reward policy; information education and training policy (among with management development); analysis of developments in employment; analysis of the labour market: regional, national compared with international; analysis of external educational and training possibilities; analysis of national income policy (including secondary and tertiary labour conditions; analysis of mutations in the personnel file; assessment of present versus potential personnel file (into capabilities, functions).
Tactical planning:	analysis of differences in present planning versus budgeted personnel numbers; analysis of actual versus budgeted personnel costs; analysis of recruitment costs, education and training costs; structure of personnel datafile (career planning, capabilities, history of employment, performance appraisal, function description, educational data, personal data); administration of reward systems; collective labour contracts; administration of education and training programmes.
Operational management:	appointments, discharges, discharge requests, suspensions, change of fees, acknowledgement of special rewards, of special relief and of advances; suitable media for recruiting (print number, reader cycle, kind of advertisement, response to advertisements); recruitment actions; personnel costs to be accounted to cost places, projects, etc.; orders to be given to payment concerning fees, other personnel payments as well as remaining personnel costs.
Transactions:	work assignments; origin data of personnel members; norms, tables, calculation rules and legal prescriptions; appointment, discharge, suspension and change decisions; absenteeism announcements.

FIS Finance and Administration

Together with information given in Chapters 5, 10 and 12, this involves the following.

Strategic planning:	long-term prognosis concerning investment plans, property needs and flows of money (liquidity); long-term indications concerning tax developments, stimulating, limiting, compared with subsidy measures of the different governments;

	prognosis about capital and money market (loan and investment capacity, interest level); the annual report, i.e. balance sheet and profit and loss statement with, as enclosure, the explanation of these papers.
Tactical planning:	financial middle- long- and short-term planning estimations and budgets, for the whole as well as for parts of the organization; norms for the review and audit of activity levels; realized activities in reality, performance levels, production figures etc.; tariffs, cost prices, coverages, ratios of distribution, taxes etc.; return calculations, costs/revenues analysis; analysis of differences between budget compared with norm and reality, subdivided into periods, in cause, in kind of difference; short-term developments concerning liquidity, credit facilities, market interests and positions in foreign currencies.
Operational management:	short-term planning of financial administrative activities (including closing dates, delivery dates of data to computer centres, holiday schedule); activities reporting of remaining company functions (utilization reports, core figures); mutations in liquidity, foreign currency transactions/ positions; age of accounts receivable, statements; mistake, delay, disruption and other exception announcements in the financial-administrative function.
Transactions:	work assignment for execution of non-recurrent activities (e.g. drawing up inventories); coding prescriptions for the reducible financial and administrative transactions to the sums of money; work procedures and techniques/operational prescriptions for routine activities and the equipment/software which are to be handled here.

11.3 ● MANAGEMENT OF INFORMATION AS PRIMARY PRODUCTION FACTOR

Information is considered as a primary production factor as soon as it serves as input for the production or servicing process. This is, for example, the case in the banking and insurance industry. Seen in this way, information is more or less an independent factor alongside labour and capital. The following characteristics are assigned to information.

- Information is multi-functional (i.e. it can be combined, accumulated and transmitted).
- Information increases in value through processing and use.
- Information can be compressed by storage.

- Information can be spread and transported very quickly.
- Information technology can replace traditional resources.
- Information can generate new products and services.

The function of information can, so to speak, be compared to the function of red blood cells in a living organism. Information provokes actions, clarifies those actions and their result, and makes supervision and comparison of actions possible.

More and more often we encounter the statement that information and the processing of it are the central issue to the practice of the banking and insurance industries. The following statements clarify this. 'Money is information in motion.' 'Besides the flow of money, financial institutions lack a movement of goods. They primarily produce information and no physical goods.'

The bank and insurance company of the future is in the mean time still typified as industrialized servicing in the area of financial information services with active control of money and risks.

Good information supply is vitally important. Banks and insurance firms would not be able to survive where computer and information systems were not able to take care of the correct spread of the necessary information. Management of the information supply contributes to:

- helping accelerate production of services;
- seeing to on-line distribution of service;
- destilling information for management decisions;
- an economic saving in energy, resources and support resources.

In order to control the enormous flows of information as efficiently as possible, banks and insurance firms have developed many systems over time. The development in administrative control of company processes with the help of information technology can be grouped into four phases.

Phase 1: Use of transaction and settlement systems for the support of the back office (e.g., processing of giro credit slips, continuation processing on security, collecting).

Phase 2: Use of information systems for the support of the front office (e.g., overviews of accounts receivable files, of policies draw up, calculation of mathematical reserves).

Phase 3: Use of customer-oriented information systems (e.g., external links such as Electronic Banking, Assurance Data Network).

Phase 4: Use of information systems for management support. These systems have to generate information for the management (e.g., a marketing information system, credit control system, risk statistics per postal code, per car brand).

These phases need not be seen as completely sequential. Even though every organization starts with phase 1, it is possible to start phase 2 before all possibilities of phase 1 are used up. In that way similarly external links of systems arise (phase 3) without a completion of phases 1 and 2. It is obvious, however, that phase 2 only starts well into phase 1 and phase 3 comes into development only after the necessary systems and processes are operational.

11.4 INFORMATION PLANNING AND PLANNING OF AUTOMATION

When introducing information systems essential elements in management and administrative control must be taken into consideration. Despite large amounts of money which often accompany the development of information systems and information supply itself, organizations may not always develop plans with regard to information systems and automation. Planning is vital since it offers possibilities in an early stage to:

- signal information needs;
- define projects;
- set priorities;
- determine personnel and organizational consequences.

Systems function within an organization. The introduction of automation can thus be considered as a more or less interventional change within that organization. The further the degree of automation within an organization goes, the larger the influence on the organization and the people employed there.

Automation never stands alone, neither do systems. If we look at the necessary integration between different systems it can be seen that automation needs to be developed from a planned approach.

11.4.1 Information planning: objectives and their reasons

Information management has to be embedded in the total policy of the organization. The technological possibilities on the one hand, and the organizational needs and demands on the other have to be finely tuned. This compels organizations to determining a long-term vision, in which clear goals and constraints have been included. This activity is called information planning, and has two goals.

1. Tuning the information supply into the need of the organization.
2. Bringing coherence into information management.

In practice this means making a relationship between information strategy, reorganization policy and developments in information technology (IT). Based on this an information structure is defined which forms a stable starting-point for future developments. This relationship also serves as a starting-point for determining plans for the development of an information system and the effective use of technology.

An information plan is derived from the information policy (which forms a partial policy of the total organization policy and directs the IT supply). From the information plan, the separate automation plans are formulated, that, in turn, consist of different system development projects. In this, planning forms the activity and the plan is the product or result.

In this way, we descend from abstract to specific: from information policy, via information planning, to automation planning. In setting up information planning and an information plan it is important, considering the time orientation, to plan in any case, in the somewhat longer term, perhaps three years. Some issues should also be contemplated in advance. These include:

- applications and priority setting (based on costs, necessity and logic);
- involvement of general and functional management;
- organizational changes in the execution of the information plan;
- technical relationships (as desired 'business relationships') with the outside world.

11.4.2 Pitfalls and failures in automation

Organizations are often faced with disappointing results in automation and as a consequence, a considerable outlay of capital, with outcomes not in accordance with original expectations.

The pitfalls and failures in automation are indicated in Fig 11.4. These pitfalls and failures can be grouped into three categories:

- those in the management structure of projects;
- those in the way projects are started and planned;
- those in the way of working in the execution of projects.

In principle, all pitfalls and failures can be influenced by the management, automateurs and users; and hence directions for solution can be pointed out with which organizations can prevent or mend the pitfalls and failures.

Pitfalls and failures in the management structure

Even though every organization which automates claims to have a project organization at its disposal, in practice it is often unclear who is responsible and accountable for what. The consequence is that those involved are difficult to approach on their performances. Procedural disagreements arise and the quality of the intended final product is put at jeopardy.

Often the automateur has more affiliation with his own specialism than with the organization and often strives for a perfect system more than worrying about whether the system supports the goals of the user. Technical orientation of system developers can hinder effective communication with users and the management. The limited

Expectations	Outcomes
Working more efficiently	Exceeding of planning and budget
Operating more flexibly	Unsatisfied users
Quality improvement	Bad acceptance
Better management information	Unintended side-effects
Better work circumstances	Premature termination
Faster communication	Worsened working climate
Competitive advantage	

Source: After Florijn *et al.*, 1993

Fig 11.4 ● Pitfalls and failures in automation at the fault line of expectations and outcomes

insight of the users into the possibilities and more particularly the limitations of the computer, contributes to an ever more yawning communication gap between the parties. Because many managers follow projects at a distance, technical arguments are decisive and if organizational and company aspects remain underexposed, the rest of the organization does not understand the outcome or does not recognize its place in it. The so-called 'gallery behaviour' (in this case of the management) ends up with the users dropping off.

Skimping on the composition of project teams leads to allowing an automation project, in which a new way of working is being designed, to be executed by automateurs: this is the guarantee of problems.

There is always resistance to change of the trusted and routine way of working. Due to there being insufficient information about goals and the consequences of the automation project, resistance remains. Ineffective use and lack of motivation in learning to use/handle a new system can be the consequences.

So conditions for the success of a project are located in:

- a clear task definition and definition of responsibility;
- involvement of management in drawing up the plan;
- representation of employees and clear goal formulation by management.

Pitfalls and failures in the start up and planning of projects

First of all one must face the fact that total commitment of all those involved is probably a utopian dream. Not everyone has the same interests. Apart from that many projects are initiated from a technological/telematic point of view, without a thorough analysis previously having taken place. Besides the complexity the vision of automation processes is confused by the tendency to run blindly after the newest technological developments.

Pitfalls in the way of working and method

An unsatisfactory result can also be caused by the use of an incorrect working method, development philosophy or project method. In practice the following ways of working are encountered.

Automation is seen as the technological solution to a business problem. By insufficient contential contribution of managers and employees in the system development project, one can speak of insufficient or wrong functionality: 'The computer does not do as we say.'

Striving for complete automation without a correct cost/revenue assessment will lead to a situation where every 'exceptional situation' has to be included, because of which the system becomes untenable.

One consciously does not choose for one's own problems, but almost without question takes over methods from external consultancy firms. Because of this the information supply in the organization will never obtain its own identity but the standard per project which is pre-determined by the system.

In the development of an automated information system, direction is towards the functionality of the system with little regard paid to the consequences of its introduction on the quality of work of the employees, for the design of tasks and functions or for the structure of organizational units and departments.

Exhibit 11.1

System failure

An insurer's new computer network does not live up to the claims made for it

Peter Howard, UK customer services director of Swiss-owned European Life Assurance Company, decides he has been too soft on Gerry Donnell, sitting opposite him in his office. Since the Swiss group bought the company two years ago, £2 million (ECU 2.6 million) has been invested in a computer system to speed up and reduce the cost of processing applications for new policies. Donnell was one of the architects of the new system, and as a reward, Howard appointed him to manage the customer service department.

So far, the results have been disappointing, and the new owners are asking, not unreasonably, where the promised improvements in productivity and customer service are to be found.

In fact, Donnell has come to the meeting hoping to persuade Howard to allow a 15% increase in his clerical staff. In spite of the new system, his department faces three weeks' backlog of work, and it is rising at the rate of a week a month. He feels he has tried everything. 'I can't push my staff any harder, Peter. They're already demotivated by the pressure.'

'But you promised a 5% productivity gain to justify buying that computer system. You've got the same staff as last year, and the workload is very little different. You should be reducing your headcount by now, not asking to raise it.'

Patiently, Donnell explains that the productivity management system he installed last year along with the order-processing system measures units of various types of customer query resolved by each member of his team per hour. Over a week, individuals can be monitored, and Donnell is proud that as a result, there are few underperformers. Even if these are eliminated, however, the productivity problem remains.

He has to admit that by his own measures, performance has declined since the new system was introduced. Units of correspondence resolved per hour are down from six to five, and the staff complain that queries are becoming more difficult to resolve. 'You've seen for yourself, Peter, that everyone is kept busy. You can't expect them to work any harder.'

Howard is not convinced. Why should customers' problems suddenly have become more complex? With the new database and processing systems, providing answers for straightforward queries should be immediate, and communication within the department over more complex ones swifter.

The question is whether the staff have a sufficient sense of urgency. Perhaps Donnell is not up to the job after all.

Source: International Management, September 1993.

11.4.3 Automation, informatization and organization

In section 11.3 four phases were distinguished with regard to the control and controllability of company processes in financial institutions. At the level of automation, in phase 1 this regards the replacement of operational work by machine labour, in phase 2 the use of data for producing more refined management information and in phases 3 and 4 the linking of one's own automated system to internal and other automated systems (i.e. 'external links').

In phase 1, one part of the operational work disappears. Human labour is replaced by machine. The nature of the operational work also changes. The consequence of that is that fewer people (especially middle management) are necessary. More generally stated, automation of operational work can lead to a flatter organization: to an organization with a lesser number of hierarchical levels.

The consequences of phases 2 and 4, that is the use of automation for production of better information for the front office and management, are totally different. This development to an extent supports the development in phase 1; less middle management demands other methods of process control; the automated processes allow the production of quantitative and qualitative data about process processing. Because of this, higher management no longer needs oral or written reports from middle management.

The consequences of phase 3, the linking of systems between separate organizations, are difficult to estimate. In the first instance, this still concerns matters which lie in the field of the payment traffic, transmittance of collected data, etc. This development is accelerated when links start to be of importance all across the line of sector chains. In the insurance industry, this chain is rather short. In the chain from consumer via intermediary to the insurer, an authorized intermediary can be between them as an extra link. In the case of 'direct writing', however, the intermediary as link is missed out. In general, phase 3 will be directed at reducing the number of administrative actions linked to intermediaries acting in the chain of activities.

Minicase 11.4

In the 1970s and 80s, automation among insurers was especially directed at the existing ways of working. The way of working was not changed. Thus, at the moment, most insurers are convinced of the fact that their organization has to be restructured. 'Transformation' and 'BPR' are the magic words. A large number of insurance companies are restructuring their primary process with the help of BPR (=Business Process Redesign).

11.5 INFORMATION TECHNOLOGY

The essence of IT is situated in the integrated use of advanced technology to link the different activities of an organization. IT influences information planning and activities of companies and institutions to a high degree, for example, in the case of banks and insurance firms.

In the financial services sector the conditions for application are often come across.

- Many activities of financial servicers lend themselves very well to automation because many processes are routine and standardized.
- A considerable amount of the traditional paper mountain can be replaced by automated input and storage.
- Many processes are, with regard to the number of sequential activities, sufficiently complex to justify the help of computers: credit granting process, risk assessment process, etc.
- Compared to past manual or even mechanical procedures, the use of a computer makes a difference in terms of time and energy.
- By the positive 'time effect' and the reduction in the number of mistakes, IT meets the standards and criteria of cost/revenue analysis. Especially where the youngest generation of computers and information systems is concerned. These can be brought into action swiftly and are more decentralized and flexible than their predecessors.

Exhibit 11.2

Publishers warned on electronics 'gap'

Traditional publishers could face great commercial danger if they hold back from entering the world of electronic publishing, a study by Andersen Consulting for the European Commission warns.

'For the majority of publishers electronic publishing is necessary to sustain long term survival and success,' the study says. The findings on the future of the total print industry in Europe, currently worth 85bn Ecu ($68bn), will be unveiled today at a press conference at the Frankfurt Book Fair.

Electronic publishing will not be a substitute for print but will become a strategic cornerstone for the industry's economic survival within the next five to eight years and an indispensable supplement by the year 2002, says the study.

'The risk for those who hesitate in starting an EP venture is that it will be increasingly difficult and expensive to make up for lost time once markets are further developed,' Andersen Consulting says. The strategy of postponing necessary investment is 'dangerous'.

At the outset, traditional publishers are well placed to take advantage of the technological opportunities offered by EP. But increasingly players from other industries such as computing, financial services and communications will enter the market in the hope of increasing sales in the emerging interactive services industry.

Andersen Consulting estimates that the electronic publishing share of the print market by the year 2000 will range between 3 per cent and 15 per cent depending on the type of publication and the speed of consumer acceptance.

The report makes a series of detailed recommendations on what the strategy should be for different sections of the print industry.

Local newspapers, for example, should concentrate on becoming the dominant local 'electronic marketplace'. Booksellers should build an innovative image by having Internet cafes in their stores and by becoming the local access point for electronic products.

Fear about security was the main obstacle to wider adoption of Internet technology among UK government organisations, according to a survey carried out for Mercury Communications.

The survey of 220 government officials by the research firm Kable found that three-quarters of those who use the Net have been doing so for more than six months, but only 28 per cent of users have a distinct security policy.

Source: Financial Times, 1 October 1996.

11.5.1 Strategic importance of IT

By IT strategy we mean the strategic/tactical decisions with regard to all applications of IT. Stated in a different way: the application of IT in the office as well as factory, that is both final product and external servicing are concerned.

With regard to information technology, three directions can be distinguished which are of strategic importance:

- cost control;
- service improvement;
- product innovation.

A low cost price is an important factor in the competitive position. Processes move faster and fewer mistakes are made because of more efficient working. This in turn provides lower costs. The cheapest supplier can win market share from the competitor. The quality of products and the process of servicing is enlarged, while the productivity increases. By means of the added value of a higher degree of service, a lot can be achieved thanks to IT. Furthermore employees gain a more complete contact with the outside world.

A third application of IT is in the development of products and distribution methods. The customer has specific needs and, regarding the costs, these are not always met via the present distribution method. Use of IT can bring about a change in that situation with more suitable products and service level.

Exhibit 11.3

Smartcards and the world market

FT

Smartcard market size

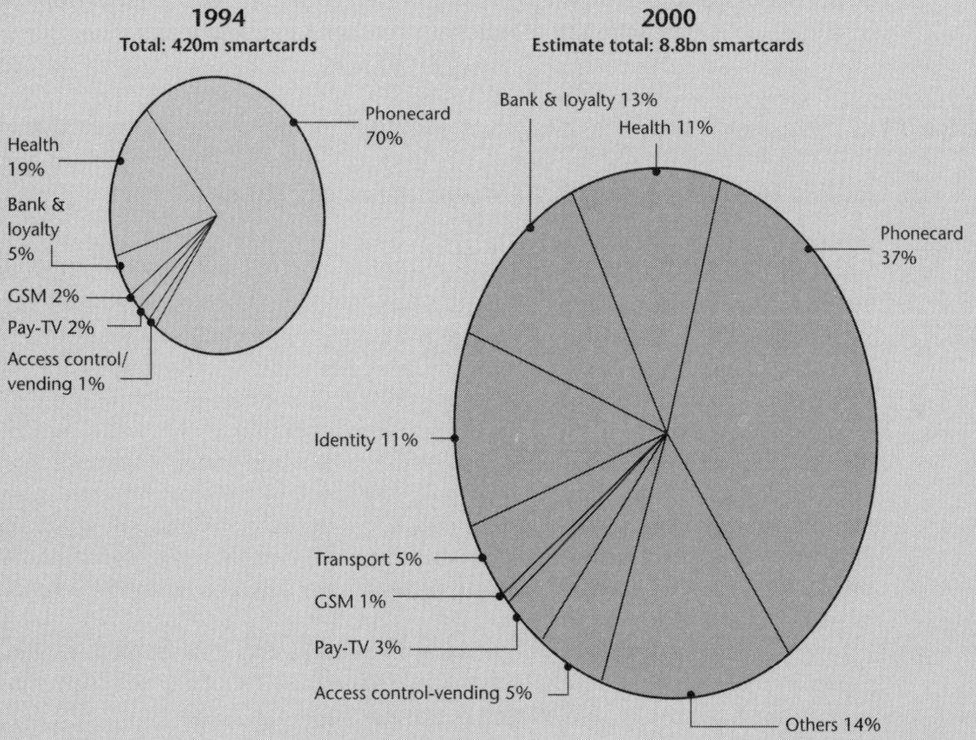

1994
Total: 420m smartcards

Phonecard 70%
Health 19%
Bank & loyalty 5%
GSM 2%
Pay-TV 2%
Access control/vending 1%

2000
Estimate total: 8.8bn smartcards

Bank & loyalty 13%
Health 11%
Phonecard 37%
Identity 11%
Transport 5%
GSM 1%
Pay-TV 3%
Access control-vending 5%
Others 14%

Source: Datamonitor, Gemplus.

Worldwide chipcard revenues*

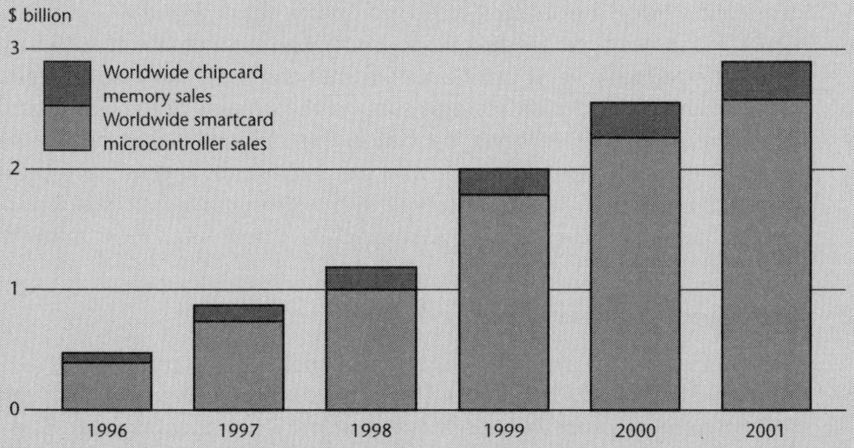

$ billion

3
2
1
0

Worldwide chipcard memory sales
Worldwide smartcard microcontroller sales

1996 1997 1998 1999 2000 2001

*Forecasts

Source: Dataquest

Source: *Financial Times*, 2 October 1996.

Influence of automation on competitive relationships

In the strategic respect and paying attention to competitive relationships, the influence of automation can be divided into three aspects, namely: line of business or sector; company; and strategy. The changes on sector level are critical according to findings from research: automation changes the rules with regard to economy of scale, entrance barriers, competition and competitive relationships. Larger organizations are, for example, capable of shifting their distribution from regional to national and even international level.

Minicase 11.5

Police in Hong Kong take computers off Internet

Hong Kong, March 5, 1995 (Reuter)

Yesterday, with the help of the local postal and telephone service, the Hong Kong Police cut about ten thousand computer users off the Internet. This happened after raids in eight of the nine organizations which supply access to the computer network.

Users in trade and industry as well as private users were shocked at the action of the police who were accused of intentionally hindering the free flow of information.

According to a police spokesman, the action was necessary in the battle against the so-called hackers, who, via Internet, break into company computers in Hong Kong. The business world states, however, that the police had become the tool of the one organization that was not raided. This one was, until lately, the only one from whom one could purchase access to the Internet. The arrival of new suppliers, however, has caused a real price war in the past months, because of which the flow of users onto the Internet increased explosively.

Lawyers in Hong Kong say that the police are not authorized to cut off the communication lines of thousands of inhabitants just like that. The telephone company was also acting against the law by co-operating with the police.

At the organizational level there are myriad examples: strategic purchase and supplier information offers advantages, as do 'computer aided manufacturing' and robot techniques. Insurance firms are directly dependent on their degree of automation.

At the strategic level it can be shown that the most successful organisations have information systems which strongly support the strategy of the organization.

From many sources, however, the conclusion repeatedly emerges that the influence of automation and of new techniques have been rather slight until now, because top management has not really become involved with it. Reasons vary: from lack of understanding to fear of the implications and the risks which may occur from those implications.

11.5.2 IT, business processes and redesign

To an increasing degree companies and institutions try to structure their work processes as efficiently as possible. The advantages connected to this can only be realized when new processes, organization and IT are combined. The IT function determines technology, applications, user level and IT management. The process design is directed at quality, flexibility and cost level. The organization is directed at control structure, culture and expertise. These factors must be in balance.

Minicase 11.6

An example of process redesign looks at the credit granting process.

Credit granting knows many risk groups: from small private credits to large company credits. Often the structure of the system for processing various credit forms is the same. It could yield large savings, however, if, in this case, distinctiveness was brought into the processes. Advantages can be attained when simple credit is structured in a simple way. Banks which do this consistently save 50% in time and costs. Here, IT provides the possibility to restructure the processes.

Another example regards an insurance company. In the old situation, policies were processed in sequential linked company processes in functionally separated departments. The policies were brought in by intermediaries. The processing takes place with technically and functionally old systems. The consequences of this are:

- higher costs, accounted for via a higher contribution;
- longer completion times, resulting in a worse service;
- more mistakes, also resulting in a worse service.

In the new situation 90% of customer contacts are handled directly by one person; because of that, the number of mistakes is reduced and the completion time is shorter. Routine matters are handled by a completely automated system. This results in fewer mistakes and work at a higher level.

The information technology which makes this possible comprises a system which reads in policy and damage data once and makes these data available to all employees in need of them. Employees are included in teams which execute all activities for clients. The better, automated support leads to a more varied task package for employees.

11.5.3 Organizational consequences of IT

IT has different consequences for the organization. In the strategy determination as well as in the personnel management rapid development of IT plays an important part. There are three consequences for the organization here.

1. Further customer orientation and direction.
2. Delayering.
3. Decentralization.

Under the influence of the mature consumer, tougher competition and technological possibilities, companies and institutions will have to direct their information systems more at the outside world. The internal systems will have to be structured more with the client as starting-point and the network will have to be reserved primarily for the improvement in communication with the outside world. The direct customer-oriented function becomes of great importance.

Computer networks have an intrinsic influence on the relationships and the assignment of work and tasks in an organization. Experiences from practice show that with the introduction of networks, a layer in the organization disappears. A 'layer' can be: inventories, warehouses, middle management or a link in the distribution chain. Through the network an intermediary can have access to customers and products and, with the help of a network there is direct dealing with the client, and the 'old' links disappear.

There is a noticeable influence of highly developed IT on the degree of decentralization. On the one hand, IT enables the organization to make good, current information available to the employees at lower levels. Through that, those employees are better enabled to take decisions, because of which their relative autonomy is enlarged.

It is possible to spread employees geographically with terminals in branch offices where all computations are conducted. This is in line with the 'profit centre' thought. Decentralization within the main office is also possible. Computers in departments are connected to the central network, so users have a high degree of autonomy, provided they adhere to the centrally determined procedures.

On the other hand, IT also enables the organization to report back to higher levels, sometimes almost in 'real time', what happens at lower levels and to inform them of developments – through this, in principle, the possibility of protecting the decentralized authorities remains.

SUMMARY

- Information supply is compared to the function the nervous system fulfils in the human organism. By means of that, all parts are connected to a whole, so that in mutual co-ordination and tuning observed signals can be reacted to. First of all information is important for employees and managers in order to be able to take well-considered decisions. In addition, information is the input of a servicing or production process: this is why information management has a two-sided character.
- The concept of 'information' has been analysed in its different aspects, namely: the syntactic, semantic, pragmatic and technical. The different functional differences have been covered and the importance of good management information has been stressed.
- Information is also seen as primary production factor.
- Based on experiences in practice, attention has been paid to pitfalls and failures in automation projects. Knowledge of these factors can possibly contribute to the prevention of the same 'mistakes' in the future.
- Information has become a strategic factor, which is why, in the framework of total organization policy, an organization has to develop information policy. Then from information policy, sequentially the information plan and automation planning are derived.
- The use of advanced information technology, and the rapid development in that, have strategic consequences for the societal and market environment (competitive relationships) and for the internal organizational environment (organizational consequences).

DISCUSSION QUESTIONS

1. With reference to *Management in action* at the beginning of this chapter: What strategic, organizational and operational changes would you indicate as being the consequences of the application of IT?

2. What requirements are there with regard to information supply?
3. What steps can be identified in the setting up of the managerial information supply?
4. In the case of management information systems, why do we sometimes speak of a 'federation' of information systems?
5. Can you name the pitfalls and failures in automation which are caused by the managerial structure of projects?
6. Is informal information a part of the management information system, or not?
7. (a) What would you advise Gerry Donnell to do in the 'System Failure' case (p560) to allow the organization to live up to the claims of the new computer network?
   (b) How would you go about encouraging staff to set its own new targets?

Management case study

Rotterdam: Information Main Port

'Rotterdam Information Main Port' stands out in the brochure of the Municipal Port Administration, the administrator of the largest port in the world. Information Port does not mean that Rotterdam now parades itself as a transit port for information besides oranges and iron ore, but that increasingly the port is making use of information technology. 'Rotterdam cannot afford to think and invest only in the physical infrastructure.'

Rotterdam Port comprises almost 3000 directly port-connected companies, that is: companies located on the territory of Rotterdam Port. Rotterdam Port is responsible for 238 000 labour years and 50 billion Dutch guilders, or rather, about 10% of the Gross National Product. Directly, 70 000 people work in the port, with total employment around 300 000. With the justice system, Rotterdam Port can be called the pivot in the Dutch economy.

Four cornerstones

The Rotterdam Port has four important cornerstones.

- *Chemistry.* All large chemical industries have establishments in Rotterdam and together they process 140 million tons of oil and oil products per year.
- *Containers.* Per year the container port processes almost three million containers. By 2010 this amount will have doubled.
- *Distribution.* Many multinationals distribute their products from Rotterdam. Rotterdam has three 'Distreparcs' and twelve trade and distribution centres.
- *Food and fruit.* Thirty million tons of food go through Rotterdam Port per year. A large part of the food is prepared in the port for consumption.

The infrastructure covers a large surface, and when the hinterland is included a large part of the urban agglomeration must be added to the processing area of Rotterdam Port.

Infrastructures pre-eminently become visible in a port: the transport of goods over water, road and rail is an impressive sight. The 'wet' infrastructure (that is: all waterways and wharves) is the property of the local authority of Rotterdam, just as is traffic control and radar system. In the flow of goods into Rotterdam many parties are involved: in one move six or seven companies are at work. The visible infrastructure is accompanied

continued overleaf

Management case study continued

increasingly by an 'invisible' infrastructure: an information flow belongs with the flow of goods with many parties.

Until 1990 initiatives for improving infrastructure were directed physically. In addition to that a new dimension arises in which competitive pressure demands a further linkage of all those involved in Rotterdam Port. This does not only mean investment in better waterways, roads and air and rail connections/links, but also in information technology, organization and telecommunications.

The Municipal Port Administration Rotterdam

How is the Port of Rotterdam organized? In all large world ports a Port Authority exists, but this is arranged differently everywhere. Singapore, for example, is a state port where everything is prescribed by the government. The containers are transshipped by the state, the state is the stevedore. In Rotterdam, for over sixty years, the Municipal Port Authority Rotterdam exists, an independent governmental authority which serves the interests of all those involved in the Port of Rotterdam. The Municipal Port Authority Rotterdam has to get the thousands of small and large companies into line. Standardization is one of those common interests which nobody takes up independently. Here, the Port Authority can steer the way. The long-term and the competitive positions are monitored. The government authority tunes employment, environment and safety into one another.

INTIS

One of the first information technology projects in the Port of Rotterdam was INTIS. When it was founded in 1985, the necessity existed to simplify communication between the companies in the port and outside. The initiative came to a dead end at the end of the 1980s. INTIS became a general software house and something new happened: trade and industry and government played into each other's hands. That is why INTIS transformed itself into a commercial organization which is now the 'electronic main post office' of the Port of Rotterdam. More and more parties in the Rotterdam Port communicate with each other electronically and INTIS intermediates in that process.

The services of INTIS are:

- conversion of networks (PTT, Telex, IBM, General Electric);
- converting message files (EDIfact, ANSI, X.12);
- cutting and pasting messages (messages are sent to customs, to company X, company Z);
- allowing parties to look into each others databases (the electronic showwindow in which companies can display their products and special offers); this now still occurs by fax, but in future all can be done electronically.

Competitors of INTIS are welcome and some are there already. It is not who offers the service that is important, as long as companies make use of information technology.

Electronic announcing

Every year 33 000 sea ships visit the Port of Rotterdam. From every sea ship, the Municipal Port Authority receives a number of announcements about ship movements, declaration of sea port money and transport of dangerous materials. Per year, more than 300 000 announcements are transmitted by skippers and ship brokers. In total, 200 kinds of announcements can be distinguished. Most of the announcements come in by mail, fax or telephone, but since 1993 it has been possible to announce ship movements and dangerous materials electronically.

The Municipal Port Authority has stimulated this by putting terminals and software at the disposal of the skippers and ship brokers and also by giving them eduction/training. Via a modem and telephone line, the software makes connections with the central 'electronic post office'. Messages can be left there and confirmations of reception can be collected. Disadvantages of the traditional method are that messages by fax are sometimes difficult to read, mistakes can be made in the announcements by telephone and that the mail sometimes arrives too late. Electronic announcement prevents a lot of these problems. Besides that the equipment delivered by the companies can be used for other purposes.

'Smartcard'

'Smartcard' is an important project of the future. Now it is a problem to follow loads. This can be solved with the help of chipcard technology: very many data can be stored on a chipcard which are nowadays taken along on paper. The 'smartcard' enables unique identification. In a few seconds a map reader can retrieve and check all data. Per year, 50 000 truck drivers come into the port. One cannot send along a container with a truck driver just like that. At the moment verification occurs by means of paper and physical checks (stamps). Sometimes a truck driver may have to wait two hours for a stamp before he is on his way again.

Twenty parties are involved in this project: large companies, transporters and ship brokers. In the first instance, the 'smartcard' directs itself at handling in the port. Later that same card can be used internally within companies. Certainly in the case of containers carrying many different products, the 'smartcard' will mean a vast simplification. The intention is that this system is operative by 1997 and it will make an important contribution to the information infrastructure in the Port of Rotterdam.

The technique of the 'smartcard' is already there: that is not the problem. For the Port of Rotterdam, identification of goods is particularly an organizational problem due to the large number of parties involved.

Source: *Management and Information*, September 1994 (adapted).

CASE QUESTIONS

1. Is information a production factor in the Port of Rotterdam?
2. What are the strategic possibilities of advanced information technology for the port company?
3. Is 'Rotterdam Information Main Port' a technical or organizational problem?

Chapter 12

Managerial process control: functional processes and process redesign

LEARNING OBJECTIVES

After studying this chapter, you should be able to:

- describe the essence of control in the process model of an organization;
- distinguish the different kinds of processes within the total of company activities;
- clarify the notion of the 'value chain';
- describe different functional processes in the case of manufacturing and servicing processes;
- describe what is meant by process redesign;
- state the characteristics and goals of redesign/re-engineering as influenced by information technology.

Management in action

How to gain a 'global' view of the business

Retailers have long used IT to boost efficiency and cut costs, but now they want to unlock the potential of technology to create a more customer-focused retailing model.

Systems integration seeks to break down information barriers, allowing retailers to pull data together to obtain a truly 'global' view of their business.

Acquisitions, multiple store formats and shortsighted investments in the past have left most retailers with a mish-mash of hardware and software 'whose whole is too often less than the sum of its parts'. The drawbacks of such systems become more apparent as retailers try to shift from an essentially paper-based culture to an integrated online environment better suited to today's fast-changing trading conditions.

'Systems integration is always an issue when you try to build a common platform,' says Jonathan Eales, the IT services controller at Woolworths, the retail group in the UK.

'Not long ago we had just a mainframe – now we also have five IBM AS/400 computer systems, a Tandem data warehouse and a number of networks.'

Integrating these different systems to work well together has proved a challenge – 'it's no good having a super data warehouse if you don't have a good system to actually deliver the merchandise or stock-tracking systems in stores,' he says. Many retailers want to move from mainframe-centred systems to distributed client-server environments that offer greater flexibility and allow powerful applications to run at both head office and store levels.

'The future is client-server with data available to all applications and a data warehouse at the heart,' says Eales.

Systems integration plays a key role in enabling this transition and it has become an attractive market for IT vendors as margins are usually higher than those from selling hardware. Olivetti was one of the first to enter the market, helped by the fact that it never made mainframes and thus had to learn to integrate its store systems into mainframe systems of other vendors.

ICL Retail Systems also emphasises its experience in multivendor environments and has a dedicated Retail Integration Centre in the UK.

IBM starts with the advantage that most retailers have an IBM mainframe, though it now claims to have the systems integration skills to help retailers maximise their technology investments regardless of source.

In the past, retail systems were designed to automate a particular function with scant regard to their wider impact or future needs.

For example, supermarkets originally installed electronic point-of-sale (Epos) scanners to automate ordering. Now, many are discovering the hidden value of their Epos data – for detailed analysis of seasonal buying patterns, for example – but their current systems do not let them fully exploit this rich information source.

'At the moment, we can't analyse the Epos data,' says Rolf Wild, an IT manager with Migros Genossenschaft, part of Swiss retail group Migros. It has invested heavily in front-of-store technology, installing ICL Epos scanners and ISS400 store management software. The terminals can handle foreign currency and electronic purses, while customers in rural areas, who cannot get to a bank, can withdraw cash without making a purchase.

In contrast with the in-store innovation, the central IT functions have lagged behind. Migros is now trying to catch up by building an Oracle-based data warehouse to allow head office staff to analyse Epos data. The company wants its new system to integrate with existing and future applications.

'We built the application programming interfaces before we built the system. This means we can put in another system without having to start from scratch,' says Rolf Wild.

continued overleaf

Management in action continued

Several software houses have developed applications to integrate store-level functions previously handled separately.

CounterPoint, from the US firm Synchronics, is an example of this new breed of tightly integrated packages and it covers the full range of retail functions, from Epos handling and order processing to inventory management and credit card processing. It also has modules to handle electronic mail, labelling and the special needs of fashion retailers. The software runs under Dos or Unix.

Nevada Bob's, a worldwide chain of golf shops, is installing CounterPoint on IBM's SureOne PC-based Epos terminals in all its US stores. The aim is to centralise Epos operations and automate stock replenishment by linking Nevada Bob's suppliers to the Epos terminals.

Another example of tightly integrated software comes from Schedule Works, a UK firm. Its Integrated Service Management System optimises staff scheduling in stores, so improving customer service and reducing staff costs. ISMS can cope with the complex shift patterns typical in retailing and integrate with a central payroll system, so reducing the need for head-office staff to manually process time sheets.

Store managers can forecast customer traffic and schedule staff to match the varying traffic during the day. The latest module in ISMS uses video cameras to count customers in the store and compare them with predicted traffic, so giving early warning when checkout queues are likely to form, for example. The video-based system was recently installed in a branch of Savacentre hypermarket, part of the Sainsbury group.

'The technology has not been available to measure store performance, so for years nobody knew anything about what customers were doing in stores,' says Michael Buckley, marketing manager at Schedule Works.

A central aim of ISMS is to give managers real-time snapshots of how the store is performing throughout the trading day.

'Key performance indicators', such as sales per hour worked, are displayed graphically on a PC. Warning messages flash when service levels drop or costs rise. Managers can be kept informed on the store floor using one of the new generation of multifunctional mobile computers for retailers, such as IBM's SurePoint.

The SurePoint is pen-based handheld device that allows managers to obtain information about the store's operations via a wireless network.

Alternatively, sales staff can use the terminal to make order enquiries for customers and process complete orders, thanks to the SurePoint's Epos functions, while an integrated scanner allows inventory management.

The ultimate in integrated software comes from the UK software house, Business Development. Fashion Yield is a suite of programs that aims to cover all the needs of a fashion store, from buying and design to merchandising and property management.

The modular software runs under Windows and can integrate with a retailer's existing accounting, Epos, stock control and executive information systems.

One module optimises merchandise management using Epos sales data, while another improves project planning and budget tracking for store refurbishments and other projects.

Fashion Yield also has two applications designed specifically for fashion retailers. The first, Yield Collage, allows buyers to view and organise garment designs and fabric swatches captured using digital cameras or scanned images.

Images can be captured on foreign buying trips using a notebook computer and transmitted back to head office via the Internet. This speeds decisions and shortens time to market – particularly important for fashion retailers. The second module, Yield Display, is aimed at visual merchandisers and allows non-artists to produce images of proposed store layouts using virtual reality techniques.

Merchandise images can be dragged and dropped on to display units and the visual impact judged from different angles by 'walking through' the virtual store.

Source: *Financial Times*, 2 October 1996.

INTRODUCTION

In this chapter the central issue is managerial process control. Structures need to stimulate the flow and progress of processes. When the 'natural' course of functional processes in an organization breaks down and the processes do not flow flexibly into each other, those processes need to be remapped.

In companies and institutions, all kinds of problems come up and decisions have to be taken based on available internal and external information. When the decisions in an organization are reduced to a few main subjects, these are usually decisions about:

- the positioning of an organization (=external tuning, positioning and adaptation);
- the organizational structure (=structuring/design);
- the daily operational process arrangements (=internal tuning and adaptation).

In Chapter 5, the first main subject has been studied in depth. In Chapters 6 and 7, the organizational structure of companies and institutions has been discussed. In Chapters 8, 9, 10 and 11, the daily operational process arrangements were discussed. We conclude this part about the daily operational process arrangement by giving a more detailed insight into different company processes. In that aspect, process control is always the most important matter. First we will pay attention to the essence of managerial process control; then different business processes will be mapped out. Starting-points can be found in Chapters 10 and 11, where methods and techniques for planning, management of action and information supply came up for discussion. Apart from that, this also offers starting-points for redesign of business processes. Here, one can state that the principle of process control, and using processes in the design of the organization as a starting-point, is an old thought. The method of redesign can, however, be regarded as 'new'.

12.1 ● PROCESS MODEL OF AN ORGANIZATION

With respect to the operational functions in an organization, the process of management and organizing fulfils a steering function. In the operational manufacturing processes, an actual transformation of the resources from the environment takes place. In other words, in manufacturing processes and processes of servicing, the technical transformation takes place and value is added, after which products or services are made available to the environment. This process is schematically depicted in Fig 12.1.

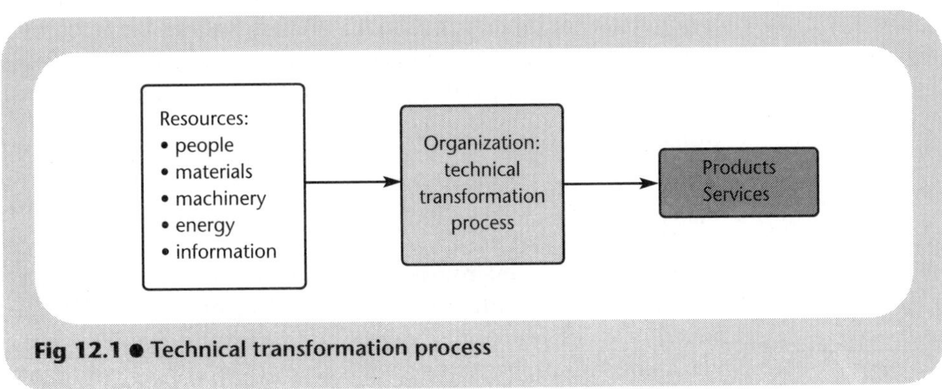

Fig 12.1 ● Technical transformation process

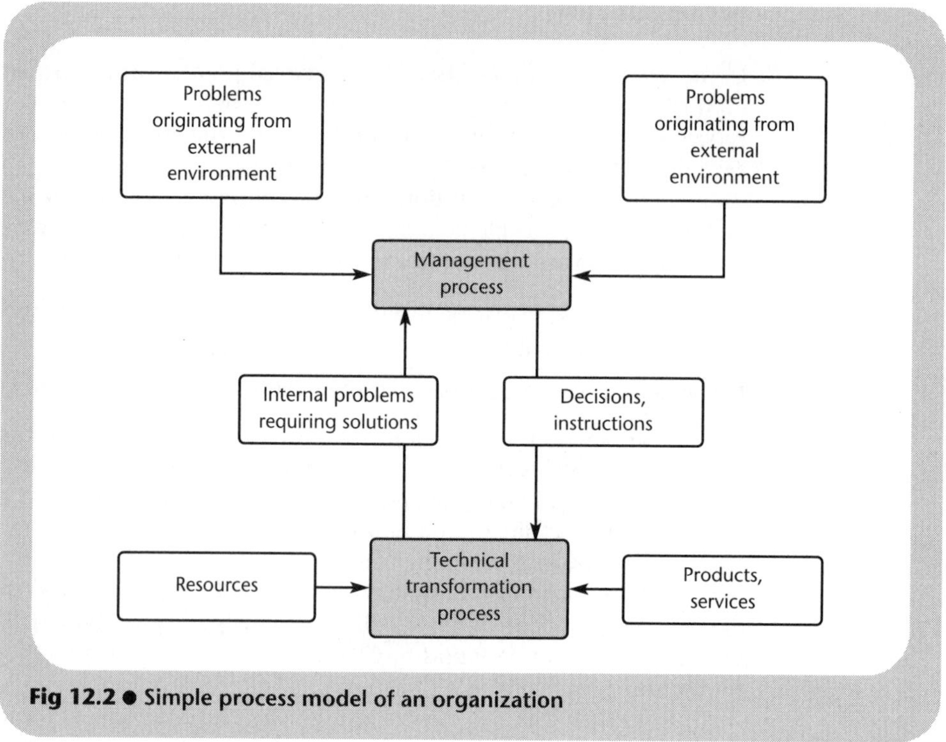

Fig 12.2 ● Simple process model of an organization

So in the technical transformation process, for example, screws are made or cars manufactured and in various processes of servicing, credits are granted, patients are taken care of or reports written.

These operational processes are managed from the process of management in which decisions are made about what products will be supplied or what services offered, and about how, by whom and where actions will be conducted. This flow of thought has been depicted in a schematic presentation in Fig 12.2.

12.2 ● A MORE DETAILED PROCESS MODEL

In other words, management process is in a steering relationship respect to the primary operational processes or main processes in an organization. This is shown in Fig 12.3 in a more detailed schematic presentation.

In the meantime, the following processes have been distinguished:

- primary or main processes;
- secondary or supporting processes;
- managerial or regulating and conditioning processes.

Primary processes or main processes comprise the activities which make a direct contribution to the coming about of a product or a service, for example: purchase, production, sales. Stated differently: the primary processes are those processes from which an organization derives its existence.

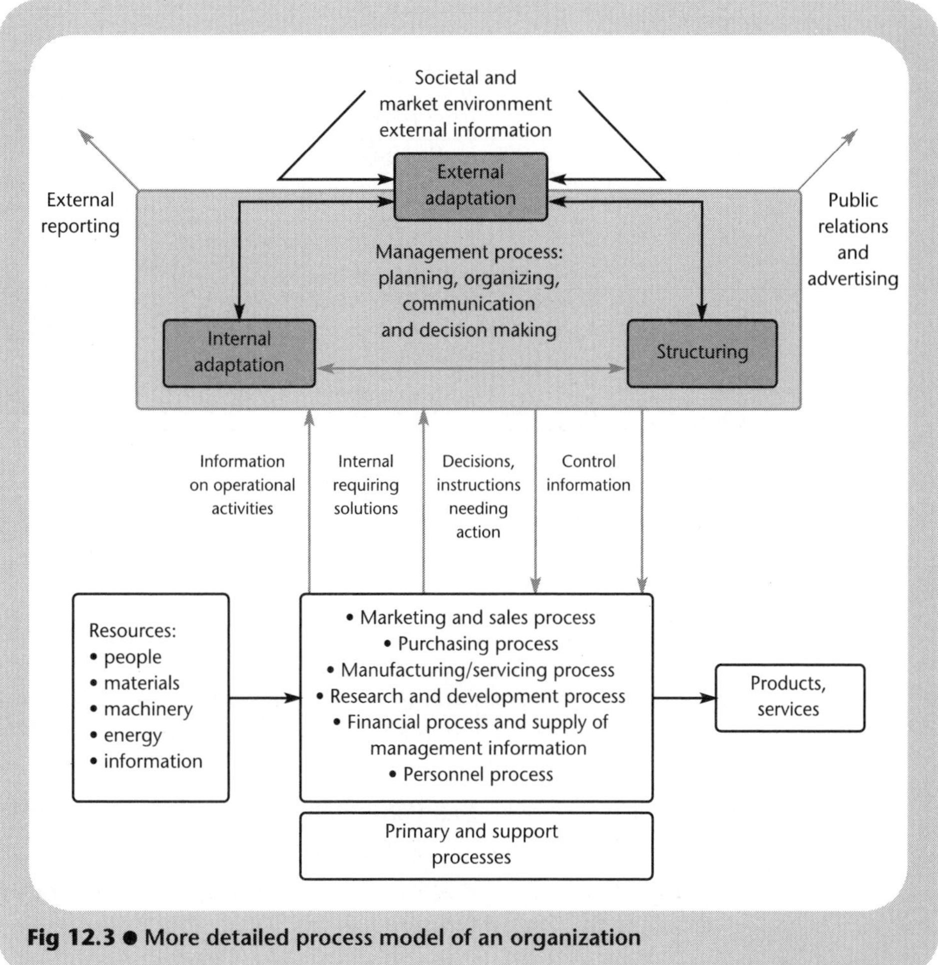

Fig 12.3 ● More detailed process model of an organization

Secondary processes or supporting processes comprise those activities conducted to maintain the primary processes, respectively letting their work be done. These do not form a goal in themselves, but render service to let the primary processes continue undisturbed and effectively.

Managerial or regulating and conditioning processes regard all those activities which determine goals for, and give direction to the primary and secondary processes. Managerial processes set the conditions to add value and direct the organization at the organization goals to be attained.

In this way the activities with which an organization creates value are divided into primary, supporting and managerial activities. These basic thoughts are recognizable in the so-called 'value chain' (Porter, 1985) (*see* Fig 12.4).

Primary activities can be divided into an incoming flow of goods, production or servicing in the widest meaning of the word, starting from flow of goods, marketing and sales and servicing. The supporting activities are the purchasing of products and services on behalf of the primary and other supporting activities, developing of technology, for example in the form of research and development, control of human potential, and the infrastructure which comprises matters such as financing, legal matters etc.

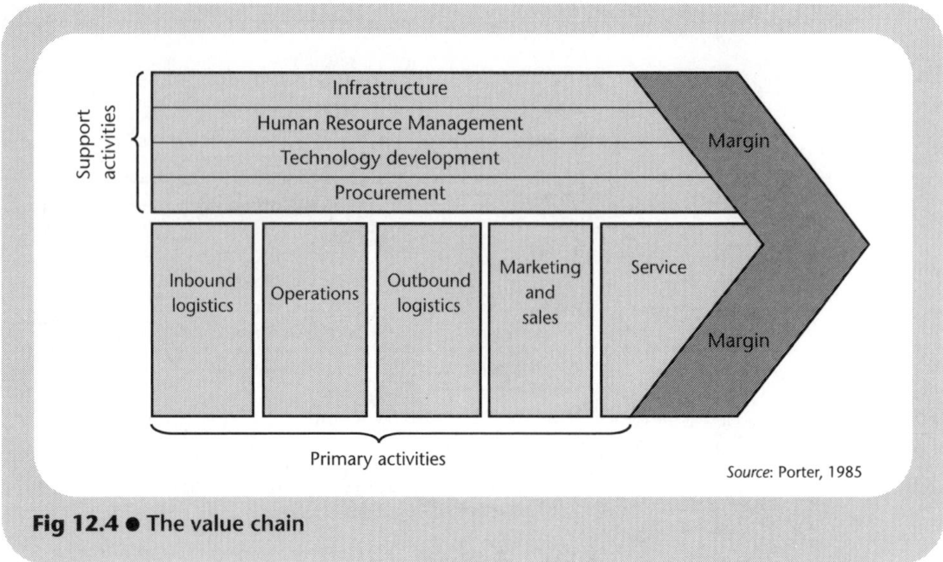

Fig 12.4 ● The value chain

Via management or managerial activities, relationships need to be optimized, cost levels kept low and revenue potential enlarged. By giving direction, form and content to operational processes and by a steering action, value is added into this chain by general management. These general management activities, which form the content of the managerial task, are:

- strategic policy making and positioning;
- design of a fitting organizational structure;
- giving of content and allowing the execution of processes in the organization including the control function.

The founder of modern management theory, Henri Fayol, represented management or rather the governing of an organization as a process as was seen in Chapter 2. Fayol (1916) broke governing up into five essential management functions, that is: 'prévoir', 'organiser', 'commander', 'coordonner' and 'contrôler'. Freely translated, this means that in the problem of management there are three core problems to be dealt with:

- external tuning and adaptation;
- structuring;
- internal tuning and adaptation.

These three managerial activities are closely related (Fig 12.5). They can be distinguished, but they are inextricably linked. Thus, in the management process they can be seen in interrelation with each other as follows.

In Fig 12.3, the following primary and secondary company processes are distinguished:

- marketing and sales process;
- purchase process;
- manufacturing process/servicing process;
- research and development process;

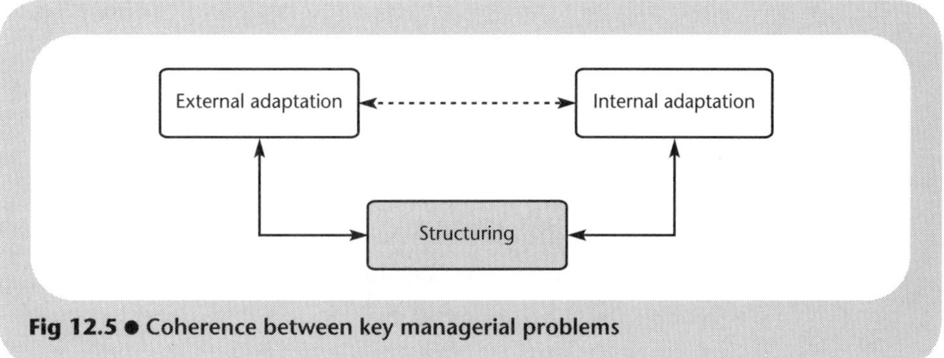

Fig 12.5 ● Coherence between key managerial problems

- financial and information supply process;
- personnel process.

Other processes often need to be linked in, for example: quality process, environmental care process, and logistic processes (both in- and outgoing).

These processes are connected via the process of management and organizing (=management process). The 'through connections' arise particularly by means of information supply and communication in an organization.

Via decision making, information is then transmitted into action, after which execution can take place in the different parts of the organization.

12.3 PROCESSES AND PROCESS CONTROL

Processes comprise the ongoing function of a company or institution. In other words, when no processes are left, an organization does not function any longer. Thus, it is of great importance to pay attention to the structuring, the making and controlling of the organizational processes. In general, the following is demanded for process control:

- mapping out the different functional or partial processes;
- fine tuning of the processes through the regulating or steering process of management.

The fine tuning comprises:

- formulating overall organizational objectives and goals;
- deriving partial goals, standards and norms from these to attain the goals;
- formulating and transmitting policy;
- determining guidelines, procedures, instructions and assignments;
- dividing tasks and assigning authority to be able to take necessary action.

12.3.1 Model for process control

In order to be able to control the process of goal actualization, it is always necessary that both during and after the execution, an examination takes place to ascertain whether everything goes according to plan. When deviations occur, one will have to make adjustments. This can be done by taking corrective actions during the execution, but can also take place afterwards by adjusting the norms set for execution.

In Fig 12.6, the control process is shown in a schematic presentation. In this cybernetic process (compared to the functioning of a thermostat in a central heating system, *see also* section 10.3), the following characteristics are always present:

- setting operational norms;
- giving an assignment or signal for execution;
- giving information to a steering organ; the managerial or operational functionary is always informed about the actual situation;
- checking, i.e. received information is tested to set norms;
- action to adjust or correct: when the actual situation deviates from the operational norm, the 'reactor' comes into action and adjusts or corrects; the information about the found deviation from a norm and the correction which follows, is also called feedback and or feedforward.

In the practice of management, we encounter such a cybernetic cycle in, for example, the application of budgeting. Deviations between the allowed and the actual costs are signalled. It is then examined how correction or adjustment can take place. In manufacturing processes, for example, we encounter numerically managed production equipment in the assembly of the coachwork of a car. Here there are built-in feedback mechanisms in a highly automated production system. When deviations exceed a certain zone of tolerance, intervention has to take place and adjustments have to be made, otherwise, the process can just carry on within the set zone of tolerance (*see also* section 10.2).

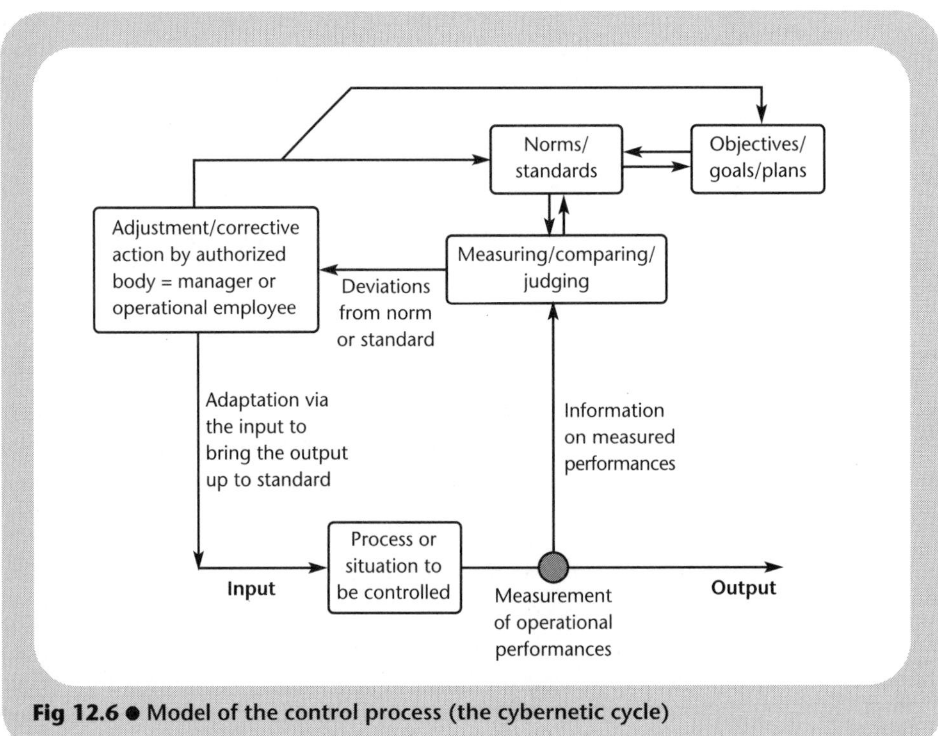

Fig 12.6 ● Model of the control process (the cybernetic cycle)

12.4 FUNCTIONAL PROCESSES AND PROCESS CONTROL

The starting-points and elements for process control described earlier hold for each of the mutual interrelating functional organizational processes, as distinguished in Fig 12.3. We will now discuss these processes briefly.

12.4.1 Manufacturing and production

Technical production and knowledge intensive transforming processes are directed at the manufacture of products or services in the desired varieties and amounts in the time available. A manufacturing process in composing process elements does not stand on its own but is dependent on the kind of product or service offered. In that regard, it makes sense to distinguish the type of manufacturing process in relation to the nature of the product. In accordance with the type of manufacturing process, and from that the types of products and services, the following can be distinguished:

- raw materials and half fabrics: in mass production in continuous processes; e.g. petroleum, paper, steel, gas, water, electricity;
- simple products or services: in series mass or series piece production; e.g. bottles, plastics, nails;
- composed/complex products: varying from simple to complex in series piece or series mass production; e.g. bicycles, dresses, cassette players, cars, locomotives, computers;
- one-off (large) works: piece production on a project base; e.g. an office building, city expansion plan, oil tanker.

Technical transformation in processes of development and manufacturing

The activities in the manufacturing processes comprise work preparation and production planning, the actual manufacturing, the maintenance of machines. The design and the development of new products are also included in the technical function of an organization.

Manufacturing, in its turn, cannot, of course, be seen in isolation from the other functions. Fine mutual tuning is required to come to the desired end result. From market research (as task of the commercial department) it will not only appear, for example, how many units of a product one will be able to sell, but also the characteristics the product should have. This includes the function of a product, the design, the packaging and so on. The desired characteristics have to be built in the product by the design and the development department. This then demands making a certain product design which, via a production development plan, has to be translated to prescriptions for composition, work drawings, manufacturing and assembly manuals and so on in order to come to a specific product.

In the phase of design and development of a product, in large, middle sized and also in small companies, use is made of Computer Aided Design (CAD), for example, in mechanical engineering, architecture, aircraft design, shipbuilding, electrotechnics, electronics and road construction and hydraulic engineering, and even in the designing of new crates and bottles.

A CAD-related application is Computer Aided Manufacturing (CAM). This uses data, which, with regard to a work piece to be manufactured, have already been determined with the help of CAD techniques, for the automatic manufacture of programs for machine tools used in the manufacturing of the work piece. On the one hand, this saves time, on the other, in principle (if the starting-point 'the computer never makes mistakes' can be applied) certainty is obtained with regard to the correctness of the processing instruction.

In another phase of product development, possibly a pilot model is built and prototypes manufactured to examine the way in which the products can be best produced on a large scale in time. In addition to product design, attention will also have to be paid to product monitoring. Signals from clients about possibilities for the use of the products, lacks, complaints and so on will have to be analysed to reach proposals for product improvement.

To control costs and time factors, progress control and cost reviewing have to be conducted in the product development phase. By means of intermediate reports, one can then make adjustments and further decisions can be made about continuation of a project and, if necessary, further budgets can be made available.

One will also have to examine the financial consequences a new product will have on the profit possibilities of the organization. What investments can be made for production on a large scale? How will the profit possibility develop in time? What price can be asked for the new product? As soon as the product appears to be commercially viable, it will start to be part of the regular assortment. Based on the composition of the product, the components and materials can be bought through the purchase department. In the manufacturing department, the production method and the layout of the machinery will now have to be determined.

Within the manufacturing department, production now needs to be planned and managed in such a way that the different products can be delivered in the desired composition and variety. In consultation with the sales department it needs to be determined therefore amounts and delivery times that will apply to the products to be manufactured. In the actual production, one can make use of different forms of process control. Process control certainly takes place in extended integrated systems, but it also occurs in partial systems.

Minicase 12.1

An example of a partial system is a pair of electronic scales, linked to a micro- or minicomputer. With the help of the computer, the weighing of goods is controlled and checked, weighing lists are printed, the weighings are determined in a file for further processing, etc. A numerically controlled lathe or milling machine is another example, the so-called NC equipment.

The management of a complete animal feed factory, staffed by four or five people and a computer, is an example of an integrated system. The computer sees to dosing, weighing, determination, failure signalling etc. and is integrated with the administrative data processing.

In the process system orders are received from the registration system. These orders form the basis for manufacturing. After shipment of the final product in bulk wagons, the actual deliverance data (especially the weights) are sent to the 'financial' computer in order to do the invoicing.

In this way it can be seen that the manufacturing process is related to the:

- purchase process and inventory process;
- sales process and inventory process;
- product design and development process;
- financial process, especially concerning costs and investment planning.

The manufacturing process as such is thus a composed process which can be looked at in more detail as a number of partial processes, for example in the work preparation process and quality control process.

Manufacturing process in partial activities

Via the manufacturing process, the organizational goal which regards the question: 'Which products are we going to make?', is further translated into production method. The production method indicates how production can take place. In the case of the actual production, it is important to watch costs of production activities. An examination must try to determine whether planning, with regard to quantities to be delivered, against the determined quality norms and against the determined costs and time norms, is attained. As soon as a deviation is found, intervention has to take place and adjustments and/or corrective actions have to be made.

Decisions in the production department

The manager of a production department will be responsible for:

- effective technical structuring and staffing of work places;
- efficient production, that is: good and accurate execution of orders, including rendering account to quality demands, time norms and cost standards.

Decisions which have to be taken concern:

- accepting production orders and settling delivery times;
- work preparation and work division over people and machines;
- ordering, storing, transporting materials, raw and help materials and final products and the control of intermediate and final warehouses;
- determining the most effective way of handling the product;
- calculation (before and afterwards) of costs and time;
- quality control;
- maintenance of machines.

Determination of optimal production programme

Determining the optimal production and sales programme not only depends on available capacity, but also on the possibilities for and the costs of the switches of productive resources: a machine, an assembly line, a shift in operational employees. In the switch from one product to another, certain changes are always necessary. Usually time is necessary. This is not only a matter of cleaning, machines also have to be reprogrammed or adjusted or an assembly line has to be rebuilt.

At the beginning of a new production series, a lot of material and speed is often lost: this is referred to as switching and adjustment costs and times. In determining an optimal production program, these costs must be included in the calculation. When another product is going to be made temporarily, in the meantime the sale of the product made earlier has to continue. To this end, that should have been produced for inventory. Inventory costs (warehouse space, interest on the inventory and so on) have to be included in the calculation. Included in these are costs of holding an extra inventory (as safety stock) in order to prevent 'negative sales' or to prevent the run of a small production series. Sales should always be able to continue.

In the determination of the optimal production program then, one has to pay close attention to the relationship between series size, adjustment and switching costs and inventory costs. In a manufacturing company, it is the task of the production manager to watch this relationship. Producing efficiently and preventing 'negative sales' form constraints on that. In striving for the lowest possible costs, sales of products (from inventory) should be able to continue as usual. It is therefore recommended that sales, production and inventory are all planned in mutual coherence.

Process activities in steps

Mapping out the process activities takes place in a number of steps.

- Process analysis: the production process is broken up into different processes, which, from the manufacturing scheme, include:
  - components, raw materials and materials from which a product is built up;
  - the necessary operations;
  - the final product.
- Analysis of operations: operations are distinguished as components of the process in which actions are conducted, for example: sawing, painting, storing.
- Analysis of actions: actions are split up into elementary motions, for example: 'Pick up component 3 with the right hand.' 'Place the component in the machine.'

In the management and control of the production process, one makes use of different management techniques to be able to prepare, plan and adjust these activities systematically and effectively. These include:

- labour study: time and motion studies, methods and action studies;
- planning techniques;
- quality control;
- internal reports, monitoring and signalling.

Determination of production methods

When what has to be produced has been determined, it will next be indicated in production methods how production will take place:

- what operations/phases are possible at the same time and/or sequentially;
- how these phases have to be executed;
- what machines, tools and possibly specialistic skills of people are necessary for this;
- how the productive resources will be set up and how work places will be laid out; e.g. formation of machines, walking distances for production employees, formation of inventory posts, walking spaces, spaces for internal transport etc. This regards routing as well as lay-out.

Lay-out and routing: mapping out the production process

In order to find the most favourable method of production, it is advisable to map out the total production process first. The goal of this is to give a handy overview of the structure of the process.

The lay-out (=spatial planning) and routing (=way or route determination) are directed at setting up the productive resources, inventory (including components and half products) in such a way (compare sections 7.2 and 7.3 for the so-called line, functional, and group-like structuring) that:

- production resources are easy to use in the execution of processes;
- cleaning, repair and maintenance can take place;
- short, wide, straight arrival and conveyance routes arise, in which internal transportation can be used;
- no unnecessary walking to and from and no unnecessary transport have to take place;
- inventories are within reach of the processing places;
- as short a waiting time as possible arises.

This is also the case in a trading company but there it is directed especially at warehouse lay-out. Furthermore, these 'basic thoughts' hold also for the lay-out of offices, repair work places, etc.

In the determination of the lay-out and the routing a map can be drawn of the room, and indicated on that the position of machinery, means of transportation, intermediate stocks and warehouse places. In this fashion, one can examine whether the chosen lay-out allows for the most efficient production route. When this is not the case, choose a more favourable lay-out.

Work preparation, progress and quality control

To allow the actual production to run efficiently and in timely fashion, work preparation will have to take place. In industrial companies, this is set up from the planning office based on data and norm studies from experience.

By means of work preparation, potential or existing orders for a certain product are transformed into indications for actual production. Through work preparation, guidelines and task assignments for different departments and operational employees arise. After that, via work dispatch, that is by giving out task assignments and instructions, materials and tools, the work is really set in motion.

Work preparation comes after making a product design but precedes the giving out of work. Work preparation comprises determining the production methods, material preparation and supply, and can include ordering raw materials, preparing components or half fabrics and so on. In this way it is ensured that these can be delivered to the processing work place from the main warehouses and the help and intermediate warehouses in time. To be able to deliver the required products in the planned time must be calculated how many production hours including both people and machines are necessary.

Then the setting of time norms for operations to be expected and the determination of the cost price (for reasons of pre- and post-calculation of materials/machinery) and time are regarded, and available capacities will have to be matched with each other. Here the challenge is to prevent peaks in utilization (under- or over-occupation) and bottlenecks in waiting times in the production. Losses of material caused by waste or refuse will have to be reduced as much as possible, while the processing places have to be chosen to be as effective as possible. In that respect, walking to and from and internal transport have to be avoided where possible.

Legal aspects of required safety, and according to legal prescriptions, for production personnel will also have to be met.

In order to control the course of the manufacturing process, it is necessary to norm the processing times based on time and method studies. These can serve as a starting-point in the determination of the standard cost price, which is itself used as norm in signalling deviations in the production costs.

In the production plan, task setting for the different departments and work places can now be indicated in terms of:

- quantity (of products);
- variety (among products);
- time of delivery (of products);
- quality (of products).

Based on the production plan drawn up by the planning office, the dispatching or assignment of work can now take place.

Progress control serves in order to determine possible deviations, and looks at timely signalling of when and where deficits, standstill or excess occur with respect to budgets and planned machine times (according to planning charts or screens). Deviations in actual costs or spent time with respect to planned costs and time can arise due to:

- complementary supply of materials, components, etc. arriving too late;
- bad materials;
- absenteeism among the personnel;
- machine standstill because of defects;
- lack of motivation.

The quality of products or services will also have to be monitored. Sometimes quality control is placed in the production department. In other cases, the Quality Control Department is quite separate, so it can operate independently from the manufacturing department. Quality control can take place by conducting random samples and testing the product to quality norms. Based on these tests, adjustment can possibly take place, either in the production design or in the actual production activity to make better products in the future (compare sections 5.10.6 and 12.5.3).

Control of manufacturing activities needs to be made possible via the registrational measurements. Data on materials used, hours worked, disruptions and so on have to be supplied in a clear way to be able to form a view on progress and state of affairs of this department rapidly.

12.4.2 Services: transformation of intangible products

In the personnel and business services in the so-called 'tertiary' sector, the central issue is the supplying of services: e.g. real estate, banking and insurance industry, retail and so on. In the nature of the function to be conducted organizations can show some marked differences. These differences in the primary, secondary and tertiary sector co-determine the structure or form of company activities, with regard for example to the possibility to automation and mechanization. Some activities will be capital intensive, while others remain labour intensive. The unique thing about the banking and insurance industry is that enormous sums of money were and are still invested in information technology, while the servicing is very labour intensive and very personally directed.

A service is an activity or a series of activities of a more or less intangible nature which usually, but not necessarily, takes place in direct interaction between the customer and the employee and/or physical resources and/or systems of the servicer. While a product is an object or a thing, a service can be described as an experience, act or performance. Thus, from its very origin, a service is intangible. Services often do have a tangible component. For example travel insurance is intangible for certainty cannot be comprised physically. The service itself, however, is delivered in such a way that the customer receives something tangible as proof: a policy, a folder, and luggage labels. Because a service is an experience or a process rather than a tangible good which one can hold or save, it cannot be kept in stock. The necessary equipment, facilities and labour can, of course, be ready to create the service, but these form only the production capacity, not the service itself. Providing a service comprises the joining and turning out of a mix of physical facilities and mental or physical labour. Customers are often involved themselves in the creating of the service. This can be done by self-service (for example, the hole-in-the-wall money machine), or by co-operating with the personnel of the servicer (e.g. determining a mortgage payment scheme with the intermediary). This is contrary to the production of most goods, in which the co-operation from the customer is minimal. A service can sometimes only be produced when the customer is present. This contact is described as 'interactive consumption'. That is why the quality of the personnel experienced by the customer determines the difference between two originally identical services. In this relation it is stated that production and consumption go together.

The consequence of the fact that people are part of servicing processes is that often standardization of the service is not simple to do. In the assessment of, for example, the quality of the service, objective as well as subjective norms will have to be handled. So here more than technical performances which can be observed objectively are regarded.

From the operational perspective we can distinguish three kinds of input for the servicing process: the customers themselves, goods (often the property of the customers) and information. Examples of the first kind are transportation, the hotel and catering industry, entertainment and the hairdresser. To be able to receive the service, the customer has to take his place in the servicing system, either physically, or by telecommunication. The 'output' can be a client who later finds himself in a different place, entertained or fed.

The input can, however, also consist of goods. The customer desires property handling. Examples of servicing process of which property is the input, are: cleaning a house, pest control, repairing computers or cars and demolishing a building. In each individual situation, the output will be some form of improvement in the experience or use of the property.

Information is the most intangible form of input for servicing. For the banking and insurance industry, information is the most important production factor. Other servicers that depend to a large degree on information are: accountants, lawyers, teachers, market researchers, consultants and physicians. The processing of information has taken a high flight because of the computer revolution. The output can be intangible (information) as well as physical (the information carriers: reports, books, tapes).

Service and production: the so-called servuction system

A servicing organization in the banking and insurance industry can be seen, for example, as a system which consists of two, partially overlapping, sub-systems.

- A producing sub-system, in which information is processed as input and the different elements of the services are created. One part of this sub-system is visible to the customer, another is not.
- A delivering sub-system, in which the desired service is made from the different elements and the services are delivered to the customers who have mutual contact with each other, the so-called servuction system.

The servuction system consists of all the elements of a servicing organization visible from the point of view of the client and are of influence on his image forming with regard to the servicer concerned, his evaluation and buying behaviour. This includes, for example, desk personnel plus direct physical support, and also the psychological effects on and appeal to other customers.

Every servicing organization must be conscious of these system elements and the mutual relationship which exists. Because of operational efficiency and ease of use for the customer, however, in many cases direct contact between servicer and customer and the physical presence of the client during the servicing process decrease. A modern example is teleshopping.

Front office and back office

In the servicing process to distinguish between the visible and the invisible parts, the terms front office and back office are used. In practice, for example, the individual back office activities in the banking and insurance industry are becoming increasingly standardized, so that front office quality is often decisive in the customer's assessment.

Productivity and quality

The distinction between the front and back office is important particularly with regard to the productivity problem. In the back office, those activities are involved into which the customer does not have insight. Here, registrational work is especially concerned which usually lends itself to automation and productivity improvement. In the front office, direct interaction with the customer does take place. This means that the principles of efficiency cannot be applied there so simply, because one has to render account to the co-producing customer and to the form of interaction which yields the best results. In this way, the notion of quality obtains content in the servicing sector through marketing thought.

Quality of service is sometimes described as the degree to which the expectations the customer has are met with regard to that service. It appears from research that there are five dimensions on which the user usually assesses quality. These five dimensions seem to appear tailor-made as well as standard services, as in case of core and additional services. The five dimensions reflect the advantages of servicing for the customer. The characteristics of these dimensions concern:

- Tangible matters: technical facilities, skilled personnel, etc.
- Reliability: being capable to execute a promised service reliably and accurately.
- Responsiveness: willingness to help clients and to deliver the service quickly.

- Care: knowledge and courtesy of personnel and the degree to which they are capable of transmitting confidence.
- Identification with the client: taking care of and paying individual attention to the customer by the personnel of the organization.

12.4.3 Research and development: aimed at innovation

Until recently it was held that in this function not much could, or indeed had to be organized. Development of new product/servicing ideas and applications of them namely demands a climate of freedom and few rules and procedures. An increasing need for renewal and product or process innovation in organizations from changing need patterns and demands from the environment, however, requires an increase in effectiveness that involves control of research and development activities in the company function too.

Subsidization, by the government or the EU, has certainly stimulated companies towards innovation; management, however, needs to take the initiative and the responsibility for this itself.

Often exercised already in large companies systematically, it is also necessary in middle sized and small organizations, both in the profit and not-for-profit sectors in society; that is research for ideas, a systematic approach to product and process development, by means of project management and in other ways.

Research and development implies a function which should occur especially in the production and service sectors, but, in fact, is also recognizable in government organizations and other not-for-profit organizations. Besides the systematic paying of attention to research for new possibilities, the further development and improvement of existing ways of working and activities also belongs to this activity. In large organizations there are special departments and/or functionaries which occupy themselves with research and development. In small organizations, production managers and other line functionaries carry out this activity. In those cases, research and development is actually a side activity, and is often therefore somewhat neglected when the current work must come first. A certain 'coincidence' in developments often passes by unrecognized, with the accompanying danger that one falls behind, or misses new possibilities. It can happen, especially with regard to more fundamental research, that an organization is too small to bear the costs of it. In certain sectors of industry and lines of business, for this reason, there are external research laboratories financed collectively.

Looking at service-intensive organizations, different 'levels' of service innovation and respectively improved servicing processes, can be distinguished.

- Services which are totally new to the organization and the market.
- New service classes or additions of services to the existing service class.
- Important changes in service forms, types of services, new brands and service varieties a company develops.
- Repositioning of certain services.
- Existing products adapted for new market segments.
- New services which yield the same result at lower costs for the company.

The relationships between these and the available options can be identified by referring to Ansoff's product – market matrix (Chapter 5).

Innovations yielding competitive advantage must anticipate both domestic and foreign needs. For example, as international concern for product safety has grown, Swedish companies like Volvo, Atlas Copco, and AGA have succeeded by anticipating the market opportunity in this area. On the other hand, innovations that respond to concerns or circumstances that are peculiar to the home market can actually retard international competitive success. The lure of the huge US defense market, for instance, has diverted the attention of US materials and machine-tool companies from attractive, global commercial markets.

Source: From *Transnational Management* by Bartlett and Ghoshal, (1992). Reproduced by permission of The McGraw-Hill Companies.

Technological innovation: product innovation and/or process innovation

New technological findings get their applications in new products more and more quickly, often realized by project organizations. Through this way of organizing the application of knowledge is speeded up, and can more quickly be passed through from research via product development, pilot production, manufacturing and sales to the market.

Technological innovation is the successful bringing to the market of new or modified products, in which new technological findings or combinations of findings are applied. The successful introduction to the market of a soap with a new colour, smell, shape or packaging does not apply here: the product innovation needs to have a certain technological content.

One can distinguish between innovations based on a 'technology push' and a 'market or application pull'. The push originates from new technological developments. The pull arises from the market or the application and is caused by the needs that exist there.

In principle a business firm can acquire technological know-how in four ways:

- by buying machinery including operating instructions and the know-how for maintenance;
- by acquisition of technologically advanced companies;
- by know-how contracts or licence agreements;
- by its own research and technological development.

In most cases companies acquire new technological knowledge by buying it, or respectively, taking it over from others. This is more so for small and medium-sized companies that are not too strong financially. Larger firms find it cheaper and easier to buy technological solutions from others.

For many successful products the pattern applies that after a phase of introduction a period of fast growth develops, after which a period of stabilization follows due to saturation of the market (*see* Fig 12.7). Through product or process innovations a firm can try to stimulate sales and volume of business. In the end there is bound to be a drop in sales, which may be caused by the introduction of a better or cheaper substitute product. The product lifecycle necessarily ends with a phasing out, which often evokes resistance both within and outside the organization.

Figure 12.7 shows the development in volume of business. In the design phase the original product (a) is designed. During the later rationalization phase the improved product (b) is prepared and modifications are included in the product design (this is product innovation) or are introduced in the manufacturing process (this is process innovation).

In a normal pattern of increasing competition quality improvement then has to be attained. At the same time the cost price has to be brought down.

In Figure 12.7 the starting-point is costing product innovation. These costs are included at Ia. Making of process innovation costs starts almost one year later. These are given at IIa. These costs are derived from costs of machinery and other equipment in manufacturing the prototypes, during the phase of pilot production or in making the so-called pilot series.

During the phase of rationalization (a) may pay close attention to the introduction of an up-graded product to the market. The costs that have to be made for this are depicted at Ib and IIb. In this figure the sales volume of the improved product is depicted (b). In cases when the market situation allows this, a second and possibly even a third and fourth improvement phase may follow in the rationalization phase.

Type of business and type of innovation

For innovation in general one has to realize, that:

- The accent is normally put on process innovation high up in the industry sector.
- In the middle of the industry sector the same attention has to be given to product as to process innovation.
- There is 'only' product innovation low in the industry sector.

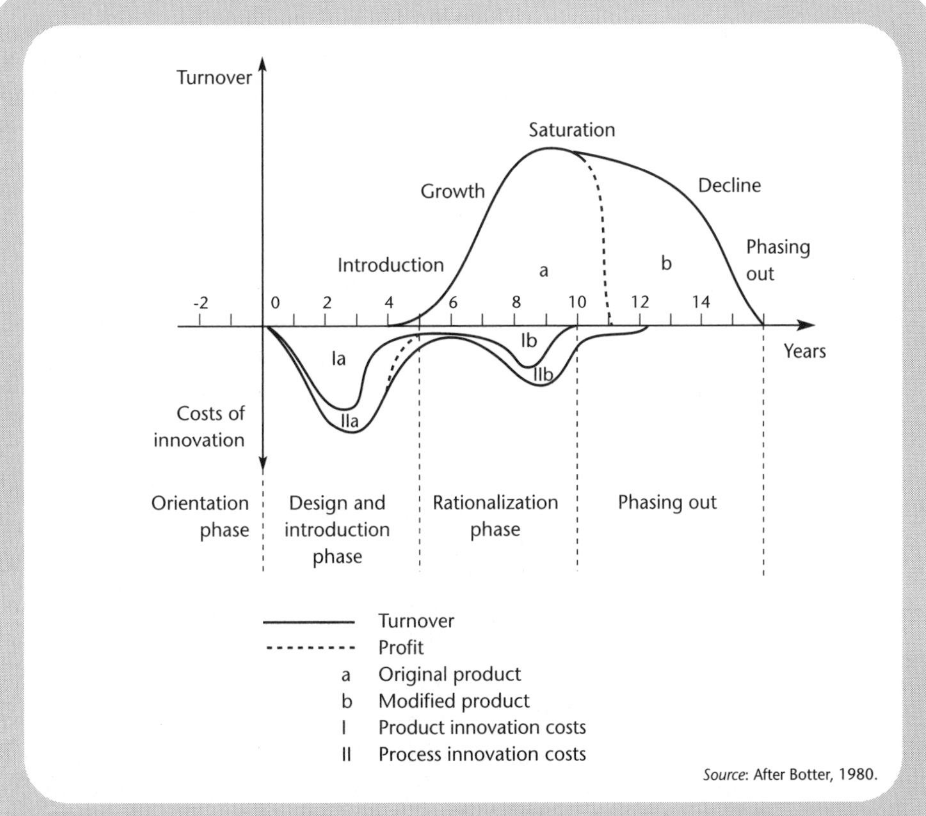

Fig 12.7 ● **Model of innovation phases and product lifecycle for simple and complex products**

For companies that design industrial installations the building of those installations is the 'product', where for the industries concerned this is the 'process'.

Companies that wish to develop their products successfully need to notice the difference between several types of R&D.

Among the many different factors that play a role in product innovation, time, capital and quantity are of particular importance. For that reason three basic categories of innovation are distinguished. These are: urgent, capital intensive and quantitative innovation.

Urgent innovation

These are usually rather uncomplicated products that cost less than 15 000 ECU: pcs, audio, video and communication equipment, camaras and household equipment. These products have a short lifecycle and are used only for short periods of time. Users rapidly want something new.

Capital intensive innovation

Capital goods with a value of more than 3 million ECU used in public or private infrastructure, for example railway systems, aeroplanes, weapons systems, satellites, process control equipment, energy works, chemical industry, telephone systems or databank systems are implied here. These products have a longer lifecycle (more than five years) and are used for longer. Depending on the somewhat costly logistics on the side of the users the starting and switching costs may rise sharply.

Quantitative innovation

This concerns mass products (low costs/large volume utility) far away from the end users and for which older technologies are used, involving the use of raw materials such as glass, plastics, resins and mineral oils or half fabrics and basic materials such as paper, card board, fibres etc. The lifecycle of these products is normally longer than ten years. Unless the market wishes otherwise, these products go through several stages in the manufacturing and the distribution process and that normally involves a lot of time.

Innovation and project management and control

An innovation project starts formally after a strategic reorientation and ends in the phase of operational maintenance. Every phase has to be a surveyable and clearly defined part of the total project. For each phase it has to be clear what activities have to be completed, who has to be informed on what, who is authorized to take certain decisions, etc.

In practice however it is characteristic for phasing projects that the phases concerned most of the time are poorly defined (*see also* section 6.3.7). Indeed it may be defined what activities have to be realized during what phase; unclear in this however is when and how one phase is followed up by the next. The only way to solve this adequately is to define the specific results – through documents and 'products' – that have to ready by the end of each phase and who may release these intermediate results or products. (*See* further in section 6.3.7 and 10.5.)

12.4.4 Quality control

Quality control requires first of all that the notion of quality is specified, for example, to performances (primary characteristics), reliability, meeting stated specifications, durability, maintenance friendliness, aesthetic quality and the subjective (perceived) quality. For specific products and situations, for example in the car industry or in aviation, these dimensions need to be more precise. Quality can be approached in different ways, which, on behalf of quality norms and control, will have to be brought in accordance with each other by management. Differences in interpretation can arise within an organization when quality of products is concerned, because in different departments different points of view always dominate. So the marketing department usually uses the 'user-directed approach' and the factory predominantly the 'production-directed approach'. The financial department will look particularly at costs and revenues thereby characterizing itself by a 'value-directed approach'.

The typically product-directed approach assumes an objectively measurable quality. Here, the product quality is based on specific characteristics which do or do not occur to a certain degree. Higher quality then means that more of a certain characteristic has been added to the product. By using this approach, quality improvement will lead to more expensive products.

In the user-directed approach, quality is determined by the eventual user in relation to the purpose for which the product is used. So the same product can be deemed a good product by a user in one situation, while in another situation, that same product is deemed bad. The user is the central issue in this approach: 'Quality is fitness for use'.

The production-directed approach starts from the fact that quality can be translated into specifications that products need to meet. The production process needs to be structured in such a way that those specifications are met as well as possible. Deviations of the specifications lead to refuse, waste, reprocessing etc. and so may mean higher costs than necessary. Improvement of the production process will then lead to lower costs. In this approach, statements such as: 'Right first time', and 'Zero defects' apply.

In the value-directed approach, the value a product or service represents for the user, is concerned. Costs, revenues and price are the central issue here.

Quality costs

Quality costs can be grouped into four categories: external costs (e.g. guarantee and repair costs); internal costs (e.g. caused by reprocessing) and assessment and prevention costs (e.g. inspection costs). Through quality management, the quality costs as a total will decrease; within the total of costs, the share of the prevention costs will usually increase. Quality costs are a good starting-point for bringing about quality policy in organizations, because:

- the size of quality problems can be made visible (becoming aware);
- priorities for improvement can be set;
- quality goals can be expressed in cost terms (improvement projects);
- with the help of cost indicators, progress control with regard to the quality policy can take place (feedback).

A strategic approach to quality means that in the product design one has already to render account to the actual production (design for manufacturing) and the product reliability (design for reliability), but also to the demands with regard to user-friendliness (design for usability) and the service (design for serviceability). Suppliers are also included in the quality improvement programmes (in the form of 'co-makership').

So in this way quality control goes further than just meeting *a priori* set norms or specifications. It also directs itself at reacting to latent expectations and needs or requirements of the customer, such as emerge from market research. In this way, a shift in the development of quality can be observed in the course of the years from 'inspecting' (first phase), via 'controlling in' (second phase) and 'building in' (third phase) to 'managing in' of quality. This shift is accompanied by a changing responsibility for quality. In the first phase, responsibility for quality is with the Department for Quality Inspection, then with the Manufacturing Department, after that with all departments for their own activities, and in conclusion with everyone in the organization, especially with top management for formulating a quality policy and the active steering of that policy.

Certification of quality systems

When the quality system of an organization meets norms and demands determined by an external authority, a certificate may be given out. By 'quality system' we then mean the total of the organizational structures, responsibilities, procedures and provisions directed at quality.

The norms and demands give a description of the conditions the quality system has to meet. Certification of quality systems is increasingly important to companies. A few reasons for this are the following.

- The ever increasing quality demands from the client/consumer. When a company has at its disposal a quality certificate, the client can be shown this as a reassurance of certainty and reliability.
- European integration with the increase in competition in different market segments. A company which has at its disposal an internationally recognized quality certificate can considerably improve its position in the market.
- New international and national legislation with regard to product liability. In this, the producer can always be held responsible for damage as a consequence of a product manufactured by him. Having a quality certificate at one's disposal could limit the amount of the claim. Insurance companies can start making demands in this area, that is requiring a company to obtain such a certificate.

Minicase 12.2

Blake Company

Blake Company produces components or half products for industrial clients. One complaint about product quality, accompanied by a considerable claim, was a cause for Blake Company to pay specific attention to product quality. Out of the Product Development Department, a project group was created. The assignment was 'improving product quality in the short term'. Three months later, the project group had not succeeded in coming up with specific proposals for improving product quality. The work group got bogged down in a few badly thought through changes in the product which would actually burden production with extra problems. The disappointing results and the remaining necessity resulted in the hire of an external consultancy firm.

Further research showed that the customer had not filed the claim because of low product quality so much, but rather that it had also been delivered late. Because of this the customer had not been capable of meeting his own delivery times. From an analysis of the complaints the late delivery came up as one of the most important causes. From a sample taken from the visiting reports from the sales field organization and conversations with the sales field organization it appeared that Blake Company performed especially badly in the aspect of delivery reliability.

Priority was thus given to improving product quality in the specific area of delivering reliability, and the method was determined by management. For this purpose a project group was composed from all logistic disciplines. This group was given a clear goal with the accompanying planning. The project group was trained by the consultancy firm, and also coached further.

In checking a sample of orders in which the delivery time was exceeded, it appeared that this was caused in most of the cases by problems with raw material deliveries. The completion time in the company itself was controlled sufficiently. The management was convinced by the intermediate results and gave the group permission to execute the proposed improvements. This started with a simplification of product design, because of which normalization of raw materials became possible. With the suppliers, the specifications the raw materials had to meet were determined anew. A system was set up for registration, collecting and analysing of the performances of the suppliers. Based on the outcomes of this and the normalization of raw materials, within three months the number of suppliers could be reduced to a third. With the remaining suppliers, a standard method for quality control was agreed on, because of which the entrance check could be simplified considerably.

Within six months after the start of the project, the raw material supplies to Blake Company were reliable. Because of this, their own delivery reliability also increased. With the reduced number of suppliers, better purchase conditions and prices could be stipulated. Some people from purchase and entrance checking could be freed from direct productive activities. In conclusion, the demands from ISO9000 were used as a guideline where possible in the improvements, because of which an advance has been made in a quality system which will be able to be certified in due course.

International quality norms

Many norms which quality systems have to meet originate from the International Organization for Standardization (ISO). The norms can be used for contractual relations between suppliers and clients.

12.4.5 Environmental control

Company internal environmental care and control regard all the measures in a company directed at gaining insight into the control of and reduction of the burdening of the environment by company activities where possible. Attention to the environment in companies and institutions is in the first phase usually directed at respecting laws, rules and prescriptions in the field of environmental care. Some laws are linked to a system of permits. The laws, permits and regulations often have a direct influence on the functioning of a company. In a later phase, the attention to the environment, in the case of an increasing awareness of environmental sense, can be expressed in one's own environmental policy.

In the further integration of environmental care into the management of internal affairs, in due time all functions within the company are involved, at least insofar as these affect the environment. This leads to the development of a form of built-in supervision on the system of internal environmental care.

Goals for internal environmental care and control

A tool for the building in of environmental care into an organization is the setting up of an environmental care system. An environmental care system is an instrument for the management to observe government rules in an efficient and effective way. Besides that such a system can also render account to future developments in the environment.

With the introduction of internal environmental care in management, different goals can be aimed at.

- **Environmental goals**. Observation of government rules in the field of environmental care, observation of company internal guidelines and instructions, controlling and/or preventing the burdening of the environment as a consequence of company activities, limitation of environmental risks, in an early stage rendering account to environmental aspects.
- **Economic goals**. Setting up an efficient environmental policy, cost savings in the long term.
- **Other goals**. Less government regulation, more effective government regulation, good relation with governments and stakeholders, better company image, anticipating future developments in the technical and societal field, appropriate handling of complaints about the environment.

Design of environmental care system and management tasks

In principle, environmental care regards all company activities: research and development, products design, the purchase of raw materials and components and the actual manufacturing process. Besides that environmental care demands a continuous effort. The organization is not occupied merely with respecting government rules, but also searches for reduction of environmental burdening continuously and systematically. This also means that via feedback as a consequence of observed deviations, necessary measures are taken, directed at the recovery of the intended situation. There is also a 'feeding forward': measures will be directed not only at the correction of deviations, but also at the prevention of deviations and problems.

Management tasks with regard to an environmental care system involve:

- drawing up an environmental policy statement, in which management indicates the meaning and position of the environmental policy in the organization;
- drawing up an environmental programme, in which management can include environmental measurements to be executed: investments and revisions, execution and revision of permit conditions, intended studies and research projects, structure of a measuring and regulating programme and special points of attention;
- a measuring and registration programme with the goal of quantifying the environmental burdening of a company, state check points and obtaining information on behalf of readjustment;
- an internal monitoring and inspection system: measuring and registration system with inspections with regard to the functioning of the system and screening with the goal of supplying insight into the execution of inspection;
- internal information, education and training to enlarge involvement of personnel;
- internal reporting about the general course of affairs in the environment;
- external reporting about the functioning and the development of the system, about the execution of the environmental programme, about the results of inspections, audits and of required reports.

In these management tasks, besides environmental policy making, embedding of environmental care into the organizational structure is also involved, as well as the giving of contents to executing and supervising or controlling of environmental care. In order to function well, the environmental care system has to be clear and simple to handle. The system should adapt to the situation in the organization as much as possible, that means that the size and complexity of the system depend on the degree (that is, nature and intensity) of the environmental burdening.

Factors of influence on the organizational measures which have to be taken are:

- size of scale and complexity;
- degree of environmental burdening;
- number of environmental laws and rules of relevance to management.

In the case of an increasing size of scale, an increasing degree of environmental burdening and a larger number of environmental laws and rules, the need arises to an increasing degree for a separate environmental department in order to support the line. For good integration of environmental care, it is important, however, that the responsibility for the execution of that is situated in the line and is stressed in the task and job descriptions of the individual company functionaries.

12.4.6 Business logistics: control of physical resources and information

Logistics management comprises all activities to do with planning, organization and operational managing of the flow of goods, including the information supply necessary for this. Within the total flow of goods, which goes from supplier to consumer, there is a subdivision between 'materials management' and 'physical distribution'. 'Materials management' comprises the total of activities conducted to run the flow of raw materials and half fabrics and the accompanying flows of data as efficiently as possible to and through the production process. Included in this are activities conducted to realize as efficient a possible use of productive resources. 'Physical distribution' is occupied with the goods and the flows of data connected with that, which start at the end of the production process and finish at/with the consumer. 'Business logistics', or rather logistics management, is the collective name for all activities executed to control the in- and outgoing flow of goods (*see* Fig 12.8).

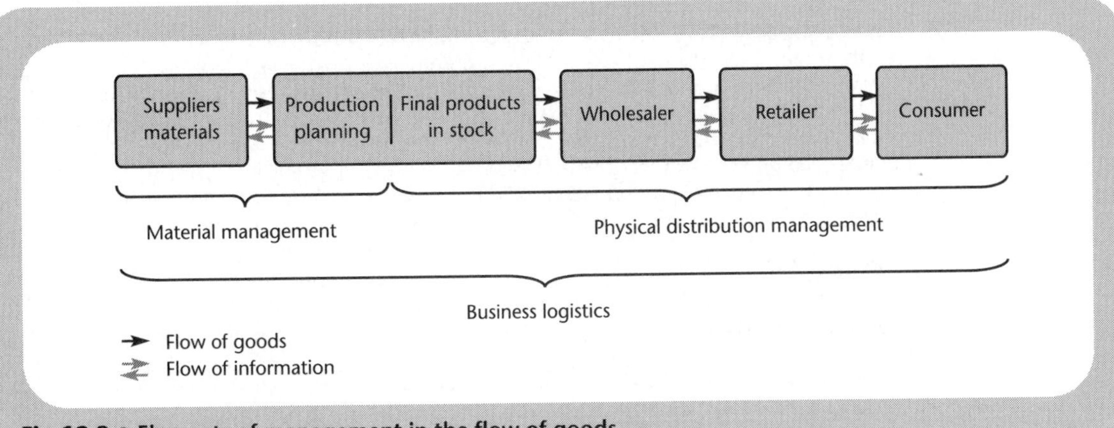

Fig 12.8 ● Elements of management in the flow of goods

Improvement in the flow of goods via logistics management

Control of logistic activities can be realized by means of improvement in inventory positions and cost control, by enlargement of flexibility and service, or by making a contribution to strengthening the competitive position of an organization. Logistics management is directed at an integrated approach and control of all aspects of the flow of goods. Thus, logistics has interfaces with almost all other functions, such as product development, marketing and sales, purchase, manufacturing (and within that, inventory control and work preparation), transportation and distribution and the financial registration systems.

In this framework, with the help of computer systems, new methods in organizations can be used, such as MRP II (Manufacturing Resources Planning), DRP (Distribution Requirements Planning) and JIT (Just In Time). MRP II is especially directed at management of the flow of goods for long running production processes of simple to complex product compositions. JIT is most suitable for organizations with short completion times, small series sizes, few materials per production step, a total production scheme and products with a relatively long lifecycle. As a management system, JIT has been introduced from Japan (*see* section 10.4.4) and is directed at reducing inventories. JIT stresses making problems visible, synchronization of products and sales and simplification of the process. Inventory is often a bad thing and usually hides underlying problems, such as machine stops, incorrect inventory data, quality problems and inflexibility of the productive resources.

A problem in the management of flow of goods is the location of inventory points in the flow of materials and from that the forming of disengaging points between customer-directed external activities and planning directed internal activities. By locating disengagement points in the logistic chain, orders can be disengaged from completion times of the logistic production chain. Optimal inventories at the disengagement points then, in a certain sense solve the ever existing tensions between production and sales in terms of stability and flexibility.

Exhibit 12.1

Nokia's signal isn't really fading

The company may bounce back quickly from its poor results

The news was a shocker. Nokia Corp., Finland's hugely successful maker of mobile phones and other electronics, announced on Feb. 28 that 1995 net earnings had dropped 43% – after a $505 million restructuring charge.

'Just a hiccup'

Part of Nokia's problem stems from three years of superheated growth. To meet soaring demand for its phones in Europe and Asia, the company added 7000 new employees last year but had difficulty digesting them. Productivity, which had climbed 15% in 1994, advanced only 3% as Nokia encountered problems with suppliers and late component deliveries. 'They lost control of logistics. They lost efficiency,' says Bill Coleman, a telecommunications analyst at James Capel & Co.

in London. In addition, the US market for digital handsets did not grow as much as anticipated because of a regulatory delay. Meanwhile, makers of analog phones cut prices as much as 50%.

Nokia Chief Executive Jorma Ollila is racing to implement new controls and make Nokia respond more quickly to regional markets. He insists all bottlenecks will be gone within six months. 'It's not an insurmountable problem,' says Ollila. He also aims for a productivity gain of up to 20% this year, so the company can endure price wars without sacrificing profits. 'This is just a hiccup,' says Johan Siberg, head of L.M. Ericsson's mobile-communications company. 'We view Nokia as a very capable competitor.'

A growing source of profit will be the sale of network equipment to telecom companies setting up cellular-phone systems. Nokia's equipment business grew 50% in 1995, to $2.3 billion in sales, while operating profits jumped 60%, to almost $600 million. In contrast, profits were flat in mobile phones, where margins of 11% are less than half those in equipment. Since January, Nokia has garnered network contracts worth $150 million with British mobile operator Cellnet and $200 million with Chicago's American Portable Telecom.

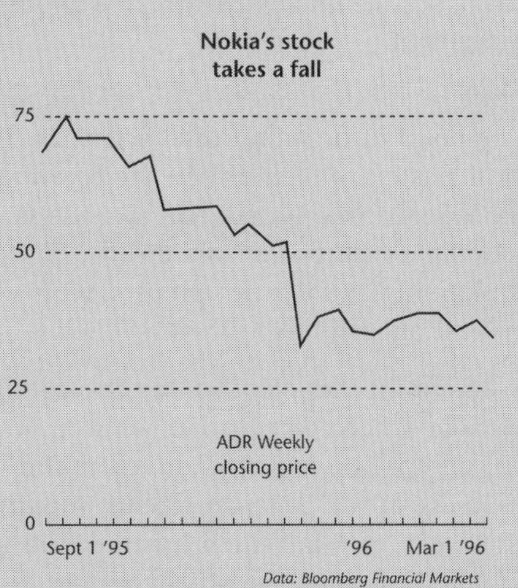

Data: Bloomberg Financial Markets

Nokia continues to gain market share in Europe, Asia, and the USA Early estimates give the Helsinki company roughly 25% of the global market in mobile phones, narrowing the gap with market leader Motorola's 36%. 'Nokia is still good at bringing innovative products to market early,' says Susan Anthony, analyst at Schroders PLC in London. Nokia's newest phone, the 1610, features a battery that outperforms rivals with seven hours of talking time and 200 hours of standby time. Nokia also leads in development of the digital technology used to transmit data over the airwaves. Despite recent bumps, manufacturing efficiency is strong, too. A study by market researcher Dataquest Inc. estimates Nokia's cost of making its 2100 series of mobile phones at $234 a phone and its selling price at $550. Only Ericsson's costs are lower.

This edge in technology should help fuel sales growth soon. 'I can't see their position [as global No.2] being threatened,' says Dataquest's Adam Zoldan. 'There is no reason to wipe a big portion of the value off the shares.' Analysts project strong earnings growth will resume in 1997 after a flat 1996.

The rebound depends on Ollila's ability to leave the TV business, smooth out production in mobile phones, and expand network-equipment sales in the USA. 'They have three levels of change going on at once,' says Susan Kalla of market researchers Soundview Financial Group. 'Any one of those issues is a big challenge.'

Ollila himself likens the speed of change in mobile phones to a bullet train. He's quick to point out that Nokia was almost bankrupt in 1992 before he bet big on cellular phones. Now, he has to prepare for more dizzying changes. Investors are watching.

Source: *Business Week*, 18 March 1996.

In servicing processes it is as well to pay separate attention to the accompanying logistics, in a physical sense (management of flow of goods in the restaurant supplies in a congress centre for example) as well as with regard to flows of information (in banking or insurance companies).

12.4.7 Marketing and sales

Marketing is the approach of thinking and doing with regard to sales and production from the market (i.e. client) point of view. The needs and wishes of the clients then form the actual starting-point for all company activities.

Marketing comprises:

- tracing needs in the market;
- indicating users' requirements for goods and services which provide for these needs;
- evoking and stimulating demand for these goods and services;
- meeting that demand by selling the goods and services in order to realize profitable management.

Marketing, and respectively sales, is actually the starting-point and indeed also the finishing-point of organizational activities. The marketing function will usually form the starting-point of planning in the organization. From the marketing plan, the sales plan for the next year is derived, from the sales plan the inventory plan, from that the production plan, purchase plan, etc.

The planning and control process, which regards the commercial activities within an organization, can be specified as follows.

- The determination of goals: for the sales policy, general organizational goals will have to be specified in market goals. In other words, one has to determine at which client groups one will start directing the sales: for example at industrial clients or consumers, at which target groups in particular: for example ladies', men's or children's wear, and in which areas: in France, in all cities with more than 25 000 inhabitants, or maybe in other countries?
- Planning in the long and the short term: for the commercial function this will result in a sales plan which comprises market goals as well as the instruments with which this has to occur, expressed in costs with respect to expected revenues.
- The organization: that regards the sales and the functioning of the marketing and sales department, as well as the way in which the external relations with the clients are maintained from there. The policy will have to be executed by this department.
- The execution: the plans have to be converted into action. Everyone will have to know what is expected of him or her and when. This means, for example, that tasks of representatives have to be formulated per region, per client group, per client or that advertising campaigns have to be executed. Provision of clear guidelines, instructions and task assignments is necessary.
- Monitoring and adjustment: activities usually do not develop completely according to plan. There are many insecurities in the market place. Deviations have to be signalled in time, so that the necessary measures and corrective actions can also be taken in time.

Exhibit 12.2

Brand awareness

Multideal's 500 brands are the jewels in the corporate crown. But only a handful sparkle

Marc-André Chapon, chief executive of Multideal, a leading European consumer goods conglomerate, was looking forward to chairing the annual marketing planning meeting. He finds the meetings, attended by general managers of different product groups and those in charge of national markets, useful forums for exchanging ideas about future opportunities.

In line with this year's theme, his opening address focuses on brands. Following an upbeat preview of the annual report, he calls Multideal's portfolio of 500 brands 'the jewels in the company's crown ... assets responsible for our 10th successive year of record profits'.

When the financial director, Daniel Drew, takes the floor he cites two intriguing facts. Five years ago, more than half of Multideal's profits came from just four brands; and last year, while the pattern was similar, three of the company's four 'star' brands had changed.

This stimulates a lively discussion, which ends when Chapon asks the country managers to name their current leading brands. Everyone names 'Mini' as their star brand. Otherwise there is little consensus and much partisan talk about new local brands. When Chapon asks about new products, several exciting ideas are put forward. However, all the managers, except Ulrike Schenk, argue that costly new brands will be needed to launch the products.

Schenk outlines her plan to align all new household cleaning products to a Mini brand-extension strategy.

Schenk explains that her ultimate goal is to develop 'Mini into a consumer lifestyle that reflects the trend towards products offering real environmental benefits'. Among Mini-branded products successfully launched with environment-friendly claims are detergent and fabric conditioner refills packaged in biodegradable cartonboard and highly-concentrated soap powder sold in small, convenient cartons. Schenk ends her presentation to loud applause.

'As Frau Schenk has demonstrated, we'd all do well to remember the old marketing adage that "People do not buy products, they buy brands and brand image",' Chapon says, as he brings the meeting to a close on a high note.

Later, Chapon reflects upon Schenk's presentation. 'To reap the benefits of the single market, we need people like her,' he says.

'Schenk is a brilliant product manager,' Drew says. 'But she has a reputation for being pushy with national managers.'

Source: International Management, February 1993.

12.4.8 Purchasing

The purchasing process comprises: closing purchase contracts, determining purchase prices, determining the order size and the sales conditions, the spread of purchases over several suppliers. Of course, these process activities are in close relationship to the primary processes of manufacturing and sales. The nature of the mutual interrelationships can differ, however. In a trading company this will be different from in an industrial company, when, for example, attention is paid to the relationship with the sales and manufacturing process.

The purchase procedures chosen must cohere with the nature of the purchase process. In this regard, for example, distinctions can be made into:

- the technical-oriented purchase; technical specifications are of great importance in this; being able to meet these specifications is decisive and is even more important than price level as such;
- the commercial-oriented purchase; this is characteristic for, for example, the trading company in which the price sensitivity is usually rather large;

- the administrative-oriented purchase; in this one purchases according to guidelines determined in advance.

In a trading company, the relationship between purchase and sales is decisive for the total business. In purchasing, all factors have to play a part which are determining for the sale of a product, including the price against which sale is possible. Thus, the commercial policy comprises purchase and sales function. An integrated policy of purchase and sales should then be seen to exist.

In an industrial company, the process of purchasing takes another form. In this, distinctions can be made into:

- purchase of main materials for the manufacturing process; these can be handled after tuning into production by the purchase department, for example in negotiation with suppliers;
- purchase of installations/plants and other long-lasting production resources; these are often handled by the managing director of a company, with advice from the technical service and the purchase department;
- purchase of help materials for the manufacturing process and materials for the support services; this can be handled according to administrative standard procedures, sometimes by the departments themselves, sometimes by the purchase department.

12.4.9 Human resources: the personnel process

Management of human resources comprises the way in which personnel is selected, hired, educated, promoted, waged, fired and retired. This decision making covers the wide area of human relations for which, from behavioural scientific and technical administrative backgrounds (compare Chapters 7, 8 and 9), systems, methods and procedures have been developed.

Control of the personnel process demands that the personnel process in management acquires content at policy level as well as at operational level. This giving of content to the personnel function is one of the responsibilities of top management board of a company or institution. The tasks which belong to this can be assigned to the Personnel Department. The execution of a part of the operational work can then be delegated to managers of departments under the supervision of the personnel department. For example, the assessment of an employee takes place in the department by the departmental chief, while the assessment system and the accompanying procedure are designed and monitored by the Personnel Department itself.

In the personnel policy, a direction or board expresses how the company or institution wants to handle matters which affect the people who work there. Since the personnel policy is a company affair, it is important that the direction or the board, as responsible authority for the content of the personnel policy, expressly also renders account to notions which emerge from the workers' council.

Besides the influence of the workers' council, a contribution from 'the line' of the work place needs to be made to the formulation of the personnel policy (*see also* sections 7.5.4 and 7.5.5). The direction or the board will itself have been advised about this by the personnel functionaries appointed in its own organization, who from their professional training, bring in the required expertise for these matters. If the organization is too small to be able to hire its own full-time personnel functionary, the management team can seek the advice of external experts, for example, from the sector organizations or management consultancy firms for small businesses.

In the formulation of the personnel policy, prescriptions determined in labour legislation, need to be respected.

The elementary matters include the registration of all personnel: the personal data and an indication of function and function content. Besides that there is rendering account to the functioning of the personnel, resulting in salary administration, social provisions such as insurances, pensions, etc. In the same area lies the registration of reimbursements, special bonuses and so on.

Education, training and personal development of the members of the organization also belong in personnel affairs. The organization which wants always to follow developments will have to manage the training and education of its own personnel. There are organizations which pay a lot of attention to this and have a department for training and development. On the one hand, in making plans one takes into account the wishes and capabilities of people, while on the other it is important to know what the organization needs in order to keep up with social developments (*see* sections 8.7–8.10).

12.4.10 Financial process and information supply

In every organization, financial and registrational processes unroll. These have to do with incoming and outgoing flows of money, as well as with reporting and information supply about the processes of adding value to the main processes, manufacturing, servicing and sales. The course and the character of these financial and information flows do of course strongly depend on these main processes.

In a financial institution, a bank for example, the incoming flow of money undergoes a process completely different from that of the incoming flow of materials in an industrial company. In all cases monitoring of the flows of money and properties or goods are regarded.

In a financial institution, the incoming flow of money trusted to the bank by the clients or created by the banking institution itself, is made available, for example, in the form of credits or loans. In that situation, with regard to the liquidity position, one will have to strive for a balance between the sums of money between the respective time periods of the incoming and outgoing flows of money.

In an industrial company one can derive the incoming and outgoing flow of money from marketing and sales plans and from the production and inventory plan. The financial process then comprises the determination of the investment policy in the long and the short term, the indicating of the financing need which goes with that, monitoring of liquidity and solvability position and the formulation of a well considered reservation policy. In this process the laws and practices of an economical nature play a relevant role.

Financial planning and budgets

For the control of the financial process, planning by making use of projections and budgets is essential. Use is made in the creation of the:

- sales budget;
- manufacturing budget;
- purchase budget;
- inventory budget;

- investment budget for fixed assets and machinery;
- cost budget;
- liquidity budget.

In this situation, one has to render account to the desired level of return, profitability and solvability. This involves not the drawing up of the budget so much, as the monitoring of it. Adjustment by calling in managerial or responsible departmental employees in combination with other departments has to fall within tolerance zones. Process control is only possible effectively by means of timely information in a clear form with a certain occurrence and/or through incidental intermediate reporting of deviations (*see also* sections 11.1 and 11.2).

12.5 ● PROCESS REDESIGN

The application of 'old' organization principles often leads to work processes being divided up. Processes such as product development, execution of an order and information supply to the client can be divided into smaller parts and spread out over several sub-units in the organization. In such a situation, slowness, rigidity and a high level of supervision are difficult to avoid.

Often the 'ownership' of a company process is not assigned in the traditional, functional-hierarchical structure of organizations and systems. So a company process such as product development (Fig 12.9) is often executed and directed by different departments (R&D, marketing and manufacturing). In practice, such a

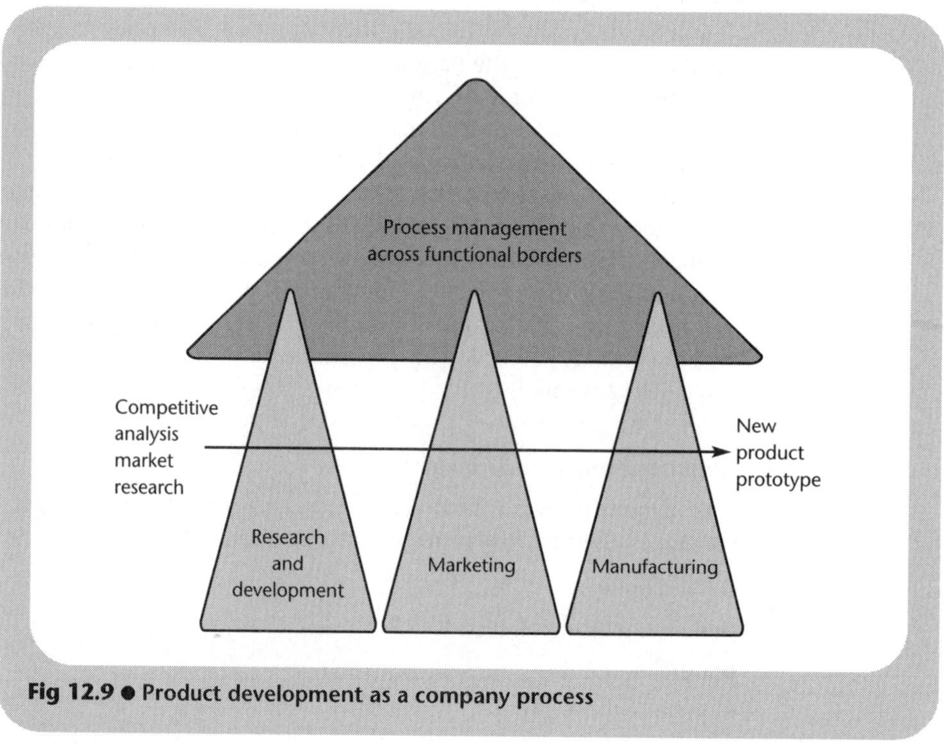

Fig 12.9 ● Product development as a company process

cross-functioning of company process can be hindered by laborious co-ordination within and especially above the involved functions, and by lack of clarity over common goals and responsibilities.

Despite stressing process orientation in the older and even classic organizational notions and concepts, in modern practice the process-oriented point of view is considered to be insufficient by many functionally structured organizations, especially where company processes are of the nature of data processing.

Company processes of the data processing type play a central part in many administrative environments: in organizations such as financial institutions and many governmental institutions and agencies, the primary processes are of a data processing nature. Michael Hammer (1991) sketches the well known image of locally optimized company processes that, through automation, are executed over many separate company functions and information systems. The completion time of those company processes is a considerable multiple of the effective processing time contained in them: 'servicing' of clients is below acceptance level. Use of information technology (IT) appears to have contributed particularly to the efficiency of certain parts of company processes. The efficiency and effectiveness of the total company process, that is a chain of activities, are not necessarily, however, served by it. On the contrary: functional-directed departments often maximize their interests at the expense of the effectiveness of the wider organization. In short, sub-optimization is the case. Inefficiency is included in the dividing lines between functional departments. These dividing lines require co-ordination mechanisms which do not add absolutely no value at all, but may work as a restraint. That is why these intermediate links have to be eliminated as far as possible by redesign or re-engineering.

12.5.1 Process orientation: a must in the IT era

A company process consists of a chain of activities, with a beginning, an end and input and output. The activities in a chain are executed, spread out in time and place, and can be temporarily organized in different ways and designed in an organizational structure (*see* Chapter 6). An integral company process can be measured much more easily than a function of the department as a small 'detached' part within this total. One can think of measuring costs, time, amount of input, quality of output and customer satisfaction.

Decades ago, Japanese business life was already fully aware of the fact that process orientation offers the best perspectives. 'Just In Time' and 'Total Quality Management' are in essence process-oriented approaches. But where these approaches direct themselves at continuous improvement, BPR (Business Process Redesign), with the use of IT (Information Technology), directs itself at radical changes: the complete redesign of processes. Where the Japanese applications originate in industry, and are later also applied in non-manufacturing processes, the examples of BPR can be found especially in the more administrative, servicing organizations, such as banks and insurance companies, or in similar parts of industrial organizations: marketing, sales and order administration.

By definition, re-engineering is radical. The primary question is not how to improve the existing situation, but why do we actually do what we do? With BPR an organization can improve its performance radically by seeing the company process not as the sum of the organized functions, but as a collection of related, customer-oriented core processes: the processes which add value for the customer. So it expressly involves a series of mutually connected activities that criss-cross through possible functional dividing lines, directed at a customer-directed output.

In the largest area of re-engineering application, 'functionally split tasks' are bundled to one cohering process and executed by one person or by a team as the process owner. It has been wrongly assumed that the complexity of labour processes is situated in individual tasks: this is no longer held to be the case. Rather it is located in the many co-ordinating activities necessary in case of further labour division.

Minicase 12.3

Some examples of BPR

By means of re-engineering, the time necessary by IBM Credit for a business transaction (the IBM daughter company which finances purchase of computers and software for IBM clients) was reduced from six days to four hours. Instead of feeding a financing problem through four specialists, all burdened with a single component of the assessment, the request is now handled by one generalist who has on-line access to datafiles and who only consults a specialist in particular cases (10 per cent of all cases). Because the forms do not have to travel from one department to the other anymore, the service is now much faster.

An insurance firm switched from an insurance request procedure consisting of thirty steps, in which twenty people and five departments were involved, with a total completion time of five to ten days, to a system with 'case managers' who handled all except the most complicated cases, with a completion time of two to five days. The processing capacity was doubled and hundreds of functions were eliminated. In this capacity, information technology played an important part.

12.5.2 Four characteristics of redesign

The redesign of company processes has the following characteristics.

- Investments (in IT among others) need to be aggragated at crucial company processes, processes which determine the success of an organization, in which processes transfer preferably from client to client, e.g. handling an order up to delivery of or collection, opening a bank account before it is ready for use.
- The goals of the organization are defined particularly in terms of specified results of process improvement. Goals in the fields of completion time, quality and costs of the company process can be distinguished. Thus the goal of a company process is first formulated in terms of the client. An example: 90 per cent of orders from fixed clients are processed within three days. Only after that comes analysis of problems and possible solutions, with the attainment of that goal in mind.
- The selected company processes are, directed at the defined, external goals, redesigned and restructured. The goal direction of the company processes is the central issue, and the structuring of a chosen company process in terms of procedures, people and resources is tuned into that. The internal organization is completely aggragated at that external result.
- Restructuring of company processes generally leads to a complex, intervening change for the organization. It often concerns the structuring of the handling of

Exhibit 12.3

Is your company ripe for re-engineering?

The following self-assessment questions have been devised by consultants Coopers & Lybrand to determine whether a company is ready to make a success of business process re-engineering. Circle either yes(Y) or no(N).

1 Do you review customer perception of your products and services more than once a year? Y/N
2 Does your company have anyone whose pay depends specifically on achieving some measure of customer satisfaction? Y/N
3 Can you define your company's basis of competition as one of cost, service, flexibility or quality? Y/N
4 Have you benchmarked your company's core business processes against those of your competitors? Y/N
5 Does your business use activity-based costing? Y/N
6 Could you write down more than three non-financial quantified targets for your company? Y/N
7 Has a new technology caused a major shift in your company's activity during the past three years? Y/N
8 Do you have a unique technical competitive advantage in any of your business processes? Y/N
9 Is your company vulnerable to a takeover? Y/N
10 For new investments do you have a return-on-capital-expenditure hurdle of at least 25%? Y/N
11 Does the head of your company pursue personal recognition ahead of recognition of your business? Y/N
12 Does the head of your company communicate personally with every employee at least once a year? Y/N
13 Does the head of your company emphasize how people are expected to act? Y/N
14 Is there a commonly held view of the likely market share which will be held by your company in five years' time? Y/N
15 Have you any business process or cross-functionally orientated teams? Y/N
16 Do you consider that teams are less successful at achieving their goals than individuals? Y/N
17 Was the last major re-organization in your company more than three years ago? Y/N
18 Has your company ever launched a new product or service which, if it failed, would destroy the business? Y/N
19 Is it difficult for individuals to make career moves between different functions in the company? Y/N
20 Is everyone in the company encouraged to undertake more than five days' training each year? Y/N

Assessment

Score 1 for each answer that tallies with the following:

1 Y; 2 Y; 3 Y; 4 Y; 5 Y; 6 Y; 7 Y; 8 Y; 9 N; 10 N; 11 Y; 12 Y; 13 Y; 14 Y; 15 Y; 16 N; 17 N; 18 Y, 19 N; 20 Y.

Interpretation

Score 0-7
You have a long way to go. So many of the conditions for success are absent that the scale of the change needed will be beyond your current capability. Instead you should undertake targeted improvement programmes in a few areas such as customer research, market share projections and cross-function teams.

Score 8-14
You have got some of the conditions – begin to think about how a re-engineering programme could make a significant difference.

Score 15-20
You have great potential for re-engineering but probably need to got senior people together to find your 'breakpoints' – those aspects of your product or service which have achieved excellence and bring a sustained leap in market share.

Source: *International Management*, November 1993.

company processes in a traditional functional-hierarchical organization, e.g.: autonomous teams which execute a company process from beginning to end with individual handling of every case. One consequence of that is that management too will change. Depending on level of ambition, willingness needs to be present in advance in order to change the organization radically, for example, to a process-directed 'horizontal' organizational form (*see* section 6.5).

IT is a powerful tool for making BPR possible. Other 'vehicles for change' in BPR projects can be of a personnel or organizational nature, for example: working in teams, company culture, training programmes, task enlargement and enrichment and production cells (*see* sections 7.2 and 7.3).

12.5.3 Objectives and business (process) redesign

Often ambitious goals are formulated in advance for BPR projects. Here goals of different natures are concerned:

- reduction of time, often completion time;
- reduction of costs, often those of man power and resources;
- improvement in quality, for example, directed at customer satisfaction by increase in speed or reliability of deliveries;
- another way of managing the organization, especially of company processes across functions.

In order to be able to realize ambitious goals regarding the overfunctioning character of company processes active involvement of the highest management of the organization is necessary. Without that involvement, the 'bottom up' change of extensive company processes will fail on questions of competence between existing organizational units. Formulating and realizing goals such as mentioned here, is sometimes made easier by accident. There are several situations which create chances to structure the company processes from a clean sheet: e.g. merger or acquisition, privatization or outsourcing of certain tasks.

12.5.4 Business process redesign: the combination of 'old' concepts with IT

Briefly stated the methods and techniques brought together by BPR are:

- thinking in terms of customer-to-customer contact;
- the critical choice of company processes to be restructured;
- measuring process performance (benchmarking) in terms of completion time, costs and quality;
- structuring activities and flows of information, directed at the realization of process goals, for example, from the point of view of logistic when the completion time is important;
- cultivating the willingness to structure the present organization radically differently;
- screening resource possibilities, e.g. IT, before or at the same time as determining goals.

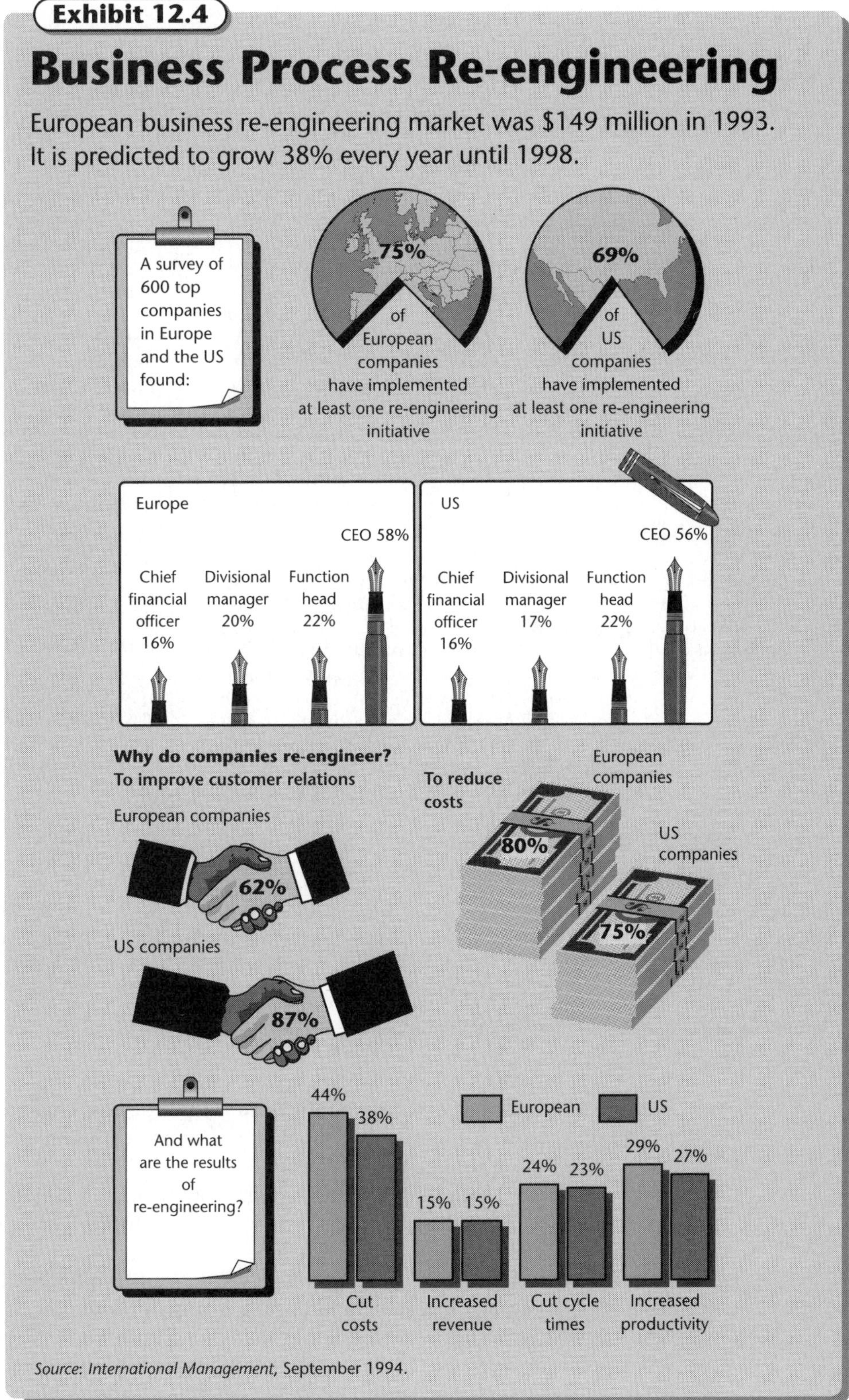

Source: International Management, September 1994.

Exhibit 12.5

American companies are worrying about corporate amnesia

A recent survey by the American Management Association (AMA) found that fewer than half of those companies that had downsized since 1990 went on to report higher operating profits in the years following the move; even fewer saw improved productivity. And unpublished research by Monitor, a consultancy based in Cambridge, Massachusetts, found that nine out of ten firms that had outperformed their industries over a ten-year period had 'stable' structures, with no more than one reorganisation and no change (or an orderly change) in chief executive.

The mechanism by which a reorganising company might lose its memory at first seems simple: by sacking Bill, the firm loses Bill's skills, commitment, knowledge, memories of what works and what doesn't, and so on. But as Lance Ealey, a consultant with McKinsey, points out, this is only the start. He believes that 're-engineering totally disrupts all of a firm's informal networks' – the contacts and relationships between employees or teams of employees, and the unofficial routines and processes that make a company tick.

Not all memory loss is a bad thing. One reason why IBM and General Motors were outwitted by younger firms is that they were unable to forget about making mainframe computers or gas-guzzling cars. For every management thinker beginning to worry about corporate amnesia, there are many more urging companies to dump their mental baggage so that they can compete in the 'nanosecond nineties'.

The whole point of re-engineering is to rethink a company's existing processes and systems from the ground up. This partly explains America's fondness for downsizing: the first three months of 1996 saw 169,000 layoffs, the most in any quarter for two years. Their processes are more perfect, their systems are sleeker and their workforces are leaner, but they are not noticeably more competitive.

Service companies are especially vulnerable to amnesia. Numerous downsized banks, insurers and retail chains have seen their customers' satisfaction plummet. One insurance group, having slimmed its claims department, found that it was settling big claims both too swiftly and too generously. Belatedly, it discovered that it had sacked a few long-term employees who had created an informal – but highly effective – way to screen claims. It was eventually forced to reinstate them.

The AMA study found that 17% of employees who had lost their jobs because of downsizing since 1990 were middle managers – even though middle managers make up no more than 8% of America's workforce. And nearly one in five lost jobs belonged to supervisors – another disproportionate share. Yet supervisors and middle managers often act as the synapses within a firm's brain, linking shop-floor workers with line managers, and line managers with senior executives. This makes them much harder to replace than easily trained shop-floor workers or line managers.

In Japan, companies have gone to unusual lengths to avoid sacking middle managers and supervisors – partly because of the tradition of lifetime employment but also because they put great stress on the importance of 'tacit' knowledge – hunches, know-how, ideals and experience.

Source: © *The Economist*, London (20 April 1996).

Information technology is a powerful tool to initiate process changes in organizations: in addition, organizational and personnel aspects almost without exception need to acquire an important place in a BPR project.

BPR comprises more than just computerization, older and still more recently developed methods and techniques come under the same heading, and here the interface between BPR and computerization is large.

In the case of redesign of company processes traditional work is still of value in describing, analysing, designing and implementing of those processes. For implementation of BPR, methods and techniques that can appropriately map out the different BPR aspects are necessary. These can include work place research, data logistics, administrative organization and so on. Besides these use is made of organizational concepts such as horizontal organizing, team forming, socio-technical system design and so on. It can still be, however, that the 'old', delicate problem of lack of a well thought out formulated strategy means that specific goals for redesign cannot be derived (in terms of time, money and quality).

Fundamental to the notion is that, across individual functional processes, BPR redesigns primary processes and links the partial processes such that they are directed at company goals.

Even though BPR is promising, changing the organization remains a difficult prospect, and possessing a new integrated view on company processes via BPR does not, in itself, make it any easier.

SUMMARY

- We have to know the company processes intimately before we can redesign the course of them. The form that course will take determines the function. When everything is right processes take their 'natural course' in a properly designed organization and they are not interrupted unnecessarily. Goals are attained in time, at low cost, within contracted delivery times, and at required service and quality levels.
- In order to ensure that this is the case, the processes need to be mapped out well and process control must be sought.
- In this Chapter, insight has been given into different company processes which as a whole are part of an industrial company or a service organization. It has been indicated what is meant by process control and those elements that play a part in this.
- Influenced by modern information technology, organization processes can sometimes be considerably accelerated. This demands an intervention in existing structures around the course of the processes. As soon as one does this, business process redesign (BPR) or re-engineering occurs. The advantages speak for themselves.
- In this way we return to the old notion that processes are the starting-point in organizations and that one has to know the processes well before restructuring. In the case that fixed and established structures hinder progress of processes, an intervention in the restructure is required.

DISCUSSION AND REVIEW QUESTIONS

1. With reference to *Management in action* at the beginning of this chapter: How would you explain the following concepts:
   (a) process redesign/re-engineering;
   (b) business redesign;
   (c) business network redesign

   at an increasing degree of complexity in redesigning activities (at three levels) in the case of a customer-focused retailing model?
2. What different approaches to 'quality' can you identify?

3. Why is it in the case of service industries, particularly the back office lends itself to automation?
4. What is the relationship between, on the one hand, 'routing' and 'lay-out' of departments, and, on the other, line, function and group formation of machinery and people?
5. (a) Is Nokia's problem simply a problem of loss of control over logistics?
   (b) How would you typify the problem(s) at Nokia?
6. What would you advise Marc-André Chapon to do to transform Multideal into a brand-centric organization?
7. What differences, if any, can you identify between the Japanese notion of continuous improvement at BPR?
8. Now that you have read this book on management what is your answer to the following question: What is the 'added value' of management within the organization?

Management case study

Albert Heijn's distribution concept for the future: 'Flexi-Flow'

Albert Heijn has begun probably the most radical logistics operation in its more than one hundred years of existence under the name 'Today for Tomorrow'. The largest retailer in the Netherlands (with substantial investments in food retail chains in the USA) thinks that a cost reduction of ten to twenty percent in the total supply chain is eventually possible. This can be realized by integration, better synchronization of manufacturing and distribution and a flexibilization of the production process.

'Today for Tomorrow' is a widely set up logistics action the goal of which is to simplify the logistics process of Albert Heijn and enlarge its efficiency. Before long stores will be delivered to more frequently, because of which service to the customers is enlarged. One rule is paramount: ordered today, delivered tomorrow.

Were things not already going well at Albert Heijn? No, not at all. In the past few years a number of important developments have occurred in the food retail industry that made new demands on the logistics. These developments were:

- erratic consumer behaviour;
- greater number of changes in the range;
- increase in the number of products;
- strong competition from discounters.

At that time there was a complex delivery structure with many different delivery frequencies and lead times, because of which it was difficult to react quickly to the changing wishes of the consumer. An important reason for logistical change, besides that, can be found in the broadening of ranges. An average Albert Heijn supermarket has over 13,000 different articles on the shelves. Of that 4000 change every year: articles disappear from the range, packaging changes and so on. So many changes clog the 'supply chain', because of which remainders and back flows arise.

Lower logistic costs

A third reason for 'Today for Tomorrow' is continual introduction of new products and product varieties which the shelves in the supermarket physically cannot contain. Only a small amount of each product can therefore be on the shelf at any one time which causes the risk of 'out of stock' to be higher.

In conclusion, a decrease in logistics costs is an important reason for changes. Even though Albert Heijn prides itself as a customer-friendly supermarket with a wide range, there is also a complete package of food articles at a low price that must remain competitive on cost. Despite the fact that the inventories of Albert Heijn are some of the lowest in the global retail business, they can decrease still further. Inventory reduction is not the main goal of 'Today for Tomorrow', and here Albert Heijn distinguishes itself from the large American supermarket chains, where in practice, under the slogan 'Efficient Consumer Response', inventory reduction in the supply chain is sought.

The operation 'Today for Tomorrow' is part of the 'Flexi-Flow' concept, the new logistics concept of Albert Heijn. As a starting-point the company wants to serve the various kinds of customers in an effective way (Fig 12.10). But before that is possible, the mainstream, i.e. the 'one-stop shoppers', have to be served in more efficiently. With the 'Flexi-Flow' concept, a distinction is made between process logistics for the 'one-stop shopper' and logistics for special groups of customers. The mainstream is structured to low costs and a high degree of routine. Machines start to play a role to an increasing degree. In the other logistics streams, service is the central issue. By means of the 'Today for Tomorrow' program the logistics stream is more efficient and effective.

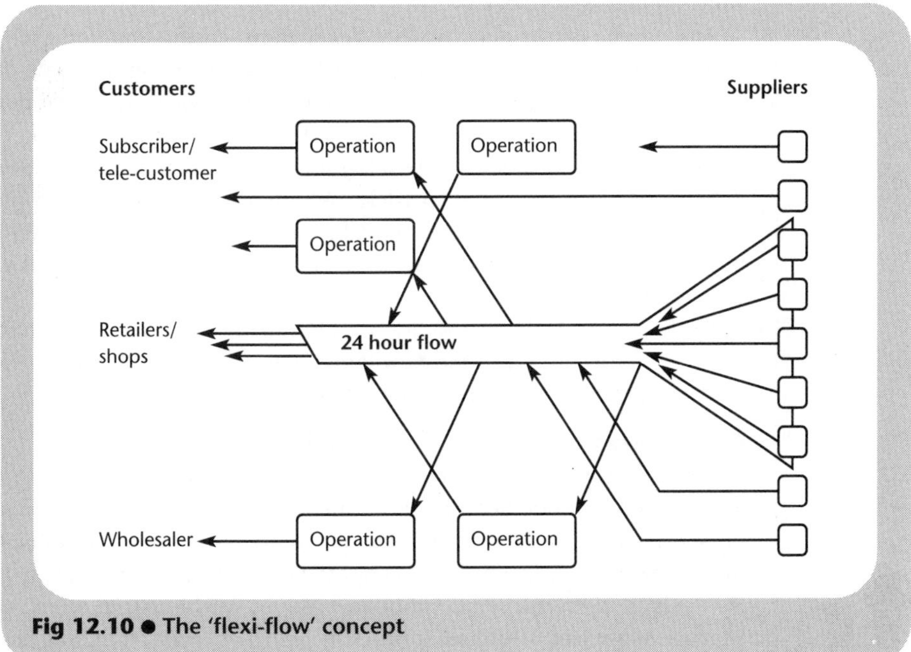

Fig 12.10 ● The 'flexi-flow' concept

From 'push' to 'pull'

Suppliers rapidly get to know exactly how much of a certain product is sold in the joint branches of Albert Heijn each day. The actual amounts sold are determined by scanning barcodes. Restocking amounts used occurs more frequently because stores are delivered to daily (or, if necessary, more times in a day) (Fig 12.11). In 'Today for Tomorrow',

continued overleaf

Management case study continued

the flow of goods is no longer pushed into the 'supply chain' ('push'), but directed by the consumer ('pull'). Until recently the shelves were kept filled up, based on available shelf-space. That is no easy task. Now the shelves are kept filled up, based on actual sales. Nowadays 92% of products at Albert Heijn are accounted for by scanner. In order to let 'Today for Tomorrow' function well 100% will have to be accounted for like this and so the barcodes need likewise to be 100% accurate. It still happens that barcodes just cannot be read, and the scanning data start to direct the whole chain: suppliers are connected to the actual sales figures and, because of this, can react quickly and with the correct goods in correct amounts. In the old system the goods, as it were, forwarded the message themselves. An employee in the store sees a shelf half-filled with shampoo and orders a new box. In the distribution centre, a box is taken off a pallet. When the pallet empties, that is the signal to the manufacturer to order. This system is now turned completely upside-down.

Just In Time (JIT)

With 'Today for Tomorrow' the time of 'economies of scale' is dead. Products are no longer delivered with long intervals between deliveries, by enormous trucks, in large quantities; but daily in exactly the right quantities. JIT thought is introduced into the Dutch food retail industry.

Albert Heijn knows only two logistics streams: cooled and non-cooled. Cooled products, vegetables, meat and dairy products, are delivered in the same truck. An average Albert Heijn supermarket moves from 50 deliveries a week to 35 combined deliveries. So because of fewer transport movements, the stores can order and receive all product groups more frequently. In the new logistics system, all branches are delivered to exactly in time according to a 'time schedule'. An important advantage of this for the branches is that they receive quantities that are handleable at fixed times. Reception and processing of goods can be organized more efficiently and deployment of morning and evening shifts can be reduced.

By the end of 1994 all 350 branches in the northern part of the Netherlands will be delivered to according to the new logistics system. By 1995 Albert Heijn stores in the southern part of the country will have followed.

Co-operation manufacturer and retailer

The manufacturers will notice the logistics changes most. 'Today for Tomorrow' will give an impulse to co-operation between manufacturer and retailer. Producers will have to deliver smaller quantities more frequently to the distribution centres of Albert Heijn. This means that the production process has to be structured more flexibly. The responsibility for the level of inventory in distribution centres will be placed more with the suppliers. Because Albert Heijn will start to stock its branches more often, but in smaller amounts, packaging will have to be smaller. Stock supply in distribution centres will soon be automated to a high degree so standardized packaging formats will be required. In time, standardized packaging influences consumer packaging. 'The first reaction of most manufacturers to "Today for Tomorrow" is panic. But when the idea has been thought through they eventually see the advantages.' In the end, a producer will be in direct contact with the consumer.

With 'Today for Tomorrow', Albert Heijn moves closer to the future. A different structuring of the supply chain is inevitable and because of that one is better off with an early

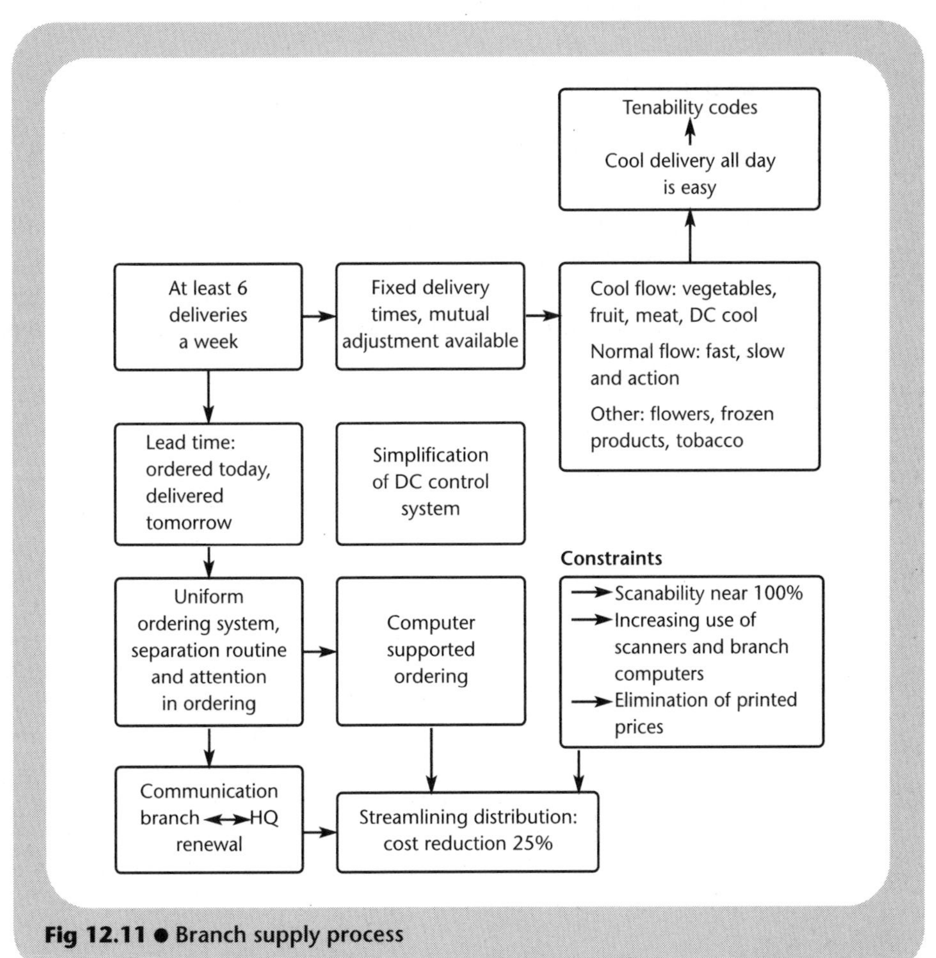

Fig 12.11 ● Branch supply process

start. Larger (brand article) manufacturers see the advantages of a flexibly structured manufacturing process: being able to switch quickly is a great advantage in changing times. Eventually costs of manufacture will decrease because of lower end-inventories, fewer remnants, lower switching costs and a more efficient supply.

Paperless 'supply chain'

Albert Heijn strives for a delivery percentage of 100 of its stores, which means that suppliers also have to deliver more fully. That is not easy. There is a danger that suppliers will react by enlarging their inventories.

At Albert Heijn they believe that it cannot be long before the suppliers are paid based on article sales determined through barcode data. The paperless 'supply chain' becomes a fact. Is this the music of the future? At Albert Heijn the future is not far away. In Japan, for example, car rim suppliers are already paid based on the number of cars sold. The reasoning is: a product takes on its value only at the moment that the consumer has paid for it.

Source: Adapted from *Tijdschrift voor Inkoop & Logistiek*, jrg 10, 1994.

continued overleaf

Management case study continued

CASE QUESTIONS

1. At Albert Heijn, with regard to the management of flows of goods, can we speak of 'materials management' or 'physical distribution management'?
2. State the relationship between the 'flexi-flow' concept and the transition in the management of the flow of goods in a 'push' to a 'pull' system?
3. What strategic possibilities and organizational consequences of application of information technology can be distinguished from the Albert Heijn example?

Bibliography

Selected references

Abell, D. F., *Defining the Business: The Starting Point of Strategic Planning,* Prentice Hall, 1980.

Algera, J.A. *et al.*, 'Prestatiesturing en teamvorming', *Gids voor Personeelsmanagement 6,* 1994.

Ansoff, H. Igor, *Corporate Strategy,* revised edn, McGraw-Hill, 1987.

Anthony, R.N., Dearden, J. and Govindarajan, V., *Management Control Systems,* 7th edn, Irwin, 1992.

Argyris, C., *Integrating the Individual and the Organisation,* Wiley, 1964.

Bartlett, C.A. and Ghoshal, S., *Transnational Management,* Irwin, 1992.

Bennis, W.G., 'Revisionist theory of leadership', *Harvard Business Review,* January–February 1961.

Berge, D. ten, *De eerste 24 uur, Handboek voor crisismanagement,* Tirion, 1989.

Bolman, L.G. and Deal, T.E., 'What makes a team work?', *Organizational Dynamics,* Fall 1992.

Bono, E. de, *Lateral Thinking for Management,* Penguin Books, 1971.

Botter, C.H., *Industrie en Organisatie,* Kluwer/ Nive, 1980.

Churchill, N. C. and Lewis, V. L., 'The five stages of small business growth', *Harvard Business Review,* May–June 1983.

Crouch, C. and Heller, F.A. (eds), *Organisational Democracy and Political Procession,* Wiley, 1983.

Dale, E., *Management: Theory and Practice,* McGraw-Hill, 1973.

Daniell, M., 'Webs we weave', *Management Today,* February 1990.

Davis, S.M. and Lawrence, P.R., *Matrix,* Addison Wesley, 1977.

Davis S.M. and Lawrence, P.R., 'Problems of matrix organizations', *Harvard Business Review,* May–June 1978.

Deming, W.E., *Quality, Productivity and Competitive Portion,* MIT, 1982.

Deming, W.E., *Out of the Crisis,* MIT, 1986.

Donaldson, G. and Lorsch, J.W., *Decision Making At The Top, The Shaping of Strategic Decision,* Basic Books, 1983.

Duyser J. and Keuning, D., 'Verplatting als vehikel voor effectiviteitsverhoging; actualiteit, mogelijkheden en voorwaarden', *Bedrijfskunde,* jrg. 66, 1994, No. 2.

Exley, M., 'Building the Empowered Organization,' *Empowerment in Organizations,* 1993, Vol. 1, No. 2.

Fayol, Henri F., *Administration Industrielle et Générale,* Dunod, 1916/1950.

Galbraith, J.R., Lawler III, E.E. *et al.*, *Organizing for the Future,* Jossey-Bass, 1993.

Graves, C.W., 'Levels of Existence: An open systems theory of values', *Journal of Humanistic Psychology,* Fall 1970.

Greiner, Larry E., 'Evolution and revolution as organisations grow', *Harvard Business Review,* July–August 1972, pp. 37–46.

Hackman, J.R., 'Work design', in Hackman, J.R. and Suttle, J.L. (eds) *Improving Life at Work*, Scott Foresman and Company, 1977.

Hackman, J.R. (ed), *Groups That Work: Creating Conditions for Effective Teamwork*, Jossey-Bass, 1990.

Hagel III, J., 'Spider versus Spider', *McKinsey Quarterly*, 1996, No. 1.

Heijmann, P.M.G., *Gids Europese medezeggenschap vergelijking wetten en regels*, FNV, Amsterdam, 1995.

Heller, F.A., *Managerial Decision Making*, Van Gorcum/Tavistock, 1971.

Hersey, P. and Blanchard, K.H., *Management of Organizational Behavior*, Prentice Hall, 1986.

Herzberg, F., 'One more time: How do you motivate employees?', *Harvard Business Review*, January–February 1968.

Herzberg, F., 'The wise old Turk', *Harvard Business Review*, September–October 1974.

Hofstede, G.H., *The Game of Budget Control*, Van Gorcum, 1967.

Hofstede, G., *Culture's Consequences, International Differences in Work-related Values*, Sage Publications, 1980.

Huyzer, S.E. *et al.*, *Strategische samenwerking*, Samsom, 1990.

Jansen, P.G.W., *Het beoordelen van managers*, Nelissen, 1991.

Johnson, H.T. and Kaplan, R.S., *Relevance lost, the rise and fall of Management Accounting*, Harvard Business School Press, 1991.

Kaplan, R.S. and Norton, D.P., 'The Balanced Scorecard-Measures that drive performance', *Harvard Business Review*, January–February 1992, pp. 71–9.

Kaplan, R.S. and Norton, D.P., 'Putting the Balanced Scorecard to Work', *Harvard Business Review*, September–October 1993, pp. 134–46.

Keuning, D., *Bedrijfskunde*, Stenfert Kroese, 1988.

Keuning, D. and Eppink, D.J., *Management en Organisatie: Theorie en toepassing*, Stenfert Kroese, 6th edn, 1996.

Keuning, D. and Opheij, W., *Delayering Organisations*, Pitman Publishing, 1994.

Keuning, D., Opheij, W. and Duyser, J., 'Herstructureren door verplatten', *Holland Management Review*, 1993, No. 35.

Kim, D.H., 'The link between Individual and Organizational Learning', *Sloan Management Review*, Autumn 1993.

Kimberley, J.R. and Quinn, R.E., *New futures: The Challenge of Managing Corporate Transitions*, Dow Jones Irwin, 1986.

Kimman, E.J.J.M., *Organisatie-ethiek*, Van Gorcum, 1991.

Kolb, D.A., *Experiential Learning: Experience as the Source of Learning and Development*, Prentice Hall, 1984.

Koopman, P.L. *et al.*, *Complexe besluitvorming n organisaties*, A&O Psychologie, 1988.

Kor, R., Wijnen, G and Weggeman, M., *Management in motiveren: inhoud geven aan leiderschap*, Kluwer Bedrijfswetenschappen, 1991.

Kotter, John P., *The General Managers*, The Free Press, 1982.

Kotter, John P., 'What effective general managers really do', *Harvard Business Review*, November–December 1982.

Kotter, John P., *The Leadership Factor*, The Free Press, 1988.

Lammers, C.J., 'Organisationele democratie', in *Men O*, 1985/6.

Lawler III, E.E., 'Substitutes for Hierarchy', *Organizational Dynamics*, 17, 1988, pp. 4–15.

Leavitt, H.J., 'Some effects of certain communication patterns on group performance', *Journal of Abnormal and Social Psychology*, Vol. 46, January 1957.

Lewin, K., 'Frontiers in group dynamics: Concept, method and reality in social science', *Human Relations*, Vol. 1, 1984, pp. 5–42.

Lievegoed, B.C.J., *Organisaties in ontwikkeling*, Lemniscaat, 1969.

Likert, R., *New Patterns of Management*, McGraw-Hill, 1961.

Luijk, H., *Waar blijft de tijd van de directeur*, Samsom, 1984.

Maccoby, M., *Why Work: Leading the new generation*, Simon & Schuster, 1988.

Mace, M., *Directors: Myth and Reality*, Harvard Business School Press, 1986.

Maslow, A.H., *Motivation and Personality*, Harper & Row, 1954.

Mastenbroek, W.F.G., *Onderhandelen*, Het Spectrum, 1984.

McGregor, D., *The Human Side of Enterprise*, McGraw-Hill, 1960.

Medezeggenschap van werknemers op ondernemingsniveau, No. 29, 1991; and *Naar Medezeggenschap op Europees Niveau*, 1989.

Miles, R.E., *Netwerk-organisaties: werkverhoudingen in de 21e eeuw, California Management Review*, Winter 1989.

Mintzberg, H., *The Nature of Managerial Work*, Harper & Row, 1973.

Mintzberg, H., 'Crafting Strategy', *Harvard Business Review*, July–August 1987.

Moerland, P.W., 'Corporate governance' in Marktwerking, *De Naamlose Vennootschap* 73, December 1995.

Mulder, M., *Conflicthantering: theorie en praktijk in organisaties*, Stenfert Kroese, 1980.

Nicholls, J., 'The paradox of managerial leadership', *Journal of General Management*, Summer 1993.

Peter, Thomas J. and Waterman, jr., Robert H., *In Search of Excellence, Lessons from America's Best-Run Companies*, Harper & Row, 1982. (Also book review: Carroll, Daniel T., 'A disappointing search for excellence', *Harvard Business Review*, November–December 1983.)

Pettigrew, A.M., *The Politics of Organizational Decision Making*, Tavistock/Van Gorcum, 1973.

Pfeffer, J., *Managing with Power*, Harvard Business School Press, 1992. (Also book review in *Men O*, 1994/5.)

Porter, M.E., *Competitive Strategy: Techniques for Analysing Industries and Competitors*, The Free Press, 1980.

Porter, M.E., *Competitive Advantage: Creating and Sustaining Superior Performance*, The Free Press, 1985.

Robbins, S.P., *Organizational Behavior: Concepts and Controversies*, Prentice Hall, 1979.

Schein, E.H., *Organizational Culture and Leadership: A dynamic view*, Jossey-Bass, 1985.

Schoenmaker, M.J.R., *Managen van mensen en prestaties: personeelsmanagement in moderne organisaties*, Kluwer Bedrijfswetenschappen, 1994.

Semler, R., *Semco-stijl*, Forum, 1993.

Shetty, Y.K., 'Aiming High: Competitive Benchmarking for Superior Performance', *Long Range Planning*, No. 1, 1993.

Simon, H.A., *Administrative Behaviour*, Macmillan, 1947.

Simon, H. A., *The Shape of Automation for Man and Management*, Harper & Row, 1965.

Snow, C., Davison, S.C., Snell, S.A. and Hambrick, D.C., 'Use Transnational Teams to Globalize your Company', *Organizational Dynamics*, Spring 1996.

Socrates, noted in Xenophon, *Memorabilia* (III. IV. 6–12) and *Oeconomicus*, Loeb Classical Library, William Heineman Ltd.

Staerkle, R., 'Der Entscheidungsprozess in der Unternehmungsorganization', *Die Unternehmung*, March 1963.

Stewart, Rosemary, *Managers and their Jobs*, Macmillan, 1967.

Stoner, J.A.F. and Freeman, R.E., *Management*, Prentice Hall, Dutch edn, 1993.

Thompson, J.D., *Organizations in Action*, McGraw-Hill, 1967.

Tracy, D., *The First Book of Common Sense Management*, William Morrow Company, 1989.

Trompenaars, F., *Riding the Waves of Culture: Understanding Cultural Diversity in Business*, Economist Books, 1983.

Turner, D. and Crawford, M., 'Managing current and future competitive performance: the role of competence', in Hamal and Heene (eds), *Competence-based Competition*, John Wiley, 1994.

Twijnstra A. and Keuning D., *Organisatie-advieswerk*, Stenfert Kroese, 2nd edn, 1995.

Vogt, G.G., *De virtuele onderneming*, originally appeared in *Der Organisator*, March 1994.

Wijnen, G., Renes, W. and Storm P., *Projectmatig werken*, Het Spectrum, 1984.

Wijnen, G., Weggeman, M. and Kor, R., *Verbeteren en vernieuwen van organisaties,* Kluwer Bedrijfswetenschappen, 1988.

Wilpert, B. and Sorge, A. (eds), *International Perspectives on Organisational Democracy*, Wiley, 1988.

Zuyderhoudt, R., 'Principes van synergie en zelfordening: Introductie in de chaos theorie binnen de organisaties', M & O, No. 1, 1992.

Further reading

General

Athos, A.G. and Pascale, R.T., *The Art of Japanese Management*, Penguin Books, 1982.

Bibeault, D.R., *Corporate Turnaround, How Managers Turn Losers into Winners*, McGraw-Hill, 1982.

Handy, C., *The Age of Unreason*, Arrow Books, 1989.

Keuning, D. and Eppink D.J., *Management en Organisatie: theorie en toepassing*, Stenfert Kroese, 6th edn, 1996.

Koning, C. de, *Goed bestuur: de regels en de kunst*, Kluwer, 1987.

Kotter, John P., 'What Effective General Managers really do', *Harvard Business Review*, November–December 1982.

Lammers, C.J., *Organiseren van bovenaf en onderop*, Spectrum, 1993.

Mintzberg, H., 'The Manager's Job: Folklore and Fact', *Harvard Business Review*, July–August 1975.

Mintzberg, H., 'Rounding out the Manager's Job', *Sloan Management Review*, Fall 1994.

Morgan, G., *Images of Organization*, Sage Publications, 1986.

Mueller, R.K., *Corporate Networking*, The Free Press, 1986.

Pascale, R., *Managing on the Edge*, Penguin Books, 1990.

Peters, T., *Liberation Management*, Macmillan, 1992.

Quinn, J.B., *Intelligent Enterprise*, The Free Press, 1992.

Senge, P.M., *The Fifth Discipline*, Doubleday/Random House, 1990.

Vanosmael, P. and Bruyn, R. de, *Handboek voor creatief denken*, DNB/Pelckmans, 1991.

Strategy

Ansoff, I., *Implanting Strategic Management*, Prentice Hall, 1990.

Buzzell, R.D. and Gale, B.T., *The PIMS Principles*, The Free Press, 1987.

Daems, H. and Douma, S., *Concurrentiestrategie en concernstrategie*, Kluwer, 1989.

Doz, Y., *Strategic Management in Multinational Companies*, Pergamon Press, 1986.

Galbraith, J.R. and Kazenjiam, P.K., *Strategy Implementation: Structure, Systems and Processes*, 2nd edn, West Publishing, 1986.

Goold, M., Campbell, A. *et al.*, *Corporate-level Strategy; Creating Volume in the Multibusiness Company*, Wiley, 1994.

Hamel, G. and Prahalad, C.K., *Competing for the Future*, Harvard Business School Press, 1994.

Haspeslagh, P.C. and Jamison, D.B., *Managing Acquistions,* The Free Press, 1991.

Mintzberg, H., *The Rise and Fall of Strategic Planning*, Prentice Hall, 1994.

Pfeffer and Salancik, *The External Control of Organizations: A Resourse Dependence Perspective*, Harper & Row, 1978.

Porter, M.E., *Competitive Strategy: Techniques for Analysing Industries and Competitors*, The Free Press, 1980.

Porter, M.E., *Competive Advantage: Creating and Sustaining Superior Performance*, The Free Press, 1985.

Porter, M.E., *The Competitive Advantage of Nations*, Macmillan, 1990.

Structure – organizational design

Brooke, M.Z., *Centralization and Autonomy*, Holt, Rinehart & Winston, 1984.

Galbraith, J.R., *Designing Complex Organizations*, Addison Wesley, 1973.

Handy, C. and Tank, A. (eds), *From Hierarchy to Network*, The Conference Board Europe, Research Monograph No. 2, 1989.

Keuning, D. and Eppink, D.J., *Management en Organisatie: theorie en toepassing*, Stenfert Kroese, 6th edn, 1996.

Keuning, D. and Opheij, W., *Delayering Organizations*, Pitman Publishing, 1994.

Lorsch, J.W. and Allen III, S., *Managing Diversity and Interdependence*, Harvard University Press, 1973.

March, J.G. and Simon, H.A., *Organizations*, Wiley, 1958.

Mintzberg, H., *The Structuring of Organizations*, Prentice Hall, 1979.

Mintzberg, H., 'Organization design: fashion or fit?', *Harvard Business Review*, January–February 1981, pp. 103–16.

Mintzberg, H., 'The effective organization: forces and forms', *Sloan Management Review*, Winter 1991, pp. 54–66.

Tank, A., *The Role of the Center: New Linkages in Fast Changing Companies,* The Conference Board Europe, Research Monograph, No. 6, 1991.

Wissema, J.G., *Unit Management: het decentraliseren van ondernemerschap*, Van Gorcum, 1987.

People, organizations and culture: Human resources management and organizational change

Bolwijn, P.T. and Kumpe T., *Marktgericht ondernemen, management van continuïteit en vernieuwing*, Van Gorcum, 1992.

Evans, P., Doz, Y. and Laurent A. (eds), *Human Resource Management in International Firms*, St. Martin's Press, 1990.

French, W.L., Bell, C.H. *et al.*, *Organizational Development*, B.P.I/Irwin, 1989.

Jong, G.R.A. de, *Personeelsmanagement: zorg voor maatwerk in de praktijk*, Kluwer Bedrijfswetenschappen, 1992.

Harrison, R., *Leiderschap en strategische planning in een nieuwe tijd*, Transformatie, Lemniscaat, 1986.

Hofstede, G., *Allemaal andersdenkenden, omgaan met cultuurverschillen*, Contact, 1991.

Korte, A.W. de and Bolweg, J.F., *De nieuwe werknemer*, Van Gorcum, 1994.

Lawler III, E.E., *Motivation in Work Organizations*, Jossey-Bass, 1994.

Lee, R. and Lawrence, P., *Organizational Behavior, Politics at Work*, Hutchinson Management Studies, 1985.

Lorsch, J.W. and Morse, J.J., *Organizations and Their Members: a Contingency Approach*, Harper & Row, 1974.

Mintzberg, H., *Power in and around Organizatiuons*, Prentice Hall, 1983.

Mintzberg, H., 'Planning on the left side and managing on the right', *Harvard Business Review*, July–August 1976, pp. 58–9.

Quinn Mills, D., *Rebirth of the Corporation*, Wiley, 1991.

Quinn Mills, D., 'The Truth About Empowerment', *Training & Development*, 1992, pp. 31–2.

Sanders, G. and Nuijen, B., *Bedrijfscultuur: diagnose en beïnvloeding*, Van Gorcum, 1987.

Schein, E.H., *Organizational Culture and Leadership*, Jossey-Bass, 1985.

Schoenmaker, M.J.R. and Geerdink, T., *Human talentmanagement, een visie op besturen, faciliteren en ontwikkelen van personeel*, Kluwer Bedrijfswetenschappen, 1991.

Scott, D.S. and Jaffe, D.T., *Empowerment: Building a Committed Workforce*, Kogan Page, 1991.

Vroom, V.H., *Work and Motivation*, Jossey-Bass, 1995.

Wissema, J.G., Messer, H.M. and Wijers, G.J., *Angst voor veranderen? een mythe?,* Van Gorcum, 1986.

Woodcock, M. and Francis, P., *Clarifying Organizational Values*, Gower, 1989.

Technology, information and organizations

Acohen, J. and Florijn, R., 'Besturen en beheersen van de kosten van automatiseringsprojecten', *Holland Management Review*, No. 35, 1993.

Batelaan, M.V. and Doorn, P. van, 'De strategische betekenis van informatietechnologie', *Harvard Holland Review*, No. 27, Summer 1991.

Bemelmans, T.M.A., *Bestuurlijke informatiesystemen en automatisering*, Stenfert Kroese, 4th edn, 1991.

Benson, R., 'Preparing IS for the 1990s: improving enterprise performance with information technology', *BIKMag, Bestuurlijk Informatiedeskundig Magazine*, August 1991.

Buitelaar, M. and Groen, U., 'Business process redesign: Een nieuwe kijk op informatisering?', *Informatie,* 1994, 36, No. 6, pp. 388–97.

Burns, T. and Stalker, G.M., *The Management of Innovation*, Tavistock Publications, 1971.

Davenport, T.H. and Short, J.E., 'The New Industrial Engineering: Information Technology and Business Process Redesign', *Sloan Management Review,* 1990, vol. 31, no. 4.

Hammer, M., 'Bedrijfsprocessen herstructureren: zet het mes erin', *Harvard Holland Review*, no. 27, Summer 1991.

Hopper, M., 'Concurreren met IT: een nieuwe benadering', *Harvard Holland Review*, no. 26, Spring 1991.

Malone, T.W., *Organizational Structure and Information Technology: Elements of Formal Theory*, Sloan School of Management, MIT, 1985.

Morris, D. and Brandon, J., *Re-engineering your business*, McGraw-Hill, 1993.

Roussel, A. *et al.* (Arthur D. Little), *Management of Research and Development*, Harvard Business School Press, 1991.

Sitter, L.U. de, *Op weg naar nieuwe fabrieken en kantoren*, Kluwer, 1987.

Tapscott, D. and Caston, A., *Paradigm Shift: the new promise of Information Technology*, McGraw-Hill, 1993.

Management consultancy and change

Bennis, W.G., Benne, K.D. and Chin, R., *The Planning of Change*, Holt, Rinehart & Winston, 1985.

Block, P., 'Dealing with Resistance', *Flawless Consulting*, U.A.C., 1981.

Feltman, C.E., *Adviseren bij organiseren*, Kreits, 1984.

Greiner, L.E. and Metzger, R.O., *Consulting to Management*, Prentice Hall, 1983.

Kubr, M. (ed.), *Management Consulting*, ILO, 1986.

Levy, A. and Merry, U., *Organizational Transformation Approaches, Strategies, Theories*, Preager Publishers, 1986.

Maister, D.H., 'Balancing the professional service firm', *CPA Journal*, November 1986, pp. 126–34.

Maister, D.H., *Managing the Professional Service Firm*, The Free Press, 1993.

Mangham, I., *The Politics of Organizational Change*, Associated Business Press, 1979.

Margerison, C.J., 'How to Raise Energy Levels', in *Managerial Consulting Skills*, Gower, 1988.

Otto, M.M. and Leeuw, A.C.J. de, *Kijken, denken, doen. Organisatieverandering: manoeuvreren met weerbarstigheid*, Van Gorcum, 1994.

Twijnstra, A. and Keuning D., *Organisatie-advieswerk*, Stenfert Kroese, 2nd edn, 1995.

Glossary

Account manager. An employee responsible for planning and policy as well as the sales of all products of an organization, directed at larger clients.

Annual report. Written report of the board to shareholders, in which a description of the events of the past year and prospects for the coming year have been included.

Annual report (fiscal). Report on behalf of the fiscal authorities, drawn up according to legal guidelines in determination of fiscal profits, including the balance sheet and the profit and loss statement of the company.

Artificial Intelligence (AI). That part of information sciences occupied with processes which produce intelligent actions.

Attitude. A tendency, formed by information and experience from the past, to react consistently to an idea, event, company or person. An attitude creates a link between feelings and ideas of a person and his behaviour. For an organization, labour satisfaction, involvement and loyalty are important people attitudes.

Autocratic leadership. A style of leadership accompanied by stringent directives, exercise of strict supervision and threats of sanctions.

Balanced Business Scorecard. A method to help management in mapping out performances. This occurs from four points of view: the customer perspective, the company processes, the organizational learning processes, the financial perspective.

Basic organization. The permanent organization for the control of the company processes. It forms the reservoir for the creation of a project organization.

Benchmarking. The continuous process of the measuring of products, services and practices in which the results are confronted with those of the toughest competitor or of the organizations which are acknowledged as business sector leaders.

Bill of material. A schematic representation of the interrelationships between components and structure of a product.

Boston Consulting Group approach. Approach of portfolio management with position determining factors being market growth and relative market share.

Bottom up approach. An approach of the planning cycle in which the initiative lies especially with the divisions and/or business units or departments.

Brainstorming. A technique to stimulate creativity in the development of new ideas.

Budget. A plan translated into sums of money which also is a task setting exercise.

Budget result. The difference between allowed and actual costs post-calculation.

Budgeting. A delegation instrument in management. By translating plans into sums of money it is possible to delegate tasks and authorities and maintain control.

Business or activity. A description of a domain of an organization which can be indicated by the client group to be worked on, the needs provided for and the technology through which that happens.

Business ethics. Systematic analysis and coverage of moral problems which occur in the course of business and organizational affairs.

Business policy. A statement of the ways and resources with which the management wants to realize the set of defined goals and objectives.

Business Process Redesign (BPR). An integral approach of functional partial processes in which, with the help of the application of new information technology, the existing course of the process is radically redesigned by means of intervention in the organizational structure.

Business unit. An organizational unit within which business activities are grouped.

Cafeteria plan. A payment system in which the employees compose their own payment package ('menu') so that this best adapts to personal needs.

Capacity planning. The component of production planning in which the planning and size of the necessary capacities (factories, machines, people) is roughly determined.

Cash cow. A business with low market growth and a high relative market share.

Cash flow. Change in the 'liquid' cash resources. Net profit + depreciation.

Cash flow control. Guarding of liquidities; and of incoming and outgoing cash flows.

Centralized functional structure. An organizational structure which arises from the combination of internal differentiation in departmentalization and centralization in decision making.

Chain of business activities. A series of organizations involved in the bringing about of goods and services, for example, from forestry to the furniture store.

Cognitive dissonance. Doubt, feeling of discomfort, which lives in an individual about the correctness of his image of reality, because certain 'cognitions' are not in agreement with each other, for example, 'holiday' and 'bad weather'.

Co-maker. A supplier who receives and accepts co-responsibility for the final product of his client.

Common Mental Model (CMM). A model which maps out the common learning process of people in an organization, via the Common Mental Model (CMM) and the learning cycle. *See* Learning cycle and Mental model.

Company. Each independent unit operating in society as an organizational unity, in which work is conducted on the basis of a labour agreement.

Competitive advantage. Relative advantage; advantage of an organization over its competitors in relation to an aspect which is considered relevant by (potential) clients.

Composed task assignment. The assignment to attain a certain result with compulsory directives with regard to the way the results have to be attained.

Conceptual learning. Starting to see a certain way of thinking or pattern of acting differently, because of which new routines can be learned from a completely new perspective. *See* Operational learning.

Conflict handling. Conflict handling can be distinguished in two dimensions: emphasis on own interest/goal (assertive) and emphasis on someone else's interest/goal (co-operative).

Consistency criteria. Criteria in the choice of a strategy, whereby it is considered whether the organization can meet the demands the strategy requires and whether the strategy accords to external developments and goals.

Constituting. Creating a regulatory framework within which the actual execution of actions can take place.

Constituting level. The level in the organization at which one determines the objectives, goals and policy of the organization in outline.

Consultation group. A temporary or permanent group within a labour organization which is composed of representatives of more than one department to prepare decisions.

Contract wage. A way of determining wages based on an agreement between employer and employee about the size of the activities to be conducted.

Control. Drawing up of norms and plans for the execution of activities, including being able to adjust/correct the execution and the planning.

Control cycle. Supervising, monitoring, checking, and if necessary, adjusting and/or correcting.

Corporatism. A societal and political system in which government, business organizations and labour organizations are stongly interwoven in the governing of society.

Costs. The value expressed in terms of money of all resources of production used in the production of goods and/or services.

Creativity. The ability to link elements and matters which, from existing perspectives or ideas, are experienced as new or unusual.

Crisis management. The active handling of sudden disruptions in the desired relationship between the internal and external environment of the organization.

Critical Success Factors (CSFs). Factors of decisive importance for the success of an organization.

Cybernetic cycle. *See* Control cycle.

Cycle lengthening, horizontal task enlargement or job enlargement. The expansion of the task cycle by preceding or subsequent activities of the same level.

Decentralization. The spreading of decision-making authority over more people and hierarchical layers in the organizations.

Decentralized division structure. An organizational structure which arises from a combination of internal specialization in the departmentalization and decentralization in decision making.

Decision making. A process which unrolls in sequential phases from the moment information identifying a problem becomes available, until the moment at which a chosen solution is executed.

Decision Support System (DSS). A decision supporting information system, for example for the making of ordering advice lists.

Delivery planning or work preparation. This takes place after planning utilization/occupation of machinery and people. It determines when raw materials and tools have to be at manufacturing departments or machine groups.

Departmentalization. The combining of work units and sub-departments into main departments and services based on managerial considerations.

Depth of control. The number of levels which one can manage (in)directly.

Detaching. The temporary or permanent assigning of organizational capacity (functionaries) to another organizational unit or department.

Detail planning or work dispatch. The division of the work on production order over different people and/or machines.

Differential piece wage. Way of paying employees in which a direct relation exists between numbers of manufacturing units and wage.

Differentiation strategy. A strategy which directs itself at supplying a product with unique characteristics.

Directing. The bringing into motion of the operational actions as well as the supervising and adjusting/correcting.

Disengagement point. An inventory whose function it is to make two partial processes within a production process less dependent on one another. By less interruption sensitivity the need for planning and co-ordination is reduced.

Diversification. A strategic choice alternative in which the organization enters new markets with new products.

Division manager. Person responsible for strategy, structure and processes within a division.

Dog. A business with low market growth and a low relative market share.

Double loop learning. Double loop learning asumes the (human) capacity to be able to take a double look at situations, not only to detect and correct errors in relation to a given set of norms, but also the capability to question the relevance of operating norms.

Earning capacity/rate of return. The revenue in relation to the invested equity capital.

Effectiveness. The degree of goal realization.

Efficiency. The relation between the planned and the actual use of resources.

Entrepreneurship. The sum of the thoughts, mentality and actions which directs itself at the conscious acceptance of risks in the supply of products or services, often with the intention to make a profit.

Environmental care. The sum of the provisions in a company, directed at the control and, where possible, at the reduction of the burdening on the environment by company activities.

Escrow agreement. An agreement between clients and suppliers of software, in which the supplier deposits the source codes of the software produced by him with a third, independent party, so that, in the case of calamity (for example fire, bankruptcy of the supplier) the software remains available to the client.

Ethics. Systematic analysis and handling of moral problems.

Exercise of power or realized power. The actual determining of behaviour to a certain degree or giving direction to the behaviour of another.

Experience effect (learning curve). The effect that in case of the increase of the volume of the production, the cost price per unit product, corrected for inflation, can decrease.

Expert power. The power someone has based on knowledge and expertise.

External adaptation. The tuning of the organization into the environment which surrounds it.

External appraisal. An investigation directed at the external societal environment and markets in order to signal opportunities and/or threats.

Extrinsic form of payment. Payments/rewards which lie outside the activities themselves, such as direct reimbursements, indirect reimbursements and non-financial reimbursements.

Flat organizational structure. The organizational form in which managers lead relatively many subordinates (i.e. there is a large span of control).

Flexible retirement. A system in which the retirement data is not fixed at the year that the employee turns 65 years of age, but in which the choice is left to the employee to work less or for longer.

Formalism. Maintenance of rigidity when rules are broken in order to maintain the structure of the organization as it was.

Formal organization. The established assignment of tasks by the management of complemented tasks and function descripti ons, guidelines and procedures.

Franchise. A form of co-operation between a franchise giver and a franchise taker. In exchange for payment, the franchise taker receives the right to make use of certain sales and distribution systems, for example shop formulae and logos.

Front-line managers. All managerial employees who are in direct contact with operational employees.

Function. *General*: the contribution to the realization of goals and values.
Sociological: the contribution of a component to the whole and the maintenance of that whole. *Organizational*: the common goal of a number of coherent tasks.

Function appraisal and evaluation. A system in which by means of the assigning of points the relative weight of a function is determined, and from which functional wage can be or is derived.

Function description. The written determination of the function content in which especially the tasks, authorities, obligations, responsibilities and interrelationships are described.

Functional area. An area within the organization which is oriented at a specialism or 'technical' aspect of functioning, for example Personnel Department, Finance Department, etc.

Functional authority. The authority to give compulsory directives/indications about how something needs to be done from a certain specialistic field and/or to execute certain tasks in this specialist area independently.

Function forming process. The division of tasks between people and groups and the formation of cohering tasks into functions.

Functional Information System (FIS). An information system for functional area in an organization, for example purchase or manufacturing.

Functional management. Managing a single specialized task as component of a complicated combined action.

Functional wage. The salary which belongs to a certain function based on function appraisal and evaluation, without considering the actual performance.

Goodwill. An extra amount of money paid for 'the good name' of the organization in case of a takeover or acquisition by another organization.

Gross profit. The difference between the sales prices and the purchase price of the goods sold.

Group morale. The sum of the unwritten notions of the members of a society or group with regard to 'the good life' and that what is 'proper/improper' behaviour, as well as with regard to '(un)fair division of pleasures and problems' (fair and just).

Hierarchy of needs. Motivation theory from Maslow which states that most people have five types of needs which, in terms of importance can be ranked in hierarchical level: physical needs, security, belonging and social contacts, respect and self-development/actualization.

Holding. A variant of the decentralized divisional structure in which there is no relationship between the activities of the different divisions than just the financial relation, so that the task of the concern top in 'the mother company' especially lies in the financial-administrative strategic 'control' over the concern.

Homo economicus. An image of human beings which starts from the assumption that the human being is always completely and objectively informed about all causes and consequences of changes in his environment. In the case of choice problems the human being chooses the alternative which yields more measurable use to him based on that information.

Horizontal organization. Dividing activities and assigning authorities at the same level of management and execution.

Horizontal relationship. The consultation relationship between functionaries at a same level with the goal of reaching co-ordinated action by direct contact.

Human Resources Management (HRM). The co-ordinated steering and development of supply and demand of human potential and skills in the organization, by integration of the personnel policy in the strategy to be followed, the structure to be designed and the desired organizational culture.

Human relations theory. Management theory based on the knowledge that there is an indirect relationship between the attention which is paid to the worker and his performances.

Identification power. Power which arises because others can identify themselves with someone or like to feel they belong to someone.

Individual Mental Model (IMM). A model which maps out the individual learning process, via the Individual Mental Model (IMM) and the learning cycle. *See* Learning cycle and Mental model.

Information management. The steering and managing of information activities. In the first place this regards the management of the flow of information on behalf of the productive, primary and supporting processes. In the second place, this also regards the information supply on behalf of the management process.

Information plan. This states the projects and the actions necessary in order to realize the information policy, in order of time and priority.

Information supply. Providing for the information needs of: members of an organization, to fulfil their own function with regard to the functioning of the organization in general; and external stakeholders with regard to the organization.

Information system. The sum of the people, machines and activities directed at collecting and processing of data in such a way that one can provide for the information needs of external and internal stakeholders.

Information technology (IT). A collective term for all knowledge and skills concerning digital and analogue transmission, storage, processing, and representation techniques, in order to manipulate data which, for the human perception, are of visual/sensual/auditive nature (from scribbling block to multimedia/virtual reality).

Instrumentality theory. Vroom's motivation theory: the strength of work motivation is the product of the strength of someone's preference for a certain outcome and the expectation that the work goal can be attained by their own knowledge, in return for the receipt of a reward.

Interactive consumption. The production of those services or servicing in which the consumer is present.

Interim manager. A temporarily appointed manager, coming from outside the organization, with line authorities in order to provide specific management expertise which is not available within the organization itself for a certain period.

Internal adaptation. The mutual tuning of the available capacities within the organization in people and other resources (machines, money, information, buildings).

Internal appraisal. A systematic analysis of the characteristics and functioning of an organization at a given point in time, in relation to a situation in either the past or the future of that organization, or in relation to another comparable organization.

Internal communication. Communication in which the target group is situated within the organization.

Internal differentiation. Grouping actions or processes by similarity with regard to expertise, knowledge, skill and attitude.

Internal environmental care. The provisions in an organization directed at obtaining insight into the control of, and where possible the reduction of, the burden placed on the environment by company activities.

Internal operational signalling. The system of internal information supply in a company or institution which provides management on different levels and in different departments, with specific and timely information for the supervision of and adjustment to planning and the execution of current company activities.

Internal or horizontal differentiation. Division of labour into phases of the operational processes (functional or F-grouping).

Internal or horizontal specialization. Division of labour based on the interrelated actions to product, geographic location or market segment (P-, G-, M-grouping).

Intrinsic form of reward/payment. Form of payment which derives from the work itself, especially the result of job satisfaction.

Intuitive approach of strategy. An approach of strategy formulation, in which the steps to be distinguished are not explicitly taken.

IT strategy. The strategic-tactical decisions with regard to all applications of information technology.

Job rotation. Frequent change of different kinds of task with other organization members.

Job share. A job that is occupied by two employees who each work, for example, half a day.

Joint venture. Two companies together found a single new organization.

Just-in-time. A way of approaching inventory control (originating in Japan), in which the necessity for inventory is eliminated by delivering just-in-time. The ideal inventory size is 'zero', because all goods are 'in process'.

Kanban. Literally 'small card'. A manufacturing management method introduced by Toyota, in which in the manufacturing department components go from phase to phase in trays with a small card attached to them. When the materials are used, the card goes back. This is the signal that a new tray of components needs to be prepared. The size of the series is standard. The consequence is minimum supply of departments.

Key factors (KFs). The key factors at tactical and operational level which can be derived from the Critical Success Factors (CSFs).

Key variables of individual behaviour. The variables which play a part in invoking the behaviour of an individual, namely values, attitudes, personality, motivation, perception, and learning.

Labour division. The grouping of activities to be conducted in tasks and functions for employees, work groups, departments, divisions and the overall structure.

Lateral thinking. A method of developing new ideas by leaving existing meaning and ways of working.

Lay-out. The spatial mapping of the method of production to be followed.

Leading. The influencing of organizational and working behaviour of employees based on personal contact.

Learning. Behavioural changes of a longer lasting nature, as a consequence of processing and interpretation of information and experiences via the learning cycle. Thus innate reactions and temporary behavioural changes are not part of 'learning'.

Learning cycle. The cycle which an individual or group goes through in the case of learning, observing, assessing, designing and applying (OADA), while making use of mental models in that process. *See* Mental model.

Learning organization. The enlarging of the capacity of an organization to reach effective action. An organization which systematically bundles the experiences of its individual members and develops new common ways of behaviour.

Line organization. The organizational form which reflects the managerial and operational functions of functionaries at different hierarchical levels.

Line relations. The authority relationship between a superior and a subordinate whereby the superior gives orders, bears responsibilities and exercises supervision, and the subordinate has to execute those orders and render account.

Line staff organization. The organizational form in which specialists in policy formulation have been added to the line organization at one or more levels of management.

Linking pin. A way of organizing and managing in which the manager consults his employees and in which the manager, as the linking pin, represents the team or the department in a higher consultation group. The use of this type of consultation implies the horizontalization of the line relation.

Logistics management. All activities which have to do with planning, organizing and managing of the flow of materials, including the flow of information necessary for this. Logistics management comprises two 'partial sections': Materials management and physical distribution.

Long-term planning. An approach of strategy formulation in which one starts from the assumption that the future developments are determined by the same forces as in the past.

Management. The collection of people who have a managerial function within an organization; the process of activities which a managerial person conducts: goal and policy determination, planning, organizing, giving of orders and support, co-ordinating, monitoring and checking and when necessary, adjusting; a scientific/specialistic field: the whole of (pure) scientific and applied knowledge and methods and techniques considering the planning, organizing and co-operation of people.

Management by exception. The organizational model in which higher management only intervenes when determined tolerance zones have been exceded.

Management by objectives. A way of managing and delegation in which the manager and the employee have reached agreements about goals and core results to be attained during a certain period.

Management consultancy. The supply of an independent and expert advice with regard to determining and solving of organizational problems.

Management development. The systematic supply and development of future management, considering the individual wishes and interests of those involved.

Management leadership. A notion which indicates that leadership always is an integral component of management via aspects of administration, stimulation, supervision and inspiration.

Management of change. Bringing an organization, by a directed effort, from the unconscious experience of a situation at T1 to the conscious experience of a new situation at T2.

Management process theory. Goal-oriented activities which give direction to the primary and supporting secondary processes in an organization.

Manager. Anyone in an organization who sets in motion and steers the actions of other people.

Managing. In the widest sense: The determining of the goals of the total organization, the designing of the fitting organizational structure and the recruiting and developing of the necessary capacities in order to be able to realize the goals.

In the narrow sense: The managing of employees by means of the giving of orders, stimulating, supporting, coaching and supervising.

Manufacturing Resources Planning (MRP II). An extension of MRP I, MRP II intends to map out the capacities (resources) by means of task setting agreements between the different functional areas with regard to the availability of their capacities. The main production plan follows from these agreements. From the main production plan, the need for materials is derived, calculated via MRP I.

Market development. A strategic alternative in which the organization directs itself at new markets with existing products.

Market penetration. A strategic alternative in which the organization, within the framework of the present activities, strives for an improvement of the results/market share. These can be attained by the reduction of competition and/or the improving of the own position.

Master budget. In this, the task setting income, cost, and expenditure budgets from the departments are processed. Expenditure which will require liquidity resources is included.

Materials management. The control of the flow of goods and the accompanying flows of information from the obtaining of raw materials up to the production phases (half fabrics/inventory goods in process). The finished product inventory belongs to physical distribution (*see also* Logistics management).

Materials Requirements Planning (MRP I). A production management method which has been developed for composed products. From the finished product one calculates backwards to the numbers of components to be ordered or produced. MRP I is material-directed and does not render account to the available capacities, thus the need for MRP II (*see above*), which considers the necessary capacities.

Matrix organization. This occurs when one can speak of dual authority and balance. Matrix organization is an extreme way of attaining co-ordination between two important goal orientations or aspects deeper in an organization.

Mental model. A deeply anchored 'world-picture' in the individual personality, which offers the basis for interpretation of reality and because of that, has large influence on action.

Mission. The role and the ambitions of the organization in the defined domain(s).

Morale. A regulating mechanism in order to stimulate the co-existance, co-operation and the group survival of people who each have their own self-interest. Individual, personal moral notions can deviate from the 'ruling' group morale, and can, in this way, be a reason for change in group or social morale. *See* Group morale and Personal morale.

Multi-factor reward. A way of rewarding/payment in which one not only considers the quantity of delivered performances, but also the quality, for example, careful use of materials, loyalty, contactual skills.

Net sales. The sales after deduction of sales tax and issued discounts.

Network organization. An organizational form in which the different functions such as product design, manufacturing, distribution and sales, are not executed in or within an organization, but by different organizations, which possibly are only linked to each other for one 'product event'.

Network planning. *See* Project planning.

Noise. Interruption of the communication process.

Non-power. The willingness and attitude of an authority in order to let himself be convinced by others during a conversation or consultation via open argumentation.

Office automation. The automation and integration of text processing and data processing processes.

Open system. The sum of the flow of material, information and energy, which can be described in terms of input, transformation (throughput) and output, which is directed at the fulfilling of functions for the environment.

Operational employees. Those employees in a labour organization who do not have managerial tasks.

Operational learning. Learning of new routines within previously learned frameworks or concepts.

Opportunity. A development from markets or the wider societal environment which provides the organization with the possibility to improve its own functioning/basis of existence.

Optimal delegation. An application of the delegation principle such that at the different levels of management and execution sufficient authority has been given to take correct and well-considered decisions.

Optimal order size/series. The size of the series, in which the sum of the ordering costs and the inventory costs are as low as possible.

Organic structure. Coherence of organs of a labour organization. In this relation, organs are the main departments and functions.

Organization. Every goal-realizing co-operative unit in which participants consistently enter into a mutual relationship and work together in order to reach common goals.

Organization culture. The common understanding of the members of an organization with regard to expected (work) behaviour of others.

Organization chart or organogram. Schematic representation of the most important characteristics of the formal division of tasks and of the formal division of authority in an organization. In short: an overview of the organic and/or personnel structure.

Organizational equilibrium. This occurs when the organization rewards its internal and external participants in such a way that they remain motivated in order to continue their contributions to the organization.

Organizational structure. The division of activities to be conducted in tasks, functions, working groups and departments; the assignment of authorities and relations in which employees, working groups and departments are related to each other in the execution of their tasks; the built-in communication mechanisms through which employees, working groups and departments are connected to each for the necessary transfer of will and co-ordination.

Organizing. The creating of effective relations between people, resources and actions in order to attain certain goals (organization in functional sense).

Outplacement. The activities to assist someone who is placed outside the organizational unit or who is fired/discharged to find another function, following their present employment.

Participation. A mutual consultation or deliberation which is experienced as legitimate, and in which a conscious influencing of the decision making of those involved takes place.

Participative leadership/management. A style of leadership in which the employee is offered space for deliberation and participation.

Perception. The process of interpreting and processing of sensory impressions so that meaning can be given to the environment.

Performance payment. Payment varies with the performance delivered. *See also* Differential piece wage and Multi-factor reward.

Personal culture. An organizational culture which is characterized by a low degree of co-operation and a high degree of spreading of power (decentralization).

Personal morale. The whole of the individual notions of a person with regard to 'the good/ideal life', '(im)proper behaviour', as well as '(un)just division of problems and pleasures'. Personal, individual notions which are shared with others, form the group morale.

Personal power or prestige. That is power assigned to someone, based on who he/she is (personality and experience) and not based on the function he or she performs.

Personnel management. A component of HRM, namely the management of the inflow, through flow, and outflow of personnel.

Personnel structure. The occupation of functions in departments by persons.

Physical distribution. The control of the materials and accompanying flow of information from inventory of finished products up to the phase of delivering the products to the final consumer (*see* Logistics management).

Planning. The process of information processing which leads to decisions in the present with regard to future actions, with co-ordination and controlling of those actions in mind.

Planning cycle. The sequential steps between analysis and budgeting (often parallel to the book year).

Policy guidelines. A complete indication of how one has to act in a given situation.

Policy intensive. The kind of work which is especially characterized by activities for developing policy.

Policy matrix (from Shell). Approach to portfolio management with the attractiveness of the sector and competitive position as policy determining factors.

Policy plan. Plan which states in which way, in what period of time and with which resources goals will have to be attained.

Pooled dependence. Mutual dependency or relatedness of parts of an organization which is limited to indirect dependency (via the hierarchy).

Post-calculation. Periodical comparison of the budgeted costs with the actual costs. The possible difference is known as the budget result.

Power or potential power. The capacity to influence the behaviour of others and to get others to act in a certain manner, possibly even forcibly.

Power culture. An organizational culture characterized by a high degree of co-operation and a low degree of spreading of power (centralization).

Power distance. Descriptive, as dimension of national culture: the degree to which the less powerful members of organizations in a country expect and accept that the power is unequally distributed. Descriptive, without taking into consideration or not accepting the power distance of those involved: the degree of inequality in power between a less powerful person or group and a more powerful person or group.

Pragmatic aspect of information. Regards the use of data by a sender of information and the intended effects by the sender in a certain context.

Preparedness or willingness to change. The degree to which the members of an organization are willing to co-operate in the changes within an organization.

Present picture of the portfolio. Survey of the present businesses with regard to the market growth and the relative market share in a figure.

Present strategic profile. A characterization of the organization in which the goals, the work domains, the competitive advantage and the synergy are determined. The profile can be seen as the starting-point from which the organization has to realize the new strategy.

Primary labour conditions. The composition of wage, salary and vacation money.

Primary process. That process from which an organization derives its existence/its 'raison d'être'.

Procedure. A series of connected tasks which form a complete whole.

Process. A number of sequential activities or events.

Product development. A strategic option in which the organization starts developing new products for the existing markets.

Productivity. The relation between results and resources used.

Product lifecycle. The period between introduction of a product and taking that product off the market.

Product/market combination. Products or services for which sales is sought in a certain market or market segment and for which a seperate strategy is developed.

Project. A series of activities to be executed by more than one specialist group acting in a temporary co-operative relation directed at a clear specified result to be attained within a limited time and with limited resources.

Project management. The managing of a set of activities, directed at a specific goal, which are executed one-time only within limited time and costs.

Project planning or network planning. A method of planning one-time only activities. The goal is the determination of the total completion time needed. The critical path indicates which partial activities are not allowed to be delayed because the completion time is influenced.

Pull system. A way of approaching the managing of production processes, in which the production is controlled, based on client order. So, the goods and the orders are, as it were, 'pulled' out of the organization by the client. The alternative is the push system (*see* below).

Push system. A way of approaching the management of production processes, in which the flow of goods/production is controlled on the basis of prognoses or marketing research. So the goods and orders are 'pushed into' the organization, based on planning. The alternative is the pull system (*see* above).

Quality. A general evaluative notion which always has to be concertized to the context within which the notion is used, for example to technical performances, extra use possibilities, user-friendliness, reliability, the meeting of specifications, durability, maintenance friendliness, aesthetical value.

Quality care. The tuning of characteristics of the product or of the service to be delivered as well as those of the organization which brings these forth, to the demands of the client, in such a way that the demands can be met continuously at acceptable costs.

Quality circles. Groups within departments which are directed at studying and attacking quality problems, production problems and other problems within that department.

Quality system. All the quality-directed organizational structures, responsibilities, procedures and provisions.

Quantitative overutilization/occupation. A workload which is clearly above the reasonable minimum performance.

Quantitative underutilization/occupation. A workload which is clearly below the reasonable minimum performance.

Question mark. A business with a high market growth and a low relative market share.

Rate of return on equity. Net profit in relation to equity.

Rate of return on total capital. Profit before tax, increased with interest to be paid over the loans, in relation to the total capital.

Ratio. A figure which relates two phenomena, with which the situation in the organization is sketched in a certain way.

Realized power. *See* Exercise of power.

Reciprocal interdependence. Mutual dependency or interrelatedness between parts of an organization in which, besides pooled interdependence, one can speak of a direct mutual interdependency. Each part supplies outputs which are inputs for the other parts and every part receives output from the other parts which are inputs for the own unit.

Relative market share. One's own market share divided by that of the largest competitor.

Resistance approach. In this approach to organizational change, resistance has a 'neutral' sound. It is a mechanism which protects the human being from an experience of 'chaos'.

Responsibility. The moral duty to execute a task to the best of one's ability and to report on the execution of that task.

Return on invested capital. Sales in relation to capital. This ratio states the relation between size of activity and the investment made for the purpose.

Return on investments (ROI). The degree of profitability expressed by: the profit margin (profit/sales) times the rotation time (sales/invested capital) of the invested capital.

Revolving budget. A budgeting system in which a budget for the initial period has a task setting character, while the figures for subsequent periods have an orientating character.

Role culture. An organizational culture characterized by a low degree of co-operation and a low degree of spreading of power (centralization).

Routing. The way or route between and within phases of manufacturing, with the optimal formation of people and machines as the goal.

Safety inventory or stock. The extra inventory of an article which one holds in order to prevent one from running out of stock, in the case of an increased demand during the ordering period.

Secondary labour conditions. Complementary payment provisions which can differ per organization, like complementary retirement insurance, life and health insurance.

Self-control. The exercising of the authority to regulate and to steer the production in a unit within previously set frameworks without direct intervention during the production process from the outside.

Self-regulating/controlling teams. Teams with operational and possibly also organizational authority to decide on planning and the manner of execution of the work in order to attain the goals which are set.

Semantics. Regards the 'meaning' which is given to a combination of data by the sender as well as the receiver of data.

Semi-autonomous working group. A working group which has authority to organize its own work.

Serial or sequential interdependence. Mutual dependency or interrelation between parts of an organization in which, besides the pooled interdependence, one can speak of a direct, one-sided dependency, in the sense that the activities have a coercive, fixed order. The output of one part is the input of the next part.

Service/servicing. An activity or a series of activities, of a more or less tangible nature, which usually take place in direct interaction between client and the employees and/or physical resources and/or systems of the supplier.

Servuction system. The part of a servicing organization which is visible from the point of view of the client, has influence on the forming of his image with regard to the supplier as well as on his valuation and purchasing behaviour.

Situational leadership. The notion that there is not one specific style of leadership which will lead to the best results in every case. The best style which has to be applied depends on the situation.

Slip chart planning board. An order planning instrument in which through coloured slips the order is indicated, set off against the time (week/day) within which the order has to be completed. Deviations of the planning can be indicated with signalling signs, like coloured triangles and green dots.

Social annual report. A summary of the general annual report rewritten in understandable language for the company's own personnel, with an emphasis on social aspects of realized business policy.

Socio-psychological factors. Besides physical factors the co-determining elements in human behaviour, which rest on the fact that human beings are social beings.

Solvency. The degree in which an organization can meet its financial obligations in case of liquidation.

Span of control. The number of employees a manager can manage directly and effectively.

Stages of growth (of an organization). Building up of existence, survival, success, expansion, optimal relations.

Standard cost price. The estimated cost price for a certain period, based on allowed costs per unit of product.

Star. A business with a high market growth and a high relative market share.

Strategic goals. Goals which the organization has to strive for, the methods of attaining these and the resources which are necessary for that.

Strategic alliance. A form of co-operation between two or more organizations, based on agreements, without any loss of identity or autonomy.

Strategic business unit (SBU). An organizational unit in which different business activities are accommodated because of an interrelated or mutual strategic relation.

Strategic management. An approach to strategic problems in which attention is paid to the choice of the product/market combinations, the development of and the maintenance of necessary skills in the future as well as the implementation of a chosen strategy and the possible adjustment of the strategy.

Strategic planning. An approach to strategy formulation in which the choice of (new) product/market combinations is stressed.

Stress. The psychological and physical situation which arises when demands are made on a person which he or she cannot meet.

Supervision/control. The testing/checking of the reality to the norms which were set.

Support department. A department which is added to the line organization in order to render certain internal services (to the whole organization or parts of it).

Synergy. The advantage which can arise when the organization starts developing new activities, in which use can be made of existing facilities.

Tall or deep organizational structure. The organizational form in which leaders manage relatively few subordinates directly (i.e. a narrow span of control).

Task culture. An organizational culture which is characterized by a high degree of co-operation and a high degree of spreading of power (decentralization).

Task enrichment. *See* Vertical enlargement.

Task enlargement. *See* Cycle lengthening.

Task maturity. The degree to which an employee is capable and willing to take responsibility for a certain task.

Technical aspect of information. Regards the way in which the data/information is transported to the 'receiver'. Here, the so-called 'information carrier' is regarded, for example CD-ROM, slide, book, X-ray.

Tertiary labour conditions. All kinds of reimbursements, for example car costs or company car, reimbursement in mortgage interest, free telephone, etc.

Time study. The method for determining the standard times for the activities to be conducted.

Timing. Criteria in the choice of a strategy in which, on the one hand, the speed of execution of the alternative is important and which, on the other, regards the question whether the organizational structure is ready for introduction of the alternative.

Tolerance zone. The zones above and under the set norm, within which one does not intervene or adjust.

Top-down approach. An approach of the planning cycle in which the top management strongly determines the direction.

Top management. The highest management level of a labour organization which bears the total or end responsibility for the management of the business and the organization.

Uncertainty avoidance. The degree to which the members of a culture feel threatened by uncertain or unknown situations; this feeling is, among others, expressed in the need for predictability: for formal and informal rules.

Unit management. A management style and an organization form which, in combination, are directed at the decentralization of entrepreneurship within an overall organization.

Unity of direction. The organization principle whereby every employee eventually accepts binding orders from one superior (or other employee) only.

Utilization or occupation planning. The part of the production planning which takes place after the capacity planning. When the capacities are known, one can plan how the flow of production will fit into the capacities.

Value. A state of affairs for an individual, group or society to strive for.

Value chain. A notion, originating from Porter, which considers activities in the primary and secondary processes as a chain of value additions.

Value system. The sum of the values, ranked in order of priority for an individual, group or society.

Vertical differentiation. The spreading of activities to a lower level of execution.

Vertical integration. Expansion of the activities of an organization in a line of business by taking over activities of supplier organizations (backward integration) or buyer organizations (forward integration).

Vertical organization. Dividing activities into different levels.

Vertical task enlargement or job enrichment. The expansion of the task with activities of higher level (work preparation, supervision, administration).

Work consultation. The institutionalized, periodical consultation within an organizational unit (department/team) between a manager and employees about the content or execution of the work and the work situation.

Work distribution. *See* Detail planning.

Work extrinsic. Those things which belong to the work environment.

Work intrinsic. Those things which belong to the content of the work itself.

Work preparation. *See* Delivery planning.

Work science. The systematic studying of the organization of the labour function and the methods of working.

Work study. The study of human action, individually or collectively in combination with machinery or tools. Special attention is paid to the improvement of the applied work methods.

Work structuring. The way of assigning or grouping of tasks to be conducted in such a way that the capacities of the members of the organization are used as fully as possible.

Works council. Organ of a company or institution involving the formal participation of the employees by means of representation.

Index